HOMAGE TO CHIAPAS

HOMAGE TO CHIAPAS

The New Indigenous Struggles in Mexico

BILL WEINBERG

VERSO

London • New York

First published by Verso 2000
© Bill Weinberg 2000
All rights reserved
The moral rights of the author have been asserted

Verso
UK: 6 Meard Street, London W1V 3HR
US: 180 Varick Street, New York, NY 10014–4606

Verso is the imprint of New Left Books

ISBN 1–85984–719–6

British Library Cataloguing in Publication Data
A catalogue record for this book is available from the British Library

Library of Congress Cataloging-in-Publication Data
A catalog record for this book is available from the Library of Congress

Typeset by The Running Head Limited, www.therunninghead.com
Printed in the USA by R. R. Donnelly & Sons Co.

Dedicated to my parents, Philip and Mary,
excellent teachers . . .

And, presumptuously, to my inspirations—George Orwell,
John Reed, John Kenneth Turner, B. Traven and
Carleton Beals

Whenever there is, in any country, uncultivated lands and unemployed poor, it is clear that the laws of property have been so far extended as to violate natural right.

Thomas Jefferson, letter to James Madison, 1785

Los Estados Unidos parecen destinados por la providencia para plagar la America de hambre y miseria a nombre de la libertad.

Simón Bolívar, *Jornadas Bolivarianas*, 1829

CONTENTS

ACKNOWLEDGEMENTS

I owe a debt of gratitude to more people than can be mentioned here. First and foremost, those who provided information, translation, transportation, contacts, logistics and analysis: Jane Guskin and David Wilson (*Weekly News Update on the Americas*, Nicaragua Solidarity Network of Greater New York); Harry Cleaver, Tamara Ford (Acción Zapatista, University of Texas, Austin); Marilyn Davis, Pat Dreger, John J. Jacq (Zapatistas Online); José Barreiro (Cornell University); Luz Martín del Campo-Hermosillo (Long Island University, Brooklyn); Dr. Scott Robinson Studebaker (Universidad Autonoma Metropolitana, Iztapalapa); Peter Dale Scott (UC Berkeley); Dino Pacio Lindin (Empire State College, ret.); Celerino Castillo III (DEA, ret.); Michelle Sforza (Public Citizen, Washington DC); Katherine Díaz (The Lindesmith Center, New York); Lluis Escartin Lara (Asociación Culturál Na Bolom, San Cristóbal de Las Casas); Randall Gingrich (Sierra Madre Alliance, Chihuahua); Brian Hill (Institute for Cultural Ecology, San Francisco); Peter Berg and Judy Goldhaft (Planet Drum Foundation, San Francisco); Carmelo Ruiz Marrero (*Claridad*, San Juan, Puerto Rico); Alex Ewen (Solidarity Foundation, New York).

Next, those who provided daily sustenance and assistance in myriad ways, first and foremost by putting up with me: Teriananda, Joanne Dittersdorf, Joe Lennon, Robbie Liben, Danny Lieberman, Sarah Hogarth, B. C. Ashmall-Liversidge, Bill Haigney, Christine Halvorson, Arun Gupta, John Veit, Michael Pahios, Michael Niman, Laura McClusky, Chesley Hicks, Matt Cassetta, Alexandra Patiño, Lauren Krivit (excellent friends and neighbors); Steve Wishnia, Dean Latimer, Gabe Kirchheimer, Peter Gorman (the High-Witness News Team); Peter Lamborn Wilson, Anne-Marie Hendrickson, Sharon Gregory (Moorish Orthodox Radio Crusade, WBAI-FM, New York); Orin Langelle, Anne Petermann, Alexis Lathem (ACERCA and fellow travellers, Burlington, VT); Maria Anguera de Sojo, Joshua

Schwartz, Andrew Lichtenstein, Teun Voeten (intrepid photographers); Claudia Jiménez, Pramila Rao, Peter Malerba, Siobhan McGrath, Bobby Lesko, Therese Chorun, Greg Ruggiero (fellow moles); Joe Wetmore, Kathleen Marie Conboy, Charlotte Rose Conboy (Autumn Leaves Used Books, Ithaca, NY); Judith Mahoney Pasternak (War Resisters League, NYC); Chris Flash (*The Shadow*, Lower East Side, NYC); Tom Ward (Pope of Radical Hedonism); Annie Miquet (in spite of everything); Matt and Susan Weinberg, and the fond memory of Josephine Healy.

And finally some brave and spirited Mexican friends (and one Chilean), for their guidance, hospitality and patience with my Spanish: Cristina Mendoza (Guardianes de la Tierra, Mexico City), Armando Mojica Toledo and Wendy Hernández Salinas (Espacio Verde, Cuernavaca), Alberto Ruz Buenfil (Huehuecoyotl, Tepoztlan), Dr. Juan Blechen Neito (Cuernavaca), Dr. Arturo Pozo (Mexico City), Carlos Ysunza (Centro de Capacitacion Integral para Promotores Comunitarios —CECIPROC, Oaxaca), Jorge Santiago Santiago (Desarrollo Economico Social de los Mexicanos Indígenas—DESMI, San Cristóbal de Las Casas), Hugo Ireta (Coordinadora de Lucha Social, Villahermosa), Luz Maria González Armenta (Defensa y Promocion de los Derechos Humanos-Emiliano Zapata—DEPRO-DHEZAC, Matamoros), Alejandro Gutiérrez (*El Diario*, Chihuahua)

A NOTE ON SOURCES

All Spanish-language newspapers cited are based in Mexico City except where otherwise noted. Most EZLN communiqués cited were received over the Internet on the Chiapas95 list maintained by Zapatistas Online at the University of Texas (www.eco.utexas.edu/faculty/Cleaver/chiapas95.html), but many are included in the anthologies listed in the bibliography.

ACRONYMS

MEXICAN GOVERNMENT AGENCIES AND PROGRAMS

CERESO	Social Rehabilitation Center
CFE	Federal Electric Commission
CIMADES	Inter-Institutional Commission for Environmental and Social Development
CNA	National Water Commission
CNDH	National Human Rights Commission
COCOPA	Concord and Pacification Commission
Conasupo	National Popular Subsistence Company
CORAT	Tabasco Radio and Television Commission
CRESET	Tabasco State Social Rehabilitation Center
INE	National Ecology Institute
INI	National Indigenous Institute
Nafinsa	*Nacional Financiera*
NCP	New Population Center
Pemex	Petróleos Mexicanos
PGR	Prosecutor General of the Republic
PJF	Federal Judicial Police
PROFEPA	Federal Prosecutor for Environmental Protection
Pronasol	National Solidarity Program
SAM	Mexican Food System
SARH	Secretariat of Agriculture and Hydraulic Resources

SCT   Secretariat of Communications and Transport
SEDENA   Secretariat of National Defense
SEMARNAP   Secretariat of the Environment, Natural Resources
                    and Fisheries
UAEM   Autonomous State University of Morelos
UNAM   National Autonomous University of Mexico

UNITED STATES GOVERNMENT AGENCIES

ACTPN   Advisory Committee for Trade Policy and Negotiations
AID   Agency for International Development
CIA   Central Intelligence Agency
DEA   Drug Enforcement Administration
EPA   Environmental Protection Agency
FBI   Federal Bureau of Investigation
FDA   Food and Drug Administration
NAO   National Administrative Office (US Labor Dept.)
USDA   United States Department of Agriculture

INTERNATIONAL AGENCIES AND PROGRAMS

BECC   Border Environment Cooperation Committee
CEC   Commission for Environmental Cooperation
CGIAR   Consultative Group on International Agricultural
                    Research
CIMMYT   International Maize and Wheat Improvement Center
FAO   Food and Agriculture Organization
FTAA   Free Trade Area of the Americas
GATT   General Agreements on Tariffs and Trade
HAZTRAKS   Hazardous Waste Tracking System
IARC   International Agricultural Research Center
ICSID   International Center for Settlement of Investment
                    Disputes
ILO   International Labor Organization

IMF	International Monetary Fund
IPR	Intellectual Property Right
MAI	Multilateral Agreements on Investment
NADBank	North American Development Bank
NAFTA	North American Free Trade Agreement
OECD	Organization for Economic Cooperation and Development
SAP	Structural Adjustment Plan
TLC	Free Trade Treaty (NAFTA)
UNESCO	United Nations Educational, Scientific and Cultural Organization
UNHCR	United Nations High Commissioner for Refugees
WTO	World Trade Organization

ORGANIZATIONS, UNIONS AND PARTIES

ACNR	National Revolutionary Civic Association
ANCIEZ	Emiliano Zapata National Independent Campesino Alliance
ARIC	Rural Association of Collective Interests
CASMAC	Sierra Madre Assessor Council
CCRI-GC	Indigenous Revolutionary Clandestine Committee-General Command
CEOIC	State Council of Indian and Campesino Organizations
CIOAC	Independent Central of Rural Workers and Campesinos
CNC	National Campesino Confederation
CND	National Democratic Convention
CNI	National Indigenous Congress
CNPA	*Plan de Ayala* National Coordinator
CNTE	National Council of Education Workers
COCEI	Worker–Campesino–Student Coalition of the Isthmus
COCES	Sosconosco Coalition of Worker–Campesino–Student Organizations
CODEHUTAB	Tabasco Human Rights Committee
CODEP	People's Human Rights Defense Committee

CONAI	National Intermediation Commission
CONPAZ	Coordinator of NGOs for Peace
COSYDDHAC	Chihuahua Commission for Solidarity and Defense of Human Rights
CTM	Mexican Workers Confederation
DESMI	Social-Economic Development of the Indigenous Mexicans
EPR	Popular Revolutionary Army
EPRI	Revolutionary Army of the Insurgent People
EZLN	Zapatista Army of National Liberation
FAC-MLN	Broad Front for the Creation of a National Liberation Movement
FALN	National Liberation Armed Forces
FAR	Revolutionary Armed Forces
FDN	National Democratic Front
FEDOMEZ	Emiliano Zapata Democratic Front of the Mexican East
FMLN	Farabundo Marti National Liberation Front (El Salvador)
FSLN	Sandinista National Liberation Front (Nicaragua)
FZLN	Zapatista National Liberation Front
GEA (1)	Environmental Study Group
GEA (2)	Armed Ecologist Group
IWW	Industrial Workers of the World
LARSEZ	Emiliano Zapata Revolutionary Agrarian League of the South
MIRA	Indigenous Revolutionary Anti-Zapatista Movement
MLN	National Liberation Movement
Modetra	Workers' Defense Movement
MPI	Independent *Petrolero* Movement
MULT	Triqui Movement of Unification and Struggle
OCEZ	Emiliano Zapata Campesino Organization
OCSS	Campesino Organization of the Sierra del Sur
OPEC	Ejidal Producers Organization of the Coast
OPEZ	Emiliano Zapata Proletarian Organization
PAN	National Action Party
PDLP	Party of the Poor
PDPR	Popular Revolutionary Democratic Party

PFCRN	Party of the Cardenista Front for National Reconstruction
PLM	Mexican Liberal Party
PP	Politica Popular
PPS	Popular Socialist Party
PRD	Party of the Democratic Revolution
PRI	Institutional Revolutionary Party
PROCUP	Clandestine Revolutionary Workers Party-Union of the People
PSS	Socialist Party of the Southeast
RAP	Pluri-ethnic Autonomous Region
SERPAJ	Peace and Justice Service
SIL	Summer Institute of Linguistics
SNTE	National Syndicate of Education Workers
STFRM	Railway Workers Syndicate of the Mexican Republic
STMMRM	Miner and Metal Workers Syndicate of the Mexican Republic
SUTAUR	Urban Passenger Auto-Transport Workers Syndicate
SUTERM	United Syndicate of Electric Workers of the Mexican Republic
SUTIN	United Syndicate of Nuclear Industry Workers
TAGIN	National Indigenous Guerilla Triple Alliance
UBISORT	Triqui Region Social Welfare Union
UCD	Democratic Campesino Union
UCPFV	Francisco Villa Popular Campesino Union
UE	United Electric Workers (USA)
UGOCP	Worker, Campesino and Popular General Union
UOCEZ	Emiliano Zapata Worker–Campesino Union
UPREZ	Emiliano Zapata Popular Revolutionary Movement
URNG	Guatemalan National Revolutionary Union

GLOSSARY

acequia	irrigation ditch
aguardiente	cane liquor
amapola	opium
amparo	a judicial order protecting the bearer from arrest
anciano	elder
apertura	opening
atole	a sweet, usually hot beverage made from *maíz*
ayuntamiento	municipal council
barranca	canyon
barrendero	street sweeper
barrio	neighborhood or district
bastón de mando	traditional Indian scepter of authority
bautizado	baptized, Christian
boca	mouth, sea opening on a barrier reef
bosque	forest, usually temperate
cabacera	municipal seat; more specifically, the municipal palace
cacicazgo	system of *cacique* privilege and power
cacique	patriarch, usually of a village
calpullec	chieftain of a *calpulli*
calpulli	basic land division of pre-Conquest Mexico
campesino	peasant
campo	countryside
cañada	canyon
capitán	captain
catequista	church lay worker

caudillismo	rule by a *caudillo*
caudillo	regional or national strongman or patriarch
cayuca	canoe
cenote	natural well found in the Yucatan, linking subterranean rivers
cerro	ridge or mountain
charro	cowboy; also, slang for corrupt and domesticated trade unionists
chilango	a native of Mexico City
chinampas	lacustrine gardens unique to Lake Xochimilco in the Federal District
chupacabras	"goat-suckers," apocryphal vampire bats
científico	"scientist," the administrative elite of the Díaz dictatorship
cofradía	village religious brotherhood
coleto	Chiapas aristocrat
colonia	neighborhood or unincorporated settlement
comisariado	local three-member commission that oversees an *ejido*
comisario	member of a *comisariado*
compadre	figure of fraternal respect; often implying political connivance
comunero	one who works communal village lands
consulta	village discussion, consensus decision-making meeting
copal	resin incense used ritually by the Maya
corrido	folk ballad
coyote	slang for middleman or smuggler who exploits *campesinos* or migrants
coyuntura	coming-together, alliance building
criollo	creole, Spaniard born in New Spain
damnificado	person left homeless by a natural disaster
dedazo	"fingering"—PRI ritual of choosing the next president
delegacion	basic administrative division of the Federal District
dueño	proprietor
ejiditario	a member of an *ejido*
ejido	communal agricultural lands; more specifically, those redistributed by the agrarian reform
encomienda	colonial system of local lordship over Indians
encuentro	meeting

expulado	internal refugee from village *cacicazgos* in Chiapas
finca	commercial farm
finquero	owner of a *finca*
frijoles	beans
gachupin	literally a spur; derogatory for a Spaniard in colonial times
gallo	rooster
gentile	pagan, unconverted
grito	war-cry, slogan
guano	bird or bat feces, used as fertilizer
guardias blancas	White Guards, rancher paramilitary groups
hacendado	owner of a *hacienda*
huaraches	leather sandals worn by *campesinos*
hacienda	plantation
huipil	traditional embroidered blouse worn by Indian women
iglesia	church
integrante	member of a political group
jefe	boss
ladino	Spanish-speaker, non-Indian
latifundio	large plantation, officially outlawed since the Revolution
latifundista	owner of a *latifundio*
maíz	corn
mariguanero	marijuana grower
merced	colonial land grant
mestizo	person of mixed Spanish and Indian ancestry
milpa	corn plot
montería	lumber camp
mota	marijuana
municipio	municipality
nahual	animal spirit
naturaleza	forest, undeveloped lands
padrino	godfather
palo	club, stick
pantano	wetland
patrón	landlord
peón	rural debt-laborer

pistolero	gunman
plantón	semi-permanent vigil or protest
posh	see *aguardiente*
pozol	soup or drink of *maíz*
predio	property, estate; often a collective of private owners
prestanombre	"name-loaner," frontman
pueblo	village or hamlet
ranchero	rancher
rancho	ranch
reales cedulas	royal certificates recognizing village land rights in colonial times
reducciones	colonial policy of "reducing" Indian lands
regidor	town councilor
repartimiento	system of debt labor that replaced the *encomienda*
selva	tropical rainforest
sierra	mountain range
sobrino	"nephew," political client
tatic	father or grandfather, a Maya honorific
teniente	lieutenant
teozintle	wild ancestor of corn
tesguino	Tarahumara corn beer
tlatoani	chieftain in Aztec times
trago	see *aguardiente*
usos y costumbres	"uses and customs," traditional system of village government
vaquero	cowboy
vega	pasture, grazing land
zócalo	central plaza or square of a village, town or city

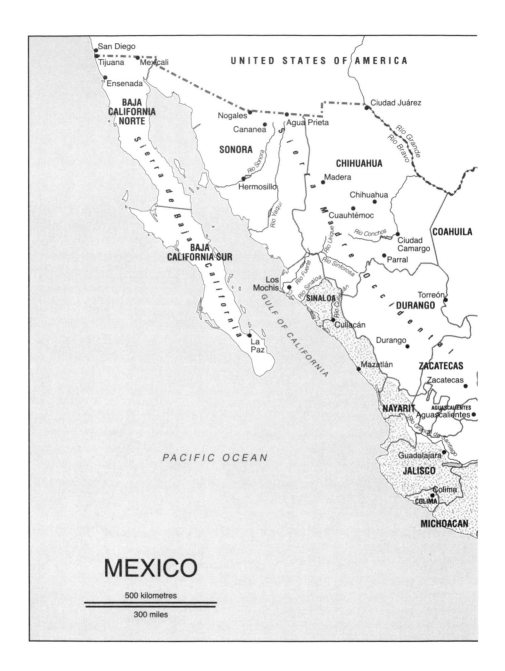

UNITED STATES OF AMERICA

San Diego
Tijuana   Mexicali
Ensenada

BAJA
CALIFORNIA
NORTE

Nogales
Cananea

Agua Prieta

Ciudad Juárez

Rio Grande

Rio Bravo

SONORA

Rio Sonora

Sierra

Hermosillo

Rio Yaqui

CHIHUAHUA

Madera

Chihuahua

Cuauhtémoc

Madre

Rio Urique

Rio Conchos

Ciudad
Camargo

COAHUILA

Parral

BAJA
CALIFORNIA SUR

Sierra de Baja California

Los
Mochis

Rio Fuerte

Rio Sinaloa

SINALOA

Rio Sinforosa

Rio Culiacán

Occidental

Torreón

DURANGO

Culiacán

Durango

Mazatlán

ZACATECAS

Zacatecas

GULF OF CALIFORNIA

La
Paz

NAYARIT

AGUASCALIENTES
Aguascalientes

Rio Grande de Santiago

PACIFIC OCEAN

Guadalajara

JALISCO

Colima

COLIMA

MICHOACAN

MEXICO

500 kilometres

300 miles

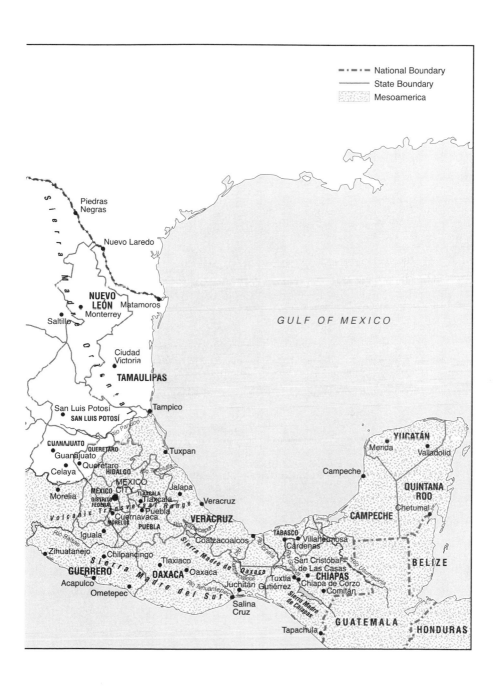

National Boundary
State Boundary
Mesoamerica

Sierra Madre Oriental

Piedras Negras

Nuevo Laredo

NUEVO LEÓN

Matamoros

Monterrey

Saltillo

Ciudad Victoria

TAMAULIPAS

GULF OF MEXICO

San Luis Potosí

SAN LUIS POTOSÍ

Tampico

Río Pánuco

GUANAJUATO

QUERÉTARO

Guanajuato

Querétaro

Celaya

HIDALGO

Río Tecolutla

Tuxpan

YUCATÁN

Merida

Valladolid

Campeche

QUINTANA ROO

MÉXICO CITY

MÉXICO

TLAXCALA

Tlaxcala

Jalapa

Morelia

DISTRITO FEDERAL

Transvolcanic Range

Cuernavaca

Puebla

Veracruz

CAMPECHE

Chetumal

Volcanic

MORELOS

PUEBLA

VERACRUZ

TABASCO

Río Papaloapan

Coatzacoalcos

Villahermosa

Cárdenas

Río Balsas

Iguala

Río Grijalva

Río Tonalá

BELIZE

Río Usumacinta

Zihuatanejo

Chilpancingo

Sierra Madre del Sur

Tlaxiaco

Oaxaca

Oaxaca

San Cristóbal de Las Casas

GUERRERO

OAXACA

Río Tehuantepec

Juchitán

Río Coatzacoalcos

Tuxtla Gutiérrez

CHIAPAS

Chiapa de Corzo

Comitán

Acapulco

Ometepec

Salina Cruz

Sierra Madre de Chiapas

QUINTANA ROO

Tapachula

GUATEMALA

HONDURAS

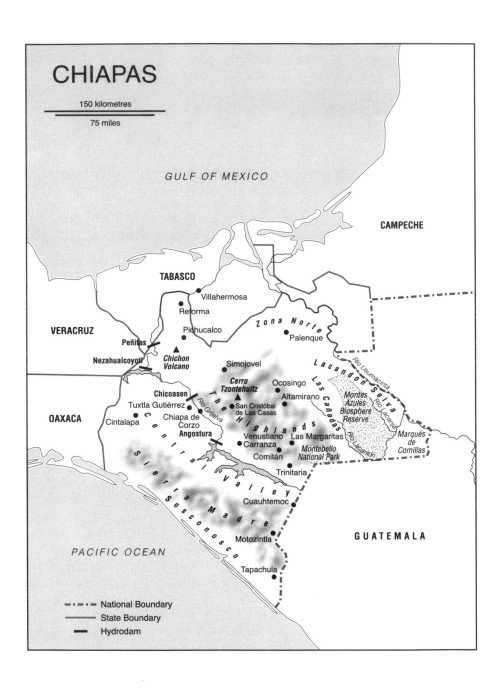

CHIAPAS

150 kilometres

75 miles

GULF OF MEXICO

CAMPECHE

TABASCO

VERACRUZ

Villahermosa

Reforma

Pichucalco

Zona Norte

Palenque

Lacandón Selva

Peñitas

Nezahualcoyotl

▲ *Chichon Volcano*

Simojovel

Cerro Tzontehuitz ▲

Ocosingo

Altamirano

Las Cañadas

Rio Usumacinta

Rio Lacantil

Chicoasen

Tuxtla Gutiérrez

Rio Grijalva

San Cristóbal de Las Casas

The Highlands

Montes Azules Biosphere Reserve

OAXACA

Cintalapa

Chiapa de Corzo

Angostura

Central Valley

Venustiano Carranza

Las Margaritas

Montebello National Park

Rio Lacantún

Marqués de Comillas

Comitán

Trinitaria

Sierra Madre de Sosconosco

Cuauhtemoc

GUATEMALA

PACIFIC OCEAN

Motozintla

Tapachula

- — · — · National Boundary
- ——— State Boundary
- ▬▬ Hydrodam

INTRODUCTION

NEW YORK CITY 1999

It is darkest February on the Lower East Side and I am late with my manuscript. I've been glued to the computer so long, I've forgotten everything else. Including the utility bills. The telephone wakes me up early after I was up all night working. It's Bell Atlantic, the communications titan that just bought out New York Telephone. Or, rather, one of their employees. Today is my last chance to pay before they cut me off. After I am informed of this pleasant news, I am asked, "Do you feel that I've treated you as a valued customer?" All I feel is sorry for the poor employee on the other end of the line for having to submit to this little humiliation.

I can't mail a check because the postage rates have just gone up, and I don't have any 33 cent stamps. I can wait on line either at the post office, or at the Bell Atlantic payment center. I recently heard on the news that the rates for corporate junk mail are going *down*—public citizens subsidizing the profligate litter of private interests.

I get on my bicycle. First stop, the bank. Next, the Bell Atlantic office. The first thing I notice when I walk in is that the customer service center is closed. That means the next time mysterious charges to China appear on my bill, I won't be able to have it out with a real live human being. I'll have to wade through forty minutes of computerized choice menus and muzak on the damn phone. My blood starts to boil as I wait on line. After I pay up, I ask the clerk through the bullet-proof glass what happened to the customer service center. She rolls her eyes. "Talk to Bell Atlantic. I guess they're trying to save money."

I say I want to pay my electricity bill too—a service they'd always provided, for a small fee. "No, we don't do that anymore. New rules."

Now I've had it. The neighborhood getting screwed by this faceless entity again. "OVERTHROW BELL ATLANTIC!" I shout as I storm out. "DOWN WITH BELL ATLANTIC!" I know the clerks are glad to hear their boss getting dissed, but I see the security guards closing in on me and shut up, hating myself for doing so.

I get back on my bike and head for the Con Edison office. I walk in, disoriented; something's out of place. "May I help you?" asks the guard. "Yeah, where's the payment center?" "There is no more payment center. It's been closed for a month."

I'm given the address of a sleazy check-cashing place where I can pay the Con Ed bill. While I wait on line again, it all becomes horribly clear. Con Ed charges the highest rates in the country. Con Ed's nuclear reactor at Indian Point, just 30 miles north of the city, is a Sword of Damocles hanging over the heads of 20 million largely oblivious residents of the greater metropolitan area. And yet, every month, they call the tune and we all dance. We reward them for their irresponsibility. We have no choice. And now this.

A reconquest of territory. The Con Ed payment center and Bell Atlantic service center were actual geographic space that was at least partially a public commons— if only for working-class neighborhood residents who prefer to pay cash to wait on despairingly long lines. Now that space is appropriated, enclosed—along with the warehoused apartments, the community gardens bulldozed for luxury developments, the public parks increasingly given over to private functions and administration, the public buildings closed to the public by the new security state.

I bicycle home certain that my generation has been cursed to witness the twilight of human freedom. My minor quotidian frustrations are paradigmatic; a microcosm of the consolidation being effected with terrifying rapidity planetwide.

And the sustenance I draw comes in messages and memories from somewhere across the Appalachians and the plains, across the high deserts and endless chaos of volcanic ranges, from a place called Chiapas where some of the most marginalized souls in the hemisphere demonstrate that resistance is still possible, the most succinct of their slogans saying everything that really needs to be said. *¡Ya Basta!*

Enough already.

CHIAPAS 1999

On August 31, the news—perhaps like the coffee I sipped over it—was from Chiapas. Coverage of the ongoing rebellion is increasingly rare, and increasingly distorted. But I was grateful for the photograph.

Deep in the Lacandon Selva, the beseiged and disappearing rainforest, at a little settlement called Amador Hernández, unarmed Maya Indians were blockading an army construction team cutting a road through the jungle. The AP shot in the *New York Times* showed a row of Tzeltal women, in traditional homemade dresses, long single black braids down their backs and bandanas masking their faces, opposing a row of military police in full riot gear across barbed-wire barricades. The MPs wielded big plastic shields, helmet visors masking their own faces.[1]

I pieced the real story together with Mexican press accounts from the Internet. The troops had arrived on the 12th, some five hundred of them. Some came with the road crew from the north—others were dropped by parachute into Amador Hernández to meet the crew. The road was to continue south, into the jungle, toward San Quintín—following the very border of the Montes Azules Biosphere Reserve, which protects Mexico's last, shrinking stretch of virgin tropical rainforest. Amador Hernández and surrounding communities immediately mobilized in protest—rebel Indians, for their own purposes and by their own available means, protecting the protected zone from its official "protectors."[2]

As the stand-off ensued, the army built a little heliport on their side of the line. Choppers came and went, bringing in more supplies and reinforcements.[3]

The community of Amador Hernández also brought in reinforcements, from La Realidad, the little settlement across the Sierra La Colmena which is the unofficial capital of the jungle's rebel zone. These unarmed volunteers marched over the low-lying, forest-cloaked La Colmena to San Quintín, and then up the Río Lacantún to Amador Hernández. They were mostly anthropology students who had been in La Realidad for the latest in an ongoing series of *encuentros*, public fora, called there by the Zapatista National Liberation Army (EZLN), the armed, clandestine, yet paradoxically democratic *avant garde* of the militant peasant movement in Chiapas.[4]

The activist soap-opera actress Ofelia Medina also accompanied the student volunteers. They joined the Tzeltal *campesinos* at the stand-off.[5]

The opposing forces in Amador Hernández exemplified the bizarre nature of the larger stand-off in the primitive region which had persisted for nearly five years. Despite the escalating militarization, the state of siege, the EZLN would not be goaded into using their weapons, into ceding any perception of the moral high ground to the government. Therefore, the army, ubiquitous and intimidating, was still bound by certain restraints. The EZLN was still able to help build and coordinate a national movement from their besieged territory, holding high-profile activist gatherings in La Realidad. The recent National Encuentro in Defense of the Cultural Patrimony was called to oppose government plans to farm out management of Mexico's multitudinous archaeological sites to private tourism interests.

(The Selva itself is especially rich in such sites, still largely undeveloped. Directly across the Montes Azules reserve from Amador Hernández, on the banks of the Rio Lacanjá, lie the Classic Maya pyramids and murals of Bonampak—only connected to the outside world by paved road within the past months.[6])

The government exploited the stalemate to encircle the Zapatistas with military roads. In May, the government announced that the Southern Frontier Highway encircling the Selva, following the Rio Usumacinta and Guatemalan border from Palenque to Comitán, had been completely paved.[7]

Closer to the Zapatista heartland, in Las Cañadas, the canyons that lead down to the rainforest, a still unpaved road now linked Ocosingo to Santa Margarita. In the Indian settlements along the way, like San Quintín and La Garrucha, the army set up makeshift bases. The rebel authorities of these settlements, the "autonomous municipalities" loyal to the EZLN, continued to function in clandestinity, in the shadow of the army. They issued press statements accusing the occupying army forces of harassing Indian women, illegal logging, and plundering the Selva's wildlife for sport and profit.[8]

Now another circle was being drawn, linking San Quintín to another artery into the forest from Ocosingo to the north. San Quintín—guarding the entrance to the deep, still-trackless interior of the Selva around Laguna Miramar—was now the site of the Selva's biggest army presence, established under the guise of fighting drug trafficking from across the Guatemalan border. The memory of the last open army offensive against the EZLN, in February 1995, made this rustic outpost strategic. Then, the Maya rebels had fled into the jungle interior, and the less agile federal army was virtually helpless to follow. Then, the army had only had positions to the north and west of the Zapatistas, toward Ocosingo, Las Margaritas and civilization. Now, with militarized San Quintín just behind the Sierra La Colmena from La Realidad, the rebel army was completely surrounded.[9]

The federal government called the road-building operation a "reforestation project" and had the troops engage in a few token tree plantings, but everybody saw the new access to San Quintín as an artery for troops and war material.[10]

The Amador Hernández face-off came to violence on August 15. When the Indians struck at plastic shields with their sticks, the MPs responded with tear gas. Two more helicopters landed, one full of camera-laden journalists, the other with more soldiers—this time combat troops, not just MPs.[11]

The next morning, high Chiapas state officials were conferring with the colonel in charge of the operation behind newly erected barbed-wire barricades.[12]

On the 18th, hundreds of Tzeltals, faces uncovered, approached the barricades, armed now both with sticks—which also helped them walk in the deep rainy-season muck—and with flowers. They had collected magnificent wild orchids and gardenias from the surrounding forest—and proceeded to festoon the barbed-wire, like the kids at the 1967 Pentagon march who stuck daisies in the MP rifle barrels. Then they sang *Las Mañanitas* to the soldiers—the Mexican "Happy Birthday"—and Catholic hymns in Tzeltal.[13]

The gesture of goodwill did not long forestall another escalation. On the 25th, in San José La Nueva Esperanza, just south of La Realidad, army troops and state Security Police opened fire on local Indians protesting their presence, masked and carrying their machetes but no guns. Seven troops were reported injured with machetes, and two Indians with bullets. The army and EZLN issued rival communiqués blaming each other for provoking the incident.[14]

The roads approaching the Selva from Ocosingo and Las Margaritas were thick with police and army roadblocks. Now, the new roads put the troops "at our backs," said Subcommander Marcos, the EZLN's mediagenic spokesman, in a communiqué issued from a clandestine location, presumably in the vicinity of La Realidad. He asserted once again that the government's long-term aim was to secure future oil exploitation in the region which is now the Zapatista zone.[15]

Federal Deputy Gilberto López y Rivas, a member of the congressional commission formed four years earlier for the long-stalled Chiapas peace talks, protested. "Congress must act fast," he pronounced, "because it is now impossible for the Zapatistas to retreat any further." This was true in a literal, geographic sense. President Ernesto Zedillo insisted the government had "infinite patience" in the search for peace in Chiapas, the road-building unrelated to military exigencies.[16]

The Fray Bartolomé de Las Casas Human Rights Center in the Chiapas Highlands town of San Cristóbal de Las Casas, 150 kilometers west and a mile above the Selva, issued a statement noting reports of *campesinos* being harassed and roughed up at roadblocks throughout the Selva and Highland regions. The center's founder, Bishop Samuel Ruiz, had four years ago led the peace dialogue, only to step down in protest of the deadlock.[17]

The unaccountable paramilitary forces were also throwing up roadblocks. A young doctor, in Chiapas fulfilling the national-service requirement of her medical training, was stopped at a roadblock by unknown men 20 kilometers outside La Realidad. A federal soldier looked on as the men tied her up, beat her, ripped her clothes and threatened to rape her, she told a *Miami Herald* reporter.[18]

But Chiapas Gobernación Secretary Luis Alfonso Utrilla pronounced: "We will not take one single step backwards in the completion of this project, the fruit of commitments by Governor Roberto Albores Guillén and the President of the Republic, Ernesto Zedillo Ponce de Leon, to ensure that education, health, communication and general development services reach all Chiapanecos, without distinction as to political leanings or social levels."[19]

Gov. Albores had his press office declare that the Indians were being "manipulated" by "*ultras*"—extreme leftists—from UNAM, the National Autonomous University of Mexico in the distant Federal District. UNAM was then being rocked by student strikes and campus occupations, the largest since 1968, in protest of the government's imposition of tuition fees for the first time. The EZLN had recently held an *encuentro* with the student leaders.[20]

Albores himself told a crowd of supporters in a pro-government village, "The patience of the people of Chiapas is running out. We can't allow a band of delinquents to hold our state hostage any longer."[21]

The *coletos*, the aristocratic elite of San Cristóbal, joined the *caciques*, the ruling party's Indian village bosses, in rallying behind the federal army. The San Cristóbal municipal council declared Ofelia Medina *persona non grata*, and ordered her to leave town on seventy-two hours notice.[22]

Thousands of Indians, many masked, marched in San Cristóbal, Ocosingo and Altamirano to protest the roadwork. The Zapatistas erected their own barricades on the roads into the Selva, facing the army roadblocks. An EZLN communiqué stated they anticipated an imminent attack.[23]

The Autonomous Municipality of San Manuel, in Las Cañadas, issued a communiqué accusing a local *PRIista*—an adherent of the government's Institutional Revolutionary Party (PRI)—of planting opium in Ejido Delicias Cascos. "We fear that through the crime of the *PRIistas* growing poppies, the government will have a pretext to invade the zone and attack the Zapatista support bases," it stated.[24]

There were many precedents for such fears. The most recent was in April, when the Mexican army announced it had destroyed twenty-five marijuana plantations in Zapatista-controlled communities in the Highlands. Three hundred soldiers backed by state and federal police uprooted marijuana fields a few kilometers from the violently divided village of El Bosque. There was "clear evidence the drugs were exchanged for armaments," said Gen. Jorge Isaac Jiménez of the 31st Military Zone. "But we can't attribute the crops to any group in specific," he conceded. Local Tzotzil Maya villagers disputed the implication. "It's a government lie and a provocation," said Roberto Garcia Pérez, representative of the nearby pro-Zapatista community of San Juan de Libertad, claiming the plantations were in an area controlled by pro-government paramilitaries.[25]

On September 1, President Zedillo was jeered by opposition legislators as he delivered a state of the union address that failed to mention the Chiapas crisis.[26]

After the Nueva Esperanza violence, COCOPA, the Congressional peace commission, had announced that construction of the San Quintín road would be halted. But an EZLN communiqué dismissed the offer as "ridiculous, since the construction of the highway had already been suspended by the resistance of the indigenous brothers and sisters of the zone of Amador Hernández." The statement warned that "federal army troops remain in Amador Hernández and continue their work of fortification, of provisioning, and of positioning arms, announcing that they are staying there for an indefinite time."[27]

Reading the *New York Times* account of the jungle stand-off over my coffee on Manhattan's Lower East Side, I wondered if Julia Preston's reportage hadn't been mangled by an editor with an ax to grind. She quoted Emilio Rabasa, President Zedillo's Chiapas pointman: "Since the Zapatistas won't talk peace, my strategy has been to press hard with our social programs to remove some of the social causes of the conflict. The policy has been so successful that the Zapatistas are trying to block it."[28]

She did not quote the Zapatista communiqué asserting that "the EZLN wants highways that bring true peace, and not war."[29]

She also repeated (as fact) Mexican government allegations that some hundred EZLN troops had defected and turned in their weapons to state authorities in 1999.[30] She did not quote any of the various communiqués from the EZLN and the autonomous municipalities asserting that these supposed defections are a "government farce," staged for the media, that the troops were actually members of the Indigenous Revolutionary Anti-Zapatista Movement (MIRA), a paramilitary group loyal to the Institutional Revolutionary Party.[31]

For three years, the dialogue had been stalled by President Zedillo's refusal to accept the San Andrés Accords which the Maya *comandantes* of the EZLN had hashed out with Congressional negotiators in a painstaking process, incorporating the rebel army's system of consultation with the base communities. The accords called for changes to the Mexican Constitution recognizing the autonomy of indigenous peoples—provisions no more radical than those in the Colombian and Nicaraguan Constitutions. Acceptance of the accords was the EZLN's one precondition for peace. But the Zedillo government called it a dangerous call for "separatism," and started pushing its own alternative autonomy plan.

Both the San Andrés Accords and the government plan called for creation of new municipalities in remote indigenous areas like the Lacandon Selva, heretofore denied self-government. But the remunicipalization of the Selva being coordinated by the Chiapas state government and federal army was aimed at undercutting the system of self-government already instated by the Zapatista base communities, the autonomous municipalities. San Quintín, under tight army control, not the nearby rebel stronghold of La Realidad, was to be the local municipal seat.[32]

The critical question of subsoil rights was a powerful if unspoken subtext for this struggle over land and autonomy. *La Jornada*, Mexico City's aggressively investigative national daily, took a cue from the Subcomandante and found that the Mexican government, for the first time since the 1994 uprising, had resumed oil exploration in the Lacandon Selva, signaling a return to long-delayed plans to push into Chiapas from the petroleum heartland of Tabasco state, on the Gulf Coast to the north. "After ten years of exploration and development, the focus of attention has moved toward the coast and the mountains of Chiapas, resulting in significant discoveries of light and condensed oil and gas," *La Jornada* quoted a June 1998 article in *Oil and Gas Journal*. "Political disturbances are more important than any geological factor" as an obstacle to oil development in Chiapas, an analyst had conceded in the pages of that trade publication in 1996.[33]

Mexico's coveted energy resources are the last to be privatized under the Free Trade regime. The EZLN had recently proclaimed its solidarity with the Mexican Electrical Workers Syndicate (SME), a dissident current which had just broken from the PRI labor apparatus to oppose privatization of the grid.[34]

The re-escalation also unfolded against the backdrop of the 2000 presidential elections—the first in which the long-ruling PRI was to hold a primary.[35] Chiapas had cost the PRI much legitimacy since the EZLN first took up arms in 1994. Analysts across the Mexican spectrum acknowledged that the rebellion in this marginal state had been critical in the nation's tentative democratic opening.

On September 12, Jacinto Arias Cruz, former ruling-party municipal president of Chenalhó in the Chiapas Highlands, was sentenced to thirty-five years in prison for his role in the massacre of dozens of unarmed fellow Tzotzils at the hamlet of Acteal. The killers, organized in a paramilitary group called Red Mask, gunned down twenty-one women, fifteen children and nine men on December 22, 1997, targeted because they were Zapatista sympathizers. All together, 102 people— including twelve police officers and a soldier—had been arrested. In December 1998, a police officer was convicted of providing guns to the killers and sentenced to nearly four years in prison. The conviction of Arias Cruz brought the number imprisoned in the incident to fifty-five. But with appeals still wending through the corrupt justice system, it was uncertain how much of their terms they would serve.[36]

Earlier in the year, Zapatista representatives, masked but unarmed, had traveled throughout Mexico, holding local *encuentros* with grassroots supporters in all thirty-one states on the issues of indigenous and municipal autonomy. In March, they had met with Chicano supporters across the fence separating Tijuana from San Diego, draping it with their red-starred rebel flag as the US Border Patrol looked on.[37] They had even met with a group of wealthy industrialists in the Federal District, urging them to pressure the government to accept the San Andrés Accords.[38]

A small publishing house in Texas actually secured a $7,500 grant from the US National Endowment for the Arts to publish a bilingual book for children authored by Subcommander Marcos, *The Story of Colors: A Folktale from the Jungles of Chiapas*— Maya creation myth retold as an allegory of multiculturalism. The NEA withdrew the grant when they realized who the author was, but the controversy only prompted private foundations to step in with double the sum![39] The book was printed—with an erratum disavowing acknowledgements to the NEA.[40]

The Mexican government had been forced to accept these humiliations.

But, simultaneously, the grisly human rights situation in Chiapas and elsewhere in the Mexican south prompted the United Nations to send a special rapporteur, Pakistani magistrate Asma Jahangir—who soon found herself isolated by both sides. The Mexican government accused her of going beyond the limits of her inquiry when she called for decentralizing power from the one-party state and international monitors for 2000 elections. The Zapatistas, in turn, refused to meet with her, asserting that the UN "has lost all credibility and legitimacy" with the NATO bombing of Yugoslavia.[41]

Two of the presidential hopefuls, the PRI's Roberto Madrazo (governor of oil-rich Tabasco) and Vicente Fox of the right-opposition National Action Party (governor of Guanajuato and a former Coca-Cola executive) were said to favor privatization of Mexico's oil resources (although they openly maintained the opposite). Most vociferously opposed was Cuauhtémoc Cárdenas of the left-opposition Party of the Democratic Revolution (PRD), whose victory had been fraudulently stolen in 1988 by (the now-exiled) Carlos Salinas. President Zedillo's purported favorite, Francisco Labastida, was a former federal Gobernación Secretary who had been appointed with the implicit mission of pacifying Chiapas.[42]

With the November 7 primary, the president's favorite won the nomination (just like in the bad old days before such extravagances as primaries). To help gain this victory, Labastida contracted the services of Stanley Greenberg, campaign consultant to Bill Clinton, Tony Blair, Gerhard Schroeder, Ehud Barak and Nelson Mandela.[43]

The primary took place in an atmosphere of escalating crisis. Weeks before, devastating floods—the latest and most deadly in a wave of alternating droughts and deluges in recent years—had claimed hundreds of lives and left thousands homeless throughout Southern and Central Mexico. In Chiapas and Tabasco, the Rio Grijalva exploded its banks, engulfing villages, towns and cities.[44]

The weeks before the primary also saw Federal District riot police attack a protest by striking UNAM students. The Federal District (*DF*) government, controlled by the PRD, had some of the officers arrested and criticized the university and federal government for not negotiating seriously with the students. *DF* Gov. Rosario Robles (who took over from Cuauhtémoc Cárdenas when he became the PRD presidential candidate) chided, "Perhaps one wants to apply the same pattern as in Chiapas, with the prolongation of the conflict."[45] Strike leaders had already been kidnapped and tortured—one by suffocation under a plastic bag. The strikers had forced UNAM's rector to resign, and the government agreed to drop the tuition proposal—but not charges pending against arrested students.[46]

On December 11, hundreds of striking UNAM students marched in support of the Seattle protests against the World Trade Organization. When riot police attacked the march, ninety-eight were arrested and ten wounded—including four police. Windows were broken at the US embassy. Some students faced serious charges.[47]

Immediately after the primary, UN High Commissioner for Human Rights Mary Robinson toured Mexico. Just as she arrived in Chiapas, Gov. Albores was under heavy pressure to step down (thus becoming the third Chiapas governor to resign in disgrace since the six-year term began in 1994) following reports that he threatened the life of the PRI's leader in the state legislature. The legislator, Oscar Alvarado Cook, went into hiding, then reappeared to form an anti-Albores splinter group and called on President Zedillo to fire the governor. Albores supporters walked off the job and blocked highways with trucks from the state fleet.[48]

On November 3, upon reaching the customary retirement age of 75, Bishop Samuel Ruiz, who for generations had been the relentless advocate and beloved "grandfather" of the Chiapas Maya, had submitted his resignation to the Vatican. He would remain at his post only until the succession was settled. On December 30, the Vatican abruptly announced that Don Samuel's presumed sucessor, Bishop Coadjutor Raul Vera, was being transferred to Saltillo, far away at the other end of Mexico in Coahuila. This sparked local protests and suspicion in the press that the "dark hand" of the government was behind the move. Mexico's new papal nuncio Justo Mullor insisted the decision was "purely ecclesiastical."[49] But the veto of Vera's ascendance to the Diocese was said to have been arranged by Mullor's long-reigning predecessor, Girolamo Prigione, whose personal mission had been to purge the Mexican church of "Marxist influences." He had succeeded in rotating the progressive Bishop Sergio Mendez Arceo out of the Diocese of Cuernavaca in Morelos state in 1983, and unseating Ruiz was his unfulfilled ambition.[50]

As was by now a tradition, the year ended—and the anniversary of the 1994 Zapatista uprising approached—on a note of paranoia. Army and state police troops flooded into the Lacandon Selva, with the Chiapas government warning that the EZLN was planning new acts of violence.[51] Federal Chiapas pointman Emilio Rabasa took the opportunity to taunt Marcos as "an anachronistic idealist who must realize the country has changed."[52]

The government also announced that hundreds of Maya settlers living within the borders of the Montes Azules reserve would be evicted—in the name of protecting biodiversity, of course.[53] The government had recently entered into "bioprospecting" deals with the University of Georgia and the California-based Diversa firm, granting them the right to scour Mexico's biosphere reserves and natural areas for potentially profitable genetic resources—with no return to local indigenous communities. The Chiapas Council of Traditional Indigenous Healers and Midwives called on the jungle communities not to cooperate with the researchers.[54]

Surreal spectacles were in the news as Mexico rolled over into the year 2000. Carlos Salinas briefly returned from exile to visit his imprisoned brother Raul, and vacation at Acapulco. His arrival at the Pacific resort city coincided with a 5.9-magnitude earthquake, which caused little damage but provided much fodder for radio talk shows.[55]

At the eleventh hour, the National Institute of Anthropology and History forced a promoter to abandon plans for a millennium rock concert at the ancient ruined city of Teotihuacan just outside the Federal District. The promoter, "Rockotitlan," had already started bulldozing areas within the ruins to facilitate the mega-event.[56]

Back at Amador Hernández, where the army still maintained a heavily fortified post, the Tzeltal jungle settlers again resorted to political theater to lampoon the hyped threat of Zapatista violence. Calling themselves the Zapatista Air Force, the Indians pelted the troops with dozens of paper airplanes. On each one was a message to the young conscripts:

Soldiers, we know that poverty has made you sell your lives and souls. I also am poor, as are millions. But you are worse off, for defending our exploiter—Zedillo and his group of moneybags.[57]

PART I

THE LEGACY OF RESISTANCE

1

FIVE HUNDRED YEARS OF
MAYA REBELLION

From Syncretism to the New Zapatismo

"*¡Tierra y Libertad!*" With this war cry an army of Indians marched out of the jungles in the south of the Republic, in order to overthrow the dictator and secure land and freedom for themselves.[1]

So opens *General from the Jungle*, a 1939 novel by B. Traven, the pseudonymous German anarchist mysteriously exiled in Mexico.[2]

An army of Maya peasants, previously unknown to the outside world, erupts from Mexico's remote southern rainforest under the leadership of an enigmatic and charismatic commander: on the morning of January 1, 1994, the day the North American Free Trade Agreement took effect, exactly this happened.

The Indians in Traven's novel, isolated in the jungle, didn't know that the Revolution was already over and the dictator overthrown; the peasant army which emerged from that jungle in 1994 claims that the Revolution has been betrayed and dictatorship restored. The demands are identical: "*¡Tierra y Libertad!*"

Whatever, in their miserable oppression and their pitiful ignorance, they sensed of poetry, of a desire for beauty, of love for mankind and living creatures, of natural faith in some absolute justice that must be found somewhere, as well as deeply felt sorrow for their comrades who had been horribly murdered or bestially tortured to death—all this, and much more that, unknown to them, slumbered within them, found its expression in that single war cry.[3]

This cry is raised anew by the Zapatista Army of National Liberation—their footsoldiers drawn from Mexico's most desperately impoverished Indians; their eloquent spokesman the urbane, mysterious Subcommander Marcos. Their cry comes like an echo from a near-forgotten past, from the twentieth century's first great revolution, the revolution before the Cold War, before Stalin, Lenin and Bolshevism—the revolution of the Mexican Robin Hood, Pancho Villa; of the anarchist, Flores Magón; of the incorruptible peasant insurrectionist, Emiliano Zapata.

The Zapatistas issued their *grito* against not only the dictatorship, but also the North American Free Trade Agreement.[4] The simultaneous treaty and uprising have sparked revolutionary struggle across southern Mexico, with indigenous peoples in the forefront. The unarmed popular movements which mobilized throughout Mexico, but especially the south, picking up the Zapatista war cry, are what really give strength and meaning to the Maya army in the rainforest.

The cultural matrix from which the new *zapatismo* emerged is a centuries-old tradition of Maya resistance to the Conquest. With a resilience that almost defies imagination, the myth of the returning Indian King remained a spiritual wellspring of resistance to domination, genocide and cultural erosion. Under the colonialists, the *caudillos* who followed them, and the new technocrats of the ruling party-state, the Maya have been the most rebellious of Mesoamerica's conquered peoples.

With the new *zapatismo*, this tradition of rebellion was wedded to a conscious revolutionary analysis. But the centrality of indigenous identity is at the heart of the new Zapatista radical democracy ethic. The first Latin American guerilla movement to emerge after the supposed death of socialism is also the first with real Indian leadership, to whom Marcos is officially subordinate. *Neo-zapatismo* is something new precisely because it is rooted in something ancient.

THE INCOMPLETE CONQUEST

Small, rooted economies based on communal *maíz* cultivation, and common mythological threads, defined Mesoamerican civilization before the Conquest. The Maya of Chiapas, Guatemala, and the Yucatan Peninsula are considered the "sister culture" of this civilization. Even during their periods of building elaborate ceremonial centers, power among the Maya was decentralized, with no city-state achieving total dominance.[5]

Meanwhile, the Nahuatl-speaking "father culture" in Central Mexico to the north and west witnessed a cycle of rising and falling empires, power and dominion expanding with each resurrection: the early Nahuas at Teotihuacan, the Toltecs at Tula, finally the Aztecs at Tenochtitlan, whose Mexica empire gave the contemporary country its name. Between the imperial eras, waves of Chichimecs—"dog people," nomadic hunter-gatherers—swept down from the deserts of the north to conquer, to establish the new dynasty, and to be absorbed by the persistent, tenacious culture of the conquered.[6]

Throughout Mesoamerica—a cultural sphere extending from the Central Mexican plateau down the Central American isthmus—the basic and oldest unit of government was the *calpulli*. At Tenochtitlan, in Central Mexico's lacustrine Valley of Anahuac, the *calpullis* were elite military orders from which the Aztec nobility and *tlatoani*—the elective Mexica emperor—were drawn. But at the regional, older level, the *calpulli* was a piece of land where local kinship groups communally worked their *maíz* plots, or *milpas*.[7]

Writes one geographer:

> To the Indian, private and individual ownership of land was as meaningless as private ownership of the sky, the weather or the sea . . . Each family of a clan group that shared the *calpulli* had a right to use part of it under conditions laid down by the local chief, the *calpullec*. No one had the right to cultivate a particular piece of land in perpetuity, and indeed the migratory nature of *milpa* farming discouraged this. The individual family was periodically alloted a plot within the area of land that a village regarded as for its own use. To this extent, there was a sense of possession of land, but only as far as the use of the land was concerned.[8]

Lying beyond the Mexica dominion, the *calpullis* of the Maya lands were not subject to payments of tribute to Tenochtitlan. They maintained their autonomy, even as they accepted Nahuatl myths and were eyed for eventual incorporation into the empire.[9] In Maya cosmology, as related in the Popul Vuh, the sacred book of the Quiché people of the Guatemalan highlands, the creator god, Gucumatz, fashioned the first humans from *maíz*.[10]

The local indigenous cultures corresponded to the bioregions of what is today Chiapas. In the southwest, the richly fertile Pacific coastal plain of Sosconosco was home of Zoques and Nahuatl-related peoples, as well as some Mams and Cakchiquels, Maya groups more numerous in Guatemala to the east. Rising to the northeast, the sparsely inhabited Sierra Madre was cloaked in lush cloud forest, forming the headwaters of tributaries that snaked down into the broad, fertile Central Valley of Chiapas, defined by the Rio Grijalva and inhabited by the Chiapaneco Indians. Continuing north and east, the alpine Highlands rise from the Grijalva plain: the Maya heart of Chiapas, inhabited by Tzotzil, Tzeltal and Tojolabal peoples. In the north, homeland of the Chol Maya, the Highlands slope toward the coastal plain along the Gulf of Mexico, home of the Chontal Maya (and the contemporary state of Tabasco). In the east, the Highlands slope down to the lowland rainforest known as the Lacandon Selva.[11]

Defined by the Rio Usumacinta basin, the Lacandon Selva is contiguous with the Peteñ rainforest of Guatemala, and was the seat of the Classic Maya civilization, which flourished from roughly 300 to 900 CE. The ceremonial cities of Yaxchilan, Palenque and Bonampak (and Tikal and Uaxactun across the Usumacinta in El Peteñ) were giant calendars, each stone temple and pyramid aligned precisely with the movements of the heavenly bodies whose cycles dictated sowing and harvest, peace and ritualized war. This civilization had fallen five centuries before the arrival of the Spanish. The inheritors of the subsequently sparsely inhabited Selva were hunter-gatherer bands known as the Lacandon Maya, who would successfully resist "conquest" well into the twentieth century. The ruins of the Classic Maya cities are still sacred to the Lacandons, who gather at them in annual pilgrimages. At Palenque, built by the king Pacal around 300 CE, on the northern edge of the rainforest, the Lacandon pilgrims today merge with international tourists. The equally majestic Yaxchilan remains even now inaccessible by road, deep in the great forest on the banks of the Usumacinta. The river is now the Guatemalan border.[12]

The decline of the Classic Maya was followed by the incursion of Toltec-related peoples into Maya realms, bringing Nahuatl, the *lingua franca* of Mesoamerica, and the myth of Quetzalcoatl, the Feathered Serpent.[13] The serpent was already a Maya symbol of fertility, sacrifice and kingship.[14]

Incursions of more militaristic peoples have been blamed, but intensive agriculture pushing the rainforest past its ecological limits may have been decisive in the Classic Maya decline. A hybrid Maya–Toltec ("Late Maya") civilization subsequently flourished in the savannas of the Yucatan Peninsula to the north, at Chichen Itza, Uxmal and Mayapan.[15]

In Chiapas, power shifted to the Highlands, where it lay with local *calpullis* rather than city-states. While the lineage of the Toltec god-king Quetzalcoatl was the Mexica empire's claim to sovereignty, and the Feathered Serpent entered the Maya pantheon (the Quiché Gucumatz), local Maya rule was linked to the kingship deity Votan.[16]

The Highland Maya from the first refused to recognize the conquistadors, who told them that their sovereign was now Carlos V, the Holy Roman Emperor in Castille. These new lords of the land imposed a feudal order, but could never quench the cycles of Maya rebellion.

The Maya realms were subjugated only after Hernándo Cortéz had conquered the Mexica empire in Anahuac, in 1521. The year he landed at Veracruz, 1519, was the year the Toltec Quetzalcoatl was prophesied to return in the Mexica calendar, signaling an end to the Aztec dynasty.[17] Unwittingly aided by the prophecy and skillfully building alliances with subjugated city-states ripe for rebellion, Cortéz simply beheaded the Mexica empire and established the Viceroyalty of New Spain in its place. The Viceroyalty's capital, Mexico City, was built on the ruins of Tenochtitlan. The Aztec island-city's great pyramid-bounded ceremonial space (where obsidian blades had thrust into numberless sacrificial victims) became Mexico City's *zócalo*, or central square, bounded by the National Palace and Cathedral. Those areas which had been beyond Mexica dominion were only tenuously brought under the Spanish heel. In these marginal areas, the Conquest and conversion of the Indians was never really complete. More so than the *mestizos* (those of mixed Spanish-Indian blood) and *ladinos* (those of Spanish culture) of the more central areas, Maya peoples remained suspended between Christianity and indigenous cosmology.[18]

The first contact came in 1522, when tax-collectors were dispatched by Cortéz to the region. They had to be followed by military units to "pacify rebellion"— exacting tribute from those communities which had refused.[19]

After pacifying the Chiapanecos at Tuxtla, Capt. Luis Marín met fierce resistance from the Tzotzil—the tough "bat people" of the highest part of the Highlands—at Chamula. Marín enlisted the aid of a neighboring Tzotzil town, Zinacantan, which had been Mexica-allied, in a siege. Chamula fell after three days, and was renamed San Juan. Just as the Spanish had allied themselves with groups opposed to the Mexica in order to defeat the empire, they now sought the aid of groups allied with the Mexica to expand the empire under their own rule.[20]

However, Marín failed to establish settlements, considering the job done after he had exacted tribute. Consequently, Cortéz had to send *another* military expedition to Chiapas next time. The Chiapas Highlands were truly conquered in 1526 by Capt. Diego de Mazariegos, who established Ciudad Real in the Valley of Jovel, below San Juan Chamula and Zinacantan.[21]

The Lacandon Selva remained wild—which is what *lacandon* means in archaic Spanish. Capt. Pedro de Solórzano was assigned the farcical task of "pacifying the Lacandon rebellion." When attacked, the Lacandons simply fled into the dense jungle. Spanish troops, with their horses, armor and cannons, were helpless to pursue.[22]

The situation was complicated by the fact that separate conquistadors had been assigned to subdue Chiapas, Yucatan and Guatemala—and each claimed the Lacandon as their own turf.[23]

In the Guatemalan Highlands, Pedro de Alvarado used the Mexica-allied Cakchiquels to help subdue their local rivals, the Quiché—and then subdued them both.[24]

By the time the conquistador Francisco de Montejo arrived in the Yucatan in 1527, the city-states such as Chichen Itza had also long since given way to a localized village society. In a book transcribed from oral tradition after the Conquest it was written that Chilam Balam, a Maya prophet in the Yucatan, had foretold that strangers would arrive from the east with new gods.[25]

Demoralized to find a region devoid of gold, or even slaves (most of the Maya had already succumbed to Spanish-introduced smallpox), Montejo departed to conquer Honduras, leaving his son Montejo the Younger to subdue Yucatan. But the Yucatecan Maya began to recover, and the young conquistador had forty years of war before him. Montejo the Younger and his priests blamed the revolt on Maya shamans; it is possible that Chilam Balam was a leader of the Yucatecan resistance.[26]

In the 1550s, as Spanish control of the peninsula was finally established, the zealous Franciscan Bishop Diego de Landa led his own Inquisition of Yucatan against "relapses into idolatry." All surviving religious texts in the ancient Maya glyphs were put to the torch.[27]

Iberian feudal society was replicated in the Chiapas Highlands—Indians as serfs under an oligarchy of *criollos*, locally born Spaniards. Cattle ranches in the Highlands and Grijalva Valley consumed Indian lands. Under the *encomienda*, the Crown's right to tribute was transferred to an individual, granting the new lords unlimited slave labor; in Sosconosco, Indians were worked to death on the cochineal plantations. It was only a full century after the Conquest that the Indian population began to recover from the dramatic demographic plunge resulting from disease, hunger and outright slaughter.[28]

The role of the Church in the Conquest was dual and contradictory. The Church was the self-appointed protector of the Indians from the abuses of conquistadors-turned-administrators and soldiers-turned-landowners. The Dominican Bartolemé de Las Casas, after witnessing the conquest of Cuba, became the unrelenting enemy of the conquistadors. In one sermon he denounced "everything we have done to the Indians so far" as "tyranny and barbarism." The Conquest itself was "against all natural law and the Law of Nations, as well as against all divine law . . . and consequently, null, void, and without any validity or legal effect." In 1519 he journeyed to Spain to plead for abolition of Indian slavery before Carlos V. After the conquest of Mexico, he wrote *The Devastation of the Indies: A Brief Account*, decrying that "kingdoms as large and more felicitous than Spain" had been destroyed and depopulated "by the sword, by fire, and enslavement."[29]

In the 1530s, Las Casas came to the Kingdom of Guatemala—really a Spanish viceroyalty, then including Chiapas—to demonstrate his belief that the Indians could be converted peacefully. He returned lands which had been usurped, and had his missionaries learn the Maya tongues. In 1542 he persuaded the Crown to pass the New Laws of the Indies, reforming the *encomienda* and abolishing Indian slavery. The New Laws were met with bitter resistance by the conquistadors, and were repealed after two years. Las Casas already faced death threats, treason charges and a denunciation before the Inquisition for sermons in which he urged soldiers to desert rather than participate in atrocities. Nonetheless, his efforts in Guatemala were so successful that in 1544 he was named Bishop of Chiapas, a position administrated from Ciudad Real.[30]

After Las Casas was forced to flee for his life back to Spain in 1547, his work was rapidly reversed. Blood-drenched campaigns against rebelling Maya followed the re-seizure of land by *criollos* in the Guatemalan Highland region Las Casas had christened Verapaz—"true peace." The official abolition of Indian slavery did little to alter the actual condition of the Indians, as debt labor and feudalism became entrenched. Additionally, the New Laws instated a policy of *reducciones*—"reducing" Indian lands by centralizing the Indians in hamlets clustered around churches. The oligarchs quickly appropriated the lands which had been "reduced."[31]

The lands ringing the hamlets remained in Indian hands, and became known as *ejidos*—"exits," because they lay on the way out of the villages. The *ejido*, adhering to a village rather than an individual, became the surviving remnant of the communal *calpulli*.[32] It persisted, protecting a degree of village autonomy, in opposition to the oligarchic system of the *encomienda*, and its successors: the *repartimiento*, in which the Indians were ostensibly paid for their labor, but lived and died working off their debt, and the *latifundio*, in which the Indians were supposedly free from obligatory labor, but lived in much the same condition.[33] The municipal powers of the Highland villages also gave them a legal autonomy recognized by Spanish tradition, if eroded by economic and political realities.[34]

The Church was central to the establishment of *criollo* Ciudad Real as the center of feudal power in the Chiapas Highlands, with outlying Indian villages such as San Juan Chamula and Zinacantan reduced to impoverished satellites. The new oligarchs co-opted the traditional system of village government into an instrument of control. Under tutelage of the reactionary Catholic hierarchy which consolidated following the flight of Las Casas, the villages established *cofradías*, religious brotherhoods responsible for collecting tribute and distributing sacraments. The families of the *cofradías* were afforded local control. The *calpullecs* became the *caciques*, the village patriarchs.[35]

The *caciques* were rewarded with land: *ejidos* became their fiefs, producing food for Ciudad Real, delivered in the form of Church tithings. As land grew scarcer, the Indians could afford these tithings ever less. By the eighteenth century, Indian pauperization and ecological degradation escalated as ever more *ejidal* land came under control of the oligarchy's cattle ranches. As cattle grazed in the fertile valleys, Maya *milpas* were forced onto the rocky mountainsides, displacing the forests. The soil eroded, gullies opened, and streams dried up.[36]

Throughout Maya lands, the clergy encouraged the preservation of indigenous lore such as the Popul Vuh and Book of Chilam Balam while playing a paradoxically indispensable role in the ethnocidal suppression of indigenous culture. Just as the conquistadors achieved a transfer of power by adapting the very political mechanisms of the Mexica empire, so the priests achieved a conversion to Christianity by exploiting the parallels to Christian symbology in the Indian traditions.

The divinely conceived Toltec prince of peace and self-sacrificing savior, Quetzalcoatl took his name from the Nahuatl creation deity who gave life to the first humans by drawing blood from his genitals. Mysteriously resurrected as Venus, the morning star of the east, the wise god-king had been overthrown by a corrupt priestly class after he abolished the cult of human sacrifice, and departed across the eastern sea with a promise to return and restore justice.[37] After the Conquest, devotion to the Feathered Serpent was transferred to the new *salvador*.[38] The Virgin of Guadalupe also became a new focus of ancient devotions, her chapels appearing where shrines to the Nahuatl earth goddess Tonantzin or the Maya moon goddess Ixchel had been.[39]

The Maya Tree of Life, the *maíz* stalk, icon of regeneration, was stylized as a cross. On the sarcophagus lid excavated from the pyramid at Palenque, it springs from the chest of Pacal in his death throes. After the Conquest, crosses appeared on Highland crags and grottos which had been sacred for centuries. Throughout Mesoamerica, churches were built on the foundations of demolished pyramids, with the very same stones.[40]

For the Maya, the masks of Christ and the Virgin were thin. For centuries the Maya region would periodically explode into rebellion—becoming the most troublesome area in the Spanish Empire, and the states that would emerge from it. The myth of the Maya king, mysteriously resurrected to restore Indian sovereignty, continued to re-emerge in the new syncretistic nomenclature of Maya "folk Catholicism."

INDIAN REVOLT AS RELIGIOUS WAR

These movements began as purely religious. Homespun cults would center around visions or miracles attributed to local icons, in open rejection of the Church of the

Spanish. Worship of idols with Indian names was reported in Chiapas as late as the 1680s; loosening of Church control over the Indians was a direct threat to the feudal system. When the Church declared the cults heresy, warfare ensued—transforming them into messianic movements to drive the Spanish from Maya lands completely.[41]

In 1708, a *ladino* hermit preaching from the trunk of a hollow oak tree near Zinacantan claimed that the Virgin was descending from Heaven to help the Indians. Large crowds of Indians from Zinacantan and Chamula gathered at the tree, bringing offerings of food and *copal* incense.[42]

In 1711, a Virgin Cult of Santa Marta emerged in a Chamula hamlet. The Virgin appeared in human form to the Santa Marta Tzotzils, wrapped in a cloak. She was brought to a chapel which was built for her; when the cloak was removed, she had been "replaced" with a wooden image. The image was carried to Chamula and other towns and worshipped before Spanish authorities confiscated it. Later that year in nearby Chenalhó, authorities burned down a chapel the Tzotzils built for saint images which had purportedly sweated and emitted rays of light.[13]

The first such movement to escalate to war was the Virgin Cult of Cancuc, a Tzeltal village north of Ciudad Real. In 1712, the Virgin appeared to a girl of San Juan Cancuc and instructed her to build a chapel in her honor. As construction commenced, the local priest ordered participating Indians flogged, accusing them of "consorting with the Devil." Indians resisted, and the priest fled for his life. Cancuc renounced Spanish priests and established an Indian priesthood. Declarations were sent to surrounding villages, claiming the authority of the Virgin and, according to some sources, the antepenultimate Mexica *tlatoani*, Moctezuma.[44]

This was the start of the Tzeltal Revolt of 1712. Participating villages sent representatives to Cancuc to be ordained in the new Indian priesthood. The cultists renamed Cancuc "Ciudad Real" (the seat of local political power), Ciudad Real "Jerusalem" (seat of the false priesthood), and the Spaniards "Jews" (the false priests).[45]

This was one of history's more amazing examples of anti-Semitism without Jews. The Holy Office of the Inquisition, executing the sadistic crusades against Muslims, Jews and heretics in Spain, had simultaneously held campaigns in New Spain— pursued more vigorously by the Franciscans in Central Mexico and Yucatan than by the Dominicans in Chiapas and Guatemala—against Indians clinging to pre-Christian traditions.[46] But the Spanish lexicon persisted among even rebel Indians for centuries; the word "Jew" conveyed evil for Maya who had never seen one.

Claiming that "the road to heaven is closed to Jews" (Spaniards), the Soldiers of the Virgin marched against villages that had disobeyed the summons from Cancuc, now rich with offerings and loot. A *ladino* army raised by Ciudad Real marched on

Cancuc—and was defeated by Indians armed with machetes and clubs. In retaliation, the Soldiers of the Virgin marched on Ocosingo and slaughtered the Spanish inhabitants—except the women, who were abducted to Cancuc and married to Indian men (in reversal of the double standard). Captured *ladinas* were forced to dress as Indian women, to grind *maíz* and make *tortillas*.[47]

The Tzotzil at Zinacantan took the opportunity to stage an uprising of their own. Ciudad Real sent for reinforcements from Guatemala. Before the revolt could spread to the Tzotzils, it was put down. San Juan Cancuc's municipal powers were dissolved, not to be officially restored until the late twentieth century.[48]

After the Virgin cults came the Indian Kings. The Indian King of Quisteil appeared in 1761 in Yucatan. A Maya named Jacinto Canek claimed the crown and mantle of the town's patron saint image, declared himself king and raised a peasant army to re-establish a "Maya Kingdom." There was a year of fighting before the movement was crushed.[49]

The revolts were part of the dynamic propelling the region toward independence. In 1701, the Habsburg dynasty was replaced by the liberal Bourbons, who instated Free Trade acts under the reign of Carlos III (1759–88). For the first time, the elites of New Spain and Guatemala could trade with other parts of the empire. A merchant class took hold in the cities, while Indian lands came under still greater pressure in the countryside.[50]

It was at the margins of New Spain, where indigenous autonomy held its strongest claim, that Indian unrest presaged the anti-colonial struggle. At the other end of Mexico, Yaqui resistance brought war to remote, arid Sonora. The Yaqui, who had been completely outside Mexica control, revolted in 1740 in response to the Bourbon efforts to break up their communal lands in the name of Liberal reform.[51]

In 1820, when Guatemala's elites began agitating for independence, a Quiché in the village of Totonicapan donned a crown and declared himself the Indian King, setting off a local crisis.[52]

The following September, Mexico won independence and Guatemala—including Chiapas and all Central America—declared its own independence the following day. Conditions only deteriorated for the Indians, with the Crown's strictures against the most blatant abuses removed.[53]

In Sonora, the Yaquis revolted again under the chieftain Banderas, declaring their *own* independence from the independent Mexico. The Banderas rebellion, joined by the neighboring Mayos, lasted well into the 1830s.[54] More such unrest would soon follow in the Maya south.

The Chiapas oligarchy elected to secede from Guatemala and join the self-proclaimed (and short-lived) Empire of Mexico with Independence, fearing the

Liberal tendencies of the Central American independence leadership. Concentration of Chiapas Maya land in oligarchic hands intensified.[55] Some one hundred *ladino* families claimed virtually all Indian lands not actually within village centers. Families already working those lands suddenly found themselves subject to monthly tributes of crops or labor to their new landlords.[56]

THE CASTE WAR OF YUCATAN

In the Yucatan, the *ladino* power structure was more Liberal, the bourgeois stronghold of Merida a center of regional commerce, growing impatient with the Conservative regime in Mexico City. The Liberals, with their ethic of industry and progress, were in general even worse from the perspective of the Indians: while the Church sometimes made paternalistic efforts to protect Indians from the worst abuses, commercial interests saw them as near slaves to exploit at will.[57]

In the Yucatan, business meant sugar. After Independence, when Mexico lost Spanish Cuba as a source, the "sugar frontier" expanded south into the savannas of the peninsula's "wild" Indian interior. In the north, the Maya were reduced to debt labor; in the interior, they remained autonomous, practicing slash-and-burn rotation agriculture in the tropical plains and dry forests. Tensions grew as sugar plantations penetrated the domain of these undomesticated Indians.[58]

In 1847, when the Conservative Dictator Santa Anna went to war with the United States over Texas, Yucatan's Liberals declared independence. An Indian army was conscripted, Maya cooperation bought with promises of land reform and abolition of debt labor, church dues and the *aguardiente* tax. But after providing the Indians with arms and military training, the Merida *ladinos* balked on their promises. Maya troops rioted in Valladolid, Yucatan's second city. Yucatan's governor executed the leaders, thereby sparking what was feared—a general Maya revolt.[59]

Wealthy *ladino* homes, shops, plantations and government offices were sacked. Early in 1848, Valladolid was evacuated as Maya troops besieged the city. Governor Miguel Barbachano met with Maya leader Jacinto Pat and agreed to his demands, appointing him Grand Cacique of all Yucatan's Indians. It was hoped the rebellion's other leader, Cecilio Chi, would respond by attacking Pat. Instead, he escalated his attacks on *ladino* targets.[60]

The peace accord was forgotten. Separatist and loyalist *ladinos*, recently embarking on a civil war, united to fight the common enemy of "civilization and religion." With the separatist revolt called off, the US Navy, theretofore defending the Yucatan coast from Mexico, started blockading Yucatan's ports.[61]

In the spring of 1848, the Maya army was advancing on Merida. An evacuation of the city was being prepared when the Maya suddenly halted their drive. The halt corresponded with the beginning of *maíz* planting season, and many Maya troops apparently returned to their villages to sow the ground. Maya leaders were probably also aware that large shipments of arms had arrived from Havana, Veracruz and New Orleans. The summer of 1848 was the turning point in the Caste War of Yucatan, and saw the deaths of both Pat and Chi.[62]

THE CRUZOB WAR

In the aftermath, *ladino* troops forcibly relocated much of the Maya south, deeper into the Yucatecan interior. Uprooted from their *maíz* plots, many died of starvation. In an effort to depopulate the region, Yucatan reinstated Indian slavery, officially outlawed for centuries, selling war captives to Cuba. Mexican and Spanish authorities turned a blind eye.[63]

In 1850, the defeated Maya sought sustenance in a cult of the "talking cross," which emerged at a remote refugee settlement called Chan Santa Cruz. A new war for control of the settlement ensued as word of the cult reached the *ladinos* and they resolved to crush it.[64]

Cholera became a weapon of the war. The *ladinos* and Indian cultists, referring to each other in hateful derision as "Jews," each did what Europe's gentiles had accused Jews of doing during the Black Death—poisoning wells.[65] The *ladinos* wrested control of Chan Santa Cruz in 1854, but the Maya succeeded in re-taking the settlement the following year. War continued.[66]

The cultists called themselves the "Cruzob"—the Spanish word for cross with the Maya plural suffix. Chan Santa Cruz (Maya for "small" and Spanish for "sacred cross") was also the site of a *cenote*, one of the open wells which dot the Yucatan karst. *Cenotes* had been sacred before the Conquest, and determined the location of such ceremonial cities as Chichen Itza.[67]

With the fall of Santa Anna in 1855, Merida and Mexico City reached accommodations. But military pressure on the Cruzob was relieved as Merida's troops put down a new separatist revolt in the poorer Yucatan region of Campeche. Cruzob power grew. The Balam Na (House of God) was built for the talking cross. By 1858, when Campeche was separated from Yucatan, the Cruzob were launching raids on *ladino* towns.[68]

In the 1860s, as the French puppet Emperor Maximilian seized Mexico and civil war erupted again, the Cruzob became a political pawn. Maximilian won the support of Merida by offering to re-attach Campeche to Yucatan. In return, Merida would aid the French in annexing Belize, the British colony to the south.[69] British gun-runners armed the Cruzob. Confused fighting spread throughout the peninsula.[70]

As Republican guerillas took Merida, Cruzob attacks escalated. Chan Santa Cruz became a warrior mini-state. The talking cross had its own priesthood (one Cruzob village, Santa Cah Tulum, had a priestess, a rare exception to Maya practice), which dictated when the miraculous cross had spoken a command for a raid. Neighboring Maya groups, armed by Merida, waged war on the Cruzob. *Ladino* "generals" offered the warring Maya groups professional military command, playing for power in whatever new order would emerge in the peninsula.[71]

British gun-runners continued to arm the Cruzob even after the fall of Maximilian in 1867, as a means of assuring that their aggression would be directed north, not south. By 1900, the long dictatorship of Gen. Porfirio Díaz had ended the warfare among the Yucatan *ladinos*, but failed to subdue the Indians in the interior. Escaped black slaves and Chinese coolies from Belize fled to the Cruzob; elements of Yoruba and other African traditions were influencing the Maya cult.[72]

Prosperity returned to Yucatan; the henequen industry throve, with the US firm International Harvester maintaining a monopolistic control over the market in this cactus fiber. The Díaz years also saw a resurgence of slavery in the Yucatan —in the form of forced labor as punishment for rebellion.[73]

The contradiction between the Yucatan's *ladino* coast and Maya interior intensified. When the Cruzob attempted to resist the building of a railroad across the Yucatan, Díaz prepared the Mexican military for a final offensive against Chan Santa Cruz. Gen. Ignacio Bravo launched a campaign of deforestation, depriving the Cruzob of the element they had successfully fought in for fifty years. Chan Santa Cruz fell, and was renamed Santa Cruz de Bravo. Decimated by casualties, epidemics and starvation, the Cruzob fled deeper into the interior. Bravo had the Federal Territory of Quintana Roo established in their former stronghold.[74]

The Mexican Revolution brought some relief, but its full impacts would not be felt in the Yucatan for a generation. In 1912, Bravo was recalled to Mexico City by the revolutionary government of Francisco Madero. The new governor of Quintana Roo made peace with the Maya, returning Chan Santa Cruz to them. The Cruzob destroyed the railroad and telegraph lines which had been built through their territory, but abandoned Chan Santa Cruz, deeming it beyond purification—Bravo had used the Balam Na as a stable. The cult survived—when the Cruzob had fled before Bravo's army, they took the cross with them and carried it from place to place in the wilderness.[75]

The 1915 invasion of Yucatan by Gen. Salvador Alvarado's Constitutionalist Army of the Southeast, representing the new revolutionary regime of Venustiano Carranza, finally put an end to outright slavery. But even a radical state regime under the Socialist Party of the Southeast (PSS) in the 1920s could not effectively challenge the planter elite. Gov. Felipe Carrillo Puerto, an agrarian populist who had fought in Emiliano Zapata's peasant army in Morelos, began expropriating land in his native Yucatan and empowering Maya "leagues of resistance" to stand up to the landlords. In 1923, a local army mutiny—supported by the planter elite and counter-revolutionaries who had seized power in Campeche—deposed Carrillo. He was assassinated while trying to escape to Cuba.[76]

Meaningful redistribution of land only came to Yucatan in the 1930s, when President Lázaro Cárdenas made the backward peninsula a showcase for his agrarian reform (and made the PSS an appendage of his one-party state).[77] Conditions improved somewhat for the Maya, and the Cruzob gradually faded. A new agricultural boom—this time chicle, the stuff of chewing gum—provided work for veteran Maya warriors. The Cruzob's *ladino* military leaders moved from leading Indian revolts to growing chicle with Indian labor, and became prosperous.[78]

THE WAR OF SAINT ROSE

The Caste War of Yucatan panicked *ladinos* in Chiapas and Guatemala. Upon independence from Spain, Ciudad Real was renamed San Cristóbal de Las Casas; but the town's spirit bore little resemblance to that of its namesake. San Cristóbal sided with Maximilian against the Liberal Republican insurgency. When the Republicans took power, in 1867, they punished San Cristóbal by relocating the Chiapas capital to the Liberal city of Tuxtla Gutiérrez in the Central Valley. But abuse of the Maya by merchants, landowners and clergy remained rampant, and included periodic slave labor (thinly disguised as "taxation" or "debt-collection").[79]

After Independence, all forests and presently uncultivated Indian land had been appropriated by private *ladino* owners under new laws passed in the name of efficiency and progress. Much of it was cleared for cattle ranches, oblivious to the fact that it was only "unused" because it was in the fallow cycle of rotation agriculture—a vital hiatus for replenishing soil fertility. This blindness to indigenous agricultural patterns again accelerated Maya pauperization. With less land, the Indians were forced to abandon rotation, and the land itself consequently grew poorer. Unable to subsist on depleted plots, the Maya sold themselves into debt labor on the coffee plantations of Sosconosco. Forced there to wear *ladino* clothes and speak Spanish, their culture eroded.[80]

In December of 1867, an Indian girl named Augustína in a Chamula hamlet found three stones that "fell from the sky" while she was tending goats. Indians reported hearing the stones "talk"; offerings of *copal*, flowers and pine needles were brought, and the girl was pronounced "Mother of God." A shrine was erected in Chamula, but removed to the hamlet as Chamula's *ladino* priest interfered. A leader named Cuscat emerged as Indians congregated on the hamlet. Local authorities arrived at the hamlet in the midst of a religious celebration and arrested Augustína.[81]

Cuscat urged the Tzotzils to cease worshipping the white Christ, and choose one of their own to worship as savior. According to local government reports, on Good Friday of 1868, a 10-year-old Tzotzil boy was crucified in the hamlet square. An account written by a San Cristóbal *ladino* twenty years later read: "We do not know what the new Jews did with the body and blood of the martyr of barbarism, although it is not improbable that they drank the latter." Some historians maintain the crucifixion was a fabrication to justify repression. In any event, that year for the first time no Chamulas arrived in San Cristóbal to worship the white Christ image at the Cathedral during Lent.[82]

The Chamulas made elaborate preparations for the Festival of Saint Rose, August 30, with Cuscat as priest and the released Augustína as priestess. During the ceremony, the two were arrested, with several others. But the Liberal governor in Tuxtla ordered Cuscat released on grounds of religious freedom, now a constitutional guarantee. Cuscat had been arrested on charges of "disobedience toward authority and attempted rebellion"—not crucifixion![83]

Newspapers wrote of an imminent "Caste War of Chiapas." An adventuresome *ladino* named Ignacio Galindo arrived from Mexico City to organize the Chamulas. San Cristóbal appealed to the federal government for help and had Cuscat and Augustína arrested yet again. On June 17, 1869, five thousand Tzotzils surrounded San Cristóbal, armed with shotguns, knives, machetes and spears, with Galindo dressed as a Chamula chieftain. Galindo offered himself in exchange for Cuscat and Augustína. The authorities accepted, because reinforcements had not yet arrived.[84]

Galindo was executed. The movement, and Chamula guerilla raids on *ladino* ranches, persisted for another year.[85]

INDIANS AS PAWNS IN REVOLUTION AND REACTION

As Liberals consolidated power in Mexico, the Chiapas oligarchy resisted, remaining loyal to the old order, like the Carlists in post-Napoleonic Spain. The Liberal Díaz dictatorship, with its official cult of economic and "scientific" progress voraciously devouring Indian land throughout Mexico, cut an implicit deal with the Chiapas oligarchy to begin integration of the marginal state into Mexico's economy. Those families which were favored by the Dictatorship—generally in Tuxtla and the Central Valley—became the dominant force in the state.[86]

With the Revolution of 1910, the corruption and brutality of the Dictatorship gave way to explosive violence throughout the country. Indians and *campesinos* rose in rebellion elsewhere in the Mexican south under Emiliano Zapata. The anarchist (and deceptively named) Mexican Liberal Party established a foothold among the Sosconosco coffee pickers, and the Industrial Workers of the World among the railroad workers in Tapachula, the region's main town—much to the horror of the landowners.[87]

In Highland Chiapas, however, Indians were manipulated into serving in the counter-revolutionary forces of the aristocracy. The Maya were organized into militias by the *ladino* oligarchy to fight against Liberal forces and Zapata-inspired insurrections. The *ladinos* effected this manipulation by telling the Maya that the revolutionary forces were anti-God and would take away their religion. If that proved insufficiently persuasive, Indians were press-ganged at gunpoint.[88]

The most powerful group in Chiapas in 1910 was the Rabasa family, representing the Liberal elite in the Grijalva Valley. The Rabasa group was loyal to the Francisco Madero government which first inherited Mexico from the ousted Dictatorship. But the San Cristóbal Diocese appealed to the Maya with promises of land and tax relief to fight the federal and Rabasa forces. The Chamulas fought fiercely under their leader Pajarito, and the Liberal army cut off the ears of captured Indians as a lesson that civilization would prevail. A fragile truce followed a 1911 battle at Chiapa de Corzo. When President Madero was removed in a counter-revolutionary *coup d'état* two years later, the dilemma was temporarily resolved.[89]

War returned in 1914, when the Carrancista forces entered Chiapas. Gen. Jesús Agustín Castro sought to abolish the privileges of the aristocracy and finally subjugate Chiapas to the central government. This time, the Rabasa elite and the Highland elite closed ranks against the invader. The San Cristóbal oligarch Alberto Pineda assumed control of an army of masked rebels called the Mapaches (raccoons), who resisted Castro's forces. The Mapaches threw their allegiance behind Félix Díaz, a nephew of the overthrown dictator then waging a counter-revolutionary insurgency.[90]

The Mapaches waged a reign of terror in the Highlands against any Indians suspected of sympathizing with the revolutionary forces. In Cancuc, they summarily hanged five hundred men, nearly the whole adult male population of the village. The hanged men had their lands taken over by the Mapache officers. Huge landholdings were consolidated in such incidents—many of which remain intact today.[91]

Even as the centralist Carranzistas consolidated power in Mexico City, Chiapas remained quasi-independent. The new federal regime was forced once again to cut a deal with the Chiapas oligarchy. This was consolidated in 1925. President Plutarco Calles had allowed Carlos Vidal of the Chiapaneco Socialist Party, with a base among the Sosconosco farmworkers, to become governor. Within two years he was killed in a general massacre of Socialist leaders in Chiapas. The federal government acquiesced in the *coup* because the Socialists had equivocated on joining with the one-party state Calles was then organizing. Land reform and anti-clerical measures which were imposed elsewhere in Mexico were overlooked in Chiapas. Even Pineda remained an important landholder. Thus, the counter-revolutionary Cristero revolt, which shook rural Mexico in the 1920s, did not affect Chiapas; it was superfluous.[92]

THE MAYA IN THE PRI ORDER

Limited reform finally began to reach Chiapas— far more tentatively than in the Yucatan—under President Cárdenas in the 1930s, at least putting an end to debt labor on the Sosconosco plantations.[93]

Cárdenas also encouraged Protestant sects from the US to convert Chiapas Indians, in an attempt to break the ecclesiastical hold on the region. The Summer Institute of Linguistics (SIL), the pioneering missionary group which was translating the Bible into Indian tongues throughout Latin America, made Chiapas their showcase, and established a Lacandon Selva "jungle camp" to train personnel for the Amazon and the whole hemisphere.[94] The evangelical message of individual salvation, hard work, teetotalism and imminent apocalypse appealed to Indians alienated from the *cacique* culture of rigid community control and ritual alcoholism.

As the new government coalesced around the hegemonic Institutional Revolutionary Party (PRI), the Chiapas oligarchy adapted once again. Under the agrarian reform, *ejidos* became the official designation for redistributed lands titled to villages, hamlets or settlements. The *cacique* system, pillar of oligarchic power over the Indians, was integrated into the new reform bureaucracies, primarily the PRI's National Campesino Confederation (CNC). With the entrenchment of corruption and patronage under the one-party state, *caciques* became intermediaries for government credit and small-farm aid, maintaining their authoritarian and often brutal control over village life and access to communal or *ejidal* lands.[95]

Cárdenas also founded the National Indigenous Institute (INI), an entity of the state rather than the party, to promote the development of Indian country and integrate it into the national agrarian sector. INI also helped transform Indians into clients of the state, although it would sometimes meet resistance from the CNC. At times, *caciques* who felt threatened by INI organizing efforts barred agents from their turf.[96]

Even as the reform bureaucracy became the new social control mechanism, the land reform still lagged behind the rest of Mexico. The Chiapas oligarchs used the subterfuge of distributing paper ownership of their holdings among family members. The federal government looked the other way, while concentration of the state's arable land in elite hands actually escalated.[97]

The post-World War II cattle boom, fueled by World Bank credit to the region's ranchers, escalated Indian landlessness dramatically. Presidents Miguel Aleman and Ruiz Cortines protected thousands of hectares from expropriation by granting prominent ranchers Certificates of Inaffectability (as allowed under a constitutional provision excluding productive commercial lands from the Agrarian Reform by presidential prerogative).[98] The resultant unrest in Chiapas prompted Gov. Efrain Aranda Osorio in the 1950s to declare a Ranchers Auxiliary Police Corps, a militia to combat *campesino* land invasions.[99]

The federal government responded to the unrest by opening up the still largely untouched Lacandon Selva to colonization by landless peasants from the Highlands. This strip of rainforest, Mexico's last true frontier, was seen as an expendable territory for use as a political safety-valve.[100]

Following the same pattern which has replicated itself on a far more massive scale in Amazonia, the first roads into the jungle were cut by loggers, and then a deluge followed. Near-slave labor in the Selva's mahogany camps, or *monterías*, was portrayed in B. Traven's novels in the 1930s—winning him death threats from Chiapas landowners.[101] Then, beginning in the 1950s, *campesinos* followed the logging roads to establish slash-and-burn settlements. Finally, cattle interests followed the relocated *campesinos* into the cleared Selva, leading to massive deforestation. It also threatened the Lacandon Maya, first "contacted" only in the 1940s, with cultural extermination as the forest they depended on for hunting and gathering was overwhelmed.[102]

In 1962, the *de facto* policy was institutionalized by passage of the Federal Colonization Law, which called for New Population Centers (NCPs) on national lands— primarily the Chiapas rainforest. The NCPs would bring the spontaneous colonization process under state control, and would become nuclei of new *ejidos* to be carved out of the forest.[103]

The threat of unrest also brought wholly unanticipated changes to Highland Chiapas. The Chamula *caciques* still maintained much power through control over production of sacraments needed for daily worship: candles and cane liquor—*aguardiente* or *trago* or (in Tzotzil) *posh*.[104] Failure to engage in ritual drunkenness still rendered the Indians vulnerable to the evil magic of witches as well as the scorn of *caciques* (who successfully resisted government efforts to establish a monopoly on rum production, blockading Highland roads in the "*posh* war" of the early 1950s).[105] This intricate, centuries-old system of community control was meticulously documented by gringo anthropologists after the founding of the Harvard Chiapas Project in 1957, when the Chamulas and Zinacantecos became perhaps the most closely studied Indians in the hemisphere.[106] But the increased role of the state precipitated an unintended ecclesiastical power shift.

As the primary control mechanism shifted from the Catholic hierarchy to the PRI bureaucracy, the local Church began to change. Father Samuel Ruiz, an idealistic young seminarian from Guanajuato, ascended to the Diocese of San Cristóbal in 1960. This antique instrument of oligarchic power was now in the hands of a man who openly saw Las Casas as his inspiration, ever more influenced by the Liberation Theology current which emerged in the Latin church in the 1960s. Although his parents were migrant laborers who met in California, the young Ruiz was deeply conservative when he first came to Chiapas. His father was a veteran of the reactionary Sinarquista movement which opposed the Revolutionary regime in Guanajuato, and the young Ruiz inherited these authoritarian and dogmatically anti-communist values. His pastoral letters warned of paganism and communist subversion, and he campaigned against the INI schools for spreading "communist propaganda." It was only after touring his Diocese (which included both the Highlands and the Selva)—often travelling on foot or by horse or mule along mountain trails with an Indian interpreter, much as Las Casas had—that he began to sense how God was already working among the Indians. One group of Indians told him "It's the will of God" after all the children in their hamlet died of measles and diarrhea, despite vain calls for a doctor. But another asked him, "Does this God of yours know how to save bodies, or is he concerned only with saving souls?" "I came to San Cristóbal to convert the poor," he would later put it, "but they ended up converting me." By the 1968 Latin American Bishops' Conference in Medellín, Colombia, his conversion was complete. "The weak and the oppressed withdraw from Christ if we appear as allies of the powerful," he warned in the paper he presented at Medellín.[107]

The October 1974 Indian Congress organized by Bishop Ruiz to celebrate the 500th birthday of Las Casas was a focus of the Diocese's new education and organizing efforts among the Maya. Indigenous delegates from across the Diocese testified on the abuses of *caciques* and the encroachments of ranchers. The Diocese's *catequistas*—lay workers—helped form land committees, agricultural collectives and local councils independent of the *caciques*. The Indians began to refer to Ruiz as *Tatic*—grandfather.[108]

Betrayed, some reactionary Catholics broke from the Diocese—and from Rome— to found a self-styled Mexican Orthodox Church, descended from that founded by President Calles as a tool against the Catholic hierarchy, and now affiliated with the Chaldean rite. The Mexican Orthodox Chaldeans succeeded in winning Indians to their orbit through control of the sacred artifacts of the Maya death cult at the Church of San Pascualito in Tuxtla. The icons of the dancing skeleton-saint King San Pascualito, "bones" of bleached wood, were ordered burned by the Church numerous times in the nineteenth century, but the Brotherhood of San Pascualito at the little Tuxtla church continued to secrete them. Indians from all Chiapas and Guatemala continue today to make annual pilgrimages to view them at specified festivals. The Chamula *caciques*, threatened by Diocese efforts to rein in their petty tyranny, also fell within the orbit of the Chaldeans. In 1984, Chamula's church broke with the Diocese to join the Chaldeans, recognizing the Brotherhood in Tuxtla rather than Ruiz and the Cathedral of San Cristóbal as their ecclesiastical authority.[109]

The Chamula *caciques* were already forcibly expelling Indian families who had converted to Protestantism. Now, even some who continued to cling to the Church of Rome faced expulsion. A new class of Chamula's *expulados* fled to urban poverty in San Cristóbal, their shanties climbing (and denuding) the mountainside on the north of town.[110]

Protestant missionaries themselves, originally seen as a progressive alternative to Catholicism, turned ultra-conservative with the rise of fundamentalism. In 1983, the SIL was briefly expelled from Mexico, and its Lacandon "jungle camp" closed. This was a play by President López Portillo to the nationalist left, which openly considered SIL a CIA front.[111]

By the late 1970s, cadres from radical left groups, including many from Monterrey and elsewhere in the Mexican north, were building upon the work of Ruiz in organizing the Indians. Militantly independent *campesino* organizations took hold as an alternative to CNC in many Highland villages—as well as among the uprooted peasants in the Selva, where the CNC had little presence to begin with.[112]

The Independent Central of Rural Workers and Campesinos (CIOAC), with a support base at the northern Tzotzil Highland village of Simojovel, was linked to the Mexican Communist Party (and successor organizations after the party's

1983 disbanding). Others, such as the Emiliano Zapata Campesino Organization (OCEZ), mostly on the Grijalva side of the Highlands, were rooted in community kinship networks, maintaining autonomy from any national structures as a matter of principle.[113]

Maoists who rejected the Communist Party as too detached and statist found a foothold in the Selva, especially the group Politica Popular. But many PP organizers, seeking more organic links to the *campesinos*, found themselves assuming leadership in the Rural Associations of Collective Interest (ARICs), which began as a government development program. Ironically, these Maoists became the most reformist, with a program of pressuring the government for credit and higher crop prices, rather than land redistribution. They began to risk reincorporation into the "pseudo-left" outer ring of the PRI machine.[114]

OCEZ remained the most uncompromising. The Tzotzil village of Venustiano Carranza was by the early 1980s the scene of frequent violence between OCEZ militants and CNC *pistoleros*. In response to the rise of militant *campesino* activity, the cattle oligarchy began forming paramilitary groups known as White Guards, a more clandestine evolution of the rancher militias established in the 1950s. By 1986, Amnesty International was documenting "disappearances" and torture in Chiapas.[115]

As the 1980s began, waves of Maya refugees from the bloody counterinsurgency campaign in Guatemala flooded Chiapas, especially the Selva. The Mexican army quickly relocated the refugees to internment camps hundreds of kilometers away in the interior Yucatan.[116] The Chiapas elites noted uneasily how the Guatemalan dictatorship's use of the Petén as a safety valve—colonized by thousands of landless *campesinos*, often in programs overseen by US AID—had merely turned the rainforest into a breeding ground for guerillas.[117]

The Mexican government launched an ambitious "Plan Chiapas," targeting the state for massive hydroelectric and oil development. A new military road was punched into the Selva, paralleling the Usumacinta and ringing the previously open territory.[118] The state oil monopoly Pemex followed, establishing test sites in the forest.[119]

In 1982, Absalon Castellanos Domínguez, oligarch rancher and former commander of the Highland's 31st Military Zone, became governor and further unleashed the security forces on Indians and militant *campesinos*. The harsh Cerro Hueco state prison outside Tuxtla swelled with arrested *campesinos*. Connivance between the army, state police and semi-clandestine White Guards became blatant, under a governor from the most reactionary sector of the local elite. Absalon was the fruit of a union between the state's two most powerful families. His father Matías Catellanos had been a Mapache counter-revolutionary guerilla leader, and his maternal family included José Pantaleón Domínguez, governor at the time of the 1868 Tzotzil revolt. (These families also had their dissidents: Absalon's grand-father Senator Belisario Domínguez was a martyr of the opposition to the counter-revolutionary Victoriano Huerta regime, killed on the dictator's orders for denouncing his *coup d'état* in 1913. Absalon's cousin Rosario Castellanos was the family's real black sheep—an artist, indigenist and feminist, who did educational work among the Indians with INI, and later became ambassador to Israel where she died in a tragic accident.)[120]

In 1988, Castellanos was succeeded by Patrocinio González Garrido, another scion of the elite, although of a somewhat more progressive sector: his father had been governor before him, and his uncle Tomas Garrido Canabal was the governor of neighboring Tabasco whose anti-clerical excesses in the 1920s were the source for Graham Greene's novel *The Power and the Glory*.[121] González attempted negotia-tions with the independent *campesino* groups. But state police with clubs and tear gas attacked a march of Selva colonists demanding clarification of their land rights at Palenque in July 1991. In September, Joel Padrón, the parish priest of Simojovel, was arrested on charges of "provocation"—clear retaliation for his defense of the village *campesinos*.[122]

On October 12, 1992, 500th anniversary of the Columbus landfall, a group of *campesinos* from the Selva, led by the Emiliano Zapata National Independent Campesino Alliance (ANCIEZ), entered San Cristóbal, carrying hammers and farm implements, and tore down the statue of the Conquistador Diego de Mazariegos outside the Church of Santo Domingo. The statue was burned to assure that it would not be erected again. The pedestal still stands empty.[123]

Few knew that the ANCIEZ had crossed the line to embrace armed struggle, had formed the nucleus of a guerilla army—and was practicing for a much more dramatic entry into San Cristóbal in the near future . . .

In early 1993, President Carlos Salinas appointed González Secretary of Gobernación, the cabinet post for the interior, leaving his *compadre* (and presumed surrogate) Elmar Setzer Marseille ruling Chiapas as interim governor. With the North American Free Trade Agreement to take effect the following January, fol-lowed by presidential elections in August, Salinas doubtless wanted an old Chiapas hand at Gobernación in case the restive state should prove troublesome.[124]

That spring, the Federal Army, apparently tipped off by ARIC leaders, combed the Lacandon Selva for guerillas. Despite rumors of clashes, González denied that there were any guerillas in Chiapas.[125]

2

"MISERY IN THE NAME OF FREEDOM"

Free Trade Mexico as a US Slave Colony

As Mexico shook off colonial rule in 1821, US President James Monroe and Secretary of State John Quincy Adams balked at recognizing the new nation.

Adams rebuked Sen. Henry Clay of Kentucky for advising recognition and friendship for an independent Latin America: "I wished well to their cause; but I had seen and yet see no prospect that they would establish free or liberal institutions of government . . . Arbitrary power, military and ecclesiastical, was stamped upon . . . all their institutions. Civil dissension was infused into all their seminal principles. War and mutual destruction was in every member of their organization, moral, political and physical."[1]

This was the council of Thomas Jefferson, who, as president in 1801, wrote to then-Virginia governor Monroe: "However our present interests may restrain us within our own limitations, it is impossible not to look forward to distant times when our rapid multiplication will expand itself beyond those limits, and cover the whole northern, if not the southern continent, with a people speaking the same language, governed in similar form, and by similar laws; nor can we contemplate with satisfaction either blot or mixture on that surface."[2]

Jefferson preferred that Spain maintain control of Latin America "till our population can be sufficiently advanced to gain from it piece by peice [sic]."[3] He justified this stance with the observation that "History . . . furnishes no example of a priest-ridden people maintaining a free civil government."[4]

There was a paradoxical unity in the contradictory democratic and imperialist character of the new American republic. Against the dominant Madisonian assumption that private property is the foundation of liberty were the Radical Dissenters and their small-farmer followers. Burdened with debt and pushed onto marginal lands by the aristocracy, they sought the abolition of inheritance and the return of private lands to the commons.[5]

This debate reached and divided the founders of the republic. In 1783, Benjamin Franklin wrote in a letter to a prominent financier: "All the Property that is necessary to a Man, for the Conservation of the Individual and the Propagation of the Species, is his natural Right, which none can justly deprive him of: But all Property superfluous to such purposes is the Property of the Publick."[6]

Jefferson wrote in a letter to a skeptical James Madison, in 1785: "The earth is given as a common stock for man to labour and live on. If, for the encouragement of industry we allow it to be appropriated, we must take care that other employment be furnished to those excluded from the appropriation. If we do not, the fundamental right to labour the earth returns to the unemployed."[7]

While conceding "that an equal division of property is impractable," Jefferson concluded that "the consequences of this enormous inequality producing so much misery to the bulk of mankind, legislators cannot invent too many devices for subdividing property."[8]

Asserting in a later letter to Madison that "the earth belongs in usufruct to the living," Jefferson weighed in on the right of society to limit inheritance of land, lest the lords of property "eat up the usufruct of the lands for several generations to come, and then the lands would belong to the dead."[9]

As president, Jefferson had extended the republic to the Rocky Mountains through the Louisiana Purchase and extended US military might to the shores of Tripoli through naval raids on pirate bases. He subsequently became a relentless advocate of local power. "As Cato concluded every speech with the words, *Carthago delenda est*, so do I every opinion with the injunction, 'divide the counties into wards,'" he was insisting by his later years.[10] Direct democracy in wards of one hundred citizens—inspired by the New England town meetings—was seen as a foundation of village-based self-rule without which freedom would fail: "Divide the counties into wards of such size as that every citizen can attend, when called on, and act in person . . . making every citizen an acting member of the government, and in the offices nearest and most interesting to him."[11]

But the westward expansion which Jefferson championed ultimately precluded the imperative to challenge wealth inequities and assert local autonomy. Just as the English peasantry disenfranchised by the Enclosure Acts were sent to the slums of London, and then to the shores of America in indentured servitude, so their grandsons and granddaughters were pushed from the fertile Atlantic coastal plains into the rocky Appalachians—and then beyond, into the Ohio Valley and across the wide Missouri. Inevitably, as they arrived at desirable lands, the inequities they were fleeing followed them. But there was still a vast continent to fill—unfortunately, for the Indian nations, and for Mexico.

The role of the western frontier as a social safety valve put the American republic on an inevitable course toward conflict with Mexico. The Arkansas River, 1,000 kilometers north of the Rio Grande, was the Mexican border then. To the west, Mexico's northern border extended to Oregon.[12]

Mexico was expanding north, much as the US was expanding west—into the same territory. US expansion followed the Platte and Arkansas Rivers, on a model of pioneer capitalism, small families clearing the wilderness, then getting bought out (or evicted) by monied interests that followed. Mexico's expansion followed the Rio Grande, on the feudalistic model of missions and manors, sprawling land grants to aristocrats for settlement by pioneer wards.[13]

The "Manifest Destiny" of the white race to fill the continent was driven by the economic imperatives of African slavery in the US South, which had to expand to survive as plantation soils were exhausted. Thus, the pioneers who were pitted against the Indians and Mexicans were unwitting pawns of the southern slavocracy. Thus, oppressions within the US were also paid for by Mexico.[14]

Slaveholder Jefferson's passage in the draft of the Declaration of Independence attacking the slave trade as contrary to the "sacred rights of life and liberty" was excised from the final document.[15] Jefferson's ethic of small government was also explicit in its inspiration from the Indians who were being displaced by the new republic's expansion: "It will be said," he wrote, "the great societies cannot exist without government. The savages, therefore, break them into small ones."[16]

In Mexico, meanwhile, an indigenous tradition of village self-rule and usufructuary land rights extending millennia into the past was being eroded—and would be eroded ever faster as US territorial and economic expansion held ever greater hegemony over the republic to the south.

"... AND SO CLOSE TO THE UNITED STATES"

The early independence revolts of the radical priests Miguel Hidalgo and José Maria Morelos fought (in the words of historian Henry Bamford Parkes) "not only for the expulsion of the *gachupines* [Spaniards] but also for racial equality, for the abolition of clerical and military privilege, and for the restoration of land to the Indians."[17]

Hidalgo's Cry of Dolores was answered by *campesinos* (peasants) who had little to lose. While village lands were often titled by the Spanish Crown, the Spanish *haciendas* illegally and increasingly encroached upon them.[18]

But independence was finally won by the Conservatives—some of the same men who had crushed the Hidalgo and Morelos revolts. Developments in Spain threatened the privileges of Mexico's landed elite. The new Liberal Constitution, imposed on the Crown by the very guerillas who had restored King Ferdinand VII after the Napoleonic occupation, curtailed the power of the Church and aristocracy. This pushed New Spain's Conservatives to take up the struggle for independence, which the Liberals favored on principle. Morelos had sought to break up the *haciendas;* the *criollo* landowners sought abolition of the Crown's strictures against encroachment upon Indian lands.[19]

Independence was initially the victory of aristocratic reaction as Augustín de Iturbide declared himself monarch of the Empire of Mexico. His manifesto, the Plan of Iguala, guaranteed existing property relations. Vicente Guerrero, the rebel leader who had brought the peasant armies which survived the execution of Hidalgo and Morelos into alliance with Iturbide, would soon return to rebellion.[20]

Secretary of State Adams responded to Mexico's independence by formally warning Simón Bolívar, liberator of South America and then Dictator of Colombia, not to extend his revolutionary movement to Cuba and Puerto Rico, which remained under Spanish rule. President Monroe was then acquiring Florida from Spain, and looking south. (Cuba, Jefferson had declared, would be "ours in the first moment of the first war."[21]) Adams told Bolívar that the Monroe Doctrine, which warned European powers against intervening in the Americas, "must not be interpreted as authorization for the weak to be insolent with the strong." Bolívar noted in his journal, "The United States appear destined by Providence to plague America with hunger and misery in the name of freedom."[22]

By the time a republic was established in 1824, Mexico faced designs on its territory. Mexico originally encouraged Anglo colonization of Texas to populate the territory and *prevent* its annexation by the US. Instead, the Mexican elites were creating what they feared. In 1829, President Vicente Guerrero realized this and issued a decree abolishing slavery—which then scarcely existed in Mexico outside Texas. The aim was discouraging further colonization by the gringos—which was barred outright the following year. The Texans started arming, demanding greater autonomy and separation from the state of Coahuila.[23]

In 1835, Mexican Dictator Antonio López de Santa Anna led a column across the Rio Grande to put down the Texas revolt. In 1829, he had defended Tampico against a Spanish expeditionary force bent on reconquest—a glory to be sullied by

Sam Houston's rebels. After exterminating the rebel defenders of the Alamo mission house at San Antonio, Santa Anna was humiliated by the Texans at San Jacinto—where the "no prisoners" policy was avenged in kind. The Texans declared independence; the captured Santa Anna was shipped to President Andrew Jackson in Washington, and agreed to withdraw from the territory in return for his life. Back in Mexico City, he was promptly overthrown in a *coup d'état*.[24]

But Santa Anna recouped his losses when the French invaded Veracruz in the 1838 Pastry War (launched by Paris to collect debts, including those incurred in the ransacking of a French pastry shop). His leg, blown off by a French cannonball, was buried with great pomp, and Santa Anna exploited the martyrdom of his severed limb to catapult himself back to power. He would, however, be overthrown again before the next Texas crisis.[25]

In 1845, Texas was formally annexed to the US—in refusal of a Mexican offer to recognize the Lone Star Republic if it resisted annexation.[26] The following year, troops under Gen. Zachary Taylor were sent to the mouth of the Rio Grande at Matamoros to patrol a "border" that Mexico did not recognize and that had never been clearly defined. As Taylor placed guns across the river from the city, some of his troops mixed it up with a Mexican patrol, supplying the desired expedient for war. One colonel among Taylor's troops wrote in his diary, "We have not one particle of right to be here." Even some in the US Congress considered the border the Nueces River, over 140 kilometers to the north. In securing the declaration of war from Congress, President James K. Polk nonetheless claimed Mexico had "invaded our territory and shed American blood upon American soil." War, he said, "notwithstanding all our efforts to avoid it, exists by the act of Mexico herself." War fever swept the US, with the expansionist press demanding annexation of "All Mexico."[27]

Polk's secret agents in Havana, where Santa Anna was exiled, arranged for him to slip past the US naval blockade into Veracruz in return for a pledge to pursue peace on terms favorable to Washington once restored to power. Santa Anna actually demanded US forces position themselves to menace Central Mexico, so his concession would be viewed as patriotic necessity. Upon his return to Mexico, the duplicitous general re-established control over the presidency through a surrogate's *coup*, and took command of the war.[28]

In the following months, US troops occupied half of Mexico. Gen. Taylor, a veteran of the Black Hawk and Seminole wars (in which whole Indian nations had been forcibly relocated), occupied Monterrey, where he acknowledged "shameful atrocities" by rampaging Texas Rangers. Gen. Stephen Kearny's Army of the West followed the Santa Fe Trail along the Arkansas to take New Mexico and California, dispatching Gen. Alexander Doniphan to Chihuahua. The nonresistance that Kearny encountered at Santa Fe was reportedly the fruit of bribes Polk's agents had lavished on New Mexico's Gov. Manuel Armijo. Gen. Winfield Scott, another Black Hawk war veteran, landed at Veracruz, bombarded the port, and followed the path of Cortéz to Mexico City. He too dutifully reported the brutality of his troops: "murder, robbery, and rape of mothers and daughters in the presense of tied-up males of the families have been common."[29]

In the unseemly intrigues among these generals—as well as John Fremont, Commodore Robert Stockton and the Bear Flag Republic rebels in California—it was Taylor who came out on top. The Norman Schwartzkopf of 1848, he rode his fame to the White House the following year. Like Polk, he was a Southerner, and was initially viewed suspiciously by Bostonians and New Yorkers who had lagged in the war fervor. But the discovery of gold in annexed California had a soothing effect on the anti-war sentiment of the Northern "free labor" elites.[30]

In the 1848 Treaty of Guadalupe-Hidalgo, the US increased its area by over a third—and Mexico, compensated $15 million, lost two fifths.[31] "Poor Mexico!" it has been said thereafter, "so far from God and so close to the United States!"[32]

Conflicting definitions of the New Mexico–Chihuahua border led to diplomatic conflicts in 1853, when US army surveying teams were sent into the annexed territory. Secretary of War Jefferson Davis dispatched railroad baron James Gadsden to settle the dispute by purchasing an additional 30,000 square kilometers. The US gained the Apache lands south of the Gila River—and a new route to California, the Cooke Wagon Road, named for one of Kearney's captains. (It is now Interstate 10.[33])

Pressure was on the Mexican government to accept the terms of the Gadsden Purchase by the presence on Mexican soil of a gringo mercenary army. This was led by the filibuster William Walker, bankrolled by San Francisco financiers and mineral speculators to seize Sonora and Baja California. His gang gained a foothold as "settlers," selling themselves to the Mexican government as guardians against the raiding Apaches. Instead, they promptly declared independence, sparking a brief local war. Jefferson Davis corresponded with Walker throughout the episode.[34]

Walker's "Sonora Republic" lasted mere days, but two years later he would seize Nicaragua (this time bankrolled by New York interests seeking a route through the isthmus to California). His filibuster regime immediately re-instituted African slavery and was recognized by President Franklin Pierce, who had entered the White House boasting he would "not be controlled by any timid forebodings of the evil of expansionism." It took an invasion of Nicaragua by the other Central American republics (backed by the rival British) to oust Walker.[35]

These grim events were observed by a German journalist then corresponding for a Vienna paper, one Karl Marx. By James Buchanan's ascendence to the White House in 1857, it was clear that the same forces which had fueled the conquest of Mexican lands would also tear the American republic asunder:

In the foreign, as in the domestic, policy of the United States, the interests of the slaveholders served as the guiding star: Buchanan had in fact obtained the office of President through the issue of the Ostend Manifesto, in which the acquisition of Cuba, whether by purchase or by force of arms, was proclaimed as the great task of national policy. Under his government northern Mexico was already divided among American land speculators, who impatiently awaited the signal to fall on Chihuahua, Coahuila and Sonora. The unceasing piratical expeditions of the filibusters against the states of Central America were directed no less from the White House at Washington. In the closest connection with this foreign policy   stood the *reopening of the slave trade*.[36]

With the outbreak of the US Civil War, a Texan Confederate army would invade the slave New Mexico Territory, scene of the westernmost battles in the war. California, with San Francisco a burgeoning outpost of Northern capital, stuck with the Union.[37]

Yet among those cheering on the gringo expansion were Marx and Friedrich Engels, who wrote:

In America, we have witnessed the conquest of Mexico and we have rejoiced in it. It is . . . an advance when a country which has hitherto been . . . perpetually rent with civil wars, and completely hindered in its development . . . is forcibly drawn into the historical process. It is to the interest of its own development that Mexico will in future be placed under the tutelage of the United States. The evolution of the whole of America will profit by the fact that the United States, by the possession of California, obtains command of the Pacific.[38]

The real winner, he conceded, was US capital: "The North Americans acquire new regions in California and New Mexico for the creation of fresh capital . . . And what about the proposed cut through the Tehuantepec isthmus? Who is likely to gain by that? Who else but the American shipping owners? Rule over the Pacific, who will gain by that but these same shipping owners?"[39]

Thus, the annexation of Hawaii, the Spanish–American War, and the rise of the US to world power status—all grew from the root of Guadalupe-Hidalgo. Ironically, it was the Northern capitalists who controlled finance and shipping, rather than the Southern slavocracy, that reaped the final gains of conquest.

The aftermath also brought civil war to Mexico. Liberals, furious at Santa Anna's betrayal, rose in Guerrero. Their Plan of Ayutla demanded a temporary dictatorship of the revolutionary forces. In 1855, Santa Anna fled again.[40]

The austere Benito Juárez, a Zapotec lawyer from Oaxaca and veteran Liberal guerilla (today Mexico's most respected president) shaped a new constitution aimed at making dictatorship impossible. The *Ley Lerdo* called for privatizing the Church lands.[41]

But the new Liberal order carried the seeds of its own destabilization. Church lands were generally not divided, but sold in whole to the new bourgeois oligarchs—including British, French and Germans. Worse, the *Ley Lerdo* ordered the sale of *ejidos* and communal village lands. Indians, correctly perceiving that the Liberal reforms worsened their position, supported Conservative rebellions against the new regime in the central provinces.[42]

The French occupation was one final attempt to restore European control over Mexico. Under cover, once again, of collecting debts, the French landed at Veracruz in 1862 and fought their way into the interior. In a deal with the Conservatives they installed the Austrian prince Maximilian as Emperor of Mexico, a personage chosen by Napoleon III because his Habsburg lineage was thought to loan him legitimacy as successor to Mexico's Spanish sovereigns. The Liberals returned to guerilla war and beat back the French. In 1867 a victorious Juárez put the puppet emperor before a firing squad.[43]

Juárez, back in power, was astute enough "to avoid any too dogmatic application of the liberal creed." He understood that landlessness was the raw material of rural unrest, whether it was exploited by Liberals or Conservatives. "As long as he remained president, the *ejidos* of the Indian villages were safe, in spite of the *Ley Lerdo* and the constitution on 1857." He also instated free secular education, and made Indian literacy a special priority.[44]

In 1872, the sudden death of Juárez brought his chief justice Sebastián Lerdo to power. When Lerdo tried to hold on to the presidency for another term, a rebellion was launched by one Porfirio Díaz, *caudillo* of Oaxaca and an old Juárez rival in the Liberal insurgency. His Plan of Tuxtepec demanded "effective suffrage" and "no re-election," Liberal-sounding principles. They won the support of Washington, largely because of Lerdo's refusal to allow US rail lines to extend across the border. Texas was the launchpad for the revolt that propelled Díaz to power.[45]

THE LIBERAL DICTATORSHIP

It was the long Liberal dictatorship of Porfirio Díaz (the most hated president in Mexican history) which first brought a "Free Trade" regime to Mexico with US support, maintaining power thirty years through blatant electoral manipulations in alliance with regional *caudillos*.[46]

Whole villages disappeared throughout Mexico as *haciendas* hypertrophied. The Dictatorship's *rurales* terrorized the countryside, executing peasants at will under the *Ley Fuga*, allowing the shooting of prisoners trying to "escape."[47]

The brutality mirrored an ostentatious allegiance to principles of pure reason. In 1893, José Ives Limantour became treasury chief, balancing Mexico's budget for the first time. Limantour's corps of *científicos* (scientists) came to dominate the government—whiz-kids committed to Social Darwinism, Free Trade and industry (and becoming millionaires).[48] The *científico* slogans of "Order and Progress" and "Little Politics, Much Administration" set the tone.[49]

The policy of increasing the number of property owners was effected by once again enforcing the *Ley Lerdo* to break up *ejidos*.[50] Water rights were given away by the government to favored landowners, depriving smallholders and *ejidos*. Rural hunger and massive food imports became the norm in a land where three quarters of the population was still engaged in agriculture.[51] Domestic *maíz* production dropped by half between 1877 and 1907.[52]

US interests—the Hearsts, Guggenheims, US Steel, Anaconda, Standard Oil, Doheny—owned three quarters of the mines and more than half the oilfields, many of the sugar plantations, and enormous ranches in the North. US investment in Mexico exceeded the total capital owned by Mexicans themselves.[53] The English shared in the oil interests; the textile mills were mainly French; the hated Spanish once again acquired vast *haciendas*, even working convict laborers in their fields.[54]

US-owned rail lines connected Sonora, Coahuila and Chihuahua to the US border, rather than to Mexico's interior.[55] By 1911, the US was receiving 75 percent of Mexico's exports.[56] The journalist John Kenneth Turner wrote, "the United States has virtually reduced Díaz to a political dependency, and by doing so has virtually transformed Mexico into a slave colony of the United States . . . The Americanization of Mexico of which Wall Street boasts is being accomplished and accomplished with a vengeance."[57]

No sooner did trade unions emerge than they were banned by the Dictatorship. At Anaconda's Cananea copper mines in Sonora, and at the Rio Blanco textile mills in Veracruz, hundreds of workers were gunned down by government troops for daring to strike.[58] Arizona Rangers volunteers were even allowed across the border to help suppress the Cananea strikes, which were organized by the Industrial Workers of the World (IWW).[59]

Sonora's Yaqui Indians provided the regime's first real challenge. The Yaqui rebelled under the chieftain Cajeme in 1875, and maintained virtual independence for the next ten years.[60] A concerted military campaign finally broke the Yaqui autonomous zone, and the US-owned Sonoran Railroad came in, bringing civilization.[61] The New York-based Sonora and Sinaloa Irrigation Company spearheaded the transformation of the dispossessed Yaqui lands into private plantations worked by captive Yaqui labor.[62] But Yaqui guerilla warfare continued for years, and the *federales* deported thousands to work as slaves on the Yucatan henequen plantations.[63]

Capitalist expansion onto *campesino* lands was propelling Mexico inexorably toward revolution. Looking at repeal of the English Corn Laws, which had protected tenant farmers from foreign imports, Marx succinctly deconstructed the euphemism of "Free Trade": "[W]hat is Free Trade under the present conditions of society? Freedom of Capital . . . Gentlemen! Do not be deluded by the abstract word Freedom! Whose freedom? Not the freedom of one individual in relation to another, but freedom of Capital to crush the worker." In his mechanistic faith, he concluded: "[T]he Protective system in these days is conservative, while the Free Trade system . . . breaks up the old nationalities and carries antagonism of the proletariat and bourgeoisie to the uttermost point. In a word, the Free Trade system hastens the Social Revolution. In this revolutionary sense alone, gentlemen, I am in favor of Free Trade."[64]

When the inevitable Revolution finally obtained in Mexico, the decades of entrenched tyranny assured a cataclysm.

THE REVOLUTION

The first revolutionary calls were raised by the anarchists Ricardo and Enrique Flores Magón, born in Oaxaca of Indian parentage. The brothers founded the opposition paper *Regeneración* and the Mexican Liberal Party (PLM) to challenge the Dictatorship in 1900. They embraced anarchism after the IWW strikes at Cananea, and were purportedly the first to raise the cry *¡Tierra y Libertad!* The PLM launched numerous insurrections in the years leading up to 1910. Released from the Dictator's prisons and exiled to California in 1904, Ricardo Flores Magón continued to organize armed expeditions across the border. The Magón brothers won solidarity from California radicals like John Kenneth Turner, but gringo filibusters attempted to co-opt their expeditions, and they were repeatedly arrested for violating US neutrality laws. In 1911 Ricardo disappeared into the US prison system for life. The struggle they had launched in Mexico was taken up by others.[65]

In 1910, when Díaz broke his promise not to run for president again, Francisco Madero, a more courageous than worldly scion of the elite, resurrected the slogan "effective suffrage, no re-election," and declared himself a disloyal candidate. This act would unleash the deluge.[66]

Francisco Madero was initially a mere reformer. His *anti-reeleccionistas* only wanted a clean vote, and did not appreciate their nation's despair. But before the election, Díaz had Madero jailed on charges of plotting rebellion; then his "official" count allotted him a mere 196 votes! Bailed out of a San Luis Potosi prison thanks to the influence of his wealthy Coahuila family, Madero slipped across the border to Texas. In San Antonio he proclaimed against the regime in his prison manifesto, the Plan of San Luis Potosi.[67]

Uprisings spread throughout the country; state capitals were seized by Maderista guerillas or mobs.[68] Upon fleeing the country from Veracruz in May 1911, Díaz famously remarked, "Madero has unleashed a tiger; let us see if he can control him."[69]

Madero took power a hero and called new elections, which he cleanly won. But troops were once again dispatched to Cananea, and to put down labor unrest elsewhere.[70] Madero also sent troops to Baja California to take the border towns back from Magonista forces—despite the fact that another Magón brother, Jesús, a defector from the anarchists, was a minister in his government.[71] Most significantly, Madero's agrarian policy continued to advocate breaking up *ejidos* and encouraging rural capitalism.[72]

This assured that Madero would have trouble with the peasant insurrectionist who had risen in his support in the South: Emiliano Zapata.

Zapata's home turf of the state of Morelos, just across the Sierra Ajusco from the Valley of Mexico, was dominated by a sugar oligarchy. By the time Zapata rose, just thirty-two men owned half of all Morelos.[73]

Morelos was the world's third sugar producer after Hawaii and Puerto Rico. Growth of the *haciendas*—fueled by the exhaustion of soils through generations of monoculture—was enforced by hired guns. Villages disappeared into sugarfields; municipal waters were redirected to *hacienda* irrigation ditches, leaving *pueblos* dry, their *milpas* and orchards shrivelling; village woodlands were denuded—all upheld by a state government whose leaders, up to and including the governor, were of the planter elite. Disenfranchised villagers were reduced to sharecropping or debt peonage. New state laws weakened village land titles; villagers with the audacity to appeal to federal authorities were arrested for their efforts. In 1876, the year Díaz took power, there were 118 *pueblos* recorded in Morelos. A decade later, despite an increase in the population, there were 105.[74]

Zapata was president of the land defense committee at the *pueblo* of Anenecuilco, and just thirty when revolution broke out. Formal petitions based on colonial-era Nahuatl documents titling Anenecuilco's communal lands, carefully secreted by the village elders, failed to win action on *hacienda* encroachment, and in 1910 Zapata began leading peasants across the fence in defiance of the authorities. "Down with the *haciendas!* Long live the *pueblos!*" was the cry of his initially unarmed movement to take back the land. When Madero proclaimed against the Dictatorship, he formed the Liberator Army of the South, which took Cuautla in May 1911—the key southern victory leading to the downfall of Díaz that month.[75]

Zapata did not long support the Madero government. Talks between the two broke down over the land question, and Zapata's refusal to disarm until it was settled. In November 1911, Zapata proclaimed his Plan of Ayala, named for the municipal seat of Anenecuilco: "Be it known: that the lands, woods and waters which have been usurped by *hacendados*, *Científicos*, or *caciques*, through tyranny and venal justice, will be restored immediately to the *pueblos* or citizens who have the corresponding titles to such properties, of which they were despoiled through the bad faith of our oppressors. They shall maintain such possession at all costs through force of arms."[76]

The Zapatista Liberator Army rose again, their sole demand acceptance of the Plan of Ayala. "I am resolved," Zapata wrote his friend Gildardo Magaña in Mexico City, "to struggle against everything and everybody."[77]

The Zapatistas burned the *haciendas* of Morelos and divided the lands among the *peónes*. They were a people in arms, a federation of free *municipios*, working their newly won lands and taking up their rifles only to repel invasion.[78] "In those days, even the stones were Zapatistas," one veteran of the movement would recall years later.[79]

By the end of 1911, the Zapatistas controlled the countryside of Morelos, with the government forces holed up in garrison towns. "We have begged from the outside not one bullet, not one rifle, not one peso; we have taken it all from the enemy," Zapata boasted.[80]

While Zapata favored boots and the black, sliver-studded *charro* (cowboy) wear of the expert horseman he was, the Zapatista troops wore the sandals and white workclothes of the *campesinos* and *peónes*. They made their decisions in big meetings where all could speak their minds. The regional commanders like José Trinidad Ruiz and Genovevo de la O (who controlled the strategic Cima pass through the

Sierra Ajusco to Mexico City, repeatedly dynamiting the rail line) owed nominal allegiance to Zapata, but were autonomous, often acting independently. While he was known as the Caudillo of the South, Zapata was more beholden to his followers than the other way around.[81]

Even with nearly all Morelos in his hands and a civilian government being elected, Zapata never organized a state police. Zapata rebuked military chiefs who interfered in village affairs, and his revolutionary Morelos decreed laws strengthening municipal land rights and autonomy.[82] A Zapata manifesto declared: "The land free, the land free for all, land without overseers and without masters, is the war cry of the Revolution."[83]

Zapatista intellectual and PLM veteran Antonio Díaz Soto y Gama said the movement sought "free land, free plot. Free cultivation . . . Without foremen, without masters in the *ejido*, without individual tyrannies exercised by the state or by the collectivity."[84] Zapatista Gen. Trinidad Ruiz, in the northeast mountains of Morelos, proclaimed: "Down with the monopolies of woods, lands and waters; down with financial extortion; down with Madero; long live General Zapata!"[85]

In Washington, the administration of William H. Taft thought that Madero was too revolutionary. Taft believed that US foreign policy should "include active intervention to secure for our merchandise and our capitalists opportunity for profitable investment." In 1912, he declared: "The day is not far distant when three Stars and Stripes at three equidistant points will mark our territory: one at the North Pole, another at the Panama Canal, and the third at the South Pole. The whole hemisphere will be ours in fact as, by virtue of our superiority of race, it is already ours morally."[86]

In this spirit, he ordered a US fleet to Mexico's Gulf Coast, intended, said Secretary of State Philander Knox, to keep the Mexicans "in a salutary equilibrium, between a dangerous and exaggerated apprehension and a proper degree of wholesome fear."[87]

Madero took the hint, and turned up the heat on Zapata. But even when his federal army was torching Morelos villages and forcibly relocating the survivors to concentration camps in the Yucatan, a *New York Times* editorial scoffed that Díaz would have crushed the Zapatistas "in a fortnight."[88]

Henry Lane Wilson, Taft's Mexico Ambassador, a man with links to the Guggenheim empire which dominated Mexican silver mining, conspired with army commander Gen. Victoriano Huerta—a holdover from the Díaz regime who was vigorously pursuing the anti-Zapatista campaign—to remove Madero in a *coup d'état*. Assured of the US embassy's support, Huerta made his move in February 1913.

Madero and his vice-president were murdered. A counter-revolutionary dictatorship was in place.[89]

This opened a new phase in the Revolution. A "Constitutionalist" army rose in the North to restore a legitimate regime. Coahuila's Gov. Venustiano Carranza declared war on Huerta, and proclaimed himself First Chief of the Constitutionalist Army. He was joined by Alvaro Obregon, *caudillo* of Sonora.[90]

These men were no more revolutionary than Madero, although they proved more wily. "We have no *agraristas* here, thank God," Obregon said of his Sonoran domain, where he reigned as Garbanzo King. "We are doing what we're doing out of patriotism and to avenge the death of Sr. Madero."[91] Yet he made an alliance with Yaqui chieftains to drive out the federal forces.[92]

In Chihuahua, the third northern state to join the rebel alliance, a very different kind of revolutionary came to power. Chihuahua's original Maderista leadership had disappeared by the time of Carranza's proclamation. The muleteer-turned-guerilla Pascual Orozco had launched a counter-revolutionary revolt, and defected to Huerta; Provisional Governor Abraham González was killed when Huerta seized power. The guerilla Doroteo Arango picked up the torch, liberated Chihuahua anew and became *caudillo*. He was better known by his *nom de guerre* Francisco ("Pancho") Villa.[93]

Born on a Durango *hacienda*, the legend goes, Villa was still a teenager when he shot the *hacendado*'s son in retaliation for the rape of his sister. He became a fabled outlaw, winning the sympathy of the poor by daring to steal the cattle of Chihuahua's reigning oligarchs, the Terrazas family.[94] With the Revolution of 1910, Orozco and González made Villa a colonel and sent his hero bandits into battle against the *federales*. Villa's forces took Ciudad Juárez in May 1911, just as Zapata took Cuautla.[95]

Jailed for insubordination on Huerta's orders even before the *coup*, Villa met Zapatista intellectual Gildardo Magaña in prison, who taught him the rudiments of literacy, and won his support for the Plan of Ayala. Upon escaping from jail, Villa raised the Constitutionalist Army's Division of the North. Attracting legions from among the disenfranchised and selling confiscated cattle for guns in Texas, Villa's Division of the North became the rebel army's most powerful. He crossed the Rio Grande into Chihuahua with eight men in March 1913. By the end of the year, he controlled Chihuahua. By the end of the next he commanded 40,000 troops.[96]

Villa did not exactly command a peasant army. Arid Chihuahua is more than twenty times the size of Morelos in area, but much more sparsely populated. The tradition of autonomous municipalities was not as strong in the North; even in pre-Columbian times the Indians there had been mostly semi-nomadic. Villa's followers were peons, cowboys, miners, lumberjacks, rustlers, bandits. But similar dynamics of land usurpation fueled unrest in the North. Vast areas of open range had been awarded to pioneer settlements brave enough to keep the raiding Apaches at bay. With the defeat of Geronimo in 1886 (by US troops who had been allowed to cross into Mexico), these military colonists had outlived their usefulness. The rangelands of Chihuahua's "free villages" were soon privatized to *hacendados* and foreign investors—reducing proud pioneers to peons and outlaws. In the 1890s, Díaz had to send troops to put down small rebellions by these free villages.[97]

Like Zapata, Villa was interested in justice and social revolution, not mere political reform. "There can never be peace as long as one man has his belly full and another is starving," Villa was quoted by a gringo biographer. "I intend to keep on fighting and killing until our country is in safe hands."[98]

Upon assuming control of Chihuahua, he expropriated the vast holdings of the Terrazas and Creel cattle barons, with 62-acre parcels distributed to the former peons and declared "inalienable" for at least ten years. John Reed, the New York journalist who would soon go on to chronicle the Russian Revolution in *Ten Days that Shook the World*, rode with Villa in 1914, dubbing him "The Mexican Robin Hood."[99]

The man who insisted he was "not educated enough to be President of Mexico" made education of Chihuahua's children his special crusade, opening new schools with funds from the seized estates. Given the Villista penchant for summary execution of war captives, Reed was surprised when Villa told him, "When the new Republic is established there will never be any more army in Mexico. Armies are the greatest support of tyranny. There can be no dictator without an army." Instead, the people themselves would receive arms and military training. "Then, when the Patria is invaded . . . in half a day all the Mexican people will rise from their fields and factories, fully armed, equipped and organized to defend their children and their homes."[100]

Reed noted that in contrast to a federal army "thoroughly saturated with conventional military theory," when the peon soldier of "Villa's army goes into battle he is not hampered by salutes, or rigid respect for officers, or trigonometrical calculations of the trajectory of projectiles, or theories of the percentage of hits in a thousand rounds of rifle fire . . . It is probable that Villa doesn't know much about those things himself. But he does know . . . that men fighting individually and of their own free will are braver than long volleying rows in the trenches, lashed to it by officers with the flat of their swords. And when the fighting is fiercest—when a ragged mob of fierce brown men with hand bombs and rifles rush the bullet-swept streets of an ambushed town—Villa is among them, like any common soldier."[101]

As Villa seized much of the North, Huerta's forces terrorized Morelos. Zapata's army dematerialized from the towns and regrouped in the hills. Its ranks swollen by the horrific abuses of the occupying generals, it would soon recover the state.[102]

By then the administration in Washington had changed, Taft's crude imperialism replaced by the more sophisticated imperialism of Woodrow Wilson, who stated, "I will teach the Latin American republics to elect good men." Along with his Open Door Policy in China, this was part of his proto-globalist agenda: "The East is to be opened and transformed. The standards of the West are to be imposed upon it; nations and people who have stood still the centuries through are to be quickened and to be made part of the Universal world of commerce and of ideas which has so steadily been a-making by the advance of European power from age to age."[103]

Wilson would face three national eruptions which challenged the capitalist world order he was bent on expanding: before the Kuomintang in China or the Bolsheviks in Russia was the anarchic explosion already underway in Mexico. And his predecessor Taft had helped put in power the thug Huerta, who was anathema to his notion of "good men."

Wilson first imposed an arms embargo on all the warring parties. But the dictates of imperialism, he would find, precluded his reluctance to use military force. Wilson was pressured by the War Department and oil interests for intervention until he complained, "I sometimes have to pause and remind myself that I am the President of the whole United States and not merely of a few property holders in the Republic of Mexico."[104]

In February 1914, Wilson lifted the embargo. US war material started flowing to Carranza's Constitutionalists. A year later, Huerta was besieged—by Zapata in the south, by Villa and the Constitutionalist Army in the north.[105]

Circumstances finally forced Wilson to directly intervene. An officer from USS *Dolphin* was arrested by Huerta troops in Tampico, just as the German *Ypiranga* was headed for Veracruz with a cargo of arms. On April 20, US ships landed at Veracruz as watching British seamen cheered, "Give 'em hell, Yanks!" After three days of bombardment and street battles, seventeen Americans and over a hundred Mexicans were dead—the corpses of the latter publicly stacked, doused with oil and burned by US troops.[106]

Wilson appeared "shaken" by the violence in Veracruz. "The thought haunts me that it was I who ordered those young men to their deaths," he confided to his biographer.[107] He would soon order more.

The pressure on Wilson only intensified after Veracruz. The Hearst press (whose William Randolph Hearst had vast Chihuahua landholdings) beat the drums for war, as it had with Spain in 1898.[108]

The fall of Huerta coincided with Villa's long-building break with Carranza and Obregon, who beat him to the capital by halting coal deliveries to the commandeered freight trains which moved Villista troops across the desert.[109]

Yaqui and Mayo chieftains broke with Obregon to join Villa. The Zapatistas took Cuernavaca in August. The Constitutionalists took the capital in July, but were losing any prospect of controlling the countryside.[110]

October's Aguascalientes Convention brought together delegates from revolutionary forces throughout Mexico and gave birth to a Sovereign Revolutionary Convention government, which embraced most points of Zapata's Plan of Ayala. "The supreme end of the Revolution is the division of lands among the peasants," the Sovereign Revolutionary Convention proclaimed; the *campesinos* "right away and by force of arms should and can recover the properties which were taken from them in the epoch of the dictatorship."[111]

In November, Carranza's isolated government evacuated the capital.[112] The US pulled out of Veracruz just in time for the Constitutionalist army to take refuge there.[113]

In December, the Villistas and Zapatistas took Mexico City. By then, these *campesino* armies controlled nearly all of the interior highlands from Morelos to Chihuahua. The cosmopolitan capital was a garrison town, much as little Cuautla had been three years ago—and it had been abandoned by its defenders.

Villa and Zapata—the "Centaur of the North" and the "Attila of the South"—met at the ancient Aztec island-gardens of Xochimilco in the south of the city. At the National Palace, they were photographed together in the presidential chambers. Villa beamed in amusement from the presidential chair; Zapata brooded sullenly. "We should burn the Chair to end ambitions," he is reported to have said. But after their troops had been masters of the capital for mere days, they withdrew. Zapata's army moved to Puebla, Villa's to Aguascalientes; the capital was left once again defenseless.[114]

Zapata returned to his headquarters at the Morelos *pueblo* of Tlaltizapan.[115] Neither he nor Villa was interested in state power. Their enemies would waste little time in filling the vacuum and recouping their losses. By the end of January, the Constitutionalists were back in the capital. Obregon had learned the lessons of the trench warfare then underway in Europe. At the battle of Celaya, Villa's waves of horsemen, who had been so effective at Juárez and Torreón, were cut down by Obregon's machine guns like the Allied forces at Gallipoli that year. The badly beaten Villistas retreated to Chihuahua—only to find that Carranzistas had assumed control there and placed a price on Villa's head. When he fled with his fast-shrinking army to Sonora, he found that Carranzista troops had been allowed to pass through US territory to reinforce their garrisons there (bypassing the arduous trek over the Sierra Madre). Villa's army was dealt a second defeat at the battle of Agua Prieta, on the Arizona border. He was reduced, once again, to guerilla insurgency.[116]

Carranza had learned that maintaining power would entail more than mere fealty to Madero's Plan of San Luis Potosi. But his "agrarian reform," which empowered military chieftains to distribute land ("fee simple" rather than as village property), was a farce. They generally distributed it to themselves. A new verb, *carrancear*, to steal, was coined to denote the most vigorous pursuit of the Provisional President's officers.[117] The old landed elite of the Díaz era was increasingly replaced by a "New Carranza Bourgeoisie."[118]

In June, Wilson issued a communiqué to the warring parties, warning that the US would soon be "constrained to decide what means should be employed to help Mexico save herself." Zapata responded via his brother Eufemio: "We are not afraid to defend our country . . . even if they [the US] send millions of soldiers. We will fight them, one man against hundreds. We may have no army and no ammunition, but we have men who will face their bullets."[119]

The US cut off Villa. Standard Oil's Mexican Petroleum Company started paying "advance taxes" to Carranza before his troops had even occupied the Tampico oilfields.[120] The Aguascalientes Villista paper *El Combate* editorialized, "Mexico must not be another Nicaragua."[121]

The pressure for US intervention was increased by the "Plan of San Diego," a conspiracy allegedly planned in a Texas town for a February 20, 1915 uprising to reclaim the lost territories of 1848.[122] The abortive rebellions and raids across South Texas (including a train derailment) were instrumented by Carranza agents as a provocation to press the US on recognition—and resulted mostly in hundreds of Mexican Americans lynched by the Texas Rangers and vigilantes. Chicano PLM militants, angered by the loss of their lands to Anglo ranchers, participated, but charged the Carranzistas with betrayal.[123]

Germany, seeking to draw Mexico (and Japan) into an alliance with promises of restoration of lost territories (and Japanese naval bases) in a dismantled United States, supported Huerta when the dictator was at odds with Wilson; then, after the US cut off arms to Villa, German agents took up the slack. When these designs were revealed in the famous "Zimmerman telegram"—sent in code from Berlin's Foreign Minister Arthur Zimmerman to his Mexico ambassador in January 1917, and intercepted by British intelligence—it only helped propel the US into World War I.[124]

Wilson's betrayal prompted Villa's notorious March 9, 1916 raid on Columbus, New Mexico. Seventeen gringos and over a hundred Villistas died in the skirmish. The day was the sixty-ninth anniversary of the first US attack on Veracruz.[125]

Wilson authorized a punitive expedition to hunt down Villa. Ten thousand US troops under General John J. "Black Jack" Pershing spent weeks fruitlessly searching the deserts and canyons, their presence merely an embarrassment to the tentative US ally Carranza. "I feel just a little bit like a man looking for a needle in a haystack," the frustrated Pershing conceded, appealing to Washington for a US occupation of all Chihuahua, or even all Mexico. One of his lieutenants, George S. Patton, wrote his father in California: "Intervention will be useless; we must take the country and keep it." Indeed, the US Army War College was drafting a plan for the "occupation and pacification of northern Mexico."[126]

The closest Pershing got to Villa was when his troops opened fire on a crowd in Parral, which had taunted them by shouting *vivas* for the fugitive rebel. Several Mexicans were killed, increasing the pressure on Carranza to expel the gringos. The only real action the expedition saw was with Constitutionalist forces at Carrizal, where the US troops refused orders to halt. Pershing's badly outnumbered men suffered seventeen dead.[127]

Back in Mexico City, Obregon was brilliantly consolidating Constitutionalist gains, playing the urban workers against the *campesinos*. He re opened the *Casa del Obrero Mundial* (House of the World Worker), an organization founded by anarcho-syndicalists in 1912 and closed by Huerta. Casa militants were recruited by Obregon into "Red Battalions" to fight Villa and Zapata.[128] Obregon, who had lost an arm fighting Villa's forces, portrayed the Villistas and Zapatistas as "reactionaries." The Casa accepted this line, despite the best efforts of Antonio Díaz Soto y Gama, Zapata's liaison to the urban movement.[129]

The movement was betrayed in the summer of 1916, when the Casa called a general strike to press the Constitutionalists on their promises. The strike was broken, the leaders threatened with execution for violating "public order."[130] Martial law was declared in Mexico City and the Casa crushed. "As soon as Carranza felt himself the master of the situation, he kicked overboard his old friends the working men," remarked Enrique Flores Magón from exile.[131]

Carranza's new constitution adopted in 1917 was nonetheless shaped by the pressure of populists and the left. Article 27 declared the nation original owner of all lands and waters, including subsoil rights. *Ejidos* and other public or communal properties were protected as "inalienable and imprescriptable." Article 123 guaranteed the eight-hour day and minimum wage, abolished child and debt labor, and upheld the right to strike.[132]

Carranza simultaneously dispatched Gen. Pablo González to finally crush the "Zapata rabble." Again, villages were burned, crops destroyed, thousands hanged, herded into detention camps, deported *en masse* to the Yucatan—as under Huerta. In May 1916, Zapatista positions outside Cuernavaca were subject to one of the first aerial bombardments in military history. Purges and dissension emerged in the Zapatista ranks; in June 1917 Eufemio Zapata was killed by a follower he had abused. But the Zapatistas would rally after the harvest season; battle-scarred Cuautla and Cuernavaca changed hands again and again.[133]

Like Madero before him, Carranza was under heavy international pressure to pacify Morelos. Opined the *New York Times:* "Order, the resumption of sugar plant-ing, the sugar industry and agricultural work generally, the revival of communica-tions, education, and peaceful life depend in Morelos upon the utter downfall, the permanent absence, or the extinction of ZAPATA . . . he is beyond amnesty."[134]

On April 10, 1919, at Chinameca *hacienda*, where he had been lured by a gov-ernment agent feigning an offer of men and guns, Zapata was gunned down in a treacherous ambush. The corpse was displayed for two days in Cuautla, where tens of thousands of *campesinos* filed past to pay last respects. Of course, rumors abounded anyway that Zapata had survived, was hiding in the hills, ready once more to return and redeem. De la O and the other Zapatista generals carried on the struggle.[135]

With the populist forces in retreat, Carranza started returning much confiscated land to former owners throughout Mexico. The "New Carranza Bourgeoisie" was closing ranks with surviving elements of the old Díaz bourgeoisie.[136]

This finally brought a split between Carranza and Obregon. Carranza was ousted by Obregonistas in May 1920, and killed in flight to Veracruz. An interim govern-ment made offers to the forces still in rebellion. The Zapatistas laid down their arms with promises of being able to keep all occupied lands. Morelos was the first part of Mexico to achieve a real agrarian reform.[137]

Villa was granted a *hacienda* in Durango in exchange for peace, where he settled with his most trusted troops. He was nonetheless assassinated in 1923, his car hit with a fusillade of machine-gun fire in an ambush at Parral.[138] Meanwhile in Chihua-hua, the regime was selling a large chunk of the land empire Villa had expropriated back to the Terrazas clan.[139]

Obregon was more adept than Carranza at exploiting populism. "The principal purpose of socialism," he declared, "is to extend a hand to the downtrodden in order to establish a greater equilibrium between capital and labor." In other words, historian James Cockcroft notes, "it could be co-opted for other than its avowed purpose."[140]

The secretive Bucareli Accords gave back to US investors much of what the "revolutionary" government appeared to take away. As the price of US recognition, Obregon agreed to minimum reimbursements on expropriated US properties and to refrain from expropriating oil companies as long as they developed their leases instead of speculating.[141]

The machine being consolidated was the foundation of the one-party state that rules Mexico today. Zapata and Villa and even Ricardo Flores Magón, all safely dead, were adopted as official heros of the Revolution. It was a revisionist history of Orwellian proportions. As one disgusted veteran put it, "This revolution has now degenerated into a government."[142]

THE REVOLUTION INSTITUTIONALIZED

Obregon was assassinated in 1928 by a Catholic zealot. He had by then ceded power to a groomed successor, Plutarco Calles, who slowed the agrarian reform and launched the National Revolutionary Party—which would be renamed the Mexican Revolutionary Party by his successor, and finally, in 1942, the Institutional Revolutionary Party (PRI).[143]

As *Jefe Maximo*, Calles controlled a succession of three puppet "interim presidents" while reliable electoral mechanisms were established. The basic elements of the PRI state were established in the 1930s: six-year presidential terms, with no re-election, but a presidential succession determined by the party elite in an obscure ritual known as the *dedazo*, or "fingering," then legitimized in a thoroughly controlled election. With the formal trappings of democracy, the PRI state would become known as "the perfect dictatorship."[144]

Calles established another presidential tradition by becoming one of the richest men in Mexico. But his real chosen successor surprised him by moving sharply to the left—and crafted the centralized leviathan. The final indispensable element of the PRI state was corporatism—"incorporation" of popular struggles into the apparatus of the ruling party. The architect of PRI corporatism, Lázaro Cárdenas —a Constitutionalist general who had fought the Villistas in Sonora, occupied the Tampico oilfields and served as governor of Michoacan—became president in 1934.[145]

Cárdenas really instated the agrarian reform, finally breaking up *haciendas* and turning them over to *ejidos*. Under Cárdenas, 18 million hectares were distributed to 814,537 *campesinos*.[146]

Cárdenas oversaw the founding of the Mexican Workers Confederation (CTM), the mammoth industrial union, and the National Campesino Confederation (CNC)— *ejiditario* membership in which was mandated by law. The CNC, built on the armed peasant organizations surviving from the Revolution, became an instrument for delivering *campesino* votes and loyalties to the PRI in exchange for access to land and credit.[147]

The greatest hour for Cárdenas was nationalization of the oil industry. The newly formed oil workers union went on strike in 1937. The companies refused to meet worker demands despite government studies that they could afford to do so. The following March 18 (thereafter a national holiday), Cárdenas seized the sixteen US and British companies. The CTM called a huge demonstration for Mexico City; workers and *campesinos* shelled out small contributions by the tens of thousands to help pay for the expropriation. Indemnification conflicts dragged on four years; foreign interests in Mexico once again called for US intervention or even annexation.[148]

Cárdenas also nationalized the railroads, established the Federal Electric Commission (CFE) to power the countryside, and made the state a partner in all mining operations. It took this kind of left-populist program to finally stabilize the regime.[149]

The regime thus stabilized, Cárdenas was followed by the more conservative Manuel Avila Camacho, and the still more conservative Miguel Aleman (the first civilian in the succession). In an indiscreet signal to the business elite, Avila Camacho's inaugural speech praised the "vital energy of private initiative" and promised to "increase the protection given to private agricultural properties."[150]

Redistribution of land, especially fertile land, was slowed again, and credit cut off to *ejidos* which worked their lands collectively. Even as the revolutionary legitimacy given the state by Cárdenas eroded, state control over the *campesinos* and workers escalated. The regime employed measured terror against dissidents from the CNC.[151]

The PRI began its "balancing act" between populist, nationalist *versus* conservative, pro-business elements—the tilt in one direction or the other mandated according to the dictates of maintaining power. The populist legacy allowed for the corporatist institutionalization of revolutionary currents, workers and *campesinos* organized in PRI-controlled "*charro*" unions.

The party cultivated a *PRIista* pseudo-left, or "satellite left." The grandfather of the satellite left, Vicente Lombardo Toledano, was purged from the CTM leadership as a "Moscow agent" in 1947. The purge launched the long, corrupt lordship of Fidel Velazquez over the CTM (the union slogan changing from "For a classless society" to "Social peace"). Lombardo broke from the PRI to found the Popular Socialist Party (PPS). But the "Lombardista thesis" of a popular front with the PRI against imperialism became PPS doctrine. PPS, in turn, would spawn more equivocal leftist entities.[152]

The disloyal opposition was on the right, reactionary forces effectively exploiting *campesino* alienation from PRI paternalism. In the Cristero rebellion of the 1920s, a backlash to anti-clerical measures, peasants took up arms to defend the Church, especially in the Bajio region, just northwest of the Valley of Mexico. This was followed by the Sinarquistas, a counter-revolutionary secret society with pro-fascist sympathies, modeled on the Spanish Falange. Sinarquistas gained a foothold in Sonora and Baja California before they were crushed, with considerable blood-shed, in the 1940s. Some Sinarquistas went on to join disaffected PRI conservatives in the National Action Party (PAN), which remains the right-wing opposition.[153]

World War II brought the PRI regime closer to the US. Mexico followed Washington in declaring war on the Axis (and sent troops with MacArthur to the Philippines), but its major contribution was economic support for the war effort. Mexican migrant workers were allowed north of the border to work US fields in the *bracero* program. Production of oil, zinc, mercury, cadmium, copper and lead spurred industrialization, while the *bracero* program allowed the regime to reduce rural areas which had supported the Sinarquistas.[154]

The US and British boycott of Petróleos Mexicanos (Pemex), the state company Cárdenas had created, was lifted for the war effort, and the discovery of vast oil-fields in a conciliatory Venezuela (then under a pro-US dictatorship) prompted Mexico to drop prices. Venezuelan and Mexican oil was critical to the Allied victory.[155] Hitler's disastrous invasion of Russia was aimed at securing the oilfields of the Caucasus for his war machine, while the attack on Pearl Harbor was Japan's bid to keep the US Pacific Fleet away from the oilfields of Southeast Asia. While these paroxysms of conquest proved reckless gambles for the Axis, the US and Britain could afford to ride out early losses with a dependable supply of Latin American oil.[156]

The *bracero* program and massive mineral exports would all outlive the war. But the PRI state's populist tradition kept Mexico from too eager an association with the institutions established at the Bretton Woods conference to expand (US-dominated) "free markets." Mexico took loans from the World Bank and International Monetary Fund (IMF), and dropped tariffs in bilateral trade agreements with the US, but resisted pressure to join the General Agreements on Tariffs and Trade (GATT).[157]

The US press hailed the post-war "Mexican miracle," while decrying the "wetback invasion"—the very existence of which was evidence that the *campesinos* were not reaping the "miraculous" benefits. The Border Patrol's Operation Wetback expelled 1 million Mexicans in 1954.[158]

A wildcat railroad strike in 1958 signaled the potential of independent labor militancy. Demetrio Vallejo, a Oaxaca rank-and-file activist with the Railway Workers Syndicate of the Mexican Republic (STFRM) issued a "Plan of the Southeast," calling for better wages than those negotiated by the STFRM bosses. Workers across Mexico shut down the national rail system. Union halls were occupied by the army, and thousands arrested. Vallejo and five other wildcat leaders were imprisoned.[159]

But the PRI regime's first real crisis came in 1968, with the emergence of a radical student movement on the eve of the Mexico City Olympics. Students at Mexico City's National Autonomous University (UNAM) denounced construction of the enormous Sports Palace near the university for the games few Mexicans could afford to attend. Incidents of police brutality provided the spark for a wave of protests.[160]

Gobernación Secretary Luis Echeverria was sent to negotiate with the students, but broadsheets denouncing the government were already being distributed to Mexico City's poor *barrios*, and workers were joining the movement—as had happened that spring in Paris. Demands for release of arrested students and resignation of the Mexico City police chief were joined by demands for release of Demetrio Vallejo and other dissident unionists imprisoned in 1959.[161]

Granaderos—riot police—were mixing it up in the streets with high school kids, but conservative President Gustavo Díaz Ordaz paranoiacally saw the movement only as a "communist plot." The presidential hopeful Echeverria could not afford to appear weak, and rejected the demands. The army occupied UNAM, hundreds were arrested, leaders tortured. But the protests only spread. On October 2, at the Plaza de Tres Culturas in Tlatelolco, where Cuauhtémoc, the last Mexica *tlatoani*, made his desperate final stand against Cortéz, a dusk demonstration of thousands was surrounded by army troops. When the shooting was over, perhaps five hundred young people were dead. The official death toll of forty-nine was believed by no one.[162]

The 1960s also saw the emergence of small *campesino* guerilla groups. Díaz Ordaz actually redistributed more land in the 1960s than Cárdenas in the 1930s—but with the critical difference that only some 10 percent of it was arable.[163]

The PRI elite decided it was time for a tilt back to the left. Echeverria, favorite of the party's populist wing, was "fingered" for the presidency. He amnestied the railway worker and student prisoners, once again stepped up the agrarian reform, spouted Third Worldist rhetoric—and successfully co-opted the student movement by offering the leaders jobs. A revival of student unrest in 1971 was met again with repression—albeit with greater discretion and deniability. Several students were murdered or "disappeared" by a clandestine paramilitary group, *Los Halcones*, the Falcons. Suspicions of a CIA hand in the strategy were supported by a February 1977 report in the *New York Times* that Echeverria had been a paid CIA operative during his tenure as Gobernación Secretary under Díaz Ordaz.[164]

The expansion of US economic hegemony continued apace. By 1970, foreign firms—principally US—controlled nearly half of Mexican industry. US corporations dominated mining and metallurgy (54 percent), automotive (57 percent), rubber (76 percent), pharmaceuticals (86 percent) and tobacco (100 percent). Remaining in state hands were oil, petrochemicals, natural gas, electricity and the railroads, with 100 percent Mexican ownership required of the banks and broadcast media.[165]

The 1973 oil shock was good news for Mexico. The resultant US shift from monolithic reliance on the Arabs to a new emphasis on domestic, Canadian and Latin American producers ushered in Mexico's boom years, just as cracks in the system had appeared.[166] The Trilateral Commission report *Energy: Managing the Transition* became the cornerstone of US energy policy under both Richard Nixon (who officially dubbed the strategic transition "Project Independence") and Jimmy Carter.[167] Mexico's subsoil had become strategic to US national security strategies.

In 1977, President José López Portillo's refusals to show up in Washington for the signing of the Panama Canal Treaty or to allow the exiled Shah of Iran to stay in his country were related to intrigues over Mexican subsoil resources. Carter's Energy Secretary (and former CIA chief) James Schlesinger (who had recently declared securing oil supplies "a military responsibility") dispatched a team to Mexico City to pressure López to lower the price on pending natural gas sales to US firms, insisting Mexico sell cheaper than Canada. López claimed he would rather burn the gas than lower the price. The new pipeline was built from the gasworks of Tabasco to the Texas border, but not on Washington's terms.[168]

On August 14, 1978, National Security Advisor Zbigniew Brzezinski (the Trilateral Commission's intellectual golden boy) signed Presidential Review Memorandum #41, "Review of US Policies Toward Mexico," to ready Carter for his upcoming trip. The top-secret document, later procured by a Mexican journalist, was the fruit of a multi-agency study "to develop a coordinated and well-integrated approach to our relations with Mexico." The Energy Secretary's commentary noted that Mexico had ignored his warnings about the gas prices. The Special Trade Representative complained that, despite the lowering of US trade barriers, the Mexican government resisted such reciprocal concessions as joining GATT.[169]

Former Secretary of State Henry Kissinger had recently joined David Rockefeller—heir to the Standard Oil fortune, president of Chase Manhattan Bank and Trilateral Commission founder—in a meeting with Mexican industrial leaders to persuade them to pressure their government on GATT.[170]

As the 1980s opened, López Portillo and Ronald Reagan were at odds over Central America. In July 1979, the Sandinista junta was flown into a liberated

Nicaragua from Costa Rican exile in López Portillo's presidential Boeing 727, *Quetzalcoatl I.* His government also loaned political recognition to El Salvador's FMLN guerillas. (Only on Guatemala, with its turmoil bordering Chiapas, did the Mexican government remain silent!)[171]

As the PRI machine judiciously tilted to the left, nearly the rest of Latin America succumbed to military dictatorships, with varying degrees of CIA involvement and direction. Mexico, equivocating on the Cold War dogma of military terror to protect the "Free World," was portrayed by the Reagan administration as the last domino of leftist revolution spreading up the isthmus from Central America. In a televised bid for Congressional approval of aid to the CIA's *contra* army in Nicaragua, Reagan said, "there is an old Communist slogan that the Sandinistas have made clear they honor: The road to victory goes through Mexico."[172]

Yet, as the pitched struggle raged in Central America, a quiet counter-revolution was actually underway in Mexico.

THE COUNTER-REVOLUTION

The oil crash of the Reagan years came just as the IMF and World Bank, having loaned heavily in the boom years of the 1970s, were calling in the chips. The resultant economic crisis and peso devaluation came just as Miguel de la Madrid was chosen as Mexico's next president—a tilt to the US-trained "neoliberal" or "technocratic" wing of the PRI, mostly ensconced in the Planning and Finance Secretariat. "Liberalizing" the economy became a condition of future credit, and the technocrats understood the game. The *tecnocratas* once again espoused an ethic of pure, apolitical administration. The results, once again, were extremely political.[173]

By 1982, the foreign debt had risen to $82 billion. In August, Finance Secretary Jesús Silva Herzog flew to Washington to plead for relief. Federal Reserve Chair Paul Volker arranged a $6.5 billion emergency package. An IMF delegation to Mexico City helped the drowning government reschedule $19.7 billion in loans, but on tough terms, above the world prime rate—with a Structural Adjustment Program imposed as a condition. The SAP demanded Mexico abandon strictures on foreign investment, privatize state-owned industries, eliminate import restrictions, cut social spending, freeze the minimum wage, reduce tariffs and join GATT.[174]

In one of his last acts as president, López Portillo nationalized the banks, his eyes welling up as he made the announcement before Mexico's Congress.[175] After this display of populist bravado, his successor de la Madrid, Mexico's first US-educated president, was well poised to begin the Free Trade transition.[176] De la Madrid immediately negotiated a $1.9 billion loan from the World Bank for an aggressive export-oriented development program.[177]

This was the beginning of the neoliberal counter-revolution: meaning, as the term is used in Latin America, a return to the *laissez-faire* capitalism of classical nineteenth-century Liberalism.

The PAN, favoring a faster pace of neoliberal reform, also proved a convenient bargaining chip against the PRI. By the 1980s, the government was resorting to blatant fraud to prevent PAN electoral victories in the northern states. A PAN delegation showed up at the 1984 Republican Convention in Dallas where Reagan was nominated for a second term.[178]

Oil prices plunged with the new Pax Americana in the Middle East, but Mexico's share of the US market continued to grow. In 1982, Mexico surpassed Saudi Arabia as the largest US supplier.[179]

The *maquiladora* sector rapidly expanded. The program, inaugurated in 1965, allowed US-owned assembly plants to import components and raw materials duty-free to a zone extending 20 kilometers in from the border for finished products re-exported back to the US. Matching factories went up on either side of the border. Mexican hourly wages have never amounted to 15 percent of those in the US, and the 1982 peso devaluation was good news for the *maquiladora* industry. In 1983, the *maquiladora* program, first conceived for the border zone, was extended to all Mexico. Between 1975 and 1987 the *maquiladora* workforce grew from 67,000 to 279,000. At $1.5 billion in 1987, the industry was Mexico's third largest source of hard currency.[180]

By the 1980s, the foreign automotive industry in Mexico, initiated by Ford in 1925, also included Chrysler, General Motors, American Motors, Volkswagen, Nissan and Renault. The US plants, mostly in the North, largely exported components to the US, while the German, Japanese and French firms concentrated on the Mexican market. Consequently, the peso crash served the interests of the US firms.[181]

US tourism became a pillar of the Mexican economy, surpassing the *maquiladoras* and vying with oil as the top currency source; it was a $2.27 billion industry by 1987.[182]

In 1986, Mexico joined GATT, and the following year entered a "US–Mexico Framework Agreement" on improved market access, which proved a precursor of the North American Free Trade Agreement.[183]

The number of Mexican millionaires rose impressively, while a 1990 World Bank study found that 41 million (nearly half) of the population lived in poverty;

17 million in extreme poverty. In Guerrero, Oaxaca and Chiapas, 80 percent of the population was without access to potable water. By 1990, the US was once again destination for 70 percent of Mexico's exports.[184]

By the time Harvard man Carlos Salinas, the Mexican NAFTA architect, took power by fraud in 1988, it was clear that the technocratic coup was less a tactical "tilt" than a permanent counter-revolution. Free Trade orthodoxy reigned.

The 1988 presidential race was a real contest for the PRI. Cuauhtémoc Cárdenas, former Michoacan governor and son of the hero Lázaro, broke with the PRI and ran as the candidate of a National Democratic Front (FDN) which briefly unified the left parties. As the votes were being counted, the fancy new computers mysteriously went down. When they came back on line, Carlos Salinas had won by just over 50 percent. The FDN charged "cybernetic fraud," but the PRI's electoral "alchemists" had also used the more traditional methods, such as dumping ballot boxes from disloyal precincts. A wave of angry protests swept the country, especially Michoacan. Followers proclaimed they were ready for a general strike to defend his victory, but Cárdenas refused the offer.[185]

The stolen elections marked the first emergence of a serious electoral opposition on the left. Many of the parties which had come together in the FDN coalesced more permanently as the Party of the Democratic Revolution (PRD). In Michoacan and Guerrero, PRD militants blocked roads, seized town halls and organized parallel municipal governments in protest of fraudulent elections. In the next six years, over two hundred *PRDistas* would be assassinated.[186]

Salinas, once de la Madrid's mentor in the Planning and Finance Secretariat, accelerated the counter-revolution. The banks were reprivatized, and sale of state enterprises to family conglomerates (*grupos*) and foreign corporations was stepped up. Tariffs were cut to rates below those demanded by the IMF.[187]

The 1990 Brady Plan, worked out between US Treasury Secretary Nicholas Brady and Salinas, brought Mexico into a "debt-for-equity" swap, allowing foreign corporations to buy Mexican debt at a cut rate, and exchange it for pesos to be invested in Mexico. Chrysler bought $100 million in Mexican debt for $65 million—in effect, gaining $100 million worth of Mexican labor and industrial assets at a 35 percent discount.[188]

The technocratic regime had still not touched state ownership of oil, or the *ejidal* lands redistributed in the agrarian reform—the two most sacred elements of the Mexican social contract, both rooted in Article 27 of the Constitution. But the *Tratado de Libre Commercio* (TLC, as NAFTA is known to Mexicans) struck at this heart of the corporatist system. Finally, in 1992, Article 27 was amended to allow privatization of the "inalienable" *ejidos.*[189]

It is no coincidence that the new Zapatistas should emerge just as the revolutionary movements of Central America were on the wane. Beating back the Central American revolutions was the necessary prerequisite for inaugurating the hemisphere's Free Trade order—and it was this inauguration which pushed the impoverished indigenous communities of southern Mexico over the brink into open rebellion.

3

SOUTHERN MEXICO IN THE
FREE TRADE ORDER

Political Ecology of the New Zapatismo

The new Zapatistas would be the first revolutionary movement to declare war not only on a government, but on an international trade agreement. An early communiqué calls the signing of NAFTA a "death sentence" for the Indians of Mexico.[1]

Under the constitutional changes Salinas pushed through in preparation for NAFTA, the *ejidos*, the surviving agrarian legacy of the Mexican Revolution, are poised to be appropriated by agribusiness. The inheritors of Zapata stand to be evicted and reduced to landlessness, or become wage slaves—picking export-bound tomatoes or strawberries on lands they once considered "inalienable," once worked to produce *maíz* for local markets.

Despite Malthusian precepts that Mexico is unable to feed itself and faces no alternative to global integration, all you have to do is go to any village in the Chiapas Highlands to understand why the people are hungry. The good land in the valleys is empty (or was, until the land occupations of the 1994 uprising), owned by an absentee speculator or rancher. The *campesinos* are left to grow their *maíz* on the rocky and sometimes near-vertical slopes—lands which in an earlier era would have been left forested to preserve watersheds. Already, nearly half of that third of Mexicans living off the land are relegated to steep slopes and other marginal lands.[2]

In the de la Madrid and Salinas years, wealth was concentrated at the top of the social pyramid in Mexico, as in the US and UK under the simultaneous Reagan–Bush and Thatcher regimes. Globalist dogma became hegemonic; the social contract which had been won through the Revolution and formalized in the Cárdenas years was betrayed. The dominant technocratic wing of the PRI saw no viable future for domestic *maíz* production.[3]

The *campesino* landbase is opened to a market dominated by global giants. In the cities, Bimbo bread (the Mexican answer to Wonder bread) displaces *tortillas*. The hypertrophied industrial zones along the US border absorb the desperately cheap labor of the displaced *ejiditarios*.

THE THIRD DEATH OF
EMILIANO ZAPATA

Carlos Salinas introduced the changes to Article 27 in late 1991. By January 1992, they had been approved by both (PRI-dominated) houses of Congress and the (PRI-dominated) legislatures of all thirty-one states. The constitutional clause mandating the government provide all petitioning "nuclei of population" with "sufficient lands and waters" was expunged. Restrictions on Church and corporate land ownership were loosened. For the first time since 1919, the agrarian reform was officially over.[4]

The amendments granted *ejiditarios* the "right" to "trade" or "grant the use of" their lands, or to "associate" with outside parties. Changes to the Agrarian Law, bringing it into conformity with the constitutional changes, interpret this to allow selling, renting, sharecropping, or mortgaging of individual parcels within an *ejido*; joint ventures or contracts between *ejidos* and private investors; or *ejiditarios* as a body to dissolve the *ejido*. The requirement that *ejiditarios* must work the land to maintain a share was terminated, along with further land redistribution.[5]

Ejiditarios could now transfer their parcels to other *ejido* members, or sell to outsiders by a majority vote, or privatize an entire *ejido* by a two-thirds vote. The *campesino* organizations protested that with restrictions lifted on use of *ejidos* as debt collateral, they are no longer "inalienable and imprescriptable," although the words remained in the text of Article 27. The *campesino* organizations questioned the claim that there was no land left to redistribute; some demanded an investigation into illegal holdings.[6]

Ejidos (lands redistributed by the agrarian reform) and communal lands (those traditionally accruing to a village since before the Revolution) together make up the "social sector," distinct from either public or private. Mexico's 28,000 *ejidos* and *tierras comunales* account for nearly half of the national territory—although generally not the most desirable half. Twenty percent of these 95 million hectares is not even considered arable. Only some 16 percent is irrigated. The majority of *ejiditarios* have parcels under 5 hectares, insufficient to support a family through either subsistence or market agriculture. Monied interests which can afford irrigation and other inputs, or which seek to exploit natural resources such as timber rather than the agricultural wealth of the soil, covet these lands. The 1993 rewriting of the *Ley*

Forestal and *Ley de Aguas*—also part of Article 27's enabling legislation—opened Mexico's forest and water resources to greater market control.[7]

The Forestry Law reforms were actually lifted directly from written proposals from International Paper VP Edward Kobacker to Luis Tellez, forestry subsecretary under Agriculture Secretary Carlos Hank González (as subsequently leaked to the Mexican daily *La Jornada*).[8]

Ejidos, which are often the only local government in remote areas of Mexico, are run by an elected three-member commission called the *comisariado* (president, secretary and treasurer)—generally controlled by PRI-affiliated *caciques*. The control of credit and inputs such as hybrid seeds and fertilizers through the CNC has entrenched this system of rural bossism for sixty years. Renting, sharecropping and even selling of *ejidal* lands by *caciques* and their favorites was already taking place quietly and illegally before the Constitution was changed.[9]

Latifundios—vast plantations owned by a single *patrón* which characterized the pre-Revolutionary era—remained ostensibly illegal under the Constitutional changes. As early as 1968, however, the young Cuauhtémoc Cárdenas had observed the illegal but widespread connivance between *caciques* and landowners: "the camouflaged *latifundios* have been established, when possible, on the best and most productive lands."[10]

In his classic *Open Veins of Latin America*, Uruguayan writer Eduardo Galeano called this betrayal of the hard-won *ejidos* "The Second Death of Emiliano Zapata."[11] With the changes to Article 27, the illegalities were honored by the law, and the Caudillo of the South died yet a third death.

Owing to pressures from the PRI's populist wing, the amended Article 27 maintained certain limits on the size of landholdings—already largely unenforced, through the use of *prestanombres* ("name-loaners") and similar subterfuge. Maximum legal property size for a single individual is 100 hectares of irrigated land or the "equivalent" in rain-fed or pasture land. Since the "equivalent" for pasture lands is determined by the territory needed to maintain a head of cattle, the permissible limit can soar in arid areas. The Article 27 changes increased the private holding limit for corporations to 2,500 hectares—which, through manipulation of the "equivalencies," could allow consolidation of vast corporate estates.[12]

The *caciques* who run *ejidos* as petty fiefdoms stand to profit from privatizations. For the *caciques*, the privatization may be a ticket to join the bourgeoisie. For *ejiditarios* who dissent from the *cacicazgo*, the system of patronage and thuggery, or whose families are at odds with those of the *caciques*, the privatization could mean entry into the ranks of the landless dispossessed in the urban shantytowns and migrant labor camps.

Depressed corn prices increase pressure to sell out, and NAFTA is virtually designed to send Mexican *maíz* prices plunging. When NAFTA took effect, all agricultural tariffs were eliminated, save those on the ancient staples of *maíz* and beans. These too are to be completely phased out by 2009. Mexico's *ejiditarios* and *comuneros*, who have traditionally fed the country, stand to be priced off the market by a flood of cheap imports.[13]

US corn producers, with access to the entire technological package of hybrid seeds, irrigation and inputs, average 6.9 tons per hectare, compared to the 1.7 of their Mexican counterparts.[14]

At the 1998 harvest season in the US corn belt, prices were at $1.75 a bushel, 65 percent below their 1996 peak, and *The Economist* reported that "silos are bursting at the seams." The depressed prices resulted from passage of the 1996 Freedom to Farm Act, which got the US government out of agricultural regulation, cut subsidies and allowed farmers to plant from fence-post to fence-post (the lessons of the Dust Bowl apparently forgotten). With the global market glutted, the US boosted exports to its NAFTA partners.[15]

The exports are mostly sold in deals brokered by the US Department of Agriculture's Commodity Credit Corporation—sometimes greased with federal loans to the purchasing countries or private grain-dealers. Prior to deregulation, the USDA heavily subsidized corn production—even paying farmers not to grow in order to regulate prices.[16]

US corn prices got a lift in 1996 by the drought that struck northern Mexico, the worst in fifty years, costing farmers millions of tons of grain.[17]

That same year, a report from the US President's Advisory Committee for Trade Policy and Negotiations (ACTPN) recommended that the Clinton administration press Mexico and Canada to accelerate elimination of tariffs on farm products.[18] ACTPN is a virtual who's who of America's corporate elite, with representatives from Chrysler, AT&T, Hewlett-Packard, General Motors, Bethlehem Steel, Eastman Kodak, Coca-Cola and Coors.[19]

An OECD report by UC Davis economist Phillip Martin predicted that 6 million rural Mexicans will flee the land for the cities and US as a result of NAFTA—unless they make a transition from *maíz* to export crops like broccoli.[20]

Mexico became dependent on corn imports from the US as *maíz* production declined during the oil boom, despite government subsidies through populist programs such as the Mexican Food System (SAM). With wage labor widely available, more *campesinos* left the land. The neoliberal counter-revolution that followed deepened this trend—even as wage labor dried up following the 1982 peso devaluation.[21]

Credit from the federal government's Banrural shifted in the 1980s from *maíz* and bean producers to growers of cattle-feed crops like soy and sorghum. This shift took place just as the devaluation made inputs more costly, further marginalizing staple producers.[22] Acreage devoted to *maíz* shrunk, while that devoted to cattle expanded. As exports of winter tomatoes and strawberries to the US grew, so did imports of US corn.[23]

In Chiapas, which produces 13 percent of Mexico's *maíz*, 67 percent of social-sector *maíz* production is sold on the market, while 33 percent is for subsistence. The National Solidarity Program (Pronasol), designed by Salinas to ease the transition to NAFTA, represented a break with programs like SAM which aimed at boosting *maíz* production. Most Pronasol funds went into public works like paving roads. What was available for agricultural credit failed to even compensate for income cut off by such neoliberal measures as the disbanding of INMECAFE, the government coffee-brokering agency which purchased from small *campesino* growers.[24] Pronasol spent more money in Chiapas than any other state, but little of it reached the struggling *campesino* cooperatives and enterprises.[25] Now price supports even on *maíz* are banned by NAFTA as "non-tariff trade barriers," and are to be phased out.[26]

While *ejidos* became far more reliant on pesticides and other such inputs during the oil boom, the contrast remains vivid between the culture and technology of the small *maíz* producer and the big agro-export producer now usurping the former's economic niche. Rigorous enforcement of FDA "cosmetic standards" at the US border—perfect, unblemished fruit—further entrenches pesticide-dependence in Mexico's export sector. A quarter of all pesticides sprayed in the fields of California are used to assure cosmetic appearance, with no effects on yields or nutrition. Corresponding studies for Mexico haven't been done, but a similar proportion can be assumed, especially on the northern NAFTA zone plantations.[27]

Researcher Angus Wright, investigating conditions on Baja California vegetable plantations contracted by the US multinational Castle and Cook, found that the local Social Security emergency clinic reported up to ten pesticide poisonings daily. The actual figure may be far higher, since workers were encouraged to go to doctors in the pay of the plantation. Wright found that overseers administered the standard organophosphate antidote, atropine (a belladonna derivative, itself a dangerous substance) at the first sign of exposure—temporarily suppressing the symptoms, keeping workers in the fields at further risk to their health.[28]

One migrant farmworker from Sinaloa's Culiacán Valley responded to Wright's questioning about whether workers there suffered from pesticide sickness: "Yes, lots of times. But it's hard to do anything about it. If you take off work to go to the doctor, they fire you . . . And if you make a complaint about the poisoning, they fire you, or they shoot you."

"Shoot you?"

"I've seen it twice. They just gun you down. The *pistoleros* who work for the growers. They'll just shoot you dead."[29]

El Bajio, a deeply fertile agricultural heartland in the states of Guanajuato, Queretaro and San Luis Potosi, for centuries provided *maíz* for Mexico City's *tortillas*. It is today a pesticide-intensive "strawberry empire."[30]

Chiapas is assigned a strategic role by the USDA to keep insect pests from spreading north from Central America. The agency maintains two plants in the state where pests are bred, sterilized with radioactive cobalt-60 and cesium-137, and released into the environment—one for the Mediterranean fruit fly outside Tapachula and one for the screw worm, a larval cattle parasite, outside Tuxtla.[31] USDA also works with the Mexican government to spray the Chiapas countryside with malathion as an additional measure against Medfly.[32] Indigenous communities have protested that they have been directly sprayed from helicopters with no warning.[33] Officials insist the programs pose no risk. But it is the prevalence of economies based on cattle and strawberries that provides a hospitable environment for these pests.

The cheap corn imports create poverty, not affordable *tortillas*.

In December 1996, the Mexican government announced steep increases in the price of *tortillas*.[34] The *tortilla* subsidy system, another populist program slated to be phased out, was already seen by the neoliberal elite as a cash cow to be milked at the cost of the public trust.

In September 1996, amid opposition charges of a cover-up, the PRI majority in Mexico's Chamber of Deputies officially ended an investigation of the National Popular Subsistence Company (Conasupo), the consumer subsidy program. The deputies voted 219 129 along party lines to send President Ernesto Zedillo a report finding no evidence of high-level corruption. Raúl Salinas, the imprisoned brother of the former president who served as a senior Conasupo official between 1985 and 1992, was cleared in the embezzlement of $40 million from the program. Zedillo, himself a target of the probe, was also cleared. Conasupo was said to have been co-opted into Raúl's money-laundering networks for narco-profits. But the allegations which raised the most anger were that Conasupo bought cut-rate corn intended for animal feed and contaminated with fungi-induced carcinogenic aflatoxins for the *tortillas* eaten by millions of Mexicans. The panel also concluded that Conasupo's importation of tons of powdered milk reportedly contaminated by the Chernobyl nuclear accident in 1986 posed no significant threat to public health.[35]

Evidence of hunger and protein-desperation could not be more blatant, and recalls the ripples of a coming social explosion that presaged the Revolution. On May 30, 1996, three hundred impoverished Mexicans held up a train hauling *maíz* for the giant *tortilla* company Maseca in Nuevo Leon, making off with 40 tons. On June 23, hundreds of residents of the poor Durango *colonias* of Flores Magón and El Consuelo held up a train loaded with wheat, carrying away tons in pick-up trucks, barrels and sacks. Just a few days earlier, Durango residents had sacked a train hauling corn.[36]

PRIVATIZING THE GENETIC COMMONS

Campesino and Indian culture merge in what anthropologist Guillermo Bonfil calls "*México profundo*." The centrality of land and *maíz* is what defines this Mexico—and the closer rural communities remain to their indigenous roots, the more "profound."[37] While *México profundo* extends to the northern border states, it is more widespread in the South. NAFTA is antithetical to the survival of *México profundo*. Yet *México profundo* is the *de facto* guardian of Mexico's biodiversity—which is now coveted as a resource by the very system which threatens it.

The chaos of forest, slopes and scrubland which had been left to *México profundo* beyond the ag-biz empires, factory zones and suburban sprawl is now recognized as a vital storehouse of genetic material. Seventy percent of Mexico's remaining forests are on *ejidos* and communal lands. *México profundo* is also the repository of knowledge on how to work this land without destroying the biodiversity: before the oil boom brought credit for pesticides, most *ejidos* were organic by default, especially in the South.[38]

The Mexican and Central American highlands are one of twelve world centers of biodiversity identified by the Russian scientist N. I. Vavilov in the 1920s. These twelve "Vavilov Centers"—all in tropical mountainous regions within the developing world—are matrices of natural evolution and the primal source of virtually all food crops. The Mesoamerican Vavilov Center is the original source of all tomatoes, most beans and chiles, many squashes—and *maíz*, which is believed to have first emerged in the plateau of Jalisco. At least hundreds and perhaps thousands of native *maíz* strains—called "land races"—have been lost, and the rate of loss is accelerating.[39]

With incursions of genetically standardized US agribusiness corn, the ancient Indian *maíz*, with its many local strains adapted to the unique conditions of each valley and micro-region, is disappearing. Uniformity, weakness and centralized corporate control replace local sustainability.

"Techno-corn," as one scholar calls it, corporate-produced hybrid strains, can produce greater bounty than unimproved land races, but is bred for dependence on petrochemical fertilizers, fungicides, herbicides, insecticides and heavy machinery. Without these inputs, it produces significantly less than native strains—or not at all. It also depletes soil fertility, petroleum-derived nitrogen replacing organic matter in the earth. With each season spent cultivating input-intensive techno-corn, the land's ability to sustain the ancient land races degrades. "Techno-corn is the product of a manipulative technology based on wresting the maximum return *out of* nature while returning the minimum *to* nature."[40]

In the nineteenth century, US farmers grew over three hundred corn varieties. Today just six hybrids dominate 70 percent of all US-grown corn, and the old native varieties have been practically eliminated.[41] Mexico, the genetic heartland of the corn plant, is now succumbing to genetic standardization imposed by the tyranny of the "free" market.

NAFTA is the culmination of an historic US mission to replace the Mexican Indian model with the US agribusiness model dating back to World War II, when Mexican progress and stability were seen as vital to the war drive. Once again, it was in the guise of populism that the devil got its foot in the door.

Henry A. Wallace was a prairie populist and scion of an Iowa agricultural dynasty. He was the grandson of Henry Wallace, an agricultural advisor to President Theodore Roosevelt, and son of Henry C. Wallace, the "father of industrialized agriculture," who developed some of the first hybrid corn strains in the 1920s, and became US Agriculture Secretary under President Warren G. Harding. Henry A. launched the Pioneer Hi-Bred Corn Company, an industry trailblazer, and became Franklin D. Roosevelt's Agriculture Secretary, and then Vice President. It was Henry A. Wallace, more than any other man, who opened Mexico to the agribusiness model.[42]

In 1940, Vice President Wallace boasted in his diary that his presence in Mexico had prevented a revolution—his rhetoric of New Deal populism and Pan-American harmony heading off an electoral revolt by the populist wing of the PRI against the Avila Camacho candidacy that year. Wallace unabashedly saw gringo know-how as the salvation of Mexico's rural poor. In 1941, back in Washington, he called a meeting with the leaders of the Rockefeller Foundation, to whom he suggested the idea of an agricultural research and education program in Mexico. Nelson Rockefeller, whose brother John D. III oversaw the Foundation, was then President Roosevelt's

Coordinator of Inter-American Affairs, a special office created to marshall Latin American resources for the US war effort.[43]

Wallace and Rockefeller Foundation President Raymond Fosdick assembled a team from Harvard, Cornell and other top US universities. Accompanied by the legendary ethnobotanist Richard Schultes, the team travelled throughout Mexico, gathering seed samples, noting agricultural methods and struggling through interviews with Indians who spoke little Spanish. The team's reports, compiled in a 1967 book, *Campaigns Against Hunger*, cited high birth rates, redistribution of land into small plots by the agrarian reform, and—most significantly—technological backwardness as the roots of Mexico's rural poverty. The report was clear on the urgency of the mission: "When persuasion fails, it is time to use compulsion . . . Hunger and ignorance and disease are so tragic that anyone who obstructs or delays their alleviation commits a gross misdemeanor against those who suffer."[44]

The program devised to correct the situation spearheaded imperialism's colonization of Mexico's vital genetic resources. In 1944, Norman Borlaug, who would win the Nobel prize for his development of hybrid wheat strains in 1970, was reassigned from his classified wartime laboratory at the DuPont company and sent to Mexico by the Rockefeller Foundation, where he led the establishment of the International Maize and Wheat Improvement Center (CIMMYT). With funds from the Rockefeller and Ford foundations and the World Bank, CIMMYT helped Mexico regain self-sufficiency in basic grains in the 1950s. Slowly turned over to administration by Mexican technicians under the direction of the UN's Food and Agriculture Organization (FAO), CIMMYT became the prototype for similar centers around the world. Today these International Agricultural Research Centers (IARCs) span from Colombia to Nigeria to India to the Philippines, overseen by the Consultative Group on International Agricultural Research (CGIAR), a UN/World Bank body. The IARCs generally conform to Vavilov centers, and specialize in "improvement" of crops indigenous to the regions where they are situated. The *Centro Internacional de la Papa* (CIP) in Peru specializes in the potato, which first emerged in the Andean Vavilov Center.[45]

IARC architect Borlaug was certain that his mission was feeding the world. "We can either use pesticides and fertilizers at our disposal or starve," he wrote.[46]

The field's dissident to the Rockefeller project in Mexico was Carl O. Sauer of UC Berkeley. Sauer had studied Mexican agriculture for twenty years, and deeply appreciated the tenacious sustainability of *maíz*, beans and squash. Sometime in the ancestral past, this ancient triculture spread from Mexico's central plateau to become the basis of indigenous cultures from the Central American isthmus to the northeastern woodlands of the Iroquois Confederacy.[47]

This triculture, Sauer wrote, "formed a symbiotic complex, without an equal elsewhere. The corn plants grow tall and have first claim on sunlight and moisture. The beans climb up the corn stalks for their share of light; their roots support colonies of nitrogen-fixing bacteria. The squashes grow mainly on the ground and complete the ground cover . . . Maize, beans and squash were grown on the lower St. Lawrence and by the Mandans on the upper Missouri. They are grown in *milpas* on the Mexican volcanoes to the highest patches of available soil. Forms were successfully selected for growing on the margins of the deserts of Sonora and Arizona where there is only an occasional summer thunderstorm. The Hopi, living in a land of little and late rain, of short summers and cold nights, depend on them and by them have maintained themselves and their fine and gentle culture, our civilization lacking the skills to match theirs for this harsh environment."[48]

Sauer saw an arrogance in the assumptions of gringo technical superiority—especially given that the US was just recovering from the Dust Bowl agricultural disaster. "The experiences of very many generations of corn growers are not to be set aside lightly by the simple and short-range interests of commerce. It is not accidental that a single native village may maintain more kinds of maize than the Corn Belt ever heard of, each having a special and proper place in the household and the field economy."[49]

In an open criticism of the Rockefeller Foundation's Mexico mission, Sauer wrote: "A good aggressive bunch of American agronomists and plant breeders could ruin the native resources for good and all by pushing their American commercial stocks . . . The example of Iowa is about the most dangerous of all for Mexico. Unless the Americans understand that, they'd better keep out of Mexico entirely."[50]

While the disappearing land races are designed by evolution for the hydrological conditions of the locale where they originate, the hybrid "miracle seeds" are designed by technicians for dependence on irrigation.[51] In Mexico's huge thrust of large-scale irrigation development in the 1950s, very little was developed for *ejido* lands. The vast majority was for large private landholders in the arid north who grow agro-exports for the US.[52]

In Sonora, agribusiness pressure for irrigation resulted in the Obregon Dam on the Rio Yaqui. The Secretariat of Water Resources, following the model of the US Bureau of Reclamation, became the regional water broker. The Yaquis, previously on a subsistence economy, now had to buy their water back from the Mexican federal government. Credit was extended by the federal government for this, but on condition that the Yaquis switch from subsistence to cash crops, to be marketed by government banks. Through such mechanisms, financial institutions such as Banrural (and the precursor National Bank of Ejidal Credit) became *de facto* regional bosses, and a minimal level of food security was exchanged for a boom-and-bust cycle.[53]

The booms erode indigenous culture further, as *ejido* bosses and their favorites accrue color TVs and other such bourgeois consumer goods as new status symbols, while the busts mean harsh deprivation.

By the 1970s, the inherent weakness of "miracle seeds" was starting to show. The 1970 Southern Corn Leaf Blight wiped out 15 percent of the US corn crop— up to 50 percent in some states. It was discovered to be due to a genetic vulnerability in the hybrid seeds in use across the country.[54]

A similar disaster struck Mexico in 1977, when air force pilots were ordered to spray carcinogenic fungicides over wheatfields nationwide to wipe out an infestation of *chahuixtle*, a disease to which the genetically uniform monocultures were similarly vulnerable.[55]

A 1972 National Academy of Sciences study, *Genetic Vulnerability of Major Crops*, found that seed patenting "adversely influenced genetic diversity," undermining food security.[56]

The solution was to find new (old) strains with the immunities, and "upgrade" the hybrid varieties every few years. But, thanks to the ubiquity of the hybrids, the old strains were disappearing. "Quite literally," Harvard botanist Garrison Wilkes lamented, "the genetic heritage of a millennium in a particular region can disappear in a single bowl of porridge."[57]

Recognizing this Achilles' heel of the Green Revolution, the USDA maintains several storehouses with samples of native seed stock from around the world—the largest the National Seed Storage Laboratory at Fort Collins, Colorado. But maintaining genetic material in refrigerated vaults is not the same as maintaining seeds *in situ*—in the field or *milpa*. A survey in the late 1980s of the 160,000 seed samples at Fort Collins and other USDA facilities found that only 5 to 10 percent were still alive and capable of generating a new plant.[58]

Meanwhile, just four companies—Pioneer Hi-Bred (bought by Du Pont in 1999), DeKalb-Pfizer, Ciba-Geigy and Sandoz of Switzerland—accounted for two-thirds of all corn seed used in the US. Five companies—Upjohn, Sandoz, Lubrizol, Shell and ITT—accounted for 30 percent of all seed patents registered with the US Office of Plant Variety Protection, with over 50 percent held by just fifteen corporations. Many of these same companies also produce the pesticides and fertilizers upon which these seeds depend. Two grain companies—Cargill and ConAgra— control 50 percent of US grain exports.[59]

Facilitation of transport and marketing, and cosmetic perfection, are prioritized as agro-genetic products are refined, at the expense of flavor and nutrition. Extra-hard tomatoes bred for mechanical harvesting and long-distance shipping have less vitamin C, and taste like styro-foam.[60]

The industry's newest generation of "miracle seeds" are those produced by recombinant DNA technology, rather than mere cross-breeding. Monsanto, both a pesticide producer and a biotech pioneer, is developing new crop strains genetically engineered to be pesticide-resistant, freeing farmers to spray even more as resistant pests are bred in a vicious cycle.[61] Monsanto's Roundup Ready soybeans are designed to be used with the company's Roundup glyphosate spray.[62] The line between crop and pesticide itself becomes blurred: Monsanto's New Leaf Superior potato, widely used in processed foods and McDonalds chains, is genetically engineered to kill any insect that nibbles it, and registered with the US Environmental Protection Agency as a pesticide.[63]

As land races disappear, US farmers and Mexican *campesinos* alike are trapped in a cycle of dependency. The corporate seeds are designed to degenerate and cannot be replanted from the last season's crop. They are designed to force farmers back to the market each season, and turn farms into seed consumers, rather than the self-sustaining biotic communities they had been for millennia. Vandana Shiva, a foremost critic of the Green Revolution, calls this "the colonization of plant regeneration."[64]

With native seed stock virtually eliminated from US agriculture, farmers who save and replant seeds from the last harvest are in violation of US patent law.[65] NAFTA now codifies internationally what the corporate manipulation of biology was doing anyway, through its protocols for protection of intellectual property rights (IPRs). NAFTA's IPR provisions include recognition by all signatories of patents on seeds, plants and new life forms created through genetic engineering.[66]

Those who speak of the coming "biotech century" and see biodiversity as "genetic capital" now support "debt-for-nature" swaps in the high-biodiversity nations of the South.[67] The United Nations Educational, Scientific and Cultural Organization (UNESCO) has established a global system of Biosphere Reserves, "representing the Earth's 200 'biotic provinces' and harboring sample communities of species."[68] Mexico has twenty-one such reserves.[69]

The importance of preserving these regions was punctuated by a remarkable discovery in the Sierra de Manantlan on the border of Jalisco and Colima in 1977, when a University of Guadalajara team discovered a previously unknown variant of *teozintle*, the wild ancestor of *maíz*. The *teozintle* was a "weed" that grew in the *ejidos* of the isolated Sierra. The Nahuatl *campesinos* crossed the *teozintle* with their own *maíz* strains to strengthen them. Upon analysis, the strain, *Zea diploperennis*, was found to have immunities to most tropical fungi and viruses—more immunities than had yet been found in any one strain. The find was written up in *Science* and *Smithsonian*, hailed as holding revolutionary possibilities.[70]

The Nahuatl communities which had been nurturing this *teozintle in situ* were at this time waging a struggle against the timber operations denuding the mountains, illegally logging *ejidal* lands and threatening the watersheds. The American Lumber Company had pulled out when the big trees were all gone in the 1930s, leaving local outlaw operations for the second-growth and final high-altitude pickings. Soon, even this would be gone, leaving the *ejidos* dry and destroyed. *Campesinos* from the communities of Ayotitlan and Cuzalapa blockaded logging roads. At one blockade, they held a banner reading, "THE WEALTH OF OUR NATURAL RESOURCES IS THE CAUSE OF OUR MISERY," echoing Eduardo Galeano's observation of "mankind's poverty as a consequence of the wealth of the land."[71]

In response to both *campesino* pressure from below and international pressure from scientists and environmentalists, the Mexican federal government declared the Sierra de Manantlan a protected area in 1987. The following year UNESCO gave it recognition as a Biosphere Reserve.[72]

Zea diploperennis samples, meanwhile, had arrived at CIMMYT and the University of Wisconsin at Madison—and thence at the laboratories of seed companies. The companies are tight-lipped about whether they have incorporated the strain into any of their products, but the South African subsidiary of the US company Asgrow is believed to have done so.[73] Incorporation of the strain through traditional hybridization was hindered by the "multifactorial" nature of its qualities: the resistance is inherited from several genes, and can be lost through the genetic reshuffling of cross-breeding. However, one scholar believes the possibilities of recombinant DNA will overcome this obstacle: "Today they can just map and tag those genes, and pull 'em out of there and put 'em into corn."[74] *Zea diploperennis* could yet become an ingredient of a new patented miracle strain.

The Nahuatl *campesinos* of Ayotitlan and Cuzalapa stand to gain no profit from any products derived from the *teozintle* they nurtured in their *milpas* for centuries before it was "discovered." Despite the declaration of the Biosphere Reserve (officially predicated on "sustainable development"), they continue to live in poverty, and face a struggle against armed *narco-caciques* who take over their lands for opium and marijuana crops.[75]

Having already been written up in the scientific literature, *Zea diploperennis* is probably now considered "public domain" and cannot itself be patented. However, under NAFTA IPR provisions, the day could arrive when *campesinos* such as those of the Sierra de Manantlan will be prohibited from cultivating an indigenous *teozintle* in their own *milpas* without paying royalties to a multinational corporation.

A final irony is the emergence of evidence that the products derived from "genetic capital" can themselves return to threaten protected biodiversity. A recent Cornell University study found that the biotoxin in the genetically engineered Bt corn (marketed to farmers throughout the Americas by both Monsanto and Pioneer Hi-Bred to poison corn-eating insects) could spread through wind-born pollen to the milkweed eaten by monarch butterflies. The study, not surprisingly, found that monarchs that eat milkweed dusted by Bt corn pollen have a higher mortality rate. The Mariposa Monarca Biosphere Reserve, the butterfly's primary wintering ground in the high pine forests of Michoacan, has seen decreasing numbers of the insects returning in recent years as a result of local deforestation, pesticide spraying—and perhaps exposure to Bt pollen in the monarch summer range (which corresponds to the US corn belt). In acknowledgement of the reserve's failure to protect the monarchs, Mexico announced in 1999 that its territory is to be slashed by over 4,000 hectares. After the study, Mexico Greenpeace held a protest at the Veracruz harbor against the importation of Bt corn, with a banner reading "IMPERIALISMO GENETICO."[76]

THE SOUTH IS PLUNDERED TO FUEL THE PLUNDER OF THE NORTH

In a lengthy, fact-filled and poetic communiqué issued within weeks of the January 1994 uprising, entitled *The Southeast in Two Winds: A Storm and a Prophecy*, the EZLN's Subcommander Marcos noted the natural wealth of Mexico's poorest state. "What does the beast leave, in exchange for everything it takes?" he asked. "Chiapas, with 75,634.4 square kilometers, some 7,500,000 hectares, is the eighth largest state . . . It is home to 40 percent of the nation's plant varieties, 36 percent of its different kinds of mammals, 34 percent of its amphibians and reptiles, 66 percent of its bird species, 20 percent of its varieties of fresh water fish, and 80 percent of its butterfly species. Exactly 9.7 percent of the nation's rain falls on Chiapas. But its greatest wealth is its 3.5 million people, two-thirds of whom live and die in the countryside. Half of the people do not have potable water, and two-thirds have no sewage systems. Ninety percent of the people in rural areas have little or no money income."[77]

The deepest part of the Lacandon Selva and the poorest part of Chiapas is the Montes Azules Biosphere Reserve, long encroached upon from the west by *campesino* colonists.[78] When the volcano Chichon in the northern Chiapas Highlands erupted in 1983, hundreds of peasant refugees from destroyed villages were relocated by the government to pre-fab housing in the Lacandon. They remain there today, fighting off malaria and the jungle, coaxing *maíz* from the thin soil.[79]

The Selva similarly serves as a receptacle for refugees from *human-made* disasters in the Highlands, or Los Altos. The expansion of the cattle industry throughout Los Altos forced thousands of Maya *campesinos* from their traditional lands to the Selva, *tierra caliente*, to clear the rainforest and build new settlements, often named after the villages they left behind in Los Altos, *tierra fria*. The acceleration of soil erosion by cattle in Los Altos was also paid for in the slash-and-burn colonization of the Selva. But it was the impoverished colonists, not the Highland cattle lords, who were demonized by TV documentaries about the disappearing Chiapas rainforest.[80]

Meanwhile, the logging operations, which cut the very first roads into the Selva, continued to take out the remaining fragments of saleable wood, to the very borders of the Biosphere Reserve.[81] Writes Marcos: "Despite the current popularity of ecology, Chiapan forests continue to be destroyed. From 1981 to 1989, 2,444,700 cubic meters of precious woods, conifers, and tropical trees were taken from Chiapas."[82]

The massive expansion of hydroelectricity in Los Altos in the 1970s sent smaller waves of Maya refugees into the Selva. Twenty-eight thousand hectares were flooded and twenty *ejidos* evicted when the Nezahualcoyotl hydro-dam at Malpaso on the Rio Grijalva went on line in 1969. This was to be the first of four giant hydro-stations in Chiapas.[83]

The Tzotzil Maya *municipio* of Venustiano Carranza, situated where the Highlands slope into the Grijalva Valley, had been petitioning for restoration of communal lands usurped by cattle lords for years. In 1974, 47,000 hectares were restored to the *comuneros*—but the next year, 5,000 were flooded by the Angostura hydro-dam.[84]

Twenty years later, the *comuneros* remain at odds with government over compensation, claiming they received only half of the 14 million pesos promised the *municipio*. In 1984, Venustiano Carranza *comuneros* in the Emiliano Zapata Campesino Organization (OCEZ) marched all the way to the Federal District to demand action on the matter.[85]

Altogether, 63,000 hectares were flooded by Angostura, and thirty-five *ejidos* displaced. At least one *ejido* relocated to the Marqués de Comillas, deep in the jungle, south of the Biosphere Reserve.[86]

The Federal Electric Commission (CFE) next unveiled the gargantuan Chicoasen hydro-dam on the Grijalva, Latin America's largest. Cut in the precipitous gorge of Sumidero Canyon where five centuries ago Chiapaneco Indians hurled themselves to their deaths rather than surrender to the Spanish, the dam flooded only 5,000 hectares—but this included three *ejidos*, among the most fertile in Chiapas.[87]

Another 5,000 hectares were flooded by the Peñitas hydro-dam further down the river in the 1980s—including three *ejidos*.[88]

Ten more hydro-dams were planned throughout the Grijalva Basin and Los Altos. But the next, on the Itzantun, a Grijalva tributary in the northern Highlands, met with resistance from the Tzotzil *campesinos* at Simojovel—some 10,000 of whom faced relocation because of the project. Three thousand members of Independent Central of Rural Workers and Campesinos (CIAOC) marched on the CFE office in Huitiupan in 1982 in protest of the project. Facing *campesino* resistance (and the peso devaluation), the CFE suspended construction of the dam.[89]

The most blatant hydro-hubris was exhibited in a plan to build a dam complex on the Rio Usumacinta, on the Guatemalan border in the heart of the Selva. To be underwritten by the World Bank and built jointly with Guatemala, the mega-scale Usumacinta Project would flood vast areas of rainforest and the Classic Maya ruins of Yaxchilan. It was conceived to generate more power than Egypt's Aswan Dam, which similarly necessitated removal of ancient cities. Environmentalist pressure halted World Bank funding for the project—and prospects for timely construction were considerably dimmed by the Zapatista uprising.[90]

Writes Marcos in *A Storm and a Prophecy:* "The tribute that capitalism demands from Chiapas has no historical parallel. Fifty-five percent of national hydroelectric energy comes from this state along with 20 percent of Mexico's total electrical energy. However, only one third of the homes in Chiapas have electricity. Where do the 12,907 kilowatts produced annually by hydroelectric plants in Chiapas go?"[91]

Increasingly, they go to the *maquiladora* zones of the Mexican North, where the gringo investment is. And Marcos, at his typewriter behind Zapatista lines "somewhere in the Lacandon Selva," underestimates the hydro-power output of Mexico's least electrified state by a factor of several hundred: the actual figure is over 3,000 *mega*watts.[92]

A strategic role for Chiapas in the NAFTA order emerges. Just as the Selva is destroyed to pay for the plunder of the Highlands, so Chiapas and southern Mexico as a whole are to be plundered to pay for the plunder of the North. As ever more Mexican resources are sent to the gringos, the marginal but resource-rich southern regions are super-exploited to maintain *Mexico*—an internal colonialism mirroring Mexico's own increasingly neo-colonial relationship with the Colossus of the North.

While northern Mexico's economic elites stand to reap the rewards of increased US and multinational investment, the oligarchs of the South are looked to as junior partners and local overseers. The indigenous inhabitants of these lands are seen as an obstacle to their efficient exploitation, when they have been able to make their presence felt at all.

Chiapas beef is mostly destined for consumption in Mexico City, while the generally higher-quality beef from the Mexican north is exported across the Rio Grande. Less than half the state's populace regularly eat meat. In a state whose hydrological resources produce power for all Mexico, only 58 percent of households have running water (compared to a national average of 79 percent).[93]

At the other end of Mexico, an industrial leviathan is spawned upon Chiapas hydro-power. At least 334 US firms moved to Mexico in the first two years of NAFTA, mainly in the North, and in highly polluting industries.[94] The toxic misery of this investment zone typifies what critics of globalization call "the race to the bottom."[95]

Despite the assurances of George Bush that NAFTA is the "greenest trade agreement ever," environmental laws can be challenged as "non-tariff trade barriers" under the treaty's "technical standards" aimed at "harmonizing" regulatory oversight in the three signatory nations.[96]

Within a year of NAFTA taking effect, there were 2,130 plants employing more than 500,000 people in the border region, a more than twentyfold increase since 1980.[97] The average *maquiladora* wage of $1.64 an hour is a tenth of the average US manufacturing wage.[98] Wages took a hit in the 1994 peso collapse, both absolutely and in terms of purchasing power. Zenith announced it intended to save "tens of millions of dollars" in 1995 as a result of the peso devaluation.[99]

In 1993, the Clinton administration's official report on NAFTA environmental concerns claimed that NAFTA would be *good* for the border region's environment: "*maquiladora* development will tend to be dispersed away from the border to other parts of Mexico" once tariffs are lowered from Chihuahua to Chiapas. Six years later, the *maquiladoras* remained overwhelmingly in the border states, but many Mexicans wonder if the treaty won't merely spread the ecological nightmare nationwide.[100]

Under Mexican law, waste from processing imported materials must be returned to the country of origin. However, the law allows *maquiladoras* to "donate" waste to charities. Since 1981, a hydrofluoric acid processing plant has "donated" mountains of calcium sulphate to cover unpaved roads in poor *barrios* of Matamoros. All it does is irritate residents' eyes, throats and skin. On windy days it blows onto their crops and into their irrigation canals.[101]

The 1983 La Paz agreement commits all US firms in Mexico to ship their wastes back out. Yet HAZTRAKS, the binational waste tracking system established by NAFTA's environmental side agreements, has been leaky at best. Almost all the

1995 data for Chihuahua were lost entirely. Where HAZTRAKS has functioned effectively, as in Mexicali, it has determined that only some 20 percent of the *maquiladoras* are in compliance with La Paz protocols.[102] Nearly a quarter of the 44 tons of hazardous waste annually produced by the *maquiladoras* has an unknown end.[103]

In 1990, the National Toxics Campaign, a US activist group, had soil and water samples taken from several sites along the *maquiladora* zones. In a canal running from the Matamoros *maquiladora* of Chicago's Stepan Chemical, the solvent xylene was detected at 52,700 times the acceptable EPA standard for factory effluent. Methylene chloride dumped in a ditch at the Rimir General Motors plant in Matamoros exceeded the EPA standard by 215,000 times.[104]

Loose environmental standards are, notwithstanding all denials, an inducement to US investment. GTE moved its plants to Juárez and Mexicali after workers at its facilities in New York, California and Ontario demanded compensation for exposure to illegal levels of cobalt dust.[105]

Maquila workers handle toxics on the job, and sometimes live in them, as at Ejido Chilpancingo, an informal settlement near Tijuana's industrial parks, littered with illegal toxic dumps.[106] In these informal communities with no running water, families often store water in used chemical drums.[107]

"I've seen the babies born with birth defects," US Treasury Secretary Lloyd Bentsen said in the prelude to the 1993 NAFTA vote. "The NAFTA package gives us the ability to assure that [these problems] will be addressed." He was referring to the wave of anencephaly—babies born with no or only semi-developed brains—along the Rio Grande, which has sparked a still-inconclusive probe by the US Centers for Disease Control.[108]

Anencephaly incidence increased after NAFTA was signed, with new cases reported in the Piedras Negras–Eagle Pass area. Few anencephalic babies are autopsied on the Mexican side, but one in Brownsville in 1991 had tissue concentrations of DDT and other pesticides banned in the US. Breakdown acids from styrene and ethylene, used in plastics manufacture, were found in the body at levels exceeding legal occupational exposure for adults in the US. In 1993, parents of anencephalic babies in the Brownsville–Matamoros area sued ninety *maquiladora* companies for damages. As a part of the settlement reached the following year, the companies admitted no wrongdoing, and the amounts paid were kept confidential.[109]

In the Brownsville–Matamoros area, where up to fifty of the fatal defects have occurred within an eighteen-month period, some locals suspect a cover-up. Among these is Paula Gómez, long-time director of the Brownsville Community Health Center, where staff physician Carmen Rocco helped expose the anencephaly wave.

Gómez told New York *Daily News* columnist Juan González that in 1991 a radiologist from Pumarejo Hospital in Matamoros showed her records of "an amazing number of birth defects." When Rocco tried to obtain those records, hospital authorities refused to cooperate, denying any unusual abnormality incidence. González wrote that a worker at the local Rimir GM plant, Hermilio Mata, said his anencephalic baby died shortly after birth in April 1992. Yet the death certificate at the Matamoros Social Security hospital said only "natural causes."[110]

Pollution does not recognize the border. Hepatitis in Texas border towns like Eagle Pass is double the state average. A persistent haze in Big Bend National Park is traced to sulfur emissions from the Carbon II power plant across the line in Coahuila, burning coal to power the factories.[111]

A case pending before the World Bank's International Center for Settlement of Investment Disputes (ICSID) illustrates NAFTA's assault on ecology and local autonomy. A complaint brought by California's Metalclad Corporation maintains the state of San Luis Potosi violated NAFTA by rezoning land the firm had purchased for a hazardous waste landfill. Residents in the local *municipio* of Naucalpan feared pollution of their groundwater—a precious resource where *campesinos* struggle to coax *maíz* from arid lands. The firm Metalclad had purchased the site from had already brought in 55,000 drums of waste. Residents wanted no more and petitioned state authorities. The state declared the area an ecologically protected zone. Metalclad called this a NAFTA-illegal expropriation, and demanded $90 million compensation—a sum far greater than the combined annual incomes of every Naucalpan family. The claim is still pending before ICSID. Metalclad insists it has the Mexican government's support; one spokesman told *The Wall Street Journal*, "I don't know of anything the federal government could have done and didn't do, short of sending the army in."[112]

The first case to go before the new trinational tribunals established by NAFTA resulted in a defeat for both ecology and sovereignty. In July 1989, Canada settled with the Ethyl Petroleum corporation of Virginia, which had sued under NAFTA to challenge a law banning one of their products, a gasoline additive found by studies to release toxins. Canada capitulated when it became obvious that the NAFTA panel reviewing the case—behind closed doors, of course—would rule against them. Not only was Ethyl Petroleum allowed to resume sales of the chemical, but Canada agreed to pay the company $13 million in compensation, and issue a statement that the product in question "poses no health risk."[113]

The NAFTA "side agreements" succeeded in winning the support of prominent US environmental groups for the treaty.[114] But Mexican NAFTA negotiator Jaime Serra Puche in 1993 assured Mexico's Senate that the "exceedingly long" dispute-resolution process "makes it very improbable that the stage of sanctions could be reached."[115]

NAFTA's Montreal-based Commission for Environmental Cooperation (CEC), made up of representatives from the US EPA and the Mexican and Canadian environment ministries, has no authority to inspect plants or toxic sites, and no subpoena power. There is a $20 million cap on CEC fines for non-enforcement of environmental laws, regardless of the extent of damage, and this is to be paid by the governments—not the offending corporations. Cases potentially resulting in fines can only be brought by a signatory government—not by a non-governmental organization. The CEC's annual budget of $9 million is significantly less than the $70 million originally proposed by the National Wildlife Federation and the Environmental Defense Fund, who were promised the side agreements as the price for their "green" stamp of approval on NAFTA.[116]

The Border Environment Cooperation Committee (BECC) and its funding arm, the North American Development Bank (NADBank), were created by the side agreements to fund a clean-up of the border zone—"to secure a better environment for the millions of Americans who live there, as well as their Mexican neighbors," the Clinton administration crowed. The NADBank is to fund recovery of contaminated areas, as well as treatment plants for the raw sewage dumped into the Rio Grande from Juárez and Nuevo Laredo. The $3 billion slated for the clean-up contrasts with the $20 billion environmental groups had asked for when the agreement was negotiated.[117] The BECC's role is to certify the clean-up projects. But the impoverished informal communities, or *colonias*, ringing the *maquiladora* zones need not apply for NADBank loans. As one NADBank credit analyst put it: "The ability to pay back loans is the most important financial consideration for NADBank."[118]

The side agreements got their first test in December 1994, when 40,000 migratory birds—ducks, egrets, ibises, stilts, sandpipers—mysteriously died on the banks of the Silva agricultural reservoir in Guanajuato. Local doctors also reported unexplained health problems among residents—rashes, headaches and intestinal disturbances, especially among children who came into contact with the water. The reservoir was drained, and the first complaint was brought before the CEC.[119]

Mexico's Secretariat of Agriculture and Hydraulic Resources first claimed a one-time dumping of endosulfan pesticide was responsible. The Mexican environmental organization Group of 100 claimed endosulfan is more toxic to fish than birds, and pointed to emissions from chemical plants, which may have mixed to turn the reservoir into a deadly cocktail. They charged Mexican authorities with a cover-up to protect industry.[120]

The CEC panel concluded the "overriding cause" of the deaths was a sewage-spawned botulism outbreak, while conceding that "exposure to heavy metals, in particular chromium, lead and mercury, was indicated in some of the birds that the panel analyzed." Environmentalists charged the CEC with complicity in the cover-up. Since the complaint was brought by the Group of 100 and the Audubon Society, rather than a government, Mexico faced no fines or sanctions.[121]

Tourism and entertainment also form a Free Trade environmental threat. In 1996, the CEC ruled the Mexican government must explain why it approved plans for a giant tourist-ship port at the island resort of Cozumel off the Yucatan without the required impact study. The Group of 100 claimed the project would damage the Paraiso coral reef, the world's second largest. But, once again, with the complaint brought by environmentalists rather than a government, the CEC was powerless to impose sanctions.[122]

In April 1998, in Playa Popotla, Baja California, fishermen held a protest at the new multimillion-dollar Twentieth Century Fox studio, where *Titanic*, the highest-grossing film ever, had just been shot. The studio was built on land claimed by the local fishing cooperative, which maintained it was sold illegally. The studio was still expanding, pushing fishing families off the beachside. To circumvent restrictions on foreign land ownership within 50 kilometers of the border, Fox magnate Rupert Murdoch resorted to the usual subterfuge of *prestanombres*. Chlorine from the giant water tank in which *Titanic* scenes were filmed leaked into the sea, poisoning aquatic life, ruining Popotla's fishing economy. After *Titanic* was filmed, local catches dropped from 15 tons a season to 2.[123]

LABOR GETS SQUASHED

Labor conditions in the *maquiladoras* are abysmal. Despite a growing number of men in the industry since NAFTA was signed, the majority of the *maquiladora* workforce remains women, and they routinely face demands for sexual favors from male overseers. Underage kids work in the *maquiladoras* with falsified documents; authorities look the other way, in violation of the Federal Labor Law and Article 123 of the Mexican Constitution.[124]

The Mexican auto industry was nearly 100 percent unionized in the 1970s; by the 1980s, the Chrysler plants were only 80 percent unionized, the Ford plants 60 percent and the GM plants 47 percent.[125] "Tijuana feels like Detroit in its heyday," writes one US reporter. "Signs advertise for workers on the gate of every plant."

But workers at a Tijuana plastics factory fired for trying to organize an independent union were blacklisted from Tijuana's other factories.[126]

NAFTA's labor side agreements created the US Labor Department's National Administrative Office (NAO), which can impose sanctions on Mexico or Canada. Shortly after NAFTA took effect, two US unions, the Teamsters and United Electric Workers (UE), petitioned the NAO to take action against Mexico for allowing General Electric and Honeywell to fire thirty-four workers attempting to organize independent unions in the Ciudad Chihuahua and Juárez plants. In October 1994, ruling in its first case, the NAO ordered no sanctions. The NAO argued that those workers not getting severance pay had a case pending before Mexico's arbitration board—a body with a seamless record in ruling against independent labor agitators.[127]

It has been a long slide down to this reality. As the neoliberal counter-revolution downsized the state's role in the economy, the federal military and police apparatus crushed worker resistance. The transition to NAFTA saw the worst labor violence and repression in Mexico since the 1959 railworkers' strike.[128]

Between 1976 and 1987, the Telephone Workers Union went on strike for better pay five times against the parastatal Telmex; in each case World War II-era legislation allowing the government to seize the means of communication was invoked, and the army sent in to break the strikes. In 1990, Telmex was privatized, and the union reduced to fighting to limit job losses. The new owner, Grupo Carso, is led by top Salinas campaign contributor Carlos Slim Helú, with investment from Southwestern Bell.[129] Government audits sparked by the post-Salinas corruption revelations would uncover $1.3 billion missing from the Telmex privatization.[130]

A 1985 reorganization of Mexico's embryonic nuclear industry similarly turned control over the sector to gringo capital while undercutting Mexican labor. The United Syndicate of Nuclear Industry Workers (SUTIN) first emerged from a "Democratic Tendency" within the United Syndicate of Electric Workers of the Mexican Republic (SUTERM), a pillar of the CTM. SUTIN broke from the giant union after a purge of SUTERM dissidents in 1977, and proved a headache as the government hurried to build a commercial nuclear reactor as a symbol of First World prestige.[131]

A 1983 strike by SUTIN was partially a political action aimed at changing development policy. SUTIN protested that the CFE's first nuclear plant, at Laguna Verde on the Veracruz coast, perpetuated dependence on the US by using a Mark II reactor designed and built under the direction of General Electric. Three Ohio utilities had even sued GE after cancelling plants over the Mark II's faulty containment system, the same model which failed at the Chernobyl disaster.[132]

Uramex, the state uranium company then exploring reserves in Oaxaca, Chihuahua and Baja California, was closed in 1985. This made Mexico's nuclear sector completely dependent on uranium imports. The consequent layoffs served to diminish and domesticate SUTIN, since the most militant factions were Uramex employees. Following the Uramex closure, *charros* consolidated leadership over SUTIN.[133]

A growing community-labor alliance against the Laguna Verde plant was defeated. On April 26, 1987, the first anniversary of the Chernobyl disaster, 10,000 protested at the gates of the plant, blocking traffic for hours on the coastal highway. The following year, the home of an outspoken Laguna Verde opponent was torched in an arson attack in Tlaxcala. The plant was subsequently opened. Protests by Purépecha *campesinos* and fishermen (and the 1982 peso crash) stopped the government from building a research reactor on the shores of Lake Patzcuaro in Michoacan.[134]

The 1986 privatization of the Fundidora steel mill in Monterrey took place with the grounds occupied by the army to intimidate the Miner and Metal Workers Syndicate of the Mexican Republic (STMMRM) into accepting massive lay-offs and eventual closure of the plant.[135]

In 1987, in the midst of a bitter two-month strike at the Cuautitlan motor works, Ford tore up its union contract, fired 3,400 workers, cut wages by 45 percent and eliminated seniority.[136]

That same year, the de la Madrid government privatized AeroMexico, laying off thousands. When the unions went on strike in protest, the army and police were sent into the workplaces, and several leaders were arrested. The strike was broken, and nearly all the strikers lost their jobs.[137]

In 1989, when Salinas privatized the Cananea Copper Mine, he secured the support of the STMMRM leadership, but nonetheless had the mine occupied by five thousand army troops. The STMMRM local, which had announced a strike in defiance of the national leadership, was broken. Hundreds were fired. Going down fighting, the local placed an ad in the national newspapers protesting the outrage: "It shall go down in history that only two presidents of the Republic have dared to send the army to Cananea: Porfirio Díaz and Carlos Salinas de Gortiari."[138]

Cananea was sold to Grupo México, whose main financier is *nouveau riche* billionaire and close Salinas crony Jorge Larrea. Over the next several years, Larrea cut over a thousand jobs at Cananea—even as the mine's production soared. Workers protested that the job cuts jeopardized proper maintenance of the mine's tailing ponds, threatening the nearby headwaters of the Rio Sonora with contamination. The miners went on strike again in November 1998, demanding a halt to the cuts. Local residents joined the protests when the mine's new owners cut off water to the municipality of Cananea—in violation of a nearly century-old deal. In March 1999, residents occupied the pumping station as Cananea was again occupied by state police, and army troops approached the town. The company hired US-based subcontractors, and the national STMMRM leadership once again capitulated, selling out the local. More lay-offs followed the breaking of the strike, with over a hundred leaders blacklisted—turned away at the mine gates as they tried to return to work.[139]

In early 1990, workers at Mexico City's Modelo brewery went on strike to demand an independent union. Federal arbitrators ruled the strike illegal; riot police surrounded the brewery, and thousands were fired.[140]

Early 1990 also saw violence at the still-simmering Cuautitlan Ford works. When the workers rallied around dissident leaders and staged an occupation of the plant, CTM *pistoleros* attacked, killing one worker and wounding nine. Others were briefly "disappeared," beaten while held incommunicado. Federal and State of Mexico police were finally sent in. As a result of public pressure, the company was forced to hold a certification vote. There was no secret ballot, and the vote took place with the plant surrounded by heavily armed police. Workers were asked, "Do you want the CTM to represent you?" Their responses were recorded on video. The vote nonetheless went only 1,328 for the CTM and 1,112 for the dissidents. Those who voted for the dissidents were sacked, and to get their jobs back had to sign a statement agreeing to "fully accept union discipline."[141]

In May 1992, the army and federal police occupied the port of Veracruz to break up labor protests against privatization of the port authority.[142]

In July 1992, 14,000 workers at the Puebla Volkswagen plant turned down a contract negotiated by the *charro* union bosses. Volkswagen fired them all, tore up the existing contract, and instated a pay cut. Federal arbitrators upheld the company's action.[143]

Business elites revel shamelessly in the race to the bottom—when they talk to each other. A 1992 ad placed in an international business magazine by the Yucatan chamber of commerce has a pensive CEO thinking out loud, "There's no way I can get my labor costs down to $1 an hour." Then the slogan and Maya-pyramid logo: "Yes You Can—Yucatan."[144]

THE GLOBAL REGIME

Beyond NAFTA's "Yukon-to-Yucatan" scope, the Bush administration in 1990 declared the aim of a Free Trade Area of the Americas (FTAA), stretching all the way to Tierra del Fuego. Chile is to be next, at which point NAFTA will become the FTAA. A "fast-track" bill on extending the pact to Chile—in which Congress could only vote the package up or down—was withdrawn by Clinton in November 1997, rather than risk its defeat. However, FTAA talks continued, and the legislation will be back.[145] Chile is already unilaterally reducing tariffs in preparation for the FTAA.[146]

Chilean farm exports to the US are at a record high, mostly brokered by multinational giants like Standard Fruit and Dole. In Chile's fruit-growing Central Valley, worker families have experienced a wave of anencephaly; researchers have found a threefold increase since the fruit industry began heavy use of pesticides.[147] In 1998, the US timber giant Boise Cascade announced new operations in temperate forests of the Chilean south, more than doubling the rate of deforestation in the region—and prompting protests from fishermen who fear degradation of salmon spawning grounds.[148]

With the establishment of the World Trade Organization (WTO) by passage of the GATT Uruguay Rounds in January 1995, an arcane and mundane set of trade agreements was transformed into a super-powerful agency of global governance, transcending the sovereignty of nations and enforcing the "race to the bottom" under threat of trade sanctions.[149]

The GATT–WTO intellectual property rights provisions sparked massive protests by peasants in India, enraged that they could be prohibited from growing their own local seed stocks without paying royalties to a transnational corporation.[150] In December 1992, hundreds of peasants overran the Cargill offices in Bangalore to announce the start of the movement.[151] In 1998, peasants set fire to cotton fields in Karnataka where Monsanto was testing "Terminator" seed technology, which enforces IPRs by preventing plants from reproducing at all.[152]

In cases involving agriculture, food products and biotechnology, the WTO relies on standards set by a UN body, the Codex Alimentarius Commission, based in Rome. Guidelines on labeling "genetically modified" food products are presently being considered by the Codex—with the US opposing any such labeling outright, even voluntary labeling stating that a product is *not* genetically modified.[153]

Many of the Codex pesticide tolerance standards are weaker than those under US law—making US law unenforceable, or at least open to WTO challenge.[154] As the Uruguay Round was negotiated, the US, EU and Japan each compiled lists of laws they intend to challenge before the WTO.[155]

In the first case heard before the WTO in 1995, Venezuela successfully challenged provisions of the US Clean Air Act barring the import of gasoline which releases more contaminants than the average from domestic refineries. Rather than face $150 million in annual trade sanctions, President Clinton ordered the EPA to rewrite the Clean Air Act. The new provisions were identical to those the oil industry had long demanded.[156]

In the next cases, in 1998, ecological principles fared no better. First, the WTO upheld complaints by India, Malaysia, Thailand and Pakistan against a US law banning importation of shrimp caught in nets that entangle endangered sea turtles. The decision slipped through a loophole in GATT's Article XX, which officially exempts laws designed to protect the environment from challenge: the WTO appellate panel ruled there was an *exemption to the exemption*, for laws which are deemed "arbitrary and discriminatory." Because the decision left open the *possibility* of upholding environmental laws, the Clinton administration actually hailed the striking down of a US environmental law as a victory. The distinction will mean nothing to the sea turtles.[157]

Next, the WTO upheld a US complaint against a European Union ban on import of beef treated with biotech growth hormones.[158] WTO Secretary-General Renato Ruggiero stated openly that environmental standards are "doomed to fail and could only damage the global trading system."[159]

The International Labor Organization (ILO), made up of government, labor and business representatives from 173 nations, is charged with setting acceptable labor guidelines for the international regime. However, ILO has no ability to impose sanctions or fines. Its declaration is explicit that it seeks to compel compliance through "shame" and "public opinion," and that labor standards should not be used for "protectionist" purposes.[160]

The Multilateral Agreements on Investment (MAI), submitted before the OECD nations in 1998, would go further than the WTO, giving corporations themselves, rather than governments, "standing" to challenge perceived threats to their investments. State, local and municipal governments would be bound to comply, with national governments held liable for local laws and regulations which run foul of the MAI. Investors could sue a nation before international tribunals to be established for this purpose, rather than in any country's courts. All economic sectors, including land ownership, natural resources and broadcasting, would be opened to foreign ownership—a provision which would go by the feel-good moniker of "non-discrimination." Uncompensated expropriation of assets—including regulatory laws which are seen as "tantamount to expropriation"—would be banned. National or local governments could be held liable for failing to crush strikes or boycotts. Once again, provisions on the "responsibilities of investors"—such as ensuring fair labor practices—are to be non-binding.[161]

In the midst of global financial turmoil, the World Bank and IMF held their international meetings in Washington DC in October 1998. British Prime Minister Tony Blair spoke of a "new Bretton Woods for the next millennium."[162] Talk was in the air of transforming the Bretton Woods institutions into an "international central bank" modeled on the US Federal Reserve—for the whole world.[163]

The architects of this system never doubt that their global dreams serve the greater good, judging by their talk. David Rockefeller, anticipating NAFTA twenty years before it was passed, said, "Broad human interests are being served best in economic terms where free market forces are able to transcend national boundaries."[164]

In the 1980s, Mexico received thirteen World Bank structural and sectoral adjustment loans, more than any other country—including a huge loan as a reward for joining GATT in 1986.[165] One US treasury official said, in reference to Mexico, "Only countries that commit to market-oriented economic reform will get the [World Bank's] help."[166]

In 1994's annual *Forbes* directory of the planet's richest men, Mexico rated an unprecedented twenty-four billionaires, up from thirteen the previous year. Only the US, Japan and Germany ranked higher.[167]

While wealth accumulated at the top, the buying power of the Mexican worker contracted by nearly half in the 1980s. The number of people living in absolute poverty rose throughout Latin America in this same period.[168] The average Mexican hourly wage in US dollars declined from $1.38 in 1982 to 0.45 in 1990.[169]

Mexican Agriculture Secretariat studies documented a decline in per capita consumption of basic grains in this period.[170] In 1996, the FAO estimated that per capita consumption of *maíz*, beans and wheat in Mexico had dropped by over 35 percent in the last ten years.[171]

IMF Managing Director Michel Camdessus told the *Wall Street Journal* in September 1995 that the new fiscally domesticated Mexico was exemplary in meeting its financial and economic targets, and was entitled to take another $1.6 billion from its credit line, on top of the $9.8 billion already extended that year. "My assessment of Mexico is very simple," crowed the chipper bureaucrat. "Their program is on track."[172]

In 1997, with Mexico deep in crisis, Exterior Secretary José Angel Gurria presided over a New York City ceremony where his country's highest honor, the Order of the Aztec Eagle, was awarded to David Rockefeller for his NAFTA advocacy. Before an audience including Carlos Slim and Henry Kissinger, he pronounced, "David Rockefeller is a vital force that has brought Mexico and the US closer together . . . he has been a firm supporter of Mexico."[173]

Estimates of the number of *campesinos* to be displaced from their lands by NAFTA run as high as 15 million.[174] The visceral refusal of these land-rooted people to be moved may provide the North American Free Trade Agreement's most serious challenge.

PART II

WAR CRY FROM CHIAPAS

4

ZAPATA LIVES: 1994

"*¡Viva el EZLN!*"

Speaker after speaker finished with this defiant battle-cry from the makeshift stage on the back of a pick-up truck, right in front of San Cristóbal's municipal palace. Each time, the cry was echoed from the throats of hundreds of gathered Indians, *campesinos* and dissident trade unionists. This was the first open display of support for the Ejército Zapatista de Liberacion Nacional since the Indian rebels took over the picturesque colonial city in the heart of the Chiapas Highlands on January 1. It was now March 6.

Before settling in the town's *zócalo*, the protestors had marched throughout San Cristóbal, blocking traffic and leaving a trail of red graffiti: "*Viva EZLN*"; "*No al TLC*"; "*Viva los caidos del 1 de Enero*"; "*Fuera los caciques de Chamula.*" The tourists were bewildered.

Now the municipal palace was under occupation. The marchers forced their way in, much as the EZLN guerillas had on January 1—only armed with spray-paint canisters instead of guns. The police were nowhere to be seen as the occupiers covered the walls with slogans, hung giant banners from the balconies overlooking the *zócalo*, and finally rolled out their blankets and settled in for the night. The banners featured giant portraits of Emiliano Zapata, Pancho Villa and Flores Magón. One of the biggest depicted Zapata holding out a rifle to the viewer. It read:

OCEZ—CNPA
¡¡POR LA DESTRUCCION DEL LATIFUNDIO!!
¡CON LA ARMA EN LA MANO
DEFIENDAN SU EJIDO!

Many of the occupiers were local Tzotzil or Tzeltal, dressed in the traditional costume distinct to each of their Highland villages: Chamula, Zinacantan, Chenalhó, Tenejapa, San Andrés Larrainzar. Others were *mestizos* from more distant Chiapas villages. Others were dissident teachers from the SNTE, the National Syndicate of Education Workers, who had marched all the way from Oaxaca. They proclaimed they would not leave until their demands were met. The teachers wanted official recognition for the democratic current within the SNTE, but they were also there in solidarity with the principal Indian and *campesino* demand: land.

The fact that neither the police nor the army—which still had a big presence in and around San Cristóbal—interfered with the occupation indicated how much things had changed in the six weeks since the January cease-fire. In the aftermath of the EZLN's take-over of the town, the federal army's planes, helicopters, artillery and tanks had rained bullets and missiles on San Cristóbal's poor outlying *barrios*. With a cease-fire declared and official dialogue initiated at San Cristóbal's cathedral, Mexico's party-state switched tactics. Repression had only sparked public protests throughout the country, especially the South. By the night of the municipal palace occupation, it was obvious the government was trying to keep the situation as invisible as possible.

This refining of the art of repressive tolerance was evident the next day. On the afternoon of March 7, the occupiers abandoned the graffiti-covered municipal palace to join an occupation of unused tracts owned by local San Cristóbal *coletos*, or aristocrats, on the town's northern periphery. The occupation had been started the previous day by Tzotzils from Chamula. Landless and reduced to urban poverty since being expelled by the *caciques*, they set up makeshift shelters and started to prepare the ground for planting *maíz*.

By relocating to the squatted land, the protestors made a tactical error. On the outskirts of town, away from the eyes (and cameras) of tourists and journalists, they were set upon by the state police and violently ejected—along with the squatting Chamulas. A fracas ensued as police tore down bivouacs and banners. In twenty minutes it was all over. With speed and efficiency, municipal authorities armed with buckets of white paint covered the graffiti which appeared to be on every wall in San Cristóbal. By nightfall, the municipal palace was spotless.

THE ROAD TO JANUARY

The PRI was in a bid to head off a revolution. The famous joke is that President Carlos Salinas went to sleep on the New Year's Eve before NAFTA took effect thinking he would wake up in the USA. Instead, he woke up in Guatemala.[1]

The EZLN did not spring fully armed from the Lacandon Selva like Athena from the head of Zeus. But the international media paid no heed as the pressures propelling Mexico's Maya toward armed revolt mounted in the 1980s. Nicaragua, El Salvador and (to a lesser extent, despite the magnitude of the bloodletting) Guatemala made headlines in the US. Chiapas, Mexico's frontier on Central America, was invisible—even as little-noted Amnesty International reports documented mounting assassinations, shoot-outs and disappearances.[2]

Government intransigence in acting on claims against ranches, *fincas* and *latifundios* which exceeded legal limits exploded the ranks of independent *campesino* organizations in opposition to the "official" CNC. These also followed the agricultural settlers into the jungle. Hopes declined along with the land. Indian peasants pushed onto Highland slopes cleared the woods, aggravating soil erosion. Those dumped in the lowland Selva cleared rainforest, cattle ranchers following in their wake. The displacements meant hunger, misery and ecological destruction in both bioregions.[3]

Seasonal migration to the coffee and cotton plantations of Sosconosco meant pesticide exposure and squalor. Those who opted for resettlement in the Selva faced incessant insect invasions on their crops, nonexistent healthcare in the face of malaria and (more recently) cholera. After early optimism, it became clear they had been dumped in the inhospitable jungle while ranchers and *caciques* dominated the good land which was their birthright.[4]

The oil boom of the 1970s paradoxically hurt the *campesinos*. When the money was good, government subsidies poured into the Highland communities for pesticides and fertilizers. With lots of wage labor available, more Maya men traveled to Sosconosco or Tuxtla to make money which could be reinvested in such agro-inputs back home. In the boom years, the land became dependent on these inputs, organic matter declining in the soil and more virulent pests being bred by successive sprayings. When the money and credit dried up, the land was less productive, and the *campesinos* were poorer than they had been before the boom. The peso crash in 1982 coincided with a *campesino* agricultural crisis in Chiapas.[5]

The introduction of techno-corn and integrated inputs in the boom years also reinforced the power of the *caciques*, as local agro-ecology became more dependent on money and credit.[6] The *caciques*, controlling distribution of government resources to their village fiefs, had greater ability to impose hunger and privation on political or personal enemies. The wave of *expulados* fled San Juan Chamula. Land occupations and contests for control of village governments violently divided Highland communities.[7]

The federal government's Plan Chiapas had goals openly as political as economic. As Indian guerillas gained ground in Guatemala, the party-state urgently sought economic integration of adjacent impoverished Chiapas. The methods were an intensification of exploitation of the Selva to relieve tensions in the Highlands. As Highland *ejidos* disappeared under the floodplains of new hydro-dams, the military roads into the Selva became new arteries for colonization. The Southern Frontier Highway, cut by army bulldozers parallel to the Rio Usumacinta, linked Palenque in the north to the Guatemalan border below the Rio Lacantún, completely encircling the Selva.[8]

As the federal government spoke of development in Chiapas, the state government of Absalon Castellanos, cattle oligarch and former army commander for the Highlands, oversaw an escalation of terror by the Judicial Police and paramilitary groups. There was also an escalation of federal army troop strength in Chiapas—officially to guard the border.[9]

Castellanos openly blamed the unrest in Chiapas on the contagion of subversion coming across the border with the thousands of Maya refugees fleeing state genocide in Guatemala.[10]

The pressures which had brought war and ethnic cleansing to Guatemala were similar to those at work in Chiapas. Pauperization of Guatemala's Maya majority by the cattle boom led to peasant support for guerillas. In 1982, the separate guerilla groups operating in the Pacific plain coffee country, the Maya Highlands and the Peteñ rainforest joined in a single front: the Guatemalan National Revolutionary Union (URNG).[11] All three of these bioregions are contiguous with their counterparts in Chiapas: Sosconosco, Los Altos and the Lacandon.

The fundamentalist dictatorship of born-again Gen. Efrain Rios Montt executed a counterinsurgency program overseen by Israeli military advisors and modeled on the US experience in Indochina. The campaign was blatant in its ethnocidal imperative. Indians were forced into military-controlled "model villages"; dependent on the army for food, they were to grow asparagus and strawberries for export by army-controlled companies. "The cult of *maíz* is finished!" thundered the generals.[12] But first came the massacres.

In the Highland departments of Huehuetenango, El Quiché and Alta Verapaz, hundreds of hamlets were destroyed and over a million people displaced as refugees or rounded up into the "model villages." Thousands fled north, into the trackless wilderness that gives way to the Lacandon Selva across the Mexican border. The Mexican army relocated the refugees away from the border area as fast as possible, but more kept coming. Throughout the early 1980s, Lacandon settlements swelled with Quiché, Cakchiquel and Mam Maya fleeing Guatemala.[13]

Chiapas was polarizing along many fronts.

Maya society was divided between Highland villages under *cacique* tyranny and Selva settlements where, even amidst a stark survival struggle, a sense of rebirth and new horizons prevailed.

In old San Juan Chamula, life revolved around ancient rituals. Burning candles in the church before the images of the saints in a state of intoxicated devotion was obligatory. Both candles and *posh* (generally mixed with Coca-Cola these days) were under control of the *caciques*. At the Carnaval festival, costumes, impersonations and songs recalled the history of the *municipio* to pre-colonial times, with references to Moctezuma, and a Judas hanged in effigy and ritually humiliated. Dancers impersonating the Jews and tormentors of Christ donned monkey-fur hats mimicking the uniforms of the French occupation troops of the 1860s; fireworks exploded like guns.[14] The tourists came every day, to be set upon by little barefoot girls selling dolls and woven bracelets with an aggression born of privation and fear. The *caciques* lay at the center of village life, and got a cut of all economic activity. Dissidents were expelled or, for lesser infractions, taken to the little municipal jail room behind the church, its dirt floor caked in feces.[15]

Meanwhile, at the settlement of Nuevo San Juan Chamula in the southern Selva, economic refugees and *expulados* from the Highland village welcomed Guatemalan refugees into their community. Nuevo Chamula was even subject to incursions by the Guatemalan army. Six were killed in one such episode in April 1984. The raids were discreetly overlooked by the Mexican government. Bishop Samuel Ruiz denounced them, and the forced relocation of the refugees to isolated camps in Quintana Roo, in the Yucatan.[16]

In the Selva, Indians from various Highland villages and regions were able to meet, learn the languages of their new neighbors, exchange experiences and organize—in the absence of *caciques*, *Guardias Blancas*, police or army troops.[17]

While many Highland *municipios* consist of no more than a small valley with a central village and a few hamlets, the Selva, considered "uninhabited" when the boundaries were drawn, lies almost entirely within the vast *municipio* of Ocosingo—with the municipal seat actually lying beyond the jungle in the Tzeltal Highlands. Smaller sections of the Selva lie within the *municipios* of Palenque, Altamirano and Las Margaritas—also towns which actually lie outside the Selva. The municipal governments had little presence in the Selva. So the new colonists were free to create their own *de facto* governments.[18]

The first region of the Selva settled by the Maya colonists was Las Cañadas, a series of broad canyons where the temperate woodlands give way to tropical rainforest. Las Cañadas run northwest to southeast, divided by forested ridges—the Sierra Corralchen, Sierra La Colmena, Sierra Livingstone—each lower than the last. These finally give way to the lush lowlands of the Usumacinta Basin, where there are still jaguars, tapirs, boas and tucans—and malaria, cholera and dengue fever.

Las Cañadas was where Bishop Ruiz and his network of *catequistas* were most successful in organizing the Indian communities. These Maya settlers were inculcated with a vision of Las Cañadas as the Promised Land, where there was more than enough land, where they could prosper free of the oligarchy's terror.[19]

But the Diocese (and the leftist organizers who followed the layworkers) were not the only ones interested in the Selva. In the 1970s, President Echeverria made expansion of the agricultural frontier into the Chiapas rainforest a national project. Landless *campesinos* from outside Chiapas were even encouraged to settle the jungle.[20] Echeverria launched a special program of *ejidal* cooperatives for the Selva, the ARICs. More than one Selva settlement bears that president's name. The government's Nafinsa bank purchased the private lumber outfits operating in the Selva, and expanded the network of logging roads through the rainforest.[21]

Simultaneously, the world scientific community began to take note of the rapid destruction of Mexico's last tropical rainforest by the slash-and-burn colonization. Anthropologists noted that the Lacandon Maya—the world's last lowland rainforest Maya culture, previously isolated and never converted—were in danger of disappearing. Conflicting agendas led to the Selva's division into a complex and overlapping patchwork of protected areas, military zones and colonization projects.

Gertrude Duby Blom, the "Grandmother of the Lacandons," was a primary voice for saving the rainforest. A socialist and pacifist exile from Nazi-occupied Europe, she had been released from a camp in France thanks to the lobbying of her native Switzerland in 1939, and settled in Mexico to pursue a photographic career. She won acclaim for a study of the women veterans of the first Zapatista movement. In 1943, she was on a Mexican government expedition to establish contact with the Lacandon Maya. In the jungle she met Frans Blom, the US archaeologist who had excavated Palenque, then on a special wartime mission from the US government to assess the Selva's potential for rubber exploitation. They married, settled in an old house in San Cristóbal, and worked to draw the world's attention to the region's threatened Maya cultures. Since their name sounded like the Maya word for jaguar, the Lacandons called their San Cristóbal home which they sometimes visisted "Na Bolom"—House of the Jaguar.[22]

The Lacandons—or Hach Winik, the "true people"—with their long hair, white cotton robes, hunting bows and "pristine" shamanic culture, were Trudy Blom's special cause. She established a friendship with Chan K'in Viejo, the elder of Nahá, the most traditional Lacandon Maya community, where hunting and gathering, augmented by a little *milpa* agriculture, still prevailed. By the 1970s, the other Hach Winik community, Lacanjá, 45 kilometers southeast, had been mostly converted to Seventh Day Adventism.[23]

In 1971, the Mexican government declared a 640,000-hectare reserve for the Lacandon Maya. The Lacandons need large areas of rainforest for their traditional lifeway—but the government simultaneously signed timber deals with their communities. The Lacandons got a cut, and started buying pick-up trucks and (eventually) diesel generators; government enterprises started taking out the reserve's last mahogany and cedar stands.[24]

With perhaps five hundred Lacandons surrounded by 200,000 Highland Maya settlers, especially to the north and west, this was a recipe for conflict. Thousands of settlers had been rendered squatters on Lacandon Maya land by the stroke of a pen. Protests and negotiations ensued, in which the government agreed to recognize some of their land rights. In exchange, however, they were made to concentrate in central communities, and abandon the scattered *milpas* they had carved out of the forest. Some of these new settlements had names like Palestina and Monte Libano, reflecting the Biblical and prophetic significance the Maya settlers attached to their new frontier homeland. Others had names as coldly bureaucratic as the Luis Echeverria New Population Center.[25]

In 1978, a Mexican presidential decree appointed 331,200 hectares of the interior Selva the Montes Azules Biosphere Reserve, with recognition by UNESCO. The Biosphere Reserve begins just south of Nahá and stretches to the banks of the Rio Lacantún, the Usumacinta's deep jungle tributary. But *campesino* encroachment reached the reserve's borders, and even penetrated it.[26]

In 1990, a World Bank study declared that the next decade would make or break the Lacandon Selva's chances for survival; it had been been "reduced to the minimum size essential for the integrity of its ecosystem."[27] Satellite photos revealed that the Mexico–Guatemala border was clearly visible from space, so completely had the forest been cleared on the Mexican side.[28]

The following year, a "debt-for nature swap" was arranged for the Lacandon Selva. The US-based Conservation International bought $4 million of Mexican debt for $1.8 million. Mexico was then obliged to spend $2.6 million on preservation programs in the Lacandon—nearly all of which was slated for a Montes Azules research station (staffed by Conservation International) to map the region's shrinking genetic wealth.[29]

The deepest parts of the Selva—Montes Azules and the Marqués de Comillas, south of the Rio Lacantún—continued to shelter a shrinking heart of virgin rainforest. This was surrounded by a growing outer ring of "jungle"—the tangled second-growth which springs from abandoned *milpas*. This, in turn, was surrounded by an expanding third ring of pastureland—areas claimed by the encroaching cattlelords.

In 1984, Trudy Blom, who had outlived Frans and was now in her eighties, wrote of a recent trip into the Selva during the burning season.

All the way from the Usumacinta to Palenque, we were enveloped in a dense cloud of smoke and dust. Everything smelled of burning, and the heat was heavy and asphyxiating. Not even the sun's rays were able to penetrate the curtain of opaque gray smoke in which we were traveling. It was an inferno of destruction . . .

The jungle is burning, the great trees are being destroyed, and the land is enveloped in a sinister darkness. No one cares; people seem to be thinking only about the cattle they are going to bring in and the profits from them. They don't stop for a moment to think that the floor of the jungle is turning into laterite, that the springs of water that the cattle need will dry up, that the level of the rivers will go down, that when the rains come, there won't be any plants or trees to stop the water's fury and the rivers will flood the fields and meadows, washing even the houses away in their mighty torrent. Everything will be swept away by the dark muddy water; and the bluish green crystalline rivers will be only a memory.

On no account should any more people be allowed to enter and settle in virgin rainforest. The solution to the problem of the landless *campesino* will not be found in the jungle.[30]

Yet, as an exile living in Mexico at the pleasure of the government, she was constrained from offering a syllable of solidarity to the *campesinos* organizing to defend their lands from enclosure by the cattlelords.

It was ecology that interfered both with the Maya's own vision of a Promised Land and with the government's strategy of using the Selva to buy peace. Rainforest land cannot be sustainably farmed with the methods the *campesinos* brought from the Highlands. The rainforest soil is rich, but thin, with organic matter decomposing rapidly in the tropical heat, nutrients recycled into the lush canopy. After a season or two of intense productivity, the settlers were forced to abandon depleted lands, and move deeper into the Selva to clear more lands. Ranchers claimed the abandoned lands—or bought them on the cheap, or seized them at gunpoint.[31]

The colonists served as the unpaid labor of the very cattle oligarchy which had pushed them into the Selva; reclaiming land from the forest, only to have it expropriated. The same social pressures and class conflicts which had pushed the colonists into the forest followed them inexorably along Las Cañadas toward its shrinking heart. The Selva communities were soon divided between the ARICs, which acquiesced in the reduction of *campesino* lands in exchange for credit, and militant groups like the ANCIEZ, which were increasingly committed to resistance. There were waves of expulsions on both sides as the Selva settlements polarized.[32]

Two hundred kilometers and a world away in Tuxtla Gutiérrez, urban Chiapas was also polarizing. Dissident elements of the SNTE broke from the *PRIista* hacks and made common cause with the militant *campesinos* whose sons and daughters they taught in the countryside. The dissident wing declared a National Council of Education Workers (CNTE) as an alternative to the state SNTE, which was dominated by a gang of *PRIista* bosses calling themselves the Vanguardia Revolucionario. Graffiti mocked it as a "Vanguardia *Robolucionario*."[33]

In spring 1987, teachers statewide went on strike for sixty-five days to demand recognition of the CNTE. On March 30, a CNTE demonstration in Tuxtla's *zócalo* was attacked by Vanguardista gunmen. One was killed and two wounded. There were no arrests.[34]

In December 1989, two CNTE teachers, Rubicel Einstein Ruiz and Oscar de Jesús Peña, were abducted on a Tuxtla street by State Judicial Police, hooded, forced into an unmarked vehicle, brought to a sheer precipice overlooking the deep Rio Grijalva gorge, and threatened with being thrown over the side. Instead, they were thrown in Cerro Hueco, where they remained for five months on charges of destroying property in a Tuxtla street protest.[35]

Tuxtla's conservative *Diario El Dia* assailed Bishop Ruiz almost daily, giving voice in front-page headlines to the Chamula *caciques* who accused him of "fomenting rebellion" in league with Communists.[36] His enemies were already deriding him as the "Red Bishop."

In 1984, I interviewed Bishop Ruiz for the first time, and unintentionally alienated him by indiscreetly asking if he was a Liberation Theologist. "I am not a 'theologist' of any sort," he replied curtly. "I am a priest doing my job. Christ has always been the God of the poor, and it is the job of his followers to work to create Heaven on Earth. I have no conflict whatsoever with traditional Christian teaching."

What about the accusations?

"The opposition is losing credibility. There is solidarity for our work with the refugees and *campesinos*, among the poor. The middle classes are ambivalent. In the upper class, there is fear."

Fear of what?

"Fear of revolution, of change, of a guerilla movement developing in Mexico."

Rumors about the Lacandon Selva were mounting.

Patrocinio González succeeded Castellanos to the governor's palace in 1988. Patrocinio was linked by arranged marriages to the family of Carlos Salinas, who assumed the presidency that year. With talk of modernization, Patrocinio actually pushed through legislation making Chiapas the first and only Mexican state to legalize abortion—to the protests of the Church. But hundreds more *campesinos* were locked up in Cerro Hueco on charges related to land conflicts under his tenure.[37] A Chol organization from Palenque called Xi'Nich—the "ant people"—marched cross-country to Mexico City to protest the repression.[38]

Two journalists were murdered during Patrocinio's term, and twelve lethal assaults on journalists were reported. A wave of anti-gay violence also swept through the Tuxtla scene, which had just begun to tentatively uncloset itself. Tuxtla transvestites, one after another, were gunned down with "police-caliber slugs to the head" on the city's cruise strips. No one was ever charged.[39]

In 1993, Guatemala, last among the Central American nations, was finally muddling toward a peace accord, signaling an end to the hemisphere's longest-running guerilla conflict. The URNG offered to lay down arms in exchange for land for its demobilized troops, and guarantees of freedom to organize politically. The UN began repatriating the refugees.[40]

But those among the Mexican elites who thought that this meant Chiapas was back from the brink were in for a rude awakening.

In October 1993, Papal Nuncio Girolamo Prigione issued an official letter accusing Bishop Ruiz of grave doctrinal and pastoral errors, and asking him to resign. Ruiz demanded to know the nature of the charges against him, and Indians marched in San Cristóbal in his support. *El Financiero* quoted sources claiming that the Nuncio had arranged for the Bishop's resignation as a pay-off for the rapprochement between the PRI state and the Catholic Church then underway. Few anticipated that in a matter of weeks Bishop Ruiz would be widely perceived as the one man standing between Chiapas and total war.[41]

In the final days of December, Trudy Blom died at the age of 92.[42] She would not live to see her beloved rainforest suddenly make world headlines.

On January 1, 1994, the Zapatista Army of National Liberation announced its existence, sealed off the Selva, and marched out to liberate the Highlands.

THE DEAD OF JANUARY

The EZLN launched its rebellion in the earliest hours of New Year's Day, 1994, precisely as NAFTA took effect.

The rebel army emerged from the Selva and occupied four towns in the Highlands: San Cristóbal de Las Casas, Ocosingo, Altamirano and Las Margaritas.[43]

Ocosingo, Altamirano and Las Margaritas are the last major towns before the drop into Las Cañadas, and are accessible to a direct surprise attack. San Cristóbal, in the heart of the Highlands, required more preparation. The troops filtered in from the Selva along Indian trails through the mountains, and converged at San Andrés Larrainzar, a Tzotzil village above San Cristóbal where PRI loyalties were less than firm. There, trucks were requisitioned from the municipal authorities for the final approach.[44]

Amado Avendaño, editor and owner of the town's primitive but spirited newspaper, *El Tiempo*, was woken at 1:00 am to reports that masked armed men had occupied the *zócalo* and municipal palace. Avendaño called the Rancho Nuevo military base outside town, and was told that they knew nothing but would look into it. He decided next to call the municipal palace itself. A man picked up the phone and told the editor that he was aware of the situation and not to worry, it was under control.

The EZLN's Insurgent Subcommander Marcos had established his first contact with the media.[45]

At the municipal palace, government records and land titles were destroyed and computers smashed. The walls were covered with graffiti. One graffito mocked Gen. Miguel Godínez Bravo, military commander for Chiapas: "NO HAY GUERILLA, DICE GODINEZ BRAVO." Indeed, all evidence indicates the good general continued to sleep soundly as the revolutionaries sacked the palace.[46]

Government stores were looted, the food distributed to the populace; prisoners were freed at the local jails. In Ocosingo, where the Zapatistas engaged the state Judicial Police in a shoot-out for control of the municipal palace, the government radio station was seized, and rebel broadcasts crackled over the valley at dawn. A slaughterhouse was burned down.[47]

The rebels distributed a manifesto called the First Declaration of the Lacandon Selva, declaring war on the "evil government," demanding recognition as a belligerent force, calling on both sides to comply with the Geneva Conventions, and for the international community to monitor the conflict. "We are the product of 500 years of struggle," the document began, invoking Hidalgo, Morelos, Villa and Zapata. The document said all legal remedies against the "seventy-year-old dictatorship" had been exhausted. It claimed legitimacy for their revolution under Article 39 of the Mexican Constitution, which affirms that sovereignty lies with the people, who have "at all times, the inalienable right to alter or modify the form of their government." Also distributed were copies of the EZLN's Revolutionary Laws for governing liberated territory, announcing intentions to take the national capital. Press accounts would tell of an articulate, green-eyed masked *ladino* in San Cristóbal who seemed to be the rebel group's spokesman.[48]

On the morning of January 2, the rebel troops withdrew from San Cristóbal to engage the army at Rancho Nuevo, rather than wait for the inevitable attack. It was a successful diversionary operation, keeping the government troops pinned down and allowing the rebels to retreat. Meanwhile, in Ocosingo things had gone badly. The rebels had gathered in the market, where they were surrounded by army troops arriving from Palenque. Numerous civilians were caught in the net as the shooting began. Scores were killed in the battle of Ocosingo.[49]

Also on the morning of the 2nd, Absalon Castellanos was seized from his ranch outside Las Margaritas by Zapatista troops, and charged with crimes against the *campesinos* and Indians.[50]

By then, the authorities realized a public statement about the situation was necessary. The statement released by President Salinas called the rebels "professionals of violence." "This is not an Indian uprising, but the action of a violent armed group, directed against the public peace and government institutions." Gobernación's statement denied the EZLN was even Mexican, but made up of Central American revolutionaries and other foreigners who have "manipulated disaffected persons." The Chiapas government's statement took a shot at Bishop Ruiz: "Direct reports from residents of these municipalities indicate that some of the Catholic priests espousing liberation theology and their deacons linked themselves to these groups."[51]

The URNG issued a statement denying any link to Mexico's new rebels. So did the Diocese.[52]

On January 4, as combat continued along the road to Rancho Nuevo, the federal army responded in force, strafing *barrios* and hamlets from the air by helicopter. At poor communities on San Cristóbal's southern outskirts like San Antonio Los Baños, bullets and rockets rained down on thatch huts. At Los Corralitos, the terrorized populace fled for the mountains. Bishop Ruiz called for a cease-fire. The government responded there would be no cease-fire unless the rebels agreed to immediately turn over their arms. By then, there was fighting at Las Margaritas and Altamirano as well.[53]

The following day, an EZLN communiqué entitled "Responses to Government Lies" was delivered to the offices of *El Tiempo:* "The EZLN does not have foreigners in its ranks or among its leadership, nor has it ever received any support or training from revolutionary forces of other countries or from foreign governments . . . The military tactics that we employ were not learned from the Central American insurgency, but rather from Mexican military history: from Hidalgo, Morelos, Guerrero, Mina, from the resistance to the Yankee invasion in 1846–47, from the popular response to the French intervention, from the heroic exploits of Villa and Zapata and from indigenous resistance struggles throughout our country's history." It denied links to the Catholic Church or to any other armed movement on the planet. It asserted that all the EZLN troops were Mexican, and most were Indians from Chiapas.[54]

The pine woods between San Cristóbal and Rancho Nuevo remained a war zone. The EZLN withdrew from their remaining positions at Ocosingo, Altamirano and Las Margaritas. "The stench of death permeates Ocosingo," a *Reforma* reporter wrote. "The vultures smell it and circle, looking for dead meat, while helicopters circle, looking for live meat."[55]

On January 7, a fax arrived at the offices of Mexico City's respected left-opposition weekly *Proceso*. It was from the rebels, and offered to establish a dialogue with the government. It proposed three possible personalities to mediate: Rigoberta Menchú, the Quiché activist from Guatemala and winner of the 1992 Nobel Peace Prize; *Proceso* publisher Julio Scherer; and Bishop Samuel Ruiz.[56]

On January 10, the world took note of Chiapas in a demonstrable way: the robust Mexican stock market plunged. President Salinas sacked former Chiapas Governor Patrocinio González from his post as Gobernación secretary for denying the guerilla threat.[57]

On January 12, a massive march, one of the largest since 1968, was held in Mexico City's *zócalo* in protest of the repression. Cuauhtémoc Cárdenas and other opposition leaders demanded a halt to the offensive. The government declared a cease-fire, pledging only to respond if attacked. After twelve days of fighting, some 150 were dead, by conservative estimates. The rebels retreated back to the Selva.[58]

The Lacandon Selva, now openly under rebel control, was surrounded by the military, and lines were established. The army put up checkpoints along all routes into the Selva, but did not attempt to enter it. Between the areas occupied by the opposing armies was the *zona franca*, a demilitarized area. Somewhere in Las Cañadas, began the liberated zone. The EZLN had carved out a niche of the national territory—the rainforest of Chiapas, newly dubbed the "dignified heart" of the Mexican nation.[59]

Absalon Castellanos was being held blindfolded under armed guard in a hut somewhere in the Selva, awaiting a Zapatista tribunal. The Diocese of San Cristóbal and the Red Cross established lines of communication to facilitate the process of establishing a dialogue.[60]

On January 15, National Human Rights Commission investigators uncovered a mass grave in Ocosingo. At least some of the bodies were of civilians. Autopsies revealed that many of the young rebels had been finished off with a *coup de grâce* while lying wounded. Accounts mounted of summary execution and torture by government troops during the fighting. The Bishop of Tapachula, Felipe Arizmendi Esquivel, released a statement calling for both sides to lay down arms, and warned of a war of ethnic extermination. "There exists a moral obligation," he addressed federal troops, "to disobey those decisions that order genocide."[61]

On January 25, five hundred San Cristóbal *coletos* held a march in support of the army. That same day, President Salinas visited Tuxtla to placate *campesino* leaders; he was met with an openly hostile response. He promised dialogue.[62]

Bishop Ruiz was named as mediator; former Mexico City mayor and federal Environment Secretary Manuel Camacho Solis as government "peace spokesman." Camacho, something of a democratic dissident within the party elite, accepted the peace assignment, but emphasized that he was acting independently, as a private citizen.[63]

On January 28, the government began freeing presumed Zapatista prisoners from Cerro Hueco.[64] Interim Gov. Javier López Moreno replaced the humiliated Elmar Setzer by a vote of the Chiapas legislature. The sole opposition legislator, from the Party of the Democratic Revolution, cast his vote for Marcos, to the applause of spectators.[65]

Gen. Godínez Bravo, commander of the Seventh Military Region in Tuxtla (covering the 31st Military Zone based at Rancho Nuevo) announced his troops were ready for a military solution. "If it has to be done, it has to be done definitively," he told the press. "Admittedly, it would be war, but a war for which our personnel are well trained. We always thought that Chiapas, well . . . could have these problems, and we thought how we could fight in this type of forest terrain. So this army is well trained, well prepared, well drilled, well equipped and, above all, with good morale."[66]

Amnesty International and other human rights groups sent teams to Chiapas. Americas Watch issued a statement in Washington DC calling on President Clinton to condemn the "grave human rights violations" in Chiapas.[67] The Internet was abuzz with reports, and San Cristóbal's hotels filled up with reporters, investigators, activists, adventurers and spies.

A wave of local rebellions spread across Chiapas. On February 7, *campesinos* occupied the municipal building in the Tzotzil town of Teopisca, throwing out the *PRIista* government and electing a new council of their own. Miguel Hernández, a Teopisca *campesino*, told the Mexico City daily *Excélsior*, "By grace, the Zapatistas have opened our eyes. We do not know them, but we must thank them. Before, we did not have the valor to do this." More would follow.[68]

The Tzeltal village of Tenejapa followed Teopisca just a week later in demanding the ouster of the PRI government there and declaring a new municipal council.[69]

A few days after that, Tzotzils in Chenalhó took possession of private lands within the *municipio*, and *ejidal* lands illegally hoarded by *caciques*. Five hundred *campesinos* took over the municipal palace in Bella Vista, in the Grijalva Valley, kicking out the incumbent *PRIistas*.[70]

Ranch and *finca* lands were occupied in Chilón, in Yajalón, and as far as Sosconosco.[71] The Francisco Villa Popular Campesino Union (UCPFV), isolated high in the Sierra Madre, occupied the sprawling ranches of Liquidambar and Prusia.[72] The rebelling *campesinos* adopted the EZLN's list of eleven demands as their own and pledged the rebels their "unconditional support."[73] On February 19, four thousand dissident teachers marched on Tuxtla in support of the *campesinos*, and to press their own demands over wages and arrest orders against their leaders.[74] Two weeks later, hundreds of teachers joined thousands of *campesinos* in simultaneous mobilizations on Tuxtla and Tapachula.[75]

On February 12, Mexico's newspapers reported a "secret" meeting between the new Gobernación secretary, former Prosecutor General Jorge Carpizo, and CIA chief James Woolsey in Mexico City to discuss Chiapas.[76]

On February 16, as a goodwill gesture, the EZLN released Absalon Castellanos to Ruiz and Camacho at Guadalupe Tepeyac on the edge of the Lacandon Selva. On handing the General over before Red Cross witnesses, the masked Zapatista troops shouted "*¡Viva el EZLN!*" Camacho rejoined, "*¡Viva México!*"[77]

DIALOGUE, STALEMATE AND THE CIVIL STRUGGLE

On February 20, masked but unarmed, a delegation of twenty Zapatistas arrived back in San Cristóbal, escorted via a Red Cross caravan. The dialogue table was established in the sixteenth-century Cathedral where Las Casas had conducted mass. Three rings of security were established around the Cathedral, twenty-four/seven. The inner ring was made up of unarmed federal MPs; then the Red Cross; and finally a human cordon made up of civil society groups.[78]

The mysterious guerillas wowed the media every time the proceedings broke for a press conference. The masked EZLN team included the charismatic Subcomandante Marcos, clearly a *ladino*, and Comandante Ramona, who wore a traditional Tzotzil *huipil* as well as trademark black ski-mask. The team made it clear that they were *not* directly negotiating peace—the dialogue team was not empowered to make decisions or accept government proposals without the participation of the people they represented in the Selva.[79]

They also made it clear that Marcos was actually the lowest ranking member of the delegation—the others were *comandantes* and members of the Indigenous Revolutionary Clandestine Committee (CCRI), the EZLN's General Command, an all-Indian body from which Marcos apparently received his orders.[80]

The Zapatistas presented the eleven demands of their program, then sequestered themselves to discuss the government's offers. The government rejected outright the resignation of Salinas, suspension of the TLC and criminal trials for every living Chiapas governor, but agreed in principle to discuss demands for Indian autonomy.[81]

"We put in eighteen-hour days," Camacho Solis told *La Reforma*. "We were constantly afraid that, if what we were doing did not bear fruit, war would break out again and many would be killed."[82]

The peace proposal at which they finally arrived called for new legislation to secure free elections, protecting Indian lands and breaking up large estates when in the "public interest." New municipalities would be drawn and laws passed to effect Indian autonomy. The EZLN would not be recognized as a belligerent force, but would be guaranteed the "right to decide on its future political and social role." Medical services and electricity would be extended to marginal rural areas.[83]

On March 2, the EZLN dialogue team ended the "first phase" of the dialogue and returned to the Lacandon Selva to bring the government proposals to their people. They shortly began holding lengthy *consultas* with the populace in their Selva villages to discuss the proposals.[84]

I arrived in Chiapas a few days before the Cathedral dialogue sessions ended. Subsequently, a visible massive troop presence withdrew from San Cristóbal, although the army still maintained checkpoints outside Rancho Nuevo on the road into town. Altamirano, Las Margaritas and Ocosingo, however, are not on the tourist trail, and the scenes there were different. Army troops patrolled the streets, armored personnel carriers and jeep-mounted machine guns waiting at the intersections. In Las Margaritas and Altamirano, the municipal auditoriums were opened as refugee camps, filled with *campesinos* who had fled fighting in the hamlets. Weeks after the cease-fire, homes throughout the region were hung with white flags, signifying neutrality.

This marginal corner of Mexico was searing in the intensity of the national spotlight. San Cristóbal's small daily *El Tiempo* became the first in the nation to print Zapatista communiqués, and aggressively covered government and White Guard repression, despite death threats and harassment. With its antiquated equipment and hand-set type, it became a symbol nationwide of a fighting press, finally defying the unofficial but universal boundaries of self-censorship.

On the equinox, a group of Tzotzils, Tzeltals, Chols and Tojolabals made a pilgrimage to Palenque, converging on the ancient ruins from their respective villages to burn *copal* and pray and sing, with their homemade harps and guitars, for peace and a restoration of Indian sovereignty. The pilgrims proclaimed the arrival of the Sixth Sun, the completion of a centuries-long Maya calendric cycle signifying an end to the time of darkness and destruction.[85]

The government's promise of dialogue with the peasants facilitated the creation of CEOIC, the State Council of Indian and Campesino Organizations. For the first time, the loose network of over two hundred village-based organizations, despite some bitter and occasionally violent factional divisions, joined in a single united front.[86] It was the CEOIC that made possible the March 6 coordinated multi-organizational march on San Cristóbal under the slogan "¡NO ESTAN SOLOS!"—They are not alone; a reference to the EZLN.

Land occupations continued to spread; it reached the point of an agrarian re-form-from-below. CEOIC declared the Chiapas *latifundios* illegal under Mexican law.[87] The state government was forced to negotiate with the squatters. By the end of March, the CEOIC agreed to suspend land occupations in exchange for a commitment not to expel *campesinos* from land already under occupation. Land-owners compensated by the government for lands ceded to squatters openly stated they were putting the money into guns to take back their properties at the first opportunity.[88]

The landowners were furious that the squatters had been legitimized by nego-tiation. *Vivas* for Jorge Constantino Kanter, the outspoken "natural leader" of the cattlelords, began appearing on San Cristóbal's walls.

Daily reports came in of spontaneous mobilizations for the Zapatistas across Mexico. Mixtecs of the Guerrero Council of 500 Years of Resistance held a "*No Estan Solos*" march—300 kilometers from Chilpancingo to Mexico City, complete with a village brass band.[89] Mixtec and Nahuatl militants of the Emiliano Zapata Revolutionary Agrarian League of the South (LARSEZ) launched protest occupa-tions of Guerrero CNC and INI offices.[90] In Michoacan, unemployed sugar work-ers, angered over the closing of a local mill, offered to join Zapatistas in armed rebellion.[91] In Hidalgo, the Emiliano Zapata Democratic Front of the Mexican East (FEDOMEZ) faced death threats after holding public protests in support of the Zapatistas.[92] Indians blocked roads in Tehuacan, Puebla.[93]

In Yucatan, students calling themselves "Zapatistas" protested at a campaign stop by Donaldo Colosio, the PRI presidential candidate; in the Guerrero *pueblo* of Xalitla, the Council of Nahua Pueblos of the Upper Balsas declared Colosio *persona non grata*.[94]

There were urban mobilizations in the shanty-towns and *barrios* of the Federal District by the Emiliano Zapata Popular Revolutionary Movement (UPREZ), which also held a ceremony for peace in the federal *zócalo;* Mexico City street gangs proclaimed for the EZLN.[95]

The CEOIC called for a national meeting of Indian and *campesino* organizations to converge on Chiapas. Held at a San Cristóbal hotel on March 13–14, the meeting brought together some five hundred representatives of groups from Chiapas, Oaxaca, Guerrero, Morelos, Michoacan, Veracruz, Puebla, Zacatecas.[96] The walls were strewn with homemade banners brought from distant villages in other states. One from the Union de Pueblos de Morelos featured a portrait of Zapata surrounded by *maíz* plants, and read: "CAMPESINO: CUIDO TU EJIDO, UNICO PATRIMONIO DE TUS HIJOS."

The Union de Pueblos de Morelos was a member of a national network of *campesino* organizations, the Coordinadora Nacional-Plan de Ayala, or CNPA. The Emiliano Zapata Campesino Organization (OCEZ), one of the more prominent Chiapas groups, was also affiliated with CNPA, which was formed in 1979 (by Zapata's own son Mateo in Morelos, among others) in response to the winding down of the agrarian reform. Numerous unaffiliated groups representing a lone valley or village were there. The CNC was also officially represented in the CEOIC, but kept a low profile at the national meeting, if they were present at all.[97]

Delegates reported on local conditions and struggles in their home villages; some fiery, some humbly heartfelt. Some recited self-penned poetic homages to Zapata and Villa, or performed political *corridos* to the accompaniment of guitars and rustic fiddles. At one particularly spirited point in the proceedings, when a real barnburner of a speaker was railing against the rural landlords, a small earthquake hit. The ground momentarily swayed beneath our feet, and the entire assembly ran in a wave from the conference room into the courtyard, shouting and laughing.

The meeting produced a statement calling for a national "*Zapata Vive*" march on Mexico City on April 10, the seventy-fifth anniversary of Zapata's death. The statement also assailed the TLC and Salinas economic program: "The *salinista* modernization has taken a high social cost in a drastic worsening of the purchasing power of the *campesinos*, economic recession, unemployment, migration, ecological degradation, decapitalization of the countryside . . ."[98]

The OCEZ–CNPA banner at the conference shared the red and black colors and five-pointed star of the EZLN. Of all the groups staging land occupations, the OCEZ–CNPA was among the most grassroots-democratic, with purely *campesino* leadership. OCEZ–CNPA insisted on rotating leadership, a decentralized structure and strict independence from all political parties. OCEZ–CNPA had in the past criticized CIOAC for a perceived lack of participatory politics, for serving primarily to deliver *campesino* votes for the Mexican Communist Party or, more recently, the Party of the Democratic Revolution. OCEZ–CNPA had assailed CIOAC for mirroring the top-down structure of the CNC, which routinely marshalls *campesino* votes for the PRI.[99] But both OCEZ–CNPA and CIOAC were now working together in CEOIC.

OCEZ–CNPA and CIOAC agreed to respect their differences, without compromising. Genaro Hernández, a *mestizo* OCEZ–CNPA militant from the village of La Trinitaria in the Frontera region of the Grijalva Valley, spoke with me as we milled in the courtyard after the earthquake. "The parties are not an alternative. We *campesinos* and Indians have to organize ourselves. Every person, every community, every *pueblo*, has to decide its own fate directly. No leader can do that for us."

Hernández said OCEZ–CNPA was occupying several thousand hectares at eight different sites in La Trinitaria, with a total of six hundred *campesinos*, including women and children, involved in the ongoing actions.[100] Hernández said OCEZ–CNPA had no direct contact with the EZLN, "but their demands are ours."

The OCEZ was also overcoming destructive internal divisions since the EZLN uprising. In 1989, the CNPA-affiliated OCEZ in La Trinitaria and the allied OCEZ in Simojovel split from the Venustiano Carranza OCEZ. The split began over whether to affiliate with national organizations and how to respond to state negotiation bids, but deepened as OCEZ activists on either side were mysteriously assassinated. Some OCEZ militants blamed White Guards; but others blamed the rival faction, and suspicions escalated.[101] Yet when I asked about the killing of OCEZ leader Mariano Pérez Díaz in Simojovel the week before the conference,[102] Genaro Hernández was unequivocal: "The government." Or *guardias blancas*? "In Chiapas, they are the same thing."

Even as the army adopted a tolerant stance toward the land take-overs, the unofficial terror network which exercised extrajudicial repression against *campesino* movements in the 1980s was re-emerging with a vengeance.

"Out with the nuns!" and "Death to Don Samuel!" rent the air at Altamirano, where local ranchers, *PRista* merchants and hired goons repeatedly held rowdy marches at the Hospital of San Carlos, run by a French-based Catholic voluntary organization, the Sisters of Charity. Public threats were issued accusing the Sisters of being "*monjas Zapatistas*."[103] There were increasing reports from remote communities on the edge of the Selva of atrocities committed—rapes, the burning of *campesino* huts with the inhabitants trapped inside—by men in black ski-masks: presumably White Guards exploiting the situation.[104]

"The White Guards have never existed," White Guard leader Jorge Kanter told an interviewer from Human Rights Watch. "The lack of government support in the face of the invasions obliged us to act."[105] Kanter, a prominent *PRista* and organizer of the Altamirano marches, had led Chiapas ranchers on a hunger strike at the Angel of Independence monument in Mexico City to demand compensation for occupied lands, and had warned the press that their "peaceful attitude" might change if the government didn't comply.[106]

The San Cristóbal *coletos* were scandalized by the March 6 spectacle at the municipal palace. As recently as the 1950s, they had run a city where Indians could not walk on the sidewalks, and had to be out of town by dark.[107]

Death threats against Bishop Ruiz predictably mounted. In a March meeting at San Cristóbal's convention center, the *coletos* promised to drive Don Samuel out of town along with the "hippies" and "communists"—a reference to the EZLN's urban supporters and international fans who flocked to San Cristóbal after the uprising.[108] A more blatant threat came in a note attached to a rock that crashed through a window of the Cathedral's parochial house, calling the Bishop the "son of Satan" and warning "your days are numbered."[109]

The Diocese continued to monitor the human rights situation in the Highlands, providing an alternative to the government monitors who set up shop to hear complaints at army checkpoints—hardly a strategy for winning the trust of terrorized *campesinos*. In February, the governmental National Human Rights Commission (CNDH) announced it had received 218 complaints about the Federal Army, and twenty against the EZLN.[110]

After several days of waiting, I was finally granted an interview with the Bishop. In the antechamber of the parochial house, where I was told to wait for Don Samuel, was hanging a portrait of the Pope. In the private chamber where I was escorted for the interview was a painting of Oscar Romero, the Archbishop of El Salvador gunned down during mass in 1980. The gunscope hairs superimposed on the face formed the cross of his martyrdom.

I'm not sure Don Samuel remembered our interview ten years earlier, despite his polite but vague assurances. Although his English was better than my Spanish (not to mention his French, Italian, German, Latin, Greek and Hebrew), he refused to speak it this time. "I am tired," he said. "We will speak in Spanish."

Don Samuel warned that it is a mistake to view the EZLN in the same light as the Central American guerillas of the 1980s.

"They don't want to seize power," he said of the EZLN. "This is something new. They want to create a democratic process that all Mexicans take part in. They want recognition of indigenous culture, history and autonomy."

Don Samuel made clear he does not advocate violence. But he called the EZLN's January uprising an example of the "Third Violence." "The First Violence," said the Bishop, is "the violence of the system—the tremendous concentration of wealth resulting in popular misery, which will only be worsened by the TLC." The

"Second Violence" is the "repression, torture and imprisonment against people organizing against the First Violence." The "Third Violence," that of revolutionary groups such as the EZLN, is "a result of the First and Second."

The Bishop emphasized that the EZLN accepted a cease-fire within days of their uprising—also unique in the history of Latin American revolutionary movements. He said he saw the rebellion as one manifestation of a larger dynamic. "The TLC represents an expansion of the system's domination. But new factors are emerging. Civil society is emerging from under the control of the political parties—seeking a human modification of the system."

The Mexican system seemed to lurch deeper into crisis in the following days, and prospects for peace narrowed. On March 23, Luis Donaldo Colosio, the PRI's presidential candidate, was assassinated at a campaign stop in Tijuana. The following day, the EZLN declared a state of "red alert" throughout their stronghold, claiming the federal army used the assassination as a cover to violate the cease-fire with aerial bombardment of a road in Zapatista-held territory. The rebels declared the dialogue indefinitely suspended.[111]

A few nights later, Easter celebration fireworks in the San Cristóbal *zócalo* formed images of giant doves and other messages of peace. It was the Diocese's message of determination.

I was arriving at my own determination: to go into the Selva and contact the rebels on their own turf.

5

BEHIND LINES WITH MARCOS: 1994

As Easter Sunday dawned over San Cristóbal de Las Casas, the stream of tourists and Indian pilgrims was already starting to trickle into town. But I was hoofing it through the chill mountain air to catch a *colectivo* Volkswagon micro-bus to Ocosingo—the first leg on an uncertain excursion into the Lacandon Selva, stronghold of the Zapatista National Liberation Army.

The rebels held Mexico enraptured. Numerous Mexican journalists had ventured behind their lines to interview Subcomandante Marcos, the man who captivated the imagination of the nation. Few gringo journalists had.

WHO *IS* THAT MASKED MAN?

I was looking at a challenge and carrying all of my food and water on my back. Some of the worst poverty in Mexico is in the Selva. Most settlements have no electricity or running water, and cholera reports were mounting. I didn't want to to get sick, and I didn't want to take from people who had nothing.

But I was mostly worried about boredom and tension. I had heard numerous stories about journalists kept waiting days fruitlessly to get an interview with the EZLN's principal military leader and eloquent spokesman.

Everyone from housewives to the Prosecutor General of the Republic (PGR) puzzled over the Marcos enigma. Never photographed without his black ski-mask and trademark pipe, the guerilla leader had a meteoric rise as a cult figure. Green eyes, beard and prodigious nose could be detected through the mask in press photos. His poetic communiqués from unknown and remote rainforest locations (always signed "from the mountains of southeast Mexico . . .") were avidly read every day in *La Jornada*, the national daily chosen by the Zapatistas. Their denunciations of the corrupt PRI hegemony, of the agonizing poverty and repression faced by Mexico's Indians, of the media's subservience to the state, of the country's impending corporate rape under the Free Trade agreement—all struck a resounding chord across Mexico.

A kind of Marcosmania prevailed. The journalists who descended on San Cristóbal during the dialogue were jokingly called the "third army," after the EZLN and the Mexican federal army. Now people were starting to chuckle about a "fourth army"— the women hoping to catch a glimpse of the mysterious Subcomandante.

Marcos t-shirts, key-chains, socks and condoms were hot items at the San Cristóbal souvenir shops. The Chamulas got in on the action by making *muñecas zapatistas*— little dolls depicting Marcos and his fellow warriors. (Ironically, the *caciques* got their cut of the proceeds!)

The government was no less obsessed. As early as January 6, a green-eyed Venezuelan aid worker was detained by the Federal Army in Ocosingo, and interrogated for over seven hours before it was determined that he was not, in fact, Marcos.[1]

While all Mexico seemed to be holding its breath to see if the rebels would accept the government peace proposal, the state was preparing for war. The Gobernación Secretariat and PGR were working with the FBI and CIA to uncover the Subcommander's identity.[2]

INTO ZAPATISTA TERRITORY

The *colectivo* stopped at the army checkpoint outside San Cristóbal. The passengers all breathed a sigh of relief that this time the troops only demanded ID instead of subjecting us to the usual frisks and searches. An hour's journey along dizzying mountain roads brought us to Ocosingo—gateway to the Lacandon Selva.

At the market in Ocosingo, I caught a bus toward Monte Libano, the jungle settlement. The old schoolbus was full of *campesinos*, mostly Tzeltals, making their way out to the Lacandon communities on one errand or another this Easter Sunday. Many of them seemed ill. The road sloped down into a valley. As we left the town behind us, we went through the final army checkpoint, ringed by armored personnel carriers and artillery.

"*Todos los hombres*," said the troops, and all the men filed off the bus to stand in line for inspection. Searches, frisks, ID checks. Then the bus was winding back down into the valley. The pavement ended and we entered a rough unimproved road. The checkpoint receded in the distance. We had entered the cease-fire zone—the *zona franca.*

I told the driver to drop me off at the little settlement where I was told journalists should go to contact the rebels. At the time, I was instructed not to print its name, but now I think it is safe. It was Ejido San Miguel.

The bus crept and heaved along through pines and occasional *milpas.* The woman next to me on the cramped seat took one swig of her beer and threw up all over her shoes. I'm definitely off the tourist trail, I thought.

A little later, the driver called out San Miguel, and I stumbled off the bus. I seemed to be in the middle of nowhere. I followed a little foot-trail up to a cluster of houses, some local children serving as my guides. They didn't seem to understand my villainous Spanish. This was Tzeltal country.

I went into the Red Cross station—part of an emergency program against the cholera break-out—and said lamely, "*Soy un periodista y estoy buscando Zapatistas.*" They pointed me vaguely down the path and told me to look for Javier. After I did some asking around, Javier appeared. He seemed all of fifteen. He took my passport and letters of introduction from *High Times* magazine and WBAI Radio in New York. He disappeared with them for several minutes, leaving me standing in the dust. He was presumably communicating with a Zapatista base. Later, when I was able to walk around more freely, I found the house he went into. A truck outside, with a line leading into the house, was mounted with a radio antenna and solar panel. The only other electricity in San Miguel came from car batteries.

Javier returned with my credentials and told me I'd have to wait until Tuesday. When I tried to ask more questions, he interrupted me and asked if I wanted to wait or not. "*¡Claro que si!*" I assured him, and shut up.

He led me to a little empty hut—one of the newer ones, made of fresh timber instead of mud and thatch—and left me there. Nobody seemed to pay me much mind.

I had a long two days ahead of me. The hut, with only a little bed in it, seemed to be part of a small compound within the settlement, run by an extended family. Gradually, some approached me over the course of the day. The men, in cowboy hats and cheap polyester clothes from the Ocosingo market, spoke some Spanish—the women, all in traditional Tzeltal dress, and children kept their distance. I didn't hear them speak a syllable of Spanish, and, except for the little girls who shyly smiled, they would not even look at me.

One old man told me how the settlement was attacked by helicopter and truck-mounted artillery one afternoon in January. There were no guns in the village, much less armed Zapatistas. A few huts went up in flames, and one 9-year-old girl fled terrified into the mountains. She hadn't reappeared.

The old man told me how the good lands in the valley are owned by a *dueño* in Comitán, who leaves them idle apart from grazing some cattle. But he protects the land with *pistoleros*, leaving the Tzeltals no choice but to clear forest on the steep slopes of the overlooking *cerros* to grow their corn and beans. At one point in the afternoon, two men on horseback passed through the settlement, heading out into the bush. The children scattered and ran for their homes. The settlement's men all looked uneasy until the riders passed. It was unnerving.

The settlement seemed to have been established in the 1950s, when the *finca* in the valley became a cattle ranch. The erstwhile laborers were thrown out of work and granted their high, rocky *ejido*. When the *ejiditarios* tried to plant on the old *finca* land in the valley, they were driven off by the *pistoleros*.

A survey of the landscape immediately confirmed this account of the valley's land tenure. *Milpas* scarred the forested slopes above the settlement and smoke from slash-and-burn clearings rose through the trees.

The valley wall behind me was part of the Sierra Corralchen. The valley stretched to the east, an expanse of brush reclaiming cleared forest. It was vacant, apart from some cattle in the distance. I now know I was at the mouth of Patihuitz Canyon.

The opposite wall of the valley was the Sierra Cruz de Plata, still verdant. On the far slopes I could make out another little *ejido*. Beyond lay Monte Libano and the Biosphere Reserve and the tropical forest.

I was told Ejido San Miguel grows barely enough *maíz* and *frijol* to get by, plus a little coffee to sell in Ocosingo for a price too low to help much.

The only government presence in the community was a schoolhouse which had been closed since January 1.

A road led southeast from the settlement, following the valley wall toward the Selva. It was blocked by a pile of rocks, watched over by a group of local kids. One wore a baseball cap with "EZLN" scrawled on it in black marker. I was awaiting the OK to go through that roadblock.

That evening, the women formed a procession into the little church for mass, wearing black veils and carrying white candles. Guitars and singing filled the air.

Late that night, I was joined in the hut by three journalists from California: Joel Simon with Pacific News Service, and Susan Ferriss and Rick Sandoval, on assignment for the *San Francisco Examiner*. They had rented a VW bug in San Cristóbal, and we formed a team, for which I was grateful. Susan was a most welcome addition. The women were not afraid (or unwilling) to talk to her, and we got coffee and *tortillas* in the morning.

On Tuesday, as promised, we got the OK to move—"*puede pasar*," Javier told us, then disappeared. A slow hour's drive—with one of the kids from the road-block, his young wife and sick baby somehow squeezing into the bug with us—brought us to another little settlement, even more primitive than the first. We were stopped by another roadblock. Here we got our first glimpse of real Zapatista troops. They wore black ski-masks and *café*-colored uniforms, and carried machine guns that looked like they'd been pried off a vehicle. They told us to wait outside the empty schoolhouse. I later found out we were in La Garrucha.

As the hours went by, we wondered if we'd actually get to Marcos that day. We were told by other journalists who had made it through that the unpredictable "*sup*" liked dramatic, unexpected entrances. We assumed that we were being watched—and being tested, felt out.

It wasn't until nightfall that a squad of young Zapatistas jogged back to the car, in uniform and single-file. They each shook hands with us. Then we were all frisked, and the vehicle searched top to bottom. I was immediately overcome with a sense of what a tremendous cultural leap had been made. The Indians in Chiapas are usually very deferential toward tourists—the women especially. It was a very strange feeling to be ordered around and efficiently searched by a teenage Tzeltal woman with a ski-mask and a machine gun.

After the search, we were told once again to wait. But as the night wore on and no one appeared, Joel and I went into the schoolhouse and rolled out our sleeping bags on beds we found there.

Perhaps an hour later I awoke to the realization that there were two figures with ski-masks and machine guns in the room. One stood at the door, rifle at the ready. The other approached me. He was puffing on a pipe and talking to me in English. "Pacifica Radio?" he asked suspiciously. It dawned upon my sleep-numbed brain that I was in the presence of Marcos.

WITH THE TROOPS

Marcos led us outside and put us into a big farm truck, telling us we must leave our car. We got into the back of the truck with two ski-masked guards and drove into the night forest. The road got worse and the forest got thicker as we went. The truck frequently had to slow down and lurch to negotiate deep ruts. The bug never would have made it.

I dimly remember the truck stopping in the forest and the two young Zapatistas leading us up a trail through the undergrowth. Marcos drove off into the night, telling us he'd be back for us in the afternoon.

We arrived at another impoverished settlement and were put in another hut. Boards attached to poles made makeshift bunks, most of which were occupied by sleeping *café*-clad bodies. We were in a Zapatista barracks.

We woke up at dawn. The Zapatista camp was on a ridge guarding the entrance to the settlement, whose name I never determined with any certainty. Banana trees were cultivated between the huts, and *milpas* crept up the slopes above. The forest on the slopes was more dense, varied and lush. We were already on the edge of the jungle.

Soon the Zapatistas were up and about, heating up rice and beans for breakfast, which they shared with us.

Over the course of the day, we got to know them. They were mostly in their teens. Capitán Nacho, among the oldest, was nineteen. I found myself surprised by their youthful innocence. They were open and playful with one another, despite saluting each other according to rank upon waking in the morning or leaving and entering the camp. At times it seemed like hanging out with boyscouts. But they carried machine guns, and there was no distinction or separation between the genders except that the women did most of the cooking.

They all seemed to trust and accept us immediately. They only put on their ski-masks when Rick was taking photos, and they even left their rifles hanging from their bunks when they were cooking or eating or carrying water.

Their rifles were AR-15s, Ruger semi-automatics and old Chinese SKS semi-autos with bayonets. No weapon was fired while we were there. "We can't waste bullets—not like the federal army," said Capt. Nacho.

Their uniforms were identical—black pants, *café* shirts, red bandanas, green caps—but clearly home-made and hand-stitched. They all wore boots—generally rubber or plastic, and cheap. The little red stars some wore on their uniforms signified rank—one for a *teniente*, two for a *capitán*, three for a *comandante* or *subcomandante*. There were two *capitánes* and a few *tenientes* among us.

Nacho told me that he and his troops had fought at Ocosingo back in January. He told us Marcos personally directed much of their military training and political education, which took place deep in the Selva. They said their political education consisted of Mexican history, especially Zapata's struggle and vision. When I asked if they had learned about the Russian or Chinese revolutions, they said no—"*solo zapatismo.*" They had each spent a few years marching around in the mountains, learning how to fight and maintain a rifle.

We were told how the Zapatista Army is divided into *insurgentes* and *milicianos*. These were *insurgentes*—full-time active-duty troops. The *milicianos* seemed to be disposed throughout the communities, guarding them while they worked their *milpas*, ready to defend. There were many more *milicianos* than *insurgentes*, although nobody would give us numbers. You have to do some time as a *miliciano* before you can become an *insurgente* in most cases. Nacho joined the EZLN when he was fourteen, and was a *miliciano* for one year. Both *insurgentes* and *milicianos*—who wear green pants instead of black in combat—participated in the January attacks.

They said it is a lie that only fourteen government troops died in the January fighting. They also said more people from the civil population than Zapatistas died, and more *milicianos* than *insurgentes*. They said some of those finished off in the Ocosingo market by federal troops were civilians—the guns beside the corpses had been staged for photographers.[3] They said they took several federal troops captive in Ocosingo, and held them for two days. "We didn't maltreat anybody," said Capt. Nacho.

"Our mothers know we are Zapatistas," said Nacho. What do they say?, I asked. "They don't say anything. They understand what we are fighting for. They understand they don't have enough food for their families. They understand the condition of exploitation we live under."

Elvia, who was fifteen, said her parents sent her to join the EZLN. "I used to be scared," she said. "But I'm not now."

"The women participate in everything," Nacho told me. "They carry the same guns we do. They have the same blood as we do." When I asked if there are both Catholics and evangelicals among their ranks, he replied, "We respect each other's religion."

"The land is pure rock in our *ejidos*," continued Nacho. "If there is no *maíz* one year, we don't eat. We've been Zapatistas eight, nine years, since we were children. There were no schools in our villages. We learned to read and speak Spanish in the EZLN."

They also learned the tongues of their fellow troops. Arturo was a Chol who also speaks Tzeltal. Whole families have joined. "Many of us have brothers who are Zapatistas," said Nacho.

"It's better to die fighting than to die of hunger. We're tired of promises and mountains of paper with meaningless signatures. We weren't prepared for dialogue. We were prepared for war."

They also told us of clashes the previous May which were never reported in the press. They said three thousand army troops were sent into this very canyon to search for Zapatistas after their whereabouts had been betrayed by the rival ARIC *campesino* union. They claimed fourteen federal troops were killed in the confrontation that ensued when they found a Zapatista camp. They said many of the deaths resulted from federal troops shooting at each other in the confusion. After the confrontation, they started planning the January attack.[4]

The troops spent most of the day maintaining the camp, playing chess, listening to the radio, talking, joking, and teasing each other. But every time a vehicle approached on the road below, they dropped everything, grabbed their guns and scrambled down the trail to be ready at the roadblock. Each time, we hoped it was Marcos returning for us.

In the afternoon, captains Nacho and Victor took us around the settlement. It was even more primitive and miserable than La Garrucha. This *ejido* was not titled, and had never received any government credit. Bombs fell around the settlement intermittently throughout the January fighting. The schoolhouse lay abandoned. They said a teacher used to come two or three days a week. In addition to working their *milpas*, many of the men sold their labor two months of the year on a *finca* outside Zapatista-held territory. On the *finca*, they worked from six to six for 5 pesos a day. Housing at the *finca* cost 3 of these.

They lived on *tortillas*, getting beans only occasionally.

Rick took on Nacho and Victor in a hoops match outside the schoolhouse. The young troops ran and dribbled with their rifles on their backs, laughing.

Back at the outpost after dark, Arturo took out a beat-up little guitar which he had rigged to hold a harmonica, and started to sing his self-penned Zapatista anthems, simple but tuneful and heartfelt.

Soldados insurgentes son
Buscando la revolución
Soldados insurgentes son
Buscando la revolución
Y ellos quieren pelear
Juntos con el miliciano
Y ellos quieren pelear
Juntos con el miliciano
Dejando su pueblo
Dejando su familia
Y dicen porque, porque
Porque, porque, porque
A pelear por la libertad.

When he handed me the guitar and asked me to sing one, I played "World Turned Upside Down," Leon Rosselson's ode to the Diggers, those peasant revolutionaries of another era. Of course, they didn't understand the words, but they listened politely.

As we turned in for the night, there was still no sign of Marcos.

VOICES IN THE DARKNESS

The next day, the truck returned to bring us back to La Garrucha, without the Subcommander.

The settlement was preparing for the April 10 celebrations commemorating the death of Zapata. A banner had been hung over the roadblock, reading, "BIENVENIDOS A LA SELVA LACANDONA, GUARDIA DE LOS TRANSGRESORES, CUNA DEL EZLN Y RINCON DIGNA DE LA PATRIA." Welcome to the Lacandon Selva, Guardian of Transgressors, Cradle of the EZLN and Dignified Home of the Fatherland.

But Marcos was nowhere in sight. We were left back at the same spot, and told to wait "for orders." By nightfall, we started to fear that Marcos had abandoned us, as we once again rolled out our sleeping bags in the schoolhouse.

As the next day crawled on, our fears deepened.

More journalists started to arrive, and some university students, mostly from Mexico City. Word had got out that the Zapatistas were planning celebrations.

Marcos was definitely somewhere in the settlement, because by afternoon he was passing notes to some of the new adventurers who had arrived. Those notes seemed to be going exclusively to young females, and were greeted with much delight. I decided that it wasn't just my imagination—there really was something flirtatious going on.

I recalled that Marcos is probably an educated, upper-class Mexican who had many years ago left his life behind to live with illiterate Indians in the jungle. It was unrealistic to expect him not to enjoy his new national popularity. But still, I felt snubbed. If I was going to make my flight back to New York out of Mexico City, I would have to leave the next morning. I had already been in Zapatista territory for six days.

Feeling unsociable, I crawled into my sleeping bag as night fell, deciding to ignore the crowd of journalists and Marcos fans milling around outside the house, waiting hopefully for a call from the *sup*. The *chilangas*—sophisticated young women from Mexico City—were overtly inebriated with the sheer excitement of being so near their idol. I closed my eyes accepting defeat, resigned to leaving in the morning without my Marcos interview.

Late at night I drifted out of sleep and became aware of loud voices filling the darkened room. An impromptu late-night party was underway. I was determined to ignore it and try to sleep.

The loudest guy seemed to be making endless wisecracks, most of which went by too fast for my limited Spanish. But they all generated a lot of laughs. He lampooned gringo culture, bragging about presumably fictitious past lives in the US, about having been a bodyguard for the Dallas Cheerleaders and a bouncer at a gay bar in San Francisco. It was almost dawn, and I wished people would shut up and go to sleep.

Some of the jokes were clearly at my expense. Mr. Wiseguy switched to English for my benefit, mimicking exactly what was going on in my brain with devastating accuracy: "Well, here I am, a New York reporter behind rebel lines in Mexico's Lacandon Selva. But there's nothing to report. The *pinche sup* has stood me up!"

I wanted to slug him. But I was impressed by his intelligence. He even blurted out the call letters of my radio station, in a mock radio-voice—"WBAI, ninety-nine-point-five FM in New York City!"

When there was enough light in the room, I decided to get up to see who the wiseguy was.

There, sprawling on one of the beds with his ski-mask on, puffing on his pipe, adoring women on every side, one under each arm—was Subcommander Marcos.

Stunned and humiliated, I could think of nothing to say. I slunk back to my corner. Finally, as the sun came up, he left the schoolhouse to resume his duties at his mobile command-post truck which waited outside. His ski masked rifle-toting guards closed ranks around him, cutting him off from the crowd of bleary-eyed journalists that had followed him outside.

After speaking with someone through the truck's radio for a few minutes, he returned to shake hands good-bye with each of us. When he approached me, I realized it was now or never. I took out my micro-recorder and said, "*Señor Subcomandante, cinco preguntas. Por favor.*"

He brought me within the cordon of his guards and told them not to let anybody disturb us. As soon as I turned on the micro-recorder, the Subcommander's demeanor instantly transformed. He became personable, respectful and serious. He spoke in halting but correct English. We talked for some fifteen minutes in the rainforest dawn.

INTERVIEW WITH THE SUBCOMMANDER

"What kind of support do you need from your sympathizers in the United States?" I asked.

"Well, the federal army has surrounded us. The civilian population here is suffering a lot. They lack necessities like food, clothes, medicine. Even the children. Our people, the civilian people here, cannot go to the city to buy such necessities, because the federal army can take them prisoner and 'disappear' them. Our people are under very strong conditions of war, even if it is not one of bullets and guns now, but the dirty war that the government is making against us." Marcos stumbled over the English grammar, but his eyes communicated intensely through the ski-mask.

"There is something you can do for us," he said. "The government of Salinas has made a big lie about our country. They say that our country is free, without serious economic or social problems, a good partner for the NAFTA. So it is imperative for us that the world know that Mexican people, especially Indian people, are not in the life condition that Salinas says—as you can see in this trip that you have made here. We need people in the United States to create counter-propaganda to that of the Mexican federal government, and get out the truth, against the lie of Salinas.

"When Salinas shook hands on the NAFTA agreement, he was playing with the lives of Indian people. You cannot shake hands on an agreement like that without staining your hands with blood. But the federal government is very sophisticated with its publicity. If the truth is known in all parts of the world, especially the United States, it would be a great help to us.

"Our movement is a true movement. There are no strangers or foreigners behind us. We are all Mexicans, and the big majority of our army are Indian people. We think the government is lying to us with their promises to solve our problems. We don't trust anymore in this government . . ."

"Is the Zapatista National Liberation Army fighting for socialism, like in Cuba?" I asked.

"The directorate of our army has never spoken about Cuban or Soviet socialism. We have always spoken about the basic rights of the human. Education, housing, health, food, land, good pay for our work, democracy, liberty. Some people may call this socialism. But it doesn't matter what name you give these demands. In Mexico there is no democracy. So it doesn't matter what you think, or what your political goal is. Because only the political goal of the government party wins—always wins.

"We say, make a democratic space, make enough liberty so that you can explain your ideas. When there is democracy, we can decide which leaders we agree with—and by we, I mean the people, not the Zapatista Army.

"The federal government does not represent us. We want to follow our own Mexican way to democracy and liberty and justice. The kind of life we want—life with good food, good land, good health, good education, good work, democracy, independence, justice and peace—if you want to call it socialism, OK, call it that. But we are not a cliché of Cuban socialism, or Castrismo or Sendero Luminoso. Basically, all of our thoughts about the workers and *campesinos* and the revolution are taken from the Mexican revolutionary heros Flores Magón, Francisco Villa, Emiliano Zapata. Their ideas about the farm workers, the workers in the cities, the hopes of liberty, are our inspiration for this movement. If you want to call it Mexican socialism or the Mexican way to liberty, that's a good name for it."

Birds were starting to call from the forest as the sun rose behind us. "You've said that you don't want any more ecological reserves for the Lacandon Selva," I said. "How do you envision protecting what remains of Mexico's last rainforest?"

"Well, look," said the Subcommander, sizing me up as a gringo vegetarian environmentalist. "We don't agree with this preoccupation with the trees over the death of our people. We say, we want trees. We want the mountains. But we also want a dignified life for our people.

"The mountain is very important for Indian people. It is a part of their tradition and their history. So we agree, we say, 'No, there should be no more cutting of trees—but give me the life conditions for another way. I will take good care of this mountain, I will take good care of these trees, and I will take care for the future of my child, from one generation to another generation. But now my people have no way to live other than to cut trees and burn them. That is the only way we can find land.'"

Marcos looked around the mud-and-thatch huts of the settlement. "Here there are no tractors, here there is no machinery, there is nothing for the Indian people. There is no option but to cut the trees, burn them, and put the seed in the land. It doesn't matter how the land is taken when you are hungry.

"This land was originally for the Indian people. The white people, the big farmers and ranchers, imposed their force over the Indian people and pushed them up into the mountains. You can see that here the good land is on the *fincas*—the plains, the valleys. The Indians have the rocky lands in the mountains. But the Indian sees the good land below and says, 'Originally, this was my land, so I have the right to recover it.' The big farmer says, 'They have stolen my land, they have stolen my cattle.' But my people say, 'Before you were even born, my grandparents made their life here.'

"Our lands cannot produce with this injustice. We need redistribution of the land. But that is not all we need."

"*Que mas?*" I asked.

"We need roads, water, schools, hospitals, technology—like tractors, like planes. Even if the land is producing, the next question is the price. You can grow a good crop of coffee, but when you take it to the city, the *coyote*, the intermediary, thinks, 'You don't speak Spanish, so I can lie to you and cheat you.' You can bring in one hundred pounds of coffee and he will say it is only fifty. He will say that the quality isn't good, and he can only pay you half price. And you have to walk four or five days from your village to get to the city, so you just take the money. You can't bear the thought of carrying your hundred pounds of coffee back to the village.

"So the Indian people face very complex structures of exploitation. I've implicated the federal government, the big farmers, the *coyotes*, the municipal governments, the police, the army. There are a lot of people who are living with the blood of Indian people. People don't understand this in other countries. They think that Mexico is Acapulco, it's Cancun, it's Puerto Vallarta, Guadalajara, Monterrey, Mexico City. They think that the Indians just make pretty clothes, they are curiosities. They cannot even imagine that these people are dying."

"There's been speculation that helicopters which were donated to Mexico by the United States for the War on Drugs have been used against the civilian population here in Chiapas," I said.

"There's no speculation," Marcos retorted. "The people saw the choppers that said 'PGR,' and we know the American government gives the PGR choppers to fight against drug dealers. A lot of people, even journalists, saw these choppers fight in San Cristóbal, fight in Ocosingo, fight in Altamirano, fight in Las Margaritas. But everybody knows that there are no drugs in our territory. The DEA knows it. The federal army knows it. The PGR knows it. All they have to do is look at their maps and their satellite pictures. The Indian people who were attacked from these helicopters with machine guns and bombs—they don't have anything. If they were trafficking drugs—well, look at their houses. Where are the big trucks, the luxury?

"We sent a letter to Bill Clinton about this problem, and we never received an answer. The choppers are even now in the airport at Tuxtla Gutiérrez, ready to strike again."

I had to ask the obligatory *High Times* question. "Do you support the legalization of drugs to undercut this kind of militarization?"

"Well, we must think about this, reflect on it. But our problems are very urgent. I mean, our problem is dire survival, and our principal work is in this direction."

I remembered the federal army's APCs and artillery at the checkpoint outside Ocosingo. "In the 1980s in Guatemala and El Salvador, after rebel movements emerged there was terrible repression," I said. "Whole villages were massacred. How do you hope to avoid this in Chiapas?"

"The only way is that our movement becomes national. If our war gains support all around the country, then the army can't take one place and make a total effort against us. If there are a lot of guerillas, or social movements against the government, we can divide their forces.

"In any case, our people are prepared for resistance. We are training the civilian people to resist an attack. But this resistance will cost a lot. So it would be better if there was civil pressure on the government to change direction, in the interests of the people of Mexico. The political exit would be better. I hope that it is possible. But if it is not possible, we will continue the war."

I asked, "What do you think is to be learned from the experience of the rebels in Guatemala, who often let the Indian civil population suffer the worst of the repression?"

"Well, we think our principal effort must be directed toward a national revolutionary movement that could incorporate a lot of forces. Not only the forces of the Zapatista National Liberation Army. I mean, other political forces, cultural forces. Our problems are the same problems faced in other parts of the country. We are learning about what happened in other parts of Latin America, in Guatemala, El Salvador, Nicaragua. When the *guerilla* provided the direction for all the movements, there were a lot of problems of division, unity became impossible. So we must find the right flag to incorporate all the ways of struggle."

"Are you optimistic that there can be a peaceful solution, or do you think that there's going to be more violence?"

"We are very skeptical about the peace process. Some parts of the government say, 'OK, make a deal.' But other parts of the government say, 'No, the strong hand is better.' The big farmers don't want peace. They just want to protect their land. The big farmers have been educated to think that they are the aristocracy. They think the Indian people should only serve the white people. Equality? They don't want to hear about it. You are dealing with very reactionary people. In their minds, it is still centuries ago. So we are making an effort for peace, but if it is impossible . . ."

"You're prepared."

"We'll fight, of course. We are prepared for a long war. I'm talking about years and years of war, throughout the mountains of the southeast of Mexico."

"Do you think there's a threat of US military intervention?" I asked.

The Subcommander's answer was disarmingly simple. "Whenever we talk to the American media, we say, 'We don't want to attack the White House. We want to live with dignity.' Our demands are the same demands of the American people— I mean, the average American people. So why should they want to fight us?"

"Because the American government has a whole lot riding on NAFTA," I reminded him.

"But do you want a NAFTA with blood on it? We don't want a NAFTA written with the blood of Indian people. If you want a NAFTA, make some kind of reform to incorporate Indian people. Because Indian people will not die without a fight. This is our message to the American people. Let us live with dignity, understand us. If you understand our situation, our reasons for fighting, the American people will not want to go to fight against Mexican people. We are trusting in this."

I turned off the tape recorder and told Marcos, only half jokingly, that after the revolution he could visit me in New York without his mask. "If I survive," said the Subcomandante. "I don't know if I'll be alive much longer."

We had an *abrazo* and parted ways—Marcos back to the Selva and the revolution; me back to Ocosingo, San Cristóbal, Mexico City and New York.

6

PARALLEL POWER: 1995

"I consider myself only an instrument of the people, who want a legitimate government," said Amado Avendaño, the "rebel governor" of Chiapas. We were speaking at his improvised headquarters in an occupied building at the National Indigenous Institute compound, just north of the market in San Cristóbal. It was the closing days of 1994, and I had just arrived back in Chiapas.

A security round of Tzotzil men kept a twenty-four-hour vigil at the gate of the occupied compound. Indian delegations from throughout the state came to speak with Avendaño about their land claims, struggles, persecution by ranchers and *caciques*. In the rebel governor's makeshift office, pine needles covered the floor. Indian supporters had set up a small altar in the reception area, with candles and *copal*. A few battered typewriters and filing cabinets were the only outward sign of administration.

"So I am here," continued Avendaño, still wearing a patch over one eye from his pre-election auto crash which he called an assassination attempt. "At the moment I no longer have that support, I am ready to go back home and continue to publish my newspaper."

Chiapas was divided by contested elections and effectively had two governments—one with administrative control in the municipal centers, and one Zapatista "government in rebellion" with territorial control in the backcountry. The EZLN and the local Party of the Democratic Revolution formed two pillars of this rebel government. The third pillar was the decentralized network of indigenous and *campesino* organizations, represented by CEOIC Independiente—the coalition minus the PRI-controlled CNC. The amiable Avendaño was the rebel government's titular head.

Avendaño published *El Tiempo*, San Cristóbal's small but feisty daily, before announcing his gubernatorial candidacy with the PRD. The first year of the Zapatista revolt took him on a personal journey from provincial newsman to rebel leader, claiming the governorship in defiance of the PRI authorities at Tuxtla and Mexico City.

FROM ELECTIONS TO CIVIL REBELLION

As 1994 came to a close, Chiapas was back at the brink of war. Avendaño's *gobierno rebelde* ruled much of the state from below in an alliance with the masked rebels who had declared "war" on the *PRI-gobierno*. Radical *campesinos* and dissident workers were challenging election results in neighboring Tabasco, Oaxaca and Veracruz as well. The EZLN added the anti-PRI struggles in these states to their demands.[1] The new President Ernesto Zedillo faced both financial crisis in the wake of December's peso collapse, and a fast-growing revolutionary movement throughout the Mexican south.

Zedillo was the Yale-educated former Education Secretary who had overseen rewriting of the textbooks to reflect the updated official history—downgrading the importance of the oil nationalization, etcetera. He had been conscripted by Salinas to replace the assassinated Colosio. Mere weeks after taking office, his predecessor's artificial inflation of the peso (a necessity to get NAFTA through the US Congress) took its inevitable toll. Zedillo was forced to oversee a dramatic devaluation.[2] However he may have felt when he accepted the nomination, by year's end he was probably starting to feel like a sucker.

On April 10, the anniversary of Zapata's death, thousands had marched crosscountry on Mexico City in solidarity with the EZLN. Clashes with police were reported when the marchers passed through Puebla.[3]

On June 10, the EZLN announced that after consultations with their people in the Selva, the government peace proposals had been rejected. Their statement urged "civil society" to take up the struggle. "Resist with us!" proclaimed the Second Declaration of the Lacandon Selva.[4]

Avendaño, already facing death threats for his reportage on the Zapatistas, answered the call.

At dawn on July 25, on a campaign swing through the Sosconosco coast, Avendaño's car was hit head on. Two Avendaño cousins and his campaign manager Agustín Rubio, a CIOAC veteran, were killed instantly. Amado suffered a fractured skull. With her husband still in a coma, Amado's wife Concepción Villafuerte, with whom he ran *El Tiempo*, accused elements in the state government of setting up the crash. The section of road was repaved the very next day. Interim Gov. López Moreno called the crash an "accident"; an alleged hit-and-run driver was eventually arrested and jailed in Tapachula. With candidate Avendaño suspended between life and death, the EZLN went back on "red alert."[5]

In this atmosphere of tension and uncertainty, the Zapatistas launched their first effort to establish a national dialogue with civil society. Thousands journeyed behind rebel lines to Guadalupe Tepeyac, a little settlement on the Selva's edge, for the "National Democratic Convention" (CND) the EZLN hosted on August 8, Zapata's birthday. The rebels built a jungle amphitheater for the occasion. Representatives from independent popular organizations throughout Mexico attended. The amphitheater was named Aguascalientes, after the Revolutionary summit of 1914. The great, crawling caravan of conventioneers was cheered by *campesinos* as it made its way to Tepeyac.[6]

A fierce rainstorm gave the affair the mixture of mud and epoch-making that marked Woodstock, and the press was quick on the analogy. Hundreds of Zapatista troops marched in procession before the assembled thousands, but with strips of white cloth affixed to the barrels of their rifles. Following much polemic, the convention reached a platform, embracing the EZLN's demands, urging Mexicans to vote, but endorsing no party or candidate until one endorsed the convention platform.[7]

At the end, Marcos presented the Mexican flag that had flown from the stage to the woman chosen as the Convention's president: longtime human rights crusader and onetime left-opposition presidential candidate Rosario Ibarra, whose own guerilla son had disappeared in Monterrey in the 1970s. Ibarra and other civil activists and intellectuals from across Mexico were chosen as advisors to the EZLN. But Marcos announced that the convention would not really disband. The CND would become a permanent body, aimed at extending *neo-zapatismo*—in some form—throughout Mexico.[8]

Four days later, before thousands in Mexico City's *zócalo*, PRD presidential candidate Cuauhtémoc Cárdenas embraced the CND platform.[9]

Defying expectations, Amado Avendaño recovered and refused to withdraw from the elections.

The elections on August 21 brought the PRI's Zedillo to the presidency and the PRI's Eduardo Robledo Rincon to the Chiapas governorship. A study revealed that the PRI had spent about $72 dollars a vote nationally—a total of $1.25 billion, including government money, exponentially exceeding both the official $40 million cap on campaign spending and the sum spent by US President Bill Clinton to get elected two years earlier.[10]

In Chiapas, a Popular Electoral Tribunal made up of representatives from Indian and *campesino* groups declared the gubernatorial results fraudulent. Upon Robledo's assumption of power on December 8, the EZLN declared the cease-fire which had held since January broken. As Robledo was sworn in, Avendaño was inaugurated in a public ceremony in the Tuxtla *zócalo*, where a council of Indians representing each of the Highland Maya groups handed him a *bastón de mando*, the traditional wooden scepter of authority. Forty thousand federal army troops poured into Chiapas, fortifying the roadblocks surrounding the Lacandon Selva.[11]

THE REBEL GOVERNMENT

Seemingly trapped, on December 19 the Zapatistas surprised the nation by filtering out of the Selva—and through the army's net—along remote mountain trails, and announcing their presence in thirty-eight of the 111 Chiapas municipalities, mostly in the Highlands. Those listed in the communiqué included Larrainzar, Chenalhó, Chamula, Zinacantan and even San Cristóbal. Blockading roads, and occupying the municipal palace in Simojovel, the Zapatistas declared the thirty-eight municipalities "in rebellion" and loyal to the "rebel transition government" of Amado Avendaño. Until this government was recognized, the war was back on.[12]

As the army moved in on the rebel positions, the Zapatistas abandoned their roadblocks and disappeared into the local populace. It was like chasing ghosts. Troops and armored personnel carriers occupied the Highland villages, often at the invitation of the municipal authorities.[13] But the *PRIista* municipal governments increasingly had control only over the village centers. In the surrounding hamlets and *ejidos*, real territorial control lay with the independent Indian and *campesino* organizations which supported Avendaño and the EZLN. "The entire rural zone of the state is Zapatista, leaving the government the cities, the municipal seats (not all) and the roads," Marcos boasted.[14]

Many hamlets and *ejidos* declared themselves self-governing "New Municipalities," breaking from the PRI-controlled municipal governments of the village centers.[15]

On December 8, as the governmental transition took place, CEOIC declared five "Pluriethnic Autonomous Regions" (RAPs) in Chiapas—the Highlands, Lacandon Selva, Zona Norte, Sosconosco and Frontera, the *campesino* region of the Grijalva Valley along the Guatemalan border. The RAPs were regional alliances of New Municipalities, explicitly including and respecting all ethnic and religious groups.[16]

Avendaño and the EZLN recognized these New Municipalities and Autonomous Regions as the local and regional foundations of the rebel government.[17]

Rebellion was again spreading across the state. In Sitalá, hundreds of *campesinos* armed with clubs and machetes seized the municipal palace, ransacking the property records.[18] In Tonalá, the Democratic Campesino Union (UCD) seized ranchlands.[19] The Regional Assembly of Pueblos of Sosconosco declared autonomy on the Pacific coast.[20] In Tapachula, the Ejidal Producers Organization of the Coast (OPEC) occupied the Banrural offices to demand debt relief, while the Sosconosco Coalition of Worker–Campesino–Student Organizations (COCES) seized the state office building.[21] In La Trinitaria, the Emiliano Zapata Proletarian Organization (OPEZ) held ranchlands until White Guards were sent in to clear them out.[22] In Santa Rosa, a Tojolabal hamlet outside Las Margaritas, several houses went up in flames in a local rebellion against *caciques*.[23] In Tenejapa, Tzeltal *PRDistas* blockaded the road to San Cristóbal.[24]

Avendaño, who had appointed an Autonomy Council made up of Indian leaders, told me, "The Tojolabals in Trinitaria, Las Margaritas and Ocosingo want their own laws, in their own language and tradition. The Chols, in the northern zone of the state, want their own system of justice in their own territory."

All of the seven councils the rebel governor had appointed included Indians. The Autonomy Council included Antonio Hernándo Cruz, a Tojolabal from Las Margaritas and a PRD federal deputy. The Economy Council included Gustavo Zarate, a *mestizo* lecturer at the Autonomous University of Chiapas who came to the attention of Amnesty International in 1983 when he was arrested on drug and arms charges, held incommunicado and tortured at Cerro Hueco. Amnesty determined that the charges were fabricated in response to his activism in Indian land struggles, and adopted him as a prisoner of conscience.[25]

Along with the PRD, EZLN and CEOIC, Avendaño counted among the pillars of his parallel government two new urban organizations, the Women's Group (which sported a portrait of Frida Kahlo and a *No a Violencia Sexual* bumpersticker on the door to its section in the occupied INI office), and Civil Society, a group which had recently come together to advocate a new politics independent of the parties.

Gov. Robledo, attempting to defuse the situation, officially left the PRI, and stacked his cabinet with leftists (or former leftists, as critics charged). Eraclio Zepeda, a writer and longtime PRD activist, accepted a post as Robledo's Gobernación Secretary—winning the scorn of his former PRD comrades.[26] Robledo's Prosecutor General Jorge Enrique Hernández was a veteran of Cerro Hueco, imprisoned in 1984 following his legal representation of *campesinos* involved in land struggles under the brutal reign of Absalon Castellanos. Robledo even created an Indigenous Issues post, headed by an Indian, Jacinto Arias. But Avendaño charged that these appointments were tokenism, pointing out that the majority of Robledo's cabinet was holdovers from the Patrocinio González administration.[27]

Robledo offered to resign if the EZLN turned in their guns.[28] Marcos, in turn, offered to intercede on Robledo's behalf when he faced a Zapatista tribunal if he would resign.[29]

The federal government declared the official agrarian reform, terminated elsewhere in the country since 1992, back on the table in Chiapas—while assuring ranchers that private property "will be absolutely respected."[30]

"Nothing has changed in Chiapas," said Avendaño. "So the Zapatistas have reason to be in the same state of war."

Samuel Ruiz remained the man who stood between peace and war. Implicitly recognizing this, the Vatican had backed off on its request for him to step down, but appointed another bishop, Raúl Vera López, to serve with him. Vera immediately surprised the hierarchy by emerging as a supporter of Don Samuel's mission.[31]

The EZLN rejected the Multi-Party Peace Commission convened by President Zedillo as bogus, and demanded recognition of the National Intermediation Commission (CONAI), convened by Ruiz. This was their one condition for declaring a cease-fire and returning to the table.[32] Bishop Ruiz insisted CONAI was the only group to have lines of communication with all parties to the conflict—Robledo, Avendaño, the federal government, the local aristocracy, CEOIC, the EZLN.

On December 19, as the truce was officially broken, the Bishop began a hunger strike—which he called a religious fast—for peace.[33] Tatic Samuel Ruiz, fasting in the Cathedral, was visited by both high-level government delegations and groups of supportive Indians from Highland villages who beat drums and danced in his honor.[34]

On December 24, the government blinked and agreed to recognize CONAI. The troops which had penetrated Zapatista territory on the edge of the Selva were withdrawn, and the EZLN responded by declaring a six-day truce beginning January 1. After ten days of tension and paranoia, Chiapas appeared, for the moment, to be back from the brink.[35]

On January 1, the EZLN announced an indefinite cease-fire. Bishop Ruiz ended his fast. On the fifteenth, federal Gobernación Secretary Esteban Moctezuma was helicoptered into a secret location in the Lacandon Selva for the first talks on the possibility of a new dialogue.[36]

But the unofficial dirty war continued. "It's a grave situation," said Marina Patricia of the Diocese's Fray Bartolemé de Las Casas Human Rights Center. She told me the center had documented 130 human rights violations in Chiapas in 1994 after the January cease-fire: killings, rapes, torture and arbitrary detention, mostly committed by the army or White Guards against local Indians. "There have been no serious investigations," she maintained. In many cases, such as that of two Tzeltal women raped at a military roadblock in Altamirano, victims were willing to report violations to the Las Casas Center, but too intimidated to pursue the cases in the legal system.[37]

Subcommander Marcos charged in a December communiqué that Kaibiles, the feared Guatemalan counterinsurgency troops, had penetrated the Lacandon Selva from across the border with the secret cooperation of the Mexican federal army.[38] But Marcos concluded that:

> Their presence does not worry us, because the EZLN is not a traditional guerilla. It controls its territory and considers itself a regular army. I think the federal army realizes that they can't use Guatemalan-style counterinsurgency. Because they know that they confront a regular army. They know that they do not face a guerilla that operates in the mountains, but a guerilla that operates everywhere.[39]

BEHIND LINES WITH TACHO AND MOISES

Since the December 19 mobilization, no journalist had been able to reach Marcos. I traveled with Avendaño's bus to the Aguascalientes amphitheater for the EZLN's New Year's Eve party. Masked troops were dancing in couples to the *ranchera*-pop tunes of a masked band up on the stage. There were amplifiers and stage lights: Guadalupe Tepeyac is one of the few Selva settlements on the electric grid, and the government, at the behest of the Red Cross, agreed to keep the power going as long as the cease-fire held. There was, of course, no alcohol. Maya *comandantes* mingled with urban intellectuals and PRD federal deputies. But Marcos was not in sight.

On January 18, I returned to Guadalupe Tepeyac in a rented VW bug with *Der Spiegel* columnist Carlos Widmann at the wheel. The last army checkpoint was just beyond Las Margaritas, just before the pavement ended. From there, the road sloped down into Las Cañadas, through forest, past little Tojolabal settlements and an abandoned, overgrown ranch. Pines gradually gave way to jungle. Some big trees, felled by the Zapatistas to block the army in December, still partially blocked the road, and the bug had to negotiate around them. Just before Tepeyac were the EZLN barricades.

We were granted entry and put up in the new hospital the government had built there, amidst much fanfare, just before the uprising. Its walls were incongruously shiny and sturdy in the mud-and-thatch settlement, but the residents told us it had been under-staffed and under-supplied from the start.

The Zapatistas maintained open control here. Men with masks and rifles aroused no more interest or concern from the *campesinos* than the pigs and turkeys foraging in the lanes. We ate beans, eggs and *tortillas* from a little stand that had been set up for visiting journalists.

After a short wait at the hospital, Carlos was getting antsy. "Do they think we came for the *cuisine?*" he fumed. Just then a masked head appeared in the window. We were ordered to follow, put in a jeep and driven a short distance to the amphitheater. There we were introduced to Major Moises, who commanded the forces that had taken Las Margaritas the previous January, and Comandante Tacho, a member of the Indigenous Revolutionary Clandestine Committee. Moises, Tacho and Marcos made up the Zapatista delegation that had met with Gobernación Secretary Moctezuma three days earlier. Like Marcos, Moises had taken to smoking a pipe; unlike Marcos, he was clearly an Indian—a Tzeltal.

Carlos asked how they felt about prospects for a renewed peace process.

"They are trying to deceive us again," Moises replied. "They had to remove the army troops under our deal for a new dialogue, and they did—but they replaced them with judicial police and highway police. That was not part of the deal. When we saw that they started to remove their troops, we retreated too. But yesterday evening we got the information that when the army was retreating, the police were coming in. So we resumed our own positions. We are ready to pull back again if we see the police withdraw. But we still don't see any sign of that. We now have a roadblock in Momón. We established one in Guerrero after the truce was broken, but agents of the ranchers came in to sell *aguardiente*, to divide the populace against the presence of our roadblock."

I asked about the communiqué asserting the EZLN is not a guerilla army, but a regular army with control of its territory. "That is clearly the case here in the Lacandon Selva," I said. "But is it really true in the Highlands too? Aren't the Highland communities more divided?"

"No, it's the same," Moises assured me. "It is not a guerilla, it is a regular army."

"But here in Guadalupe, in the Selva, the Zapatistas are the open authority," I persisted, "while the municipal authorities in the Highlands are *PRIistas* and *caciques.*"

"It is a process," came the Major's reply. "We will follow what the population says. When they say it is time to announce our presence to the municipal authorities, it is done. We don't want to impose our position. We follow what the people want.

They are aware of their own situation—the balance of power with the ranchers, the *caciques*. They will know the right moment. And then we will be the authority in the Highlands too. The Highlands are in a different stage of the same process."

Carlos asked Moises to tell us how he became a Zapatista.

"I was a *campesino*," he began. "I was born here in Chiapas. Since I was a little child, I participated in the meetings of the community where I lived. We talked about the land conflicts, transportation, credit. I participated in the big marches for land, and in one march we were met with repression. That was in 1975. Later, Zapatista political representatives started to show up in the Indian communities, locating people they could work with in the struggle. One representative got in touch with me. We spoke about the situation in my community.

"After that I started to study, to read about the Indian struggles of 1521, of Hidalgo in 1810, of Zapata in 1910, of Rubén Jaramillo in the 1950s and Lucio Cabañas between 1970 and 1975. I realized that the problem of land and the *campesinos* is on a national level, and that peaceful struggle was not the solution. Why? Because the government makes the laws and violates them at will. That is justice for them, not for us. If the *campesino* doesn't obey, he faces the judicial police, while the landowners break the law with impunity. So I realized that the way was not through peaceful struggle."

"When did the Zapatista representatives first contact you?" I asked.

"In 1980. They were still a nucleus of politicization and consciousness-raising then. They started calling themselves Zapatistas and drew up the program for forming an army of national liberation in 1983."

"In the community where you grew up, what language did they speak?"

"They spoke Tzeltal."

"What kind of education did you have in the village of your youth back in the 1970s?"

"There were six teachers in our village. Three of them really tried to educate us, the other three only taught us bourgeois ideas. There were two groups of teachers—the democrats and the *charros*. The *charros* were on the side of the rich, the government. They just got drunk, and the communities rejected them. The teachers themselves were violently divided, so I was only in school for six months and I didn't learn anything. But when I arrived in the EZLN, there I really began to learn. The EZLN taught me to read, to write, to add, to subtract."

"Did you speak Spanish before you joined the EZLN?"

"It was very difficult for me. I couldn't speak well with the *compañeros*. But they taught us through readings and lectures, political conversations about the situation in our country. Now in the Zapatista communities, the democratic teachers can stay, but the *charros* have to go. And those who know how to read and write have to teach the others."

"What about other armed movements in Mexico?" I asked. "There are rumors about armed groups in the Sierra Madre."

"We think so. The *campesinos* in Mexico have a tradition of struggle against their exploiters. This is the logical process. Always the *campesinos* struggle against the conditions of misery. We know there are many armed groups in the Mexican south, but let's see what is their purpose. Sometimes they are *narcotraficantes*. But sometimes they are *campesinos* who are arming themselves against the gunmen of the landlords. There are some armed groups which have approached us and are now under the command of the EZLN. How many and where, we can't say."

"Outside of Chiapas?"

"Outside of Chiapas. There are also other groups not under the command of the EZLN, but who share the same struggles as the EZLN. We don't want war. But the evil government obligates us to take up arms. Education is our right. Dignified work is our right. Healthcare is our right. Access to the communications media is our right. This is what we were saying when we took up arms on January 1, 1994, that Salinas was responsible for the situation facing Indian people in Mexico. That's why we demanded the resignation of Salinas. Now if Señor Zedillo is following the same idea, the same plan as Salinas, he will lose the reins of power. The war will continue until this system comes to an end. The Mexican people are waking up."

"But you are willing to talk with the government," Carlos reminded.

"Words are one thing; deeds are another. The government's deeds will show us what is really true. Right now there is just one small group that imposes its will on Mexico. We want the people to govern themselves. We cannot call the conditions we live under now peace. We face persecution, imprisonment, torture, assassination, disappearance. This is not peace. We are dying from diarrhea, vomit, parasites. We live in sadness, in pain. This is not peace. Meanwhile, the rich—they have everything. They aren't missing anything, at all. For them, there is peace. For us, the *campesinos* and poor of Mexico—what? There is no peace, there is no justice, there is no democracy. So we will fight, and if necessary, we will die."

I asked about the Zapatista demand for Indian autonomy in Mexico, and how this might look. This time Comandante Tacho answered.

"The communities have declared New Municipalities throughout Chiapas and are already governing themselves. In the first days of 1994, when we declared war against the evil government of Salinas, the New Municipalities began to organize, and gave rights to people who had never had rights before—the right to participate in running their own communities.

"Autonomy is protection of indigenous culture; indigenous communities deciding how they want to live, and having a respected place in Mexican society. Where they speak Tzeltal, Chol, Tojolabal or other Indian languages, they cannot understand the language of the bureaucrats, and the government exploits this situation. So the EZLN, from our First Declaration of the Lacandon Selva, has demanded the right of Indians to elect their own governments, and now we are defending that right.

"But that doesn't signify independence from Mexico. It means a dignified place for Indians within Mexico. The evil government makes money off the folklore and archeology of the Indians, but deceives the rest of the world about the condition of Indians in Mexico. They can't do that any more. We have shown that Indian communities can govern themselves. That is what we are fighting for. Chiapas exports electricity to the rest of Mexico, but we don't have electricity. We don't have roads, we don't have education. We don't exist for the government. This is the just demand of the EZLN—for the dignity of every Indian and every indigenous community."

"The EZLN also speaks of democracy," I said. "But this notion of regional autonomy is different from the concept of two-party democracy that we have in my country, the United States."

Tacho responded, shifting the AR-15 he held in his lap. "Our thought is that the people in our own communities can run our own affairs, and be able to elect and recall our own leaders at any time, both locally and nationally. Autonomy means communities arguing, discussing, planning, deciding how we want to live, how we want to share the wealth, and presenting our plans to the national government. This has never happened before in the history of our country. Always the authorities, the government, make their own plans to control the national wealth and resources as they wish.

"For example, the changes to Article 27, the privatization of the *ejidos* and state companies, the Free Trade Treaty, the famous modernization of the farms and the cities—there was no previous discussion with the Indians and *campesinos*. Why privatization? Who will benefit? The change to Article 27 shows no respect for *campesino* communities. So we say there needs to be real democracy and free dialogue over these issues. Why didn't Salinas step down when the people demanded it? Because the oligarchic group in Mexico has power, and Salinas protects their interests."

"In most countries, the legislature has the right to remove the president, not the people," I pointed out.

"But our elected officials do not represent us," Tacho retorted. "Let me give you the example of the municipal president in Las Margaritas, Romeo Suarez. He's been elected four times, despite all the protests and accusations against him. Clearly, the people don't want him, they are demanding that he step down. He says all the roads in Margaritas are paved, but the people know this isn't true. Where are the millions of pesos he received to pave those roads? And how is it possible that Salinas believed him? The federal government doesn't have a helicopter to see how many roads in Margaritas are really paved? But they had helicopters to drop bombs on Indian people last January. It isn't correct. It isn't just."

"Tell us about the role of the Clandestine Committee," Carlos said.

"Our work in the Clandestine Committee is with the base of the people, to talk and develop the struggle for democracy and liberty. We always go to the base for our decisions in the struggle. We've known the people we work with for years. We are a part of the communities we work in."

Despite the denials of Moises, it was clear that the PRI had more of a foothold in the Highland communities than in the Selva. Two weeks earlier, hiking through outlying woods and *milpas* in San Andrés Larrainzar, once again with Joel Simon of Pacific News, we met a group of PRI loyalists loading harvested *maíz* into a truck. When questioned, they bitterly complained that Don Samuel's diocese was a Zapatista front, incredibly claiming that nuns and church workers were training with guns in the mountains. They pointed out, not a hundred yards away, three local men who they said were Zapatistas guarding a trail leading to an EZLN camp. When approached, these men refused to talk, but their taciturn, disciplined, no-nonsense demeanor indicated that they were the Real McCoy.

It was clear that, as Bishop Ruiz had warned, if war came to these Highland villages, it was likely to be fratricidal.[40]

THE HUNT FOR MARCOS

The return to the brink was not long in coming. On February 8, the federal author-ities announced that warrants had been issued for the arrest of Marcos and other figures alleged to be in the Zapatista leadership. The Subcommander's identity was "revealed" as one Rafael Sebastián Guillén Vicente, a UNAM graduate and long-missing philosophy professor of petit-bourgeois origins in Tampico. An old photo of the somber, bearded young academic was splashed across the nation's and the world's front pages.[41]

A Zapatista safehouse in Mexico City had reportedly been busted, and a woman arrested there, a supposed Subcommander Elisa, was said to have confirmed the secret identity under "interrogation." At a Veracruz safehouse, an "arsenal" of weapons and explosives was reportedly found, providing Zedillo with the rationale for breaking the cease-fire.[42]

Marcos was the only one among those under arrest orders who was behind Zapatista lines. Maria Gloria Benavides, the former medical student seized in the Mexico City raid, "confessed" to arms trafficking under the tender ministrations of the Federal Judicial Police. The next arrested were Jorge Javier Elorriaga, a Chiapas-based video-journalist, and Jorge Santiago Santiago. A CONAI member and director of a San Cristóbal non-governmental organization, Social-Economic Development of the Indigenous Mexicans (DESMI), Santiago was purported to be the EZLN's liaison to Bishop Ruiz. Fernando Yañez, a veteran of a 1970s guerilla effort, remained at large.[43]

Not one Indian was on the list. The government's statement to the press said, "We know that there is no Indigenous Revolutionary Clandestine Committee, but a command comprised of people with clear tendencies to use . . . violence as a solution."[44]

Federal army troops flooded past the roadblocks, through the *zona franca* and into Las Cañadas. The rebels retreated into the jungle, some twenty thousand Indians abandoning their settlements to follow them, fearing reprisals. Troops sealed off the Selva to journalists, who were unable to confirm accounts of aerial bombardment and terrorization of settlements. Guadalupe Tepeyac and the Aguascalientes amphitheater, La Garrucha and other strongholds fell into government hands with little exchange of fire. But the federal troops were unable to follow the Zapatistas in the dense and trackless rainforest.[45]

If the heart of the Selva provided refuge, the refugees were trapped, facing hunger and disease at makeshift camps. There were reports that Indians who stayed behind were threatened and tortured for information. But with the Selva declared a "restricted zone," there were no witnesses.[46]

Tens of thousands marched on Mexico City's *zócalo* to protest the aggression. The favored chant was *"todos somos Marcos"*—we are all Marcos.[47]

On February 2, just a week before Zedillo ordered the army into Zapatista territory, President Bill Clinton went over the head of his own Congress by executive order to bail out the Mexican peso to the tune of $50 billion in loan guarantees and outright loans. The peso immediately began to rise in response to the announcement.[48] Amidst speculation about secret protocols of the bail-out, Marcos issued a communiqué, written on the run deep in the Selva: "The only price which has remained high in the rise and fall of the financial markets is that on the head of the Zapatistas. Señor Zedillo has already begun paying back the loans."[49]

A simultaneous communiqué signed by the CCRI rejected Zedillo's offer of amnesty to the EZLN's Indian footsoldiers if they would turn over Marcos and surrender their arms. Claiming the aggression was aimed at "the satisfaction of big foreign capital," the communiqué said Zedillo "has chosen to be humble and servile with the powerful and haughty and arrogant with the humble." It stated: "The surrender of the wealth of the national subsoil, especially petroleum, is what actually lies at the bottom of the government's decision. The existence of rich petroleum deposits of high quality in Chiapanecan lands is known in high government spheres in Mexico and the United States. The EZLN is an obstacle to the treasonous plans of the supreme government. This is the price of the loan; the payments can be made in Mexican blood, and especially with indigenous blood."[50]

The statement refuted the "calumny" that the Zapatista leadership is not Indian: "The EZLN declares that it has no supreme command other than the Indigenous Revolutionary Clandestine Committee-General Command, which is composed, in its totality, of indigenous Chiapanecos." It asserted Marcos "obeys our political and organizational command," maintaining "direct authority" only over "military questions." It denied that there was any other member of the Zapatista Army with the rank of Subcommander.[51]

The US State Department responded dryly: "The United States continues to call for moderation, respect for human rights and full compliance with legal process."[52]

But the paranoid view was fueled by public release of a January memo entitled "Mexico—Political Update" from the Chase Manhattan Bank's Emerging Markets Group, by analyst Riordan Roett. The report to investors at the Rockefeller financial mainstay directly addressed the impasse in Chiapas:

[I]t is difficult to imagine that the current environment will yield a peaceful solution. Moreover, to the degree that the monetary crisis limits the resources available to the government for social and economic reforms, it may be difficult to win popular support for the Zedillo administration's plans for Chiapas. More relevant, Marcos and his supporters may decide to embarrass the government with an increase in local violence and force the administration to cede to Zapatista demands and accept an embarrassing political defeat. The alternative is a military offensive to defeat the insurgency which would create an international outcry over the use of violence and the suppression of indigenous rights . . . While Chiapas, in our opinion, does not pose a fundamental threat to Mexican political stability, it is perceived to be so by many in the investment community. The government will need to eliminate the Zapatistas to demonstrate their effective control of the national territory and of security policy.[53]

The last sentence was the punch line, interpreted by the regime's critics as a veiled instruction from Wall Street to Zedillo. The reference to the "increase in local violence" was also prescient. Real or contrived Zapatista plans for "new acts of violence and terrorism" was Zedillo's excuse for launching the offensive.[54]

Chase "disavowed" the controversial memo, calling it the work of an "independent scholar" (author Roett was director of Latin American Studies at Johns Hopkins University).[55] But La Jornada reported that Wall Street was monitoring the situation "minute by minute," quoting a Salomon Brothers analyst that while markets reacted favorably to the initial move by Zedillo they were likely to react negatively if the crisis dragged on.[56] An OECD spokesman warned of an "international contagion" if the peso didn't recover, with Argentina and Brazil next to collapse, potentially sparking a global crisis.[57]

The offensive was called off within a week, as the government realized it now had no option but to wait the rebels out. CONAI issued an "urgent call" for the government and EZLN to return to the dialogue table, exhorting that "it is still possible to avoid war and genocide." The EZLN demanded a withdrawal of federal troops from the Selva as an "indispensable" condition of resuming dialogue. The "authentic coletos," now calling themselves the San Cristóbal Civil Front, held a march demanding the army remain in their positions.[58]

Outmaneuvered again, the government blinked, abruptly agreeing to drop the remaining warrants if the EZLN returned to the table. On February 14, the same day Zedillo made the announcement, Gov. Robledo Rincon resigned. The state legislature named another PRIista, Julio César Ruiz Ferro, as interim governor.[59]

The Zapatistas re-emerged from the jungle interior into Las Cañadas. In one of his first interviews since the government "revealed" his identity, Marcos complained to La Jornada reporter Carmen Libra that "the guy from Tampico" was very ugly and had "ruined my correspondence with women." He told her, "Write there that I am taller, stronger and more handsome than what the Prosecutor General says, so that the girls will start writing me again. OK?" Given the circumstances, the reporter found his sense of humor "hard to understand."[60]

DIALOGUE AT SAN ANDRÉS

On March 9, a federal Dialogue Law was passed barring government attacks or arrests as long as the peace process was in effect. The Highland village of San Andrés Larrainzar, a stronghold of Zapatista sympathies an hour north of San Cristóbal, was established as the talks site. This time, the EZLN representatives would be meeting with a team of federal legislators—not only from the PRI, but also from the opposition PRD and PAN. This legislative team—dubbed the Commission of Concord and Pacification (COCOPA)—would then pass on the peace proposals to the executive branch. CONAI would mediate.[61]

The EZLN was in a weakened position. The rebels had lost much territory in the February offensive. Worse still, the *campesinos* who had fled into the jungle were unable to plant their *milpas* on time, before the rains. Las Cañadas faced at least a year of hunger. The returning refugees often found their homes had been ransacked by the federal troops.[62]

The Zapatistas were able to re-establish a presence in some of their settlements. But now—in violation of the new dialogue agreement—there were no clear lines between rebel and government-held territory. Instead, government troops and Zapatistas had camps in neighboring settlements. La Realidad became the rebel army's new visible base of operations—beyond Guadalupe Tepeyac at the end of the road, just before the Sierra La Colmena and the Selva interior. Guadalupe Tepeyac was held by federal troops, the amphitheater dismantled.[63]

As freedom of transit was restored, observers returned to the Selva. In army-occupied communities, CONPAZ, the NGO network which had coalesced to monitor the peace process, reported prostitution, alcoholism, military vehicles invading *ejidos*, troops ordering local women to make *tortillas* for them and interrogating residents about the presence of Zapatistas.[64]

On April 15, Jorge Santiago Santiago was released after two months in Cerro Hueco, the charges against him dropped when the prosecution witness failed to show up in court. Javier Elorriaga and Sebastián Entzin, a Tzeltal man arrested along with him, remained in prison, awaiting sentencing, as did Gloria Benavides at a top-security facility near Mexico City.[65]

Things began tensely at San Andrés Larrainzar in April. The *cabacera*, or municipal building, was surrounded by four cordons—army MPs, the Red Cross, NGO volunteers and San Andrés Tzotzils. All four maintained a stoic, round-the-clock discipline, even through rain. The federal army and international media maintained large encampments in the little village. The Tzotzils burned *copal* as each day's talks initiated in the morning; in the wee hours of the night, the delegations would emerge from the *cabacera* to report on the progress—or lack thereof.

This time Marcos stayed behind lines, stating self-deprecatingly that his "pronounced nose will go back to sneezing more and talking less."[66] The eight *comandantes* of the Zapatista delegation included David, who wore a traditional ribbon-festooned Tzotzil sombrero over his ski-mask, and Trinidad, a 65-year-old Tojolabal woman with long gray-streaked hair who the Indians called Grandmother Trini.[67]

The government refused to comply with the EZLN's demand that federal troops withdraw to the positions they had occupied before the February offensive, but finally dropped its initial refusal to discuss national issues.[68] Slow progress was made. Between sessions at San Andrés, the EZLN delegation took the proposals back to their communities in the Selva. The EZLN scored a media coup by inviting federal negotiators to observe the *consultas*, undermining the government's claim that the *consultas* were a myth and all decisions were really made by Marcos and his cabal of violent extremists.[69]

THE NATIONAL *CONSULTA*

Campesinos and dissident workers nationwide continued to rally around the Maya rebels as the talks ground on.

On May 1, the dissident unionists won a political victory. The CTM's *caudillo*, Fidel Velazquez, afraid of trouble, for the first time officially cancelled the annual Mayday spectacle in Mexico City. The dissidents marched by the tens of thousands, and were saluted in an EZLN communiqué. Instead of the usual CTM-produced banners reading "GRACIAS, SEÑOR PRESIDENTE," many bore hand-made signs advocating a firing squad for Zedillo.[70]

The EZLN established mutual solidarity with a local of Mexico City's bus-drivers' union, the Urban Passenger Auto-Transport Workers Syndicate (SUTAUR). The Ruta 100 line was shut down by the government after the drivers broke with the official labor bureaucracy. The government called it an austerity move; the workers claimed it was politically motivated. Twelve SUTAUR-100 leaders were accused of embezzling union funds. A federal judge, Abraham Polo Uzcanga, refused to sentence them for lack of evidence. He was promptly kidnapped and killed. Immediately, the government found a new judge willing to carry out the sentencing.[71]

Vows of mutual solidarity were also exchanged between the EZLN and El Barzón, a union of debtors whose ability to pay back was decimated by the devaluation. Many Barzonistas were commercial farmers from El Bajio and the North, or downwardly mobile members of the middle class. Named after the leather plough-strap which had been immortalized in a popular song of the 1930s as the symbol of the struggling farmer, El Barzón declared a moratorium on debt payments pending renegotiation. The banks, bailed out by Washington, remained intransigent.[72]

The national *campesino* movement remained localized and fragmented—peasants taking over land and seizing control of village governments, Indians declaring autonomy, all under the auspices of a confusing alphabet soup of organizations, mostly rooted in kinship networks, and only sometimes affiliated with national coalitions. These local struggles generally viewed each other with a sense of solidarity, but were unable to find ways to act in concert.

In July, the EZLN called for a national and international *consulta* to determine the future direction of the Zapatista movement—an effort to replicate their village-based democracy on a national level.[73]

The CND's work to extend the Zapatista movement was mired in factionalism, and becoming moribund. Marcos accused the leadership in the DF of "trying to convert the CND into a solidarity committee with the Chiapaneco people. This isn't Central America, it's Mexico."[74] In January's Third Declaration of the Lacandon Selva, the EZLN had called on Cuauhtémoc Cárdenas to join with the CND to form a National Liberation Movement.[75] (Cuauhtémoc's legendary father had led an identically named organization after he broke from the PRI in 1961.[76]) But this failed to materialize. The *consulta* aimed to take the debate on the movement's shape directly to the people.

The EZLN produced a short survey on what *zapatismo* should look like if there was to be peace. The options did not include a return to war. They asked for support of the eleven demands, and the idea of a new national civil organization. Activists with the CND and Alianza Civica distributed the survey in *pueblos*, *ejidos*, *colonias* and *barrios* throughout Mexico.[77]

Over one million Mexicans voted—*campesinos*, Indians, migrant laborers, dissident workers, debtor farmers, students, teachers, intellectuals, activists, artists, housewives, prostitutes. International supporters mailed in ballots from nearly every country in the Americas and Europe. Critics said the questions were so general that they invited only positive responses, but in fact they were cautiously worded to sound out questions dividing the Mexican left on civil society's relation to the organized opposition.[78]

In September, the *consulta* results were in. The eleven demands were virtually unanimously embraced; even a final question asking if women should have "an equitable presence and participation" in political life was overwhelmingly approved. The notion of the "democratizing forces" joining in a "broad majority opposition front" was approved. In the two questions apparently considered mutually exclusive, a majority favored the EZLN becoming an "independent political force" as opposed to uniting "with other forces and organizations" to form a "new political organization."[79]

Although the confused *New York Times* incorrectly reported that the *consulta* called for the Zapatistas to become a "political party," the rebels were clear that their new civil organization would *not* be a party or participate in the electoral arena. It would pursue a third option, still vaguely determined, which was neither armed nor electoral struggle.[80]

TERROR AND RESURGENCE

The October municipal elections in Chiapas precipitated more violence. Abductions and assassinations were reported from all over the state. The elections were cancelled on account of violence in Ocosingo, the state's largest *municipio* in area. In several others, especially in the Highlands, *campesinos* supporting PRD candidates proclaimed the PRI victories fraudulent. While the PRI retained a majority of municipalities, it was the party's worst showing in Chiapas ever, even by the official count.[81]

The government game continued with the arrest of Fernando Yañez, the supposed "Comandante German," by federal police in Mexico City. The Monterrey architect's car was surrounded by police vehicles on October 23 on a DF street. He admitted he was a veteran of a brief 1970s guerilla effort in Chiapas, the National Liberation Armed Forces (FALN). But he denied he had weapons in the car as charged, or links to the EZLN, "though it would be an honor." He was sent to the top-security Reclusorio Oriente prison. Major Moises told reporters in La Realidad the arrest was in violation of the Dialogue Law, and that the rebel army was going on "red alert."[82]

A judge ordered Yañez released after four days of protests. The PGR dropped all charges. "They arrested me for political reasons," Yañez told reporters as he left Reclusorio Oriente, accompanied by Rosario Ibarra, "and I suppose they got me out for political reasons."[83]

Days later, Cecilia Rodriguez of the National Commission for Democracy in Mexico, the EZLN-recognized solidarity group based in Texas, reported at an LA press conference that she had been abducted and gang-raped at Lagunas de Montebello National Park, on the western edge of the Lacandon Selva just above the Guatemalan line, where she was visiting following a Chiapas networking trip. She had recently put out a call for pressure from the US citizenry to release Fernando Yañez.[84]

The Mexican government refused to investigate the rape unless Rodriguez returned to Comitán *municipio* to file a complaint there. She had fled Chiapas after the attack on the advice of human rights observers, and complained to the US embassy in Mexico City.[85] Curiously, within weeks of the attack, the *New York Times* travel section reported that tourists were "venturing back" to Chiapas two years after the uprising. It even recommended a "day trip to the lovely—but bracingly cold—Montebello Lakes" (since it "skirts around the conflict zone"). The paper never reported on the attack there.[86]

On December 16, Julieta Flores Hernández, a young Tojolabal woman, was raped and tortured by state Judicial Police officially looking for her father, who was accused of blocking roads and killing a *cacique*. Flores was charged with the murder and taken to Cerro Hueco after the rape, but freed owing to lack of evidence. This was one of a growing number of politically motivated rapes the Chiapas Women's Group documented.[87]

On December 1, Zedillo made an unprecedented tour of the government-held settlements in Las Cañadas, which he called a gesture of "good will." Immediately thereafter, an increase in army patrols in the vicinity of La Realidad provoked the EZLN into declaring an alert and cancelling the next round of dialogue then scheduled for Larrainzar.[88]

The government was moving against radical *campesino* groups throughout Chiapas. State Public Security Police evicted OCEZ squatters at Las Nubes ranch in Sosconosco. State police and federal army troops evicted UCPFV squatters on ranchlands in the Sierra Madre.[89] The UCD responded by blockading the Chiapas offices of the federal Agrarian Tribunals in protest of the government's failure to break up the illegal *latifundios*.[90]

In Chamula, a local revolt broke out against the *caciques*, resulting in six dead. The state attempted to mediate, and the municipal government was reshuffled to appease the opposition.[91]

The Zapatistas were also asserting their presence in the heart of the Highlands. At Oventic, one of San Andrés Larrainzar's hamlets, the residents announced they were rebuilding the Aguascalientes amphitheater. They started a trend. Three more New Aguascalientes centers, now conceived as local meeting places for *consultas*, were soon under construction at Morelia (a hamlet of Altamirano) and at La Realidad, La Garrucha and Roberto Barrios, in Las Cañadas. The EZLN established a separate General Command for the Highlands.[92]

As the second anniversary of the uprising approached, troop movements were reported toward San Andrés Larrainzar and La Realidad, the most significant Zapatista strongholds in the Highlands and Selva, respectively. The EZLN once again charged the government with breaking the dialogue, and went back on red alert.[93]

The EZLN's communiqués now emphasized (in contrast to the situation a year earlier) that they were not interested in war, but raising the level of the civil struggle.[94] However (precisely as a year earlier), the government appeared to be gearing up for a new military offensive—in violation of stated policy.

7

THE CHALLENGE OF
SAN ANDRÉS: 1996

Army troops and *campesinos* faced off over New Years in Oventic, Morelia, La Realidad, La Garrucha and Roberto Barrios, the five communities where New Aguascalientes centers were under construction. Army encampments were established alongside the construction sites, with *campesinos* blocking the troops and shouting "*¡Fuera soldados!*"[1]

Hundreds of Indian protestors seized the *cabaceras* to prevent new *PRIista* governments from taking office at San Andrés Larrainzar and Chenalhó, and at La Libertad in the Zona Norte. There were also protests in Ocosingo, where the elections had been cancelled and an Indian council was demanding power.[2] As soldiers were rushed in, Indians lined the roads with hoes and machetes to yell "Buzzards go home!" In San Andrés, a group of children attempted to blockade an APC column.[3]

On January 3, Indians lined the roads to cheer as Marcos made his first public re-emergence since federal troops sent him fleeing deep into the Selva eleven months earlier. He was picked up by the Red Cross at La Realidad, and delivered to San Cristóbal for an appearance at a National Indigenous Forum convened there. The forum was organized by the EZLN and the National Indigenous Congress (CNI), and attended by Indian groups from throughout Mexico. Comandante Tacho presided. Marcos walked the city freely, masked but unarmed.[4]

At the forum, indigenous groups hashed out a common position on "autonomy," both for their local struggles and for the EZLN's peace talks.[5]

The government had an overwhelming troop presence in Chiapas. Yet Indians were taking over village governments, and the Zapatistas boogied in public in San Cristóbal.

Like the EZLN, the rebel councils in San Andrés, Chenalhó and La Libertad governed through *consultas* with the base. The rebel councils in Chenalhó and La Libertad were shortly evicted by the state Public Security Police. But San Andrés Larrainzar, site of the dialogue, was merely surrounded by the army. The rebel council renamed the town Sakamchem de Los Pobres, reviving, and politicizing, the place's original Tztotzil name.[6]

The EZLN's Fourth Declaration of the Lacandon Selva called for a Zapatista National Liberation Front (FZLN). The communiqué said the FZLN "will fight not to take political power, but rather for a democracy in which leaders will lead by obeying" the people. It called, again, for a National Liberation Movement, a broad-based opposition front of which the FZLN would be part—a synthesis of the two options broached in the national *consulta*.[7] Repudiating vanguardist aspirations, the Zapatistas made clear the FZLN was to be separate from EZLN; Marcos and the Clandestine Committee would not be joining.[8]

In February, the army pulled back from the communities occupied on the New Year, and the rebels once again returned to the table. The EZLN team and COCOPA reconvened at San Andrés/Sakamchem to complete a document on Indian autonomy which became known as the San Andrés Accords. The Accords on Indigenous Rights and Culture, as they are formally known, called for changes to Article Four of the Mexican Constitution, obliging the State to "recognize the right of Indian peoples to freely determine their own internal forms of social, economic, political and cultural organization."[9]

As a national model, the Accords called for changes to the Chiapas constitution, under which municipalities with an Indian majority would govern themselves according to their traditions, maintaining a bilingual justice system based on indigenous modes of conflict-resolution. Municipal boundaries were to be redrawn, creating more Indian-majority *municipios* (as hamlets and settlements are often wholly indigenous, while *ladino* merchants in the larger municipal centers wield political power). The San Andrés Accords were based on the system of parallel power which already existed in Chiapas—the New Municipalities and Pluriethnic Autonomous Regions.[10]

As President Zedillo prepared a response to the San Andrés Accords, the EZLN team and COCOPA prepared for the next table of discussion, on political reform.[11] Zedillo was in a dilemma: to approve the Accords would legitimize the parallel power system in Chiapas. Failure to approve would place the onus on the government if war returned. The PRI hardliners saw an obvious way out: provoke the Zapatistas into breaking the cease-fire.

MOTA AND MILITARIZATION

Despite the Dialogue Law, violence escalated. In March, eight were killed in evictions of rebel *campesinos* from occupied ranchlands. Near the Highland village of Nicolas Ruiz, state police fired tear gas on the squatters, then set the grass on fire to drive them off. Three *campesinos* and two police were killed in the ensuing gun battle. In Pichucalco, CIOAC militants seized the estate of Tabasco narco-banker Carlos Cabal Peniche, then hiding from the law overseas. The eviction turned into a confrontation, leaving two *campesinos* and one police agent dead.[12] In Tapachula, the OPEZ occupied the Federal Electricity Commission offices in protest of high rates.[13]

The White Guards of the ranchers were now joined by paramilitary groups organized by *caciques* who felt power slipping away. These paramilitaries, often affecting a "revolutionary" posture to co-opt and confuse in traditional *PRIista* manner, were able to maintain a closer reign of terror in the Highland villages.

One such outfit, the "Chinchulines"—officially the Donaldo Colosio Civic Front, a community development group—effected a virtual counter-revolution in the Northern Zone *municipio* of Chilón following a PRD electoral victory. The PRD municipal president fled for his life following a violent attack on PRD-loyalists in the hamlet of Bachajón on May 5. The Chinchulines burnt homes and a Jesuit convent, leaving six dead. They said the *presidente* would be next.[14]

The situation was again deteriorating toward open war. On May 2, two Zapatista sympathizers arrested in the February 1995 offensive were found guilty of "terrorism" by a federal court. Javier Elorriaga, the video-journalist, was sentenced to thirteen years. Sebastián Entzin, a Tzeltal *campesino*, received six. The EZLN issued a communiqué denouncing the sentences as a violation of the Dialogue Law. The talks were broken off yet again.[15]

On May 4, COCOPA's most respected member, the PRD's Sen. Heberto Castillo of Veracruz, veteran of the 1968 student movement and silver-haired patriarch of the Mexican left, stepped down from the Commission, saying he wouldn't return unless "the boys are set free."[16]

May 7, FZLN supporters seized a San Cristóbal radio station for thirty minutes to broadcast a statement demanding the release of Elorriaga and Entzin. "The real terrorists are in the government," proclaimed rebel governor Avendaño.[17]

The government announced major new military mobilizations in the Highlands and Selva. This time, with aggression against the EZLN barred by the Dialogue Law, the army had to use a subterfuge. This was readily provided by the presence of marijuana crops in the hills surrounding the Highland Zapatista strongholds, and purported cocaine trafficking routes through the Selva.

As the dialogue broke down, troops were once again scouring San Andrés *municipio*—under guise of hunting down *mota* plantations. The EZLN declared a "maximum alert" on May 19.[18]

The tension centered around Oventic, the heart of Zapatista country in the Highlands. San Andrés *municipio* remained divided, with an "official" *PRIista* junta and an Indian council supporting the PRD candidate both claiming legitimacy. The PRD forces occupied the *cabacera*, and declared the entire municipality "in rebellion."[19]

Oventic was openly Zapatista; *campesinos* worked the *milpas* with bandanas over their faces; banners announced to the visitor that this was rebel territory. The trucks and APCs of the "counter-narcotics" forces rumbled up the mountain road from San Cristóbal, through the San Andrés village center to Oventic—right past the banners and the Nuevo Aguascalientes. The troops established encampments and fanned out over the mountains and *milpas* in search of *mota*, the evil weed.[20]

Under the command of Col. José Ernesto Ledín, the troops were part of the ironically named *Fuerza de Tarea Arcoiris*—Rainbow Taskforce—Rancho Nuevo's crack unit.

On May 21, Hermann Bellinghausen of *La Jornada* reported from the army encampments just outside Oventic. He overheard Rainbow Taskforce troops chanting their special code-word for the anti-*mota* operation into their radios: "*Bosnia, Bosnia, Bosnia.*"

This "left no doubt" of their intentions, marked Bellinghausen.[21]

But Col. Ledín denied any provocation. "Let's not try and invent any kind of conflict," he told *La Jornada*. "This is exclusively part of the permanent anti-drug campaign."[22] He boasted that his troops had found twelve *mariguana* plantations and a few opium crops in the environs of Oventic—and burned them on the spot. Each *mota* field was up to 4,000 square meters and filled with plants over a meter high, claimed Ledín.[23]

By May 31, CONPAZ stated that Oventic was "deserted," the homes "abandoned," the inhabitants having fled to San Andrés or the mountains. "The new military camp is located 2 kilometers from Oventic in two communities, Jolbash and Sikilucum," reported CONPAZ. "The few families that were residing in the community of Jolbash left in fear, after approximately 153 soldiers entered their community to set up camp."[24]

The ranking Zapatista at Oventic, Capt. Noe, told CONPAZ, "the pretext is to look for drugs, but that is not true. What they are looking for is a strategic position against us."[25]

The government remained unyielding. The next round of talks had been scheduled for June 5. A spokesman for Gobernación told the press: "If the Zapatistas don't show up on June 5, then we will carry out the arrest warrants against them and everything will be ruined."[26]

Federal troops were also moving on the Highland Zapatista strongholds of El Bosque, Simojovel and Bochil to search for *mota*.[27] In Palenque, *campesinos* sent a letter to the new federal Gobernación Secretary Emilio Chuayffet, protesting that 150 soldiers had set up camp in their *ejido* and were searching their homes.[28] In Altamirano, the Tzoman Campesino Organization sent a letter to the state and federal governments protesting the invasion of their *ejido* by a convoy of eight trucks and three tanks on anti-marijuana ops.[29] A communiqué from the EZLN's new command wing, the CCRI of the Highlands, warned of the "threat of war."[30]

Troops also moved into the Selva. At San Quintín, military engineers were building a bridge and expanding the road to facilitate anti-drug operations. San Quintín lies just over the Sierra La Colmena from La Realidad. It is also where the Ocosingo–La Garrucha road ends, on the border of the Biosphere Reserve. It was a strategic place to bar the Zapatistas at both La Realidad and La Garrucha from taking refuge in the interior of the Selva, as they had the previous February. The army established San Quintín as a Special Training Camp for Jungle Operations.[31]

Chiapas "has long been a thoroughfare for drug traffickers who have tried to introduce huge quantities of cocaine," Gen. Renan Castillo, new head of the Seventh Military Region, told the press. He said the Marqués de Comillas region, in the south of the rainforest, had become a key transfer point for drugs from Guatemala.[32]

The EZLN interpreted the erratic shifts from dialogue to provocation as indicative of divisions within the regime. "In some places military pressure has dropped. But in others, under the drug trafficking pretext, the soldiers are harassing civilians. That makes us think there are some in the military that want peace and others that want war," Comandante Tacho said in a jungle news conference.[33]

In the first days of June, as the anti-*mota* operations ended and the deadline for resumption of talks neared, I was sufficiently recovered from a bout of salmonella to leave my San Cristóbal hotel room. Joined by two adventuring friends from New York, I hopped on a *colectivo* at the market for San Andrés Larrainzar. The usual vertiginous trip along mountain roads brought us to the military encampment overlooking the entrance to the village. Soldiers surveyed the passing traffic, but didn't stop our vehicle. When we came to a halt in the *zócalo* it was clear we were in rebel territory. On one side of the square, Indians prayed and burned *copal* among the ancient images of saints and virgins in the town church. At the other end, the occupied *cabacera*, which had hosted the dialogue, was hung with a banner:

> IMPORTANT WARNING:
> IN THIS MUNICIPALITY IN REBELLION IT IS PROHIBITED TO CULTIVATE, TRAFFIC OR
> CONSUME DRUGS. HE WHO IS DISCOVERED DOING SO WILL BE EXPELLED FROM THE
> COMMUNITY.

The anti-*mota* militarization only deepened the EZLN's own puritanical instincts. Alcohol had always been banned in Zapatista territory. Ritual abuse of *posh* has helped keep the Indians down for centuries. Especially on holy days, they can get terrifyingly drunk on the stuff, and the *caciques* maintained a monopoly on production. Now, with many *caciques* driving shiny new four-wheel-drive pick-ups, it was clear they had moved into more lucrative contraband enterprises as well. In response, the Zapatistas banned *mota* from their territories too.

From San Andrés, a second *colectivo* took us up the road to Oventic.

On the wood fence around the little community was a banner reading "MAIZ Y PAZ, SI; DROGAS Y SOLDADOS, NO." The Nuevo Aguascalientes sported a mural featuring portraits of Che Guevara, Emiliano Zapata, Pancho Villa—and the Virgin of Guadalupe wearing a Zapatista-style face mask.

Standing guard at the gate was a young Tzotzil man with a cowboy hat, dark sunglasses and a bandana over his face. He was a Zapatista *miliciano*. He said his code-name was Noe, like the *insurgente* captain at Oventic. Since the Rainbow Taskforce pulled out, the inhabitants of Oventic had mostly returned, and the *insurgente* troops under Capt. Noe had withdrawn. *Miliciano* Noe invited us into the Nuevo Aguascalientes to talk.

Noe told us the Rainbow Taskforce had passed on the road right by the gates of Oventic. "To come into our camp is a violation of the Law of the Dialogue," he said. "If they come here, we could immediately go to CONAI, the press. They don't come here. But they put troops on all the *cerros* and all the ways in and out. So the people left for fear of an attack. We have received no order to suspend the red alert. We are still surrounded by the military on all sides."

"Were they really looking for *mota?*"

"That is what they say. But in reality they were looking for a confrontation with us. It was a provocation."

"But they did find *mota*," I said. "Who grows the stuff?"

"The same *PRIistas*. We organizers of the EZLN—we don't allow any drugs or alcohol in our territory. We have a law—corn and peace, yes; drugs and soldiers, no. It's a campaign we have throughout our communities. We have eliminated alcoholism and prostitution from our areas. It's the *PRIistas* that grow, with payments to the local authorities."

Since the operation ended, said Noe, every day army helicopters passed directly over Oventic—once at dawn, once at dusk. As we spoke, Noe pointed out that some kind of unconventional aircraft was passing high and directly above. He said it was a military surveillance plane.

Noe and a fellow *miliciano* took us on a tour of Oventic—little plots of *maíz*, thatch huts with no plumbing or electricity. Our guides pointed out the surrounding mountains where the Rainbow Taskforce had combed for marijuana. The army still had their encampment just the other side of San Andrés and could re-assume these positions any time.

"Your military position seems very bad here," I remarked.

Miliciano Noe gave the reply of a disciplined soldier: "That's a question for the CCRI—not for me."

REPRIEVE AND PARANOIA

Yet again, just as open war approached, the government blinked. On June 6, Elorriaga and Entzin were freed. A federal appeals judge dropped all charges against Elorriaga and reduced Entzin's charges from "terrorism" to "rebellion," instating a 300-peso fine.[34]

Upon his release, Elorriaga demanded freedom for the other accused Zapatistas still languishing in Cerro Hueco: "I'll be truly free when they are all free. As long as they are in jail, there are obstacles to the peace process." Entzin said he would return to Altamirano "to work in the *maíz* and the *café*" and join the FZLN "to follow the struggle and the movement of the Zapatista Army on the civil path."[35]

The EZLN called off the red alert, and on June 9 Zapatistas met with government negotiators at La Realidad to discuss re-establishing the dialogue. Chiapas was back from the brink once again.[36]

But the narco-subterfuge remained available for the next tactical escalation. Northern Mexico's drug mafias had clearly targeted Chiapas as a new operations sphere. On June 2, the Maya ruins at Palenque were hit by armed robbers who made off with thirty-seven pre-Columbian artifacts—these, together with endangered species from the rainforest, make up a local cartel sideline.[37] The following weekend, the local press reported, the personal (unnamed) chauffeur of the Arellano Felix brothers, kingpins of the Tijuana Cartel, was blown away in Palenque by unknown gunmen wielding AK-47s.[38]

San Cristóbal's conservative newspapers warned of a "narco-satanic" cult performing "macabre rituals" in the city, linked to the human sacrifices reportedly carried out by drug gangs in northern Mexico.[39] At a May press conference, San Cristóbal's Municipal President Rolando Villafuerte warned that local *mariguana* use was on the rise, blaming the "contagious presence" of "a minority who use drugs"—a barely veiled reference to San Cristóbal's community of hippies, expatriates and international lefties drawn by the romance of the Zapatista struggle.[40]

THE INTERGALACTIC ENCUENTRO AND OTHER ADVENTURES

In the months to come, San Cristóbal would be swamped with an onslaught of these "*zapaturistas.*" Among the more prominent was Régis Debray, the French intellectual who had accompanied Che Guevara on his final adventure in Bolivia (and later became an advisor to Socialist President François Mitterand). In April he traveled to La Realidad for a meeting of minds with Marcos, and came away impressed. "I think the tactics of the Zapatistas are better, more peaceful and more realistic than ours in the 1960s," he told the press.[41]

Later that month, the EZLN held a Continental Encuentro at La Realidad, bringing together activists from throughout the Americas. In addition to the slew of unionists, ecologists, feminists, poets and Marxist academics were a handful of Hollywood celebrities, including Oliver Stone, who happily never chose to immortalize his experiences there for the silver screen. (Marcos "made the most dramatic entrance I've ever seen in my life," he gushed to *La Jornada*). Marcos announced that this was building for a still larger Intercontinental Encuentro, to be held at the start of August.[42]

In July, the EZLN held a San Cristóbal forum with NGOs and civic groups on reform of the Mexican state, organized jointly with CONAI and COCOPA. The panel at the Convento del Carmen included both Cuauhtémoc Cárdenas and Marcos, who concluded with a call for a "big rainbow of political forces . . . which everyone can give the color they think is most appropriate."[43]

In August, the EZLN held the Intercontinental Encuentro for Humanity and Against Neoliberalism, for their supporters from around the world. Emphasizing the event's multicultural character in his typically flamboyant style, Marcos dubbed it the "Intergalactic Encuentro."[44]

Gringo journalist John Ross called it a "monumentally eclectic gathering of young European anarchists, aging Latin American guerrilleros, US cybernauts and the *indígenas* of Mexico Profundo . . ."[45] Eduardo Galeano was there from Uruguay, as was Danielle Mitterand, the French president's widow, and Douglas Bravo, the Venezuelan guerilla veteran.[46] Even representatives from Cuba's left-dissident Democratic Socialist Current were in attendance, testing the tolerance of the doctrinaire Fidelistas.[47]

Once again held in the rainy season, the assemblage got a taste not only of romance and heroism, but of the rebel army's daily struggle with the rivers of paralyzing mud into which every unpaved road in Chiapas is annually transformed.

Although Latin Americans, Europeans and gringos predominated, every continent was represented. Marcos addressed the political pilgrims from some fifty countries at La Realidad: "Who can say in what precise locale, and at what exact hour and date this Intercontinental Encounter for Humanity and Against Neoliberalism began? We don't know. But we do know who initiated it. All the rebels around the world started it. Here, we are only a small part of those rebels, it's true. But to all the many walls that all the rebels of the world break every day, you have added one more rupture—that of the wall around the Zapatista Reality." The last line was a double entendre on the name of the little jungle settlement where the proceedings were held, encircled by government troops.[48]

The Intergalactica was the springboard for an International Network Against Neoliberalism, which pledged to build cross-border resistance to the Free Trade order, that the Intergalactica would "continue on every continent, in every country, in every countryside and city, in every home, school or workplace where human beings want a better world."[49]

In November, Javier Elorriaga visited France on a speaking tour with his wife Gloria Benavides, the presumed "Comandante Elisa," recently released from prison.[50]

At the Odeon National Theater in Paris, the team's speaking gig got so exuberant that a riot threatened and the seventeenth-century building was surrounded by gendarmes. The theater was swamped past capacity with hundreds of undocumented Arab, African and Asian immigrants who proclaimed their solidarity with the Zapatistas, accused the Jacques Chirac government of persecution, and demanded the assemblage adopt their cause. The anarchists, meanwhile, jeered Danielle

Mitterand. Elorriaga and Benavides did their best to maintain calm as chaos reigned in several languages.[51]

Before they had moved on from the city, the working-class Paris suburbs of St. Denis, Pantin, Bagnolet, Trembloy-en-France and Aubervilliers announced sister-city relationships with Oventic, La Realidad, Morelia, Altamirano and Roberto Barrios, "for the ideals of justice, democracy and liberty that gave rise to the French Revolution and today give life to the noble struggle of the EZLN."[52]

In October, the CNI held a second indigenous forum in Mexico City. An intense national debate surrounded the question of whether the Zapatistas could travel to the Federal District for the event. The government claimed that the EZLN's confinement to the state of Chiapas was a condition of the cease-fire. After winning the right to dispatch a ten-member (unarmed) delegation following intricate negotiations and a national campaign, the EZLN decided to send only one—their "most bellicose, most aggressive and most intransigent" leader, said Marcos: Comandante Ramona, now gravely ill with kidney cancer.[53]

COCOPA sent a team to meet Ramona at La Realidad, where she emerged from a hut on the arm of Marcos. She was driven to Tuxtla for a special flight to Mexico City. Her arrival in the Federal District brought tens of thousands to the *zócalo*. In a small voice before the multitudes, she read a message from the EZLN to tears and thunderous applause: "We have come to Mexico City. This is the first of many journeys . . ." At the Indigenous Congress, in her red San Andrés *huipil* and ski-mask, she presented a Mexican flag, the EZLN's gift to the Congress, as *copal* was burnt in her honor. Accepting the flag on behalf of the Congress was Félix Serdán, a Nahua from Morelos. Serdán was an old fighter who rode with Rubén Jaramillo, the veteran of Zapata's army who waged a new insurgency in the 1950s. An historical cycle had been completed.[54]

DRUG WAR OR DIRTY WAR?

The Intergalactica, after some discussion, had issued a call to end the War on Drugs and support "legalization of soft drugs throughout the planet." The question I had asked Marcos in my interview two years earlier now seemed more relevant. The statement said the War on Drugs "has converted narcotrafficking into one of the most successful clandestine means of obtaining extraordinary profits" and called for "channelling the resources destined for combatting narcotrafficking into programs of development and social welfare."[55]

The EZLN was massively outgunned by sixty thousand federal army troops, detachments of state and federal police—and White Guards and paramilitaries.[56] Unlike the army, these semi-official forces felt no compunction to resort to an "anti-drug" cover for their activities.

The San Andrés dialogue reconvened after the Intergalactica, but the EZLN delegates insisted they would not move on to the next table, the Accords on Democracy and Justice, until the government freed the remaining Zapatista political prisoners and moved to "end the climate of persecution."[57]

Human rights monitors themselves were targeted for reprisals. Late on the night of November 4, the San Cristóbal offices of CONPAZ were ransacked and firebombed. Computers and files were burned, the telephone lines cut, and material aid intended for besieged *campesino* communities destroyed. That same night, CONPAZ administrator Javier López Montoya was kidnapped with his wife Eva Lara and their two children from their home. Held by unknown men at an unknown location for forty-eight hours, Javier was tortured, his wife molested, and his daughter's hair cut off. Two evenings later, they were released outside Chiapa de Corzo, some 60 kilometers from San Cristóbal.[58]

On November 9 in Venustiano Carranza, an OCEZ march for better *maíz* prices was attacked by combined state police and army forces, with machine guns, tear gas and helicopters, leaving three unarmed protestors dead. Hundreds were arrested.[59]

At this moment, Marcos and other EZLN leaders had returned to San Cristóbal to mark the formation of a legislative Verification Commission to ascertain that the peace agreements were being applied on the ground. Marcos strolled arm-in-arm through the *zócalo* with Amalia Solórzano, the widow of President Lázaro Cárdenas and mother of Cuauhtémoc.[60]

But the new commission would have little to do. In fact, the San Andrés dialogue had ended for the last time.

8

STEALTH
COUNTERINSURGENCY:
1997

As the year began, President Zedillo issued his long-awaited response to the San Andrés Accords. Zedillo's executive branch offered a new version of the Accords, with subtle yet significant changes throughout.

The EZLN–COCOPA version called for the Constitution to "recognize" indigenous rights; the federal executive version would "grant" rights. The EZLN–COCOPA version established the right of indigenous peoples to "the sustainable use" and a share of "all benefits derived from the use and development of natural resources in the territories they occupy." The executive version deleted the reference to indigenous "territories" and restricted use of natural resources to "the forms and modalities of property delineated in Article 27 of this Constitution" (private, state, *ejidal* and communal). The EZLN–COCOPA version recognized the right of indigenous peoples to determine the forms of development in their territories; the executive version obliged the government to "take account of" indigenous peoples in development programs. Finally, the executive version rejected the remunicipalization proposal, instead restricting the powers of indigenous communities to economic and social spheres, excluding the juridical and political.[1]

On January 11, almost a year after the original Accords were signed, the CCRI–GC issued a communiqué rejecting the presidential rewrite, saying the changes constituted a "categorical no" to the EZLN's one precondition for laying down arms and becoming a civil movement. The communiqué called Zedillo's proposal "racist, ethnocentric and discriminatory." The dialogue was declared once again "indefinitely suspended."[2] Zedillo countered that the original proposal was "separatist," granted Indians "special powers," and would lead to the "Balkanization" of Mexico.[3]

Tensions immediately escalated. In a January 24 communiqué, Marcos warned: "The pre-military campaign of the government has begun. The Mexican federal army is saturating its barracks with troops and armaments; the military patrols have doubled in size; planes and helicopters are practicing time and again for the surgical attack; the public ministers are preparing to count the captured and dead. The division leaders of the Rainbow Taskforce have their orders sitting on their desks."[4]

FRESH BLOOD AT NIXTALUCUM

On March 14, for the first time since the early days of 1994, armed conflict broke out between EZLN and government forces. The violence, which left four Indians dead, was centered around the Tzotzil hamlet of San Pedro Nixtalucum in the Highland *municipio* of El Bosque.[5]

The conflict started in a land dispute between Zapatista and *PRIista* villagers. State police said they were responding to a call in the hamlet and were ambushed. But residents told *La Jornada* police fired first, from helicopter gunships. After strafing the village from the air, the two choppers then dropped troops who continued the gun battle. Comandante David, the CCRI member responsible for the region, concurred with this account.[6]

Many Nixtalucum residents were members of the Zapatista militia, although no EZLN *insurgentes* appear to have been based at the hamlet. Four Tzotzils and six police were also wounded in the incident.[7]

In subsequent days, twenty-five Nixtalucum Tzotzils were arrested and hauled off to Cerro Hueco for alleged involvement in the fracas, and over three hundred fled the hamlet. Villagers charged that two residents "disappeared" after the attack.[8]

Just a week earlier, two state police were slain in a shoot-out with armed Chol *campesinos* staging a land occupation in Palenque. The violence broke out as police were evicting members of Xi'Nich, the ant-people—although Xi'Nich leaders denied their militants were responsible for the killings. Two Jesuit priests were arrested for involvement in the incident, and released following protests by Indians and human rights activists. One of the priests, Gonzalo Rosas, claimed he was beaten and pistol-whipped while in custody.[9]

Xi'Nich was among the *campesino* groups which had armed themselves in response to escalating paramilitary terror. By the time of the incident, there had been over three hundred deaths in Chiapas political violence since the end of open warfare on January 12, 1994.[10]

"FREE" ELECTIONS CLOUDED
BY TERROR

The July 6 midterm federal elections were immediately hailed as historic, the "freest" and "fairest" in Mexican history. For the first time, the PRI lost its grip on the lower-house Chamber of Deputies. The PRD, PAN and resurgent Mexican Ecological Green Party (PVEM) now shared control of the legislative branch with the PRI, breaking the party's sixty-eight-year hegemony. The PVEM was a former satellite breaking free of the PRI's orbit. In doing so it joined the PRD in being targeted for terror. In the three weeks before the elections, two PVEM leaders were murdered—one in Guerrero and one in the State of Mexico.[11]

The Federal District, 20 million people theretofore under direct federal rule, also elected its first governor, having recently passed a referendum for home rule. The victor was the PRD's leading light, Cuauhtémoc Cárdenas.[12] Immediately after the election, an unprecedented wave of violent crime shook Mexico City. The DF police forces were themselves implicated in attacks, leading many to smell a conspiracy against the Cárdenas administration. In November, an elite SWAT team called Los Zorros mutinied rather than face arrest for the torture-killing of six *barrio* youths, and had to be evicted from their compound by army troops.[13]

In Chiapas, the elections were business as usual: fraud, patronage and terror. Many indigenous communities were under military siege throughout the elections in Chiapas, and CONAI called the results "extremely confused, manipulated and in doubt."[14]

The Chiapas results showed a PRI victory in ten districts, and a narrow PRD victory in just two, Tuxtla and Tapachula. A 70 percent statewide abstention rate was reported. Military presence on election day was reported in Ocosingo, San Andrés Larrainzar, Altamirano and other communities, with some reports of direct intimidation of voters. Paramilitaries were reported intimidating voters in Palenque, Simojovel—and Tila, where PRD-stronghold hamlets were kept from the polls by threats from a new and powerful paramilitary with the Orwellian name of "Peace and Justice."[15]

One hundred and sixty of 610 ballot boxes slated statewide were never installed. Over a hundred were either burned or stolen by Zapatista supporters who barred the elections from their "communities in rebellion," including areas of Ocosingo, San Andrés, Altamirano, Simojovel, Chenalhó and Tenejapa. The Zapatistas cited military occupation of the communities as cause for the decision.[16] The OCEZ blocked roads and marched on Comitán and Tapachula to demonstrate their support for Zapatista abstentionism.[17]

Both the PAN and PRD demanded nullification of the results in the conflicted communities. The PRI retaliated by demanding nullification of the PRD victories in Tuxtla and Tapachula.[18]

On July 8, in San Andrés Larrainzar, *PRIistas* armed with pistols, clubs and machetes violently evicted the *PRDistas* who had been occupying the *cabacera*. That same day, armed UCPFV militants were dispersed from ranchland they were occupying at Liquidambar in the Sierra Madre by eight hundred federal police and army troops. Human rights groups protested the "disappearance" of fifteen *campesinos* in the incident; authorities admitted arresting only six.[19]

On July 18, in Venustiano Carranza, hundreds of state riot police attacked OCEZ squatters, who were dispersed by machine-gun bursts from truck and helicopter.[20]

After the elections, the papers ran a photo of PRD leader Porfirio Muñoz Ledo, fiery leftist and defected PRI *jefe*, shaking hands with Zedillo, pledging to work together. In a communiqué analyzing the election results, Subcommander Marcos decried that the PRD leadership had joined the PRI in calling for the "pacification" of Chiapas despite the fact that the government and EZLN remained completely at odds on the issue of indigenous autonomy.[21]

A PROMISE IS KEPT

September once again witnessed pitched debate over whether the Zapatistas could travel to the Federal District to march with the National Indigenous Congress and inaugurate the FZLN. Once again, the government was initially intransigent, and finally capitulated following a national campaign in support of the EZLN's freedom of transit. The government then demanded that they remove their masks if they leave Chiapas, but was finally outmaneuvered on this as well. A contingent of 1,111 Zapatista troops—masked but unarmed—drove in a caravan of 159 buses and trucks, with civil supporters and NGOs, from Chiapas to the DF, stopping for rallies and celebrations along the way, hosted by local *campesino* groups. "For the first time in eighty years, the cry of 'Here come the Zapatistas' is really true," Juan Juárez, a nonagenarian survivor of the first Zapatista generation, proudly told a reporter in Tepoztlan, Morelos.[22]

The Special Groupation Emiliano Zapata, as the contingent was known, arrived in Mexico City on September 12. At the national indigenous march, the troops were joined by tens of thousands despite rain. It fulfilled the EZLN's preposterous promise of January 1994 to march on the national capital.[23]

Special Groupation Emiliano Zapata representative Claribel told the crowd that if Zedillo did not intend to comply with the peace accords, "then we're telling him to say so clearly to the people of Mexico. If he wants war . . . we Zapatistas know how to fight with honor and bravery, because we have a powerful weapon the government doesn't have. This weapon is called dignity."[24]

Two months later, the Federal District witnessed a very different kind of gathering, as top Wall Street investors converged to review Mexico's financial climate. The meeting warned that the opposition wasn't leaving Zedillo enough "maneuverability for establishing his structural reforms" and that markets "are going to react very negatively if the budget isn't balanced." But Santander Investment Securities president José Antonio Díaz dismissed the Zapatista threat. "We're already forgetting about Marcos," he said.[25]

Just two weeks after that, on November 29, the rebel army and supporters held an unarmed march through the streets of San Cristóbal, more than ten thousand strong, to demand compliance with the San Andrés Accords. Roads were blocked in the Chiapas countryside, halting all traffic to the city for five hours. It was the largest gathering of ski-masked Indians in the city since 1994.[26]

NEITHER PEACE NOR JUSTICE

The outside world continued to pay little notice as the dirty war unfolded in Chiapas. Paz y Justicia was the most notorious of the new *PRIista* paramilitaries. Over the past year, it had killed upwards of a hundred civilians in the Chol Maya northern zone of the state, and forced hundreds more from their homes, the Diocese reported. Pro-Zapatista families in Tila and Salto de Agua took refuge in remote hamlets high in the mountains.[27]

On November 4, Bishop Ruiz was the target of an assassination attempt—his motorcade sprayed with gunfire in the Zona Norte, wounding three church workers. Two days later, the Bishop's sister, Maria de la Luz Ruiz, was attacked with a hammer at the Diocese offices in San Cristóbal, and hospitalized with a fractured skull. One man was arrested in the attack on Maria, but the Tila attack on Don Samuel and his Bishop Coadjutor Raúl Vera remained unsolved. The Diocese officially protested to federal authorities that the PGR agent on the case, "instead of investigating the facts of the attack against the bishops, has dedicated his efforts to interrogating the witnesses regarding the work of the Diocese in the northern region."[28] The Bishop took to wearing a metal helmet when he visited hostile villages.[29]

A network of *PRIista* paramilitaries was spreading throughout the Highlands. Paz y Justicia and Los Chinchulines dominated the Chol lands of the Zona Norte.[30] Moving south, the Indigenous Revolutionary Anti-Zapatista Movement (MIRA) emerged in the Tzeltal *municipios* of Ocosingo and Oxchuc, organizing patrols of the routes into Las Cañadas. The MIRA was reported guarding access to Las Cañadas in the Tojolabal lands of Las Margaritas as well.[31] In the central Tzotzil Highlands, a group called Mascara Roja—red mask—brought terror to Larrainzar and Chamula, leaving menacing graffiti warning *PRDistas* and *catequistas* that they were marked for death.[32] The Alianza San Bartolemé de Los Llanos armed in Venustiano Carranza, and engaged a violent struggle with the OCEZ for control of the *municipio*. A spate of shoot-outs between the groups left twenty dead and nearly a thousand displaced in February and March.[33]

Strange names for death squads, perhaps. *PRIista caciques* arming their wards to terrorize rebel *campesinos* back into submission shrewdly exploited populism and even revolutionary sympathies. Both the automatic rifles and the sophisticated political imagery indicated that the *caciques* were being groomed as counterinsurgency surrogates. As the year drew to a close, an horrific bloodletting would finally, if briefly, draw the world media's attention to the Chiapas violence—and reveal something of the forces shaping the paramilitary network.

THE MARTYRS OF ACTEAL

On December 22, Red Mask went too far. The massacre at Acteal, an outlying hamlet of the Tzotzil *municipio* Chenalhó, left forty-five dead—nine men, twenty one women (four of whom were pregnant) and fifteen children. Almost all were shot in the back. The attack began as the victims were praying for peace in a semi-enclosed chapel near Acteal's church. Others were gunned down with automatic weapons as they attempted to flee into the mountains. The bodies were horribly mutilated with machetes. "We need to finish off the seed!" one traumatized survivor told investigators the gunmen had said before slicing open the womb of a pregnant victim.[34]

The "fratricidal war" the Bishop had warned of seemed very near.

The warning signs were there. Violence had been building in Chenalhó for months, and had been amply documented by the Diocese. In November, as *PRIistas* reconsolidated control over the *municipio*, several villagers were assassinated, disappeared or raped, their houses burnt, and over a thousand expelled from the community. Many took refuge in hamlets loyal to the rebel government, such as Polhó and Acteal.[35]

On the morning of December 22, gunmen entered Acteal, attacking homes and the chapel, targeting members of Las Abejas—the bees—an Indian group sympathetic to the rebel government, but Christian-based and committed to nonviolence. *Catequistas* with Las Abejas were even translating Gandhi into Tzotzil.[36]

The community was unarmed. Thatch huts were no shelter from machine-gun rounds. Many dived into a ravine beside the hamlet, to hide among the rocks and crevices. The gunmen fired into the ravine, leaving the bodies piled at the bottom—some dead, some wounded.[37] The killing went on for five hours, as the gunmen chased down those who fled. It wasn't until five hours after that—ten hours after the slaughter began—that state police were mobilized to Acteal.[38]

As first reports of the carnage reached San Cristóbal, the Diocese immediately alerted state authorities. Police did not respond, despite maintaining a post just outside Chenalhó's municipal center. Red Cross workers recovered the bodies at Acteal early the following morning. More corpses had been dumped in the ravine in an effort to hide them. Wounded survivors were still hiding in terror under the pile.[39]

That day, with thousands of new refugees from the area hiding in the cold and misty mountains without adequate food or shelter, Acteal was occupied by federal police and army troops. Fifty people were shortly arrested in connection with the killings, including the PRI mayor of Chenalhó, Jacinto Arias Cruz. The Red Cross announced to the authorities that their radio transmitter on Cerro Tzontehuitz overlooking San Cristóbal had been stolen on the morning of the massacre, an apparent effort to keep reports from getting out and buy time to hide the grisly evidence.[40]

Zedillo, solemnly addressing the nation on television, called the massacre "an absurd, indefensible criminal act."[41] His fellow regime technocrats and pragmatists doubtless viewed this ritual distancing as a shrewd prerogative of power. Many hardliners and dinosaurs doubtless perceived weakness and betrayal.

Federal Prosecutor General Jorge Madrazo's initial report blamed the massacre on family feuds and "intercommunal conflicts."[42]

In January, the National Human Rights Commission (CNDH) issued a report on the massacre after extensive investigations and interviews with survivors. It asserted that elements of the state government were complicit.

"The gunfire was perfectly audible from . . . police stations, and their intervention could not only have halted the massacre, but would have in all likelihood helped three of the wounded victims survive," the report said.[43]

The CNDH quoted one eyewitness, his name withheld for safety, saying he saw police chase and capture some fifty armed men dressed in black uniforms and led by an unnamed ex-army official. A state police commander who arrived at that moment "ordered his agents to return the weapons to the men, letting them free."[44]

One police patrol in the hamlet during two hours of the massacre told the CNDH they heard shots and saw that all the houses had been hastily abandoned. But the commander's official record noted that the patrol had "nothing new to report" from Acteal.[45] Later, the CNDH found, higher police officials altered the reports with crude smudges to make it appear that the patrols had been in Acteal much later than they were.[46]

After the CNDH report, the PGR was forced to bring federal charges against a state police official. The indicted commander, Felipe Vázquez Espinosa, was in charge of a Public Security Police post a few kilometers from Acteal. According to the warrant, he loaned the killers police patrol cars to help them stockpile guns and ammo near Acteal.[47]

In mid-February, *federales* arrested two more state police commanders. The PGR concluded that Roberto Garcia Rivas, in command of forty Public Security officers stationed in Chenalhó, and Roberto Martín Mendez, his deputy, must have heard the gunfire at Acteal but did nothing. They brought the number arrested in relation to the massacre to fifty-eight.[48]

The state police "decided, at least, to remain passive," read the PGR's preliminary report, released in early February. Their statements to federal investigators were "contradictory and false," and indicated they had conspired to fabricate a cover story.[49]

Another five men were arrested by Chenalhó municipal authorities in February after attempting to smash the windows of a *colectivo* micro-bus operated by anti-*PRIistas*. Refugees from Acteal charged they were among the gunmen. They were handed over to federal authorities who delivered them to Cerro Hueco. All were former soldiers.[50]

The federal investigations sought to foist the complicity entirely onto the state government. But investigations by the independent press soon documented that complicity also extended to the federal army.

"CAMPAIGN CHIAPAS 94"

Human rights observers maintained that former and active military and police officers were arming and training the Chiapas paramilitaries—which would explain how they had been able to get AK-47s and other automatic weapons that outshone the EZLN's largely antiquated rifles.

These claims were given further credence by a story which ran in *Proceso* on January 4, extensively quoting an army document reporters had uncovered entitled "Plan of Campaign Chiapas 94." The document, drawn up shortly after the January 1994 uprising, called for S-2, the Defense Secretariat's Military Intelligence Section, to "secretly organize certain sectors of the civilian population, including ranchers, property owners and individuals characterized by a high sense of patriotism, who will be employed in support of our operations."[51]

The October 1994 document was ordered by the Defense Secretariat, and co-authored by officers based at Rancho Nuevo, who had long been studying the rise of militant *campesino* groups in Chiapas. It identified local elements who could be used as clandestine counterinsurgency forces. One paragraph noted: "The friendly population defends what is theirs, and this is especially valid for the ranchers and small property owners."[52]

The state government and army had been working in concert. After the Acteal massacre it was revealed that Gov. César Ruiz Ferro donated $500,000 to Paz y Justicia for "community development projects" during the previous July's federal elections.[53]

Ruiz Ferro resigned in the wake of the massacre. However, his replacement chosen by the state legislature, Roberto Albores Guillén, the state's fourth governor in as many years, was a grandson of former Governor Absalon Castellanos Dominguez[54]—the same briefly held by the EZLN and charged with crimes against the Indian population of Chiapas.

Castellanos himself, as Rancho Nuevo commander in 1980, had overseen a massacre of Tojolabal squatters at Golonchan ranch near Comitán—where more Indians may have died than at Acteal seventeen years later. Then, as governor, he oversaw development of the semi-official *Guardias Blancas*.[55]

Campaign Chiapas 94 cemented what had already been at least an informal relationship between the paramilitaries and the federal army. When the stakes got higher after the EZLN uprising, it was predictable that the Pentagon's fingerprints would emerge in the counterinsurgency plan.

THE PENTAGON CONNECTION

After the massacre, Chenalhó was occupied by the elite army troops of GAFE—the Special Airborne Forces Groups. In 1996, US Army Special Forces began a training program for GAFE, bringing some 3,200 Mexican officers to Fort Bragg, North Carolina. There the GAFE officers received instruction from the Seventh Special Forces Group—including veterans of the counterinsurgencies in El Salvador and Guatemala. GAFE troops poured into Chiapas after the massacre, setting up road-blocks throughout the Highlands.[56]

On December 26, just days after the massacre, *La Jornada* reported on a recent GAFE anti-drug operation in Jalisco, in which over a dozen young men were abducted and tortured. One of the youths, Salvador López Jiménez, died in GAFE custody.[57]

It is ironic that US-trained elite troops should be sent into Chiapas to restore order. One of the masterminds behind the counterinsurgency program was Gen. Mario Renan Castillo, who, as Rancho Nuevo commander, was an "honorary witness" in the ceremony where the state government forked out a half-million dollars to Paz y Justicia. Gen. Renan Castillo was also a Fort Bragg-trained expert in "psychological warfare," and creator of Rancho Nuevo's elite Rainbow Taskforce.[58]

Wrote columnist Jaime Aviles in *La Jornada*: "The creation of paramilitary militias in the Highlands was the responsibility of General Mario Renan Castillo Fernandez . . . Experts under his command, trained, like him, at the counterinsurgency school in Fort Bragg, North Carolina, took on the detailed task of finding out . . . just how big the EZLN areas of influence were in the mountain chains that surround the city of San Cristóbal."[59]

In November 1997, when Gen. Renan Castillo was transferred out of the Seventh Military Region, Paz y Justicia sent a delegation to his farewell party in Tuxtla. The delegation was headed by Paz y Justicia leader Samuel Sánchez, a PRI state deputy from the Zona Norte, who touchingly told the General, "We shall never forget you, sir . . . Everything you did for us motivates our gratitude."[60]

Many of the army officers overseeing the Chiapas campaign were trained for drug enforcement by the US Army's School of the Americas (SOA).

As President Clinton went through the ritual condemnation of the massacre, on January 12 Rep. Joe Kennedy of Massachusetts sent a letter to his colleagues in the House entitled "SOA Graduates' Fingerprints on Mexico's Chiapas Policy." The letter mentioned three Mexican SOA graduates implicated in human rights abuses.[61]

Col. Julian Guerrero Barrios (SOA Class of 1981) was commander of the unit in the grisly Jalisco incident.[62]

Gen. José Rubén Rivas Peña (SOA Class of 1980), a Rancho Nuevo officer, contributed "historical, sociological, political, religious and economic analysis" to the Campaign Chiapas 94 document. Rivas Peña was later sent to command the

28th Military Zone in Oaxaca when the Popular Revolutionary Army, a second guerilla group, appeared there in 1996. Under his tenure in Oaxaca, paramilitary groups began to appear.[63]

Gen. Juan López Ortíz (SOA Class of 1980) was commander of the January 1994 operation in Ocosingo, where EZLN troops and suspected sympathizers were rounded up and summarily shot in the town market.[64]

As growing evidence implicated the military, the PGR detained two army personnel in the Acteal investigation—although neither was initially charged. Retired Gen. Julio César Santiago Díaz, serving as a director of the Chiapas Auxiliary Police, was apparently in Acteal while the massacre was in progress, "listened to gunfire and machine-gun bursts, failing to intervene and ask for help from the closest Public Security detachments." Instead, he hid in the schoolhouse and told his superiors he had "nothing unusual" to report. Soldier Mariano Pérez Ruiz, a native of Chenalhó, was reported by the PGR to have used his November furlough "to instruct family and friends in the use of .22 caliber rifles," and helped import AK-47s to the village.[65]

FIRE AND SHADOW

The PGR report also predictably blamed the presence of Zapatista sympathizers for escalating violence in the region. "When the Zapatista National Liberation Army began its strategy of founding autonomous local governments . . . attacks, threats, robberies, and killings became ever more common and serious," the report read.[66]

PGR chief Madrazo told TV Azteca that the EZLN as well as the paramilitaries were operating in Chenalhó. "[M]any people indicate that the EZLN had eleven camps in the area," he said.[67]

Facing a national outcry for disarmament of the paramilitaries, federal Gobernación Secretary Emilio Chuayffet declared on December 29 that the disarming of Chiapas must include the EZLN. The thousands of fresh federal police and army troops flooding into Chiapas for the ostensible task of disarming the warring parties predictably targeted those regions known to be EZLN strongholds. Paz y Justicia's northern fiefdom was overlooked.[68]

Within days of Chuayffet's declaration, a purported EZLN arms cache was "discovered" by the army near Altamirano. The EZLN denied the arms were theirs. Marcos said "the weapons of the Zapatistas consist largely of sticks, taken from various types of jungle trees . . . The EZLN has not obtained arms in almost four years. We entered a peace dialogue process and, in consequence, haven't accumulated military force." Local residents claimed the arms had been buried by a local landowner who fled the area after the Zapatista revolt.[69]

Manipulation of paramilitaries allowed the government and party deniability. Then, the government militarization in response to the violence was aimed at the Zapatistas. It was counterinsurgency by stealth.

In his communiqué denying responsibility for the Altamirano arms cache, Marcos again warned that the federal troop build-up in Chiapas signaled an imminent attack on the Zapatistas: "It's a question of days, the most cautious say. Of hours, say the most nervous."[70]

9

DIRTY WAR OF ATTRITION:
1998

On January 3, two hundred army troops advanced on La Realidad, the principal EZLN-controlled settlement in the Lacandon Selva.[1]

At this precise moment in Mexico City, President Zedillo had the hardline Gobernación Secretary Emilio Chuayffet replaced by Francisco Labastida, the former Agriculture Secretary and a reputed moderate. The troops in the Selva merely surrounded La Realidad rather than entering it, and the feared bloodbath was averted. It remains unknown whether the troops got a change of orders from Mexico City.[2]

Other Zapatista strongholds were occupied by the army, including Morelia and Oventic, where the rebels had just held a *fiesta* to celebrate the fourth anniversary of their uprising. Reports again mounted of Indians being roughed up by army troops demanding to know the whereabouts of Marcos. Oventic was again abandoned, and Marcos dropped out of sight.[3]

The seven thousand who had fled Acteal and Chenalhó's municipal center following the massacre took refuge in the mountain hamlet of Polhó, a stronghold of the rebel government. Polhó's meagre resources were quickly overwhelmed. Hunger and illness inevitably followed. Polhó nonetheless refused government aid. Hamlet leaders accused the government of distributing expired medicine, more concerned with looking good before the media and world opinion than with actual aid.[4]

Indian women, some with babies slung across their backs, confronted armed troops in hamlets, villages and settlements throughout the Highlands and Cañadas, linking arms to bar them entry to their communities. Tense pushing matches ensued between unarmed mothers and tough soldiers young enough to be their sons. In a Chenalhó hamlet, military police beat Tzotzil women back with batons.[5]

On January 12, an unarmed march commemorating the 1994 cease-fire approached state police barricades in Ocosingo. Police opened fire. Guadalupe Mendez, a Tzeltal woman, was shot dead and her baby injured as the crowd scattered. Twenty-two state police officers were arrested in the incident. One would eventually be convicted.[6]

ZEDILLO ON THE HIGHWIRE

Also on January 12, nearly 100,000 came to Mexico City's *zócalo* to protest the massacre, many carrying cardboard coffins emblazoned with the names of the Acteal martyrs.[7]

Mere months after the Acteal massacre, the thirtieth anniversary of the Tlatelolco massacre in October would spark a national reckoning—and a special Congressional commission to uncover the truth of what really happened on that blood-drenched day in 1968. Many (not all) of the secret files on the massacre were finally made public, from both Mexican and US intelligence agencies. They clearly implicated provocateurs and pseudo-left shadow organizations in providing an expedient for the repression: if any initial shots came from the demonstrators in the Plaza de Tres Culturas (still far from certain), they likely came from government agents.[8]

Mexican officials had evidently warned the US embassy of a hardline Trotskyist "Olympic Brigade" bent on creating chaos during the games, while US Defense Intelligence Agency documents refer to an identically named "Olympic Brigade" of Mexican crack troops assigned to keep order during the games. Documents also established that an "Olympic Battalion" of armed undercover agents had infiltrated the plaza, and fired shots.[9]

Astute observers noted similarities between the Tlatelolco revelations and the dynamics which had led to mass murder in the Chiapas Highlands. Red Mask, the group that carried out the Acteal massacre, was actually made up of both *PRIistas* and adherents of a psuedo-left organization called the Party of the Cardenista Front for National Reconstruction (PFCRN), commonly known as the Frente Cardenista.[10]

The PRI's most insidious satellite, the PFCRN's opportunistic adoption of the Cárdenas name succeeded in confusing voters. Critics called the PFCRN "*marxista-salinista*" for splitting the PRD vote in the 1991 midterm elections.[11] In the Chiapas Highlands, the Frente Cardenista had even led land occupations[12] to establish a populist base—which could then be incorporated into the apparatus of counterinsurgency.

Zedillo, who had himself been a minor figure in the 1968 student movement,[13] ceded to the opposition on the Tlatelolco investigation—while doubtless once again facing the opprobrium of his own party dinosaurs.

International pressure also mounted on Zedillo to make a just peace with the Zapatistas. Even the International Labor Organization issued a statement demanding an explanation for Mexico's failure to approve the San Andrés Accords despite signatory obligations under ILO 169, the new international protocol recognizing the right of indigenous peoples "to participate in the decision-making process in all questions and programs directly affecting them."[14]

A distraction was called for to divert the attentions of Zedillo's enemies both to the left and right from the actual issues.

THE XENOPHOBIA CARD

This was provided by the presence of numerous gringo and European Zapatista supporters in Chiapas.

On February 13, Lolita de Vega, talkshow anchor for TV Azteca, did what even the army had never attempted—she descended, without warning, on La Realidad in a helicopter, loaned by the Chiapas government. The chopper was immediately surrounded by angry residents who demanded that it immediately depart. After some minutes of haggling, her crew took off—but ascended diagonally, catching the roof of the settlement's schoolhouse and tearing it off. Sheet metal rained down, injuring two children. In the show produced from the episode, Lolita claimed she had been ordered to leave by arrogant, armed foreigners, who barked orders in English, French and German. She said they "spoke to us like Zapatista commanders" and were "manipulating our Indians."[15]

The foreigners in La Realidad were members of a Civil Peace Encampment established by NGOs to monitor the cease-fire. Lolita claimed the Zapatista movement had been usurped by foreign revolutionaries who "exploit the authentic indigenous struggle."[16]

The appropriate atmosphere of xenophobia in place, the federal government stepped up harassment of foreign activists, journalists and human rights observers.

On February 19, Thomas Hansen Alfred, an official of the Minneapolis-based Pastors for Peace, was detained by *federales* during a visit to the hospital in Altamirano. He was taken to a San Cristóbal jail cell, and from there to Mexico City for deportation. A government statement accused him of illegally working for the EZLN. Hansen said he was teaching Indians how to use video equipment to document human rights abuses. He had served as an observer at the San Andrés dialogue with full government credentials. A federal judge ruled the expulsion illegal after the fact.[17]

Immigration officials also deported Robert Schweitzer of Factoryville, Pennsylvania, accused of violating his tourist visa on an earlier visit when he photographed the peace talks at San Andrés. Days earlier, on February 9, Maria Darlington of North Carolina was deported on charges of having joined a Zapatista demonstration the previous year.[18]

On February 26, Father Michel Henri Jean Chanteau, who had served as the parish priest of Chenalhó for over thirty years, was detained at the village by federal police, driven to Tuxtla, flown to Mexico City and summarily deported back to France.[19]

Then came the showdown with Italy. The previous September, Venice had bestowed its highest order, the Lion of Gold, on the EZLN. Two Zapatista women, Maribel and Mecias, traveled to accept the honor. Handed the statuette by the vice-mayor, they greeted him with a *bastón de mando*. The affair was the climax of an anti-racist conference arranged by the city's left-coalition government to counter a rally by northern Italy's right-wing Padania separatists. Maribel and Mecias said the money from the award would be used for a hydro generator in La Realidad.[20]

In May, Mexico retaliated by summarily expelling 134 Italian "peace observers," including left-wing parliamentarians. The Mexicans derided them as "revolutionary tourists" and banned them from the country for life. Italy launched a diplomatic inquiry into the matter.[21]

AFTERMATH AND CONSOLIDATION

Under Gov. Ruiz Ferro a total of some twelve thousand had been displaced by paramilitary violence.[22] Since the 1994 uprising, forty churches or chapels had been burned, destroyed or closed by opponents of the Diocese.[23]

In the post-massacre damage-control, Zedillo rotated a new crop of purported progressives and Chiapas hands into the federal bureaucracy, as well as mandating the resignation of Ruiz Ferro. Adolfo Orive, a veteran PP Maoist and one of the first radical organizers to enter Chiapas a generation earlier, was even appointed a high-level advisor to the Gobernación secretary.[24]

But Secretary Labastida and Gov. Albores worked to consolidate the gains of their more overtly hardline predecessors. Albores announced that no new autonomous municipalities would be tolerated. "Until the San Andrés Accords become law, it would be politically irresponsible to permit the formation of town councils that usurp the legitimate authority of existing municipal governments," Albores told the press.[25]

When the deep Selva settlement of Taniperlas declared itself Autonomous Municipality Ricardo Flores Magón, Albores pounded his fist on his desk before an AP reporter. "It's incredible. I don't understand it. It was a provocation."[26]

On April 11, state and federal police and army troops occupied Taniperlas/Flores Magón. The foreigners serving as observers there were summarily deported.[27]

Two months later, the troops were still there. A statement by the Autonomous Municipality protested, "The schoolhouse and the community school grounds are occupied by Public Security, and the army use them like barracks and it has been three months now since the children have been able to study . . ."[28]

Another statement complained that even with the troops there, MIRA terrorized the settlement with impunity—shooting at homes and threatening women with rape to reveal the whereabouts of their men who had fled with the April raid.[29]

On May 1, a thousand federal and state police backed up by half as many army troops raided Autonomous Municipality Tierra y Libertad (formerly Agua Tinta, near the Guatemalan border in the official municipality of Las Margaritas). Over fifty Indians were arrested, and eight were held at Cerro Hueco on charges of "rebellion."[30]

Gov. Albores first claimed the Tierra y Libertad raid had been requested by the UN High Commissioner for Refugees to rescue a Guatemalan refugee who had apparently been detained by the settlement's rebel authorities for illegally felling trees on communal woodlands. The UNHCR issued a prompt denial.[31]

A state government press release purported that the Autonomous Municipalities were prepared to disband, citing documents signed by *ejiditarios* stating their intent to return to a "state of legality."[32] Rebel municipal authorities claimed the signatures had been forged, or were of residents who fled in the 1994 uprising and hadn't returned since.[33]

On June 3, a thousand police officers and soldiers swarmed into the small Highland *municipio* of Nicolas Ruiz, firing tear gas, breaking down doors and arresting 167 Zapatista sympathizers they said had "held the town hostage." State authorities charged there had been a wave of expulsions of *PRIista* families by the town's PRD authorities—who in turn countercharged that the expelled residents were MIRA members who had threatened and violently attacked members of the community.[34]

On June 10, a thousand soldiers and police entered Autonomous Municipality San Juan de La Libertad (formerly Unión Progreso and surrounding hamlets) in the official *municipio* of El Bosque. When the Tzotzil residents tried to block their way, the troops responded with tear gas and machine guns. When the shooting was over, eight *campesinos* and one police agent were dead. Residents fled into the mountains. Gov. Albores claimed his troops had been fired on first by ski-masked men. Residents said government troops had forced local youths at gunpoint to put on ski-masks, hold rifles—and pose for police cameras.[35]

The authorities were knocking over the autonomous municipalities one by one, with piecemeal bloodshed rather than the wholesale type exhibited at Acteal, so as to avoid unseemly international attention.

In July, Bishop Ruiz announced at a mass in the Cathedral that he was stepping down as mediator of the peace process. The government and rebels had not met in nearly two years. "Clearly a stage in the process of peace has ended," Ruiz told the press. He also decried the "constant and growing aggression" against him.[36]

Zedillo countered that the CONAI commissioners were "apostles of hypocrisy" who were "defrauding" the government by siding with the Zapatistas.[37]

In January, Gen. José Gómez Salazar, the new commander of the Seventh Military Region, had publicly accused Bishop Ruiz of involvement with the EZLN. The General said troops had discovered evidence with the Altamirano arms cache "proving" Ruiz was an EZLN operative who went by the code word *Caminante*—the walker, a term of respect long bestowed on the Bishop by his admirers. A manuscript on Liberation Theology uncovered in the raid had been thus signed. The General did not question why Ruiz would use a code word so obvious that it was immediately detected. He also speculated that Ruiz was actually the EZLN's long-sought "Comandante German."[38]

WANTED posters with Don Samuel's face, accusing him of being a "Red Bishop" and "corrupter of nuns," appeared on San Cristóbal's walls, produced by an "Iberoamerican Solidarity Movement," local organ of the neo-fascist cult controlled by Lyndon LaRouche in the US.[39]

Chiapas municipal elections on October 4 were typically confused. The autonomous municipalities abstained. The PRI kept nearly all of its official municipalities, but some of the victories were highly dubious—such as the *unanimous* one in San Andrés Larrainzar. Elections were postponed in eight flood-stricken *municipios*, as well as in Chamula—where the PRI's own militants refused to allow authorities to set up polling stations until demands were met for the freeing of *caciques* charged with killing evangelical converts.[40]

While beating back the Zapatistas on the ground in Chiapas, the government attempted to undercut their sympathy on the national stage. In March, Zedillo introduced his own Indian autonomy proposal to Congress. It was essentially the same proposal the Zapatistas had already rejected, but if he could get it passed, he could appear to set the unresolved issue of the San Andrés Accords to rest.[41]

A federal initiative also called upon Mexico's thirty-two states to add autonomy clauses to their constitutions. Chiapas Gov. Albores Guillén responded with a remunicipalization plan which bore a superficial resemblance to what the Zapatistas themselves were calling for—but aimed precisely at undercutting the actually existing autonomous municipalities. Ocosingo, the state's biggest *municipio*, and among the most conflictive, would be carved up into thirteen new municipalities designed to maximize PRI strength. Eleven of the proposed new jurisdictions overlapped with (and divided) already-declared autonomous municipalities.[42]

TLALOC BETRAYED

The earth itself was the next to strike at suffering Chiapas. In the spring—*maíz* planting time at the end of the dry season—fires raged out of control throughout the mountains of Mexico, from the Altos of Chiapas to the Sierra Tarahumara of Chihuahua, cloaking the skies in a carboniferous haze from Guatemala to Texas.

In May, US AID chief Brian Atwood announced an emergency loan of fire-fighting, security and communications equipment to the Mexican army troops battling flames which had already destroyed 400,000 hectares of forest.[43] The army was said to be concerned the US was planning infrared heat-detection flights over areas with massive troop deployments against the Zapatistas.[44] Environment Secretary Julia Carabias said Chiapas suffered most from the fires.[45]

With the Houston skyline engulfed, Texas declared an air pollution alert on May 15. The media blamed the drought conditions which nurtured the fires on El Niño, while environmentalists warned that the severity of the atmospheric phenomenon was a harbinger of the greenhouse effect—itself aggravated by global deforestation, in a vicious cycle. "This may be a wake-up call for what global warming is going to bring in the twenty-first century," Sierra Club clean-air director Neil Carman told the *New York Times*.[46]

Then, in September, late in the rainy season, just before the harvest, came the floods. Sosconosco was hardest hit. Hundreds were killed as water and mud engulfed whole communities. In Motozintla, in the Pacific-facing foothills of the Sierra Madre, over 170 bodies were dug out.[47]

Of course, the two disasters were linked. The fires that swept through the mountains were started by *campesinos* who had no choice but to clear forested slopes for their *milpas*. The more forest is destroyed, the more the hydrological cycle is disrupted; with no canopy for transpiration, local rainfall and cloud cover decline; drought makes surviving forest vulnerable to wildfires. Then, when the rains do come, sweeping in from the Caribbean on the trade winds, there are no roots to hold down the soil and absorb the water. Millennia's accumulated wealth of organic matter is swept from the mountainsides in deluges of mud. The titanic hurricanes of recent years are themselves purportedly sparked by global warming, closing the grim circle.[48] Tlaloc, the revered Nahua rain god who the Maya called Chac Mool, brings destruction instead of abundance.

President Zedillo described the disaster as the worst since the devastating 1995 earthquake, and authorized emergency relief for the region.[49]

Criticisms soon mounted that government aid was dispensed only to PRI supporters and the party's local machine. An EZLN communiqué charged that the state government, "with the complicity of federal employees, is perpetrating a scandalous theft," comparing it to that of "the Nicaraguan dictator Anastasio Somoza, who profited from aid sent to the victims of the earthquake in Managua" in 1972.[50]

October saw angry street protests in Tapachula, with thousands of *damnificados*—people left homeless by the destruction—charging that "the thousands of tons of food, potable water, clothing and medicines have existed only in the official speeches." While corrupt bureaucrats and their patrons misappropriated the aid, rural communities remained cut off where roads and bridges had been washed away in the torrents. The protestors asserted that over five hundred were dead, two hundred still missing and some 100,000 homeless from the disaster—far in excess of official estimates.[51]

In November, small coffee-producers in Motozintla and nearby *municipios* protested that earth-moving equipment donated by the federal government to local authorities to dig out mud-locked communities had found its way into the hands of prominent *finqueros*, and never aided the intended beneficiaries.[52]

As forests decline, corporate power seeks to reclaim land with monoculture tree farms. Alfonso Romo of the Mexican timber giant Pulsar, who had toured Chiapas with World Bank President James Wolfensohn in 1994, proposed pacifying the region with giant eucalyptus plantations, providing employment for deforested regions, especially in the Lacandon Selva. He began aggressively pitching the World Bank, Mexican government and International Paper on the idea after the Acteal massacre. Louisiana Pacific was also said to be considering pulp farms in a pacified Chiapas.[53]

DIALOGUE RESUMED; STRUGGLE CONTINUES

In October, the EZLN announced that it was seeking a renewed dialogue. This time, talks with COCOPA in San Cristóbal would coincide with an *encuentro* with civil society—popular organizations, NGOs and individuals. The Zapatistas continued to maintain they would not lay down arms until the government accepted the San Andrés Accords, disarmed the paramilitaries, demilitarized their territories, released accused Zapatista prisoners, and made serious proposals on the long-stalled Democracy and Justice phase of the dialogue.[54]

The talks started badly, with the Zapatista delegates complaining that inadequate accommodations and security had been arranged for them—not even beds, much less guards and fax machines. With CONAI out of the picture, COCOPA was responsible for logistics, and the *comandantes* were apparently expected to sleep on the floor of the San Cristóbal municipal auditorium. The delegates accused their COCOPA hosts of "racism." The army maintained little visible presence in San Cristóbal during the talks, and the Diocese remained silent throughout. Marcos was present only via a video address pre-recorded in the jungle.[55]

Beds were brought in, and both sides ultimately called the talks a success. Comandantes Tacho and Zebedeo and Major Moises presided over the sessions. The civil talks, alternating with the EZLN–COCOPA talks, were attended by three thousand. The Zapatistas decided on a new strategy in their ongoing effort to extend their movement: they would appoint five thousand Zapatista delegates to visit every *municipio* in Mexico, convening local *consultas* on their civil initiatives.[56]

On November 26, the COCOPA delegation left La Realidad after escorting the EZLN delegation back there from San Cristóbal. Within hours of COCOPA's departure, another convoy of some forty military vehicles was rumbling down the road to La Realidad. The game continued.[57]

The settlement was again surrounded, and troops approached the Nuevo Aguascalientes, shooting at it with video cameras instead of rifles. Although the troops withdrew without incident, the EZLN called it a "mock take-over" and a provocation—and perhaps a warning from the executive branch, which the Zapatistas had explicitly excluded from the new dialogue.[58]

Just days before the anniversary of the Acteal massacre, masked gunmen ambushed a truck in the hamlet of Los Platanos in El Bosque. A young child was killed and seven were injured. The government immediately blamed the Zapatistas. The EZLN responded in a communiqué, condemning the attack and denying responsibility: "The EZLN does not attack civilians. The government does." The statement insisted that Los Platanos was "under the complete control of paramilitary groups, Chiapas state public security forces and federal soldiers. Nothing happens in that community and its surroundings without the knowledge of those paramilitaries, and no one can move about those areas without their approval." Most Zapatista sympathizers had already been expelled from Los Platanos. The rebels portrayed the incident as an internecine conflict between *PRIista* groups vying for government aid.[59]

There had been plenty of evidence, once again, that trouble was brewing in El Bosque. In July, two military attachés from the US Embassy, on a "fact-finding mission" in the Chiapas Highlands, had been detained by a *PRIista* crowd at Los Platanos for four hours. Witnesses reported seeing sophisticated communications equipment in their vehicle. The mission's cover blown, the Mexican government was embarrassed into an official protest of the USA's "unacceptable interventionist attitude."[60] A Pentagon statement initially said the attachés were detained by "villagers affiliated with a paramilitary group organized by the Institutional Revolutionary Party," although this was later denied by incoming US Ambassador Jeffrey Davidow, who insisted Chiapas was not "a national security problem" for the US.[61]

In the days following the shootings at Los Platanos, the neighboring hamlet of Unión Progreso, scene of the killings in June, was occupied by fifty state police backed up by paramilitaries from Los Platanos. Fearing a second massacre, some forty families fled to the mountains, remaining in the cold and mist for six days, with babies growing ill and only dry *tortillas* to eat.[62]

A year after the Acteal massacre, ninety-seven people, including eleven police officers, were still detained in the investigation. There had still been no convictions—although several Chiapas government officials were barred from holding office for eight years.[63]

At the massacre commemoration in Acteal, masked Zapatistas joined the grieving villagers, as an army helicopter circled overhead.[64]

Bishop Samuel Ruiz delivered a special homily for the occasion:

Human blood, all human blood, always is precious before God's heart. It contains and it means life itself, which God gives. The perception of this truth is common among all cultures, at all times and in all places. For this reason, shed human blood hits like a hard blow to the gut of people and of God, even if it is the blood of a criminal who dies in the act of committing a crime.

If it is the blood of an honest and good person, it hits with special force. If the blood is shed as a consequence of an injustice suffered, it has an added quality. And if the blood has run through the veins of one actively struggling for freedom, justice and equality among men, then it is the blood of a hero.

But if that blood is the innocent blood of someone who, in the middle of a war, has decided to set out on the radical path of the Gospel, with no other arm than the force of love and truth; and it is offered generously, accompanied by prayers for the benefit of the one who sheds it, we have before us the precious blood of a martyr, a witness to the redeeming love of Christ, someone who has had the privilege of mixing their own blood with that of the Lamb of God.

And if we are speaking of forty-five lives offered up in this way, including those of children, then we have reached a peak moment in the history of salvation.

This is Acteal.

And this is why we are here: Because we are witnesses and beneficiaries of the fecundity of this blood that has saturated the earth here. So we should take our shoes off, because, truly, we are standing on the holy ground of Acteal.[65]

10

"A REVOLUTION TO MAKE A REVOLUTION POSSIBLE"

One of the EZLN's first communiqués after the Acteal massacre was full of black humor. Marcos poked fun at the paramilitaries by name, and suggested the government investigate Cervantes, Saavedra, Shakespeare, Euripides, Socrates, Heraclitus and Homer because books they had written were found in a Zapatista camp.

Strangely, he signed it "Sup Speedy González," and followed it with a characteristically cryptic postscript quoting the cartoon mouse's signature line: "*Yepa, yepa, yepa! Andele, andele! Yepa, yepa, yepa!*"[1]

This peculiar phrase re-emerged as the complete text of an extremely succinct July 1998 communiqué, the EZLN's first in many months, along with an urgent postscript in Nahuatl: "!!NEMI ZAPATA! !NICAN CA NAMOTATA, AYEMO MIQUI! !NEMI ZAPATA!"—Viva Zapata! Your father isn't dead yet, he still lives! Viva Zapata![2]

Nahuatl, rather than a local Maya tongue. These were calls to their supporters beyond their territories, cries to the unmasked who made an implicit commitment to the Zapatistas when they called upon the rebel army to pursue peaceful struggle.

"Why is everyone so quiet?" the Subcomandante asked in an early communiqué. "Is this the democracy you wanted?"[3]

THE ZAPATISTA DREAM

In his 1997 book *Subcomandante Marcos: El Sueño Zapatista*, French journalist Yvon LeBot presents a series of interviews from La Realidad in which Marcos discusses how the Zapatistas viewed their 1994 insurrection. Marcos insisted that the EZLN actually intended to advance toward the Federal District—first, toward Tuxtla and Tabasco, taking the war as far from the Zapatista support zones as possible, so as to "gain time for these communities to organize the resistance." He also told LeBot, "This history hasn't ended, we are going to arrive in Mexico City. We haven't abandoned our march on Mexico City."[4]

The envisioned means of arriving there have changed: circumstances almost immediately caused the Zapatistas to rethink the traditional precepts of armed struggle. Marcos told LeBot:

> We met with this other force that appeared; it wasn't the government which wanted us to dialogue, but the people. We thought the people would either not pay attention to us, or come together with us to fight. But they did not react in either of these two manners. It resulted that all of these people, who were thousands, tens of thousands, hundreds of thousands, perhaps millions, did not want to rise up with us, but ... neither did they want us to be annihilated. They wanted us to dialogue. This completely broke our scheme and ended up defining *zapatismo*, the *neo-zapatismo*.[5]

Since then, the Zapatistas have sought to extend the "armed *zapatismo*" of the Chiapas indigenous communities to a "civil *zapatismo*" throughout Mexico, and even "international *zapatismo*."[6]

If the Zapatistas were to return to the military option, they would win international headlines again. Instead, they have continued to opt for peaceful struggle. They haven't surrendered their weapons, and they still face organized terror, but in the court of Mexican public opinion they are overwhelmingly perceived as occupying the moral high ground.

The Zapatista rebel government continues, even after significant setbacks, to rule from below throughout much of Chiapas. It has stood up to the cattle oligarchy goons and instated its own agrarian reform; outmaneuvered the state and federal governments into accepting at least some land take-overs; instigated the fall of numerous local governments; challenged the institutional subservience of women; and changed the nature of political discourse in Mexico. It has made Indian autonomy a national issue, brought revolutionary ideas to the mainstream, and accelerated the rupture between organized labor and the ruling party. *New York Times* reporter Alan Riding admitted the Zapatista uprising "had thrown the entire political system into disarray and given Mexico a hefty shove toward becoming a real democracy."[7]

The Zapatistas have effected all this despite hardly firing a shot in anger since January 12, 1994, and largely without visible leadership: Marcos and Ramona and Avendaño are spokespeople and inspiring figures, but they do not control the *campesino* organizations which are the actual structures of the rebel government on the ground.

These "post-modern" guerillas have been remarkably nonviolent and anti-authoritarian, effecting their advances less through military than moral means. Their rifles—and they have never had enough rifles to go around, as evidenced by the young rebel troops of January 1994 marching into battle with sticks symbolically shaped like rifles—have, to an extent, been props in a highly effective political theater.

THE LEGACY OF CHE

The face of Che Guevara appears alongside Zapata and Villa in the murals of Zapatista territory. "Che is closer to us than many people think," Marcos told a reporter in 1997. "He is still around and alive thirty years on from his death . . . One way or another, all rebel movements in Latin America are the heirs to Che's rebellion."[8]

But the EZLN's relationship with the iconic guerilla is a subtle and critical one. Autonomous Municipality Ernesto Che Guevara in Las Cañadas has its seat at a settlement which the community has renamed Moses-Gandhi, a juxtaposition indicating different currents within the Zapatista base on the role of armed struggle. Marcos also discussed the EZLN's relationship with Che in his talks with Yvon LeBot, who noted that Che is "essentially defined" by "the armed seizure of power." Marcos responded:

This is an aspect of Che, but for the Zapatista National Liberation Army the reference is to the Che who left Cuba and went to Bolivia. The Che who continued to struggle, who chose to continue being a rebel, who decided to abandon everything and begin anew . . . with all the difficulties that this represents and all the failures or mistakes that were committed . . . Not, at the moment, the guerilla method, the Guevarista *foco* . . . In the end, that is not the part that *Zapatismo* takes from Guevara, but the human part . . . Independent of whether his ideas are correct or erroneous . . . Guevara . . . has with us the similarity of being a *guerrillero* who went, against all odds, to raise a dream, a utopia . . .[9]

Since the 1994 Aguascalientes conference, the Zapatistas, contrasting the Guevarista vanguard model, have attempted to work out a revolutionary program in an open and organic dialogue-of-equals with the Mexican democratic left—dissident union-ists, independent *campesino* groups, radical students, middle-class organizations like El Barzón, and the PRD.

Of necessity, this is a slow and sloppy process (as real democracy always is), and certainly hasn't been completely successful. But the break with vanguardism is implicit in the Zapatista slogan "everything for everyone, nothing for us," and their principle of "leading by obeying," with the Clandestine Committee deriving its orders from the *consultas*.[10]

"We don't want to seize power, we want to exercise it," Marcos put it in one communiqué.[11] The EZLN state that they do not seek state power, but rather seek to open a democratic space or *apertura*,[12] "to liberate politics from the trap set by the politicians."[13]

Marcos elaborated in one of his peculiar series of (presumably) imaginary con-versations with a jungle beetle named Durito, who plays the role of the Sub-commander's alter-ego, sounding board and Devil's advocate. The hallucinatory beetle informed the Subcommander that his revolution

> is not about the taking of Power or the imposition (by peaceful or violent means) of a new social system, but about something which precedes all this. It is about the construction of the ante-chamber of the new world, a space where each of the different political forces, with equal responsibilities and rights, can struggle for the support of the majority of society. Does this confirm the hypothesis that we Zapatistas are "armed reformists"? We don't think so. We just point out that a revolution which is imposed, without the support of the majority, even-tually turns against itself . . . [W]e are not proposing an orthodox revolution, but something even more difficult: a revolution which will make a revolution possible.[14]

DEMOCRATIC OPENING *VERSUS* CIVIL WAR

"Globalization, neoliberalism as a global system, should be understood as a new war of conquest for territories," Marcos wrote in a 1997 communiqué analyzing the planetary context of *neo-zapatismo*. He postulated a "Fourth World War" which has recontextualized the polarity of "World War III," or the Cold War. The capitalist powers now vie for hegemony over the "liberated" markets in the former colonies.

It is a "world order returned to the old epochs of the conquests of America, Africa and Oceania. This is a strange modernity that moves forward by going backward. The dusk of the twentieth century has more similarities with previous brutal centuries than with the placid and rational future of some science-fiction novel. In the world of the post-Cold War, vast territories, wealth and above all, a qualified labor force await a new owner."[15]

In the privatization of Mexico's communal lands and *ejidos*, this reconquest of territory can be seen in a literal sense. Global capitalism is poised to deal the last remnants of the Mexican Revolution a *coup de grace*, finishing off the work started with the peso devaluation and de la Madrid election in 1982; the transformation from a corporatist state to a corporate state—a system of governance by, for and of private power.

The same Chase Manhattan Bank memo which advised President Zedillo to "eliminate" the Zapatistas also warned of the dangers of "splitting the governing party." The memo stated: "The Zedillo administration will need to consider carefully whether or not to allow opposition victories if fairly won at the ballot box."[16]

There are inherent obstacles to Mexico's orderly transition to modern capitalist democracy supposedly envisioned by NAFTA's boosters. Three rival currents are seen within the PRI: the US-educated, globalist "technocrats"; the nationalist-corporatist "dinosaurs"; and the left-leaning "democrats" who support devolution from a centralist machine to a legitimate party in a pluralist system. Many in this last category have already defected to the PRD. It is the more populist *dinosaurios* who tend to be the most hardline anti-Zapatistas. The long-reigning CTM union boss Fidel Velazquez—who finally died at the helm in 1997 at the age of 96—publicly called for "annihilation" of the EZLN (winning him the epithet "Fidel Schwarzenegger," a reference to the muscle-bound Arnold of *The Terminator* movies).[17]

The game of brinkmanship in Chiapas reflects these divisions. Dinosaur hardliners seek to provoke a return to total warfare; technocrats hold out for co-optation. These divisions permeate the federal army itself.

In a 1997 interview, Marcos warned that a military solution to the Zapatista dilemma would open the "possibility of a civil war in Mexico . . . very similar to the Yugoslavia of today and to Lebanon of the last decade, where there are so many groups that they don't know who to shoot at, or where, or who to negotiate with or to dialogue with." He cautioned that the only way to avoid this was "if Mexico would open the channels of political participation in a way that the differences or the discords that exist in social sectors could have causeways of political participation."[18]

DEMOCRACY: POPULAR *VERSUS* TECHNOCRATIC

In light of the local context of rootedness in indigenous identity, the continental context of rebellion against a free trade pact, and the global context of continuing the revolutionary project after the collapse of the socialist world, the description by *New York Times* reporter Tim Golden of Marcos as Latin America's "first post-modern guerilla hero"[19] is meaningful, perhaps in spite of itself. Mexican political analyst Gustavo Esteva has called the Zapatista movement the "first revolution of the twenty-first century."[20] Historian Lorenzo Meyer termed the EZLN the first "post-Cold War" guerillas.[21]

Marcos acknowledged both *neo-zapatismo*'s continuity and its break with its fore-bears of the previous decade when he responded in a later interview: "Some say it is the first post-modern revolution, others say that it is the last Central American revolution, even geographically speaking." He laughed that, "What upsets the Pentagon is that when you punch 'Zapatista' into the computer, nothing comes out that says, 'Moscow' or 'Havana' or 'Libya,' 'Tripoli,' 'Bosnia,' or any other group. And the left, accustomed to the same way of thinking, says, 'Well, they don't fit in anywhere.' It doesn't occur to them that there might be something new, that you have to re-theorize."[22]

Their insistence on organic process as opposed to authoritarian vanguardism places the Zapatistas in a post-Leninist left; their insistence on democratic praxis as opposed to an autocratic program places them in a post-ideological left.

The EZLN's first demand of democracy does not refer to formalistic rotation of suited politicians. In Mexico, the shrinkage of the corporatist party-state creates a political vacuum among the disfranchised, increasingly filled by the new popular movements. The old/new Zapatista slogan *Tierra y Libertad* implies that the strug-gles for land and democracy are indivisible. Enclosure of the *campesino* lands was instated by the Liberal dictatorship of Díaz—and now by the neoliberal dictator-ship of the PRI. "It seems to me that what most radicalized the *compañeros*," said Marcos in an early interview, "was the reform of Article 27; that was the door that was closed on the indigenous to survive in a legal and peaceful manner."[23]

That door is also closing on Mexican workers and the middle class in such "reforms" as the government's 1998 lifting of all subsidies on *maíz* production and price controls on *tortillas*.[24] In Mexico, formalistic technocratic democracy finds its most serious challenge in an emerging popular democracy.

This new democracy, seen as inclusive of local control over local resources, is antithetical to the neoliberal order which delivers these to remote multinational control. Technocratic democracy is based on the extinction of indigenous cultures, with the corporate media considered the appropriate fora for debate, and decision-making power relegated to the managerial caste. Popular democracy is rooted in surviving traditions from land-based cultures, with local communities considered the appropriate fora both for debate and for seeking ways to exercise decision-making power.

PLURIETHNIC AUTONOMY *VERSUS* NEOLIBERAL ETHNOCIDE AND SEPARATISM

Ethnic survival is central *neo-zapatismo*, but the movement seeks inclusion, not exclusion. While the leadership, footsoldiers and civil base of the EZLN are proudly indigenous, the Zapatistas call upon *mestizos* to join the movement as equals, as long as they respect indigenous dignity. This is an antidote to the internal racism which has traditionally divided Mexico's *mestizo campesinos*, however miserable, from the Indians. Popular organizations in Chiapas such as the OCEZ now embrace Indian and *mestizo* as equals, and the Autonomous Regions which govern much of Chiapas from below are explicitly "pluriethnic."

The ethnic identity of an oppressed people—the Maya—is embraced proudly, but not exalted to the exclusion of common class concerns.

The Zapatista autonomy slogan is "never again a Mexico without us."[25] When the Pluriethnic Autonomous Regions marched on San Cristóbal to press for approval of the San Andrés Accords in 1997, they chose February 24 because it is Mexico's Day of the Flag. Their official statement read: "Autonomy and free determination are not separatism, it is not independence, it is not to create States within the State, it does not overturn national sovereignty, because autonomy . . . conforms to the tradition historically called customary right."[26]

The slogan *todos somos Marcos*, spontaneously popularized after the government launched the manhunt in February 1995, was not only an expression of solidarity with the fugitive Subcommander, but an assertion that his fight was the fight of all Mexicans outside the power elite.

There has been speculation that there is more than one "Marcos," and that he is not Mexican, but Nicaraguan, European or gringo—all of which he has denied. There has also been speculation that he is gay—and he, to his credit, has refused to give the question a "straight" answer. He again joked to a *Houston Chronicle* reporter, "I was working as a waiter in San Francisco until they sacked me for being gay." The pro-government papers seized on the gaffe, with headlines screaming: "MARCOS ADMITS TO BEING HOMOSEXUAL!"²⁷

Marcos responded in his next communiqué with a typically lengthy PS, expounding his brand of radical multiculturalism:

> Marcos is gay in San Francisco, black in South Africa, an Asian in Europe, a Chicano in San Ysidro, an anarchist in Spain, a Palestinian in Israel, an Indian in the streets of San Cristóbal, a gang member in Neza [a Mexico City slum], a rocker in the CU [the DF's University City], a Jew in Germany, an ombudsman in SEDENA [the Defense Secretariat], a feminist in the political parties, a Communist in the post-Cold War era, a prisoner in Cintalapa [a fly-blown town near the Chiapas–Oaxaca border], a pacifist in Bosnia, a Mapuche in the Andes, a teacher in the CNTE, an artist without gallery or portfolio, a housewife alone on a Saturday night in any neighborhood of any city anywhere in Mexico, a guerilla in Mexico at the end of the twentieth century, a striker in the CTM, a reporter assigned to filler stories for the back pages, a sexist in the feminist movement, a woman alone on the Metro at 10 pm, a pensioner protesting in the *zócalo*, a *campesino* without land, a fringe editor, an unemployed worker, a doctor without a practice, a rebellious student, a dissident under neoliberalism, a writer without books or readers, and, of course, a Zapatista in the mountains of southeast Mexico. In sum, Marcos is a human being, any human being in the world. Marcos is every minority who is untolerated, oppressed, resisting, exploding, saying "Enough!"²⁸

This spirit stands in contrast to Pancho Villa's xenophobic hatred of the Chinese, and his army's violent attacks on Chinese immigrants.²⁹ The Zapatistas have manifestly learned from the failings of their role models, even if they choose not to speak of those failings for propagandistic reasons.

Zapatista ethnic politics challenge patronizing and racist tendencies on the left. The EZLN's Indian leadership breaks with the tradition of a *ladino* vanguard directing Indian rebellion, which characterized the more traditional Guevarism of Guatemala's URNG, as well as the extremist Maoism of Peru's Shining Path. *Neozapatismo* rejects the orthodox notion of "proletarianizing" Indians and *campesinos*, which has often turned land-based peoples against revolutionaries with disastrous results—the Miskitos in Nicaragua being an obvious example.³⁰ *Neo-zapatismo* affirms the radical notion that indigenous peoples, with adequate resources, can best manage their own lands.

REVOLUTIONARY ECOLOGY *VERSUS* GLOBAL MANAGEMENT

This affirmation is related to Zapatista reinventing of the politics of ecology. The Zapatistas do not use the language of the environmental movement. They state that they want no more ecological reserves in the Lacandon Selva, and view the timber-cutting ban in the Montes Azules Biosphere Reserve as a betrayal: the Indians had been encouraged to settle the jungle when it was viewed as expendable, then sealed off from it when Mexico needed to appease international environmentalists.[31]

But the centrality of land and indigenous identity to Zapatista demands manifests a new ecological ethic. The EZLN's Revolutionary Agrarian Law, part of the code governing all Zapatista territory, calls for breaking up large ranches and estates, expropriating tractors and fertilizers—and preserving all "zones of virgin *selva*."[32] This is a recognition both that the Selva is being destroyed by oligarchically imposed land-poverty, and that the proximity of thriving forests is necessary to keep liberated lands productive.

The besieged Lacandon is a microcosm of dynamics at work in rainforests throughout the hemisphere. In contrast to precepts of "pristine wilderness" preserved within policed boundaries, rendering indigenous peoples invisible, the new *zapatismo* sees the rainforest's dwellers as the protagonists of its protection.

Biosphere Reserves are theoretically designed to incorporate small populations of indigenous peoples, and integrate them into local management.[33] Instead, the Mexican state's globally managed environmental policy only pitted the Highland Maya settlers in the Selva against their cousins, the Lacandons—and made the settlers hostile to the notion of "environmentalism."

The role of transnational corporations and international finance in the creation and management of "debt-for-nature" reserves in Latin America's rainforests has been assailed as a "privatization" of genetic resources and a further erosion of local control.[34] This technocratic environmentalism, imposed from above, contrasts with the radical localism of rainforest struggles such as *neo-zapatismo*, the *empate* movement in Brazilian Amazonia,[35] and the resistance of Indians in Ecuador's Oriente to the rape of their homeland by international oil companies.[36]

Alejandro Toledo Ocampo, a scholar of *campesino* ecology struggles in southern Mexico, poses a "bioimperialism" predicated on "capitalization of nature, and its management and control at the service of the market," against a "biodemocracy" based on "the ecological culture" of land-rooted peoples, "control of resources by local communities," and "restoring the co-evolution of human societies and eco-systems, interrupted, destroyed and fragmented by industrial civilization."[37]

Zapatista ecology is necessarily predicated on revolutionary ambitions. Less radical solutions will continue to pit ecologists against revolutionaries. Zapatista demands for paved roads and transportation to the impoverished Selva communities could result in accelerated destruction of the forest, facilitating further colonization. A more profound transformation would address the inequitable land distribution in the Highlands, which is the driving force behind colonization of the Selva.

VOTAN-ZAPATA

If the new *zapatismo* breaks with ways in which the revolutionary left has replicated the structures it opposes, it also breaks with ways in which Indian culture has adapted to oppression. Many factors which had held back Maya rebellion for centuries were overcome in the matrix of *neo-zapatismo*.

Rivalries and suspicions between Maya ethnicities were eroded by the geographic mobility imposed by the enclosure of traditional lands, with linguistic groups previously isolated in Highland valleys thrown together in the rainforest.

Another factor is oppression of women. In the culture of *cacique* tyranny, women go barefoot as a sign of inferiority, marriages are arranged by village politics with zero regard for their desires, enforced by the ubiquitous threat of violence. The EZLN's Revolutionary Women's Law, instating "severe punishment" for rape and abuse, recognizes and defends the right of women to "participate in the revolutionary struggle in a way determined by their desire and capacity"; to "work and receive a just salary"; to "decide the number of children they will have and care for"; to "participate in the affairs of the community and hold positions of authority"; and "not to be forced into marriage."[38]

The inclusion of the Women's Law was apparently the work of a Tzotzil Insurgent Susana, who organized women in dozens of communities to produce the code, according to an early communiqué. "After the Women's Law was approved unanimously, a Tzeltal man was heard saying, 'The good thing is that my wife doesn't understand Spanish . . .' A female Tzotzil insurgent with the rank of major in the infantry started in at him: 'You're screwed, because we're going to translate it into all of our dialects' . . ."[39]

Neo-zapatismo broke the centuries-long tendency for revolt to be cloaked in the ultimately recuperable form of syncretistic obscurantism. A legacy of rebellion nurtured for five centuries in mystical realms is wedded to a conscious revolutionary analysis; the Maya have become protagonists rather than pawns.

Some of these changes are traced to the influence of the *ladino* cadre which entered the Selva to organize the Indians in the early 1980s. But this cadre was itself influenced by the Indians it sought to organize.

Marcos told a group of young anarchists who journeyed to interview him in Las Cañadas in May 1994 about the cultural cross-fertilization which took place when he and his clique of leftists first arrived to offer military training and political leadership to the Maya:

> In this initial political work, a connection began to take place between the proposals of the guerilla group, the initial group of the EZLN, and the communities . . . There began a confrontation, a relationship of convenience, between two ways of making decisions. On one hand, there was the initial proposal of the EZLN: a completely undemocratic and authoritarian proposal . . . On the other hand there was the indigenous tradition that before the Conquest was a way of life, and that after the Conquest became their only way of surviving . . . making decisions in common about problems that affect the entire community . . .
>
> I want you to understand me; we didn't arrive and say, "It is necessary that the collective and democracy guide us" . . . This wasn't our conception. Our conception was vertical: "What is necessary is a group of strong men and women, with ideological and physical strength . . . to carry out this task." Our conception was that we were few but of high quality. Well, I'm not saying we were of that high quality, but we sure were few.
>
> Finally, I can't say exactly when—it's not something that's planned—the moment arrived in which the EZLN had to consult the communities in order to make a decision . . . A moment arrives in which you can't do anything without the approval of the people with whom you work. It was something understood by both parties: they understood that we wouldn't do anything without consulting them, and we understood that if we did anything without consulting them, we would lose them . . .
>
> When we reflect on this now its isn't a question of "us" and "them"—now "we" are the entire community . . . Strategic decisions have to be made democratically, from below, not from above . . . The Clandestine Committee cannot decide which path the organization is going to follow until every *compañero* is consulted.[40]

While the EZLN make brilliant use of the verbose Subcommander's powerful charisma, they make it clear that he is (at least officially) answerable at all times to the CCRI, that the EZLN reject any form of *caudillo*. The use of ski-masks, according to one early communiqué, was adopted not only for security, but as an equalizing measure, a "vaccine against *caudillismo*."[41]

On the April 10, 1995 commemoration of the martyrdom of Emiliano Zapata, the EZLN issued a communiqué which evoked both Zapata and Votan, the ancient culture hero of the Highland Maya.

Today we again remember the struggle which gave us our name and face. We remember the day in which betrayal killed General Emiliano Zapata when he was struggling for justice. Emiliano died, but not his struggle or his thinking . . . In us, in our weapons, in our covered faces, in our true words, Zapata became one with the wisdom and the struggle of our oldest ancestors. United with Votan, Guardian and Heart of the People, Zapata rose up again to struggle for democracy, liberty and justice for all Mexicans.

The powerful and great monies do not understand why Votan-Zapata does not die, they do not understand why he returns and rises from death to life in the words of true men and women . . .

Today, wisdom says that the indigenous cannot be Votan-Zapata, that there is a foreign step in his walk. With the weapon of betrayal, with sweet and false words, with the threat of their humiliating war, with lies, the powerful want to fell and crush Votan-Zapata . . .

The powerful failed in 1521; dignity is sheltered deep in the hearts of the indigenous, it was nurtured and cultivated, waiting for the time to plant and grow. The betrayal failed in 1919; dignity did not die with the death . . .

Today, lies, betrayals and power return to fail . . . The powerful say that the people of light skin bring bad ideas to the indigenous because they talk to them of struggle against injustice . . . That the indigenous were fine and content with dying as they died of poverty, that by talking of dying to live, the people of light skin brought discontent and disgrace to the indigenous. These gentlemen of money don't understand that when only one color painted the skins of the inhabitants of these lands, they were struggling and fighting for truth. That the struggle for democracy, liberty and justice does not come from one color of skin or from one language; it comes from the land, from our dead who seek a dignified life for their death . . . They can kill us, drive us into the mountains to shut up our voices, make big lies like prisons to hide our truth. But we are all the eternal dead, who died to live. Our voice will continue coming down, through the many people and many paths, from the mountain to the hearts of all Mexican brothers and sisters.[42]

Quetzalcoatl, the Toltec god-king whose myth was linked to the Maya Votan in the Mesoamerican cosmology of sacrifice and sovereignty, was, by tradition, born in the same region, the contemporary state of Morelos, as Emiliano Zapata—the redeemer of Indian and *campesino* dignity. Zapata, like the mythical Quetzalcoatl, was persecuted and betrayed by an illegitimate and tyrannical regime based in Anahuac, the central Valley of Mexico, which he courageously resisted.[43]

Octavio Paz analyzed the original Zapatista movement in *The Labyrinth of Solitude*, noting the pre-Columbian indigenous roots of the *ejido*, Emiliano Zapata's contribution to the Revolutionary order. "When the Zapatistas made the *calpulli* the basic element in our economic and social structure, they . . . affirmed that any political construction, if it is to be truly productive, must derive from the most ancient, stable and lasting part of our national being: the indigenous past."[44]

As soon as this element of the social order was betrayed, the Zapatistas returned. The early Marcos communiqué *The Southeast in Two Winds: A Storm and a Prophecy* (actually written two years before the 1994 revolt) grappled with the post-socialist despair of the revolutionary left, and how hope comes in an echo from Zapata:

There is nothing to struggle for. Socialism is dead. Long live resignation, reformism, modernity, capitalism and a whole list of cruel etceteras. The viceroy and the feudal lords dance and laugh joyfully in their palaces, great and small . . . Radio, television and the newspapers proclaim it, and some ex-socialists, now sensibly repentant, repeat it.

But not everyone listens to the voices of hopelessness and conformity . . . Most, the millions, continue on, not hearing the voice of the powerful and the timid as they are deafened by the lament and the blood that death and misery cry in their ears. But in moments of rest . . . another voice is heard, not the one that comes from above, but the one that the wind brings from below, that is born in the indigenous heart of the mountains, that speaks of justice and liberty, that speaks of socialism, that speaks of hope . . . the only hope in this earthly world. And the very oldest among the old in the communities tell that there was a Zapata who rose up for them, and that his voice sang more than cried, *¡Tierra y Libertad!* And these old ones tell how he didn't die, how he will return. And the oldest of the old ones tell that the wind and the rain and the sun tell the *campesino* when to prepare the earth, when to plant and when to harvest . . . And the old ones say the wind and the rain and the sun are speaking of another form of the earth, that such poverty cannot continue harvesting death, that it is time to harvest rebellion. So say the old. The powerful don't listen, the words don't reach them, deafened by the wizardry that the empires shout in their ears. "Zapata," the youth of the poor repeat. "Zapata" insists the wind, the wind from below, our wind.[45]

The communiqué ends in chilling poetry that draws simultaneously from the Western revolutionary tradition and indigenous Mesoamerican cosmology that tells of the end of our cycle of creation and the coming of the Sixth Sun when the world is tired and worn:[46]

> THE STORM . . . It will be born of the clash of the two winds, it arrives in its time, the kiln of history is stirred. Now the wind from above reigns, soon will come the wind from below, soon the storm will come . . .
> THE PROPHECY . . . When the storm subsides, when the rain and fire again leave the earth in peace, the world will no longer be the world, but something better.[47]

THE CALL TO CIVIL SOCIETY

The obstacles that *zapatismo* faced in 1919 remain, have in fact grown larger, and restrict *neo-zapatismo*'s ability to live up to its own intrinsic demands. The challenge posed by *zapatismo* to the reign of the local oligarchy, the rule of the authoritarian national state, and, ultimately, consolidation of the hemispheric trade bloc, risks unleashing a bloodbath. It is this reality which helped the PRI maintain power in 1994. Fundamentally identical realities across the hemisphere drive the most intransigent and ambitious revolutionary movements to view bloodletting as a ritual cleansing, to adopt the totalitarian structures and ideology conducive to ruthless instrumentality.

For the Zapatistas to remain committed to their profound challenge without betraying their democratic sensitivity will require that local repressive forces, the Mexican state, and foreign powers—principally the US—be constrained by effective, militant and uncompromising civil solidarity with *zapatismo*. The Zapatistas recognize this reality in their call for civil society to take up the struggle, both within Mexico and abroad, for people to find ways to act in their own locales.

The "*ultras*" of Mexico's extreme left criticize the Zapatistas as "armed reformists." The term was also disdainfully used by political analyst Jorge Castañeda, a veteran of the Mexican left drifting fashionably centerward.[48] The Zapatistas inconveniently emerged immediately following Castañeda's declaration that the Latin American revolutionary left was dead in his 1993 book *Utopia Unarmed*.[49]

1   Subcomandante Marcos with Zapatista troops in Las Cañadas of Chiapas, March 1994.
© Joshua Schwartz

2   Indians march in support of the EZLN, San Cristóbal de las Casas, Chiapas, March 1994.
© Joshua Schwartz

3   Peace dialogue with the EZLN in the Cathedral, San Cristóbal de las Casas, March 1994. © Joshua Schwartz

4 Chontal fisher-
man at Campo Sen
oil field, Tabasco,
January 1997.
© Joshua Schwartz

5 Polluted lagoon at Campo Sen,
Tabasco, January 1997.
© Joshua Schwartz

6 Municipal palace rooftop, occupied Zapotec village of San Augustín Loxicha, Oaxaca, November 1998. © Maria Anguera de Sojo

7 Triqui-Mixtec market, Tlaxiaco, Oaxaca, November 1998. © Maria Anguera de Sojo

8   Tarahumara elder Fidel Torres Valdenegro stands by the grave of his son, killed by *narco-caciques*, Coloradas de la Virgen, Chihuahua, May 1998. © Andrew Lichtenstein

9   Guadalupe Rivas Vega, fugitive from *cacique* terror in the Sierra Tarahumara, May 1998.
© Andrew Lichtenstein

10   Opium poppies in the Sierra Tarahumara, May 1998. © Andrew Lichtenstein

11   ERPI fighter in Guerrero, May 1999. © Luz Maria Gonzalez A.

Marcos poked fun at himself and his critics on all sides in a communiqué in which he played the prosecutor at his own political trial:

The *machistas* accuse him of being feminist: guilty
The feminists accuse him of being *machista*: guilty
The Communists accuse him of being anarchist: guilty
The anarchists accuse him of being orthodox: guilty
The reformists accuse him of being an *ultra*: guilty
The *ultras* accuse him of being a reformist: guilty
The "historic vanguard" accuses him of appealing to civil society and not the
    proletariat: guilty
Civil society accuses him of disturbing their tranquility: guilty
The serious accuse him being a joker: guilty
The jokers accuse him of being serious: guilty
The adults accuse him of being a child: guilty
The children accuse him of being an adult: guilty
The orthodox leftists accuse him of not condemning homosexuals and
    lesbians: guilty
The theorists accuse him of being practical: guilty
The practical accuse him of being a theorist: guilty . . .[50]

Neither the *ultras* nor the moderates share the Zapatista faith in the transformative power of self-organized people. But there are millions of Mexicans, indigenous and *mestizo*, rural and urban, who fall between the ultra-left and those who have abdicated revolutionary aspirations.

The EZLN's original eleven demands—"work, land, shelter, food, health, education, independence, freedom, democracy, justice and peace"—became fifteen when dialogue with civil groups organizing the 1995 national *consulta* resulted in the addition of "security, anti-corruption, information and environmental protection."[51]

These demands are not pleas to the government; nor are they visions of future utopia "after the revolution." The Zapatistas are struggling for these demands within the actually existing *human* system, the only system there really is. The demand for land is answered in land occupations. The demand for information and access to media is answered in a network of rebel radio micro-transmitters throughout the Zapatista zones,[52] and indigenous news services like Melel Xojobal that get statements from the most remote jungle settlements immediately posted on the Internet.[53]

The demand for democracy is answered, first of all, by practicing it.

As Bishop Ruiz put it to me, the Zapatistas are seeking a "human modification of the system"—militantly independent of the state, but stopping short of a utopian-apocalyptic call for its imminent destruction; seeking to influence and pressure it in the sense of *wresting* a better deal from it. This was much the same stance of Emiliano Zapata three generations earlier.

The earthquake of 1985, which caused such destruction in Mexico City, was a turning point for Mexico's popular movements. With government resources stretched and mired in the usual corruption, civil society organized almost spontaneously, forming citizen rescue brigades and self-help groups. Since then, Mexico has seen a renaissance of popular movements linked to neither the ruling nor the opposition parties.[54]

Throughout Mexico, but especially in the Indian south, the EZLN uprising sparked a civil revolutionary upsurge. The guerillas served as a catalyst (not a vanguard) for rapidly advancing struggles for land and democracy. The EZLN still seeks to consolidate these into a national movement—*la coyuntura*, or coming together, as it is dubbed.[55]

In Tabasco, in the Tehuantepec, in Tepoztlan, *campesinos* have taken the EZLN's lead in challenging the state, the local authorities and elites, spontaneously spreading the Zapatista vision. Struggles already underway in states and *pueblos* and regions beyond Chiapas were given greater urgency by the 1994 uprising. The Maya of Chiapas had put their lives on the line, and it was immediately perceived that they had done so for all the Indians and *campesinos* of Mexico. It was understood that the most effective solidarity was to raise the level of the local struggles. By seizing land, staging municipal revolts, blockading oil wells, Indians throughout Mexico were paying their own homage to Chiapas.

PART III

THE FLAME CATCHES

11

OIL AND RESISTANCE IN TABASCO

The Chontal Maya Survival Struggle in Mexico's Land of Black Gold

The militant Maya movement in Tabasco, just north of Chiapas on the Gulf of Mexico, lacking sexy ski-masks and rifles, has been overlooked by the world media. Yet the future of Mexico's most lucrative resource is at the heart of the struggle: black gold.

Tabasco is Mexico's most oil-rich region, seen by the ruling elites in the Federal District as strategic to the country's national security and economic future. With US corporations hoping to open the Mexican oil industry under NAFTA—and with Mexico's role as supplier to the US Strategic Reserves—Tabasco is likewise viewed by Washington as vital to US national security.

Tabasco is also Mexico's most water-rich region in an arid and rapidly drying country. As Tabasco's wealth of water is poisoned by breakneck oil exploitation, the Chontal Maya, whose homeland is the state's heart, organize to protect their resources and their future. Joining with local *mestizo campesinos* and fishermen, the Chontal have repeatedly blockaded the oil wells—and met with repression from federal police and army troops.

In early 1997, when I traveled there, demands for reparations for degraded lands and waters had been outstanding for years. So had civil resistance to the political machine of Roberto Madrazo, the state's *PRIista* governor. Madrazo and the state oil monopoly Pemex were unyielding before Chontal and *campesino* demands. In the aftermath of the Chiapas revolt, Tabasco was one of Mexico's most polarized states.

LAND AND WATER *VERSUS* OIL AND BUREAUCRACY

Auldarico Hernández Geronimo, a Chontal poet, was the only *PRDista* of Tabasco's four federal senators, and the PRD's only indigenous senator at that time. He hailed from the *municipio* of Nacajuca, in La Chontalpa, Tabasco's Indian heartland, a region of fertile plains, *pantanos*—wetlands—and rivers that drain slowly north to the Gulf Coast.[1]

At a January 13, 1997 rally in Villahermosa's Plaza de Armas, Auldarico spoke to the assemblage of Indians and *campesinos* who had come in from the countryside: "The Madrazo government is completely corrupt and illegitimate. We know that it took power through electoral fraud. It is violating constitutional rights. It dominates the news media and buys votes. It is responsible for escalating drug addiction, and now must face the conscience of the people in defense of our rights and economy, our hunger for justice and respect for constitutional order. We must build a civil resistance movement throughout the state of Tabasco."

The Villahermosa rally was part of a *plantón*, a campaign of daily protests, which began January 1 to demand release of the thirty-five political prisoners held statewide: mostly Indians and *campesinos* arrested at oil wells on "riot" or "sabotage" charges. Some faced up to twenty years. At least two, both Chontals, were already seventy. Thirteen Nacajuca residents were facing arrest orders.[2]

The Coordinadora de Lucha Social (Coordinator of Social Struggle), representing communities demanding indemnification for despoiled lands, had entered a dialogue with Pemex and the federal government in February 1996, following huge blockades at the oilfields. Nearly a year later, demands were still outstanding for indemnification, a halt to the repression, and a moratorium on moves to privatize Pemex—one of the most controversial issues facing President Ernesto Zedillo.

The Chontal and their allies found themselves on the frontline of Mexico's hottest national debate because of an accident of geography: their homeland sits on a sea of petroleum.

Tabasco is pervaded by a complicated network of pipelines terminating at Puerto Dos Bocas, Pemex's exit port for the region. La Chontalpa, the state's principal agricultural zone, is one of the most heavily impacted—second only to the coastal zone just to the north, once sustained by abundant aquatic resources, now the heavily contaminated nexus of the duct network.

Pemex began operations in Tabasco in the late 1950s. The Ciudad Pemex complex in Macuspana was built, the first *lagunas* drained and rivers dredged for barge traffic. In the valley of the Rio Tonalá, on the Veracruz border, chemical accumulations in the soil quickly reached dangerous levels as waste storage reservoirs overflowed in the rainy season. This valley was the seat of the ancient Olmec "mother culture" of Mesoamerica. The Olmec ruins at La Venta, on the river's east bank, were renowned for their mysterious giant stone heads. The megaliths were relocated 100 kilometers to a Villahermosa city park to make way for Pemex development, an act that evokes Nasser's transplanting of Nubian temples for the Aswan Dam.[3]

But it was in the boom years of the 1970s that expansion from Pemex's stronghold up the coast in Veracruz and Tamaulipas began in earnest. The money flowed in, the cacao and banana industries were eclipsed, sleepy Villahermosa hyperdeveloped—and the Indian, *campesino* and fishing communities found their lands and lives radically altered.[4]

The first impacts were felt on the coast. Boca de Panteones in Cárdenas *municipio*, a narrow opening on the sea, was 15 meters wide before Pemex arrived. This gap in the outer bank regulated salinity levels in Laguna del Carmen and Laguna Machona. Then Pemex opened wells in the *lagunas*. The Boca was widened to 150 meters in 1974 to facilitate sea access to the wells. Subsequent hurricanes blew the damaged *boca* open to over 1.5 kilometers wide. The *lagunas* and hundreds of thousands of acres were inundated with salt water. "An ecosystem was instantly and drastically altered," according to Raymundo Sauri of Villahermosa's Santo Tomas Ecological Association, which supports the indigenous movement.[5]

The development spread east to Campeche in the Yucatan Peninsula, where numerous oil platforms were built off the coast. Campeche's Laguna Pom—since incorporated into the Laguna de Terminos Protected Area—was contaminated, causing extinction of mollusk species local fishermen had harvested for generations.[6]

Tabasco became Mexico's first natural gas producer and second oil producer, after the Campeche sea platforms. Tabasco, which was 30 percent *selva* (rainforest) in 1940, was only 3 percent in 1970 and zero percent in 1990. The *selva* was eaten by ranching and oil.[7]

A 1977 reform to the Regulatory Law of the Mexican Constitution's Article 27 gave Pemex the right to exploration and exploitation on *ejidos* and smallholder lands with only after-the-fact indemnification. Oil wells encroached onto the *ejidos* of La Chontalpa; the Chontals started organizing to defend their lands.[8]

The first *campesino*–fisherman alliance to confront Pemex was the Pacto Ribereño of the late 1970s, which launched over twenty thousand indemnification demands. Pemex paid over $2 million. The pressure prompted government agricultural development programs like the Plan Chontalpa, with World Bank funding—mostly focused on spurring the cattle industry.[9]

But the breakneck petro-development continued.

Wells were drilled within 15 meters of homes; residents woke up at night coughing and vomiting from fumes. Foam appeared on the surface of wells for drinking water. Researchers at Juárez Autonomous University of Tabasco (UJAT) documented the rise of leukemia as a cause of child mortality, from sixth to third place between 1991 and 1995—a thousandfold increase. In 1991, eighty-seven cases were registered in *municipios* with Pemex installations—and only six in Emiliano Zapata, El Triunfo, Balancán and Tenosique, the four without (all in the isolated southeast corner of the state near the Guatemalan border).[10]

Pemex has over a thousand functional gas and oil wells in Tabasco, with twice as many exhausted and thousands more planned or under construction. The company also has fifty-three separation batteries, thirty-one compression stations, eight water-injection plants, three pumping stations, thirteen natural gas collection centers, two petrochemical plants, and a duct network traveling 8,000 kilometers of legal rights-of-way through villages, *ejidos* and *pantanos*. 450,000 barrels leave Puerto Dos Bocas daily, representing 20 percent of Mexico's national production and generating an annual $4.6 billion.[11]

The complex hydrological system at the confluence of the Grijalva and Usumacinta, the two great rivers of the Mexican southeast, covers much of Tabasco and contains a third of Mexico's fresh water.[12] Yet 400,000 Tabasqueños have no access to potable water.[13] In the supermarkets, a bottle of water costs three times more than a bottle of milk.[14]

The Rio Mezcalapa, as the Grijalva is known as it enters Tabasco's lowlands, was the largest to have its course altered by oil development. In 1996, the Secretariat of Agriculture and Hydraulic Resources (SARH) recommended local residents "avoid use of water from the Rio Mezcalapa for human, animal and agricultural consumption."[15]

There is an ever-present risk of explosions. Over eight hundred people have been killed and ten times as many injured in Pemex accidents throughout Mexico since the 1984 San Juan Ixhuatepec disaster left over five hundred dead in a single fiery blast, incinerating a whole *barrio* on the outskirts of Mexico City.[16] Another spectacular Pemex disaster was the sewer explosion which killed over two hundred in Guadalajara in 1992, caused by oil leaking into the lines. Guadalajara's mayor and several Pemex employees faced charges in the debacle.[17] Corrupt Pemex managers routinely purchase equipment below international standards, billing the company for industry-standard and pocketing the difference. The accident rate in Mexico's oil industry is three times the world average.[18]

There is an annual average of fifteen explosions in Tabasco, and as old equipment deteriorates, the situation is getting worse. Many pipes are over twenty years old, and they decay quickly in the moist, tropical climate. There were 73 duct leaks in Tabasco in 1993, 99 in 1994 and 139 in 1995. By March 1996 there had already been 25.[19]

The independent Tabasco Human Rights Committee, CODEHUTAB, was founded in 1990 by the Jesuit Padre Francisco Goitia, whose own home in Platano y Cacao was damaged by a Pemex blast in 1986. Father Goitia testified before the National Human Rights Commission (CNDH) in 1996 that Pemex's "negligence and lack of maintenance" had caused "the death of many people and incalculable damages to homes, fields and rivers."[20]

The indemnification movement was reinvigorated in the 1990s after ambitious-seeming bureaucratic responses failed to deliver. In November 1990, attorney Remigio Ulín denounced Pemex before the CNDH on behalf of Tabasco *campesinos* and fishing communities. Two years later, the CNDH issued Recommendation 100/92, finding Pemex guilty of human rights abuses in Tabasco.[21]

> Nearly 800 hectares, property of *ejiditarios*, *comuneros* and smallholders, have been totally destroyed with hydrocarbon residues. The damage has affected sub-terranean waterways, and domestic wells in the affected zone only produce salt water and are contaminated with hydrocarbons. Diverse species of fish have been extinguished or are in danger of disappearing . . . Much of La Chontalpa has been irreversibly lost, converted into barren land; gastrointestinal illnesses have severely affected the young population of the region and have caused the death of some children, predominantly due to consumption of contaminated water.[22]

The Recommendation called upon Pemex and the government to repair damages to the "*patrimonio*" of *ejiditarios*, *comuneros* and small-holders. It also mandated formation of an Inter-institutional Commission of Attention to Reclamations, dubbed CIAR/100, to coordinate state and federal agencies with Pemex in the restitution.[23] Pemex protested "politicization of a technical problem," generally only paying indemnifications after protests and blockades of oil wells forced their hand.[24]

In 1992, Pemex paid $5.9 million to *campesinos* and fishermen after five thousand marched from Villahermosa to Mexico City for a *plantón* at the CNDH offices. In 1994, the company paid another $3.9 million following blockades at three hundred wells. The agreements stipulated that the indemnified peasants were signing away their rights to demand further payments, even in the event of further deterioration of their lands. And only a fraction of those demanding indemnification were recognized by Pemex.[25]

In 1995, Pemex paid $39.6 million for remedial efforts after more blockades, in addition to $50,000 to maintain and repair oilducts, and a $3 million-a-year environmental review of its Tabasco facilities.[26]

In January 1995, a gasduct near Platano y Cacao exploded again, killing nine people and gravely burning twenty-two, damaging crops and homes.[27] The explosion sparked a new wave of mobilizations. In September 1996—more than a year and a half after the fact—the CNDH released Recommendation 86/96, calling on Pemex and the state and federal government to investigate the causes of the explosion and take measures to avoid environmental damages. The government responded by forming, and funding, yet another commission—the Inter-institutional Commission for Environmental and Social Development (CIMADES).[28]

CIMADES was also supposed to coordinate Pemex, the state government, and federal agencies like the Secretariat of the Environment, Natural Resources and Fisheries (SEMARNAP) and the National Water Commission (CNA). But Andrés Manuel López Obrador, the Tabasco PRD leader who claimed his gubernatorial victory was stolen by Madrazo through fraud, charged CIMADES with doling out jobs and money to buy off opponents and win votes for the PRI. (CIMADES coordinator Juan Molina Becerra was a secretary in Madrazo's gubernatorial campaign.)[29]

"The money was robbed," concurred Raymundo Sauri. "There's no other word. At least half of the money went to buy votes, buy local leaders—the usual PRI game."

THE BLOCKADES OF 1996

The situation came to a head in early 1996. By then there were 63,000 outstanding indemnification demands on Pemex. Of these, Pemex recognized only six thousand.[30]

In January 1996, a Popular Assembly of forty thousand convened by the charismatic PRD militant López Obrador proclaimed Tabasco a "territory in resistance" and announced a statewide campaign of blockades: "In our region, there is misery all around the wells producing Mexico's black gold. We will not allow Pemex to drill a single new well in this state if the company does not cede benefits to the people of Tabasco and pledge to respect and restore our environment."[31]

On January 29, blockades began at Pemex's Campo Sen in Nacajuca, the highest producing oilfield in the state. Authorities mobilized the Mixed Operations Group (BOM), an enforcement unit coordinating federal and state police with army troops. Two thousand Chontals, mostly women, were attacked by full half as many BOM troops on February 7. Helicopters sprayed tear gas. But waves of Chontal protestors re-occupied the sites after the dispersals. Tabasco PRD director Rafael López Cruz was arrested, and López Obrador himself had his head clubbed bloody by police at a blockade of the bridge leading to Campo Sen. The Villahermosa left-opposition *Verdad del Sureste* headline screamed *"Madrazo ¡Fascista!"*[32]

The BOM also broke up blockades at Pemex's El Castaño administrative offices in Cárdenas, arresting fifty. At Pemex's Villahermosa headquarters, company guards attacked protestors demanding to speak to officials. Tree trunks were dragged across Pemex access roads. Newspapers reported a federal arrest warrant had been drawn up for López Obrador, and awaited President Zedillo's orders.[33]

Pemex protestations that the Tabasco contamination "is not a catastrophe" were contradicted by the Federal Prosecutor for Environmental Protection (PROFEPA), which called the ecological situation in the state "extremely grave." Hector Leyva, Pemex's Exploration and Production Subdirector for Region Sur, which includes Tabasco, warned that the blockades were jeopardizing investment in the company. PRI federal legislators accused Tabasco *PRDistas* of "violating the rule of law" through "destabilization and confrontation." Pemex demanded that Auldarico Hernández be expelled from the federal Senate.[34] PRD locals, meanwhile, held solidarity protests at Pemex offices in Sonora, Guerrero and Veracruz.[35]

Nacajuca's PRD municipal government expressed full support for the blockades. Many Nacajuca municipal functionaries were arrested at the actions. PRD officials from Cárdenas *municipio* were arrested by the BOM at El Castaño. Cárdenas *presidente* Hector Muñoz Rodriguez was threatened with federal charges by Pemex for his role in the blockades.[36]

Raymundo Sauri called use of the BOM to break up the blockades "blatantly unconstitutional. There is no war going on here. The army shouldn't be involved in civil law enforcement."

On February 11, the headlines in the *PRIista* press cried *"¡Sabotage!"* as Pemex accused PRD militants of closing the valves at the Caparroso 192 well in the Chontalpa *municipio* of Centla. The Pemex statement read: "Those who have taken the oil installations have assumed a grave responsibility. An accident, or the loss of control at a well, could mean petroleum leaks or uncontrolled gas emissions into the atmosphere, accidents that could put people and property in danger." The PRD leadership denied any sabotage was carried out by party militants.[37]

On February 12, at a special presentation before the federal Chamber of Deputies entitled *Energia 1995–2000*, President Zedillo condemned the blockades, stating, "Nobody has the right to use the energy resources, their exploitation and their development, for personal ends, nor as an instrument of pressure or political quarrels."[38]

Pemex Director General Adrian Lajous Vargas claimed Pemex had lost $8.5 million dollars since the blockades started, about $450,000 (30,000 barrels) a day.[39]

On February 23, *Verdad del Sureste* reported that arrestees held at the Tabasco State Social Rehabilitation Center (CRESET) were being violently attacked by inmates in the pay of prison authorities. Amnesty International called for an investigation into the Tabasco situation.[40]

On March 5, over eight hundred fishermen from the *municipios* of Jalpa de Mendez, Paraiso and Centla blockaded a Jalpa worksite where the Protexa firm was building a Pemex gas duct linking Campo Sen to Puerto Dos Bocas through *lagunas* where they fished.[41]

By mid-March, when the blockades were called off pending negotiations, there had been 102 arrests on riot, sabotage, sedition and criminal association charges. Amnesty International reported that many of the detained were injured and denied medical care. Citing CODEHUTAB, Amnesty stated "they are reportedly being held in appalling conditions, which may amount to cruel, inhuman and degrading treatment."[42]

All the 102 were released by the month's end, following protests by CODEHUTAB. Thirty thousand marched from fishing and farming communities all over Tabasco on Villahermosa's Plaza de Armas in support of the Coordinadora de Lucha Social in the negotiations.[43]

On June 5, Campo Sen was blockaded again for twelve hours in recognition of World Environment Day.[44]

Two weeks later, when President Zedillo visited Tabasco, roads were blocked along his route through the state. The blockades were attacked by *PRIista* gangs with clubs and guns. At Macuspana, state Preventative Police threw gas canisters to break up a roadblock. Campo Sen was yet again occupied by Nacajuca Chontals. La Venta petrochemical plant and Puerto Dos Bocas were both closed by protests. In Centla *municipio*, a caravan on its way to a presidential appearance in the coastal fishing town of Frontera was blocked and had to turn back to Villahermosa— despite gunfire over the heads of the protesting Indians by the *PRIista* guards. Zedillo flew over the blockade in his helicopter. Thirty were wounded and as many arrested in the actions. A bus carrying seats for the presidential audience was burned, and other vehicles were damaged.[45]

Afterwards, state PRD director Rafael López Cruz appeared at a press conference with shell casings and empty gas canisters swept up from the scene of the confrontation.[46]

The accidents continued. On July 27, three explosions rocked the Pemex gas plant in Cactus, Chiapas, just south of the Tabasco line, straddling the Zoque *municipios* of Juárez and Reforma. Pemex claimed seven deaths, but municipal authorities claimed seventeen, with forty-two wounded.[47]

In November 1996 (just three days after another explosion at a Pemex tank in the Federal District's San Juan Ixhuatepec left four dead), an accident at Puerto Dos Bocas killed two workers.[48] On January 25, 1997, a Pemex worker was killed and another gravely injured when a pipeline exploded at Cárdenas.[49]

The year 1997 began with the campaign to free the thirty-five political prisoners. On January 20, marchers stormed the entrance to the governor's palace overlooking Villahermosa's Plaza de Armas, demanding that Madrazo come down to address their demands—nearly provoking a confrontation with the black-clad state police guarding the building. Speakers at the PA system in the Plaza pleaded for nonviolence, and the situation de-escalated just in time.[50]

On April 8, 1997, *mestizo campesinos* blockaded Campo Samaria in Cunduacan *municipio* to press indemnification demands. They were attacked by BOM troops who threw gas canisters and arrested eight, including women, children and elders.[51]

LA CHONTALPA IN RESISTANCE

I found Mercedes Gordillo at the PRD office in Nacajuca, a quiet village on the verdant plains in the very heart of La Chontalpa. Gordillo was the Nacajuca representative of the Coordinadora de Lucha Social, which shared the PRD's modest office—a few typewriters, party posters protesting the pending Pemex privatization. The Coordinadora was openly supported by the Nacajuca municipal government. The *municipio* had then been in PRD hands for nine years. When I arrived with my photographer Joshua Schwartz to see the Sen oilfields, Gordillo took us to the municipal palace and filled out requisition forms to borrow a vehicle. It turned out to be a police car, and soon we were driving through the fields and swamps in a shiny new Nissan patrol cruiser—one of several ironically supplied to the *municipio* by the state government it militantly opposed. A representative from the municipal presidency joined us.

"The *municipio* gets nothing from the oil," said Gordillo. "Madrazo and his friends get the benefits. There is only misery for us from the oil—it destroys our land, our *campo*, and brings no benefit. The land doesn't produce like it did before the oil."

Gordillo cited Article 115 of the Mexican Constitution, claiming that Pemex's development of the region without local consultation is an unconstitutional violation of municipal autonomy.

"A great social contradiction exists here," he said as we passed mud-and-thatch homes with no indoor plumbing. "This is one of the richest zones of the country."

Many little rivers wound through the plains, flowing languidly toward the *lagunas* and *pantanos* to the north. "There are very few fish in the rivers now," said Gordillo. "The water is full of Pemex's wastes." Are the fish still eaten?, I asked. "Of course. The people here have no other manner of living."

We crossed the bridge over the Rio Calzada toward the oilfields, and left the pavement behind. Federal army trucks followed us into Campo Sen. Oil rigs towered over *lagunas* traversed with pipelines and surrounded by open tar pits, bubbling and black. Fishermen skimmed back and forth along waterways in hand-carved *cayucas*. Egrets and herons passed overhead. Pemex bulldozers and tank trucks rumbled back and forth, raising dust.

Chontals still fish in the *lagunas* of what is now Campo Sen, and are among those demanding indemnification. Discovered in 1984, Campo Sen had fifty-six wells—though few were as big as the two giant rigs that dominated the lush, scarred landscape.

When we passed the BOM outpost guarding the oilfields—a permanent fixture since the blockades—our police cruiser was stopped by army troops. Unimpressed by our vehicle, they questioned us and demanded our papers. They wrote down our names before finally waving us on. The BOM vehicles and olive-drab tent-barracks were painted in big white letters with the names of the participating agencies—PGR (Prosecutor General of the Republic), PJF (Federal Judicial Police), SEDENA (National Defense Secretariat). It was clear that this federal presence was openly at odds with the local, Indian *municipio*.

"We have been protesting for eight years and we still have no response from the government," said Gordillo as we drove on from the BOM camp.

Sen was producing 40,000 barrels daily of Olmeca crude, earning the Mexican state $600,000 a day. Adan Magaña Gómez, the *PRDista* municipal president of Nacajuca, had told *Proceso* the *municipio* received just 15 million pesos a year from the federal government—about what Campo Sen generates in two days.[52]

Four of Tabasco's seventeen *municipios* were then PRD-controlled. Of these, two were in La Chontalpa: Jalpa and Nacajuca. But all of La Chontalpa was a PRD stronghold, thanks to popular discontent over the region's industrial colonization.

Our next excursion was to visit Hector Sánchez de La Cruz of Simón Sarlat in Centla, just to the north of Nacajuca. A PRD militant and veteran Pemex worker, Sánchez used his degree from Villahermosa's Technical Agronomy Institute to assess damages throughout Tabasco with the Coordinadora de Lucha Social. But he could mostly be found in Simón Sarlat, where we arrived unannounced, as his home has no phone. He was watching kiddie movies on TV with his children, and greeted us with a broad smile, immediately offering fresh oranges while his wife made us coffee. I could tell he was impressed that we had come to his turf; when we were introduced a few days earlier in Villahermosa by Raymundo, his greeting had been perfunctory and almost suspicious.

Hector Sánchez was born into the struggle. Simón Sarlat is on the Rio González, near Laguna Santa Anita. Pemex opened operations there in 1970. The wells of Campo Caparroso now dot the *pantanos* and *ejidos* outside Simón Sarlat. "The contamination is growing every day," said Hector as we crossed the swamps and fields toward the rig looming over the landscape.

The Caparroso 5 well in the middle of Simón Sarlat's *ejido* ruptured in December 1996, spilling oil into the *pantano* for ten hours. The Chontal villagers blockaded the road to Caparroso 5 for a week following. Tension grew as the area was sealed off by police and army troops.[53]

"Before Pemex came, we were poor, but we could eat," said Hector. "We were poor because we had no money, but we had *maíz*, *frijol*, *yucca*, *camote*, *pescado*, *tortuga*. Now the turtles are all gone. There isn't one left. There are still fish, but few and small."

Local fish include the bass, or *robalo*, and the *pejelagarto*, distinct to the region, and so named for its gator-like snout. The fish decline is due less to oil spills than to sedimentation of the rivers and *lagunas* by dredging of canals through them.[54]

Hector reflected on how Simón Sarlat had changed—for better and worse—since his childhood. "When I was a kid there was no electricity here. People went to sleep at seven and woke up at three in the morning to work their *milpa* or fish in the river. There was abundance then. We lived without money. My father would take *maíz* to Frontera to trade for clothes. We ate our own *maíz*—we had *pozol*, *tortillas*. We got good and fat. The land my father worked is still in our family, but it doesn't produce like it did twenty years ago."

In addition to the *ejido*, Hector's family worked the mixed orchard on his father's private smallholding, adjacent to the *ejidal* wetlands surrounding Caparroso 5. The orchard is within a kilometer of the rig, and Hector claimed that the roads Pemex built through the *pantano* blocked drainage, saturating the soil. "Our mango and orange trees are dying because of the flooding," he says.

Auldarico Sánchez Valencia, Hector's father, who accompanied us to the orchard, agreed. "*Mandarinos, guanabana, coco—todo murio.*"

Most of the trees still bore fruit—but Auldarico said the harvest diminishes each year. Standing by one completely dead tree, he said, "The avocado is the most affected by the water retention. It's all gone. *No hay.*"

"We are waiting for indemnification from Pemex," said Hector. "But they say our land is not affected."

ALLIANCE-BUILDING FROM THE COAST TO THE HIGHLANDS

The Chontals have forged an alliance with neighbors affected by Pemex contamination—the *mestizo* fishermen in the coastal zone to the north, and the Chol Maya and Zoque *campesinos* in the foothills of the Chiapas Highlands to the south.

At Laguna Mecoacan near Puerto Dos Bocas in Paraiso, the economy of the local fishing communities has been devastated. Between 1991 and 1993, the oyster catch in Laguna Mecoacan dropped from a daily seven thousand per fisherman to practically nothing, and the drop in *mojarra* (porgie) was nearly as precipitous. Those same years saw numerous oil spills in the *laguna* and surrounding *pantanos*. The nearby ocean waters have been fouled by leaks from pipelines connecting Puerto Dos Bocas to the Campeche marine platforms. Pemex also widened the Rio Cuxcuchapa in the 1970s, lowering salinity in Laguna Mecoacan beyond that necessary to sustain the shellfish. The shellfish decline was documented in a 1992 study by the federal Secretariat of Fisheries. Pemex claimed the decline was due to an outbreak of the disease *Perkinsus marinus*.[55]

In 1993, a thousand Mecoacan fishermen and their families marched cross-country to Villahermosa for a *plantón* in the Plaza de Armas, and fishermen blockaded Puerto Dos Bocas. The next year, Pemex paid $2,500 to each of the 530 members of the four fishing cooperatives using the laguna—once again on condition that they sign away their right to press for further damages in the future. But promises to rehabilitate the barrier reef and relocate the nearby smokestacks that burn off excess gas over the *laguna* have seen no action.[56]

Campesino lands straddling the Tabasco-Chiapas border to the south of La Chontalpa first mobilized against Pemex in 1962, when construction of a gasduct linking Chiapas with Tabasco's Ciudad Pemex plant blocked irrigation drainage channels, flooding *ejidos*. In May 1978, the Chiapas *municipio* of Juárez demanded indemnification for the contamination of local waters, which had resulted in the death of twenty-six head of cattle, and the illness of scores more. This Zoque zone of northwest Chiapas saw numerous protests against Pemex in the late 1970s, when local residents first joined with Tabasqueños in the Pacto Ribereño.[57]

The Chol territory of the Highland foothills is intercepted by the state line. Chol communities north of the line have formed a Tabasco Indigenous Forum to participate in the Zapatista autonomy struggle. The army has beefed up its presence in Tabasco's southern *municipios* of Teapa and Macuspana (usually under guise of drug enforcement) every time the dialogue has broken down in Chiapas. At a Macuspana protest for liberation of political prisoners in May 1996, Chols marched with ski-masks and wooden mock rifles.[58]

Sen. Auldarico Hernández and Raymundo Sauri joined Chontal representatives to attend the EZLN's Aguascalientes conference in 1994. And in July 1996, Chontals attended the EZLN-called Forum on Reform of the State, held at the Convento del Carmen in San Cristóbal de Las Casas.[59]

The PRD leadership has been ambivalent on committing to solidarity with the Zapatistas, torn between the party's popular base and electoral aspirations. While the EZLN built an alliance with the Chiapas PRD following the contested 1994 elections, Marcos has criticized the national PRD leadership for seeking an "impossible political 'center.'"[60] Marcos met with PRD leader López Obrador at the Convento del Carmen. After discussion of a possible "alliance" with the Zapatistas, the PRD leadership agreed in principle to a "formal relationship" with the rebels.[61]

Another feature of the struggle in Tabasco is an at least formal commitment to nonviolence by the PRD and Coordinadora, and even a reverence for Mohandas Gandhi in some communities. Rafael Landerreche of the Latin American pacifist group Servicio Paz y Justicia (SERPAJ) is among those who have worked to instill this sensitivity in the Tabasco movement. "We work with the PRD, but we are not in the PRD," Landerreche told me, admitting that the militants have sometimes responded to provocation in less than Gandhian fashion—as when the bus was burned on the road to Frontera during Zedillo's 1996 visit.

The movement is fundamentally about democracy, said Landerreche, which is what unites the tendencies and ethnicities. "There can be no defense of the environment without the participation of the indigenous people who live there."

LA CENTLA: BIOSPHERE OR PETROSPHERE?

Simón Sarlat and the Caparroso oilfields are just outside La Centla Biosphere Reserve—the broad wetlands at the confluence of the Grijalva and Usumacinta, the most remote area of Tabasco, teeming with bird and aquatic life. An important winter feeding ground for migratory birds from North America, La Centla was declared a protected area by President Salinas in 1992, and shortly received UN recognition.[62]

But Pemex actually has numerous oil and gas wells *within* the borders of La Centla. The Chontal who live and fish within the reserve—the most marginal people in Tabasco—claim that Pemex's dredging of La Centla's canals is leading to siltation of the *lagunas* and declining fish populations.

La Centla is among several biosphere reserves declared by Salinas as part of his agenda to further integrate Mexico into global institutions. He also had an eye toward incorporating Tabasco—which, with its ubiquitous oil infrastructure, is often less than picturesque—into the Ruta Maya "ecotourism" program which has boomed in Chiapas and the Yucatan.[63]

La Centla still attracts few tourists because of its inaccessibility. It is divided into three sections—a "buffer zone" forming an outer ring around two high-biodiversity "nuclear zones" at the heart of the reserve. Permanent settlements, roads and high-impact exploitation are ostensibly barred in the nuclear zones, which are separated by a strip of buffer zone that follows the Rio Usumacinta, dotted with little Chontal settlements. These Chontals fish and farm on *ejidos* in the nuclear zones. Nuclear Zone One is to the south of the Usumacinta; Nuclear Zone Two to the north. The reserve abuts the Campeche border and the Laguna de Terminos Protected Area to the east. Together, the two reserves make up Mexico's largest expanse of wetlands and mangroves.[64]

The Chontal, who have depended on the waters of La Centla for millennia, charge that it is Pemex operations rather than biodiversity that the reserve protects. Humberto Leon Garcia, a leader of Ejido Lázaro Cárdenas in Nuclear Zone Two, met us when we arrived at his settlement of Chichicastle. He and his fellow *ejiditarios* live in the cluster of huts clinging to the north bank of the Usumacinta, near the very center of the reserve. He bitterly resented the presence of Pemex within the reserve's borders. "Our struggle to have money depends on the fish," he said. "The wealth of the oil doesn't help us. It's the wealth of the ecology, the *fauna*, that interests us. If they connect the wells, it will bring us only misery."

Most of the wells in La Centla were already drilled when Salinas declared the reserve, but those at Ejido Lázaro Cárdenas had still not been connected because of local protest. "We don't even have a decent road to our villages. This road is useless," said Humberto, indicating the gulley-ridden strip of rock and dirt that follows the Usumacinta from Frontera. Gasoline for river transport to Frontera from Chichicastle costs more than the Chontal fishermen make in a month. "The government is a bunch of bandits," Humberto concluded.

We had come to Chichicastle with Hugo Ireta, a PRD activist working with the Chontals of La Centla. The reserve merely allows the Mexican state to score points with global environmentalists while the real activity in La Centla is invisible to the outside world, he asserted. "The buffer area is supposed to protect the reserve—and Pemex is in the nuclear zone."

Our little outboard headed from Chichicastle into Nuclear Zone One. A shallow, narrow canal leading south from the Usumacinta finally opened onto the wide Laguna Chichicastle. Across the expanse of sun-drenched water, Chontal fishermen cast lines and nets from *cayucas* and outboards. On the banks, thick with vegetation, other waterways led to other *lagunas*, other *ejidos*—and Pemex's Campo Usumacinta.

We turned down the channel to Campo Usumacinta, which the local fishermen had blockaded in June 1993. Under the blazing sun, a Pemex crew was working on a huge barge hauling a piece of drilling equipment, pumping up earth and water as it re-perforated old wells in the *pantano*. Noise and diesel fumes filled the air. The canal was brown and churning.

The canal was dotted with small natural gas wells—some with herons lazing atop them. The pipes from each well merged at Campo Usumacinta—where there was a cluster of still more wells, amounting to some twenty-five. The gas was sent to an on site separation battery, and then piped to Ciudad Pemex and processed for domestic electricity generation. *Ejidos* near Campo Usumacinta have had their waters contaminated with salts and heavy metals from the battery, according to a 1993 PROFEPA report.[65]

There were other Pemex camps in the reserve. Campo Hormiguero, also in Nuclear Zone One, has thirty gas wells and a separation battery. At Ejido Lázaro Cárdenas in Nuclear Zone Two, another thirty gas wells were waiting to go on line. Sector Petrolera Los Naranjos includes the Gualas exploratory oil rig, just within the buffer zone (and just down the Frontera road from Simón Sarlat). The nearby Escuintle oil rig was also waiting to go on line. Campo Los Almendros, also in the buffer zone, had ten functioning oil wells, and several others waiting to go on line. Altogether there were 109 wells in the reserve.[66]

A 1993 report by the Commission for the Development of the Petrol Zones of the State of Tabasco (yet another "interinstitutional" body called to study the problem) in response to an indemnification request by Ejido San José found that "the levels of grease and acid detected at Campo Usumacinta, even if high, are not attributed to petrol activities because the wells located in the area are producers of gas."[67] But Hugo Ireta charged that the area is affected by the nearby Almendros oil wells.

In October 1993, PROFEPA found that Caparroso 45, just across the Frontera road from the buffer zone, was in violation of the General Law of Ecological Equilibrium through contamination of waters with "dangerous residues." There was no fine—only a "recommendation" to correct the damage.[68] Hugo denied that there was any real oversight: "The judgement is on paper only. It's the same government—Pemex and the Prosecutor."

Back in Villahermosa, I paid a visit to Fabian Dominguez Cervantes, Tabasco subdelegate at SEMARNAP, which administrates the biosphere reserves. He said he was disturbed about Pemex in La Centla. "Under the decree creating the reserve there can be no public or private development activities in the nuclear zones. There can only be development in the buffer zone, and then only with an impact statement. But the wells already existed when the reserve was declared."

He also had a sort of solution to the contradiction. "SEMARNAP has a proposal to redraw the border so the Pemex camps will not be in the nuclear zone."

He also objected to the dredging of channels to *lagunas* by Chontal fishing communities in La Centla, which have sometimes themselves contracted heavy equipment with government credit.

He did not deny that Pemex may seek to open new wells within La Centla. "Pemex may have plans to expand in the reserve, but SEMARNAP is in opposition to this and we will maintain our vigilance."

In 1996, the Gualas exploratory well was opened in La Centla's buffer zone—and two exploratory wells opened across the Campeche border in Laguna de Terminos Protected Area. Pemex engineers are said to believe Gualas has more oil than Sen.

A 1996 internal Pemex map of the region, covering the Gualas and Escuintle camps in the western part of La Centla's buffer zone and the Caparroso fields just outside the zone, is entitled "Program of Perforation." It shows several spots marked "locations to perforate in 1998–2010."[69]

THE MADRAZO REGIME

The crisis over Pemex's degradation of indigenous lands was compounded by that over the legitimacy of the Roberto Madrazo government. Acquiescing in the national elite's super-exploitation of Tabasco's petroleum, local elites exploit the state's strategic geographic position as a transfer point for cocaine coming up Central America's Caribbean coast and across the Yucatan toward northern markets. As revelations of the Madrazo regime's corruption unfolded after his election, the Mexican press naturally dubbed the mess Tabascogate.[70]

On January 19, 1995, *PRDistas* occupying Villahermosa's Plaza de Armas to protest Madrazo's purported electoral fraud the previous year were violently attacked by *PRIistas*, resulting in hours of street battles—and some of the few international headlines the Tabasco situation has received.[71] A quiet but grisly wave of repression followed throughout the state. In May, the bodies of two PRD militants were found on the banks of the Rio Usumacinta in Jonuta, shot in the head and tortured.[72]

Three months after the January violence, the PRD organized a forty-day march from Villahermosa to Mexico City to press the fraud claims. The march grew to several thousand by the time it reached the Federal District. The protestors set up an encampment outside the Chamber of Deputies. On June 5, shortly after their arrival, some twenty boxes of documents were anonymously delivered to the camp in the middle of the night: original records detailing Madrazo campaign expenditures, totalling more than $70 million. In a state of 3 million—with a $4 million legal spending limit—Madrazo had spent more than Bill Clinton did to get elected president of the US. Only $1 million had been officially reported by the Madrazo campaign. After furious photocopying, the protestors handed the documents over to the PGR. The PRD demanded that charges be brought, and the PGR was forced to launch an investigation.[73]

Madrazo launched a suit against the PGR and Zedillo, charging interference with state affairs. In August, Madrazo claimed he was kidnapped by federal agents and held for several hours outside Mexico City. The PGR denied the claim, but the fact that the PGR was then headed by Zedillo's token cabinet member from the opposition—Antonio Lozano Gracia of the National Action Party—helped loan Madrazo's claims credibility.[74]

The federal Finance Secretariat (the "Hacienda"), at behest of the PGR, opened an investigation of Madrazo's connections to the notorious Carlos Cabal Peniche— then on the lam in Europe. A hard-charging, ruthless ultra-yuppie on the make, Cabal at forty had been the single biggest pillar of the Tabasco economy after Pemex. Then his financial empire crashed under the weight of its own corruption just after Madrazo's election, mired in money-laundering and international intrigues.[75]

The records mysteriously delivered to the protestors documented over $4 million illegally transferred through Cabal Peniche's Banco Unión, Lomas Mil and San Carlos World Trade companies to Madrazo's political machine. Madrazo accused the PGR of "fabricating" the links with Cabal.[76]

But Madrazo could no more have consolidated his machine without the connivance of Cabal than without the acquiescence of the "petrol mafia." By 1993, when Madrazo started running for governor, Cabal controlled 50 percent of all private investment in Tabasco.[77]

Then, in September 1994, mere weeks after Madrazo's election, Cabal's Grupo Financiero Cremi-Unión (Mexico's fifth largest financial group) was seized by the Hacienda, and the PGR issued a warrant for Cabal's arrest. He immediately fled the country—and Madrazo immediately disavowed associations with him.[78]

Cabal was snared on regulation-skirting in his elaborate shell games—loaning himself money from his own banks through dummy companies, in order to buy other businesses and expand his empire. Eleven officers of Banco Unión's leasing division, Arrendora Pragma, were arrested. Trading in Banco Cremi, the only public company in the Cabal empire, was suspended by federal authorities.[79]

Cabal's banks, with combined assets of over $11 billion, were popular among Mexico's scandal-ridden political elite. Current and former government officials filled the boards of his companies. He co-owned a Florida shrimp importer with Federico de la Madrid, son of the former president and a frequent visitor to his Tabasco plantations.[80]

Cabal's empire included thousands of acres of prime agricultural land through-out Mexico's southeast, Villahermosa's *El Sureste* newspaper and an interest in the Camino Real luxury hotel chain. But his real prize was Del Monte Fresh Produce, the world's third largest fresh fruit trader. In 1992 Cabal purchased the Florida-based enterprise for $550 million, then made a down-payment on a $277 million buy-out of the San Francisco-based Del Monte Foods.[81] The two divisions were separated when parent company RJR Nabisco sold Del Monte off to pay back junk-bond investors after a 1989 $25 million hostile take-over by corporate raiders Kohlberg, Kravis.[82] Before the break-up, Del Monte was a global agribusiness titan, with holdings throughout Central America,[83] and Cabal aspired to reunite these sprawling properties under his ownership.

Cabal was already mired in the scandal surrounding the collapse of Pakistan's Bank of Credit and Commerce International (BCCI)—top laundromat of Panama's Noriega dictatorship, Colombia's cocaine cartels and terrorist organizations world-wide. Cabal received loans through BCCI to expand his Tabasco shrimp and banana interests. One BCCI-infused New York merchant bank, Eastman, sued Cabal after he defaulted on one such loan. Cabal was also sued in Manhattan federal court by Prince Khalid bin Maffouz, Saudi director of the BCCI, over another $70 million loan. Manhattan District Attorney Robert Morgenthau probed Cabal in his BCCI case, but ultimately cleared him—thereby freeing Morgan Stanley and Co. to finance his Del Monte deal. Eastman then dropped its suit when he offered the bank a share in Del Monte.[84]

Cabal's interests in US fruit and shrimp importers point to plans to turn Tabasco into a cocaine export hub and build a Tabasco Cartel to rival those in the border cities of Tijuana, Juárez and Matamoros. Cabal's Tabasco banana plantations were implicated in drug running when two cargo trucks from his San Carlos trading company were caught transporting cocaine. Cabal predictably denied any involvement in the incidents.[85]

Cabal's "synergy" strategy was an incestuous web: Banco Unión lent money to his plantations to supply Del Monte, which then expanded its business to other product lines to which Banco Unión would lend more money. Even while he was committing fraud at Cremi-Unión, the federal Nafinsa development bank loaned him over $130 million to buy Del Monte Fresh Produce from the London bankruptcy court which had taken it over from its financially troubled former owners.[86]

Cabal's Banco Cremi was fingered by Mexican, US and Swiss investigators as a conduit for laundering at least $200 million in drug cartel protection money by Raúl Salinas, the imprisoned brother of ex-President Carlos Salinas. Investigators traced Raúl's network from Citibank's Mexico City branch to accounts at the financial titan's New York headquarters in the name of Salinas-owned dummy companies in the Cayman Islands—and from there to secret Swiss accounts. The checks deposited in Citibank were drawn on Banco Cremi, initial depository of the cartel grease.[87]

Mexican investigators also explored claims that Cabal Peniche had established a secret political fund for the Salinas brothers with laundered narco-dollars. They sited Cabal's "godfather" in the federal apparatus as Emilio Gamboa Patrón, communications secretary under Salinas (and personal secretary to Miguel de La Madrid). Cabal launched his financial empire in the Salinas years, when he purchased privatized state banking assets to start Cremi-Unión.[88]

The former Mexico chief for Interpol was dispatched to Europe to hunt down the elusive Cabal, who continued to manage the remnants of his empire while dancing from plush hotel to high-security mansion in Spain, France and Monaco, his New York lawyer wiring him money from his JP Morgan escrow account. At least one property was seized by Spanish authorities, and Swiss authorities froze $10 million of his funds.[89] The Mexican government was also trying to unload the majority interest in Del Monte Fresh Produce it seized from Cabal, and hired Shearson Lehman of New York to manage the sale.[90]

Closing this dark circle, Mexican investigators claimed Raúl Salinas turned to Citibank at the suggestion of his friend Carlos Hank Rohn, son and business manager of Mexican billionaire Carlos Hank González, who was agriculture secretary under Salinas. The family's network of businesses is under the umbrella of Grupo Hank—of which Roberto Madrazo is a member.[91]

INTRIGUE AND CLAMPDOWN

The most embarrassing moral challenge to the Madrazo regime was launched by the *barrenderos*—Villahermosa's municipal street cleaners who risked death in a hunger strike in 1997 to press their labor demands.

Madrazo had 360 *barrenderos* fired in 1995 in retaliation for protests against low pay and unhealthy working conditions. Aquiles Magaña Garcia, the Chontal *barrendero* leader, was arrested on numerous occasions for such crimes as "stealing water" from the municipal government. In the fall of 1996, two *barrenderos* started a public hunger strike in Mexico City, erecting encampments outside the Chamber of Deputies and CNDH offices.[92] Several other *barrenderos* joined the strike later, and received a letter of solidarity from the EZLN.[93] After such mediagenic actions as occupying the Chamber of Deputies in their underwear, on January 19, 1997 the strikers had their encampment broken up by riot police, and were forcibly hospitalized. The two original hunger strikers, Venancio Jiménez Martínez and Luis Magaña Alamilla, were near death, having refused nourishment for almost a hundred days. Madrazo finally blinked, agreeing to a compromise in which some of the fired *barrenderos* were rehired, and the others granted severance benefits.[94] Another crisis had passed.

Much to Madrazo's chagrin, as soon as the *barrenderos* ended their protest encampment, nearly a hundred Tabasco sugar cane workers immediately started a new vigil in Mexico City's *zócalo*, demanding government action on the illegal withholding of their benefits—which they charge were embezzled by the local union bureaucracy.[95]

Among the thirty-five claimed by the Tabasco opposition as political prisoners were six Chontals from Buenavista, in *municipio* Centro, accused of burning buses during a conflict between two rival lines linked to the political parties; six ex-Pemex workers accused of "sabotage" in an occupation of Pemex's regional headquarters; Villahermosa street vendors; *campesino* leaders from the countryside and even six former state police officers arrested at protests for a better labor contract. Some, such as Iturbide Villamil—leader of the street merchants, who protested for their right to public space and were arrested on the usual "riot" and "sabotage" charges—have held prison hunger strikes. In response to Villamil's hunger strike, Madrazo told the press in January 1997, "there are no political prisoners" in Tabasco.[96]

Throughout the crisis, Tabasco's villages have been periodically shaken by repressive violence—the seeds, CODEHUTAB fears, of the kind of dirty war which obtains in Chiapas. In February 1996, just after the Pemex blockades, state Preventative Police in Macuspana fired on PRD protestors, killing one, Oscar Hernández

Arellano—the fifth *PRDista* killed in political violence in the *municipio* under the *PRIista presidente* Alexis Falcon Aguirre. Oscar's two brothers were also wounded in the incident.[97] In April 1996, thirty were wounded in a confrontation between PRD militants and a *PRIista* gang in Nacajuca.[98]

To counter the movement for his resignation, the Madrazo machine formed a "Civil Society" group which, purporting to be independent, was actually an appendage of the Tabasco PRI. In June 1996, when President Zedillo visited, "Civil Society" called a big march in Villahermosa against the Pemex blockades and for "social peace," with *de rigueur* attendance by virtually the state's entire formidable bureaucracy. Madrazo proclaimed to the press that "everything is tranquil" in Tabasco.[99]

Attacks on the press escalated. The offices of Villahermosa's one thin but un-compromising opposition paper, *La Verdad del Sureste*, were fire-bombed in May 1996, damaging a printing press.[100] Villahermosa's independent radio XEVA was forcibly taken over by *PRIista* gangs during the popular morning news analysis program *Telereportaje* three times in 1996.[101]

The most puzzling intrigues surrounded the supposed presence in Tabasco of Mexico's new and enigmatic guerilla group, the Popular Revolutionary Army (EPR), which poses itself as more orthodox than the EZLN.

On August 28, 1996, masked gunmen claiming to be *EPRistas* took over the radio station of the Tabasco Radio and Television Commission (CORAT) to read a proclamation addressed to the federal government.[102] A subsequent state police search, centered on La Chontalpa, turned up EPR propaganda in homes in outlying Nacajuca *pueblos*, including a banner reading "¡*Vivan los campesinos pobres!*"[103]

On September 2, Madrazo announced that four Tabasco *EPRistas* had been arrested: José Garcia Marín (code-named "El Calao"), Juan Gómez Mendez ("El Cepillin"), Francisco Alfaro Flores and Salomon González Caceres. All were said to have been caught with "subversive" EPR propaganda. They all denied involvement in the CORAT take-over, and claimed the material was planted. Most embarrassingly, they insisted they were all PRI militants. "It's a lie that I'm a guerilla, I'm *PRIista!*" cried "El Calao" to reporters.[104]

In the following edition of *La Verdad del Sureste*, an article on the accused El Calao's links to Madrazo himself was published—with a picture of the two men together! The presumed "El Cepellin" lurked in the background of the photo. El Calao/Garcia Marín apparently worked on Madrazo's 1991 campaign for federal deputy in the Nacajuca *pueblo* of Ocuiltzapotlan. PRD deputy Nicolas Geredia produced a 1994 letter from Madrazo to Garcia Marín, soliciting his aid in organizing a Tabasco campaign stop for then-presidential candidate Ernesto Zedillo.[105]

The EPR, for its part, issued a communiqué stating: "those who have been detained by the *PRIistas* have no relation whatsoever with our political-military structure."[106]

The four were released on bail, but still faced charges. The affair raised eyebrows among those who suspected the EPR of being manipulated by the party-state for provocation purposes.[107]

These bizarre contradictions did not slow the militarization of Tabasco in response to the supposed EPR threat. The Villahermosa-based Thirtieth Military Zone installed roadblocks along the Chiapas border and initiated patrols in Nacajuca. State police interrogated residents in Ocuiltzapotlan. Federal police beefed up security at Puerto Dos Bocas.[108]

The Madrazo corruption put the ecological destruction in a stark light. Sewage treatment is virtually nonexistent in Tabasco, with municipal waste contaminating the Grijalva and other waterways. The $70 million Madrazo spent on his campaign could have paid for a water treatment plant in each *municipio*.[109]

In 1996, the state government cut electricity to sixty communities across Tabasco which had declared a state of "civil resistance," refusing to pay electric bills, a protest of high rates despite the sacrifice of their lands to the energy sector. These communities joined the widespread *campesino* electricity strike in Chiapas, strongest in the Grijalva Valley where Indian lands have been sacrificed to hydro-power.[110]

The National Supreme Court of Justice turned down Madrazo's challenge to the federal Tabascogate probe.[111] President Zedillo at first broached the possibility of calling for new elections in Tabasco, but backed down from this position.[112] The campaign spending limit is a state law, so the PGR remanded that investigation back to Madrazo's own state prosecutor—which, in July 1996, predictably cleared him. Days later, the Hacienda said it would not seek charges against Madrazo for his links to Cabal Peniche. López Obrador protested the Hacienda exoneration as "an order of the Executive."[113]

The PGR's own investigation into the Cabal money machine remained nominally open. The PGR opened an investigation of Madrazo campaign finance secretary Oscar Saenz Jurado, suspected of laundering dirty money through campaign contributions. But the PRI national leadership insisted Madrazo was the legitimate constitutional governor for his full six-year term, ending, conveniently enough, in 2000.[114] Madrazo was soon openly angling for the presidency.[115]

STEALTH PRIVATIZATION OF PEMEX?

Lurking behind the Tabasco turmoil is the pending privatization of Pemex, a potent symbol of national pride since Lázaro Cárdenas seized the foreign oil operations in

1938. With the banks, telecoms, rail lines, sea terminals, airports, TV networks and other state assets already privatized,[116] Pemex is the most precious plum remaining to fall into corporate hands. Mexico is the world's fourth oil producer, and Tabasco is the country's most productive land region.[117]

The political taboo on talk of privatizing Pemex was broken in the Salinas administration, when the company was opened to foreign subcontractors for the first time. Shell and Exxon began providing technical assistance in Pemex exploratory work. Pemex's subcontracting of private US firms started in 1991 as a condition of a $1.3 billion loan from the US Export-Import Bank. Houston's Triton International is drilling new sea wells for Pemex in the Gulf of Mexico; the firms Halliburton, Baker and Hughes direct construction at Tabasco rigs; Diamond Shamrock oversees refinery construction. The private contractors increasingly bring in their own crews instead of hiring local labor. Shell also refines Pemex crude at a plant in Deer Park, Texas, for re-export back to Mexico.[118]

Foreign firms are also seeking a share of Pemex's natural gas, now mostly used for internal consumption. Canada's Gaz Metropolitan gained a contract with Mexico to aid Pemex in natural gas exploitation. Chevron runs the gas pipeline linking Tabasco to the Federal District—part of the network which links to the Texas border.[119]

An unprecedented step toward foreign control of Pemex was taken following the December 1994 peso devaluation. Under the February 1995 $50 billion rescue package deal, Pemex's profits were delivered directly to the US Federal Reserve as collateral.[120] Opponents in the Chamber of Deputies from PRI, PRD and PAN alike charged that a "simulated sale" of Pemex had already begun.[121]

Silvia Whizar of the Santo Tomas Ecological Association links the increasing US control over Pemex to the ecological destruction in Tabasco: "The Mexican petrol industry is controlled by the demands of the US economy's need for oil. The velocity of exploitation is an obligation mandated by the bail-out accords. There is no interest in protecting the ecology."

At the CODEHUTAB offices I met Francisco Castillo, a dissident Pemex worker and member of Alianza Civica, a non-governmental organization which monitors elections and corruption. Castillo, a technician at the Gualas rig in La Centla, said the oil workers movement was largely destroyed in a union purge disguised as a corruption crackdown.

The 1989 crackdown was dramatic. Joaquin Hernández Galicia (aka "La Quina"), notorious political boss of the Petrol Workers Syndicate of the Mexican Republic (STPRM), was arrested on the orders of President Salinas. Following a shoot-out with army troops at his Tamaulipas headquarters, hundreds of automatic weapons were found. Thirty other STPRM leaders were arrested on gun-running and corruption charges. Army troops were mobilized to protect Pemex installations against sabotage as refinery workers walked off their jobs in protest. Panicked Mexicans hoarded gasoline, with long lines at Pemex stations reminiscent of those in the US during the 1973 oil crisis.[122] La Quina would be granted parole in 1997, but by then the STPRM was the proverbial shadow of its former self.[123]

"La Quina was very corrupt, but he had the nationalist spirit," said Castillo. "Since he was ousted the union is much weaker. It obeys the government unconditionally."

Castillo claimed that among the hundreds of workers sacked following La Quina's arrest were dissident leaders who had *opposed* La Quina, such as Salvador Hernández Ayala of the Independent Petrolero Movement (MPI).

"Some of the dissidents were among the best workers at the wells," said Castillo. "Many of them were technical workers too."

Under the new contract worked out in the wake of the purge, technical workers could no longer be part of the union. Ten thousand Pemex workers marched from Villahermosa to Mexico City in protest of the changes. In January 1994, dissident workers went on hunger strike and blockaded the gates of the Coatzacoalcos plants in Veracruz. But new STPRM chief Sebastián Guzmán Cabrera accepted the contract change. Locals who resisted Guzmán's imposition were violently attacked by *charro* goons.[124]

"The union movement was killed," said Castillo. "The technical workers are now considered *de confianza*—in the 'confidence' of the company. As a worker, I have no right to be part of the union. It was all worked out by Salinas and the petrol mafia."

De confianza workers are special contract laborers whose ranks increased as a part of the Salinas drive for a more "flexible" workforce. The Federal Labor Law distinguishes between *de confianza* and regular *de base* workers, with the former barred from unionizing or collective bargaining.[125]

De base workers were laid off in the Salinas "modernization" of Pemex which followed the purge. The ex-Pemex worker political prisoners in Tabasco were arrested in protests over severance benefits. Workers claiming they had been denied the twelve days salary for every year worked mandated by the Labor Law blocked roads in Tabasco, and even took over Villahermosa's Pemex offices.[126]

Carlos Romero, the latest STPRM *jefe*, was also a PRI senator from Hidalgo—where Pemex's Tula refinery employs legions. The STPRM still opposed privatization in principle, but had lost much of its clout to oppose it in reality.[127]

Pemex is an inefficient, lumbering giant of the global oil business. Churning out 3 million barrels a day, Pemex is the world's sixth largest oil company by production. Half of this output is exported, of which up to 80 percent goes to the US. Pemex employs 135,000, and has its own worker health system and company-wide telecom branch. Since the oil boom, it has provided between a fourth and half of the Mexican government's annual income—up to $20 billion a year. But Pemex has allowed its refineries to deteriorate in the rush to export crude; Mexico has had to import refined oil from Venezuela and elsewhere in recent years.[128]

With Mexico's oil wealth concentrated overwhelmingly along the Gulf Coast, Pemex is divided into three regions: Region Norte, consisting of Tamaulipas and northern Veracruz; Region Sur, consisting of southern Veracruz, Tabasco, Chiapas and the Yucatan; and Region Marina, covering the sea platforms.[129]

The Mexican oil industry has been moving south since it was established a century ago by such firms as (Exxon predecessor) Standard Oil and Royal Dutch Shell at Tampico, Tamaulipas. Region Sur was largely responsible for the 1970s boom, and accounts for 70 percent of national production. The proven reserves of Region Sur alone equal 30 percent of total US reserves, and surpass those of Canada by 16 percent.[130]

Region Sur also has the country's most important petrochemical plants—the first Pemex sector openly slated for privatization. The petrochemical division raises nearly 10 percent of Pemex's profits. Tabasco has petrochemical plants at La Venta and Ciudad Pemex, but the biggest—Cosoleacaque, La Cangrejera, Morelos and Pajaritos—are all just over the state line around Coatzacoalcos, Veracruz, where they have long since destroyed the local fishing economy.[131] The Rio Coatzacoalcos is more polluted with hydrocarbons than any waterway in the world.[132] A new on-site waste incinerator at Pajaritos spews dioxin into the atmosphere.[133]

Exxon, Shell, Chevron, British Petroleum and Sumitomo have all expressed interest in the petrochemical plants.[134] Sixty-one petrochemical plants were initially slated for privatization by Zedillo in 1995, opening a 49 percent stake in each plant to foreign firms.[135]

Getting the new policy to conform to the federal Petroleum Law, as mandated by the Constitution, took some bureaucratic subterfuge. Under the *Ley de Petróleo*, "basic petrochemicals" which are of "fundamental economic interest to the state" must remain entirely in national hands. Those listed as "secondary petrochemicals" can be open to foreign investment. In 1992, President Salinas had the list reorganized. The number of basic petrochemicals was reduced from twenty to eight. This followed a 1986 reorganization by President de la Madrid which had already reduced the number from thirty-four to twenty. Those removed from the list included ammonia, used in fertilizers, and methanol, considered an alternative fuel by the US Energy Department. Critics charged that the current eight—such as butane, used in cigarette lighters—are not basic petrochemicals at all. None of the current eight were on the original list drawn up in 1960. Critics also pointed out that the same plants—particularly the four giants of Coatzacoalcos—produce both the "basic" and "secondary" petrochemicals.[136]

In March, 1996, when bidding started on the petrochemical plants, the PRD's Francisco Curi, Energy Commission chair, called for a halt to the process on the floor of the Chamber of Deputies.[137]

Pemex Director Adrian Lajous Vargas backed up Zedillo in insisting the plan was legal. But the STPRM sued to stop the petrochemical privatization, arguing that the reorganization of the list was unconstitutional.[138]

In September 1996, US Ambassador James Jones was quoted in the Mexican press as warning that any retreat on the petrochemical privatization would cause Wall Street to pull billions of dollars out of Mexico's financial markets. Following the requisite outcry from Mexican officials, Jones quickly said he had been misquoted. But later that month, a rank-and-file rebellion at the national PRI congress demanded that Zedillo abandon the privatization plan.[139]

The plan remained under review by the Zedillo administration—reportedly under the contracted consultation of JP Morgan.[140]

Meanwhile, the PRD charged that the Oil Proceeds Facility Agreement (OPFA) Mexico had signed as a part of the $50 billion bail-out accords had already unconstitutionally compromised national control over Pemex. What the privatization forces failed to get through NAFTA, opponents said, they actually got through the 1995 bail-out accords.[141]

Under Article 605 of NAFTA, the three parties to the agreement cannot allow the percentage of total oil production exported to the other parties to fall below levels established in the three years prior to the Agreement taking effect (1991 to 1993). Since the US exports practically no oil to Canada or Mexico, the article really serves as a guarantee of minimum imports to the US. In the three-year period, Mexico exported 30 percent of its total crude production to the US. However, because of the likely political backlash and the Article's questionable legality under the Mexican Constitution, at Mexican insistence an annex to Article 605 stipulated that it is non-binding on Mexico.[142]

The PRD and nationalist elements of the PRI said Article 27, placing oil and mineral reserves under the "inalienable and imprescriptable direct dominion" of the nation, had already been weakened by the 1995 reform allowing foreign firms to exploit natural gas. They also said allowing Shell to refine Pemex crude violates the *Ley de Petróleo*, part of Article 27's enabling legislation. But the OPFA went much further.[143]

Under the OPFA, Pemex profits were deposited into a joint New York account of the Bank of Mexico and the US Federal Reserve to back up the loans. Under the package, Washington put up $12.5 billion and guaranteed the remainder provided by the International Monetary Fund and other multilateral agencies.[144] The agreement, signed before a New York judge, obliged Pemex to inform the US of any actions which might affect profits—such as reducing production or exports below minimum levels established at the time of the agreement.[145]

At the time of the agreement, Pemex's director assured the Mexican public that use of the funds to actually pay back the US was an "absolutely remote possibility."[146]

But during the 1996 US presidential campaign, Mexico announced that it would pay back $7 million to the US ahead of schedule—boosting Clinton and depriving populist rival H. Ross Perot of propaganda ammo. More payments were made over the summer, leaving just $3.5 billion of debt.[147] In January 1997, days after Clinton's inauguration, the payback was completed—the US Treasury Department removed $3.5 billion from the joint account. Hacienda Secretary Guillermo Ortíz then stated the Pemex profits were not merely collateral, but an "alternative mechanism of payment."[148]

The US Treasury made $500 million profit on the interest.[149]

Mexican oil is a critical US national security concern—especially since the official shift to western hemisphere sources after the 1973 Arab embargo. During the second oil shock of 1979, sparked by the Iranian revolution, the Pentagon drew up contingency plans for securing the Mexican oilfields in the event of a national crisis.[150]

In 1982, Pemex signed a long-term agreement to supply the US Energy Department's Strategic Reserves—emergency supplies of millions of barrels stored in Texas and Louisiana salt domes—established after the 1973 crisis. The 1982 deal was itself a condition of a Washington bail-out following the peso crash that year. The devaluation sparked by the drop in global oil prices marked the end of the boom years and the beginning of the neoliberal counter-revolution.[151]

The stipulation instated in 1980, at the height of the boom, that no more than 50 percent of oil exports would go to any one country, was quietly forgotten. Jorge Díaz Serrano, the Pemex director who compliantly dropped prices, slashed personnel and struck the first deals with the US Strategic Reserves, also presided over one of the oil industry's most spectacular ecological disasters. In June 1979, the Ixtoc I well in Campeche Sound went out of control, spewing 30,000 barrels a day into the sea for nine months before it was finally capped. Some of it washed up on Texas beaches, sparking a diplomatic row. Díaz Serrano subsequently served as a convenient scapegoat, and was arrested in 1983 for skimming astronomical sums off the purchase of oil tankers. It was also revealed that in the 1960s he was a partner in a Mexican oil venture called Permargo with a prominent Texas oilman who was represented on the board by *prestanombres*—a practice which, if common, violated the clear spirit of Article 27 and the Petroleum Law. The Texan in question was future US president and NAFTA architect George Bush.[152]

Pemex boosted oil sales to the US during Operation Desert Storm at White House behest. The suddenly rocketing prices netted Pemex its first windfall in over a decade. The additional output became permanent. Exports have increased steadily ever since—despite the Salinas administration's much-touted but little-realized plan for "depetrolization" of the Mexican economy.[153] The 1994 peso crash coincided with the leveling off of global oil prices, imposing further budgetary austerity and placing Mexico once again in a position for imperialism to wrest concessions.[154]

In a 1988 *New York Times* op-ed, Benjamin Weiner of the elite consulting firm Probe International had responded to Washington's latest Mexican debt-relief plan: "There is no novocaine solution to the third world debt problem; eventually, much of it could become the responsibility of American taxpayers. However, I believe Americans would accept this burden if they were assured of parallel concessions from the debtor nations. What sort of concessions? If there were oil shortages like the one in 1973, the Mexicans could guarantee us an unfettered supply of crude oil."[155]

In the immediate aftermath of the 1994 crash, Jaime Serra Puche, the Yale-trained Hacienda Secretary who had negotiated NAFTA and was a favorite for the 2000 presidency, was forced to resign. His replacement, Stanford-trained Guillermo Ortíz, immediately flew to New York, where he promised a group of Wall Street investors that Mexico's previously sacrosanct energy sector would soon be up for privatization. He stopped just short of confirming rumors that Pemex would be auctioned off.[156]

During the February 1996 blockades, Sandra Scott of Cambridge Energy Associates dismissed the Tabasco turmoil in the *New York Times:* "From the perspective of the world oil market, this is not making a blink."[157]

But the Villahermosa daily *Presente* reported during the blockades that an "observer from Washington" in Tabasco, insisting on anonymity, said that there is "much preoccupation" about the Tabasco situation among US companies interested in the petrochemical privatization.[158]

Before the 1982 oil/peso crash, Pemex had been planning for the next phase of expansion—south from Tabasco into the Lacandon Selva of Chiapas. Pemex estimated 250 billion barrels of oil lying under the soils of Tabasco and Chiapas.[159]

In 1978, Pemex established an exploratory camp in the Marqués de Comillas, in the heart of the Lacandon Selva. Test wells were also drilled along the Sierra de

Corralchen, the Selva's outer wall. Pemex worked closely with the army in con-quering this frontier, and was among the first to exploit the new military road through the jungle.[160] The oil expansion plans were put on hold by the 1982 crisis —and were revived again with the North American Free Trade Agreement.[161]

It was in the Sierra Corralchen, in May 1993, that army troops on patrol to protect Pemex operations first encountered Zapatista guerillas. The shoot-out, which left at least one soldier dead, was hushed up, with NAFTA still pending in the US Congress. "This could not have been just a military error," Marcos later told *Proceso*. "This was a political decision and it was made very high in the regime. I'm sure the decision had to be made in the office of the President of the Republic. There is no other explanation . . ." This ironically allowed the Zapatistas to take the world by surprise when they launched their rebellion on New Year's Day 1994, the moment NAFTA took effect. At that point, the Pemex exploration teams, with their US and French subcontractors, beat a hasty retreat from the Lacandon Selva.[162]

In March 1997, Marcos told Italian journalists that US subcontractors doing exploratory work for Pemex in the Lacandon Selva had discovered uranium. He said he had found out through a Pemex engineer who was a Zapatista mole.[163]

Later, the Energy Secretariat would confirm that uranium traces had been detected in Chiapas (while denying evidence of exploitable quantities).[164]

There have been efforts to link the remnants of the oil workers' movement to the *campesino* indemnification movement in Tabasco. The MPI, a dissident oil worker current, has participated in Villahermosa rallies for release of political prisoners. In June 1996, Santo Tomas organized a meeting between *campesino* leaders and dissi-dent oil workers at Coatzacoalcos. But Raymundo Sauri admitted, "There does not exist a strategy of common struggle."[165]

In March 1996, when Pemex Director Lajous Vargas visited Tabasco to preside over the inauguration of the parastatal's International Congress and Exposition, two hundred Pemex workers, retirees and widows staged an occupation of the company's Villahermosa headquarters in protest of privatization, union corruption and denial of severance benefits. Raúl Drouaillet Patiño, coordinator of the Work-ers' Defense Movement (Modetra) organized the protest.[166] Drouaillet was also Tabasco spokesman for the Broad Front for the Creation of a National Liberation Movement (FAC-MLN), a new militant alliance in southern Mexico—which the federal authorities linked to the EPR. Facing "sabotage" charges related to the Pemex protest, Drouaillet went into hiding.[167]

Despite such efforts to build alliances, the decline of the workers movement left the Indian, *campesino* and fishing communities on the frontline of the struggle against the privatization of Pemex.

TABASCO IN ATTRITION

After negotiating a maze of security checks, I found Mario Martínez Rubio, chief of Public Relations for Pemex's Region Sur, at his office in the company's futuristic Villahermosa HQ. He dismissed the 57,000 outstanding indemnification claims as a non-issue. "The Pemex policy is, if we damage, we pay or restore the damaged areas. The pasture, the fruit trees, whatever. But political parties have assumed the issue of indemnification as a banner. They should protest before the National Water Commission or the Agriculture Secretariat, not Pemex. Our position is that Pemex is not responsible for retention of water, for example. Federal authorities have determined that Pemex is not to blame."

How can the question be resolved? He shrugged his shoulders. "It's a complicated problem. Demagogues are exploiting the issue for their own personal gain."

When I asked him about the wells in La Centla, Martínez responded, "There are none."

"But I saw them at Campo Usumacinta," I pressed.

"They don't affect the reserve," he responded this time. "They predate the reserve. Campo Usumacinta was there twenty years before the reserve was declared."

Martínez also assured me "there are absolutely no plans for new wells in the reserve."

The struggle in Tabasco was turning into one of attrition, with Madrazo using measured repression, and the opposition pressing for release of political prisoners and payment of indemnification with more or less continuous actions.

The Tabasco PRD was increasingly divided, revealing the group's own internal contradiction, simultaneously a local popular movement based on direct action and part of a national political party with aspirations to the top levels of power. PRD leader López Obrador was a longtime Tabasco PRI militant before he broke with the state-party, and Tabasco's rank-and-file PRD dissidents accused the party elite of mirroring the PRI's corrupt and authoritarian style.

In July 1996, the PRD held internal elections. López Obrador, representing the militant southern wing of the party, ran against Amalia Garcia, representing the moderates, and Heberto Castillo, a federal legislator from Veracruz and a longtime pillar of the Mexican left opposition. López Obrador claimed a victory by 70 percent. But Castillo accused López Obrador supporters of stealing ballot boxes and other manipulations.[168]

On January 24, 1997, Fidel Hernández Geronimo, brother of Sen. Auldarico Hernández, announced a public hunger strike in a Villahermosa plaza to protest his expulsion from the PRD. Claiming to speak for a group of "authentic militants," he charged the party with a "witch-hunt" against dissident elements.[169]

That same day, dissident *PRDistas* in Nacajuca briefly occupied the municipal palace to protest lack of accountability for public funds by *PRDista presidente* Magaña Gómez. The PRD leadership, rather predictably, blamed PRI provocation for the actions.[170]

In the 1997 elections, the PRI took back all seventeen Tabasco *municipios*—amidst the usual charges of fraud.[171]

The national controversy over the Pemex privatization has gained the ecological devastation some attention. In March 1997, Mexican Greenpeace activists threw buckets of oil, contaminated water and dead animals at the Pemex building in Veracruz to protest a 264-gallon spill of oil-contaminated water into the Rio Tecolutla from the San Andrés II plant in the north of the state.[172]

In 1998, the blockades slowed, but the contest of repression and resistance in Tabasco continued. In February, the *barrendero* leader Aquiles Magaña was kidnapped by unknown men in Villahermosa.[173] In December, José Dolores Cordova Hernández, a SERPAJ adherent and *comisario* at Ejido Carrillo Puerto in Centla was "disappeared." Cordova was leading a legal challenge to an attempted grab of part of the *ejido* by local landowners, winning him death threats. Police were posted on the road to the *ejido* at the request of the landowners, but a search of the hospitals, police stations, jails, and morgues by Cordova's family was fruitless.[174] A month later, he sent a letter to a Tabasco radio producer stating that he had escaped his captors and was in hiding.[175]

And 1998 also saw a public thirty-day hunger strike by ex-Pemex employees in front of the company's Villahermosa offices.[176]

Madrazo stepped down in 1999, a little ahead of his term's expiration, to devote himself to seeking the presidency, running as a populist challenger to the PRI's Mexico City elite. But his grim legacy lived on in Tabasco, and he reserved the right to take over from his hand-picked interim governor if he failed to gain the PRI presidential candidacy.[177]

In November 1999, José Angel Martinez, commander of the Beta Group, a Mexican border police unit created to aid immigrants, handed his superiors a report claiming he had uncovered Madrazo involvement in drug smuggling across the Guatemalan frontier into Tabasco. Sensing he was in danger, he contacted human rights groups and UN High Commissioner for Human Rights Mary Robinson, who was then touring Mexico. But within a few days, while making his rounds along the Guatemalan border, Martinez was shot through the heart at close range. Authorities charged a colleague of Martinez with the murder. But Jorge Canel, a top federal immigration official in Tabasco, said it is likely "somebody paid [the killer] to be the trigger man."[178]

Ecological crises continued to cost the PRI legitimacy in Tabasco. In October, when torrential rains caused devastating floods across Southern and Central Mexico, federal authorities opened the floodgates of the Peñitas Dam, up the Grijalva in Chiapas, without warning. In Villahermosa, neighborhoods straddling the river were instantly swamped, leaving thousands homeless.[179] Victims protested the government's failure to provide relief by opening drainage ditches, sending water rushing over a main highway, stranding cars. In the city, the rising waters were contaminated with human waste; in the countryside by petrol.[180] Shortly after this disaster, Madrazo, having lost in the PRI's historic first primary, returned to power in Tabasco.

Santo Tomas Ecological Association questions the prevailing logic which conflates democratization of the political sphere with privatization in the economic. The group seeks to expand public oversight of institutions like Pemex which profoundly affect the lives of local citizens. Santo Tomas calls for creation of a Civil Vigilance Committee to regulate the industry in Tabasco, with democratic representation by all the affected groups.[181]

Silvia Whizar of Santo Tomas was willing to concede the possibility of a clean oil industry in the state. "Technically it is possible to considerably reduce the impacts, if they could pursue a clean industry with the same force that they are pursuing money. Our work is to advocate the participation of the local communities in shaping the future development of Tabasco, and to ensure that the boundaries of protected areas are respected."

Until Pemex moves on these demands, Mexico's land of black gold is likely to remain divided.

12

GUARDIANS OF
TEHUANTEPEC

Campesino Struggle and Revolutionary Echoes in Oaxaca and Guerrero

Between Morelos, heartland of the first Zapatistas, and Chiapas, that of their heirs, lie the poor, heavily Indian states of Guerrero and Oaxaca. The Sierra Madre del Sur, the mountain spine of these states, has followed Chiapas toward revolution faster than any other part of Mexico.

The doomed guerilla leaders of the 1970s are still local legends in these mountains, their spirits revived by the EZLN rebellion across the Isthmus of Tehuantepec. Just an hour outside the international tourist paradise of Acapulco, hamlets are violently divided from official authorities and municipal centers, the backroads patrolled by army convoys.

North of Guerrero's mountains, in the broad valley of the Rio Balsas, Nahuatl *campesinos* work *ejidos* first liberated by their Zapatista grandparents. Poverty and indigenous identity deepen as the mountains rise to the south. Following the Sierra southeast through Oaxaca, the rugged lands of the Mixtec, Amuzgo, Triqui and Zapotec give way to the lower Isthmus of Tehuantepec, separating the region from the Zoque and Maya realms of Chiapas. The isthmus is the site of the neoliberal regime's most ambitious development schemes for the next millennium.

Oaxaca's capital is situated in the state's central plateau, north of the Sierra and southeast of the Balsas plain—lands Mixtec and Zapotec dynasties once ruled from the city-state whose ruins are now the tourist destination of Monte Alban. North of the plateau rises the Sierra Madre de Oaxaca, high homeland of the Mazatec and Chinantec peoples, which drains into the low Gulf Coast plain of Veracruz. Both the Sierra del Sur and the Sierra de Oaxaca are made up of regional *sierras*, usually named for the local indigenous ethnicity.

A Mixtec and Zapotec cultural revival has been underway for two generations, vitalizing a movement for indigenous local rule. The wave of municipal uprisings and land occupations swept up the *sierras* from Chiapas in 1994. Two years later, the *sierras* of Oaxaca and Guerrero, separating Central Mexico from the strategic Isthmus of Tehuantepec, would follow Chiapas into armed rebellion.

UP THE SPINE OF THE ISTHMUS

From December 2 through 8, 1994, Oaxaca City's *zócalo* was occupied by thousands of dissident teachers demanding the resignation of the PRI's Gov. Diodoro Carrasco, who they accused of repression and fraud in his election two years earlier. This followed a November strike in which teachers occupied the city's airport, and two were mysteriously killed.[1]

Subsequent municipal elections would divide village after village in the Sierra del Sur, in both Oaxaca and Guerrero.

In November 1995, Mixtec and Amuzgo militants of the Guerrero Council of 500 Years of Indigenous Resistance occupied the municipal palace of Tlacoachist-lahuaca, a small town in an isolated valley near the Oaxaca border. The Indians vowed to block the elections because of *PRIistas* buying the vote with "gifts" of alcohol, *tortilla* meal and fertilizers. The local PRD agreed that no clean elections were possible, and actually joined with the Indigenous Resistance Council in demanding a municipal government based on Indian traditions, with no political parties—*usos y costumbres*, as the system is called in the Sierra del Sur.[2] Until their demands were met, they declared the Zapatista-style Autonomous Municipality of Rancho Nuevo de la Democracia.[3]

In January, army troops moved on the occupied *cabacera*. The Indians responded by setting the hall ablaze and retreating to their own communities, where they declared a Popular Municipal Council in Rebellion. In the following months, numerous lives were claimed in violence by the *caciques* against the rebel council and its followers.[4] Marcelino Isidro de los Santos, President of the Autonomous Municipality, was imprisoned for his role in the *cabacera* occupation.[5]

Throughout 1996, Nahuatl residents of Xalitla, a *pueblo* in the central Guerrero *municipio* of Huitzuco, on the Balsas plains, repeatedly blocked the Mexico City–Acapulco road. Marcelino Díaz de Jesús, a leader of the 500 Years of Resistance Council, was PRD candidate for state deputy that year. His supporters claimed his victory was stolen by *caciques*, and given to a "*sobrino politico*" of Guerrero's despised Gov. Rubén Figueroa.[6]

Marcelino Díaz had earlier organized blockades of the highway in protest of the planned federal hydroelectric dam at San Juan Tetelcingo on the Balsas, which would flood both communal lands and archaeological sites.[7]

Just as the *campesinos* of remote Tlacoachistlahuaca were radicalized by their marginalization, those of the Upper Balsas had been radicalized by federal "development" projects. The giant Caracol hydro-dam on the Balsas, some 40 kilometers downstream from the Tetelcingo site, was built in the 1980s with a loan from the Interamerican Development Bank, and flooded several *pueblos* and *ejidos*. The "compensation" deals were cut with *caciques*, who were rewarded with government contracts and jobs for their cooperation. The displaced *campesinos* received little or nothing. Several communities disappeared entirely, their inhabitants scattered to the slums of Mexico City, Los Angeles and Chicago. The debacle accelerated the break of local *campesinos* from the *PRIista* system.[8]

The San Juan Tetelcingo project was suspended in 1993, after the local *pueblos* declared autonomy over the issue. The Council of Nahua Pueblos of the Upper Balsas challenged the *caciques* who had acceded to the project for control of the *pueblos*. One of the leaders of this struggle, Sabino Estrada Guadalupe, was killed in a car accident near Chilpancingo, Guerrero's capital, in 1996—widely assumed to be a political hit. Marcelino Díaz carried on the cause.[9]

Marcelino became a federal deputy in the 1997 elections, one of a growing but still small number of Indians in the Chamber of Deputies. Leading the Indigenous Issues Committee, Marcelino alone refused to take off his sombrero in the Chamber as a symbol of pride in his Nahuatl *campesino* roots.[10]

Demands for indigenous and municipal autonomy spread throughout Guerrero and Oaxaca. Clashes between *PRIistas* and *PRDistas* left four dead following contested elections in Santa Catarina Juquila, in the Sierra de Oaxaca in April 1996.[11] On January 26, 1997, hundreds of *PRDistas* blockaded Guerrero's coastal highway to demand action on disputed municipal election results in Cuautepec and Cruz Grande.[12] In June 1997, the Emiliano Zapata Revolutionary Agrarian League of the South (LARSEZ) staged a *plantón* in Acapulco's *zócalo* to demand bilingual education for the Mixteca *municipio* of Malinaltepec, and freedom for imprisoned militants.[13]

With the San Andrés Accords stalled, the government had to appease autonomist sentiment in the restive region. Following the federal government's request that state constitutions be amended to appease indigenous autonomy demands, in June 1998 Oaxaca's Gov. Carrasco (as one of his last acts in office before becoming federal Gobernación secretary) led a revision allowing Indian-majority municipalities to govern themselves according to *usos y costumbres*, deciding their leaders in communal assemblies according to indigenous traditions. The changes were made just in time for municipal elections—although those *municipios* opting for *usos y costumbres* were not bound by the state elections calendar.[14]

The elections in those 153 *municipios* which voted to remain with the party system went overwhelmingly to the PRI. In the remaining 417 *municipios*, there was an immediate and violent backlash from *PRIista caciques*.[15]

At Mazatlan Villa de Flores, in Oaxaca's northern Sierra Mazateca, PRI gunmen seized the *cabacera*. A four-hour shoot-out ended with the traditional Mazatec leaders expelled from the *cabacera*. In a letter they appealed to the state authorities to restore a legitimate municipal government—an *ayuntamiento constitucional*.[16]

On January 19, 1998, on the Oaxaca side of the Sierra Mixteca (which straddles the Guerrero border), in the hamlet of San Juan Copala, members of a Triqui Indian organization and their families were attacked by presumed members of a *PRIista* paramilitary group, the Triqui Region Social Welfare Union (UBISORT). Four were left dead, including children. This was the latest in a wave of gunplay in Triqui country. Earlier, a truckful of UBISORT militants was shot at on the road to Tlaxiaco, leaving two wounded—in retaliation for previous violence.[17]

The organization under attack was the Triqui Movement of Unification and Struggle (MULT), which had declared self-governing zones in the backcountry, based on the traditional system of "elders" and "natural leaders." The contest went back to the early 1980s, when MULT leaders were assassinated after attempting to run for municipal seats.[18] Along the unpaved road to San Juan Copala, sequestered in a steep valley, the adobe walls were covered with pro-EZLN graffiti.

"We named our own authorities according to our traditional laws," said MULT militant Rufino Merino Zaragoza when I interviewed him there in November 1998. "We took justice into our own hands, because there was no justice from the ruling authorities of the PRI."

Merino said twenty-three of the twenty-five Triqui communities were with the MULT. The council of the local *municipio* of Juxtlajuaca was made up of both *PRIistas* and MULT adherents with no party affiliation. MULT was building schools, small-scale hydro-energy and potable water projects in its communities, and had in recent years secured some state funding for this work.

"After eighteen years of struggle, with *compañeros* imprisoned, assassinated, our women raped, we have established a political space, and won some respect from the state government," Merino told me. "It isn't because the government says the Triquis are very beautiful. We have won this respect through much sacrifice."

The local PRI bosses, however, remained bitterly opposed to the MULT. Four MULT *integrantes* were in jail in Juxtlajuaca on robbery and homicide charges, with many others under orders of apprehension. "They invent things," Merino said.

As in Chiapas, inequitous land tenure lay at the root of the violent political contest. The walls of the valley were green with communal orchards and coffee crops, but little forest remained. Merino told me proudly that their land was good, with enough for everybody. But many Triqui travel to Sinaloa and California for work. Merino had worked in restaurants and laundries in Phoenix, Arizona.

THE CYCLE COMES ROUND AGAIN

These mountains have nurtured the legacy of Zapata for three generations. The revolutionary currents that now come up the Sierra from Chiapas meet with those which generations earlier filtered down from Morelos. The link in the lineage between the Caudillo of the South and the new revolutionaries was Rubén Jaramillo.

At the age of 15, Rubén Jaramillo was a captain in Emiliano Zapata's Liberator Army of the South.[19] By the 1940s, he was once again organizing strikes and land occupations against the Morelos sugar barons. Already, politicians, retired generals and businessmen favored by the party were consolidating new *de facto latifundios*. Watching increasing bureaucratic control over the *ejidos* and cooperatives, Jaramillo was suspicious even of the populist Lázaro Cárdenas. When the party tilted back to the business elite after Lázaro's term, Jaramillo announced, "the counter-revolution has begun."[20]

In April 1943, when workers with the Mexican Communist Party went on strike at the Zacatepec sugar mill, Jaramillo organized the *campesinos* in his rural coopera-tive to stop producing cane for the mill. The Morelos state government ordered Jaramillo's arrest. He fled to the hills with a group of comrades from his coopera-tive, and launched the first guerilla insurgency of the post-Revolutionary era. Jaramillo and his band succeeded in briefly taking his hometown of Tlaquiltenango before they accepted an amnesty offer in June 1944.[21]

Refusing a government offer of land in Baja California, Jaramillo founded the Agrarian Labor Party of Morelos and ran for governor in 1945. The newspapers briefly acknowledged his victory, but retracted it when the ruling party announced that it had won. In the wake of the election, Jaramillo's followers were abducted, tortured and assassinated by the state Judicial Police and private gunmen of the sugar lords. In August 1946, an attempt on Jaramillo's own life led to a shoot-out near Jojutla. The federal army was called in, and Jaramillo for a second time fled to the hills. He reissued his 1943 call to insurrection, the Plan of Cerro Prieto, and amassed his forces for a drive on Cuernavaca.[22]

The attack on Cuernavaca failed, and the Jaramillistas were driven back into the hills. But this time the insurgency was to last years. After months of eluding government troops in the tortuous Sierra Ajusco above Tepoztlan, Jaramillo and his followers finally accepted another amnesty in 1958. With the election of Adolfo López Mateos that year, there was a slight tilt back to the left—in part, a response to the *campesino* upsurge in Morelos.[23]

But 1960 saw Jaramillo again leading land occupations in Morelos. New federal irrigation projects on the Rio Amacuzac made dry rocky lands which had been parcelled out as *ejidos* suddenly desirable. Cattle interests moved in, evicting *ejiditarios* through terror and fraud. Thousands of *campesinos* led by Jaramillo began "squatting" their alienated lands.[24]

On May 23, 1962, Jaramillo's home in Tlaquiltenango was surrounded by federal soldiers and the Judicial Police, machine guns placed at the entrance and rear. When Jaramillo resisted, the soldiers forced their way in and seized him. His wife and three sons refused to abandon him, so they too were forced into the waiting car. Hours later, the bullet-ridden corpses of the entire family were found on the roadside near Xochicalco, the Toltec ceremonial center where Quetzalcoatl was said to have received his education. The irrigation project is today visible from the mountaintop pyramids.[25]

Before the decade was out, radical *campesinos* in Guerrero's mountains, just across the Balsas plains to the south, would pick up the torch. Lucio Cabañas Barrientos was a rural schoolteacher and veteran of the National Liberation Movement (MLN), founded by Lázaro Cárdenas in 1961 to pressure the PRI back to the left. A year after returning to his hometown of Atoyac de Alvarez to teach, he was transferred out by the Guerrero state government to put an end to his organizing popular assemblies and challenging the *charro* teachers. On May 13, 1967, a *campesino* demonstration in Atoyac demanding his reinstatement was fired upon by the federal police. Some protestors returned fire, leaving seven villagers and two police dead.[26]

Cabañas fled to the mountains, where he organized his Armed Commandos of Guerrero. In a string of executions and kidnappings, the Armed Commandos took revenge on the federal police, local political bosses who terrorized the *campesinos*, and particularly hated army officers.[27]

The following year, after a jailbreak from his Iguala prison cell, another radical schoolteacher, Genaro Vázquez Rojas, launched a loosely allied revolt. As a young militant of the Popular Socialist Party, Vázquez had several years earlier interviewed Rubén Jaramillo for the Cuernavaca paper *¡Presente!* Vázquez began building his National Revolutionary Civic Association (ACNR) in the early 1960s. After one march was fired on by the state police in Chilpancingo, leaving several dead, the ACNR was forced underground and took up arms. Its 1971 kidnapping of a Coca-Cola bottler won the release of nine political prisoners to Cuba.[28]

1968 also saw Lucio's Armed Commandos joined by a Campesino Brigade of Adjustment, the military and judicial wings of a new clandestine vanguard, the Party of the Poor (PDLP). Unlike the Zapatistas before and after them, these were guerillas of the Cold War—although Mexico's unique geopolitical posture kept them somewhat isolated. Rumors that the PDLP received aid from Cuba are denied by Jorge Castañeda in *Utopia Unarmed*, who maintains Havana kept a fastidious distance from the revolutionaries so as to remain in the good graces of the left-tilting PRI. Some radical students who joined the PDLP guerillas had apparently received training in North Korea.[29]

Other legacies persisted as well. The Figueroa brothers, Ambrosio, Francisco and Romulo, were the regional *caudillos* who kept Emiliano Zapata from spreading his revolution south into Guerrero.[30] Lords of a ranching empire, they made an alliance with the Morelos planter oligarchy against the peasant rebels. Ambrosio finagled himself to be appointed governor of Morelos in 1911 in an effort to purge *zapatismo* and extend the family domain. The Zapatistas made his Morelos ungovernable, and he was forced by President Francisco Madero to resign.[31] The Figueroas later revolted against Madero, and were themselves overthrown by Guerrero's peasant insurrectionist Heliodoro Castillo, a Zapata loyalist.[32] In the 1920s, the Figueroas, scrambling to get back on top, supported abortive rightist rebellions against the Revolutionary regime.[33]

Rubén Figueroa Figueroa, the next heir to this dynasty, was a federal senator and the PRI's candidate for Guerrero governor when he was kidnapped by Lucio's Armed Commandos in May 1974. As a dangerous campaign stunt, Figueroa went into the mountains uninvited to negotiate an end to the insurgency. Cabañas seized him to demand liberation of political prisoners. In September, he was freed in an army raid—but Lucio escaped.[34]

Two months later, following a military occupation of the Sierra del Sur, with *campesinos* bribed and tortured to betray Cabañas, the whereabouts of his hideout was revealed. Cabañas met his death in the resultant shoot-out. Rubén Figueroa Figueroa became governor.[35]

The PDLP was shortly crushed. The ACNR declined after the death of Genaro Vázquez in a car accident—possibly while fleeing the authorities.[36] But their insurgencies served as a crucible for numerous small guerilla efforts which remained active throughout the 1970s.

One PDLP veteran, Carmelo Cortés, brought the struggle to the cities under the banner of the Revolutionary Armed Forces (FAR). In September 1975, days after a Cuernavaca bank heist, Cortés was killed in a gun battle with the Judicial Police in Mexico City.[37]

Florencio "El Güero" Medrano took the struggle back to the heartland of Zapata. An admirer of Mao Zedong, in 1969 the young militant was invited to China to witness life on the agricultural collectives (and attend a banquet where Chou En-Lai officiated).[38] Near Temixco, Morelos, he established an autonomous commune, conceived as heir to the settlement project Jaramillo had planned for Michapa and El Guarín, the last land invasions he organized before his death. The commune, dubbed Colonia Rubén Jaramillo, actually considered itself independent from the state of Morelos and a staging ground for "prolonged people's war." The Armed Forces of Colonia Rubén Jaramillo launched attacks in the surrounding countryside, and deep in the Sierra. In October 1978, El Güero was mortally wounded in a gunfight with the army in Oaxaca. Two weeks earlier, he had told a reporter: "If I'm eliminated, I'll die in peace because nobody can stop the movement of the indigenous villages and *ejidos* of Guerrero, Oaxaca, Veracruz, Chiapas, Campeche, Michoacan and Durango."[39]

Another group to pick up the torch was the Armed Forces of National Liberation (FALN) in Chiapas, which was crushed by the army following skirmishes near Ocosingo in 1974.[40] Nine years later, a new cadre of aspiring revolutionaries would follow the FALN into the Chiapas jungles to organize the kernel of what would become the EZLN.[41]

Guerrero's governor at the time of the 1994 Chiapas revolt was Rubén Figueroa Alcocer, son of Figueroa Figueroa. As a spirit of rebellion reanimated the mountains of southern Mexico, an inexorable cycle would soon be playing itself out. Ghosts were returning to haunt the Sierra del Sur.

THE BLOOD OF AGUAS BLANCAS

In the 1990s, the Campesino Organization of the Sierra del Sur (OCSS) emerged in the former heartland of Lucio's insurgency. The OCSS began with demands for credit, fertilizers and pesticides, but, facing government repression of its protests and catalyzed by the events in Chiapas, moved to a more oppositional stance.

On June 28, 1995, a truckload of OCSS militants was stopped by a combined detachment of state police units, some three hundred strong, on a mountain road at a place called Aguas Blancas in Coyuca de Benitez *municipio*, just east of Atoyac de Alvarez. They were headed to a rally at Coyuca's *zócalo* to demand authorities produce one of their comrades, Gilberto Romero Vázquez, who had been missing four days (and still remains unaccounted for). They never made it to the rally. The state police opened fire, leaving seventeen dead in the mud.[42]

Angry *campesinos* gathered around the coffins of their slain comrades in the Coyuca *zócalo* the next day, demanding justice. PRD militants seized Coyuca's municipal palace, and the *PRIista* authorities fled.[43]

Figueroa first displayed a police video which was taken at the massacre, which made it seem as if the OCSS militants had been armed and engaged in a firefight with the police. The OCSS insisted the *campesinos* were armed only with their machetes. In August 1995, the National Human Rights Commission accused Guerrero state officials of hiding, altering and manufacturing evidence in the massacre. The CNDH report concluded the videotape had been manipulated and edited. Guns photographed in the hands of some of the dead victims were "almost certainly" planted after the shooting, and there was no evidence that *campesinos* fired weapons.[44]

The report denied OCSS claims that the police "ambushed" the *campesinos*, but portrayed an intimidating and gratuitous police roadblock which escalated to violence. One of the *campesinos* had struck an officer with a machete, inflicting a minor wound. Gunfire broke out no more than five seconds later. At least one and probably three of the victims were killed at close range, execution-style.[45]

A special prosecutor imprisoned twenty-eight police officers and seven high-level state officials. The controversy prompted Figueroa to step down in March 1996. He was exonerated of all crimes despite being determined responsible for "grave human rights violations" by the federal Supreme Court of Justice.[46]

A dirty war was starting to unfold again in Guerrero. June 1995, the month of the Aguas Blancas massacre, had also seen the murder of three 500 Years of Resistance militants in Tlacoachistlahuaca, whose cases remained unsolved.[47] Over five hundred had disappeared in Guerrero under two generations of Figueroas, the opposition claimed.[48] The PRD claimed eighty-four party *integrantes* were murdered in Guerrero during Figueroa Alcocer's term.[49]

In February 1996, just before Figueroa's resignation, nine *campesinos* were gunned down by the state police at a small *rancho* near El Paraiso in Atoyac de Alvarez. According to the testimony of family and witnesses, the *campesinos* had been attempting to resist a kidnapping. Police said they were trying to arrest "delinquents"; the survivors said the police were operating in league with gangsters, and finished the victims off with a *coup de grace*.[50]

Figueroa's replacement by a *PRIista* interim governor did little to slow the repression. Dissident schoolteachers marched in Acapulco in January 1997, accusing Eladio Aguirre Rivero's interim government of blocking investigations into the assassination of one of their leaders, René Jaramillo Pineda.[51]

Military and federal police troops stepped up patrols in Guerrero, ostensibly searching for drug gangs. In May 1998, one such detachment intercepted truckloads

of marijuana on the coastal highway. The implicated truckline, Autotransportes
Figueroa, belonged to none other than the deposed governor.[52]

TIMBER EXPLOITS TERROR

The imperative of protecting NAFTA investments from radical *campesino* movements may have more to do with the troop presence than with narcotics enforcement. The US timber giant Boise Cascade signed a five-year agreement with the
Figueroa government in the spring of 1995 to log in the Sierra del Sur. Boise
Cascade was granted rights to contract with *ejidos* for exploitation of their woodlands, under a program instated for NAFTA.[53] Boise closed mills in Idaho, Washington, Oregon and Louisiana after the trade agreement was passed.[54] But that
rugged Mexican range where they chose to relocate operations was the OCSS
stronghold.

Timber exploitation was already a source of local rage. OCSS maintained local
timber contracts were cut with corrupt *caciques*, and illegal. As Boise signed the
Guerrero deal, OCSS and loggers backed by state police faced off near Tepetixtla,
a mountain hamlet in Coyuca de Benitez. A logging truck was blockaded, its load
of cedar and pine cut free with machetes. Militants involved in the incident later
disappeared.[55]

Figueroa agreed to suspend logging in the Tepetixtla area. Boise nonetheless
rented a privatized sawmill at Papanoa and started negotiating for a second mill in
nearby Tecpan. Logs started pouring into the Papanoa mill from twenty-four *ejidos*
throughout the Sierra. "We are the salvation of the *ejidos*," boasted Papanoa super-
intendent Carlos Vega to gringo journalist John Ross.[56]

Timber exploitation compounds the "spontaneous" deforestation caused by
campesinos clearing lands for their *milpas*. Ecological decline is already leading to an
increase of tropical diseases. Dr. Juan Blechen Nieto, a Cuernavaca physician, traveled
through the Sierra del Sur on a survey of local health conditions in November 1998,
and found an alarming incidence of dengue fever and malaria. "These are diseases
which are traditionally associated with lowland coastal regions, and are now appearing in the Sierra del Sur," he told me. "They are also moving north from Central America and Chiapas into Oaxaca and Guerrero. Indians in highland Oaxaca
communities tell me they have mosquitos now, for the first time." Dr. Blechen
believes, "This has to do with deforestation impacting local and regional climate. It
gets hotter, and the undergrowth that comes up after forests are destroyed provides
a habitat for pests."

In October 1997, deforestation took a deadly toll when Hurricane Paulina hit the Sierra Madre del Sur. Mudslides off the denuded mountainsides left scores dead and thousands homeless, especially in Zapotec country.[57]

THE SPECTER OF THE CANAL

The Isthmus of Tehuantepec has been assigned a far more ambitious and strategic role in the Free Trade order. Like Panama and Nicaragua, it has for over a century been eyed by US elites as a likely site for an inter-oceanic passage—another history now returning like a *fin de siècle* boomerang.

US designs on the Isthmus go back at least to the time of Benito Juárez. In 1859, the threat of US intervention in his war with the French extorted the McLane-Ocampo Treaty from the Oaxaca native son, granting Washington perpetual transit rights across the Tehuantepec—and the right to send troops to defend it. US engineers had already mapped the Isthmus, tracing its rivers, the Tehuantepec, Coatzacoalcos and Papaloapan, to the mountain lakes which are their sources, concluding that they could be dredged and linked.[58]

The Isthmus was also a special concern of Juárez: nine years earlier, as Oaxaca governor, he had sent troops to put down a localist insurrection in the Tehuantepec. An unprecedentedly ambitious development scheme there would serve to colonize and pacify the region.[59]

The treaty was rejected by the US Senate, whose Northerners regarded it as an expansionist scheme of the Southern slavocracy.[60] Subsequent intrigues over establishing an inter-oceanic trade route shifted to weaker Nicaragua and Panama.[61]

The Trans-Isthmus Railroad was built in lieu of the canal. By the time it was completed in 1907, much tenuously titled Indian land had been lost to the economic interests that followed it.[62] In the 1950s, a Trans-Isthmus Highway was built parallel to the rail line.[63] But the Isthmus was not even a close second to Panama as a passage for inter-oceanic trade.

However, the Panama Canal is today approaching obsolescence. The US, obligated by treaty, ceded it back to Panama at the end of 1999—now that it can no longer accommodate modern supertankers. Worse still, the canal's giant fresh-water locks are threatened by deforestation of the mountain watersheds that feed them. One Panamanian ecologist warns the canal is fast becoming "a worthless ditch."[64]

Elite eyes once again turn to the Tehuantepec. Mexican and US investors now float proposals to build a new inter-oceanic canal through the Isthmus to facilitate NAFTA-boosted trade and replace Panama.[65]

In 1996, the Zedillo administration embraced the slightly more modest idea to build a giant overland trade route, a "dry canal" of expanded freight lines and superhighways linking new sea terminals, replacing the old Trans-Isthmus Railroad. The new artery would connect the Gulf port of Coatzacoalcos, Veracruz, with the Pacific port of Salina Cruz, Oaxaca. High-speed rail and automated loading pods would shorten the trip to forty-five minutes. Promoters envision new *maquiladora* zones springing up around the project, rivalling those of the border states—this time, for Asian goods to be assembled on the Isthmus before shipment to the US.[66]

"What worries us is a dividing of the country in two, with creation of a band across this strategic area where sovereignty could be lost and control left in the hands of international companies," Hector Sánchez López, PRD senator from Oaxaca told *The Christian Science Monitor*. Sánchez invoked "the old dream of the United States" to control a Mexican inter-oceanic route, but said concerns remain regardless of what foreign interests gained control of the Isthmus—"Japan or Canada or any other country."[67]

Sánchez emphasized he would support a mega-project across the Tehuantepec if it was "nationalist and patriotic," with foreign participation limited to 49 percent, spread among several countries. Zedillo's Transportation Secretary Carlos Ruiz Sacristan acknowledged a 1996 Congressional vote for majority Mexican participation in the project, but called it only a "recommendation."[68]

Proposals for the land bridge and associated industrial development were drawn up by the Mexico City engineering consultants Ochoa and Associates under contract to the Secretariat of Communications and Transport (SCT). The largest budget item was reported to be a new petrochemical plant for the Oaxaca coast, extending the Pemex leviathan south from Coatzacoalcos.[69]

But the proposal, officially dubbed the Isthmus of Tehuantepec Integrated Regional Development Plan, was not released to the public. The press reported that the Zedillo administration was seeking to interest the California engineering giant Bechtel in the project, and potential investors in the United Arab Emirates.[70] *Proceso* claimed the Mexican embassy in Japan was discussing the project with *zaibatsu* investors.[71]

Ochoa and Associates president Felipe Ochoa, in a comment to the press, acknowledged that similar "dry canal" schemes were being floated in Colombia, Panama, Costa Rica and Nicaragua, but said, "The one closest to the US will have an edge . . ."[72]

Meanwhile, the government announced privatization of the existing trans-Isthmus rail lines, and the port facilities at either end. A new four-lane highway was scheduled for completion the year 2000. Construction of new container storage yards commenced in Salina Cruz—also to be privatized for the right price.[73]

The SCT plan was also said to include new Salina Cruz assembly plants, exploiting hydroelectric power from future dams on Rio Coatzacoalcos headwaters in the Chimalapas, a region of tropical highland forest that rises toward the Chiapas border east of the Isthmus, inhabited by isolated Zoque communities and under consideration as a potential Biosphere Reserve.[74] Forests in the region are apparently slated to be converted into water-intensive eucalyptus plantations and opened to mining under the SCT proposal.[75]

Just 20 kilometers down the coast from the proposed global trade pod of still-sleepy Salina Cruz, across the mouth of the Rio Tehuantepec, lies Juchitan, a Zapotec town with a distinct matriarchal culture and a long tradition of autonomy and resistance. In February 1997, *campesinos* and ecologists held a conference at Juchitan entitled "*El Istmo es Nuestro.*" The conference demanded recognition of the San Andrés Accords and popular participation in any development plans for the region.[76]

Miguel Angel García of the National Committee for Defense of Los Chimalapas accused authorities of keeping the Indians in the dark about the mega-project slated for their territory. "The Oaxaca government promotes meetings with the municipal presidents of the zone to seek their approval, and does not inform the communities."[77]

The scheme will certainly require overturning popular advances in the region. The history of the Isthmus in this century is a dynamic of centralized development *versus* local resistance.

In the Revolution, the Isthmus peasant leader Francisco "Che" Gómez fought both the rival Juárez and Díaz clans which vied for power in Oaxaca (the families of the twin titans of nineteenth-century Liberal Mexico). The Díaz clan was fiercely reactionary, and allied with the counter-Revolutionary forces in Chiapas, but both opposed the Zapotec revolutionaries of the Isthmus. The honor of assassinating Gómez actually fell to the Juárez faction.[78]

The post-Revolutionary order brought stability to the Isthmus. But once again federal "development" schemes only sparked a *campesino* backlash. The Benito Juárez Dam on the Rio Tehuantepec and an associated Federal Irrigation District escalated land values, leading to waves of land evictions in the 1960s. The Worker–Campesino–Student Coalition of the Isthmus (COCEI) emerged from the struggle of these Zapotec smallholders to keep their lands.[79]

The COCEI was born in 1973, staging land occupations, blockading highways and demanding municipal autonomy. Protests and actions were modelled on traditional *fiestas* and ceremonial processions; banners were written in Zapotec. In 1981, COCEI won the Juchitan government in alliance with the Communist Party. This *ayuntamiento* was impeached in August 1983, following violence (reportedly sparked by PRI provocateurs). COCEI called the impeachment illegal, and was forcibly evicted from the *cabacera* that December by the army. The subsequent repression only swelled the COCEI's ranks. The group resumed power in 1986, eventually worked out a coalition with the PRI, and in 1989 returned to power outright. The COCEI has held Juchitan ever since.[80]

Even in alliance with the CP, the proudly localist COCEI criticized the party for its electoralist focus and national ambitions. COCEI boasted that "Juchitan is to the Mexican government what Central America is to the White House." In 1983, Juchitan's COCEI Municipal President Leopoldo de Gyves told *La Jornada*'s Blanche Petrich: "A socialist government in the Isthmus of Tehuantepec, with the Nicaraguan, Salvadoran and Guatemalan experiences just a few kilometers to the south, is a possibility that makes the *PRIista* military authorities of the state of Oaxaca fear undesirable contagion."[81]

Juchitan sits at the mouth of the strategic isthmus which, besides being a natural canal site, also separates the greatest Mexican petroleum reserves from the national capital and the rest of the country. The Mexican left paradoxically came to see the localist COCEI as the defender of national sovereignty over the Tehuantepec.[82]

Private investors were first floating the dry canal scheme under the name of the Alfa-Omega Project when de Gyves pledged to Blanche Petrich that COCEI would resist it. Alfa-Omega, he said, would "impose a development model based on the seizure of communal lands, exploitation of the region's cheap peasant labor, and the depredation of fishing resources. COCEI is the only force capable of opposing this antipopular project."[83]

Construction of an actual trans-Isthmus canal, currently ruled out as too costly by the Mexican government, has been repeatedly fielded by private investors. Industrial colonization of the Tehuantepec's fresh-water sources is imperative if they are to feed the locks of a future canal. This process is already underway, if for reasons ostensibly unrelated to the canal scheme. It can be seen in the federal developments on both the Rio Tehuantepec, which flows south from the Sierra del Sur to the Pacific, and the larger Rio Papaloapan, draining the Sierra Madre de Oaxaca north to the Gulf of Mexico. The Papaloapan schemes have bred *campesino* resistance in the high Sierra.

In 1947, the federal government appointed a Rio Papaloapan Commission to chart the development of this rural backwater, modeled on the Tennessee Valley Authority. First the giant hydro-dam at Temascal and then the ambitious Cerro de

Oro irrigation dam, funded by the World Bank to the tune of $1.6 billion, brought the Papaloapan under centralized industrial control. Vast areas of forest were opened to logging in the 1970s as the lands were slated to disappear beneath Cerro de Oro's floodplains. Nearly forty thousand Mazatec and Chinantec Indians were displaced by the Cerro de Oro project, which was finally completed in the early 1990s.[84]

Of course the government promised new lands as compensation—colonization of the tropical forests of the Uxpanapa Valley, a remote area extending north into Veracruz from Los Chimalapas, over 200 kilometers away from the flooded Chinantec homelands. The Uxpanapa was second only to the Lacandon Selva of Chiapas in the jungle colonization drive of the 1970s. But with promised aid for the colonization projects mired in the usual bureaucracy and corruption, the Chinantec hydro-refugees faced desperate conditions in their new homes along the Rio Uxpanapa (a Coatzacoalcos tributary). In their hydro-colonized homeland, some resisted relocation, affiliated with the Worker, Campesino and Popular General Union (UGOCP)—and began invading the large irrigation-fed landholdings of the *ladinos* who had truly benefited from Cerro de Oro. One disillusioned observer of the development project termed the process one of "engineered ethnocide."[85]

Today, three thousand Chinantec families isolated in the Uxpanapa without roads, electricity, phone lines or political power, are demanding that their settlements be named the 204th *municipio* of Veracruz.[86]

GROPING TOWARD REVOLUTION

The *campesino* movement of Oaxaca and Guerrero is militant but geographically fragmented, its organizations based on regional and family loyalties. Escalating repression has provided an imperative for inter-regional unity and coordination. The 500 Years Council recently expanded its name to 500 Years of Black, Indigenous and Popular Resistance, in recognition of the strong African element in the populace of coastal Guerrero, and to include *mestizos*.[87]

In January 1996, the OCSS held a meeting of *campesino* groups in Acapulco to form a Broad Front for the Creation of a National Liberation Movement (FAC-MLN). This was an answer to the EZLN's call for the forging of such a movement to unite common but still-isolated struggles. Over two hundred organizations were represented, including the 500 Years of Resistance Council, the LARSEZ, OCEZ, FZLN and the National Indigenous Congress. There were representatives from the Tepoztlan struggle in Morelos, where *campesinos* were resisting real estate developers; and from urban groups such as the Francisco Villa Patriotic Front, Mexico City's largest slum organizing committee.[88]

In May, the FAC-MLN coordinated occupations of the municipal palaces in the Guerrero villages of Ahuacuotzingo, Coyuca de Benitez and Copanatoyac—where the *presidente* was held to press demands on land claims, and the state government sent officials to negotiate his release.[89]

FAC-MLN, however, failed to ally with either the EZLN or FZLN.[90] Many influential FAC-MLN militants were critical of Zapatista willingness to dialogue with the government.[91] This division, along with the presence of heavily armed drug gangs in the Sierra del Sur, made the region ripe for intrigue and manipulation. These would not be long in coming.

But before new armed clandestine organizations would make their presence known in the Sierra del Sur, the militant *campesino* struggle would return to haunt even the fast-industrializing and suburbanizing state of Morelos, the one-time heartland of Zapata, just 80 kilometers over the Sierra Ajusco from Mexico City.

13

THE GOLF WAR OF
TEPOZTLAN

Popular Defense and Ecological Struggle in the Heartland of Zapata

It came at the cost of Indian lives—especially that of a 65-year-old *campesino*, killed by police seventy-seven years to the day after the slaying of Emiliano Zapata. But in the spring of 1996, the Mexican village of Tepoztlan won its struggle against the real estate developers who had appropriated municipal lands and waters, held in common by the Tepoztecos according to a tradition that predates the Spanish Conquest.

Tepoztlan declared itself "in rebellion" against the corrupt and increasingly brutal political regime in the state of Morelos. The developers pulled out, but both sides remained unyielding. The rebel Tepoztecos wanted their land rights clarified, their prisoners released and the governor to step down. The governor, in turn, wanted Tepoztlan's rebel "Municipio Libre" dissolved and its leaders arrested. Resistance spread throughout Morelos—the land of Quetzalcoatl and Zapata, where the ancient traditions of a people rooted in the Indian past are confronted by the super-development dreams of a Mexican elite pursuing the NAFTA millennium.

THEFT OF THE SACRED WATERS

Morelos, perhaps even more so than Mexico City just to the north, is the spiritual heart of Mexico. The Tlahuicas, the indigenous Nahuatl people of the region, shared the high culture of the Valley of Mexico over the Ajusco mountains. The Tlahuicas called their land Cuauhnahuac, Land of Trees; the current state capital Cuernavaca is a corruption of this word. In the southern foothills of the Ajuscos lies Tepoztlan, one of Mexico's oldest towns. In one of its outlying *pueblos*, Amatlan, the Toltec god-king Quetzalcoatl is said to have been born. El Tepozteco, the protective god of the ancient *municipio*, is associated with the youthful Quetzalcoatl.[1]

Morelos/Cuauhnahuac lies at the north of a mountain-intersected basin between the Ajuscos and the Sierra Madre del Sur. The forested Ajuscos receive the highest rainfall in the state and drain into the basin's Rio Amacuzac, a tributary of the Balsas, watering some of Mexico's best farmland.[2]

The heartland of Quetzalcoatl is a triangle delineated by three archaeological sites: El Tepozteco, the little *cerro*-top pyramid overlooking Tepoztlan; the foreboding ceremonial center of Xochicalco to the south; and Malinalco just across the line in the State of Mexico to the west. Every February, Indian pilgrims still follow waterways through the Ajuscos to bathe in the sacred waters of Chalma, near Malinalco. But the mountain streams they follow ran all year in the time of the Tlahuicas. Today they only run in the wet summers.[3]

The shrinking of water resources is due to centuries of deforestation—for the sugar plantations of the old oligarchy and, recently, for the luxury homes, corporate complexes and golf clubs of the new oligarchy. Just as Mexico City's smog now comes over the Ajuscos into Morelos, investment and development schemes aim to make Cuauhnahuac a suburban appendage of the megalopolis to the north.

There is now a golf club at Malinalco. But when Tepoztlan was targeted for golf and corporate development, the town rose in rebellion against the local PRI functionaries and state government.

The entire *municipio* of Tepoztlan is made up of communal lands which the Tepozteco Indians have defended for centuries. These include both farmlands in the valley, and forested slopes in the mountains above, which protect the watershed. King Philip II of sixteenth-century Spain issued *reales cedulas* recognizing Tepoztlan's land rights dating back to the "*antiguo imperio megicano*"—the Aztecs.[4]

Encroachment of plantations onto Tepoztlan's *tierras comunales* made the town a focus of rebel activity in the Liberal Revolution against Santa Anna in the 1850s—and, two generations later, in the insurgency of Emiliano Zapata. Tepoztlan's loyalty made it an important base in Zapata's climb to power in Morelos, and it remained loyal to the end. Zapatista troops used the caves in the *cerros* north of town as a hideout to the last days of the insurgency, protected by the local populace. Finally, nearly the whole town fled to the mountains rather than submit.[5]

After Zapata was assassinated in the famous ambush at Chinameca on April 10, 1919, the new "revolutionary" government still had to buy peace. In 1929, Tepoztlan's communal lands were officially recognized by a decree of President Emilio Portes Gil.[6]

Certain of these lands received another level of protection when President Lázaro Cárdenas declared Tepozteco National Park in 1937, covering El Tepozteco pyramid and the chaotic mountains of pine forest and weather-sculpted rock beyond it to the north. Much of the lower part of the park overlaps with Tepoztlan's communal lands, providing a second barrier against private encroachment.[7]

Across the Ajuscos, to the east and west respectively, Popocatepetl and Lagunas de Zempoala national parks were also established in 1937. The first protects the towering snow-capped volcano, "El Popo," which forms the border of Morelos, Mexico and Puebla states (and whose deadly spewings have prompted the evacuation of nearby villages with alarming frequency in recent years). El Popo's sister peak, Ixtaccihuatl, the "Sleeping Lady" of Aztec legend, also lies within this park. The second park, Lagunas de Zempoala, straddling the border of Morelos and Mexico 60 kilometers to the west, protects the mountain lakes which provide water for Cuernavaca.[8]

In 1988, El Tepozteco and Lagunas de Zempoala national parks were linked by the Ajusco-Chichinautzin Biological Corridor, traversing the Ajuscos, incorporating Chichinautzin volcano, and affording another layer of protection to many of Tepoztlan's forested communal lands.[9]

The corridor was established both to protect the biota of the Ajuscos, and to slow the disappearance of water. There were seven lakes at Zempoala in 1937. In 1997, there were two.[10]

In addition to Tepoztlan's 25,000 hectares of communal lands, the *municipio* has 2,100 hectares of *ejidal* lands, areas redistributed from private landlords by the Revolution. The *ejidal* lands are in the *municipio*'s agricultural Amilcingo Valley, to the east of town, while a new ring of residential lands has sprung up in the closer Atongo Valley. Even the *chilangos ricos*—wealthy Mexico City residents, who started building expensive second homes in Atongo Valley in the 1970s—are on communal lands, and officially only have usufruct rights. Tepoztecos hold meetings on the first Sunday of each month to hash out land use decisions.[11]

In 1995, Grupo KS, a fashionable Cuernavaca real estate developer with properties as far as Acapulco, unveiled plans for Tepoztlan communal lands with the backing of the state's governor, Gen. Jorge Carrillo Olea.[12]

Grupo KS had an ambitious project for its 300 hectares to the west of town: eight hundred luxury homes, a heliport and "data center and business park" to be built by the gringo communications giant GTE Data Services, conceived as a nerve center in Mexico's newly privatized telecom system. For the executive's pleasure, the corporate center would be adjacent to a golf lodge complete with a world-class eighteen-hole course designed by international golf champ Jack Nicklaus and his

Golden Bear Course Management. Perversely, the whole development was dubbed "El Tepozteco."[13]

Twelve thousand construction jobs and three thousand service jobs were promised. But the 70 hectares for the golf green at a place of scattered trees and fallow ground called Monte Castillo were within the protected area—in the "buffer zone" between the Ajusco–Chichinautzin Corridor's "nuclear zone" and Tepoztlan's agricultural lands. Tepozteco opponents of the project called it blatantly illegal.[14]

The overriding concern was water. In a town already facing seasonal shortages, the specter of the water-guzzling golf course spurred formation of the Comité de Unidad Tepozteco (CUT) to defend local land rights. It was calculated that the water consumed daily by a golf course of that size in the dry season exceeded that consumed daily by Tepoztlan's six thousand families. The CUT was joined by the environmentally minded among Tepoztlan's *chilango* colonists, "Tepoztizos" in local parlance, in opposing the project.[15]

Water is at the social and geographical center of Tepoztlan—the market next to the *zócalo*, where *campesinos* from throughout the *municipio* daily gather to sell their produce and prepare meals in little stalls, is arranged around a big round fountain that provides water for all. Even within the town there is still plenty of agriculture, with many families growing avocados, mangos or *maíz* in their backyards.

The contamination of local water with the agro-chemicals needed to keep the golf green nicely manicured also raised fears. The US EPA has determined that golf uses an annual 4 kilos of pesticides per acre, compared to agriculture's 0.5 kilos.[16]

A CUT statement against the golf project did not dismiss the problem of pesticide use by Tepozteco *comuneros:* "This argument does not free from guilt the agricultural methods promoted by the dominant development model with extremely high inputs. It simply shows the awful example of a private enterprise which, allowing a handful of foreigners to chase a little ball with a stick, will pollute the soil and water to a much greater degree than does the current farming population of Tepoztlan in the production of food and respectable jobs."[17]

Moreover, KS's land rights were unclear. When approval of construction at Monte Castillo slipped through federal, state and municipal bureaucracies, the CUT charged the *pueblo* had been betrayed. Claiming legality and the Mexican Constitution on its side, the rebellion was on.

THE ANTI-GOLF UPRISING

In August 1995, KS bulldozers uprooted trees at Monte Castillo to plant experimental grass plots for the golf course.[18]

On August 24, Tepoztlan's municipal president Alejandro Morales Barragan approved the land-use change at Monte Castillo. It had been voted down many times before. Just a few days earlier, an angry CUT march had passed the homes of both Morales and Abraham López, the Tepoztlan *comunero* leader. López capitulated with Morales, signing on with some other *comunero* leaders to the land-use change. Like most local public officials, Morales and López were *PRIistas*. The PRI majority among the *regidores*, the town councilors, signed on for the project as well.[19]

That same day, Tepoztlan was participating in the national *consulta* called by the new Zapatista rebels in Chiapas when word spread that the town's leaders had caved in. The municipal palace was immediately surrounded by thousands of Tepoztecos, many armed with *palos* and machetes. The CUT militants finally seized the building, along with the *regidores* and officials there. The *regidores* were expelled, while six state officials were held captive, their hands bound behind them.[20]

The siege began. A permanent vigil was maintained in the *zócalo* outside the municipal palace. The "seven traitors"—the *regidores* and *comuneros* who had voted for the project—were hung in effigy outside the palace. The palace itself was hung with anti-golf banners.[21]

The special anti-riot forces of the state Preventative Police—the Granaderos—were mobilized to Tepoztlan. On September 3, Granaderos surrounded the home of Abraham López, and were confronted by protesting Tepoztecos. The police were driven off, and a high state official was discovered in a meeting with López in the house. Gov. Carrillo's Gobernación subsecretary Victor Manuel Saucedo joined the hostages in the occupied municipal palace.[22]

CUT barricades went up on the two main roads into Tepoztlan—one at San Miguel *barrio* on the road to Cuernavaca, the other just outside the *pueblo* of Santiago on the Cuautla road to the east.[23]

September 5, the hostages were released in exchange for the resignation of Alejandro Morales as municipal president. Morales and the *regidores* who had voted with him fled into exile in Cuernavaca. The state police pulled out of Tepoztlan, withdrawing to kilometer 17 on the Cuernavaca road, the *municipio*'s border. The *Ayuntamiento Libre, Constitucional y Popular de Tepoztlan* was declared—the Free, Constitutional and Popular Town Council.[24]

The state government presence in Tepoztlan disappeared. The Ayuntamiento Libre took over all municipal duties.

September 24, the Ayuntamiento Libre held new municipal elections. It was determined that no member of any political party could run—neither PRI, PRD, PAN, nor any other.[25]

As the election was held, a mysterious Cessna flew overhead, dropping anti-CUT leaflets on Tepoztlan.[26]

Undaunted, Tepoztecos came out in unprecedented numbers to vote for the candidates selected by each *barrio*. The Alianza Civica observed the elections, and affirmed they were perhaps the cleanest ever held in Tepoztlan. There were no "carrousels" (voters taken from polling place to polling place to vote multiple times) or "tacos" (several ballots rolled together and deposited in the ballot box as one), or any other such tricks.[27]

After new *regidores* were elected, one among them was voted in as municipal president. This was Lázaro Rodriguez Castañeda of Santo Domingo *barrio*. Alianza Civica held Lázaro was elected by a higher proportion of the vote and with a higher voter turn-out than any in Tepoztlan's recent history.[28]

The ancient King Tepozteco ceremony, which had lapsed for generations, was revived, the passing of the *bastón de mando*, the staff of authority, to the new *presidente*. The village priest, Padre Filberto González, ritually cleansed the municipal palace. The oath of office was spoken in Nahuatl as well as Spanish. Lázaro Rodriguez vowed that Tepoztlan would be "the patrimony of no oligarchy."[29]

The state government cut the phone lines to the municipal palace, and the place was now guarded round the clock by a citizen vigil. The famous Mexican cartoonist Rius, a Tepoztizo, painted murals on the walls of the municipal palace. In one, a *campesino* in traditional garb said, "*¡La dignidad vale mas que un pinche club de golf!*"— Dignity is worth more than a damn golf club![30]

The system established by the CUT for popular democracy and defense of the Municipio Libre was organized *barrio* by *barrio*. Each of the seven Tepoztlan *barrios* has for centuries had its own organization for making costumes and music in the town's annual *fiestas*—elaborate affairs in which the Christian reconquest of Spain from the Moors and other such historical memories are re-enacted. Each *barrio* is represented by an animal totem dating back to the *nahuals*, or guardian spirits, of local *calpullis*. Barrio Santo Domingo, where Lázaro lived, is represented by the toad, *cacame* in Nahuatl. Ancient stone toads adorn the fences and walls of the *barrio*'s church and homes. La Santisima has the ant (*tzicame*); San Miguel the lizard (*techihehicame*); Los Reyes the maguey worm (*metzalcuanime*); San Pedro the opossum (*tlacuache*); Santa Cruz the bassarisk (*cacomixtle*).[31]

Under the rebel *ayuntamiento*, each day of the week a different *barrio* organization had responsibility for maintaining the roadblocks and guard at the municipal palace, as well as providing food at these locations and patrolling the streets for public security. Every midnight, in a ceremony called the Changing of the Guard, the Tepoztecos gathered in front of the municipal palace. The Mexican national anthem was sung and responsibility officially passed to the next *barrio*. The gathering was also an opportunity to publicly hash out problems and issues. There were frequently live music and speakers, representatives from Morelos *campesino* groups pledging solidarity with the Tepoztecos.[32]

A radio micro-transmitter, La Voz de Tepozteco, was set up in the *zócalo*, spreading word of new developments throughout the *municipio*.[33]

The rebel *municipio* functioned with a deceptive normalcy. The tourists with their cameras came and went, *chilango* hippies climbed the ancient steps to the pyramid on the weekends. The municipal truck fleet was painted with an official and unassuming "*Ayuntamiento Libre, Constitucional y Popular de Tepoztlan*." The Ayuntamiento Libre carried out all services, from waste disposal to providing water. A private company was contracted to fix the water system's antiquated pumps and pipes. An organic waste composting program at the municipal dump was launched by Tepoztizo environmentalists. A full accounting of municipal funds was posted monthly in the *zócalo*. With no money coming in from either the state or feds for the municipal budget, the Tepoztecos stopped paying taxes. No police, state or federal government officials were allowed to set foot in the town.[34]

Presidente Lázaro Rodriguez was something of a Tepozteco environmentalist. He had founded Los Tejones, a reforestation, search-and-rescue and fire-fighting volunteer group, made up of Tepoztecos who have known the surrounding mountain trails all their lives. The animal they take their name from, the *tejon*, or badger, is one inhabitant of the tortuous, narrow canyons and pine-clad *cerros* above Tepoztlan. A carpenter and craftsman by trade, Lázaro sold furniture in Tepoztlan's market before his election as rebel *presidente*. He also worked as a local primary school teacher. With his muscular build, handle-bar moustache and impeccable *campesino* garb, he bore a striking resemblance to Emiliano Zapata—whose portrait adorned his office in the municipal palace.[35]

I asked Presidente Rodriguez in what sense the rebel Ayuntamiento was "constitutional."

"The government doesn't recognize our constitutionality," he replied. "But we didn't have participation in decisions over our own resources at either federal or state level, so we had no choice but to declare our own free municipality." He cited two articles of the Mexican Constitution from which the Ayuntamiento Libre derived its legitimacy: Article 115, recognizing municipal autonomy as the basis of legitimate government, and Article 39, stating that national sovereignty resides with the people, who have the right to change the government when it does not represent their interests.

Lázaro was openly proud of Tepoztlan's experiment in direct democracy. I asked how Tepoztlan managed without police. "The police disturbed the tranquillity of the *pueblo*," he replied. "Thieves are now brought to kilometer 17 and turned over to the authorities."

He was equally vehement in his dismissal of Grupo KS's purported land rights. "How can a few people take lands needed for aquifers and subsistence for all the people of Tepoztlan?" he asked rhetorically. "Fortunately, the community does not accept this."

I asked what economic future Tepoztlan held without KS and GTE.

"We want development in agreement with the people and their traditions and the characteristics of the town. The government says we don't want progress. But we want progress which is appropriate for Tepoztlan, our *pueblo*."

"We have to take this responsibility," said Lázaro. "We are near the year 2000. If we don't protect the *naturaleza*, we will die. If there are no trees, there is no rain, and the land dries. The forests which protect biodiversity also protect our water. We need the bats and badgers because they spread the forest, carrying the seeds. I've seen the fauna of the Ajuscos move to different territories as water dries up. In this *municipio* we grow tomatoes, *maíz*, every type of *frijol*, peanuts, chile—just no rice because we don't have enough water. The water is our future."

Lázaro had a special message for me to bring back to *los estados unidos*. "El Tepozteco is a reserve for all humanity—the *naturaleza*, the archaeological artifacts. We are the guardians. Tell your readers to write President Zedillo and demand a resolution to the problem of Tepoztlan. We will say thank you for listening."

GEOGRAPHY WARS

Grupo KS traced its ownership of Monte Castillo to a 1961 sale of the land by a group of Tepoztlan *comuneros*—this despite the fact that the Agrarian Law and Article 27 of the Mexican Constitution hold communal lands as "inalienable, imprescriptable, unsalable and untransmissable."[36]

A Tepozteco schoolteacher, Esteban Flores Uribe, was killed by *pistoleros* in the conflict over development at Monte Castillo in 1962. Due to opposition, the development plans were dropped. But the Morelos agrarian bureaucracy continued to recognize KS's rights to the land. For the next generation, Tepoztlan's *comuneros* continued to work the land in question, with actual ownership contested and ambiguous.[37]

Then, in 1994, the National Water Commission (CNA) approved KS's request to drill three wells on the Monte Castillo site, and the new development plans were unveiled. The Tepoztecos filed suit with the federal Agrarian Tribunals challenging KS's right to the land. But with the case pending, development continued.[38]

KS maintained they owned the land legally. Armando Mojica of the Cuernavaca environmental group Espacio Verde, which supported the Tepoztlan rebellion, called the title transfer "obscure, dirty and illegal."

An Espacio Verde study predicted that water consumption by the golf course would lower aquifer levels in Tepoztlan, and the total needed for the project (including the "industrial park") would be five times the village's total consumption. The study also found that the mining of the surrounding lands for the 150,000 cubic meters of soil needed for the golf project would exacerbate local erosion.[39]

The nearly 28,000 inhabitants of Tepoztlan rely on wells to around March; then cistern water collected in the May–September rainy season must be used. With the golf course emerald-green even in the dry season, the wells would start drying out earlier in the year, residents feared. The CUT statement distributed to the Ayuntamiento Libre's supporters and visitors read: "The water which is found within Tepoztlan should be used, first of all, to satisfy the needs of the community, and the use of the surplus should be decided by the community itself."[40]

But KS countered that the development would not affect Tepoztlan's waters at all.[41]

Tepoztlan lies in a geologically complicated zone between the Cuernavaca and Cuautla aquifers. South of the *pueblo*, the division is clearly defined by the Sierra de Yautepec which extends down from the Ajuscos; Tepoztlan lies above these low mountains, straddling the divide. Both sides of the Sierra de Yautepec drain south to the Amacuzac, through different tributaries. Depletion of the Cuernavaca aquifer was less of an issue, since the city pipes in water from Lagunas de Zempoala. The wells which supply Tepoztlan's water system draw from the Cuautla aquifer. Monte Castillo was believed to lie above the Cuernavaca aquifer to the west. Whether these two aquifers are linked was subject to heated debate.[42]

The environmental impact study for El Tepozteco golf club and industrial park, drawn up by Dr. Oscar Dorado Ramírez of the Autonomous State University of Morelos (UAEM), found that the aquifers were not linked, and that the "economic and development impact" of the complex would be "positive for the state of Morelos and especially in the region of Tepoztlan." The swimming pools likely to be built in the eight hundred luxury units were not mentioned in the study. The project was approved by the National Ecology Institute (INE), the appropriate office in the Environment Secretariat, in a record four days on July 31, 1995.[43]

Salvador Aguilar Benitez, a geographer with the National Autonomous University of Mexico (UNAM) who helped draw up the borders of the Ajusco–Chichinautzin Biological Corridor, believed INE acted too quickly. "We don't know if the aquifers are linked," he told me at his suburban Cuernavaca home. "There are insufficient studies. But we do know that Chichinautzin's geology is extraordinarily porous."

Aguilar pulled out a 1991 UAEM report by geographer Henryk Niedzielski, *Results of the Elaboration of the Hydrological Map of Cuautla*, which found that the two aquifers are linked. "If this study is accurate, the golf project would lower the aquifer that provides water to Tepoztlan," he said. "KS has an interest in saying the aquifers are separate. It solves the problem." He had already spoken to the press about the conflicting study.[44]

September 9, in response to the Tepoztlan uprising, the Federal Prosecutor for Environmental Protection (PROFEPA) instated a permanent ban on development in the wooded northern section of Monte Castillo where the luxury units were planned, and a temporary ban in the fallow southern and central zones slated for the golf club and corporate complex.[45] The Ayuntamiento Libre decided to maintain the rebellion until permanent closure of the project. The temporary ban was lifted in November when KS promised to use "non-toxic" chemicals for the golf course.[46]

While some pointed out that the Monte Castillo site was far from pristine, Aguilar stressed its biological importance. He pointed to its position within the transition zone between the two types of forest found in Morelos: *bosque* and *selva caducifolia*—the highland coniferous forest of the Ajuscos and the lowland tropical brush of the Amacuzac Basin. Some species move from the *bosque* to the *selva* in the winter and back again in summer. This transition zone is home to pumas, deer, such local birds as the *jacaranda* and the *quetzal café*, and migratory birds from the US and Canada. *Cordonis* (roadrunners), whose eggs are eaten by the Tepoztecos, nested in the development site. There were also *cuajiote* trees growing there, used by the Tepoztecos for medicinal purposes.[47]

The Ajuscos are a part of Mexico's Volcanic Transversal Range, which separates the Sierra Madre Oriental and Occidental to the north from the Sierra Madre del Sur across the Balsas basin. The Oriental and Occidental are largely contiguous with the Rocky Mountains, while the Sierra del Sur jumps the Isthmus of Tehuantepec to become the Sierra Madre of Chiapas, contiguous with the mountain spine of Central America. The *bosque* is similar to northern temperate forests; the *selva* is related to the Mesoamerican rainforests.

"Monte Castillo is one of the only places in Morelos where there is a continuous corridor between the *bosque* and the *selva*, where animals can migrate between the two," said Salvador Aguilar as we pored over maps in his study. "This is the critical meeting place of the biological zones of North and South America."

RAISING THE STAKES

In October, with Gov. Carrillo and the Ayuntamiento Libre still at odds, hundreds of Tepoztecos marched cross-country on Mexico City to demand the federal government act on the situation. The marchers blockaded Bucareli Avenue outside of the Gobernación offices. The government agreed to broker a dialogue between the CUT and the State of Morelos.[48]

October 26, Carillo attempted to install the old *regidores* (minus Morales) in power in Santa Catarina, the *pueblo* near the *municipio*'s western border, as a parallel municipal government. The entrance of the *regidores* met with a thousand Tepoztecos armed with *palos* and machetes; the *regidores* retreated back to Cuernavaca.[49] The Bishop of Cuernavaca, Luis Reynoso Cervantes, an adherent of the secretive and reactionary Opus Dei, who called the golf project a "blessing of God" in one sermon,[50] had his car attacked in the incident.

The Consejo de Comunidades Tepoztecos (CCT) was formed as a *PRIista* alternative to CUT. Its base was more among the Tepozteco exiles in Cuernavaca than in the *municipio*'s communities, but the CCT's emergence indicated that Gov. Carrillo was about to raise the stakes.[51]

The move came with an escalation of violence. Two young Tepoztecos were shot and wounded by state Judicial Police on the edge of the *municipio*, reportedly while attempting to stop a clandestine arms shipment to supporters of the CCT parallel government.[52]

On November 3, the women of Tepoztlan marched in Cuernavaca, demanding recognition of the rebel Ayuntamiento. The state government responded that same day by officially declaring a "dissolution" of Tepoztlan's municipal powers.[53]

Then, on December 2, as the *municipio* was preparing for the following day's Tepozteco Cultural Festival, Pedro Barragan Gutiérrez, uncle of the deposed municipal president Morales, was killed in a gun-battle that erupted between *PRIistas* and CUT militants.[54]

The conflict began in a local struggle between *PRIista* merchants and CUT supporters for street stall space. It escalated as a *PRIista* paramilitary group formed in response to the crisis, the Ratones, jumped in. Five Ratones, armed with automatic pistols and an Uzi, appeared in the fracas, which may have been a provocation. CUT and the Ayuntamiento Libre claimed Pedro Barragan was killed by his own men, who fired erratically behind them as they fled a Tepozteco security patrol. The fleeing gunmen were disarmed and apprehended by the patrol after they took refuge in a house, and were handed over to the state authorities at kilometer 17. They were shortly released—to join the other Tepoztlan exiles in Cuernavaca.[55]

Gen. Carrillo Olea shortly announced that he had fourteen orders of apprehension for Tepoztecos suspected in the slaying—on top of those already in place for the rebel *regidores* and various collaborators (including the village priest) for usurpation of powers.[56]

On December 26, CUT militant Fortino Mendoza was arrested by Judicial Police at a road checkpoint.[57]

On January 4, CUT's José Carrillo Conde was similarly stopped and arrested—despite the *amparo*, procured by attorneys for the Tepoztecos, suspending penal action against the shooting suspects pending a federal investigation. Carrillo Conde said the police tore up the *amparo* when he displayed it.[58]

On January 18, Gerardo Demesa Padilla, a CUT militant and schoolteacher active in the National Education Workers Syndicate (SNTE), was arrested at the union office in Cuernavaca. Demesa insisted Barragan had been shot by his own men: they had been running uphill, and the bullet entered from above. A Washington DC human rights group, the Center for the Study of Responsive Law, found "disturbing signs that the three men imprisoned in Cuernavaca . . . were deprived of their liberty solely because they oppose a large development project that enjoys the backing of powerful Mexican investors and politicians."[59]

José Carrillo and Gerardo Demesa both claimed they were beaten after their arrests.[60] The Tepozteco prisoners were on hunger strike for fifteen days. On January 26, while the prisoners were fasting, twenty thousand marched in Cuernavaca to protest the arrests—the biggest since the Mexican Revolution, and possibly in the city's history.[61] In other actions that week, SNTE and CUT militants joined forces to block traffic in central Cuernavaca for hours.[62]

Gov. Carrillo's proposal for new elections in Tepoztlan was repeatedly turned down by the Tepoztecos in their nightly *zócalo* meetings, which brought out up to five thousand. "NO ELECCIONES" joined "NO AL CLUB DE GOLF" as ubiquitous Tepoztlan graffiti.[63]

Grupo KS remained equally unyielding in their development plans. But the situation was approaching a grisly climax.

AN ECHO FROM CHINAMECA

When it came, it resonated like an echo from the Mexican Revolution, history repeating itself out of refusal to die.

The memory of Emiliano Zapata is vivid and passionate in Morelos. On April 10, 1979, President José López Portillo attempted to move Zapata's remains from his Morelos grave to a Federal District monument. Hundreds of *campesinos* gathered in Cuautla's *zócalo* to stop federal officials from removing the bones.[64]

April 10, 1996, President Zedillo was to be at Tlaltizapan to commemorate the seventy-seventh anniversary of Zapata's slaying. The Tepoztecos planned to deliver him a letter demanding action on their situation, incorporating the political message into their own annual Zapata commemoration.[65]

Ritual became protest as the caravan of buses and cars pulled out of Tepoztlan. The elders and children were there, the boys dressed as Zapatistas (the 1910 version, with outsized sombreros, painted handle-bar moustaches and cardboard rifles), the girls as *adelitas*, village maidens in traditional 1910s garb.[66]

Hundreds strong, the caravan retraced Zapata's route through Morelos to Chinameca Hacienda, where he fell. In the morning, the procession was at Cuautla to leave flowers at the feet of Zapata's statue. At 1:30 pm it stopped outside Tlaltizapan—where Zapata had his headquarters, just a few kilometers from Chinameca. It was there that ritual re-enactment of history became the real thing.[67]

At Barrio San Rafael, just outside town, the Tepoztecos found their way barred by some two hundred Granaderos in full riot gear. Refusing to turn back, the Tepoztecos started to argue with the police, asserting their right to free passage. The troops charged, dispersing them with beatings—and bullets.[68]

The road remained blocked for hours afterwards. Only at night, after the official commemoration presided over by Zedillo and Carrillo was finished, did the road open, allowing through ambulances to take away the wounded.[69]

Thirty-four arrested Tepoztecos were released that night in Cuernavaca.[70]

Seven hours after the violence, the body of Marcos Olmeda Gutiérrez was found in Jojutla, 15 kilometers from Tlaltizapan where he fell. There were two pistol bullets in his head.[71]

Marcos Olmeda was a *comunero* and a PRD supporter from the Tepoztlan *pueblo* of Santo Domingo Ocotitlan. He was 65 years old and had five children.[72]

A state government press release issued on April 10 before Olmeda's body was found said the police at Tlaltizapan had no firearms. But a Tepozteco on the scene at Tlaltizapan caught the whole thing on video. The tape, released to the press and broadcast, showed Granaderos wading into the crowd with rifles. Juan Manuel Ariño, director of the Preventative Police, was shown menacing Tepoztecos with a pistol.[73]

Of the fifteen wounded in the incident, two remained in the hospital weeks later. One, a Tepozteca schoolteacher, had her womb removed.[74]

Fifty-four police were arrested. Preventative Police Director Ariño, also a captain in the federal army, was among them. Some of his own men testified against him for provoking the incident.[75]

Marcos Olmeda was buried in Santo Domingo Ocotitlan. His coffin was draped with the yellow field and Aztec sun insignia of the PRD. A banner read "FUERA CARRILLO ASESINO."[76]

April 29, Marcos Olmeda's birthday, was proclaimed International Anti-Golf Day by the Malaysia-based Global Anti-Golf Movement, which networks peasant struggles against golf development worldwide.[77]

In the wake of the killing, Grupo KS, citing the situation of "ungovernability" in Morelos, announced they had found a new location for the project, in Sonora—where there is even less water.[78]

MORELOS IN RESISTANCE

After KS pulled out, the struggle only escalated. On May 13, one hundred Tepozteco *ejiditarios* seized Quinta Piedra, a sprawling luxury home they claimed was illegally built on *ejidal* lands. The house belonged to one of Tepoztlan's more high-profile investors—Guillermo Occelli, brother-in-law of former President Carlos Salinas. A complaint about the land grab had been filed with federal authorities, but the Tepoztecos were tired of waiting. The Occellis, their guests and staff fled as the *campesinos* pounded on the gate with machetes and *palos*. The *ejiditarios* said Quinta Piedra would become a community center for the Tepoztecos.[79]

There was again a sense of history repeating. The *ejido* had been granted in 1929, returning Tepozteco lands which had been usurped from the *municipio* generations earlier by the Hacienda de Oacalco, a long nemesis of the village.[80] Now the usurpers were back.

A Tepozteco roadblock barred the long driveway to Quinta Piedra. Where Occelli's armed guards once stood was a patrol of *campesinos* with machetes. The outer gate of the estate was hung with a banner:

EJIDO TEPOZTLAN
CASA DEL PUEBLO
AREA EJIDAL

Guillermo, the *ejiditario* who guided me through the occupied complex, asked me not to use his last name. He carefully unlocked the gate and we stepped into a deserted playground of Mexico's elite. There was a swimming pool on one side of the house, a huge jacuzzi and ornamental fountain on the other, now dry. A new extension was still under construction, with its own pool and jacuzzi. But work had been abruptly halted, obviously. A bulldozer and pick-up truck lay abandoned nearby, and batshit accumulated on the floor of the half-built extension.

Water came gushing out of a pipe on the lawn with the turn of a faucet. "That's more water than we have in our houses," said the wife of one of the *ejiditarios* with a sad, ironic chuckle. An artificial lake was also left mid-construction, a dock suspended over a pit.

Occelli obtained permission from the CNA to dig the well for Quinta Piedra in just two weeks in 1993. The *ejiditarios* had been trying to obtain permission to dig another well nearby for several years.[81]

Occelli owned 30 hectares in Tepoztlan, on top of the 10 hectares of Quinta Piedra. There were two more wells on his other Tepoztlan lands, awaiting development.[82]

As we entered the big house, the *ejiditarios* secured each door behind them with their own locks and chains. Plush furniture, a wide-screen television in the master bedroom, food in the refrigerator (including a big, long-wilted salad)—all untouched.

"We don't want to be accused of stealing," explained Guillermo. Although the federal authorities had yet to act on the case, Gov. Carrillo had nonetheless issued arrest orders for the *ejiditarios* occupying Quinta Piedra.[83]

Tepoztlan was (before the rebellion) the fashionable place for the Mexican elite to invest in real estate. Raúl Salinas also had a house in Tepoztlan. So had Donaldo Colosio. Carlos Salinas, from his unknown exile location, ordered his own luxurious vacation home in Tlaltizapan vacated—just in case.[84] There were an estimated two hundred illegal wells in the Valley of Atongo for the gardens and swimming pools of the rich.[85]

Tepoztlan had been slated by the federal machine's urban planning bureaucracy to become an upscale suburb for Mexico City yuppies. In 1991, Tepoztlan saw protests against a "scenic train" monorail proposed by former president Luis Echeverria and a group of Japanese investors. The plan was embraced by President

Salinas and then-Mexico City Mayor Manuel Camacho Solis, who saw Tepoztlan as a *ciudad dormitorio*—bedroom community—for Federal District commuters. The scenic train would go directly over the wild Ajuscos, bypassing the ancient route of the Cima Divide between the peaks of Chichinautzin and Zempoala to the west, where the roads and exisiting rail line go.[86]

This came on the heels of a struggle against a proposed *funicula* which would bring tourists up to El Tepozteco pyramid.[87]

Gov. Jorge Carrillo Olea repeatedly complained, "The Tepoztecos don't want progress."[88] He was echoed by Grupo KS, whose José de los Rios told the press: "You can't stay isolated in this world anymore. This project would be progress for Tepoztlan."[89] He asked a question that lies at the heart of NAFTA's future: "How are foreigners going to invest in Mexico if there are problems like this?"[90]

México profundo clashes with the cultural encroachment of the technocratic elite over the landscape throughout Morelos. Most of the land in Morelos is communal or *ejidal*. But much of it has come under private or state control, either through institutionalized corruption or outright government grabs for highway construction.

The Cuernavaca Valley Industrial City (CIVAC) was declared in 1977, and foreign firms like Nissan, Upjohn and Syntex started moving into the outer urban ring. Morelos was to make the leap from an agricultural to an industrial society.[91]

Fifteen years later, the state government announced a new highway circumscribing the Cuernavaca industrial belt. The Periferico Industrial was to cut right through the Tepozteco *pueblo* of Santa Catarina. On August 8, 1994, Santa Catarina *campesino* leader Mauricio Franco Sánchez was arrested for blockading bulldozers and detaining workers at the construction site, and sentenced to twenty years. The highway was eventually cancelled because of opposition, but Franco remained in prison.[92]

As Morelos made the next leap to a post-industrial economy, new highways were to be the arteries for suburbanization. In 1994, the giant Mexican firm Civil Engineers Associated (ICA), which had started construction of the "scenic train" before the project was dropped, completed a new privately maintained highway linking Mexico City and Acapulco through Morelos, the Autopista del Sol—with much higher tolls than the old federal highway. The federal government indemnified much *campesino* land for the Autopista del Sol, then turned it over to the private interest that ran the project. When the Autopista's prohibitively high rates failed to turn a profit, the private interests turned it back over to the government, penalty-free.[93]

Autopista Siglo XXI, yet another artery under construction through Morelos— linking Puebla and Veracruz to the Pacific coast—also met *campesino* opposition.[94]

Environmental degradation drives unrest throughout Morelos. The Texcal Ecological Zone is a water-rich patch of *selva* under official protection near the Cuernavaca industrial park, now contaminated by seepage of wastes from CIVAC's pharmaceutical and chemical plants. In Emiliano Zapata and other local communities which take their water from Texcal, residents are plagued by health problems.[95]

With Tepoztlan still in rebellion, other civil revolts broke out. The palace was occupied by angry *campesinos* in Temixco, a small *municipio* south of Cuernavaca, where the city's garbage dump is located and local water is contaminated by the state capital's sewage. Agriculture persisted there, but the *campesinos* had long switched to roses since contamination made growing food impossible. After the *PRIista* municipal president was jailed for fraud, local party *jefes* and Gov. Carrillo attempted to impose a new *PRIista*, and the people revolted.[96]

The municipal palace was also seized in Huitzilac, near Zempoala National Park, when Carrillo Olea imposed an interim municipal president in response to internal conflicts. In Xoxocotla, a deeply traditional Nahuatl *pueblo* in Puente de Ixtla, the elders declared themselves "in rebellion" against the Carrillo Olea government, in solidarity with Tepoztlan, and in defiance of the municipal authorities.[97]

The SNTE, CUT, PRD and other opposition groups joined in demanding the resignation of Carrillo. The Zapatista Army expressed full solidarity with the Morelos movement. A September 10, 1995 EZLN public communiqué to the CUT read, "Your struggle is our struggle."[98]

A popular Tepozteco t-shirt during the rebellion read "tEpoZtl aN."

THE CARRILLO REGIME

Grupo KS announced development of El Tepozteco golf club and corporate complex three weeks before the March 1994 elections that brought Gov. Jorge Carrillo Olea to power.

Under President Salinas, Gen. Carrillo Olea was chief of the National Institute to Combat Drugs. A few short years later, the suburbanization of the state he governed was fueled by drug investments, numerous press accounts asserted. And Grupo KS was at the heart of the allegations. The respected Mexico City daily *El Financiero* reported on April 28 that it had procured a DEA document calling El Tepozteco project "the biggest system for laundering drug profits" in Mexico.[99]

David Ibarra Muñoz, KS financial manager and father of a KS partner, was linked by the DEA investigation to money laundering. He was Finance Secretary under President José López Portillo, when *El Financiero* says the DEA suspects he had numerous "business connections" with Panamanian narco-dictator Manuel Noriega.[100]

The KS partners, who collectively put up $300 million for the project, were a virtual who's-who of Mexico's corporate elite. Ricardo Salinas was majority-owner of TV Azteca, Mexico's recently privatized number two network, in a "strategic partnership" with NBC. Although he was not a member of the former presidential family, federal officials then looking into the source of the secret millions of Raúl Salinas were investigating nearly $30 million in Swiss bank transactions by Ricardo Salinas. KS partner David Ibarra Cardona, son of David Ibarra Muñoz, was a convicted trafficker in endangered species. Another partner, Luis Slim Sayeg, was a cousin of Carlos Slim, the Mexican billionaire who owns most of the privatized Telmex. Another, Enrique González Garrido, was brother of Patrocinio González Garrido, the former Chiapas governor and Gobernación chief. Another, José de los Rios Hernández, was private secretary of former President Luis Echeverria and purported *prestanombre* for various Echeverria business interests. Rafael Haran Achar was an engineer who had done construction work for Echeverria. Juan and Francisco Kladt Sobrino, finally, were scions of the family for whom the corporation is named. Francisco, the president of Grupo KS, was married to the daughter of David Ibarra Muñoz.[101]

El Financiero cited the "real brain" behind the Monte Castillo project as Sicilian mafia *capo* Maurizio Raggio, once based in Cuernavaca and then on the lam from Italian money-laundering charges in Tunisia. *El Financiero* named the *capo*'s "accomplice" as one Pablo Antonio Hernández Garza, who worked in the federal police herbicide-spraying program against marijuana and opium when Carrillo was Mexican Drug Czar. The DEA characterized Garza as "rude, dangerous and violent."[102]

El Financiero named Salinas' brother-in-law Guillermo Occelli as the top lobbyist for the Monte Castillo project with the federal authorities.[103]

Another KS partner, Hugo Salgado, was a veteran attorney in the service of Luis Echeverria, Guillermo Ocelli and Cuernavaca real estate figures linked to Maurizio Raggio by Mexican federal authorities. His father, Margarito Salgado, another KS partner, was the target of an attempted kidnapping in 1996. The kidnappers only got his brother, Bernardo.[104]

Ex-President Luis Echeverria, now a top Morelos real estate investor, developed suburban Cuernavaca's Hacienda San Gaspar golf club and Sumiya luxury housing complex, with KS investment.[105]

Jorge Carillo Olea is credited with saving Echeverria's life when he served as head of his presidential guard. In 1971, President Echeverria went to UNAM to placate angry students after a massacre of some thirty protestors by Los Halcones, a paramilitary group linked to the security forces—and was attacked with rocks. It was the timely intervention of Carrillo that saved the president.[106]

Jesús Miyazawa Alvarez, Gov. Carrillo's Judicial Police chief, resigned from his post in the federal security apparatus in 1979 after he was linked to the clandestine "White Brigade" and the Rio Tula scandal, in which federal police summarily slaughtered a band of criminals (including ex-federal police) and dumped the bodies in a riverbed. Miyazawa worked closely at that time with Carrillo, then a Gobernación subsecretary under President López Portillo.[107]

The KS partners were also well ensconced in the Morelos state environmental bureaucracy. David Ibarra Muñoz's ex-girlfriend, Ursula Oswald Spring, was the Morelos state Ecology Secretary who approved the Monte Castillo development. She was also the top investigator for Luis Echeverria's private eco-thinktank, the Centro de Investigaciones del Tercer Mundo.[108]

Environmentalists on the wrong side of these elite circles were targeted by the state security forces. Armando Mojica of Espacio Verde had his Cuernavaca home fired on after he started distributing information on golf's environmental impacts in Tepoztlan. He received the Morelos version of a telephone death threat—the Scott Joplin music from *The Sting*. The break fluid was drained from his car in September 1995 as the Tepoztlan struggle escalated. This prompted him to hold a press conference, and the threats stopped. But Judicial Police vehicles still lurked on the street outside his house with disturbing frequency.[109]

Gov. Carrillo, undisturbed by the rebellions over narco-fueled suburbanization in his state, introduced legislation to the PRI-controlled state legislature to "deregulate" urban development from cumbersome environmental and health standards.[110]

Carrillo continued to insist that the Tepoztlan elections and Municipio Libre were invalid, and that the arrest orders against nearly all the CUT militants would be carried out. The rebel *ayuntamiento*, in turn, demanded written documentation of the golf project's cancellation, freedom for the political prisoners, lifting of the warrants, official recognition of the Municipio Libre, and damages to be paid to the family of Marcos Olmeda and others hurt in the struggle.

Rebel Municipal President Lázaro Rodriguez was among those wanted for usurpation of government functions, kidnapping and several other charges. "I have no fear because I am struggling for a just cause," he told me. "If these demands are met, possibly we can have new elections. This situation will persist until the government agrees to resolve it in favor of the people."

THE REGIME COLLAPSES

The Carrillo Olea regime began to teeter when it was linked by the press and law enforcement to Amado Carrillo Fuentes (no blood relation), the notorious "Lord of the Skies," kingpin of the powerful Juárez Cartel—and Morelos real estate investor.[111]

As Salinas administration Drug Czar, Carrillo Olea helped establish a radar network linking the DEA's El Paso intelligence center with a new Federal District "war room" at Gobernación headquarters, where unidentified planes could be followed on a wall-size screen. But "human intelligence" reports at the El Paso center shortly alleged that Carrillo Olea was actually serving as the Juárez Cartel's mole in the Drug War apparatus. One DEA document, leaked to the *New York Times*, read: "Reporting from 1992 indicates that the former Mexican coordinator against narcotics trafficking, Jorge Carrillo Olea, was at that time the most influential associate of Amado Carrillo Fuentes in the Mexican Government. Carrillo Olea was in charge of controlling the radar detection in Mexico, and by utilizing the information provided to him, he was able to insure the safe passage of Carrillo Fuentes's aircraft."[112]

La Reforma revealed that Amado Carrillo Fuentes, who managed to run his multi-million dollar machine from a life of opulent luxury even while running from the police, was making special use of the Cuernavaca airport. He and his family moved in and out to various residences around the city—including a walled "bunker"—with no interference from local authorities. The PGR concluded that "in no other place in the country could Amado Carrillo be as secure as in the entity governed by Jorge Carrillo Olea." The opposition in Morelos started to claim openly that Carrillo Olea had been given the governorship by Salinas as a reward for cooperating with the president's own narco-money operations as Drug Czar.[113]

It was the kidnapping scandal which finally pushed Carrillo Olea over the edge. In February 1998, federal police arrested Armando Martínez Salgado, head of the Morelos state anti-kidnapping squad, and two of his agents, parked just over the Guerrero line in a vehicle carrying the tortured and lifeless body of a 17-year-old boy, later identified as part of a kidnapping gang. Martínez and his agents were accused of crossing state lines to dump the body. The PGR investigation found, "it appears these individuals are involved in protection of gangs dedicated to kidnapping and narcotics trafficking." Shortly thereafter, Morelos Judicial Police chief Jesús Miyazawa resigned.[114]

Guanajuato Prosecutor General Felipe Arturo Caballero announced that his officers investigating a local kidnapping had observed Martínez personally retrieving $36,000 in ransom from a highway drop point. He claimed Morelos Prosecutor General Carlos Perefo Merlo would not cooperate in the investigation.[115]

Protests demanding the governor's ouster again mounted in Cuernavaca as an impeachment proceeding was finally launched. In May 1998, like Richard Nixon before him, Jorge Carrillo Olea ceded power rather than submit to this indignity.[116]

AFTERMATH

By then the Tepoztlan situation had been normalized. In March 1997, Tepoztlan agreed to participate in the regularly scheduled Morelos municipal races, and a PRD *ayuntamiento* was elected. After a year and a half, the rebellion had come to an end. The divided *municipios* of Temixco and Huitzilac too accepted new governments. The PRD also gained control of the state legislature—a key development toward Carrillo's ouster.[117]

The PRI interim governor who took over in 1998, Jorge Morales Barud, faced a state which had lost an unprecedented fourteen *municipios* to the left opposition, and Cuernavaca itself to the right-opposition PAN. All the officers arrested in the April 1996 violence at Tlaltizapan were exonerated, but all orders of apprehension against the Tepoztecos were dropped. The new government also freed the four Tepozteco political prisoners: Gerardo Demesa, Fortino Mendoza, José Carrillo Conde and Mauricio Franco.[118]

Morelos had been to the brink and back, and the resistance had made significant enough gains to end the rebellion with dignity. One wonders how long they could have held out.

By the time I arrived in Tepoztlan to cover the story, just after the Tlaltizapan violence, the initial euphoria of the uprising had faded. Divisions were beginning to emerge in the ecologist–*campesino* alliance, and in the *municipio*'s populace generally.

"CUT has made mistakes," Armando Mojica told me then. "That's normal; they were unprepared for this situation and they are under siege. These are very tense and difficult moments. The CUT is working with people they know well. The one big mistake is the failure to include the *pueblos*. Now the government is trying to play the people of the *municipio* against each other like roosters in a chicken fight."

In the outlying *pueblos* of San Juan Tlacotenco, Amatlan, Santo Domingo Ocotitlan, Santiago, San Andrés, San Pedro and Santa Catarina, Nahuatl is spoken more frequently and folk traditions are stronger, but the *PRIista* pretender *ayuntamiento*, the CCT, gained a following, exploiting the ancient envy of the municipal center.

For generations, the more sophisticated Tepoztecos (mostly in the municipal center) considered themselves *los correctos*, while those who clung to the old ways (mostly in the *pueblos*) were *los tontos*, the fools. This nomenclature persisted into the 1920s.[119]

One afternoon I took the bus up to San Juan Tlacotenco, in the mountains directly above Tepoztlan. There I struck up a conversation with Zenon Cuevas Medina, a *campesino* who grows *nopales*, the edible cactus which is San Juan's economic mainstay. He said San Juan was 90 percent *PRIista*, and complained bitterly of the CUT. He said the barricades blocked his *pueblo*'s freedom of transit. The *pueblo*'s women had to go all the way to the Cuernavaca market to sell their *nopales* since they were thrown out of their place at the Tepoztlan market, he said.

There were obvious divide-and-conquer angles being played over control of water. San Juan has no indoor plumbing or pipes for potable water. The *pueblo* is dependent on a weekly tank truck. KS offered to build the *pueblo* a water system, and to pipe up any water left over from Monte Castillo's three wells after keeping the golf course green.[120]

Canadian aid workers developed a project for San Juan to provide a rainwater catchment system. San Juan *campesinos* complained these workers couldn't get to the *pueblo* because of the Tepozteco barricades. The CUT, meanwhile, maintained that San Juan's own *caciques* kicked out the aid workers.

Like San Juan, Santo Domingo Ocotitlan is dependent on tank trucks for water. Amatlan only has limited piped water. Distant Amatlan also remained largely isolated from the rebellion. In this sense, Tepoztlan was the reverse of the Chiapas model, in which revolutionary hamlets are divided from ruling-party municipal centers.

There were also tensions within the *pueblo* of Tepoztlan. Along with the "¡NO AL CLUB DE GOLF!" (or simply "NO") which covered the *pueblo*'s walls, the words "FUERA TRAIDORES"—traitors out—were scrawled on certain homes and businesses.

The artists, hippies, back-to-nature *chilangos*, New Age types, UFO freaks and guru-worshippers who live alongside the Tepoztecos initially supported the rebellion. But these transplants, the "Tepoztizos," increasingly complained of CUT xenophobia and dogmatism.

The Tepoztizos come in many sub-categories: Tepoztricos (the rich), Jipitecos (the hippies), Tepoztposas (the gays). As always, the hippies and artists came first, back when it was still cheap, and made Tepoztlan fashionable for the yuppies who followed.

The indigenous Tepoztecos also have a sub-category: the Tepoztercos, the most hardcore and intransigent Tepoztecos.

Rebel Presidente Lázaro Rodriguez didn't make much of the elaborate local lingo, or the tensions. "Everybody who lives here is Tepozteco, as long as they are in the struggle with us," he said.

Tensions notwithstanding, all categories but the Tepoztricos stood as one against KS and Carrillo Olea to the end.

Armando Mojica said the Carrillo Olea government had lost all legitimacy. "It's absurd. It's Kafkaesque. Quinta Piedra is private land even though it's on *ejidal* territory."

In contrast, he believed that everything the CUT and the Municipio Libre did was within the law. "There is an illegal roadblock outside the governor's building in Cuernavaca," he said. Preventative Police were then barring access to the public building, with protests in the city becoming frequent. "The roadblocks in Tepoztlan are not illegal or unconstitutional. They are a form of popular defense."

A POSTSCRIPT: XOCHIMILCO

Just as the situation in Tepoztlan began to de-escalate, a second anti-golf rebellion was nearing just over the Ajuscos in the Federal District *delegacion* of Xochimilco, where an ancient lifeway struggles to survive in one of the largest super-developed cities on the planet.

Lago de Xochimilco is a surviving fragment of the giant Lago de Texcoco which once surrounded the Aztec island-city of Tenochtitlan, and was drained by the Spanish (or, rather, their Indian slaves) after the Conquest. The unique system of lacustrine agriculture which once fed Tenochtitlan still survives at Xochimilco— the "floating gardens" or *chinampas*, constructed in the lake from *guano*-enriched soil. Some *chinampas* grow flowers and serve as a curiosity for the tourists, but some still grow food for the local populace. The local Environmental Studies Group (GEA) monitors the water quality and works with the urban *campesinos* of Xochimilco to develop methods of filtering toxins from the water and soil.[121]

In October 1996, a group of real estate developers announced plans to build a golf course and luxury country club at Santa Cecilia Tepetlapa in Xochimilco. The Xochimilco Citizen Council unanimously rejected the proposal, but the Federal District's *delegaciones*, unlike *municipios*, have no powers of self-government. The Citizen Council appealed to the Federal District authorities to cancel the project, claiming it would suck up water, further degrade soil quality, and violate the stated policy of maintaining Xochimilco as an urban agricultural zone. The promise of jobs at the country club was dismissed as "an insult to the Xochimilcas; they want us to have the category of servants."[122]

The issue of profligate water consumption is especially salient in the Valley of Mexico, where the biggest city of the hemisphere is sinking at an alarming rate—10 meters in the twentieth century—as the remnants of Lake Texcoco, lying below the concrete, are pumped up for urban use.[123]

Protests were held, and vows of solidarity exchanged with the anti-golf rebels in Tepoztlan. In January 1997, José Antonio Vital Galicia, one of the leaders of the Xochimilco struggle, was forced into a car at gunpoint by unknown and non-uniformed men who beat him and threatened him for hours before finally bringing him to a police station. He was released after an outcry from human rights groups, and the Federal District agreed to further study before going ahead with the development project—although it was never cancelled.[124]

Just as the technocratic culture of Mexico's new elite crosses the Ajuscos to colonize the heartland of Zapata, so does *México profundo* and the renewed spirit of resistance persist even within Mexico's central megalopolis.

PART IV

SHADOW DANCES

14

FIRE IN THE SIERRA MADRE DEL SUR

Who Is the Popular Revolutionary Army?

In the summer of 1996, federal troops and tanks on narcotics patrols were combing the mountains of Guerrero in growing numbers.

In this militarized atmosphere, the Campesino Organization of the Sierra del Sur (OCSS) held a commemoration marking the one-year anniversary of the Aguas Blancas massacre. On June 28, Cuauhtémoc Cárdenas was among the speakers on the makeshift stage erected at the site of the bloodletting. So he was among the two thousand to witness a group of masked men and women in olive uniforms with AK-47s emerge from the brush.

Bandanas cut with eye-slits veiled their faces. They took over the stage, left wildflowers from the mountains at the spot of the killings, and read their Manifesto of Aguas Blancas to the assembled—first in Spanish, then in Nahuatl. Then they withdrew back up the slope, firing in the air as they ran—seventeen shots in honor of each of the fallen.[1]

Contemporary Mexico's second significant guerilla effort, the Popular Revolutionary Army (EPR), had announced its presence to the world.

Escalated militarization and sporadic firefights between the EPR and government troops followed.

On three occasions in August, army convoys in Guerrero were ambushed by AK-47 fire. One soldier was killed, and a civilian killed in the crossfire. On August 30, men in fatigues with AKs attacked an army convoy across the Rio Balsas in Michoacan, killing one soldier. The army sent helicopter gunships, combat planes and armored vehicles into the Sierra. Troops occupied villages and hamlets.[2]

If the EPR emulated the Guevarista strategy of forcing the enemy to show its repressive nature, they had succeeded.

A "GROTESQUE PANTOMIME"?

The Mexican press was filled with speculation as to whether the EPR was a guerilla group, a narco-gang or even a creation of *PRIistas* to justify a crackdown.

Cuauhtémoc Cárdenas was among those for whom the olive uniforms and profligate display of Soviet assault rifles smelled more slick than authentic. He called the new rebels a "grotesque pantomime."[3]

In August, as skirmishes spread in Guerrero, a group of journalists attended an EPR press conference. The location, a three-day march through mountains, was kept secret as a condition of the meeting, but it was somewhere in the Sierra Madre Oriental—far from the EPR's presumed stronghold in the Sierra del Sur. Photos showed a rough podium under the trees, hung with three flags—one Mexican; two red-and-green, emblazoned with five-pointed stars and the EPR's letters. Four rebel commanders presided, in identical olive uniforms with "EPR" arm patches, their faces concealed by the distinctive bandanas. Their masked and uniformed guards stood silently at attention behind them, wielding AKs.[4]

Comandante Francisco told the reporters the EPR was born in May 1994, when fourteen organizations came together to build a clandestine army. The *comandantes* read a potentially reformist list of demands, including nationalization of US holdings in Mexico, cancellation of foreign debt, and debt relief for the struggling middle class. But they also called for President Zedillo to cede power to a "socialist transition government." Comandante Victoria said the EPR would never agree to talks with the government. Comandante José Arturo said "We do not consider the state is invulnerable. We believe we can strike it and defeat it."[5]

José Arturo said the group financed their arms purchases through "bank expropriations and the kidnapping of big businesspeople."[6]

Simultaneous with the press conference, masked and armed men—presumably *EPRistas*—attacked an army patrol back in Coyuca de Benitez, leaving one soldier dead.[7]

The government claimed the EPR was controlled by the Clandestine Revolutionary Workers Party-Union of the People (PROCUP), a deep-underground remnant of the 1970s guerilla movement with a penchant for bomb scares and as many enemies on the left as in the government.[8] PROCUP was purported by many in the above-ground left to be a "pseudo-revolutionary" group, heavily infiltrated, if not controlled, by government agents and provocateurs.[9] The government, in turn, blamed PROCUP for the 1994 kidnapping of Mexican banking magnate Alfredo Harp Helú, who netted his captors a $30 million ransom.[10]

PROCUP could claim a lineage back to Lucio Cabañas. In 1975, David Cabañas, Lucio's brother, founded the Union of the People as a successor to Lucio's Party of the Poor (PDLP). While a hardcore few nurtured the PDLP in the mountains of Guerrero, the Union of the People merged with various Maoist factions, expanded its name to PROCUP, and became an urban underground cell.[11]

PROCUP outlived the various revolutionary efforts of the 1970s—but most of its exploits were against enemies on the left. In 1984, PROCUP kidnapped Mexican Communist Party leader Arnaldo Martínez Verdugo. In 1990, PROCUP re-emerged from inactivity, seemingly to attack the offices of *La Jornada*, which had recently criticized the group. Two guards were killed, but a PROCUP statement later claimed they had been shot while attempting to chase down operatives who had dropped off a communiqué, calling it a "lamentable occurrence" and "not part of our strategy or tactics."[12]

David Cabañas and Felipe Martínez Soriano, former rector of the Autonomous University of Oaxaca, were arrested in the investigation of the incident. Martínez Soriano denied any link to PROCUP—but his release was secured later that year when PROCUP kidnapped a German consular official. Martínez Soriano was arrested again two years later, following a wave of bomb attacks on US-owned business outlets in Mexico City, including Citibank, IBM and McDonalds.[13] David Cabañas, although never formally sentenced, remained in federal prison.[14]

On January 7, 1994, with the Zapatistas engaging government troops in Chiapas, a car bomb exploded in Mexico City's University Plaza. On January 8, power lines and other targets were bombed elsewhere in the country, including the federal building in Acapulco. Because of the timing, they were erroneously reported as EZLN actions. PROCUP subsequently took responsibility for them.[15] The EZLN later disavowed "any relationship or link" with PROCUP.[16]

The situation got still murkier when *Proceso* reported that it had learned its own employees were under investigation by Federal District police for the Plaza Universidad bomb.[17]

If PROCUP first attempted to steal the EZLN's fire with the January bombings in 1994, they worked with impressive efficiency to quickly establish a new rural vanguard in the Sierra del Sur. After the Aguas Blancas massacre, many *campesinos* in Guerrero doubtless decided peaceful struggle was no longer an option; PROCUP cadres deemed the time right to resurrect the guerilla movement right in Lucio's old turf.

ESCALATION AND REPRESSION

They were, initially at least, more successful than their forebear Lucio. It was only after the Cold War and history itself had been declared over that the Sierra Madre birthed its most ambitious guerilla army of the post-Revolutionary era. The EPR dramatically demonstrated its power on the night of August 28, 1996 with coordinated attacks on military and police targets in five southern and central states, leaving thirteen dead.

At ten o'clock, two officers were killed in an attack on the state police barracks in Tlaxiaco, in the Sierra Mixteca of Oaxaca. Graffiti were left on Tlaxiaco's colonial-era walls, *vivas* for the EPR and *lucha popular*. An hour later, a similar attack was carried out at the Oaxaca beach town of Huatulco (site of a Club Med), leaving nine dead—five police, two rebels and two civilians caught in the crossfire. Meanwhile in Oaxaca's capital, the rebels took over a radio station and read a communiqué.[18]

Virtually simultaneously, armed attacks were carried out in three widely separated locations in Guerrero. Two police were killed in the villages of Tixtla and Ciudad Altamirano, while a home-made grenade blew up a police station on the outskirts of Acapulco, leaving an officer wounded.[19]

On a federal highway in the State of Mexico, also simultaneously, an army detachment guarding an electrical substation was attacked, leaving three soldiers wounded.[20]

That same night in Chiapas, the EPR set up armed barricades on the road through the Highlands, stopping traffic and distributing a manifesto. A phone call to the Tuxtla daily *Expreso* said the EPR would refrain from military attacks in Chiapas "because we don't want to interfere with the dialogue of the EZLN with the government."[21]

Near dawn in the mountains of Puebla, the army base guarding the federal hydro-dam at Necaxa was attacked. A thirty-minute gun battle ensued, miraculously leaving no casualties.[22]

Proceso wrote that the EPR had "destroyed the myth of a pantomime."[23]

Others clung to the pantomime hypothesis. M. Delal Baer, an analyst with the Center for Strategic and International Studies (CSIS)—a Washington DC think-tank run by Henry Kissinger, Zbigniew Brzezinski and James Schlesinger—told *The Wall Street Journal* he didn't believe such a sophisticated fighting force could emerge from peasants. "The vital question is: Who is yanking the string?" The *Journal* raised the usual suspects: "drug-traffickers, rogue police gangs or even disaffected factions within Mexico's political elite." It quoted PAN official Carlos Castillo Peraza, who blamed dinosaurs attempting to hold back the free-market transition: "It seems like quite a coincidence that each time we are ready to reap an economic advance, we face some new shock, like the EPR."[24]

Other observers recalled the involvement of Raúl Salinas in the Maoist current Politica Popular in the 1970s, before he became top middleman between the drug cartels and Mexico's political elite. Perhaps he kept some of his old connections to manipulate for new purposes.[25]

The EPR and the government each ruled out any possibility of dialogue, with President Zedillo deriding the new guerillas as "terrorists."[26] The *Wall Street Journal* headline called the EPR "brutal"; the *New York Times* preferred "fanatical."[27]

Gobernación Subsecretary Arturo Nuñez insisted the EPR was a "mini-group left over from the 1970s." He told the *New York Times*, "We can definitely affirm that they have no popular base."[28]

Immediately after the dramatic August raids, the EPR declared a month-long cease-fire to allow Guerrero state elections to take place. Military patrols were officially suspended, and the PRD won control of nineteen of the state's seventy-six *municipios*—up from twelve.[29]

The cease-fire was broken in October with an ambush on a police patrol in Oaxaca's mountains, leaving five officers dead. Most alarmingly, there were several attacks within the Federal District and State of Mexico—including a spray of gunfire on the army barracks outside the pyramids of Teotihuacan, a top tourist attraction.[30]

There was also a wave of bomb threats in Acapulco, mostly targeting US businesses such as Wal-Marts, although the EPR denied responsibility.[31]

President Zedillo vowed to fight the new guerillas with the "full force of the state" in a nationally broadcast address. "Today less than ever can violence be justified."[32]

In this spirit of fastidiously avoiding violence, Zedillo immediately boosted military spending and the army's troop strength by 15 percent to a respective $2 billion and 180,000 men, in spite of the economic downturn.[33] The army asked the government to suspend civil rights "in specific zones where the presence of subversive groups is suspected," applying Article 29 of the Mexican Constitution for the first time.[34]

For the EPR's second press conference, in February, reporters were led on a tortuous route around the teeming Federal District, and finally guided to a safehouse with their eyes covered. "As long as the Mexican people remain trapped in intolerable misery, it is logical and natural for an armed movement to develop," said Comandante Victoria in a room with draped walls. Perplexingly, a Comandante Oscar said, "We have not declared war yet."[35]

In the 1997 Congressional elections, which were devastating for the PRI, the EPR again called a truce, but promised to escalate attacks if there was evidence of fraud.[36]

A Comandante Antonio reiterated to CNN reporter Harris Whitbeck at a Oaxaca mountain camp press conference just before the elections that the group was not ready to declare war. "We believe that should not be our decision, it should be a product of current social conditions."[37]

But it seemed ever clearer the EPR was following the Guevarista doctrine of *creating* conditions where the government—in Che's words—"breaks its own contracts, its own appearance of 'democracy,' and attacks the people . . ."[38]

The center of federal power now appeared ringed by zones of guerilla sympathy. It was no longer necessary to drive all the way to Chiapas or Guerrero to see tanks on the roads and sullen peasants going about their business under the watchful eye of federal troops.

The Sierra Huasteca, an arm of the Oriental between Hidalgo and Veracruz, only an hour's drive from Mexico City, was nearly as militarized following army discoveries of arms caches there. There were reports of Huastec Indians roughed up in army "interrogations," their homes ransacked. The army singled out *pueblos* where the Emiliano Zapata Democratic Front of the Mexican East (FEDOMEZ), a civil *campesino* group, had a following.[39]

But the Sierra del Sur got the worst of it. Tlacoachistlahuaca, already in rebellion, faced escalated terror. On March 26, 1988, army troops entered the community of Barrio Nuevo San José to conduct searches for weapons and EPR propaganda. Homes were ransacked, meagre possessions destroyed or confiscated. When residents protested, the troops became more violent. Seventeen-year-old Cenobio Sixto Santos was beaten to death. Four others were detained without charge and evacuated at gunpoint to an unknown destination by helicopter.[40]

In Guerrero's Ahuacuotzingo *municipio*, local militants of the Emiliano Zapata Worker–Campesino Union (UOCEZ) accused a motorized column of army and Judicial Police of entering Xitopotla and Tehuaxtiltlan *pueblos* shooting machine guns into the air, bursting down doors and ransacking homes.[41]

Tlaxiaco, Oaxaca, was occupied by army and police following the August 1996 attack there, but their presence predictably failed to prevent extra-judicial revenge against perceived guerilla sympathizers. Two months later, with the *cabacera* sandbagged and bristling with machine guns, Manuel Ramírez Santiago of the local People's Human Rights Defense Committee (CODEP) was kidnapped.[42]

But the most profound impacts from the August attacks were felt in San Augustín Loxicha, an isolated Zapotec village high in Oaxaca's mountains.

COUP D'ÉTAT AT SAN AUGUSTÍN LOXICHA

Loxicha was quiet during the August attacks, but the very next day army troops occupied the little town. Over the following days, over 125 residents were arrested on charges of colluding in the attacks. They were taken to the top-security state Social Rehabilitation Center (CERESO) at Ixcotel. Forty-four were tortured, and several held incommunicado, according to Adrina Carmona of Oaxaca's Fray Francisco de Vitoria Human Rights Center. She cited testimonies smuggled from the prison and dismissed the confessions as extracted through fear.[43] The Mexican League for the Defense of Human Rights reported that when some of the prisoners were interrogated, there were gringos present wearing caps that said "FBI."[44]

Among the arrested were not only local *campesinos* and teachers—but the town's municipal president, Agustin Luna Valencia, and entire *ayuntamiento*.[45]

Hundreds of Loxicha residents marched all the way to Mexico City to petition the government for their release—to no avail.[46] School service at Loxicha was interrupted as the state government instrumented a purge of teachers suspected of supporting the guerillas.[47]

An EPR communiqué denied any link to the Loxicha prisoners, and twelve of the prisoners announced an indefinite hunger strike.[48] The National Indigenous Congress called on COCOPA, the federal body convened for the Chiapas peace process, to act on the Loxicha situation.[49]

Ironically, the deposed Loxicha government was *PRIista*, but had also won the support of the FAC-MLN, the new radical *campesino* alliance.[50] The government alleged that Loxicha residents formed the backbone of the eighty-man EPR force that attacked the tourist town of Huatulco, and that municipal leaders had recruited for the guerillas in the hamlets.[51]

The situation at remote Loxicha began to attract some international attention. A *New York Times* reporter who secured an interview with one of the accused Loxichas at CERESO wrote that Francisco Valencia, looking "dazed and worried, and straining to express himself in Spanish . . . was not even certain of the name of the organization he is accused of fighting for."[52]

Guadencia Garcia Martínez, Loxicha's new interim *presidente*, admitted it was really the army that was running the town. He told a visiting *Washington Post* reporter he was afraid to be seen wearing boots on the street. "You wear boots and the army arrests you for being a guerilla," he said. "The entire town is scared."[53]

The following March, schoolteachers from Oaxaca's dissident Section 22 of the SNTE joined with other civil organizations to establish a peace camp in the town. Within hours, they were attacked by masked men with rifles, *palos*, rocks and machetes. Several suffered blows and gunshot wounds before the state police finally intervened. The group, including the wounded, were evacuated from Loxicha and dumped back on the main road through the high sierra. They made their way back to Oaxaca City by bus, on their own.[54]

In November 1998, my photographer Maria Anguera and I drove into San Augustín Loxicha, a deceptively long trek on terrible roads, to find army and police check-points at the entrance to town. We were stopped and questioned, and finally allowed to proceed. The town clings to the side of a mountain, overlooking a spectacular vista to the south; the distant Pacific gleamed through the morning fog. Hummers ringed the *zócalo*, and armed troops surveyed the town from the church steeples and the *cabacera* rooftop. Few people would talk to us. When we got back to our rented VW bug, someone had scrawled in the dust on the windshield, "move on gringo, you are not wanted here."

Maybe we'd have done better to stay in *el DF*. At that moment, Loxicha children were holding a vigil in front of the federal Chamber of Deputies demanding release of their parents from prison, afforded freedom to speak in the metropolitan center that they did not have in their besieged home.[55]

The regional press also faced terror and reprisals. Razhy González, principal reporter and editor at the Oaxaca weekly *Contrapunto*, was abducted at his office by masked men and held for two days after attending an EPR press conference. His captors roughed him up and interrogated him on the location of the press conference.[56]

THE EPR AND THE CIVIL STRUGGLE

The EPR threat provided the government with the appropriate atmosphere to crack down on civil *campesino* movements—especially the OCSS and FAC-MLN. This, of course, played into the EPR's hands by making civil struggle increasingly untenable.

Tepetixtla and other OCSS strongholds in Coyuca de Benitez were occupied by the army immediately after the EPR's appearance. Eight OCSS militants were ar-rested as EPR members, and apprehension orders issued for OCSS leader Benigno Guzmán Martínez. As soon as the press and human rights workers were able to establish contact with them, half the prisoners recanted their confessions, stating they were extracted through torture—suffocation with plastic bags and electro-shock to the testicles.[57]

Hilario Mesino Acosta, one of the arrested men, said he was threatened with the disappearance and death of his family.[58] Held for almost a year, he was finally released for lack of evidence.[59]

By February 1997, the FAC-MLN claimed it had nearly a hundred militants being held as political prisoners.[60]

Benigno Guzmán Martínez had been contacted by a Reuters reporter in Guerrero's mountains in November 1995, when he was already wanted on "public disorder" charges. Benigno denied he was preparing for armed struggle and said he wanted to see a "peaceful revolution" in Mexico.[61]

The struggle apparently divided Guzmán's family. In December 1996, Bartolo Guzmán, Benigno's brother, was killed by unknown gunmen in Tepetixtla, and suspicion fell on the OCSS. Bartolo had been *jefe* of the Benito Juárez Campesino Organization, which Benigno accused of being set up by the PRI to divide the OCSS.[62]

Benigno Guzmán was arrested January 1997 at a house in Mexico City, where he was hiding with his wife Sonia and their children, awaiting plastic surgery.[63] He maintained his innocence, and went on a hunger strike for weeks in Acapulco's state prison. An EPR statement denied any link to Guzmán.[64]

That same month, attacks were launched on party bosses in Guerrero. The locally notorious *cacique* Eleuterio Aguilar was ambushed in Tepetixtla, probably in revenge for recent killings of OCSS supporters. Another political boss was gunned down at his Petatlan logging mill by presumed *EPRistas*.[65]

The EPR grew as increasingly desperate *campesinos* came to see it as the legitimate successor to the Cabañas insurgency. On February 5, 1998, EPR troops, clutching their AKs, held a march in the Tecoanapa *zócalo*, in Guerrero's mountains. Reporters wrote that villagers stepped forward to press *maíz* and money into the hands of the veiled men and women.[66]

If the militarization drew many *campesinos* to the EPR, it alienated others. In January 1997, the Oaxaca OCEZ held a *plantón* in the state capital to demand demilitarization of their Sierra Mixteca villages. "We are an organization that struggles openly, which is democratic but does not agree with the taking of arms to achieve its demands," said OCEZ leader José Santiago Cruz.[67]

ALPHABET SOUP IN THE SIERRA MADRE

In April 1998, a Popular Revolutionary Democratic Party (PDPR) pronounced as General Command of the EPR. Communiqués arrived by Internet at Mexico's newspapers, complete with directions to the PDPR-EPR website (maintained by supporters in Italy). The communiqués decried the Mexican state's "Low Intensity Warfare" campaign, claimed the legacy of the Cabañas brothers and embraced

Lenin. But they also invoked two heretical Frenchmen, the anarchist Pierre Joseph Proudhon and Auguste Blanqui, conspiratist of the Paris Commune. They noted "the lessons of anarchism."[68]

The documents also listed the fourteen constituent organizations of the EPR: the Communist Cells-Chiapas, the Francisco Javier Mina Self-Defense Group, the Union of Revolutionary Commandos, the Revolutionary Commandos of Mexico, the Francisco Villa Armed Commando, the Commando Morelos, the Workers Self-Defense Brigade (BOA), the Campesino Brigade of Adjustment, the May 18 Brigade, the Genaro Vázquez Rojas Brigade, the Vicente Guerrero Brigade, the Ricardo Flores Magón Revolutionary Workers Organization (ORO-RFM), the People's Armed Revolutionary Organization (ORAP) and PROCUP-PDLP.[69]

These are presumably local groups formed to defend against *caciques* and police, each with a small armed force in its own valley or region, brought together around the nucleus of PROCUP-PDLP.

But the movement evidenced a centrifugal as well as centripetal dynamic.

Divisions became clear following an army raid on a schoolhouse in the Guerrero mountain *pueblo* of El Charco on June 7, 1998. When the shooting was over, eleven were dead, both guerillas and civilians. The army claimed the guerillas had opened fire when surrounded and ordered to surrender, but Miguel Angel Godínez, a local PRD militant, told a *Miami Herald* reporter the army had opened fire without provocation: "There were no clashes, it was massacre."[70]

A previously unknown group, the Revolutionary Army of the Insurgent People (ERPI), came forward to claim the fallen. Antonio, a defected EPR commander, later told a Mexican journalist in a secret-location interview "those responsible for the El Charco massacre will be punished."[71]

However, an EPR communiqué also claimed the rebels who died in El Charco.[72]

Two arrested at El Charco, university student Erika Zamora Pardo and PRD militant Efrén Cortés, retracted their "confessions" in an Acapulco prison interview with a *La Jornada* reporter, claiming they had signed under threat of torture. The two prisoners also confirmed charges by El Charco residents that the morning assault was unprovoked, and some of the dead had been executed in the school basket-ball court after surrendering.[73]

On July 4, a Guerrero state police convoy near La Montaña was attacked, and two officers were killed. Authorities were stumped as to which faction to blame.[74]

The breakaway faction was first known as EPR Autonomo, accusing the EPR leadership of being "dogmatic, anti-democratic, conservative and intolerant." In *Proceso*, Carlos Marín rendered the "I" in ERPI as standing for "Indígena" rather than

"Insurgente," and claimed to have seen documents revealing plans for a nation-wide insurrection in the year 2000.[75]

A pair of reporters from *El Universal*, after meeting with ERPI insurgents at an undisclosed location within Chilpancingo, offered that the split represented a generation-old difference between PROCUP and the PDLP. The EPR, closer to the hardline PROCUP, believed armed struggle the only path, while the ERPI, closer to the PDLP, conceived their role as an armed wing of the civil struggle, and was open to dialogue.[76]

There were still other armed groups with uncertain loyalties to the EPR.

In January 1995, a Clandestine Indigenous National Liberation Army (ECILN) sent a communiqué announcing its presence in Oaxaca's northern Sierra Juárez. The government implicated it in the kidnapping of a PRI federal deputy.[77]

Later that year, an Armed Revolutionary Commando of the South (CARS) issued a communiqué blaming the "Salinista-Zedillista usurpers" for Guerrero's misery, and proclaiming, "We are now ready for prolonged popular war!"[78]

In December 1996, an Armed Front for the Liberation of the Marginalized People of Guerrero (FALPMG) issued a communiqué to the press.[79]

A year later, just after the Acteal massacre, a police post in the Guerrero mountains was attacked by armed men, leaving two officers wounded. An Army of Justice of the Defenseless People (EJPI) claimed responsibility as retaliation for the blood spilled in Chiapas. The communiqué ended, "No more crimes against indigenous people!"[80]

FEAR IN ATOYAC

Despite the seeming fragmentation, and in the absence of official declaration, the war zones requested by the federal army were already really in effect.

At dawn on November 10, 1998, Maria and I were searching the Sierra del Sur for some trace of the guerillas when the EPR launched its first attack since the bloody El Charco incident. The rebel troops sealed off the entrances to San Juan de las Flores, a *pueblo* in Atoyac de Alvarez. They cut the electrical and telephone lines before setting upon the state Motorized Police detachment stationed there. One officer and two guerillas were killed before the *EPRistas* retreated, leaving *vivas* for Lucio Cabañas scrawled on the schoolhouse wall.[81]

Gen. Humberto López Portillo Leal, commander of the Ninth Military Region, announced an intensive search of rugged Atoyac *municipio*.[82]

With Hummer convoys combing the backroads, the Motorized Police in San Juan de Las Flores were "practically expelled" by the *pueblo*'s residents, according to *El Sol de Acapulco*, which we picked up while racing along the coastal highway toward Atoyac. The detachment withdrew at the demand of San Juan's *ejidal* and traditional authorities, who feared their presence would draw more bloodshed.[83]

Gen. López Portillo simultaneously announced that troops were being sent into several Sierra *municipios* to search out and destroy opium and marijuana crops. He boasted that his troops had already eradicated nearly 1,000 hectares of illegal crops that year, and mentioned Atoyac as one of the top marijuana-producing *municipios*.[84]

As we progressed, the army and PGR checkpoints became more numerous, inquisitive and intimidating. Helicopters flitted overhead. Late in the day we reached Atoyac. We drove up a terrible dirt road into the mountains, parallel to the similar road leading to San Juan de Las Flores. Some of the guerillas must have approached San Juan through the forested canyon between the two roads. Far enough up the road, high in the Sierra, we surmised, small communities protected their camps.

The road passed El Paraiso, where Lucio Cabañas had his earliest following as a radical schoolteacher. We were warned not to stop there, as it was now the domain of grim *narco-caciques* who do not welcome outsiders. We kept going, through mist-shrouded tropical forest.

As it got darker and the road got progressively worse, the next spot on the map, which had appeared deceptively close, seemed to recede into an unfathomable distance. We decided to turn around and take our chances with the *narcos* in Paraiso, or the army back in the municipal center.

As we returned through the dusk, eyes peered out uneasily from every *campesino* cabin we passed, to see if our headlights signified friend or foe. Every time a pick-up passed us on the road, there was the wary exchange of suspicious glances with the occupants. The primal origin of the custom of waving—to show that you are unarmed—took on a new significance. It broke the tension palpably.

When we were flagged down at one cabin, we were relieved to find it was a *campesino* who needed a ride down the road to Paraiso. He had harrowing stories about bandits holding people up on the road, raping women. Some operated with the cooperation of the police, he said. Between bandits, police, army, *narcos*, guerillas and paramilitaries, you never knew who armed men might be.

Our passenger said the *narcos* plant on communal lands without consulting the communities—marijuana in the hotter valleys, opium high on the slopes. The police protect some *narcos*, while hunting down others. He said the PGR had twice picked him up to question him about opium that had been planted in his *milpa*. Once, he had a knife held to his nose and a gun stuck in his mouth; the next time they took him up in a helicopter and threatened to throw him out over the mountains.

When we dropped him off at Paraiso and continued back down toward the main road—where we would be subjected to a thorough search by the army, which was fortunately rougher on our possessions than our persons—we asked our passenger if people still remember Lucio.

Without hesitation, he insisted, "Lucio Cabañas didn't die. They got the wrong man. Lucio is still alive. Perhaps in Cuba."

WITH THE ERPI

We drove all over the mountains of Guerrero and Oaxaca, but people were generally afraid to talk—and perhaps the movement was in a state of retrenchment. But we did plant a few seeds. In April, back in New York, came the phone call: the ERPI was ready to meet me.

Back in Mexico City again, I was given the nascent guerilla organization's first internal document, entitled: *Proposal: Thesis for Change (Our Basic Principles)*.

The 24-point manifesto mostly seemed to address the ERPI's differences with the EPR. Read point one: "The fundamental commitment of the revolutionary is with the people. No other commitment, neither personal nor group, is above that." It rejected "the messianic conception by which revolutionary organizations have seen themselves as the representatives of the people, who can only participate in the revolution through their own intermediation."

Point two demanded "construction of Popular Power, beginning now, in every aspect and until the ultimate consequences." It called for formation of Insurgent Councils to wield executive power, and the preparation of "organs of legislative and judicial power in every zone, region and state," eventually readying a national Insurgent Popular Assembly. Admitting that "it is easy to say, but not so easy to achieve," it stated that "PP" should be "directed effectively by the people," through representatives who "lead by obeying," that the revolutionary organization "should be subordinate" to "the base." It credited the EZLN with "establishing a different relation" with the base, and cited the "obligation" to "find new and always better forms of applying this norm."

Point three stated: "Until now we have been concerned to build the Army of the Party; it is now the hour to build the Army of the People." Point four: "The liberty of the people cannot be conquered by any supposed vanguard, but by the people themselves. For this reason, we do not aspire to be a vanguard marching before the people, but to march together with the people in the struggle for democracy, justice and liberty." Five: "It is the hour to build a party of the people, and not a 'party of revolutionaries' who consider themselves above the people."

Point six decried the tendency of revolutionary organizations to "prioritize discipline of a military character and diminish the weight of democracy . . . It is now the hour to give greater weight to democracy." Point seven: "Revolutionary theory, the arm of the Revolution, has in some cases been converted into an . . . arm against the Revolution." It noted with irony that fighting with World War I-vintage arms would be considered absurd by revolutionaries who cling to "theoretical conceptions" from the same era. "Yes, our ideology has Marxism as a base, but not the dogmatic, rigid, wizened vision . . . Our theoretical position is impregnated with a critical, practical, creative and flexible vision."

Point eight: "The methods of organizing, like theory, have been delayed with respect to reality . . . It is time to reset the pace." Point nine pointed toward new methods: "The *coyunturas* are opportunities that history has offered the revolutionary forces."

Point ten, noting the "necessity of clandestinity" and "the political-military character of our struggle," stated: "Nonetheless, we have to take into account that even when the organizational principles elaborated by the classics, and in particular by Lenin, were adequate for the conditions in which they struggled, the actual conditions in our nation are different . . . Democratic centralism as traditionally applied emphasizes centralism while diminishing democracy . . . [T]he principal enemy of the Mexican people is the financial oligarchy and the anti-democratic government, so the principal demand of society is democracy . . . Those who struggle for democracy cannot be anti-democratic, on pain of isolating themselves from the people for their inconsistency . . ." The experience "in countries where bureaucratic socialism has fallen" demonstrates the "negative effects of centralism even when applied with revolutionary aims."

Point eleven: "The revolutionary process in Mexico requires the combination of all forms of struggle . . . [A]rmed struggle is necessary, yes, but subordinate to the political struggle."

Point twelve: "The tactic utilized in the present stage" is to "guarantee the people's self-defense and, simultaneously, to advance toward the construction of popular power" and "preparation of insurrectionary forces."

Point thirteen called for a "Popular Army," an "army of the masses whose maximum expression is the people in arms. It is the hour to undertake its construction." Point fourteen stated that "strategic planning" should "respond to the concrete and immediate needs of the population."

Fifteen decried the "hegemonist conception" of certain revolutionary organizations: "[H]istorical experience can help us comprehend that a revolution in contemporary Mexico, as in the Revolution of Independence and the Revolution of 1910, cannot be a product of the action of only one force or organization, but of an entirety [conjunto] of all . . . Our principal aspiration is to form a part of the conjunto of forces that contribute to the transformation of the country . . ."

Sixteen: "Self-defense is a legitimate right of the people . . . No argument is valid for not exercising it. No aggression against the people should go unpunished."

Seventeen called for "unity in diversity" as an alternative to demanding "interior homogeneity" of revolutionary forces, asserting that "unity is possible even when we have divergent positions in some aspects."

Eighteen: "The truth is revolutionary. To be a revolutionary is to speak with truth, to affirm it . . . It is the hour to leave behind the 'reason of party' that serves to justify lies." Nineteen: "It is the hour to take democracy to its ultimate consequences, within the organization as without."

Twenty attacked "preconceived ideas," asserting: "Reality should recover its role as the principal source of revolutionary conceptions."

Twenty-one warned against elites concerned with the "great general theories of the revolution," and called for leaders to "engage actively and directly in work" at "every level."

Twenty-two warned against seeing the reality of "unequal development" within the "revolutionary camp" as a need for imposed homogeneity, calling instead for accepting "a law of unequal and combined development."

Twenty-three warned against "dehumanization, considering revolutionaries as objects, their conversion into machines, and their submission to the interests of the party. We should recuperate our human relation between revolutionaries and with the people."

Twenty-four stated: "Liberty, democracy and justice are only complete if they are realized in the political terrain as in the economic. We should recognize the aspirations of the people in both aspects and struggle together to achieve them."[85]

As a condition of my meeting with the ERPI, I am constrained from revealing the location, but it was in the mountains of Guerrero. The state was more divided than ever. In February's elections, the PRI's René Juárez won a narrow gubernatorial victory that the PRD challenger Felix Salgado charged was fraudulent. Federal authorities affirmed the victory, but thousands marched from Chilpancingo to the DF in protest, eleven days cross-country. There was still a permanent blockade of the governor's palace in Chilpancingo by PRD militants, forcing Juárez to work out of an ad hoc office in the governor's mansion.[86]

A long, dusty ride in the back of a truck from a coastal farmtown brought us to a small Indian *pueblo* far beyond where the pavement ends. It was on the electric grid, but water was piped down from the mountains to communal spigots. The women wore traditional dress, and spent much of the day weaving. The men mostly wore white *campesino* pajamas, and worked in the *milpa* and sugarcane. It was clear that the *pueblo* was sharply divided. We stayed on the generally poorer PRD side of town, and waited. Our hosts fed us well on bean soup and *atole* and *tortillas*, but I sensed they were eating better than usual because of our presence.

After a week of waiting, we were led through the dusk to a rendezvous just outside the *pueblo*. Ten masked men with rifles, led by a Comandante Arturo, shook hands and saluted me and my companions. They were all young Indians, with a better command of their indigenous tongues than Spanish. They wore no uniforms, but a patchwork of ragged civies and camo. Their masks were bandanas, some cut with eye-slits. Their arms were also a patchwork—.22s, a shotgun, two *cuernos de chivo* ("goat horns"; AKs).

We marched up the mountainside, into the night. Near the summit I got winded, and was grateful when they slowed to accommodate me. As we descended the other side, pastureland gave way to bush. A big fire burned on an opposing slope, hanging like a beacon in the night. We descended steeply, toward the sound of running water, forded a river, and were told to make camp.

We woke up in a hidden valley, a pocket of tropical forest along the river that plunged in on a waterfall. The troops lined up for review by Comandante Arturo. I could tell he was smiling through his mask when he asked how I was feeling.

We were waiting for another *columna*—this one members of the support base or militia, as opposed to Arturo's column of active combatants.

Comandante Arturo told me; "We make *reuniones* with the people, guard the people against thieves, rustlers, highwaymen. We are ready to defend the people. Thievery has stopped since the column was formed." Arturo said his column had already been in combat with bandits, but not government troops.

"I grew up witnessing the injustice," said Arturo, who was perhaps twenty. "The army and police stopped the buses and robbed the *campesinos*. Since we formed our army, this is not as much of a problem. They don't want to die."

He called this work "propaganda armada."

"We take our orders from the communities," Arturo said. "The high command supports us, gives us supplies, boots, food." He said there were other columns throughout the mountains. Each column has a *comandante*—a rotating position. Their troops are called *combatientes*, and their own superiors are *capitánes,* who oversee several columns. Arturo said some *capitánes* are "people of the city," but many are Indian as well.

Their army is "pure indigenous people," Arturo said. "We want the *gente indígena* to have respect and to govern themselves as they want to. Now the local governments are imposed by the rich, by outsiders. If the government doesn't want war, it must answer us. They should change the *cabacera*, have a clean election."

My questions about ideology always met answers about day-to-day reality. "We are struggling to change the government to one which will aid the poor people here, all the people of Mexico," Arturo stated. "People need credit. People may have land but no tractor, no seeds."

Is there enough land here for the people? I asked.

"There is great territory. The land can support us. But the *PRIistas*, the *caciques*, steal all the aid that comes to our communities. They go to Chilpancingo to get money for irrigation, roads, and it all goes right into their pockets."

I asked if they supported Felix Salgado as Guerrero's legitimate governor.

"Yes. We are ready to offer any kind of support."

I asked their thoughts on EZLN.

"We support their struggle. They are also fighting for the poor. Their struggle is equal with ours."

I asked if they had links to other guerilas.

"There are various other armed groups with other names. We want to talk with them, bring ourselves together. We want to be united with all who are struggling against the evil government."

I asked about the EPR.

"The EPR don't do anything. They exist only in name. They were accustomed to work only with money. Us, without money—here we go."

The second column joined us a few hours after dawn, entering the valley from another direction, another *pueblo*. They wore *campesino* garb, pajamas rather than camo, *huaraches* rather than boots. Two carried rifles, but most only machetes. There were two women—one thick and gray-haired; one a young mother, breast-feeding a baby, a pistol stuck in her belt. All wore bandanas over their faces.

Manuel was "director" of the committee that supports the column. In a soft, almost shy Indian voice, he said; "The *indígenas* here don't have electricity, health centers, potable water. We want a municipal presidency that fulfills its promises. René's people bought votes here—ten pesos and a machete for each vote. For certain there will be war, because the government will not give in."

Outside the municipal center, he said, practically everybody supports the *columna*. "The *cabacera* doesn't work with the communities. The majority of the people here are with our struggle."

José, another member of the committee, had been working with the armed movement for four years—first the EPR, then the ERPI. "Here in the indigenous zones of Mexico, there is no justice, no human rights. Every day the poverty advances. The government wants indigenous people to disappear. They want to impose the policy of modernity, promote consumerism. We want an economy that supports the family, that doesn't exploit. We want work with a just salary. Indian people have the ability to govern their own communities. But the government does not respect the vote. We are in arms because there is no other remedy."

They said they mostly grew corn and beans for their own families—what they sold was in their own *pueblos*. *PRIistas* maintained a near-monopoly on spaces in the *cabacera* market.

Government aid "is used only as propaganda for the PRI," José claimed. "You don't get aid if you don't support the PRI. If you oppose them, the police and the judge are the same *PRIistas*. We have land—but if you are sick or in jail you can't work it. You are forced to sell it, and it is all you have."

The meeting lasted into the afternoon, and was followed by some instruction in fighting skills. The two columns parted with salutes and handshakes in an orderly line, and the slogan—*"Con la lucha popular, el pueblo vencerá."*

As the sun set, my companion and I were given an escort back over the mountain to our *pueblo*.

A SIGH OF GRIM RELIEF

Once during our wait, some army trucks had rumbled through the *pueblo*, and I had been concerned about the possibility of encountering them with the *columna*, of course. When I picked up the newspapers after returning to Mexico City, I was doubly glad this had not passed. There had been several violent incidents in the mountains of Guerrero.

On April 20, soldiers had entered Barrio Nuevo San José (Autonomous Municipality Rancho Nuevo de la Democracia) in Tlacoachistlahuaca. That day, a 12-year-old boy, Antonio Mendoza Olivero, and the *campesino* Evaristo Albino Tellez disappeared. Two women searching for Albino and Antonio, who had never returned from the *milpa*, were accosted by soldiers and raped. Neighbors, family and community leaders denounced the incident before the authorities in Ometepec. It wasn't until May 7 that the state Human Rights Defense Commission announced that the two bodies had been found in an Acapulco morgue. The army's version claimed the *campesinos* attacked them with firearms, and didn't mention the rapes. Tlacoachistlahuaca was subsequently occupied by hundreds of troops.[87]

On May 2, army and state police at Pizotla, in Ajuchitlan del Progresso, had exchanged fire with men guarding opium and marijuana crops, leaving one dead. Two others were arrested, and several firearms seized. According to a Guerrero state police report, the men belonged to a new faction, the Armed Ecologist Group (GEA), who were growing *mota* to buy arms to defend the communal forests from timber exploitation. The army insisted the men were only *narcotraficantes*, but police sources in Ciudad Altamirano leaked the version that the detainees were "members of an ecologist guerilla organization."[88] Rodolfo Montiel Flores, a *campesino* who had been leading blockades of Boise-Cascade's logging trucks with the Organization of Campesinos and Ecologists of the Sierra de Petatlan, was arrested. Montiel denied links to arms or drugs, and his family protested he was being held incommunicado.[89]

On May 7, another confrontation in Ajuchitlan del Progreso drew new blood. Army troops searching for "*estupificantes*" (drug crops) encountered ten armed men and exchanged fire, leaving one dead on each side. The following day, state police arrested a 20-year-old man after finding two AKs in his home. The *ejidal* authorities in Coacoyul y Tizotla, where the incident took place, demanded his release and issued a statement accusing the army, police and René Juárez of "every repressive act against the population of the sierra."[90]

Violence was also escalating in Oaxaca. On May 9, PRD Sen. Hector Sánchez, COCEI leader Oscar Cruz López and reporter Isaac Valdez were all shot and wounded by *caciques* in Chalcatongo de Hidalgo. Sánchez, hit in the leg, accused Oaxaca Gov. José Murat of being the "intellectual author" of the attack, and demanded his resignation. "The intention was to kill me; that is very clear," Sánchez said from his wheelchair at a hospital press conference. The PRD had won the last election in Chalcatongo, but *PRIistas* seized the *cabacera*, and were still occupying it. Sánchez was on his way to a PRD meeting when the attack took place. Days after the attack, MULT leader Heriberto Pazos Ortíz was wounded and two companions killed in a drive-by shooting in Oaxaca City—where the MULT had just held a march to protest the Sánchez shooting.[91]

THE TRIPLE ALLIANCE

I had one more meeting before returning to New York. This one was in the mountains of Morelos. At a *pueblo* back in the land of Zapata, I was guided blindfolded into a little adobe house and greeted by two elderly men and one young woman, all wearing bandanas over their faces. These were Don Miguel, Don Pepe and

Combatiente Cecilia—representatives of the most indigenist of Mexico's new in-surgents: the National Indigenous Guerilla Triple Alliance (TAGIN).

The Triple Alliance is a joint command of three armed groups active in the Sierra del Sur, Morelos and Mexico state—the Indigenous Campesino Revolutionary Army (ERIC), the Nationalist Army of Insurgent Indigenous Mexico (ENMII), and the Armed Campesino Command of Indigenous Liberation (COACUAUHTLI). The last acronym forms the name of the Serpent Eagle, a high-ranking Aztec military order.

The guerilla federation's name also refers to the Triple Alliance of Anahuac city-states that ruled the Mexica empire—Tenochtitlan, Texcoco and Tlacopan (today all absorbed into the capital megalopolis). Each constituent group of the TAGIN contributes a member to the command triumvirate, each with a code name taken from Mexica myth and history: Mixcoatl (a Nahuatl creation god, and the early Toltec warrior-king who fathered Quetzalcoatl), Ilhuicamina (the Nahuatl archer god and name assumed by the Aztec *tlatoani* Moctezuma I) and Tlacaélel (Moctezuma I's brother and co-founder of the Mexica empire). The insignia of the guerilla alliance is the shield of Cuitlahuac, the penultimate *tlatoani* who rose against Cortéz.

TAGIN's manifesto states, "we want a reformed constitution, based on the indigenous valors and rights of Anahuac." It offers greetings and solidarity to the EZLN, EPR and ERPI, and calls upon them to "reactivate the armed struggle," as "twelve days of war is not sufficient to intimidate the government."[92]

TAGIN's *comandancia* answers to a Council of Elders from each community represented in the alliance. The minimum age to be a member of the Council of Elders is fifty-two years—the basic cycle in the ancient Nahuatl calendar. TAGIN is seeking representatives on the Council of Elders from every indigenous ethnicity in Mexico. TAGIN's proposed constitutional changes call for the *Consejo de Ancianos* to share federal legislative power with the Senate and the Chamber of Deputies.

Don Pepe and Don Miguel were both on the Council of Elders. Their complaints were familiar ones. Said Don Miguel: "We need money for tractors, fertilizers, pumps, but there is no credit, and without it, the land won't produce, so we can't buy." Don Pepe stated: "We are concerned to conserve the traditions of our peo-ple, to be able to practice our ceremonies freely, to defend our autochthonous rights. The modern culture is destroying our *pueblos*."

When I tried to ask questions, they turned the interview over to Combatiente Cecilia, whose responses were terse and staccato.

What is TAGIN's proposal for governing Mexico?

"*Usos y costumbres.*"

Do you support the San Andrés Accords?

"Yes."

What are the principles of your internal structure?

"Democracy and military discipline."

Do you see any possibilities for dialogue with the government?

"No. We intend to take power."

When are you ready to take up arms?

"When the Council of Elders orders."

THE CHALLENGE TO *ZAPATISMO*

The EPR poses itself as more radical and uncompromising than the EZLN. EPR Comandante José Arturo openly said at one clandestine-location press conference: "We seek power. We won't carry on a dialogue with the murderous government. The government is illegitimate."[93]

In an interview with *Proceso*, EPR Comandante José Arturo took a more obvious stab at the EZLN's Marcos, stating "poetry cannot be the continuation of politics by other means"—a reference to the Clausewitzian definition of war and the Subcommander's verbose, sometimes obscurantist communiqués.[94]

Marcos rebuffed an EPR offer of solidarity. Addressing the EPR in a communiqué, he expressed "respect" for their military tactics of "combined surprise and forceful-ness," but stated: "You fight to take power. We fight for democracy, freedom and justice. It's not the same thing. Even if you are successful and win power, we will go on fighting for democracy, freedom and justice."[95]

But he also warned against any "game that promotes confrontation between the 'good' guerillas and 'bad' guerillas."[96]

The fact that Zapata was betrayed by a bourgeois state which only adapted ele-ments of his program as a tactic of co-optation informs the EPR's rejection of the EZLN's "armed reformism." While the EZLN has evidenced greater internal cohesiveness in the long run, there were reports in 1996 of Chiapas *campesinos* growing frustrated with the stalemate and seeking contacts with the EPR.

The emergence of the ERPI points to a tilt back toward the Zapatista ethic in the Sierra del Sur. By 1999 there were reports that EPR was seeking to eliminate the ERPI leadership.

On October 22, 1999, the Federal Preventative Police announced that they had arrested four *ERPIstas* at a safehouse in Chilpancingo, including two leaders of the organization—Carlos Garcia Rosales ("Comandante Antonio") and Gloria Arenas Ajís ("Colonel Aurora").[97] Rosales was said to be a founding member of the EPR and author of an ERPI document entitled *Rumbo al 2000* calling for a nationwide insurrection.[98] Police also claimed to have confiscated a computer containing plans for developing ERPI cells in eight states.[99] Col. Aurora was said to have been working in the Sierra de Zongolica in Veracruz.[100] Police warned that they had identified fourteen guerilla organizations operating in twelve states from Chiapas to Chihuahua.[101] But the prognosis on violent factionalism was optimistic: they purported that the ERPI leadership, having won over 60 percent of the guerilla support base in Guerrero, "are threatened with death by the EPR."[102]

Regardless of which tendency prevails, and regardless of whether elements in the federal security apparatus view the EPR as useful provocateurs, the unrest creeping north along Mexico's spine is a threat to the stability of the continental Free Trade regime—and assures that the US–Mexican economic integration will be mirrored in closer military cooperation.

15

ANATOMY OF THE NARCO-DICTATORSHIP

The Counter-Revolution Devours Its Children

The infallibility of the great patriarch in Los Pinos, the presidential palace, is a fundamental of the Mexican party-state. Today, in the federal *zócalo*, street vendors hawk caricatured masks of Carlos Salinas de Gortari, favored protest wear. They are tolerated. The disgraced and exiled president makes a convenient scapegoat for the current administration.

Since NAFTA, scandal after scandal has revealed a PRI regime riven with narco-vendettas at the highest levels of power. Salinas, the USA's candidate for first chief of the World Trade Organization, became the most hated Mexican president since Porfirio Díaz. It is universally assumed he inflated the peso by recycling laundered narco-dollars into the treasury in order to get NAFTA passed. His brother Raúl Salinas was acquitted of laundering but convicted of the murder of a top PRI *jefe.* Investigators scoured Switzerland, Panama and the Caymans for the secret bank accounts where the Salinas brothers sequestered their illegal fortune. This unprecedented investigation of a former president would itself be compromised by involvement of Zedillo administration figures in the narco-corruption web.

As the scandals wore on, Carlos globetrotted from his new home in Dublin, occasionally coming to New York for Dow Jones board meetings. Each time, the company's futuristic downtown Manhattan headquarters were staked out by Mexican photographers hoping to get a shot of the elusive pariah. Finally, it got too embarrassing; he took the hint and resigned from the board.[1] The White House withdrew his WTO candidacy.[2]

Under NAFTA, Mexican cartels based in the border cities have established hegemony over the hemispheric dope industry. Colombia's vanquished Cali and Medellín cartels had been positioned for hegemony by their control of the cocaine production zones; now the Gulf, Juárez and Tijuana cartels are so positioned by their control of the entrepôts.

"Cocaine trafficking in the United States is now dominated by organized criminal groups from Mexico who operate on both sides of the 2,000 mile border," DEA Chief of Operations Donnie Marshall told a Congressional subcommittee on immigration in 1998. The Mexican syndicates "are far more sophisticated and wealthy than their predecessors, using their wealth to corrupt and intimidate citizens and law enforcement officials in Mexico, and to a lesser extent in the United States."[3]

Of course, Washington continued to pour money and weapons into this regime in the name of fighting drugs and crime—a matter which has been elevated to a "national security" concern since the end of the Cold War. Mounting evidence of the Mexican regime's co-optation has only caused US Drug Czar Barry McCaffrey, a top advocate of US–Mexico "bilateral cooperation," to become more shrill. In May 1999, he told reporters that the threat from Mexican drug trafficking is "more serious than the Germans in World War II."[4]

While critics term Mexico a "narco-democracy," others have called the *PRI-gobierno* "the perfect dictatorship" precisely because it successfully masquerades as a democracy. The violence of the Mexican cartel wars now approaches that of Latin America's old military regimes. "There's just no parallel to what's happening in Mexico's northern states," Amnesty International's Latin America chief Morris Tidball Binz told the *New York Times* in 1997. "We're seeing disappearances of the type seen in the 1970s, and the number of reported cases has shot up over the last year and a half."[5]

NAFTA Mexico emerges, with Orwellian irony, as a narco-dictatorship whose militarization is pursued in the name of waging a War on Drugs.

"EVERYBODY COULD BE BRIBED"

On February 18, 1997, the National Defense Secretariat announced that Brig. Gen. Jesús Gutiérrez Rebollo, Mexico's "Drug Czar"—head of the National Institute to Combat Drugs—had been arrested as a paid protector of the Juárez Cartel. The revelation came at a bad time. President Bill Clinton was just then facing a decision on "certifying" Mexico as a reliable Drug War ally to receive US aid. Barry McCaffrey had weeks earlier called Gen. Gutiérrez "a guy of absolute unquestioned integrity." The Clinton administration was forced to admit that a Cartel mole had received intelligence briefing in the US.[6]

It got worse. Less than a month after the Drug Czar's arrest, the chief of a CIA-trained army intelligence unit, Brig. Gen. Alfredo Navarro Lara, was arrested—on charges of offering a $1 million-a-month bribe to a brigadier general in Baja California on behalf of the rival Tijuana Cartel (and threatening to have his family killed if he refused).[7]

The previous year, Colombia had been decertified for US aid—although US military assistance (in counter-narcotics guise, of course) continued to flow to the Colombian army.[8] Decertifying Mexico would be trickier, with the future of NAFTA at stake. Clinton was in the unenviable position of having to stand by a Mexican regime apparently subject to a wholesale take-over by the cartels.

The Juárez Cartel, led by Amado "Lord of the Skies" Carrillo Fuentes, was then Mexico's most powerful cocaine syndicate. The honor had previously gone to the Matamoros-based Gulf Cartel, which fell into decline after kingpin Juan Garcia Abrego was captured by *federales* in January 1996, and—in an unprecedented example of bilateral cooperation—flown to Houston for trial. Prosecutors said he shipped up to a third of all coke consumed in the US.[9]

But cocaine exports did not fall. A wave of gangland murders followed the decline of the Gulf Cartel, as the rival Juárez and Tijuana cartels jockeyed for the new top position. In September 1996, a month after he took office with promises of crushing the Tijuana Cartel, Ernesto Ibarra Santes, Baja California commander of Federal Judicial Police (PJF), was assassinated (along with two colleagues) when gunmen pulled up alongside his taxi in Mexico City. A suitcase containing $50,000 in US currency was found in the taxi.[10] Days earlier, he had proclaimed that some of his men were "not just friends of traffickers, but their servants."[11]

After Tijuana's *Zeta* magazine fingered Cartel hitmen in the Ibarra assassination, *Zeta* publisher Jesús Blancornelas was shot on his way to work by the same gunmen—one of whom was killed when the newsman's bodyguard returned fire just before taking a fatal bullet himself. Blancornelas, critically injured, survived to win the Freedom of Expression Prize from New York's Committee to Protect Journalists.[12]

The Juárez murder rate soared to double that of New York City. In one unexplained pattern, seemingly random young women were targeted, their corpses dumped in the desert outside town—over a hundred by the end of 1997.[13] Thousands staged a brave protest against the violence in August 1997 at the town's plaza. An hour later, gunmen shot three men on the same spot. The press warned of Mexico's "Colombianization."[14]

The Juárez Cartel emerged victorious from this struggle, and for a while Carrillo Fuentes was the undisputed master of the multi-billion dollar Mexican coke trade.

He earned his appellation Lord of the Skies by using jumbo jetliner fleets to ferry his product up from the Andes. Then, in July 1997, doctors performing plastic surgery on the Lord of the Skies to alter his appearance at a swank Mexico City clinic injected him with a lethal drug. Their own mutilated corpses were subsequently discovered in barrels of concrete along the Mexico City–Acapulco highway.[15]

Within weeks, of course, there were reports that Carrillo Fuentes was still alive. *The Washington Post* cited a Chilean newspaper's statement that the Lord of the Skies was being hidden by the DEA.[16] It was documented that the kingpin had purchased millions of dollars in Chilean real estate in case he should have to disappear from Mexico.[17]

The Juárez Cartel, of course, had an heir apparent. A year after the supposed death of *El Señor de los Cielos*, the US Justice Department filed drug and money-laundering charges against his brother, Vicente Carrillo Fuentes, claiming he had inherited the Cartel.[18]

But the Tijuana Cartel, led by the Arellano Felix brothers, saw the fall of *El Señor* as a signal that their own time had come. Every region of Mexico has its own crime machine, each with a kept network of police and army officials. The big three in the border cities battled to bring the regional cartels under their control.

In 1998, the Tijuana Cartel won the strategic Guadalajara franchise. A new pact between Guadalajara's Caro Quintero family and Tijuana's Arellano Felix brothers created "the most powerful and sophisticated network for distributing drugs in the United States," a DEA report stated. The new organization, dubbed "The Federation," stood to streamline operations and end the violent struggle for hegemony.[19]

Through it all President Ernesto Zedillo strived to maintain the image of a rigorous clean-up, his oedipal struggle against his own mentor the birthpangs of Mexican democracy.

In December 1995, Cuauhtémoc Cárdenas filed treason charges against Salinas on corruption surrounding the privatization of Telmex.[20] Bouncing from Toronto to Havana to Dublin, Salinas responded to the charges in a bitter nine-page fax to the Mexican media, accusing former president Luis Echeverria of plotting against his family.[21]

Zedillo's desire to portray a clean break made the Gutiérrez affair all the more agonizing. After military investigators placed a wiretap on Gutiérrez's phone, they learned that his bank accounts, vehicles, plush DF apartment and secret high-tech encryption devices had all been furnished by Cartel handlers.[22] His offices were a hornets' nest of intrigue. On January 13, a month before his arrest, *La Reforma* reported that four volumes of evidence against the Gulf Cartel had mysteriously disappeared from the files of his National Institute to Combat Drugs.[23]

"Everybody could be bribed," said Juan Antonio Ortíz, a Gulf Cartel *jefe* who cut his prison time down by cooperating with US authorities. "From what I know, everybody was being paid all the way to the top."[24]

THE RUIZ MASSIEU CASE: MURDER IN THE FAMILY

Ortíz was testifying in a civil case against Mario Ruiz Massieu, the former Mexican deputy prosecutor general, in which the US sought to confiscate over $9 million in Gulf Cartel protection money Mario had reportedly funneled out of Mexico City in suitcases to deposit in Texas banks. One witness, the bodyguard of a federal police commander, testified he had delivered suitcases of cash into the trunk of Mario's car. But receiving pay-offs may be the least of Mario's crimes. His case opened a window into the string of high-level assassinations which has decimated the Mexican elite.[25]

Mario Ruiz Massieu, former Drug Czar, was the PGR investigator into the slaying of his own brother, José Francisco Ruiz Massieu, PRI national secretary-treasurer, gunned down with a Tec 9 on a Mexico City street on September 28, 1994.[26]

Mario fled Mexico when the PGR opened an investigation into his own investigation. He was arrested by US authorities at Newark airport on March 3, 1995, *en route* to Europe.[27]

As the hapless Mario sat under house arrest in New Jersey, periodically flown down to Houston to testify in his money laundering case, Mexican federal authorities attempted to extradite him back home. On March 16, a Houston federal jury ruled that $7.9 million of Mario's $9 million in the city's banks was cartel grease to be confiscated by Uncle Sam.[28]

The case of the Ruiz Massieu brothers betrayed the degree to which the *PRI-gobierno* had become a cash machine for corrupt elites. By the time of José Francisco's death, he had amassed over $20 million, beginning with his 1987 election as Guerrero governor. He had also married into the ruling dynasty, his assassination widowing Adriana Salinas, sister of the notorious duo.[29]

Raul Salinas was already in prison on charges of slaying Tamaulipas federal deputy Manuel Muñoz Rocha. He had allegedly paid Muñoz Rocha to murder José Francisco Ruiz Massieu, then decided that dead men tell no tales and had *him* offed as well. At least, this was the theory of Antonio Lozano Gracia, Zedillo's prosecutor general and the lone representative in his cabinet of the right-opposition PAN.[30]

The accused gunman in the Ruiz Massieu hit had "confessed" (under the ministrations of Lozano's interrogators) that he had been hired by Muñoz. By then, Muñoz had conveniently disappeared.[31]

In October 1996, Lozano's investigators unearthed a cadaver at Raúl's private ranch, El Encanto. They had allegedly been guided to the spot by a psychic (and confidante of the Mexican elite), Francisca ("La Paca") Zetina Chavez, enlisted by Lozano to the tune of a half-million dollars. The PGR announced that the body was that of Manuel Muñoz Rocha.[32]

But on February 1, 1997, after the requisite forensic tests inconveniently demonstrated that the body was *not* that of Muñoz Rocha, La Paca admitted that it was really that of her son-in-law's father—which she had exhumed and planted on the ranch![33]

Pablo Chapa Bezanilla, Lozano's investigator on the case, disappeared, and a nationwide manhunt was announced.[34] La Paca, Mexico's *bruja*-to-the-stars who counted John F. Kennedy and the Pharaoh Tutankamon among her "spiritual protectors," was imprisoned.[35]

By then, Lozano had been ousted. His replacement, Jorge Madrazo Cuellar, had creds as former head of the government's new National Human Rights Commission, but was a loyal *PRIista*. Madrazo claimed to have a video of La Paca and Chapa meeting at her home in December 1995, plotting to frame Raúl.[36]

Mario Ruiz Massieu still faced federal charges in Mexico of altering documents to divert evidence away from Raúl in the death of his brother. He continued to insist that the machine was obstructing his investigation (and that the suitcases of cash he shipped to Houston were all clean money).[37]

Documents provided to Mario's defense team by US prosecutors and published in *Proceso* alleged direct Salinas involvement in Mario's dirty money. One read that "in 1993, Raúl Salinas ranch, four (4) million" was delivered to Mario Massieu and other officials to "relieve" certain *narcotraficantes* "from public scrutiny after the seizure of 1,200 kilos of cocaine from Tampico, Mexico."[38]

A secret 369-page report by the Swiss police (leaked to the *New York Times*) singled out Raúl as top middleman for cartel grease to Mexico's political elite. Raúl "assumed control over practically all drug shipments through Mexico" when his brother became president. "Through his influence and bribes paid with drug money, officials of the army and the police supported and protected the flourishing drug business." The Swiss put Raúl's narco-fortune at $500 million, and questioned the "probability" that Carlos "did not learn about criminal activities of this extent" by his own brother.[39] In October 1998, Swiss authorities announced they had seized $114 million Raúl had stashed in their banks.[40]

The Mexican courts cleared Raúl on money-laundering, but in January 1999 convicted him as intellectual author of the Ruiz Massieu assassination.[41] The key evidence was the taped interrogation of the Muñoz Rocha aide who hired the assassin, a Tamaulipas ranch hand. The hapless aide was worked over by the Salinas federal police in Mexico City until a broken rib convinced him to discreetly refrain from any mention of Raúl in his testimony. But the tape was recorded days earlier, when he was first picked up in Matamoros—and named "Raúl Salinas and his father" as issuing the orders to kill. The father, clan patriarch Raúl Salinas Lozano, a veteran cabinet member from the 1960s, was silent throughout the affair.[42]

In September, days before he was to be arraigned in Texas on money laundering charges, Mario Ruiz Massieu was found dead in his New Jersey apartment—overdosed on pharmaceuticals, an apparent suicide.[43]

THE COLOSIO CASE: TIJUANA GETS A ZAPRUDER FILM

In January 1997, a Baja California state prosecutor in Tijuana, Hodín Gutiérrez Rico, was gunned down in a hail of bullets by unknown assailants. The eighth Tijuana prosecutor murdered in the past year, Gutiérrez had been investigating the murder of former Tijuana police chief Federico Benitez—who, in turn, was investigating the most colossal murder case in Mexico, the apparent catalyst of countless more violent deaths: the slaying of PRI presidential candidate Luis Donaldo Colosio at a Tijuana *barrio* campaign stop.[44]

Colosio was felled by pistol fire on March 23, 1994. Suspicion initially fell on Grupo Tucan, the security firm hired by local *PRIistas* to police the fatal campaign stop, made up almost entirely of ex-State Judicial Police—an agency notoriously mixed up with the Tijuana Cartel. On March 3, not three weeks before the Colosio assassination, State Judicial Police protecting bigshot Tijuana *narcotraficante* Ismael Higuera Guerrero got into a gun battle with Federal Judicial Police attempting to arrest him, leaving five officers dead.[45]

Then, on April 28, 1994, Police Chief Benitez—who headed his own investigation of the Colosio assassination—was shot dead while responding to a bomb hoax at the city's airport.[46] And then Gutiérrez Rico was assassinated while investigating *his* death. Small wonder that Oliver Stone was soon seen in Tijuana collecting material for a movie idea.[47]

The Benitez slaying left only the federal investigation into the Colosio case. The Federal Judicial Police on the Tijuana Cartel's turf were hardly less co-opted than the state police. In November 1995, the entire PJF force in Baja California Sur was rotated out after witnesses reported seeing a detachment of uniformed federal agents unloading tons of cocaine from a disabled jet in the desert—and then using bulldozers to dismantle and bury the jet.[48]

One Mario Aburto, fingered by federal investigators as the gunman in the Colosio case, was sentenced to forty-five years at the top-security Almoloya federal prison west of Mexico City, sharing the illustrious facility with such luminaries as Raúl Salinas and Guadalajara narco-*jefe* Rafael Caro Quintero. The feds dropped investigations into accomplices and closed ranks around the lone assassin theory—despite an initial broader probe sparked by a video of the killing which appeared to show Grupo Tucan men clearing a path for the gunman.[49]

Earlier arrests in the case—including such Tijuana bigshots as José Rodolfo Rivapalacio, an ex-State Judicial Police investigator with a reputation for torture—were released one by one. The day before his own assassination, Federico Benitez gave an interview to *Washington Post* reporter Tod Robinson. Reaching into a desk drawer for his file on Rivapalacio, he exclaimed "It's gone!"[50]

Another man released after being arrested in the slaying was Fernando de la Sota, a former agent of the elite Federal Security Directorate (DFS) on the Grupo Tucan team. The *New York Times* cited unnamed US "intelligence officials" as saying de la Sota was a paid CIA informant.[51]

Yet another was Jorge Antonio Sánchez, an agent for Gobernación's Center for Investigation and National Security (CISEN). Aburto claimed under oath that Jorge Antonio Sánchez was his "double" and the real gunman. Sánchez was released despite the fact that his shirt was bloodied and he tested positive for having fired a gun after being arrested at the scene of the crime. DEA agent Enrique Plascencia also told *El Financiero* Sánchez was the real gunman.[52]

Still another Aburto "double" was federal police agent Antonio Martínez "El Guamuchi" Estrada, reported by *El Financiero* to have killed himself after killing Colosio. The PGR shortly produced a live Martín Antonio Gutiérrez, claiming he was the real El Guamuchi, and had been stationed in Guadalajara on the day of the killing.[53]

Eduardo Valle (aka "El Bujo," the owl), a top PGR investigator, fled to the US after the Colosio killing and started claiming that Cartel-linked PRI officials were behind the hit. It was El Bujo who coined the term "narcodemocracy" to describe the co-opted Mexican state.[54]

Eduardo Valle claimed Colosio had earned the wrath of both the cartels and Carlos Salinas by acting too independently—even having the Garcia Abrego brothers ejected by security men from a Monterrey fundraiser. He also alleged that Colosio and Salinas had had a screaming argument mere days before the assassination.[55]

The Colosio assassination came just as military incursions into Las Cañadas of Chiapas prompted the EZLN to reject the government's peace proposal. The timing led many to suspect a narco-dinosaur intrigue, possibly with the complicity of Colosio's own mentor, Carlos Salinas. El Bujo claimed the "narco-homicide" was a conspiracy between Raúl Salinas and the Gulf Cartel.[56]

Former PRI chief Colosio was to have been the third consecutive president from the party's technocratic faction. Chiapas peace negotiator Manuel Camacho, a hopeful from the democratic faction, was passed by. The dinosaur faction of old-line nationalists was completely overlooked. Well ensconced in the security apparatus, and hence more likely to have useful connections in the drug under-world, the dinosaurs may have sought to use the assassination as a pretext for a cease-fire violation and renewal of repression against the Zapatistas, as well as to intimidate Salinas into handing the candidacy over to their faction. If El Bujo was correct, Colosio had betrayed Salinas by drifting unacceptably close to the demo-cratic current, and the *jefe maximo* himself approved the assassination.

However, in choosing a replacement for Colosio, Salinas turned to Colosio campaign manager Ernesto Zedillo, another technocrat—rather than tilting to the rival faction as mandated under the old "balancing act."

In 1996, just as the twisted revelations were reaching a climax, all Mexico developed a seemingly spontaneous lurid obsession with the *chupacabras*—the dread "goat-suckers," alienesque vampire bats that terrorized the countryside. Intellec-tuals speculated the stories were being planted in the prole press as a diversion. The atrocious creatures were the perfect metaphor for the malevolence at the very pinnacle of the social pyramid.[57]

THE POSADAS CASE: ECHOES OF EL SALVADOR

In May 1996, an arrest was finally made in the killing of Cardinal Juan Jesús Posadas Ocampo, Archbishop of Guadalajara, hit by a blast of AK-47 fire on May 24, 1993 as he sat in his car at the city's airport. He had previously been Bishop of Tijuana, and was an outspoken foe of the Cartel. One Alvaro Osorio Osuna ("El Nahual," the trickster spirit), a Tijuana Cartel soldier, was the accused assassin. El Nahual admitted he was at the airport—but on orders to kill "El Chapo" Guzmán, a traf-ficker who had apparently crossed the Cartel. The PGR maintained El Nahual had mistaken the Bishop's car for that of El Chapo.[58]

The month of the arrest, new Guadalajara Archbishop Juan Sandoval Iñiguez went on national TV to demand that Carlos Salinas be investigated in the death of his predecessor. Rejecting the official line that Posadas Ocampo had been killed accidentally, he claimed the Cardinal had been in a heated argument with Salinas days before the slaying. Baggage handlers and other airport witnesses had been threatened by federal police to keep quiet about what they really saw, he asserted.[59]

Posadas Ocampo's personal assistant of many years, Felisa Sánchez, directly accused Carlos Salinas of ordering the murder—because the Cardinal knew too much about the Tijuana Cartel's involvement at the top levels of power. Days before the hit, she said, the Cardinal met at Los Pinos with Salinas, Colosio, Manuel Camacho, Gobernación Secretary Patrocinio González and Papal Nuncio Girolamo Prigione. The Cardinal apparently challenged the assembled power-brokers with facts about how the Cartel war had penetrated the political elite. Felisa Sánchez told the scandal-mongering monthly *Ahi*, "From that moment, Cardinal Posadas and Colosio were sentenced to death."[60]

Following these allegations, the press may have wanted to question the federal prosecutor in the Posadas case, who had established the mistaken-car thesis. This, alas, was not possible. Leobardo Larios Guzmán, former Jalisco prosecutor general, had already been gunned down on a Guadalajara street in a burst of automatic fire from a passing car.[61]

ASSASSIN NATION

The culture of assassination permeates every level of Mexican politics.

In September 1996, the same month that Judicial Police Commander Ernesto Ibarra was gunned down, came the case Ian Fleming might have titled "You Only Die Twice." First, authorities announced they had found the body of PJF agent Jorge Garcia Vargas, missing Tijuana director of the National Institute to Combat Drugs, with those of three other police agents and aides in a Mexico City neighborhood. Then, just days later, they said that they had found another body—also tortured to death, and also believed to be Garcia's—in a car in another Mexico City *barrio*. The PJF now said the man buried under Garcia's name was another msyterious double.[62]

All the bodies were mutilated, one had a marijuana leaf tattoo and two were unofficial police aides—*madrinas*, or "godmothers," notorious for brutality and corruption.[63]

By 1988, the case against ex-Drug Czar Gutiérrez was turning up corpses. Gen. Gutiérrez was sentenced to thirteen years at Almoloya on illegal arms possession and abuse of authority, while military courts-martial and civilian drug and bribery cases continued. In the midst of the case, the General's lawyer, Tomas Arturo González Velazquez, was slain by unknown gunmen as he drove from his Guadalajara offices.[64]

González had portrayed the General's arrest as part of a power struggle between military commanders loyal to the Tijuana and Juárez Cartels. Defense Secretary Enrique Cervantes made furious public denials of González's charges. Five months into the trial, military police detained González at a court hearing and accused him of orchestrating an attack on a witness. González was released without charge, but distanced himself from the case. Gutiérrez Rebollo's daughter, Teresa Gutiérrez Ramírez, told reporters González had received death threats. "They're trying to intimidate the defense," she said.[65]

Attorney González himself had belonged to Gutiérrez Rebollo's circle of collaborators when the General served as commander of the Guadalajara Military Region. González acknowledged he had participated in many of Gutiérrez Rebollo's operations, including brutal interrogations. Prosecutors claimed the General protected the Juárez Cartel while acting in aggressive pursuit of the Tijuana Cartel.[66]

Gutiérrez was also linked to ransom kidnappings. A notebook dropped in a car recovered from the abduction of a Sinaloa businessman was traced to a military officer investigating the Ernesto Ibarra slaying—an investigation headed by Gen. Gutiérrez. Subsequently, numerous other northern Mexican families came forward to allege government complicity in the abduction of their loved ones. Human rights workers looking into the cases received death threats.[67]

Mexico's anti-kidnapping units expanded as the kidnapping wave terrorized the nation—first the elites, then even the common folk. These state and federal Delta Force clones receive training from the FBI and Israeli, French and Colombian experts.[68] This expertise has been used in some unanticipated ways.

In January 1998, PGR chief Jorge Madrazo announced that federal agents assigned to kidnapping investigations on Juárez Cartel turf had been compromised. PJF commander Hector Mario Varela was executed in Juárez by gunmen who shouted, "This will teach you to keep your word!" as they pumped twenty bullets into him. "It's absolutely clear that he was a narco-policeman," Madrazo said. He also questioned the integrity of Valera's local collaborators, announcing that "the state investigations into the disappeared in Chihuahua were carried out in a very deficient and irregular fashion. In some cases it appears that after people reported the disappearances, nothing was investigated."[69]

In 1999, human rights workers reported that poor Juárez *colonias* had become "ghost towns" following Cartel terror against residents who resisted their control.[70]

Human rights monitors are themselves targeted for repression, of course. Attorney Jorge Aguirre Meza, president of the Sinaloa bar who had been demanding a crackdown on drug corruption in the state, was shot to death by four masked men dressed in black outside his home in January 1999. He had also led the campaign with four colleagues for establishment of the National Human Rights Commission. He was the third among the four to be killed.[71]

The cartel wars even had a grim echo of the Acteal and Aguas Blancas massacres. On the night of September 17, 1998, twenty members of the Castro Ramírez family—including young children and a pregnant woman—were forced from their ranch outside Ensenada by black-clad men with AK-47s, rounded up in the driveway, tortured and executed. Family patriarch Fermin Castro Ramírez clung comatose in a hospital before expiring several days later. The only survivors were two children who hid under a bed. The Fermin Castro family were members of the small Paipai Indian group, whose *ejido* in Baja California's Trinidad Valley, inland from Ensenada, has been almost completely colonized by the Tijuana Cartel for marijuana cultivation.[72]

Castro Ramírez was said to be the regional marijuana provider, middleman between the growers on the *ejido* and Cartel overseer Ismael Higuera Guerrero. The press portrayed the massacre as retaliation for the slaying of Juárez Cartel boss Rafael Muñoz Talavera. Others said Paipai patriarch Castro Ramírez got into a money dispute with Higuera. Two men arrested in the killings, on the testimony of the child survivors, were members of a Tijuana street gang that provides soldiers for the Cartel.[73]

That the Paipai should be convenient targets for the Cartel's enemies is especially bitter. Marcelino Murillo Alvarez, a Paipai *comisario* who protested the Cartel's encroachment on the *ejido*, was gunned down on a roadside in 1996. Cartel enforcers also shot up a Paipai rodeo, leaving another recalcitrant *ejiditario* dead. The Paipai numbered some fifty thousand at the time of the Conquest; they today constitute barely a thousand. "We're not many Paipai, and this has devastated our community," the new *comisario*, Armando González, told a reporter.[74]

THE IMPERIUM TANGLED IN THE FINANCIAL WEB

Pillars of the global financial establishment played prominently in the Mexican scandals.

Mexican and Swiss investigators traced the dirty millions of Raúl Salinas from Banco Cremi through Citibank's Mexico City and New York branches, and thence to Geneva and Zurich.[75] Chase Manhattan was the next implicated New York titan. Fifteen million in Chase accounts controlled by Juárez Cartel treasurer Rigoberto Gaxiola Medina (then facing federal charges in the US) was traced by a binational investigation along a tortuous route through Banca Serfin, Mexico's third largest, and Banco Unión—the other half of Tabasco narco-banker Cabal Peniche's Grupo Cremi-Unión.[76]

The Gaxiola case took another embarrassing turn for Clinton just before the 1997 certification deadline. The US demanded Mexican authorities expropriate $184 million Gaxiola had stashed in banks in Hermosillo, just south of Arizona. Sonora police were sent to seize Gaxiola's Hermosillo properties in high-profile raids, and the US consul wrote a congratulatory letter to Sonora's Gov. Manlio Fabio Beltrones Rivera. Then, the day before the certification, the US embassy in Mexico City received a phone call from a Hacienda official claiming only $16 million had been confiscated! A probe verified this, prompting the White House to apply yet more pressure on Mexican authorities—and the media to raise questions about the loyalties of Gov. Beltrones.[77]

Subsequent reports by DEA informants said Beltrones took part in secret meetings between Juárez Cartel representatives and high-level politicians. Raúl Salinas is said to have arrived at one meeting with suitcases full of cash to distribute.[78]

The next fiasco was the US Justice Department's three-year, ultra-secret "Operation Casablanca," the largest money laundering case in US history. May 18, 1998 was "a very bad day for drug dealers in this hemisphere," boasted US Attorney General Janet Reno, announcing an unprecedented sting on the cream of the Mexican banking establishment. A Los Angeles federal grand jury had brought charges against three top Mexican banks for laundering Cali and Juárez cartel profits.[79]

Charges were brought against Bancomer and Banca Serfin, Mexico's second and third largest banks, as well as Banca Confia. Cease-and-desist orders were brought against Mexico's top Banco Nacional (Banamex) and Banco Internacional, and Banco Santander of Spain. The banks could face multi-million dollar fines and have their US branches shut. Twenty-two bank officials were arrested after being lured to the US to attend such staged events as the opening of a Nevada casino seeking narco-investments. Thirty-five million dollars in assets, 2 tons of cocaine and 4 tons of marijuana were seized.[80] The investigation began as LA Customs officials identified local branches near the US border which were receiving narco-proceeds. The banks were then linked to overseers in Juárez, Cali and US cities like Las Vegas.[81]

The case was remarkable for its secrecy from NAFTA partner and "Drug War ally" Mexico. Reno and Treasury Secretary Robert Rubin only alerted their

Mexican counterparts—Madrazo and Hacienda Secretary José Angel Gurria Treviño—after the indictments were handed down and the arrests made.[82]

The sting predictably stopped short of following the network stateside through the financial arteries of NAFTA—even with Banca Confia recently purchased by Citibank, and ex-Citibank VP Amy C. Elliott under investigation by the Justice Department for laundering the narco-accounts of Raúl Salinas.[83]

With Clinton under fire for certification, a show like this was worth alienating Mexico's elite. But the US agents apparently held out for a high-profile sum to make big headlines rather than shutting the laundromat when they discovered it. Customs acknowledged that their agents carried out millions of dollars worth of laundering operations, often using accounts at Bank of America and other US banks.[84]

The lack of coordination prompted protests from Mexico, and within days, Reno, Rubin and McCaffrey had apologized to Mexican authorities for keeping them in the dark.[85]

Next month, following Clinton's address to the much-hyped United Nations "Drug Summit," Zedillo's rejoinder made an obvious reference to Operation Casablanca: "We all must respect the sovereignty of each nation so that no one becomes a judge of others, so that no one feels entitled to violate other countries' laws for the sake of enforcing its own."[86]

Next, US Customs agents involved in the sting claimed the operation was called off to protect Mexican cabinet members from indictment. The agents, posing as corrupt bankers, were promised introductions to new clients—including Defense Secretary Enrique Cervantes. But just at that point, the White House ordered the operation shut down. No further effort was ever made to investigate the offer. "Why are they sitting on this kind of information?" asked Customs agent William Gately. US Customs Director Raymond Kelly stammered in his defense: "There was skepticism about it. Was it puffing? It just was not seen as being—I won't use the word credible—but it wasn't verified."[87]

NARCO-NAFTA

Sometimes even heads of state inadvertently spill the beans about the real nature of the Free Trade order. At a White House news conference in April 1997, Canadian Prime Minister Jean Chretien responded matter-of-factly to a reporter's question about drugs coming across the US–Canada border: "It's more trade." The incredulous look on President Clinton's face prompted him to backtrack: "I heard 'trucks.' I'm sorry."[88]

The $50 billion-a-year cross-border drug trade (by the DEA's own estimates) indicates that, perceptions aside, cocaine, heroin, methamphetamine and marijuana are major NAFTA imports, far outstripping profits from such legal ag-biz commodities as winter strawberries, and even significantly surpassing those from Pemex oil exports.[89]

Marijuana has grown in Mexico for centuries. Opium was first introduced to Sinaloa's Culiacán Valley by US agents to produce morphine for the war effort in the 1940s, traditional sources then cut off by Japan's occupation of Southeast Asia. Production continued, illegally, in the high canyons of the Sierra Madre Occidental after this special wartime arrangement ended. Mafias started turning the stuff into black tar heroin for black market export. Heroin had the advantage over marijuana of being easier to conceal, and delivering more bang for the buck.[90]

With the cocaine boom of the 1980s, Mexican mafia smuggling routes were exploited by the Colombian cartels to deliver their product to market. The Mexicans welcomed the addition of another high-return alternative to bulky, smelly marijuana. One kilo of cocaine has the same market value as one ton of *mota*—"which means," writes analyst Jorge Casteñeda, "that a car filled with marijuana is equivalent in value to a two-pound flour bag filled with cocaine." Cocaine seizures by US Customs at the California crossings jumped 700 percent between 1986 and 1987.[91]

Ex-DEA agent Michael Levine left the agency in 1989 to become its most vocal dissident after repeatedly finding his efforts to snare Latin America's top drug lords bottlenecked by what he calls the Washington "suits." In his memoir *Deep Cover*, he relates how Operation Trifecta, aimed at Bolivia's coca cartel, "*La Corporacion*," led to the top levels of power in Mexico. Among those indicted was Col. Jorge Carranza—son of Venustiano Carranza, founder of the modern Mexican state.[92]

In July 1998, ten years after Operation Trifecta, I interviewed Levine at the studios of New York's WBAI radio, where he hosts *The Expert Witness Show*. He said the sting spread from Bolivia to indict *La Corporacion* operatives abroad. "We also targeted their Panama money-laundering center, and practically the entire Mexican government up to the incoming Carlos Salinas administration. And once again, we found that the Justice Department was doing everything possible to kill the case— including Attorney General Edwin Meese himself telephoning the attorney general of Mexico and warning him of an ongoing undercover case!"

"Why?" I asked.

"Well, that time it was NAFTA. Incoming President Salinas was telling our politicians he was gonna deliver NAFTA as law in Mexico. At the same time, his people were telling me, 'Luis Miguel Garcia,' half-Sicilian mafia chief, that when Salinas is in, Mexico's wide open."

"And it turned out to be . . ."

"Exactly! And that's on video. I guess the problem Meese had was that if the American people knew this—no NAFTA."

Levine said Col. Carranza "sat in uniform and told me I could have the whole Mexican government. On camera. I wrote a memo on how the government had just done everything it could to destroy the case. If we had gone through with the deal, which would have cost the US government $5 million for a 1,000 kilos of coke, my next meeting would have been with the secretary of defense of Mexico!"

Col. Carranza and his co-defendants won on appeal, NAFTA was signed, and Levine quit the DEA in disgust.[93]

The subsequent NAFTA narco-boom even touched the controversy around the environmental impacts of the Free Trade Agreement. A 1990 US statute, the Marine Mammal Protection Act, barred import of tuna from ships using the deadly "purse-seine" drift-nets which inadvertently killed up to 100,000 dolphins a year in the Pacific. In 1995, Mexico charged that this "Dolphin-Safe Tuna" law was illegal under NAFTA and GATT, and threatened to take the case to the World Trade Organization. A GATT panel had already ruled for Mexico.[94]

Dropping the law would jack up US imports of Mexican tuna—and open a new artery for cocaine. Just as Honduras-based lobster fleets ferry cocaine up to Mexico through the Caribbean,[95] Colombian, Panamanian and Mexican tuna fleets conceal the Pacific maritime routes. Numerous tuna boats have been busted with huge hauls of cocaine along Mexico's Pacific coast. The country's largest fleet, Pescadora Azteca, was targeted by investigators as a secret holding of Raúl Salinas.[96]

But the issue of *atun blanco* ("white tuna," as the trafficker code-word goes) failed to enter the debate as the Salinas administration sicced its big-bucks New York PR firm, Burston-Marsteller, on the Dolphin-Safe Tuna law. Vice President Al Gore, recently demonized as the eco-extremist "Ozone Man" by George Bush, went to bat for Salinas to have the law overturned. He proposed a "compromise" calling for on-board observers to assure that no dolphins die. The debate split the environmental movement, with San Francisco's Earth Island Institute campaigning to keep the Marine Mammal Protection Act, joined by Sierra Club and Public Citizen. The Environmental Defense Fund, National Wildlife Federation, World Wildlife Fund and (surprisingly) Greenpeace chose to loan a cover of "green" legitimacy to the Free Trade regime's reversal of the law.[97]

In 1997, the law was overturned. Barry McCaffrey, who also went to bat for the repeal, insisted observers on the boats would assure that no drugs were onboard. But Earth Island Institute compiled letters from observers themselves contradicting this, stating they are not onboard during loading, transport and unloading.[98]

Mexican scientists claimed that the dolphins and whales mysteriously washing up on the Sinaloa coast were killed by the cyanide-based NK-19 chemical used by smugglers to mark ocean drop-off sites.[99] But some environmentalists pointed to discharges from the nearby Mena San Felipe gold-mining operation—reportedly owned by a consortium including Raúl Salinas and Carlos Slim.[100]

Raul was also rumored to be a silent partner in the gargantuan salt mine slated for Laguna San Ignacio on the Baja California coast, a joint venture by Mitsubishi and the Mexican state. Mexico's leading environmental organization, the Group of 100, protested the project's placement within the Vizcaino Biosphere Reserve, the Pacific's grey whale calving area—and asserted the project was a cover for cocaine traffic. "There is reason to believe that more than salt will be laundered at Laguna San Ignacio," said Group of 100 president, the poet Homero Ardjis.[101]

Gringo tourists are no less useful than tuna, lobster and salt in masking NAFTA's booming contraband sector. In the Yucatan, where a coastal tourist paradise rings an impoverished Maya interior, luxury resorts proved an expedient means of hiding cocaine profits. In 1998, the PGR seized three Cancun hotels, valued at $200 million. Tourists were bewildered as their playground was surrounded by armed agents. Quintana Roo Gov. Mario "El Chueco" (The Crook) Villanueva Madrid promptly flew to Mexico City to complain to Zedillo.[102]

The investigation began when a union leader at the Cancun airport reported that thousands of gallons of fuel were being diverted to clandestine airstrips. The whistle-blower was shortly murdered. State prosecutors determined the airport manager hired the assassin, but Villanueva would not bring charges. Villanueva had an opposition activist jailed on defamation charges after he distributed copies of newspaper articles on the governor's purported drug ties. The interception of a rig loaded with cocaine at Chetumal, the state capital on the Belizean border, finally sparked the federal probe.[103]

Gov. Villanueva disappeared just days before his term was to run out, missing a scheduled appearance before Mexican Drug Czar Mariano Herran Salvatti in the Federal District. Villanueva never showed up, instead sending a letter restating his denials. The second-ranking official in Quintana Roo, Raúl Santana, told *El Universal*, "If anybody knows where the governor is, please tell me." Because Mexican law makes prosecuting a sitting governor difficult, media speculated Villanueva might be arrested when he was due to leave office.[104]

Demonization of the narco threat on the USA's southern border has predictably not caused Yankee power to examine its own complicity in the Mexican mafia's rise to hemispheric hegemony.

In the 1980s, the CIA collaborated with Colombia's Medellín Cartel and Panama's narco-dictator Manuel Noriega to overthrow the Sandinista regime in Nicaragua. "Privatized" CIA assets maintained Honduran and Costa Rican airstrips as transfer points for coke going north and guns coming south for the Nicaraguan *contra* rebels. Officially derided as "conspiracy theory," this fact has been abundantly documented since the Contragate scandal broke in 1986.[105]

Following the scandal, Noriega became more useful as a scapegoat than a client. At Christmas 1989, Panama was invaded and the technocratic client regime of Guillermo Endara installed. Endara immediately jumped in bed with the rival Cali Cartel, moving more coke and dirty money through Panama than Noriega ever did.[106]

The CIA, DEA and Colombian government began cooperating with the Cali Cartel front group People Persecuted by Pablo Escobar (PEPE) to hunt down the Medellín Cartel bosses. In 1994, Medellín kingpin Pablo Escobar was blown away by a CIA/DEA-trained Colombian military hit squad. The Medellín Cartel was crushed and the Cali Cartel became the new top dog.[107] With the cash-starved outlaw regime of Raúl Cedras in Haiti an eager junior partner, the Caribbean became a top transshipment route.[108]

Colombia's President Ernesto Samper was decertified by Washington, and to get back in Uncle Sam's good graces launched a real crackdown on the Cali bosses.[109] The creation of the South Florida Task Force had already made things difficult at the traditional Medellín Cartel entrepôt of Miami, squeezing the trade inland—strategically positioning the Mexican mafias.[110] More significantly, NAFTA took effect: the implosion of the Colombian cartels combined with the loosening of trade restrictions along the US border precipitated Mexico's rise to dominance. Now, the top cartel was not in the Andes, but just a few kilometers below San Diego.

"The Mexicans are now the single most powerful trafficking groups," DEA chief Thomas Constantine, whose agency had helped create this reality, luridly warned *US News and World Report*. In the same article, Gen. McCaffrey stressed the new bilateral front with the Mexican regime against this insidious new threat on the southern border. "We see steady, concrete forms of cooperation," he said; but cautioned, "We're talking about a decade-long effort."[111]

NARCO-MILITARIZATION

When seven hundred PGR agents were fired in a much-touted "clean-up" under Prosecutor General Lozano Gracia in 1996, McCaffrey called Lozano "a man of tremendous courage and integrity"—mere months before he was ousted for incompetence and probable corruption.[112]

New Prosecutor General Jorge Madrazo symbolically initiated his term by announcing a reorganization of the National Institute to Combat Drugs.[113] McCaffrey lost no time in heaping praise upon the new boss: "I applaud the current leadership; Mexico's new attorney general, the president, the secretary of defense . . . all of those who are involved in this. That includes all the brave soldiers in the Mexican armed forces who have destroyed more illegal drugs this year than any other force in Mexico. We are proud of what they have done."[114]

Madrazo quickly accelerated the transfer of military officers to anti-drug posts previously held by civilians, calling the policy a matter of "national security." The Pentagon joined the FBI in training Mexican forces for the Drug War. The CIA began training and equipping a new army intelligence unit, the Counter-Narcotics Intelligence Center.[115]

This militarization and CIA oversight follows the rise of revolutionary movements in southern Mexico as well as drug cartels in northern Mexico.

In January 1995, sources within the National Institute to Combat Drugs told *El Financiero* that cocaine was being flown into Mexico in cartel fleets of second-hand Boeing 727s. *El Financiero* reported that federal surveillance and enforcement were being beefed up in the south by decree of President Zedillo—to intercept not only drugs bound for clandestine cartel airfields, but also the flow of arms "presumably for the Zapatista Army of National Liberation."[116]

However, the cartels, unlike the Zapatistas, were equipped to run rings around the government. Mexico's drug-interception aircraft were mostly Cessnas—no match for pirate 727s with no radar transponders. The US began pressuring Mexico to use its military F-5 fighters against the Cartel fleet.[117]

Officials first became aware of the new Cartel air force in May 1994, when a coke-laden 727 touched down at a private Jalisco airport operated by Taesa, a Mexican airline favored by millionaires and politicians. Taesa personnel told police that gunmen forced them to light the airstrip for the jet, then released them after the cargo was unloaded. Taesa was founded in 1988 by Carlos Hank Rohn, son and business manager of Mexican billionaire Carlos Hank González, Salinas-era Agriculture Secretary. The elder Hank, who has sprawling properties throughout Mexico, was also Zedillo's campaign manager.[118] Both Hanks were also reported by the *Washington Post* to be under investigation by the US Justice Department for involvement in the Raúl Salinas network.[119] Another brother, Jorge Hank Rohn, is a Tijuana real estate developer and convicted trafficker in endangered species whose bodyguard was convicted of killing *Zeta* reporter Hector Felix Miranda after he had revealed money-laundering at his Agua Caliente race track.[120]

Militarization proponents argue that the army is less corrupt than the police. Conveniently forgotten are such incidents as that on the Veracruz coast in November 1991, when alerted PJF agents intercepted an aircraft tracked by DEA surveillance—only to find that the secluded airstrip was being guarded by over a hundred army troops. In the ensuing three-hour shoot-out, seven PJF officers were killed and the smugglers escaped with their cocaine.[121]

Little seems to have changed since then. As President Clinton once again "certified" Mexico in 1999, Mexican authorities announced a new $500 million two-year counter-narcotics program, including aircraft, ships, satellite surveillance, and high-tech military hardware. Gobernación Secretary Francisco Labastida, who met with Clinton immediately before the certification deadline, said the new program meant "total war" on drug trafficking. Just then, evidence emerged that the Mexican army's CIA-coordinated Counter-Narcotics Intelligence Center, created the previous year to replace corrupted agencies, had already been co-opted by the Cartels. "We give them houses, we give them phone numbers—and nothing happens," one anonymous US official told the *New York Times*. "Cases go nowhere." In October, the army unit captured Gilberto Garza Garcia, the Juárez Cartel *jefe* who oversaw cocaine shipments from Cancun up the Gulf Coast to Texas. The very next day, he escaped while in the custody of two federal detectives. Garza was recaptured, and the detectives placed under investigation after being found with more than $20,000 apparently given to them by the trafficker.[122]

Mexico undertook an aggressive lobbying effort in Washington, spending $100,000 a month on PR firms to push for certification. Despite bluster, Congress failed to overturn the White House's certification of Mexico. Only Iran, Nigeria, Afghanistan and Burma remained uncertified. McCaffrey continued to defend his Mexican colleagues. "Do we think that partnership with Mexico is important to us and is beginning to show signs of substantial cooperation? My own advice is they should be certified."[123]

The 1999 certification also came just as fugitive narco-banker Carlos Cabal Peniche had been tracked down. From a prison in Australia, where he was fighting extradition, Cabal Peniche revealed in written statements his $25 million donations to the PRI—including $20 million donated during the 1994 campaign of President Ernesto Zedillo, and $5 million for the campaign of Tabasco's Gov. Roberto Madrazo. The sum far exceeds the total campaign spending declared by the PRI in 1994. Zedillo claimed he had no personal knowledge of Cabal's contributions. However, in a written response to questions transmitted through his Australian spokesman, Cabal said he had discussed the donations personally in a face-to-face encounter with Zedillo. He said he met Zedillo at the PRI's Mexico City headquarters on

January 12, 1994, when Zedillo was still campaign coordinator for Colosio. "I remember the meeting well," Cabal said.[124]

McCaffrey's perennial gullibility becomes hard to swallow.

DEA chief Thomas Constantine told *The Washington Post* just before retiring in May 1999: "There has been explosive growth of criminal drug mafias from Mexico. We just turned around and they were everywhere, in New York, in Baltimore, in Atlanta . . . What is frustrating is that we know who the 20 or 25 top drug dealers in Mexico are, but Mexican law enforcement is so weak it seems unable even to find them, never mind arrest them or extradite them."[125]

TERROR *VERSUS* TRADITION IN THE SIERRA DE HUICHOLES

As always, it is the indigenous peoples who bear the harshest burden of Mexico's narco-militarization.

In December 1998, Philip True, a Mexico-based reporter for the *San Antonio Express-News*, was found dead in a remote canyon in Jalisco. The US Embassy first said True had fallen to his death while hiking, but later admitted the autopsy revealed he had been strangled and sexually assaulted. True was reporting on the region's Huichol Indians, who are forced to grow marijuana and opium by local drug lords. "I'm afraid that there are strong suggestions that this was carried out because of his work," my Chiapas colleague Joel Simon, now with the Committee to Protect Journalists, told the press. "He wasn't robbed." True's wallet, watch and wedding ring were all intact when his body was recovered.[126]

On December 20, army troops entered the indigenous community of San Sebastián Teponahuaxtlan, where they tortured a community leader, to discover the whereabouts of two Huichol men, Juan Chivarras and Miguel Hernández de la Cruz. After their arrest, the two men confessed to strangling True. Subsequently, a second autopsy, observed by an official US forensic expert, found the journalist had been beaten, not strangled. Amnesty International warned that this could indicate the confessions had been obtained under torture to fit the initial thesis.[127]

The contradictory nature of the narco-dictatorship's Drug War had become sadly surreal in one incident in this severe domain during Holy Week 1998. From their homes high in the canyonlands between Jalisco and Zacatecas, the Huichol have for millennia made the pilgrimage 500 kilometers across the desert plateau to the peyote fields of Wirikuta in San Luis Potosi. The Mexican Constitution and international law protect the native right to ritual use of the sacred cactus.[128]

But on Easter Sunday, twenty-one Huichols, including women and children, were stopped at an army drug checkpoint on the pilgrimage route and detained for gathering peyote. "It's like putting a Catholic in jail for taking holy communion," Susana Valadez of the Huichol Indigenous Center in Huejuquilla told a reporter. The Indians were held for two days. Fifty kilograms of peyote and religious artifacts were seized, the army reported officiously—in blatant violation of Article 23 of Mexico's Agreement on Psychotropic Substances, which exempts traditional use of wild plants by indigenous peoples from the drug laws imposed by the United Nations Single Convention Treaty.[129]

16

OPIUM FIELDS OF THE TARAHUMARA

Narco-Colonialism in the Sierra Madre Occidental

A 45-minute bush plane flight west from the old mining-boomtown-turned-timber-boomtown of Parral lies Baborigame: a squalid, paranoid settlement of five thousand in a high valley surrounded by forested (and deforested) hills and mesas. Separated from the industrial sprawl of central Chihuahua by twisting, yawning canyonlands (and, seemingly, several centuries), primitive Baborigame, with its unpaved lanes and rustic wooden church, is the gateway to the heartland of the Tarahumara, Mexico's most populous and isolated Indian people. This same remote and rugged territory is also the heartland of Mexican drug cultivation.

Baborigame is Tepehuan land, southern cousins of the Tarahumara. The army is there to meet you when you step off the plane into the cold mountain morning, and they are never far out of sight in the valley. The army "fort" at Baborigame—more like a compound behind a wall of pine stakes—issues raw sewage that flows along a ditch down the middle of the *pueblo*. It also issues Humvees affixed with machine guns manned by menacing young men in masks and green uniforms, which rumble through town at breakneck speed, splashing mud and raising dust. Old Tepehuans who speak no Spanish and have never been outside the valley herd goats and grow *maíz* on the outlying slopes. Young Indians are fast becoming hip to the outside world's ways. Vendors at the Pemex station sell *narco-corrido* cassettes, gangsta polkas. A local Tepehuan kid wears a cap that reads "LA PIÑATA"—with images of a marijuana leaf, syringe, razor blade and three white lines.

The Sierra Tarahumara, an arm of the Sierra Madre Occidental, is critical for that large chunk of Mexico's foreign exchange earnings derived from illegal crops. The Tarahumara and Tepehuan are besieged by violence and pushed from traditional lands by the drug mafias much as the Tzotzil and Tzeltal are by the cattle oligarchy in Chiapas, far away at the other end of Mexico.

Three interlocking interests impose their order on the Sierra Tarahumara. First, the drug lords recruit Indians for opium and marijuana cultivation, and take their lands for plantations. The *caciques* in the Tarahumara are not Indians at all, but *mestizo* enforcers for the mafias. Then, police and military sent in to chase the drug gangs more often target small Indian cultivators. Finally, logging operations, often controlled by the same *caciques*, denude the timber of Indian communal lands in deals of dubious legality—terrorizing those who resist.

Some *narco-caciques* have been beaten into retreat by an Indian–ecologist alliance. But the struggle for the strategic region brings the conflict which defines Indian country in Mexico to a state that borders New Mexico and Texas.

THE OUTLAW REGIME

The forest fires which raged from one end of Mexico to the other in the spring of 1998 were started in this arm of the Sierra Madre by the clearing of wooded lands for opium and marijuana cultivation.

The Sierra Tarahumara defines Mexico's *Triángulo Dorado*, the majestic and lawless lands where the states of Chihuahua, Durango and Sinaloa meet. Settled mesas and forested plateaux are separated by massive canyons—*barrancas*—which drain to the Pacific, 240 kilometers to the west. In Chiapas the desirable lands are in the valleys, and Indians are pushed up onto mountainsides; here the good lands are on the plateaux, and the Indians are pushed down into the vertiginous *barrancas*. The settled valley of Baborigame and the mesas surrounding it sit atop a plateau with *barrancas* falling away on either side—into the Rio Los Loera to the east, the Rio Baborigame to the west.

Somewhere in this wilderness, Guadalupe Rivas Vega—"Lupe"—appeared from the woods with a rifle on his back and sat down at our campfire, a meeting we'd hoped would be possible. It was May of 1998, the end of the dry season, and fires could still be seen burning on some of the surrounding slopes. For the past four years, the young Tepehuan had been on the run, leaving his wife and children to hide in the forests and *barrancas*. The crime he is running from arose from a situation typical of the outlaw regime confronting the Sierra's Indians, goaded by drug and timber profits.

Lupe was among a group that uncovered how local *caciques* were ripping off Baborigame's *ejido*. Elsewhere in Mexico, these usufructuary lands can be small agricultural strips encircling villages. But like much in the vast-scaled geography of the Tarahumara, the *ejidos* of this region go on for miles, encompassing several small communities and large expanses of forest. Ejido Baborigame is among many contracting with timber outfits to exploit these forests.

In 1994, Lupe discovered that timber profits were being fraudulently diverted from the *ejiditarios* into private hands, leaving Ejido Baborigame in debt. After he spoke out, he received threats. In November, Lupe was at a traditional gathering where the Indians drink *tesguino*, their *maíz* beer, at the settlement of Tupuri. Lupe says the meeting was interrupted by a group of young knife-wielding Tepehuans drunk on tequila, who had been enticed to attack him. As he tells it, Lupe pulled his pistol, but didn't get a shot off before he was disarmed. He wrestled away an opponent's knife, stabbed him in the stomach, and ran. The stabbed Indian lived, but Lupe wasn't home free. Two more were waiting for him—one with a .22. Lupe dove at him, disarmed him and killed him with his own rifle. He is certain the men were in the pay of Gilberto Molina, a local *cacique*.[1]

Federal police moved against drug plantations that year at nearby Mesa de Los Martínez, and Lupe was accused of betraying the whereabouts of plantations—a well-placed rumor to make him a target.[2]

Gilberto Molina was still grabbing land around Baborigame, corrupting younger Tepehuans to "sell" him land that isn't really theirs to sell, and even getting elders to sell at gunpoint. Molina's gang of hired *pistoleros* were accused in several such incidents. Baborigame Tepehuans filed official complaints—some signed with a thumbprint—before the municipal authorities in distant Guadalupe y Calvo. Nearly a year later, they had received no response.[3]

Despite Indian protest, Molina remained free. Lupe, facing first-degree murder charges, was on the run from both outlaw gunmen and the law. When someone approached from the woods, he reflexively assumed a fighting stance and leveled his rifle. He relaxed when he saw it was a friend, and not *pistoleros*, *mariguaneros*, army or police.

On the run from drug-related violence, Lupe nonetheless decried the police and military incursions into the Sierra to chase drugs.

"Half Mexico is surviving from the narco trade," he said. "The government is getting rich off it."

"Is opium a good thing for the Indians?" I asked him.

"Yes and no. Some of us have more *maíz* to eat from selling *amapola*. But others are given alcohol and cocaine and pistols by the *narcos* and get drunk and crazy and kill each other. And more and more land is controlled by the big plantations of the *caciques*."

The next *pueblo* to the north from Baborigame, Coloradas de la Virgen, suffered the most under the *narco-cacique* seige. Rusty-bearded gringo Randy Gingrich of the Sierra Madre Alliance, based in Chihuahua City, was one of the small group of urban supporters who helped bring the situation there to the attention of the outside world. He flew in with us to introduce us to the Indians, and we used the four-wheel-drive pick-up he kept at Baborigame to get to the lonely Tarahumara settlement, far beyond the last electric lines and the last Pemex station.

Coloradas de la Virgen lies just over a ridge from the mile-deep *barranca* cut by the Rio Baborigame. This runs north to the Sinforosa, one of the great rivers that drain the Sierra. We drove to the little *pueblo* over dusty dirt roads through forests of ponderosa, oak and piñon, Lupe's brother Loreto at the wheel. The roads followed the ridges, skirting the canyon-edge. When the forest cleared and mesa-top vistas appeared, we could see the gap in the sheer and imposing canyon wall where the Baborigame and Sinforosa rivers meet, far in the distance. That became my signal for which way was north, allowing me to reorient myself in this vast, tortuous landscape.

In Coloradas de la Virgen, the air seemed freer than in Baborigame. The adobe homes were spread out over the little valley, and the only authorities present were the Tarahumara traditional government. Fidel Torres Valdenegro, the *capitán-general* of the *pueblo*, came to greet us shortly after our arrival. His Spanish was halting, his leather-sandled feet were rough from scores of harsh winters without boots. It was then six years since Fidel saw his son killed in the *pueblo* church.

Luis Torres was twenty-seven when he was gunned down during the Matachines dance ceremony in November 1992. The stone church's inner wall was pockmarked from the bullets. Just before the shooting started, a fight broke out on the church steps between Luis and some Tarahumara henchmen who had arrived with Augustín Fontes, *cacique* of Ejido Coloradas de la Virgen. Pistols were drawn, but it was broken up before anyone fired. Luis and his brother Gumercindo went into the church for the festivities. Augustín Fontes followed him in with an AR-15. Luis was shot in front of his family, getting off one shot with his pistol before he died. Gumercindo ran across the church to his aid, and was himself shot in the hip and shoulder.[4]

Augustín Fontes, who killed Luis, was still in prison in Ciudad Chihuahua—but for shooting Gumercindo, who lived. As part of a bargain, he got a shorter term by copping to the lesser crime. The fact that anyone did time at all indicated that the Fontes gang was in decline. The real boss of the family, Artemio Fontes (Augustín's cousin), remained free.[5]

Fidel fled with his wife to Baborigame after his son's murder. He had recently returned, now that the Fontes ranch sat semi-abandoned in the forest. "I think they've repented," said Fidel. "A little bit."

Randy described the reign of terror in Coloradas de la Virgen: "You couldn't get any government help here. You couldn't get a cop here. You couldn't get a doctor. You couldn't get any material aid. It took over a year and a half before they arrested Augustín. And that was a deal set up with the drug runners, because it was getting too hot with all the media coverage we were generating." The Fontes clan backed off after they were mentioned in both the *New York Times* and *Los Angeles Times*.[6]

The Sierra Madre Alliance and allied Sierra Madre Assessor Council (CASMAC), a private aid and development group, held a forest conservation meeting in Coloradas de la Virgen in April, just a month before we arrived. Said Randy: "If we'd held an open meeting like that two years ago, we all would have been shot."

Artemio Fontes was the *pueblo*'s enforcer for over a generation. Locals speak of three decades of "*Ley Fontes*" in Ejido Coloradas de la Virgen. But the real reign of terror lasted ten years, from the mid-1980s to the mid-1990s. Nearly forty of Coloradas de la Virgen's twelve hundred residents died violently in those years.[7] "Many families left, they went to live in Baborigame, or into the *barrancas* to hide," recounted Fidel. Most had returned now. Teachers wouldn't come during the terror, so the school closed in 1992, and only reopened in 1996.[8]

Isidro Valdenegro, a Coloradas de la Virgen resident who works with CASMAC, recalled, "When they started exploiting the forest, that's when the violence started. They started killing the *comisarios* who opposed them." Isidro's father, Julio Valdenegro Peña, a *comisario* of the *ejido*, was assassinated by the Fontes gang in 1986.[9]

Lucinda Torres Molina, Isidro's wife, piled the table high with fresh, thick, hot *tortillas* as we ate—big Tarahumara *tortillas*, almost flapjacks. She wore a cap with a marijuana leaf image, reading "EL VERDE ES LA VIDA." Her first husband had been killed five years ago, leaving her with four children. "They killed my husband, my two cousins in the *barranca*, practically my whole family," she said in response to our questions. "They killed my father thirty years ago when they were carving the forest into *ejidos*."

Lucinda and Salvador López Pérez, traditional *gobernador* of Coloradas de la Virgen, stayed throughout the reign of terror—virtually alone. They kept a base for the annual festivals and dances, when the scattered inhabitants would reconverge on the *pueblo*, preserving a sense of community and continuity. September 8 is the festival of the Virgen de Loreto, honoring the image of Mary in the *pueblo*'s church (there was no male figure in the church at all). In November is the Matachines dance. December 12 is the Virgen de Guadalupe; February 2, Dia de La Candalaria. These festivals contain the *pueblo*'s history, and the nucleus that maintained them in defiance of *cacique* terror was critical to its survival and recovery.[10]

The Sierra Tarahumara represents Mexico's most blatant corruption of the *ejido* system. Throughout Mexico *ejidos* are controlled by *caciques* who protect a system of patronage. But in the Tarahumara, the situation is worse. The arrival of *ejidos* actually served to break up Indian communal lands, and deliver them to outsiders.

The *caciques*, local ranchers like the Fontes, drew the *ejidal* lines. They also started trading liquor or *maíz* or cash with the Indians for opium and marijuana. Their cousins and friends from as far away as Los Mochis, on the coast in Sinaloa, were written into the *ejido*, while many local Tarahumara whose families had used the land since time immemorial were excluded.[11]

Three hundred and sixty Coloradas de la Virgen families had been working the land, but only some thirty were granted access to the *ejido*. Many had practiced semi-nomadic seasonal migration with their goat herds—spending dry winters in the *barrancas* to collect wild plants and fish, and summers on the mesas growing beans and *maíz* with the rains. They had to abandon this lifeway after being cut off from the mesa tops when they were enclosed by the *ejido*. These are now the most marginalized Tarahumara, living deep in the *barrancas*.[12]

Francisco Fontes, Artemio's father, drew up the *ejido* boundaries in 1957 with the connivance of the authorities. The *ejido* was completely corrupted in the 1970s and 1980s, when *mestizo* outsiders became *ejiditarios* in large numbers.[13]

Artemio Fontes became *comisario* after Isidro's father was killed, stepping down in 1990. Having established his local machine, he then got into timber. The influence of his personal friend, *PRlista* Gov. Fernando Baeza, helped secure World Bank funding to improve logging roads. A pilot road improvement from Baborigame to Coloradas de la Virgen was part of a $90 million World Bank project approved in 1989.[14]

In the 1980s, Alexandro Fontes (Artemio's brother) became regional commander of the *rurales*, a local militia under the formal command of the Chihuahua state police. He was later killed in a mysterious plane crash near the Texas border, an incident immortalized by the *narco-corrido* group Los Tigres del Norte in the "*Corrido de Alexandro Fontes*." ("The army shot him down in a plane stuffed with marijuana," said the *Los Angeles Times*.)[15]

Documentation of Coloradas de la Virgen's communal land rights, dating to the 1930s, was stolen from the *pueblo* during the violence in the 1980s. CASMAC attorneys were searching historical archives in the Federal District for this documentation.

The *cacique* terror coincided with the militarization of the Sierra. The army came in the late 1970s, officially to crack down on the drug trade. The first big army counter-narcotics campaign was Operation Condor, combining search-and-destroy tactics with aerial eradication. The Mexican army contracted for training with private US firms run by veterans of CIA operations in Southeast Asia—firms which were, in fact, privatized CIA assets left over from the war in Laos.[16] Troops tortured and raped Indians, but never caught up with the Fontes gang.[17]

This era also saw the beginnings of outside solidarity with the Tarahumara. Human rights groups started organizing in Ciudad Chihuahua, the state capital, helping put an end to the worst abuses. Founded by Father Camilo Daniel Pérez, the Chihuahua Commission for Solidarity and Defense of Human Rights (COSYDDHAC) continues to document intimidation, torture and killings of Indians by police and military forces in the Sierra.[18]

Aerial herbicide sprayings began in Mexico under DEA direction in the early 1970s. Paraquat, while far more toxic than the glyphosate currently used in Colombia, was adopted later in the decade as a "safer" alternative to the first product used—2,4-D, a defoliant similar to Agent Orange.[19]

Although the outcry over it faded twenty years ago, Mexico still sprays paraquat. The outcry in the US press was entirely driven by sensationalized fears of stateside marijuana tokers getting poisoned—a slim risk, given that no vegetation can survive a paraquat spraying in acceptable condition to be exported. When poisonings failed to occur, the issue died. There was virtually no concern for the poisoning of *campesinos* in the Sierra.[20]

Studies of paraquat's health effects on Mexican *campesinos* have focused on its agricultural use rather than anti-drug application. One study found that paraquat's "development was considered to be a major advance in herbicide safety because the chemical decomposed rapidly . . . and left no toxic residue. Despite its theoretical safety, however, poisonings have been described virtually everywhere Paraquat has been used."[21] Another study reads: "Paraquat in the quantities to which farm workers may easily be exposed is capable of killing people in a matter of hours or days after contact. It can also cause various illnesses that may not show up for several years, including the proliferation of tissue in the lungs leading to suffocation and, in severe cases, death."[22]

The PGR, often backed up with troops from the army's Fifth Military Zone, carries out the fumigation program.[23] In May 1997, PGR helicopters sprayed paraquat and glyphosate on Coloradas de la Virgen *ejidal* lands at Barril.[24] In the 1998 spring harvest, there was spraying in Durango and Sinaloa, but not Chihuahua. "This year, Chihuahua was completely free for production of drugs," Isidro said. "They only fumigate the plantations not run by their friends."

Opium—*amapola*—is frequently intercropped with marijuana, which comes up later. While the *caciques* can get away with plantations on the mesas, the Indians maintain small plots hidden deep in the winding *barrancas*. *Amapola* is planted in December, and is ready for harvest in May. Marijuana is planted in June, and harvested in October, along with the beans and *maíz*.

Two hundred grams of *amapola*, the yearly yield from a small patch, gets the Indian grower 1,600 pesos—about $200. Tarahumara *mota* fetches 200 pesos a kilo, with a patch yielding 15 kilos, or 20 on a good year. This isn't much, but it is more economical than growing traditional beans, *maíz* and squash. Economy is more pressing as lands are degraded by erosion from deforestation—or stolen altogether.

How much is annual US anti-drug aid to Mexico?, asked Loreto as he led us along a canyon trail, discussing Indian survival in the narco economy.

Around $100 million, including helicopters and equipment, I told him.

"Give us $100 million," he responded without hesitation. "We'll completely destroy the drug traffick."

BETWEEN THE ARMY AND THE CHIHUAHUA CARTEL

Before flying to Baborigame, we spoke with Edwin Bustillos, technical director of CASMAC, in Ciudad Chihuahua. Bustillos was winner of the 1996 Goldman Prize, awarded each year to the world's bravest environmental activists on five continents.[25] He risked his life to get out the truth about the Sierra Tarahumara, and survived violent attacks. Wearing gold chains and obviously blind in one eye from a childhood injury, Bustillos was surprisingly soft-spoken and personable.

A *mestizo* who grew up in the Sierra, Bustillos founded CASMAC after years of frustrated efforts to get the bureaucracy to respond at the National Indian Institute, where he worked. INI was then conducting a study with the World Bank as a prelude to the development loan. Edwin's documentation of misery and terror in the Sierra was iced from official reports, he accuses.

Bustillos documented the various "*trucos legales*"—legal tricks used by *caciques* to illegally "buy" *ejidal* lands. "Indians signed contracts they didn't understand because they didn't know Spanish," he said. "The contracts were illegal." Then the *caciques* fence off a huge area—bigger then what they "bought"—with barbed wire. Thus *chabochis*—as the Tarahumara call whites or *mestizos*—have come to control more and more traditionally indigenous land.

It was largely due to Edwin's efforts that Artemio Fontes was investigated by federal authorities. In 1994, Teresa Jardi, the particularly hardcore PGR prosecutor then assigned to Chihuahua, slapped Artemio with a seven-count indictment for drugs, arms and murder. But he was protected from arrest by an *amparo*. A decree issued by a judge, officially to protect victims of persecution, an *amparo* can be more like a get-out-of-jail-free card for sale to the highest bidder.[26] Artemio is still seen around Ciudad Chihuahua, Edwin told me.

Meanwhile dozens, perhaps hundreds, of Indians were in local jails in the Sierra for crimes related to land and timber conflicts.[27] In 1995, of the ninety thousand Indians in Chihuahua, there were 223 in the jails of Guadalupe y Calvo, Guachochi, Parral and other Sierra *municipios*—a rate nearly triple the state per capita average.[28]

Rejecting the US media label of the "Juárez Cartel," Edwin calls the state's narco mafia the Chihuahua Cartel. "Maybe the *jefes* are in Juárez," he said. "But the cops never find opium or labs there."

Juárez/El Paso is the main entrepôt for the Cartel's exports, but the machine has operations throughout the state. Most profits come from moving Colombian cocaine, but lucrative sidelines are provided by the harvest of the Sierra: compressed bricks of marijuana and big balls of opium gum carefully scraped from the ripe poppies. The labs that process Sierra opium gum into the potent black tar which floods California's streets are in Ciudad Cuauhtémoc and Camargo. Cuauhtémoc, 80 kilometers west of Ciudad Chihuahua, hides a Cartel communications hub, with radios, satellite antennas and computers, said Bustillos.

The rival cartels have divided the Sierra Tarahumara between them. Edwin says Artemio Fontes was the *padrino* who oversaw Chihuahua Cartel operations for the region. The rival Tijuana Cartel's turf is on the Sinaloa and Durango side of the *Triángulo Dorado*. The Tijuana Cartel's heroin labs are in Culiacán, Sinaloa, according to Edwin.

In Balleza *municipio*, in the Sierra's eastern foothills on the road to Parral, an old prop-jet passenger plane lies abandoned in an open field, rusting and covered with graffiti. We would pass it when we drove back from Baborigame. Locals said for four years there was a flight up from South America into the field each month before it crashed there in 1991. At this time, *El Diario de Chihuahua* reported that Cartel enforcers with AK-47s were forcing local *campesinos* to grow drugs—and assassinating *ejido* leaders who resisted.[29]

Abelardo Payan Villalobos ("El Guante") was the Balleza municipal president then, and locals say he coordinated the multi-ton cocaine flights. "El Guante" had disappeared and was now believed to be controlling drug shipments in Denver, Colorado. His uncle Servando Payan Halquín was the new *presidente*. Violence continued to shake the municipality. Raúl Fernandez Villalobos, the new PRI *presidente* candidate, was gunned down in June 1998.[30]

Chihuahua's *PANista* Gov. Francisco Barrio cooperated closely with the Fifth Military Zone in beefing up anti-drug operations in the Sierra. Since the PAN had openly accused the *PRIista* ex-governor, Fernando Baeza, of protecting the drug trade, this show of force was politically necessitated.[31]

Barrio had come to Baborigame on a campaign stop in 1992 and made a speech extolling roads and timber exploitation. In October of that year, soldiers from Baborigame's fort burned Tepehuan houses and tortured some Tepehuans, including women and elders, in the outlying communities of Arroyo de la Huerta, Pino Redondo and El Hundido. These were reprisals after a sub-lieutenant was killed by a Tepehuan. The army claimed the Tepehuan, who disappeared after the incident, was guarding a drug plantation. Tepehuans said the killing was revenge after the sub-lieutenant had raped the man's wife and daughter.[32]

Despite the highly visible army presence in the Tarahumara, Edwin, who worked as an advisor to PGR eradication efforts in 1992 and 1993, said most of the federal helicopters are in southern Mexico—where guerillas have emerged.

According to the PGR's own information, the Chihuahua–Durango–Sinaloa triangle has 24,000 hectares under drug production. The five central and southern states involved in drug production—Jalisco, Michoacan, Guerrero, Oaxaca and Chiapas—have only 8,000 altogether. Yet there are three times as many PGR and army helicopters assigned to these states.[33]

The comparative lack of paraquat use in the South is an implicit admission that there is considerably less to spray. In southern Mexico, the anti-drug campaign disguises counterinsurgency, Bustillos said, while in the *Triángulo Dorado* the big drug plantations are protected by the government.

During the ten days I spent in the Sierra Tarahumara with Randy and my photographer Andrew Lichtenstein, we didn't see a single helicopter. Many of the Sierra Tarahumara opium fields are conveniently at altitudes too high for helicopters to manage. Federal Prosecutor Teresa Jardi confirmed to the press what Isidro told me at Coloradas de la Virgen about the spraying being highly selective. She told the *New York Times* that "army helicopters sometimes spray only water" and "for every field that is supposedly destroyed, several others are untouched."[34]

THE TIMBER MAFIA

In Palos Muertos, a Tepehuan community outside Baborigame, we drank *tesguino* with the *ejiditarios*. The stuff was passed around in a gourd, and it was apparently considered insulting to refuse a round. Despite my initial suspicions, it was entirely more palatable than many a homebrew I'd sampled on Manhattan's Lower East Side, and only slightly inebriating.

The community's land, within Ejido Baborigame, is a patchwork of cornfields and pine forest. Rafael Herrera, a traditional Palos Muertos leader, told how for years *caciques* tricked the *comisarios* to sign logging contracts under false terms—or even just forged signatures—and then pocketed the difference. Of 430 Palos Muertos *ejiditarios*, only twenty or so speak sufficient Spanish to understand contract terms, he said.

He said *caciques* control the judges in Guadalupe y Calvo, the municipal seat some 60 kilometers distant over terrible roads. "With money, they can pay the judge. And there's no justice."

Herrera was the new *capitán-general*, and had wrested a better deal from the timber outfits. He is "*mas listo*" —sharper—than his predecessors, said the men at Palos Muertos.

Herrera's leadership as *capitán-general* extended to various Tepehuan communities around Baborigame. "Our territories have been much smaller since they brought in the maps and divided the land into *ejidos*," he said, echoing the same complaint we heard in Coloradas de la Virgen.

The timber mill in Baborigame was one year old. Big pines were cut into boards by twenty-four fulltime workers without even such rudimentary safety gear as gloves and goggles. The mill processed perhaps half the wood cut in the *ejido*. The other half was trucked out to sawmills beyond the Sierra, to firms like Maderas de Parral. From there, some was export-bound. These outfits were still cutting new roads through the forested mesas and valleys of Ejido Baborigame. Randy was furious upon discovering a new road atop Mesa de Los Martínez.

The timber mafia is closely integrated with the drug mafias, timber proceeds often being used to launder drug profits. The machine pervades local governments. Even municipalities, Mexico's smallest units of official government, are seen by the Indians as distant bureaucracies, while the real power in their communities is divided between traditional Indian structures and the *caciques.*

In the Tarahumara, municipalities cover vast areas which have little contact with the municipal seat, and are divided into sections for administrative purposes. But the sectional presidents often have no closer link to the isolated Sierra communities they ostensibly represent.

Manuel Rubio, the *PANista* sectional president for Baborigame, was elected December 1995 in a race called fraudulent by the Tepehuan—up to eight hundred boycotted out of five thousand in the section. The election site was unilaterally moved to a schoolhouse from the traditional ceremonial ground where the Tepehuans elect their *capitán-general*, and the traditional open vote with community discussion changed to a closed vote with no discussion. The changes were made the day of the election, with no prior notice. A Tepehuan schoolteacher who ran independently and a local doctor who ran on the PRI ticket both protested the move. A letter signed by representatives from Baborigame's traditional government protested the "imposed election" to municipal authorities. Three years later, there had been no response.[35]

Rubio had been charged in shootings, and arms and drug trafficking in recent years, and convicted on cocaine charges just before the election. He never served more than a month. Legally he shouldn't be able to hold office, but Gov. Barrio did not interfere—despite 1,400 Tepehuan petitions. Rubio said thumbprints on the petitions were forged.[36]

Rubio owned land at Soledad Vieja, where he was accused of illegally representing other landholders from his *predio* (cooperative of private owners) in a deal with the timber operations of another regional powerbroker, Ismael Díaz Carrillo. Old-growth pine forest was logged out before the protests of the spurned *predio* partners halted the operation. Rubio apparently pocketed the proceeds.[37]

Timber lord Ismael Díaz Carrillo was also a *PRIista* state deputy. As a bank official in Guachochi, the *municipio* which covers Coloradas de la Virgen, he reportedly laundered drug money for the Fontes gang. He later became a Guachochi sectional president. It was in this capacity that he sent two municipal police and three hired thugs to the Tarahumara community of Caborachi on December 12, 1993 to break up a Dia de La Virgen *fiesta*. Eight Indians were beaten, and six hauled off to the Guachochi jail—where Carrillo's nurse wife certified they were OK. Edwin Bustillos, then working with the PGR's Community Aid and Crime Prevention Department in the Tarahumara, pressured for a federal investigation and started talking to the local papers about the incident. Threatening phone calls from Carrillo followed: "Now we'll see who is more powerful." On Christmas Day, Edwin was stopped by state police in his car near Guachochi, pistol-whipped in his good eye, and left for dead by the road.[38]

Díaz Carrillo's personal secretary eventually went to prison in the Caborachi incident (reportedly in a deal Carrillo cut to have the secretary take the fall). Díaz became immune from prosecution when he was elected state deputy.[39]

NAFTA has been very good for the timber mafia. There are *ejido*-owned sawmills in the Sierra, but most are closed down, or in disrepair and marginal use. They declined because of past overcutting, and then couldn't afford upgrades. Outside firms came in and took over in the 1990s. Simultaneously, parastatal timber firms which had managed several *ejidos* in government programs were privatized. The *ejidos* were left to the mercy of a market in which they were very small players.[40]

Foreign multinationals are also getting in on the action. International Paper of Dallas started cutting Ejido San Alonzo near Barranca del Cobre to the north of the Sinforosa in 1996, and was said to be applying for a Mexican federal subsidy. Local firms were already receiving federal subsidies to log the Sierra.[41]

In 1989, the World Bank approved $45.5 million to Mexico as part of the $90 million Forestry Development Project in the Sierra Tarahumara. The Mexican government matched the World Bank's half—but most of the funding never came through.[42]

The loan was mired in controversy almost immediately. Edwin Bustillos claimed the project's Pino Gordo road—linking that Tarahumara *ejido* to Baborigame—was built under the false pretext of improving an "existing road" which didn't really exist. The equally dubious Pino Gordo logging contracts with Impulsora Forestal Durango were subsequently suspended. Artemio Fontes was said to be a silent partner in Impulsora Forestal Durango.[43]

Jaime González, the federal government's Chihuahua director for the Forestry Development Project, stepped down in 1993, facing corruption allegations. In May 1995, the World Bank officially announced that the project was dead, and demanded that Mexico account for all funds.[44]

Said Gingrich: "Officially the reason was inter-agency conflict which paralyzed the program, but in reality it was international pressure and growing evidence that the credits were facilitating illegal road building, illegal logging and violent drug traffickers. The Fontes gang were silent partners in timber outfits. There were two or three murders a week in Guadalupe y Calvo *municipio* at this time, half of which were indigenous leaders protesting illegal logging and other abuses."

The community of Pino Gordo, even more remote than Coloradas de la Virgen, was relieved when the logging scheme fell through. "Ejido Pino Gordo became a community-declared reserve," said Edwin Bustillos. However, the neighboring *mestizo* community of Coloradas de los Chavez subsequently invaded Ejido Pino Gordo and claimed much of it as theirs to contract out to loggers (purportedly linked to the Balleza drug mafia). A 1992 federal court decision found in favor of the Indian *ejiditarios* and against the invaders.[45]

Fraudulent timber contracts are challenged in the courts, while *ejidal* land disputes are heard by the Agrarian Tribunals. Coloradas de la Virgen still has a case pending before the Tribunals on the illegal naming of outsiders as *ejiditarios*. But such rulings often mean little. In 1997, SEMARNAP approved a logging plan for the same Pino Gordo contracts the court had ruled against—which Gingrich called "a blatant violation of federal law."[46]

The *mestizo* invaders started logging Pino Gordo lands in June 1998. Now the situation was complicated by the fact that Pino Gordo's *comisario* had sold out to the timber interests—and changed the *ejido* registry, replacing Indian residents with outsiders. In April 1999, Pino Gordo *ejiditarios* actually occupied the governor's palace in Ciudad Chihuahua to demand action. PROFEPA subsequently issued a temporary halt to the logging. By then, 5,000 trees, worth over $2 million, had been taken out—with no benefit to impoverished Pino Gordo.[47]

TARAHUMARA CULTURAL RESISTANCE

"The state and federal deputies will come to Baborigame, but never here," Isidro Valdenegro told us at Coloradas de la Virgen. "They are afraid. They don't recognize the indigenous laws. We don't have written laws, like the federal and state governments. We have our own way of resolving conflicts within our community."

Isidro said the community wants government recognition of this system—and the ancient patterns of land use it protects. He said Coloradas de la Virgen must have communal rights over 63,000 hectares.

"We want legal recognition of our lands, with clear territorial limits. The *ejido* doesn't do that for us. The *ejido* was a complete fraud, but it was very well done."

The plunder of the Sierra Tarahumara's forests now meets increased Indian vigilance. International Paper's operations have been slowed by indigenous communities challenging unclear contracts, with cases currently before courts and Agrarian Tribunals.[48]

CASMAC's work with Coloradas de la Virgen and Pino Gordo has preserved remaining old-growth stands on these *ejidos*. "We have a *de facto* protected area— not because of recognition from the government," Bustillos put it.

CASMAC and the Sierra Madre Alliance envision expanding this protected area into a Barranca Sinforosa Biosphere Reserve, to be managed by the Tarahumara and Tepehuan. International funds for programs in forestry, ecology, community history and wildlife preservation would help develop local indigenous management of the land.[49]

The CASMAC agro-ecology program at Agua Azul in Ejido Caborachi is based on preservation and restoration of indigenous seed stock. Indigenous plant varieties are disappearing from the Sierra as Indians are introduced to agribusiness hybrids— and as drug crops squeeze out traditional crops. In 1997, CASMAC reintroduced Tarahumara white sunflower seeds, provided by the distributor Seeds of Change in Santa Fe, New Mexico. The samples had been originally collected by researchers with Native Seed Search of Tucson, Arizona. The white sunflowers are now being grown in the Sierra again, after a hiatus of possibly generations.[50]

CASMAC is attempting to document the presence of endangered species like jaguars, ocelots and thick-billed parrots—locally called *guacamayas*—in the region to apply for UN biosphere status. These species once extended into the US Southwest; now the Sierra Tarahumara is their northernmost or—as for the *guacamaya*—final range.[51]

CASMAC and the Alliance also document the Tarahumara's wealth of wild medicinal plants. Traditional Tarahumara medicinals still widely used include *hierba de la virgen* to calm the stomach, the aromatic *guachichile* for colds, *patabuja* for diarrhea and menstrual problems, to name but three of many we were shown in Coloradas de la Virgen. The drug crops have been added to this pharmacopeia. The Tarahumara never smoke pot or opium (except some of the young men), but use both medicinally. Marijuana is soaked in alcohol to treat rheumatism; opium gum is applied to an aching tooth.

This work has gained some international support. The Nature Conservancy and World Wildlife Fund, with some money from US AID's Biodiversity Support Program, have funded the Sierra Madre Alliance, which pools resources with CASMAC. The Ciudad Chihuahua office the two groups share has at times been under open surveillance by mysterious armed men.[52]

CASMAC, which has two Tarahumara and two Tepehuans among its six board members, advocates reparations from *caciques* and timber outfits for damaged communal lands through civil penalties. CASMAC and the Sierra Madre Alliance are both based on recognition of traditional Indian authority.[53]

"We're trying to empower the Indians to get out from under the thumb of the *caciques*," Randy said. "Justice is bought and sold here. So the alternative is to give them some economic self-sufficiency and the ability to manage their own forests. We'd like to see the emergence of Indian-managed forestry based on sustainably harvested timber. Nobody's piling money into these communities to help them with their legal problems."

The next major canyon system to the north of the Sinforosa is the world-famous Barranca del Cobre, Copper Canyon. It is cut by the Rio Urique, like the Sinforosa a tributary of the Fuerte, which meets the Pacific in Sinaloa. On the same gargantuan scale as the Sinforosa, Barranca del Cobre is better known because the Chihuahua-Pacific Railroad twists through its time-sculpted arteries on its way down to the Sinaloa port of Los Mochis. It is shown on tourist maps as a "natural park," but Randy Gingrich calls this a "paper park," pointing to timber contracts on *ejidos* within the park's borders.

Barranca del Cobre is now the site of a major development project promoted under the specious label of "eco-tourism." With funding from Japanese investors and the Mexican government, the scheme envisions huge hotels, swimming pools and golf courses in the spectacular canyon, skirting the border of the park. The "next Cancun," they are calling it. An international airport is planned for Creel, the old canyon-edge railroad stop and northern gateway to the Tarahumara. Union-Pacific and the Mexican engineering giant ICA, co-owners of the Chihuahua-Pacific since its 1996 privatization, are also involved. Tarahumara lands were expropriated by the state government for the scheme in 1996. The project is opposed by Padre José Luis Dibildox, Bishop of the Tarahumara.[54]

As the tourists play and photograph the Indians, sold on the allure of an ancient culture, just 100 kilometers across the canyonscapes to the south, in the Sinforosa, in the *ejidos* of Baborigame and Pino Gordo and Coloradas de la Virgen, lies another NAFTA, another reality.

THE AUTONOMY QUESTION IN THE *TRIÁNGULO DORADO*

The Tarahumara—or Rarámuri, in their tongue—are part of what anthropologists call the Uto-Aztecan language group, which also includes Nahuatl. But the Tarahumara, unlike the Nahuatl-speaking Indians of classical Mesoamerica to the south, were a semi-nomadic people with no central settlements before the Spaniards arrived—a lifeway better suited to the harsh environment. In the seventeenth century, the Spanish finally moved to bring the largely unconquered region under control. But the Tarahumara and Tepehuan resisted the *reducciones* more effectively than any indigenous groups in Mexico.[55]

The Tepehuans revolted at Balleza under the chieftain Quantlas in 1616. In 1648, the Tarahumara rose under the chieftain Teporame to eject ranchers, miners, soldiers and priests from their territory. Unlike the Yaquis, who held more desirable lands below on the Pacific coast, the Tarahumara did not pose an obstacle to imperial expansion. But the Jesuit missionaries found they had to adapt elements of the Tarahumara traditional self-governance system in order to maintain control. Even after the Indians were induced to settle in *pueblos*, they maintained a high degree of autonomy, and access to much of their lands. Those Indians who accepted Christianity were the *bautizados;* the more isolated groups which resisted conversion, such as Pino Gordo, were *gentiles*—a minority, but still numerous. This terminology persisted into the twentieth century.[56]

While long-abandoned gold and silver mines litter the *barrancas* and mesas of the Sierra Tarahumara, the region never yielded the bonanzas of Parral or Durango, partially because of its inaccessibility.[57] The Sierra Tarahumara served as a welcoming refuge for Pancho Villa when he had to hide and turn to guerilla warfare, and Indians from the Sierra served very effectively as scouts in his army.[58] The Tarahumara and Tepehuan were largely left to their own devices until Mexico's dope lords discovered the new treasure of the Sierra Madre.

When I was in Chihuahua, the gubernatorial campaign was in full swing, and legal recognition of traditional government in the Tarahumara had actually become, at least, a minor issue in the race. This was largely because the Zapatistas in far Chiapas had made Indian autonomy a national issue, and prompted President Zedillo to pressure state governments to enact their own autonomy statutes.

Just before the state elections, the Diocese of the Tarahumara formally protested the government's effort to seek Indian signatures for the government autonomy plans before alternative plans had been discussed in their communities. *Caciques* and sectional presidents were collecting the signatures. Bishop José Luis Dibildox issued the statement from the Diocese seat at Sisoguichi, noting that the San Andrés Accords had not been presented to the communities.[59]

Timber lord Díaz Carrillo then headed the Indigenous Affairs Committee in Chihuahua's Chamber of Deputies, and developed the state autonomy plan. It closely mirrored the federal autonomy proposal pushed by President Zedillo, which the Zapatistas rejected. If Carrillo's plan was accepted, it would halt reforms long advocated by CASMAC, COSYDDHAC and certain allies in the state Chamber of Deputies.[60]

Ricardo Robles, a Jesuit priest with the Tarahumara Diocese and an advisor to the EZLN, was the most outspoken critic of Díaz Carrillo's plan. He emphasized that it would leave the Indians at the mercy of the *mestizo*-dominated courts under which they now have no justice.[61]

In the July elections, the PRI recovered the governorship of Chihuahua— the first time the party ever recovered a state it had lost.[62] Timber lord Díaz Carrillo's *diputado* term ended and he returned to private life, but the new governor, Patricio Martínez Garcia, adopted his autonomy plan. The PRI and PAN fought a dirty campaign—the prior on a populist line, the latter on an anti-corruption platform—but both supported the Díaz Carrillo plan. The small PRD minority in the Chamber of Deputies began working on a new plan, in conjunction with grass-roots organizations.[63]

The Sierra's Indians recently began to take their protests to the city. May 1997, two hundred Tarahumara from Ejido Monterde in Guazapares were attacked and beaten by Ciudad Chihuahua police at a march demanding action on swindles by timber *caciques*. Photos of bloodied Indians ran in the national press, and the National Human Rights Commission condemned the attack. But the corruption they were protesting was never addressed.[64]

In 1989, Juan Gardea became the first Tarahumara to be elected to office in Mexico's official political system, winning the sectional presidency for Norogachi in Guachochi *municipio*. He ran as an independent and won on the strength of his leadership in the struggle to defend Norogachi's lands. Norogachi is the next *pueblo* across the Sinforosa from Coloradas de la Virgen, and faced a similar reign of terror. The Gardea family was subject to threats and physical attacks after the election. In January 1996, Juan Gardea was Tarahumara delegate to the National Indigenous Forum held by the Zapatistas in San Cristóbal de Las Casas. Six months later, his younger brother José Gardea, who had succeeded him as sectional president, was shot dead by unknown gunmen in Norogachi.[65]

The federal army is certainly aware that the Sierra Tarahumara, with sparsely inhabited forests and convoluted geography intimately known by the Indians, is ideal country for waging a guerilla struggle. The Tarahumara are famous for running inconceivable distances over precarious goat trails in phenomenal time. Of necessity, many of them are already armed.

The Sierra Tarahumara, now isolated from the struggles in Chiapas and the Sierra del Sur, at the far end of Mexico's mountain spine, was actually a crucible of the guerilla movement which shook Mexico in the 1960s and 1970s—and can claim a lineage to the new rebels of the 1990s.

The schoolteacher Arturo Gámiz witnessed a contest for disputed land grow increasingly violent at Madera, in the Sierra's northern foothills not 300 kilometers south of the US border. In early 1964, after two *campesinos* were murdered on orders of the big landholder, Gámiz organized armed raids onto the disputed property.[66] On September 23, Gámiz launched an audacious if suicidal attack on the Madera army barracks. The attack left six soldiers and eight guerillas dead— including Gámiz. But survivors regrouped in the Sierra and kept the insurgency alive for another four years. The Madera attack became legendary. The group, formerly the Armed Commandos of Chihuahua, became the September 23 Movement.[67]

The name was resurrected in 1969 as the September 23 Communist League, which succeeded the Madera veterans and sought to unite Mexico's emerging guerilla factions. Their Chihuahua cadre established contacts with radical *campesinos* throughout the mountains of Mexico, and with the urban campus movement. Some were reportedly trained in North Korea, and joined the Guerrero insurgency of

Lucio Cabañas and Genaro Vázquez. Others formed the early Chiapas guerilla effort, the FALN.[68]

One veteran of the September 23 Movement was apparently among a group of twelve militants who entered Las Cañadas of Chiapas in 1983, deeming the region ripe for revolution. This old veteran was gunned down at a police stop in Ocosingo, and one of his comrades, who stuck it out in the jungle to build the rebel army, adopted his code name: Marcos.[69]

In June 1996, there were rumors of a cell of Mexico's second and still mysterious guerilla group, the Popular Revolutionary Army, organizing in Ciudad Juárez. There was also talk of a new "Ejercito Villista." The federal and state authorities announced formation of a joint army–police "anti-guerilla committee" for Chihuahua.[70] Army patrols in the Sierra Tarahumara were stepped up.[71]

But the Indians and those who work with them, like Randy and Edwin, say the only armed groups in the Sierra Tarahumara are drug traffickers.

PART V

INTERVENTION AND SOLIDARITY IN THE FREE TRADE ORDER

17

NARCO-IMPERIALISM

The New Interventionism

In the NAFTA-mandated bilateral integration, the Mexican military is abandoning its traditional distance from the Pentagon. Ever more Mexican officers receive training in the US, and ever more US war material heads south of the Rio Grande. Officers assigned to counterinsurgency in Chiapas, Oaxaca and Guerrero are gradu ates of the Pentagon's School of the Americas—notorious in Latin America as the "School of the Assassins" for its instruction of death-squad bosses from Bolivia to Guatemala.[1] Increasingly, this training takes place under cover of the War on Drugs.

US military aid to Mexico is growing fast. In 1997, the US granted Mexico $37 million in helicopters and surveillance aircraft, and an additional $10 million for command-and-control electronics.[2] In meetings in Merida in February 1999, President Bill Clinton and Ernesto Zedillo discussed a $500 million package of dramatically more such *matériel*.[3]

In the first such summit of their respective administrations, on October 22, 1995, US Defense Secretary William Perry met in the Federal District with his Mexican counterpart, Gen. Enrique Cervantes Aguirre, to discuss a $70 million loan for Mexico's radar system, and a doubling of the Pentagon's $500,000 budget for training Mexican officers. That same day in that same city, Fernando Yañez, the supposed Zapatista Comandante German, was arrested by federal police.[4]

In his visit, the first by a US Defense Secretary to Mexico since 1948, Perry posed a "third link" in the bilateral integration—political, economic, and now military.[5]

Also in Perry's entourage was Gen. Barry R. McCaffrey, chief of the Pentagon's Southern Command. Gen. McCaffrey would within weeks become the first military man to be appointed director of the US National Office of Drug Control Policy—the "Drug Czar."[6]

McCaffrey, a top Pentagon counterinsurgency expert and theorist of "narco-terrorism" as the post-Communist threat in Latin America, came up through the ranks. He led a platoon in the 1965 invasion of the Dominican Republic, and won a chestful of medals for combat heroics in Vietnam. In 1969 he was transferred to the elite strategy think-tanks of the Panama Canal Zone. The School of the Americas was based in the Zone until it was relocated to Fort Benning, Georgia, in 1984 as a treaty obligation. From the Zone, McCaffrey supervised clandestine operations against Nicaragua in the 1980s, and was a top planner of the 1989 invasion of Panama—the first US military intervention in the name of the War on Drugs.[7]

After commanding an infantry division in Operation Desert Storm, McCaffrey was appointed a top-level aide to the Joint Chiefs of Staff. In 1994, he became head of the Southern Command, which was by then spending an annual $155 million—over 20 percent of its total budget—on counter-narcotics efforts.[8]

Shortly after he was named as Drug Czar he addressed the Heritage Foundation on the Pentagon's new mission in Latin America: "The new problems are obvious—they're counterterrorism, they're counterdrugs, they're illegal movements of peoples, they're arms smuggling, they're transnational Marxist movements that have now become international criminal conspiracies, narco-guerilla forces."[9]

He would assume a guiding role in Mexico's Drug War militarization.

The next high-level US Drug War delegation to Mexico would coincide with an even bigger crisis for the Zapatistas.

TOWARDS GRINGO INTERVENTION?

On May 6, 1996, just as tensions were mounting in Chiapas, with the dialogue stalled and army troops invading Zapatista zones under guise of chasing drug crops, US Secretary of State Warren Christopher flew into Mexico City. In his entourage were Attorney General Janet Reno, DEA chief Thomas Constantine and Gen. McCaffrey. In the following days, pacts were signed on immigration, pollution, and Drug War cooperation.[10]

"The US can support the military and police forces with technical assistance, radar, the cooperation of the Coast Guard, and other mechanisms," said Gen. McCaffrey. "We are committed to cooperating on intelligence matters. We're going to give Mexican authorities the information they need to form an even better defense of their own sovereign air space and sea frontiers."[11]

McCaffrey, the first Drug Czar to serve as US liaison to the US–Mexico Binational Commission for Military Issues, had two months earlier testified to Congress that 70 percent of drugs in the US come in from Mexico.[12]

Simultaneous with the DF meeting, President Bill Clinton issued a directive to his cabinet to outline steps for Drug War integration, ordering McCaffrey's Office of National Drug Control Policy to produce a "white paper" on the Mexican problem, to be presented to the new US–Mexico High-Level Contact Group.[13]

A week earlier, William Perry had met with Gen. Enrique Cervantes on expanding training of Mexican troops on US bases: primarily Fort Benning and North Carolina's Fort Bragg, home to the elite Special Forces units known as the Green Berets. Fifteen fresh Mexican officers were to begin anti-narcotics training at these bases, in turn imparting this expertise to their own troops. "We are using a training-to-train concept," said Pentagon spokesperson Brian Sheridan.[14]

Christopher's meeting with Cervantes arranged the immediate transfer of twenty UH-1H ("Huey") helicopters to the Mexican Air Force, as well as training of helicopter pilots and mechanics for the new Rapid Reaction Units. The choppers were the first of seventy to be delivered that year, augmenting some thirty delivered since 1989—on top of another twenty for the PGR. Most of the Hueys had seen action in the skies of Vietnam. The army also got six newer Blackhawk helicopters, and the army and PGR each got some Bell 212 twin-engines.[15]

The helicopter transfer met criticism on Capitol Hill. California's liberal Democrat Sen. Dianne Feinstein joined New York's conservative Republican Sen. Alphonse D'Amato in demanding the White House decertify Mexico for further US aid. North Carolina's ultra-conservative Sen. Jesse Helms actually warned that the Drug War choppers would be used for counterinsurgency campaigns.[16]

A 1996 report by the US General Accounting Office (the Congressional investigative arm), "Drug Control: Counternarcotics Efforts in Mexico," found that "US personnel have little way of knowing if the helicopters are being properly used" and that use of the PGR choppers in Chiapas in January 1994 "was a violation of the transfer agreement."[17]

The US State Department confirmed that the helicopters would not be used exclusively in anti-drug operations. A US embassy "aviation advisor" would travel periodically around the country to inspect the equipment. But these visits will never be conducted without prior notice.[18]

The new cooperation also met opposition in Mexico. There was an outcry in the press in March 1996, when it was reported that Perry, in a meeting with Mexican military officials on a US nuclear aircraft carrier off the Pacific coast, raised the possibility of joint military maneuvers. Mexico's National Defense Secretariat

(SEDENA) immediately denied that joint maneuvers were being considered, saying the new cooperation would be limited to training, intelligence and equipment.[19]

In January 1994, the EZLN had sent President Clinton a letter protesting the use of US military aid in Chiapas: "Troops, planes, helicopters, radar, communications technology, weapons and military supplies are currently being used not to pursue drug traffickers . . . but rather to repress the righteous struggle of the people of Mexico . . . The support that the North American people and government offer the Mexican federal government does nothing but stain your hands with indigenous blood."[20] As Marcos told me three months later, they never received a response.

Rumors abounded that there were already US troops in Chiapas. In 1995, Marcos told a Uruguayan publication that the Pentagon had sent "a group of advisors" on a covert mission to Chiapas, and that one gringo lieutenant colonel was among the Mexican federal troops occupying Guadalupe Tepeyac.[21]

"We know from the prostitutes that service the army that they had been taking care of a group of soldiers we assume were from the US, because they were tall, blond, blue-eyed, and they spoke in English. Obviously we did not see their passports," said Marcos.[22]

Marcos claimed that many of the same elements who masterminded the 1980s terror campaigns in Central America were now at work in Chiapas: "Another bit of information we have is that the US army was functioning as an intermediary in bringing the Argentine mercenaries who are present in Chiapas. There are those who claim they are with the paramilitary squadrons, the White Guards. The federal army denies that it has Argentine advisors. We have pictures of some of those advisors, from when they were training others in Honduras. We located one of them here, preparing explosives and training people on the use of mortars."[23]

Veterans of the Argentine dictatorship's "dirty war" in the 1970s had been brought to Honduras by the CIA to train the Nicaraguan *contras* in the early 1980s.[24] Later, clandestine US Green Beret detachments took over this training, and even entered Nicaragua to back up *contra* operations.[25]

In May 1994, just months after the Zapatista revolt, the Mexican government announced a new Anti-Terrorist Group (GAT). Decried by the opposition as an "Orwellian superagency," the GAT was to be overseen by special trainers from the US, Argentina and Spain (where the security forces were soon mired in a scandal over torture and abduction of Basque separatists). Argentina, which simultaneously launched an identically named agency, dispatched elite troops to Mexico for GAT counterinsurgency training, *La Reforma* reported.[26]

Marcos also told the Uruguayans, "we did confirm that the Mexican army received counterinsurgency training from the Guatemalan Kaibiles."[27]

Elite Guatemalan veterans of the genocidal campaigns of the early 1980s, the Green Beret-trained Kaibiles established bases near the border with Mexico's Lacandon Selva immediately after the 1994 uprising.[28] The Zapatistas claimed that Kaibiles had actually crossed into the Selva to aid the Mexican army—and that Green Berets may have come with them. It would be two years before existence of the training program would be independently corroborated by the Mexican press.

Just as Mexico was stepping up the number of officers sent for training at Fort Benning, media reports confirmed that the SOA explicitly instructed foreign troops in torture, assassination and blackmail in the 1980s.

"Counterintelligence" (CI) manuals used at the SOA between 1982 and 1991 were released by the Pentagon following a long activist campaign—and a suit under the US Freedom of Information Act. With names like *Handling Sources* and *Terrorism and the Urban Guerilla*, the manuals instructed in such tactics as imprisonment and beating of "sources" and arrest of their families. One passage reads: "Another function of CI agents is recommending CI targets for neutralizing. The CI targets can include personalities, installations, organizations, documents and materials." Examples of "personality targets" are "governmental officials, political leaders and members of the infrastructure." "Neutralizing" is an intelligence euphemism for assassination.[29]

Among the masterminds of murder and torture trained at the SOA in the 1970s and 1980s are Guatemalan counterinsurgency leaders Col. Julio Roberto Alpirez and Gen. Hector Gramejo, deposed Haitian despot Col. Michel François, imprisoned Panamanian narco-dictator Manuel Noriega and the late Salvadoran death-squad boss Roberto D'Aubuisson (author of the Archbishop's assassination).[30] Serving on the official SOA Hall of Fame is Gen. Hugo Banzer of Bolivia, whose blood-drenched dictatorship in the 1970s availed itself of the expertise of Gestapo agent Klaus Barbie (and who returned to Bolivia's presidency, this time by electoral means, in 1996).[31]

Mexico's Green Beret-trained Special Airborne Forces Groups (GAFE) are the special brainchild of Gen. McCaffrey.

GAFE operations are coordinated with an office in the US embassy, the Information Analysis Center (IAC), which exchanges intelligence with the DEA, FBI, National Office of Drug Control Policy, and PGR. IAC computer links to DEA command-and-control centers along the international border are supposed to tip GAFE troops off to narco-trafficking activities in Mexican territory. But some observers in the Mexican press ask if the training is really "anti-narcos" or "anti-Marcos."[32]

A 1994 Pentagon intelligence study (procured via the Freedom of Information Act and reprinted in *La Jornada*) noted that anti-gringo sentiment in the Mexican army made US military intervention "improbable," but also stated: "It is conceivable that an eventual deployment of US troops in Mexico might be received favorably if Mexico's government is confronted with the threat of being overthrown as the result of widespread economic and social chaos."[33]

This conception was echoed by Donald Schulz, Latin America expert at the US Army War College in Carlisle, Pennsylvania, who told *El Financiero*'s international edition: "If there were major instability in Mexico of the kind that the country was getting too close to in 1994, this would provoke large-scale immigration and could carry with it violence to the United States—this is what we have to consider." Schulz admitted that "some of the training and equipment that has been provided to the Mexican military can be used for counterinsurgency purposes."[34]

In June 1998, PRD federal deputy Gilberto López y Rivas requested a Mexican Congressional probe of a report by a US veteran's group purporting to name US military advisors in Chiapas. The report, *Slippery Slope: US Military Intervention in the Chiapas Conflict*, was produced by Brian Willson, an Air Force veteran who in 1987 had his legs sliced off while blockading a trainload of weapons bound for Central America at California's Port Chicago Naval Station. He was now working with Veterans for Peace, and had spent several months investigating in Chiapas. The report mentioned three officers by name, intelligence presumably provided by Marcos: lieutenant colonels Alan Hassam Sánchez, John Kevin Kord, and Propp.[35]

FASCISM AND THE NEW SECURITY STATE

The Mexican state's response to the Chiapas revolt has brought Mexico within the fold of US-directed hemispheric policing. This fundamental transition had been building for fifteen years.

After the hiatus of the much-touted "return to democracy," a post-Cold War version of "national security doctrine" is once again being embraced throughout Latin America: this time in the name of combatting drugs and terrorism rather than Communism, and carried out under the auspices of technocratic "democracies" rather than military dictatorships—often with hardly less bloodshed.

The Mexican National Army (by official appellation) has traditionally been a closed institution, closely linked to the PRI. The Federal Judicial Police (PJF) and Prosecutor General of the Republic (PGR) have since the mid-1980s been more integrated into the hemispheric policing directed from Washington.[36] These civilian agencies led the way toward rapprochement as the counter-revolution consolidated under President Miguel de la Madrid.

The February 1985 torture-killing of DEA agent Enrique "Kiki" Camarena on the Michoacan ranch of Guadalajara Cartel *jefe* Rafael Caro Quintero proved critical in the transition from a nationalist to integrationist stance. The DEA team sent to Guadalajara to search for Camarena shortly reported that local police were frustrating their efforts; a diplomatic row ensued. The Federal Security Directorate (DFS), the "Mexican CIA," purportedly stepped in to block Caro Quintero's arrest after he was spotted at Guadalajara's airport. Washington retaliated by instructing Customs to slow the traffic flow at the border with extensive vehicle searches. De la Madrid personally phoned President Ronald Reagan to protest.[37]

Three days later, the DFS made arrests in the case. Camarena's body was discovered on March 5. A month later, Quintero himself was arrested by Costa Rican authorities, alerted by the DEA.[38] There was also the standard collateral damage: an innocent family was massacred when Mexican *federales* hit the wrong ranch.[39]

Guadalajara's police commander was sentenced to prison for accepting a $300,000 bribe to allow Quintero to flee the city.[40]

Tensions deepened when a Dr. Humberto Alvarez Machain was abducted by US bounty hunters and dispatched to Texas on charges of overseeing the three-day torture session. Mexico again protested, but the US Supreme Court upheld the kidnapping. The PGR capitulated, turning over the tapes of the torture. Mexican law enforcement had been appropriated by Washington's objectives.[41]

As usual, these objectives evidenced schizophrenic tendencies. A prosecution witness at the Los Angeles trial of Rubén Zuno Arce, a brother-in-law of former President Luis Echeverría arrested on charges related to the Kiki Camarena killing, testified that the CIA had established a training camp for Mexican law enforcement agents—and some Nicaraguan *contras*—on a Veracruz ranch owned by Caro Quintero. He claimed Caro Quintero targeted Camarena after the DEA busted his giant slave-labor marijuana plantation in Chihuahua because the CIA had given him reason to believe he was protected.[42] Two Mexican journalists who reported that *contras* were being trained at the Veracruz ranch were murdered.[43]

The co-opted DFS chief was Miguel Nazar Haro, reputed author of the White Brigade, a clandestine death squad which emerged in the 1970s. He was also said to be "protector" of the legendary kingpin Alberto Sicilia-Falcon, a Cuban exile and veteran of commando raids against the Fidel Castro government who settled in Tijuana and was among the first to establish Mexico as a cocaine transshipment point. He also controlled vast opium and marijuana operations in the Sierra Madre. When

Sicilia-Falcon was arrested in 1975, he claimed his plantations and smuggling routes were protected by the CIA, the proceeds bound for clandestine operations in Central America. These claims were given credence when he managed to escape. The PJF recaptured him, but before he could betray more, Nazar Haro magnanimously stepped in to protect him from torture.[44]

Following the Kiki Camarena crisis, the DFS was disbanded and reorganized as CISEN, the Center for Investigation and National Security, which remains Mexico's top civilian intelligence agency.[45]

Fallout from the episode is still felt. In February 1998, Puebla Gov. Manuel Bartlett Díaz, a crusty dinosaur and Gobernación secretary during the Camarena affair, launched an early presidential bid to reclaim Mexico from the technocrats, breaking with the protocol of waiting quietly for the *dedazo*. In the Los Angeles trial of the two charged in the Camarena murder, DEA informers testified Bartlett was among senior Mexican officials present at the agent's torture sessions. Bartlett and two former US ambassadors to Mexico ridiculed the accusation, but the US Justice Department said it would continue to seek his testimony before an LA grand jury. Bartlett conveniently avoided travel to the US.[46]

The Mexican state, with its corporatist and populist tradition, never adopted anti-Communist national security doctrine in the Cold War, seeking to co-opt rather than repress popular movements, employing only measured doses of terror. Mexico was the only Latin American country (apart from, arguably, Costa Rica) never to experience a Cold War military coup. This was due to the Mexican National Army's unique relationship to the civil government. President Cárdenas incorporated the army as an official sector of the ruling party. Until 1940, the army had a quota of congressional seats. In exchange for this access to political power, the army acceded to such doctrines as regular rotation of zone commanders, to prevent regional *caudillos* from emerging.[47] This rule was loosely enforced in Chiapas, considered an exceptional case, and fiefdoms such as that of Gen. Absalon Castellanos did emerge.

But the new anti-drug and anti-crime security doctrine Washington now promotes throughout the hemisphere is applicable to Mexico as well as Central and South America. Use of the PGR helicopters in the January 1994 repression speaks to the obvious reality that expanded security prowess in Drug War guise is nonetheless targeted against popular movements and the civil population.

US ambassador James Jones admitted that US-provided choppers were used in Chiapas, but denied they had been used inappropriately. He claimed he had been assured that they were only deployed logistically, rather than in direct combat. Marcos, for his part, contradicted this.[48]

Following the Zapatista revolt, the army followed the police forces into hemispheric integration. Immediately after the uprising, Mexico initiated imports of new armored vehicles and crowd-control weapons from the US, as well as cut-rate Russian war material.[49]

Mexican army troops are now replacing civilian police in domestic enforcement. In July 1999, Gobernación Secretary Diodoro Carrasco said SEDENA was freeing up 4,899 soldiers, 352 military vehicles, 1,862 weapons and 99 dogs to collaborate with the new Federal Preventative Police for "a head-on fight, with no concessions, against crime." The government denied it was militarizing police functions, saying the soldiers would be deployed for intelligence and surveillance operations.[50]

The Mexican prison system has also witnessed an unprecedented expansion. The new Almoloya federal prison was opened in 1992, incorporating sophisticated "control units" modeled on those in the US, and state-of-the-art behavior modification techniques.[51] Old dungeons like Cerro Hueco persist in many states, while the federal government pioneers the high-tech Reclusorio archipelago around the Federal District. These are emulated in the new system of state prisons known as the Social Rehabilitation Centers, a euphemism bordering on the hilarious.[52]

In January 1994, the spouses and mothers of Almoloya inmates—nearly all of them drug convicts—formally protested conditions at the prison in an open letter to Gobernación. They charged their loved ones were denied sufficient food, exercise, visiting rights and medical treatment—even following torture sessions. The statement compared the new elite facility to the Bastille of 1789.[53]

Adding insult to injury, the Mexican press shortly published photos of "luxury cells" at the Reclusorios—sprawling, carpeted and well-appointed for members of the political elite.[54]

Disappearances or extrajudicial arrests often involve the army's Military Camp One in the Federal District.[55] There are also reports of clandestine prisons operated by the unofficial security forces.[56]

In another chilling echo of the Central American counterinsurgency campaigns of the 1980s, the Independent Organization of Mixtec and Tlapanec Pueblos (OIPMT) recently announced that it had documented through interviews with local peasants in the Sierra del Sur that the Guerrero State Health Services began a systematic campaign of sterilization abuse in the region after the emergence of the EPR in 1996. Indian women are apparently offered food, clothing or money to submit to having their fallopian tubes tied. Sometimes threats of a cut-off of government farm aid are used, and in most cases the women are not made to understand that the procedure is permanent.[57]

A minority current in Mexican ruling circles sought to bring the country into conformity with hemispheric anti-Communist doctrine during the Cold War. Such elements formed the White Brigade in response to the guerilla emergence of the 1970s—never officially acknowledged, but responsible for some four hundred disappearances in the 1970s and early 1980s.[58]

In 1989, Zacarias Osorio Cruz, a deserter from the Mexican army, sought refuge in Montreal, where he told an Immigration Board he had participated in the execution of sixty political prisoners. He said his unit had official orders from SEDENA "to make these people disappear." He flew in military aircraft to several Mexican states to bring hooded, handcuffed prisoners back to Military Camp One, where they were riddled with gunfire until "the bodies were practically torn apart." These included some thirty *campesinos* involved in a land dispute in Guerrero.[59]

Influential in this current were Los Tecos, "the owls," a fascist secret society ensconced in the Guadalajara business elite. Los Tecos developed from extremist elements in the Cristero opposition of the 1920s, and congealed under the leadership of Carlos Cuesta Gallardo, a World War II Nazi agent whose mission was to factionalize the army and develop paramilitary groups to attack the US border. After the war, Los Tecos established the Mexican Anti-Communist Federation (FEMACO), the Mexican chapter of the World Anti-Communist League (WACL), and became a clearinghouse for anti-Semitic literature, such as their *Conspiracy Against the Church*. They also established control over the Autonomous University of Guadalajara, loaning their name to the school *fútbol* team.[60]

In spring 1984, Mexico's foremost muckraking journalist, Manuel Buendia, in a series on CIA intrigues in Mexico for *El Día*, reported that US AID funds for the University were being diverted to Los Tecos coffers. In May, weeks after the series had run, Buendia was shot dead by unknown gunmen at his office. The murder remains unsolved.[61]

Los Tecos maintained a network of "men of action"—rightist paramilitaries and generals—which offered its services to El Salvador's death squads. Operating under (or within) a Mexican regime still maintaining leftist postures, they worked under the slogan, "Against the Red guerilla, the White guerilla."[62]

Los Tecos remain linked via WACL to the veteran Central American death squad leaders, rightist Southern Cone generals and their CIA collaborators. In the 1980s, under the leadership of Gen. John K. Singlaub, former commander of US forces in South Korea, WACL was a prime source of private funding for the Nicaraguan *contras*.[63]

The Mexican fascist right predictably saw conspiracies galore in the 1994 peso devaluation, and even put forth the theory that the Zapatistas were funded by Wall

Street, H. Ross Perot or the CIA to destabilize the peso and enable the gringos (read: Jews) to take back the oil.[64]

The Movimiento de Solidaridad Iberoamericano (MSIA), Mexican wing of the far-right cult led by Lyndon LaRouche, links the local Chiapas reactionaries and the national fascist right. The MSIA's rancher and *coleto* followers in Chiapas distribute propaganda portraying the Zapatistas as "separatists" and "narco-terrorist" pawns in a world domination conspiracy by the KGB, Jewish bankers and the Queen of England. The EZLN is "Sendero Luminoso Norte," and Samuel Ruiz is the "corrupter of nuns." The MSIA was also active in the historic 1997 DF governor's race, distributing propaganda portraying Cuauhtémoc Cárdenas as a violent extremist and the PRD as "the arm of narco-terrorism."[65]

The LaRouche cult has long cultivated ties to the intelligence community, providing "executive reports" to the CIA and Noriega dictatorship in the early 1980s. LaRouche's liaison to the CIA was Mitch Livingstone WerBell III, a veteran of mercenary work in Guatemala who ran a paramilitary training camp in Georgia. In 1982, Gen. Singlaub addressed a group of LaRouche followers at the Georgia camp— although the general later became a bitter detractor of the cult leader.[66]

The International White terror network's fingerprints are already on the Chiapas violence. Following allegations in the Mexican press in January 1998, the Guatemalan Public Ministry opened an investigation into several current and former military officers (including at least two SOA graduates) for diverting arms to paramilitary groups in Chiapas.[67]

In the immediate aftermath of the 1994 uprising, *La Jornada* received what it called an "implicit threat" in the form of a "Communiqué Number One" from a "Mexican Anti-Communist Front": "The war has started . . . The dog pack of communists will be stopped, along with its mouthpiece *La Jornada*, apologist for the red insult . . . Death to the PRD! Exemplary punishment for subversives! Out with Rigoberta Menchú and foreigners! No to the political clergy! Viva Mexico!"[68]

DRUG WAR AS COUNTERINSURGENCY

In 1996, the annual US State Department report *Patterns in Global Terrorism* invoked both the EZLN and the EPR: "In Mexico, the Popular Revolutionary Army (EPR) carried out a series of small-scale attacks, killing 17 persons including several civilians, and the Zapatista National Liberation Army (EZLN) signed an agreement on indigenous peoples' rights with the government." This information is accurate, but implicitly assigns the label "terrorist."[69]

Former CIA Director John Deutch, writing on the global terrorist threat in *Foreign Policy* in 1997, stated: "Drawing the line between terrorism and insurgency can be difficult. In Mexico, for example, dissident groups such as the Popular Revolutionary Army in Guerrero and the Zapatista National Liberation Army in Chiapas seek to change the country's political and economic system."[70]

Drawing the line between counterinsurgency and drug enforcement can also be difficult. The report *Law Enforcement and the Mexican Armed Forces: The Military Undertakes New Internal Security Missions*, produced by the US Army Foreign Military Studies Office at Fort Leavenworth in 1997, once again invoked the EZLN and the EPR: "Mexican internal security concerns began to intensify more than three years ago with the January 1994 appearance of the Zapatista National Liberation Army . . . " It acknowledged that anti-drug aid will be used for other purposes: "The distinction among drug traffickers, arms traffickers, other heavily armed criminal groups and bandits, or insurgents is often not a clear one. As a consequence, military support to law enforcement will certainly be directed against a variety of targets."[71]

The EZLN's use of the Internet to build support for their movement outside Chiapas was noted by RAND Corporation analyst David Ronfeldt, who wrote in a 1995 report: "The country that produced the prototype social revolution of the twentieth century may now be giving rise to the prototype social netwar of the twentyfirst century."[72]

SEDENA has traditionally had one document discussing guerilla warfare, *Manual of Irregular War*. Under SEDENA doctrine, Mexico is a "revolutionary country"; therefore any rebel movement is considered "counter-revolutionary." The document ostensibly studies guerilla tactics to be adopted by the Mexican Army in the event of foreign occupation. In 1995, after the Chiapas revolt, SEDENA produced a second volume of the manual, entitled *Counterguerilla Operations, or Restoration of Order*, maintaining that Mexicans "who take arms against legally constituted institutions . . . cannot be considered *guerrilleros* or belligerents, but can be treated as rebels . . . in this case, the armed forces conduct restoration of order operations."[73]

Counterguerilla Operations seeks to adopt the doctrine of *Guerra de Baja Intensidad* (GBI) to the Mexican reality. This doctrine, developed by the Pentagon in the Central America experience of the 1980s, is referred to in gringo military culture as Low Intensity Conflict (LIC). The 1986 Pentagon document defining the doctrine, the *Joint Low-Intensity Conflict Project Final Report*, openly stated the term "emerged as a euphemism for 'counterinsurgency' when that term lost favor" after the Vietnam War.[74]

The Pentagon document states: "Low-intensity conflict is neither war nor peace . . . The term 'low-intensity' suggests . . . a spectrum of warfare. Low-intensity conflict, however, cannot be understood to mean simply the degree of violence involved. Low-intensity conflict has more to do with the nature of the violence— the strategy that guides it and the way individuals engage each other in it—than with level or numbers . . . Low-intensity conflict is a limited politico-military struggle to achieve political, social, economic, or psychological objectives. It is often pro- tracted and ranges from diplomatic, economic, and psychological pressures through terrorism and insurgency. Low-intensity conflict is generally confined to a geo- graphical area and is often characterized by constraints on the weaponry, tactics, and the level of violence."[75]

The document openly places LIC in the context of Free Trade: "As a super- power in the nuclear age with an economy largely dependent upon an extensive, vulnerable overseas trade system, this country faces challenges that are far more troubling and complicated than those it faced before World War II." It discusses both terrorism and insurgency, stating that the latter "poses an open and direct threat to the ordering of society . . . For the United States, with extensive global interests and an economy increasingly reliant on a stable world order, the chronic instability in the third world is a serious concern."[76]

Since the "chronic instability" reached the USA's southern neighbor in no uncer- tain terms, the Pentagon has busily imparted this doctrine to the Mexican National Army. Between 1996 and 1997, the number of Mexican military officers receiving Pentagon training jumped from 300 to 1,500. A September 1997 report to Con- gress on the program by Drug Czar McCaffrey's office stated: "Central to the development of Mexico's counterdrug capability is the training of GAFE . . . elite Mexican Army units that have received Special Forces and air assault training for use in counterdrug interdiction operations."[77]

However, the January 1996 issue of *Special Warfare*, the Fort Bragg base maga- zine, boasting that GAFE represents an advance in the development of Mexican special forces, made no mention of counterdrug training. It stated: "particularly heavy emphasis is being placed on those forces that will be located in the states of Chiapas and Guerrero, where 'special airborne forces' will be set up."[78]

Fort Bragg is the home of the Seventh Special Forces group—veterans of the Panama invasion, the Nicaraguan *contra* insurgency, counterdrug missions in Bolivia and counterinsurgency campaigns in Vietnam, El Salvador, Colombia and Peru. According to their Web site: "Today we are continuously engaged in Foreign In- ternal Defense throughout Central and South America wherever SocSouth [Special Operations Command South] and SouthCom [Southern Command] may direct."[79]

Secretary of State Madeline Albright told Congress in response to criticisms: "We are not involved in any counterinsurgency training and the Mexican government has not requested said training."[80]

In addition to the Fort Bragg and Fort Benning programs, Mexican officers are trained in counterintelligence at Bolling Air Force Base in Washington DC; in helicopter maneuvers at Fort Rucker, Alabama; in helicopter maintenance at Fort Sam Houston, Texas; and in related programs at twelve other US military bases.[81]

The torture of abducted drug suspects by GAFE troops in Jalisco was revealed after the force was sent to "restore order" in Chiapas following the Acteal massacre. The Pentagon and McCaffrey were embarrassed once again in August 1998 when twenty GAFE troops (including majors and captains) were arrested on charges of trafficking in drugs and undocumented immigrants at the Mexico City airport.[82]

The CIA, which once coordinated with the now-discredited DFS, has also shifted its efforts to the military. SEDENA's CIA-trained Counter-Narcotics Intelligence Center is overseen by Col. Augusto Moises Garcia Ochoa, a 1997 SOA graduate in Jungle Operations.[83]

Realities of CIA complicity in the 1980s Central America atrocities were documented in the 1990s. CIA "interrogation" training manuals used in Latin America were released to the *Baltimore Sun* in 1997. The paper, pursuing a Freedom of Information Act request in an investigation of the Battalion 316 death squad in Honduras, threatened to sue the Agency. The 1963 "KUBARK Counterintelligence Interrogation" manual included suggestions on "medical, chemical or electrical methods." Tip for torturers: "If a new safehouse is to be used, the electric current should be known in advance, so that transformers or other modifying devices will be on hand if needed."[84]

In January 1998, just after the revelation of links between Guatemala's army and the Chiapas paramilitaries, former Guatemalan Chief-of-Staff Otto Pérez Molina admitted to *El Financiero* that, after 1994, some fifty Mexican army officers began training with the feared Kaibiles in the Peteñ rainforest. The Subcomandante's intelligence had once again been vindicated by the press.[85]

THE NEW DISSIDENTS

Until the new realignment, SEDENA had made a point of looking elsewhere than the US for military gear. But US Foreign Military Sales to Mexico jumped from $4.8 million in 1996 to $28 million in 1997—this on top of outright Pentagon donations, and at least $12 million in sales from private US arms companies. This placed Mexico as Latin America's third purchaser of US war material, behind Colombia and Venezuela.[86]

A New United States Strategy for Mexico, a report by Lt. Col. Joseph Nuñez for the US Army War College, actually advocates a joint command for US, Mexican and Canadian forces. It also calls for a North American peacekeeping force, headquartered in the US, with deputy commander positions rotating between Canada and Mexico. It urges a hemispheric military organization that "reflects regional economic and security concerns . . . particularly considering our burgeoning trade through NAFTA, and the growing threat of terrorism that can penetrate through our borders." The document details current revolutionary movements in Mexico and concludes: "If we fail to change our current strategy, the country could become less stable, thus jeopardizing the viability of NAFTA and the Free Trade Area of the Americas."[87]

With this new alignment, left-leaning nationalists within the Mexican military are the new dissidents. There are already suggestions that the army may be fracturing under the pressures of the transition to an integrationist counterinsurgency stance.

On December 18, 1998, fifty soldiers in dress uniforms marched on Mexico City's Paseo de la Reforma, halting traffic to protest the "obsolete, absurd, corrupt, painful and ignorant" military justice system. The group's leader, Lt. Col. Hildegardo Bacilio Gómez, went into hiding after the march and was charged with desertion. Other soldiers who had attended later reported they had been detained at Military Camp One and subjected to physical and psychological abuse. Lt. Col. Bacilio Gómez issued communiqués from hiding via fax and Internet, announcing the formation of a "Patriotic Command of the People's Consciousness" (CPCP). Demanding dismissal of Enrique Cervantes, he called on Mexico's generals to elect their own defense secretary, and attacked civilian control over the military. He also attacked the Free Trade economic model that has brought a "Mexico . . . in flames, living a Dantesque inferno."[88]

The CPCP called for the release of Brig. Gen. José Francisco Gallardo Rodriguez, imprisoned at Military Camp One since 1993, when he published an article calling for the creation of a human rights ombudsman within the army. Amnesty International declared Gallardo a prisoner of conscience, claiming the corruption charges against him fraudulent, and protesting that he has been subject to psychological torture.[89]

Lt. Col. Bacilio Gómez also expressed admiration for Subcommander Marcos. "Marcos is in a trench where many of us should be. If he at some time reads me or sees me on the Internet, he should feel that he was a real inspiration to my thinking," wrote Gómez, adding that he was proud of his Otomi indigenous background.[90]

This was not the first manifestation of unrest among the ranks. In January 1997, eleven retired high-ranking army officers publicly defected to the PRD, announcing they considered it closer to the ideals of the Revolution.[91]

The 1994 Ocosingo bloodletting resulted in an unprecedented humiliation for SEDENA. In July 1999, former Mexican army captain Jesús Valle won a two-year legal battle for political asylum in Texas by convincing US immigration judges he had a "well founded fear of persecution" if deported back to Mexico. Capt. Valle was sent into Chiapas when the uprising began. Valle said he was ordered to kill "anyone who looks like a Zapatista" at Ocosingo once the press were out of sight. He refused to obey the order and was transferred to Puebla, where fellow soldiers warned him to "disappear" before someone did it for him. He fled to his home state of Chihuahua, and crossed the border in February 1995. The ruling made Capt. Valle the first Mexican soldier granted political asylum in the US.[92]

The emergence of dissent within the military may strengthen the resolve and conscience of those Mexican troops already inclined to disobey orders for repression. But if the army actually splits, US pressures to integrate SEDENA into hemispheric policing may only augment the forces propelling Mexico toward civil war.

18

B O R D E R   W A R S

Scapegoating or Solidarity?

As revolutionary movements re-emerge in Mexico, political debate in the US is dominated by invective between the corporate right and the populist right. Populist billionaire H. Ross Perot, rather than a labor or environmental leader, came forward to debate Vice President Al Gore on NAFTA in 1993. The ascendant right wing populists link their rejection of Free Trade to xenophobia, and the federal government finds it expedient to appease them with militarization of the Mexican border as the trade barriers fall.

But tendrils of the culture which animates *zapatismo* extend north of the border, through surviving land-rooted Mexican-American communities of the US Southwest, and immigrants who still remember the soil of Oaxaca. Border militarization can only presage a generalized militarization of the US, because the cultural divide does not conform to the neat colors on the map. Mexico and the United States permeate each other in myriad ways. The effectiveness of grassroots opposition to the transnational Free Trade regime will depend on whether it is rooted in scapegoating or solidarity.

WHO WATCHES THE WATCHMEN?

Under President Bill Clinton, baited as a liberal by his opponents, the US Border Patrol beefed up troop strength by the hundreds, launched big special operations to intercept drugs and migrants, conducted unprecedented joint exercises with the National Guard, brought Pentagon troops massively into border enforcement, and built miles of wall along the international line.

There are now 62 miles of wall—"fences," authorities like to say—along the USA's southern border. They first went up at California's major crossing, San

Ysidro; then at the inland desert outposts of Jacumba and Calexico. El Paso was next, the big Texas crossing where the Rio Grande veers north and the border becomes an arbitrary line drawn west across the Chihuahuan Desert. In 1997, at the major Arizona crossing, Nogales, pains were taken to avoid the distasteful welded metal of the California and Texas sites. Official dictates for a structure that will "allow light and a feeling of openness" resulted in an Orwellian construction captured by the *New York Times* as "forbidding yet friendly."[1]

Visions of a high-tech Great Wall spanning 2,000 miles from San Ysidro to Brownsville, bristling with electronic sensors, dance in the head of Pat Buchanan, who vowed in his 1996 bid for the Republican presidential candidacy, "I will stop this massive illegal immigration cold. Period. Paragraph." He told one Iowa crowd: "I'll build that security fence, and we'll close it, and we'll say, 'Listen José, you're not coming in!' "[2]

Buchanan explicitly scapegoats Mexican migrants for the economic pain of NAFTA. Two-term California Governor Pete Wilson, advocate of 1994's Proposition 187 which bars undocumented immigrants from public services, does so implicitly. In reality, it is manufacturing and industrial jobs which head south under the NAFTA regime, corporate bosses eager to pay wages in devalued pesos. The migrants heading north usually wind up washing dishes or doing domestic labor for below minimum wage, or toiling under toxic clouds of pesticide in the broccoli and lettuce fields of Kern County and the Imperial Valley.

This dirt-cheap labor floats California's economy. As Mexican *campesino* lands are enclosed by the ag-biz expansion, the migrants keep coming—driven by desperation to risk their lives for jobs that pay dollars. Federal sanctions against employers who hire undocumented workers drive down wages. The job pool shrinks (slightly), but—militarization notwithstanding—not the numbers coming over the border. So employers who depend on undocumented labor can get away with paying less and less.

In the age of NAFTA, the border becomes ultra-permeable to goods and capital—licit and illicit—and ever less permeable to *people*.

The militarization is great for the gringo politicians and the Mexican cartel *jefes*. It is the poor, the powerless and ordinary folks who pay for the massive effort with their lives and freedom—on both sides of the border.

A DEATH IN TEXAS

On May 20, 1997, 18-year-old goat herder Ezequiel Hernández, Jr. was shot dead by a hiding, camouflaged US Marine on the Texas side of the Rio Grande. Within two weeks of the killing, discrepancies began to appear in the military's explanation of the incident. The angry and grieving citizens of Redford (population: 107), about 40 kilometers from Big Bend National Park, demanded information and justice, and local authorities were pitted against the Pentagon.[3]

Presidio County District Attorney Albert Valadez didn't buy the preliminary conclusion by Marine Col. Thomas R. Kelly of self-defense in "strict compliance" with military rules of engagement. A grand jury prepared to probe the first shooting of a US citizen by a military drug-surveillance team on the border, raising the specter of a US Marine standing trial in a state court. Conflicting versions battled it out in the press: on one side, Presidio County and the Texas Rangers; on the other, Joint Task Force Six, a new counter-narcotics unit coordinating Border Patrol and Pentagon troops.[4]

It was early evening, and Hernández, his schoolwork done, was grazing the goats he tended as part of a church project in the plains outside Redford, along the banks of the ancient river that forms the Texas–Chihuahua border. Hernández carried an old .22 rifle to defend against a wild dog pack which had mutilated one of his goats. We don't know if he ever got a shot off, or knew he was being tracked by duck-walking, camouflaged Marines with M-16s. He was shot in the side from a hundred yards and knocked backwards into a fire pit, where he bled to death.[5]

Joint Task Force Six said Hernández had fired in the direction of the four Marines. Texas Rangers investigator Capt. Barry Caver claimed forensic evidence contradicted this version, asserting Hernández was unaware he was shooting at US Marines—who were in heavy camo, their faces blackened and bodies covered in burlap and leaves.[6]

Rangers found Hernández was facing away from the Marines when he was shot, and that no medical aid was given to the dying youth—even though the Marine team included a medic. The accused Marine's attorney countered that it took the team almost ten minutes to make their way to Hernández, and they didn't want to move him for fear of a spinal wound. Residents suggested the Marines let Hernández die to keep him from telling his side of the story.[7]

The Rangers found the Marines had radioed that they were observing a young man herding goats and carrying a rifle, and followed him for twenty minutes before one corporal fired through brush and mesquite trees.[8]

Marine Cpl. Clemente Bañuelos of California (who bore an eerie resemblance to the young Hernández) apparently fired the fatal shot. DA Valadez announced his intention to try Bañuelos for murder. The Hernández family hired an attorney to pursue a wrongful death suit against the Pentagon. Local residents launched a campaign to get the military out of border enforcement.[9]

Joint Task Force Six was created by Pentagon Joint Chiefs of Staff Chair Colin Powell, celebrated hero of Operation Desert Storm, who pioneered an expanded military role in the federal Drug War. Fort Bliss was nerve-center in the operation, with Army troops providing intelligence, fence building, mapping and training for Border Patrol. Military LP/OPs—for "listening posts/observation posts"—were established upon Border Patrol request. It was one LP/OP which got into the fatal incident at Redford.[10]

After the Border Patrol's Marfa Sector requested LP/OPs for the Redford area, a message went out to every Army and Marine base in the US, soliciting volunteers. The Fifth Battalion, 11th Marine Regiment from Camp Pendleton near San Diego was the first unit that volunteered. It was dispatched to Fort Bliss, then to Border Patrol's Marfa HQ, and then Redford. There, it hid out along the banks of the Rio Grande as JTF 6 Unit 513.[11]

Unit 513 was looking for the human "mule train" of smugglers paid $1,500 a shot to haul 200-pound backpacks of marijuana across the border by a mid-level Chihuahua *jefe* called "El Cubano." Presidio County residents were not told of Marines patrolling the area.[12]

Unit 513 never sighted any of El Cubano's backpackers. But on the evening of May 20 a Marine radioed they were under fire. Texas Rangers forensics experts contested the JTF 6 assertion that Hernández was hit as he raised his .22 to fire. They allege he was hit as he was turning to go back home with his goats. The Marines did not identify themselves. Marine Col. Thomas Kelly told journalist Robert Draper who covered the incident for the *Texas Monthly*, "In order to get the attention of the individual, they would've had to expose themselves. And there was no requirement under the rules of engagement about having to do that."[13]

The Hernández family and neighbors founded the Redford Citizens Committee for Justice and launched their own investigation, backed by the DC-based Common Sense for Drug Policy. This investigation found more discrepancies. Residents reported hearing only one shot that evening. "Nobody interviewed any local citizens, and we don't know why," said Redford's Rev. Mel LaFollette. There was no ballistic report on the last time Ezequiel's rifle was fired, which was not even secured until after heavy rain had fallen on it. Bill Elliott, the Houston private investigator hired by the Redford citizens, found the official probe tainted by "tampering of key evidence."[14]

In a letter to DA Valadez, the Citizens Committee stressed that they did not want Bañuelos to be made a scapegoat. "This community has been grievously wounded by the actions of Cpl. Bañuelos and his team. Nevertheless, the community feels that there are others in the chain of command . . . who should be sought out and made to admit responsibility for the sorry desecration of traditional American values."[15]

On August 14, the grand jury brought back a decision not to indict Bañuelos—after an emotional appearance by Lance Cpl. James Michael Blood, who testified that Bañuelos "possibly saved my life" by shooting Hernández. Marines told the jurors Hernández fired twice in their direction—although he may well have thought he was firing on wild dogs. The grand jury found Bañuelos "acted reasonably" in firing on him.[16]

One of the twelve grand jurors was a Border Patrol agent and part of the command chain that assigned Marines to the border. "This is not the end," Rev. LaFollette told the press. "This is the beginning."[17]

"I think somebody should be held responsible for the death of my brother," Ezequiel's surviving sibling Margarito Hernández told a reporter. "They made it look like it was his fault. I don't know, the only mistake he did was to go to pasture his goats on that day."[18]

While millions poured into border militarization , Redford homes only got running water in 1995. "We are not drug dealers in Redford," said Enrique Madrid, an archaeological steward for the Texas Historical Commission who worked with Ezequiel on a school history project. "We are not terrorists. This is what Redford really is—hardworking, humble farmers and families . . ."[19]

Ezequiel's bedroom wall had been decorated with pictures of Pancho Villa, the Virgin of Guadalupe—and a Marines recruiting poster. After he found out his brother had been killed, Margarito went into the bedroom and tore down the recruiting poster.[20]

MILITIAS, VIGILANTES AND FEDERAL POWER

The military suspended its drug-fighting activities in the Marfa sector of West Texas after the Hernández shooting. As the outcry grew, military troops were officially removed from border drug enforcement altogether by Defense Secretary William Cohen—although it is hard to say where drug enforcement ends and migration enforcement begins. The shooting came as the Clinton administration was preparing an unprecedented increase in the Border Patrol, ostensibly phasing out Pentagon troops and reversing the policy inherited from the Bush administration.[21]

The militarization had been building for a generation. President Richard Nixon's 1968 Operation Intercept brought traffic at the crossings to a crawl with car searches for marijuana, prompting diplomatic protests from Mexico. The operation's architect was Nixon aide and future Watergate defendant G. Gordon Liddy, who also was instrumental in launching the Mexico herbicide program (even suggesting direct US aerial eradication of the marijuana fields regardless of Mexico's approval).[22] Reagan policy brought military troops into border control, opening loopholes in the post-Civil War Posse Comitatus Act which bars the military from domestic enforcement. In 1983, Vice President George Bush, former CIA chief who was simultaneously organizing the secret war in Nicaragua, was appointed head of the National Narcotics Border Interdiction System.[23]

Although the military was officially confined to surveillance and training—barred from making arrests or searches—many protested the historic loosening of Posse Comitatus. Lawrence Korb, a Reagan-era assistant defense secretary, said the Redford incident demonstrated the incompatibility of military and police duties. "The military, to put it bluntly, is trained to vaporize, not Mirandize," Korb told the *Dallas Morning News*, referring to the Supreme Court decision protecting the rights of arrested suspects.[24]

It looked like the Redford tragedy would spell the policy's end. Common Sense for Drug Policy's Kevin Zeese told the *Washington Post* that the removal of military from border drug enforcement was "a good first step . . . We are not at war with Mexico."[25]

Then, the empire struck back.

In an unprecedented move, Drug Czar Barry McCaffrey announced that he would exercise his veto power over the Pentagon's 1999 budget unless the Defense Department boosted anti-drug spending by $141 million (over the Pentagon's proposed $809 million). This would include, in addition to training of Mexican officers and special operations in the Andes and Caribbean, an increase to $162 million (from $132 million) for National Guard anti-drug missions on the Mexican border.[26]

McCaffrey was not slow to play the fundamentally linked cards of Free Trade and xenophobia. "Mexico is our second-biggest trading partner today," he told reporters. "If Mexico doesn't make it, if they go down the tubes, then we ought to assume we're going to have 20 million Mexicans in the United States."[27]

The Drug Warriors backed him up. Phil Jordan, former head of the DEA's El Paso Intelligence Center, told the *Dallas Morning News* that border military operations just level the playing field. "The American people don't have any idea of the sophistication of countersurveillance and intelligence that the traffickers based in Mexico have," he said. "When you're dealing with an army of smugglers, you need to respond accordingly."[28]

Border agents were threatened with firearms or shot at 110 times from October 1996 to April 1997, reported the Immigration and Naturalization Service (INS), which oversees the Border Patrol. Three days before the Redford shooting, a Border Patrol agent in California was fired on by a sniper from the Mexican side and wounded in the shoulder.[29]

Clinton was also under long-building pressure from the weekend warriors of the grassroots radical right.

Dean Compton of National Alliance of Christian Militia, based in the Northern California mountain outpost of Shingletown, had issued a call in October 1995—dubbed "Operation Protect America"—for a February national militia mobilization on the southern border "to fight illegal immigration and traffic in illegal drugs." The call actually quoted an article by Mexican analyst Jorge Castañeda in the July 1995 *Atlantic Monthly*:

> During the NAFTA debate and at the height of his credibility in the United States, Carlos Salinas argued that failure to ratify the treaty would bring about an economic collapse in Mexico, which in turn would bring about a wave of undocumented immigration to the north. The economic collapse came about anyway, but the wave looks more like a steadily rising tide. Were the Clinton administration in its obsession with re-election politics to try to stem that tide, it would threaten the only true deterrent to the proverbial wave: Mexican stability. Any attempt to clamp down on immigration from the south—by sealing the border militarily, by forcing Mexico to deter its citizens from emigrating, or through some federal version of Proposition 187—will make social peace in the *barrios* and *pueblos* of Mexico untenable.

Then Compton picked up his call:

> Ladies and Gentlemen, what Castañeda is saying here is we have two choices. Either we accept large-scale "illegal immigration" in order to allow Mexico to avoid chaos in their country [sic], or we can increase our efforts to arrest the tide and face a full-scale invasion as a result! Neither of these two scenarios is acceptable. Under the Constitution . . . the President as Commander in Chief . . . has a responsibility to defend the Sovereign Borders of the Union from invasion by foreign forces . . . We still have the world's greatest army. We have the best trained men and women and the best equipment that a Free, Taxpaying Country can buy. We have the will of our Soldiers in Arms to defend our borders from

invasion. But, it seems as though the will of our elected officials is just not quite as strong . . . The people of the state Republic of California have begged and pleaded, we've cried and died, and we have Voted! And still the problem magnifies . . . WE THE PEOPLE will no longer tolerate our brothers and sisters, mothers and fathers, sons and daughters, our friends and fellow citizens being destroyed by a foreign invader . . ."

Compton urged "the UNORGANIZED MILITIA to be at DEFCON level 2" by February 1, 1996. "Defense Condition Level 2 means 'ready for deployment' . . . When we are deployed, there will be nothing and no one that crosses that border EXCEPT in a LAWFUL MANNER! Nothing larger than a gopher will make its way past!" Invoking Vietnam, Compton wrote: "We lost that war. We will not lose this war!"[30]

At the precise moment Compton issued his call, the federal government was making similar sounds. In October 1995, Attorney General Janet Reno created a "Border Czar" post, mirroring the Drug Czar. Alan Bersin, US Attorney for San Diego, was appointed to the new office.[31]

Simultaneously, the Clinton administration released a contingency plan to contain a human surge across the border, with deployment of Army units and detention of immigrants on inactive military bases. INS chief Doris Meissner said the Army "is the only force that could be counted on once the civilian agencies' capacities are surpassed."[32]

Training exercises for the plan were immediately launched in Nogales, Arizona, and McAllen, Texas. The Nogales exercise, originally planned for October, was postponed to November because it would have embarrassingly coincided with President Zedillo's visit to Washington![33]

Border Patrol erected tent cities behind barbed wire in the desert as "temporary collection points" for the imaginary detainees. National Guard units erected new "fences" along the frontier.[34] A pilot project was initiated to detain migrants at Miramar Naval Station, near San Diego.[35]

After this, Dean Compton's militia mobilization seemed anti-climactic.

But there may be a role for the radical-right militias in the darkest corners of federal emergency response plans for the Southwest border.

The precedent for the October 1995 exercises was 1984's REX 84 ALPHA— a "readiness exercise" in which the INS and Federal Emergency Management Agency (FEMA) prepared for a domestic crisis sparked by a US invasion of Central America. In the REX 84 ALPHA scenario, paramilitary State Defense Forces would be deputized by FEMA to help round up 400,000 refugees in a six-hour period. State Defense Forces participated in REX 84 ALPHA's "Operation Nightrain," a dry-run for the round-up, marching in the desert to intercept imaginary refugees. Ten military bases around the country were designated as detainment centers.[36]

REX 84 ALPHA was drawn up by Lt. Col. Oliver North (then the National Security Council's liaison to FEMA), as part of a contingency plan to suspend the Constitution and declare martial law as the Marines hit the beaches of Nicaragua. These plans were outlined in the *Miami Herald* during the 1987 Congressional hearings on the "Contragate" scandal.[37] However, when the matter was brought before Congress, hearings chair Sen. Daniel Inouye scuttled the discussion to the "executive session," closed to the press and public.[38] FEMA chief at that time was Louis O. Giuffrida, who in 1970 had authored a document entitled "National Survival—Racial Imperative" at the US Army War College, examining the feasibility of mass round-ups of African Americans on military bases in the event of urban unrest.[39]

The State Defense Forces (SDFs) were created across the US by state legislatures at federal behest in the 1980s, and attracted participation from various unseemly elements. Among these was the Aryan Nations, which calls for a racially pure secessionist "white homeland" in the Northwest Rockies and has a violent underground arm called The Order which has carried out a string of bank heists across the West. In 1987, the Utah State Guard (the state's SDF) was purged following revelations that members had diverted arms to the Aryan Nations and that State Guardsmen had trained at the group's compound in Hayden Lake, Idaho.[40]

Another precedent for the Clinton plan was the military detainment of Haitian "boat people" in the 1980s, who were fleeing the brutal regime of President-for-Life Jean-Claude "Baby Doc" Duvalier. Florida's Camp Krome, one of the ten bases named in REX 84 ALPHA, was actually used to hold thousands of these refugees— in appalling conditions that drew protest from human rights organizations and hunger strikes from the detainees.[41]

The pattern of federal power following, appeasing and ultimately incorporating elements of the radical right continued. In October 1996, after a month of Southern California vigilantism in which illegal migrants were shot and held captive by local ranchers, the US and Mexico launched a joint enforcement operation to police the area. One migrant, wanted by local police for robbery, was shot and wounded by vigilantes. Another six were rounded up and held at gunpoint until Border Patrol arrived.[42]

A self-declared Airport Posse started patrolling San Diego's Lindbergh Field. Authorities went to court to stop the patrols[43]—but once again stepped in with their own programs, bringing more powerful resources to work pioneered by unofficial forces.

Finally, McCaffrey's maneuver assured that even if active-duty Pentagon troops were to be demobilized from the border, National Guard troops would take their place. A November 1997 article in *Soldiers* ("The Official US Army Magazine") boasted of the California National Guard's role as "frontline participants in America's war on drugs." The Guard's elite Team Wolf puts "their land navigation, intelligence gathering and tactical movement skills to good use" in "anti-smuggling ground reconnaissance missions." Team Eagle provides law enforcement aerial support with their OH-58 Kiowa helicopters. Thermal sights from decommissioned tanks are fitted on Border Patrol vehicles. Guard light armored vehicles (LAVs, basically mini-tanks) ferry law enforcement around the desert. Troops are also involved in school "drug prevention" programs. The article concluded, "the California Guard is striving for nothing less than the elimination of illegal drugs."[44]

Meanwhile, even ultra-hardened elite Pentagon units—designed to first penetrate enemy lines in wartime and carry out covert operations—have found their way into border enforcement. In January 1997, Mexican citizen Cesario Vasquez was shot in an exchange of gunfire with a Special Forces unit conducting surveillance along the Rio Grande near Brownsville. Vasquez, hospitalized with a chest wound, was believed to be part of a bandit gang preying on migrants.[45]

FREE TRADE FOR THE CARTELS, POLICE STATE FOR THE POOR

Mexican federal border police are now trained by the FBI at Quantico, Virginia. The Southwest Border Initiative (SWBI), launched by the Clinton administration to coordinate DEA, FBI, Customs, Border Patrol and local law enforcement against the flow of drugs across the international line, was conceived as a binational effort.[46]

But relations between US and Mexican border authorities are as much suspicious as cooperative. In January 1997, seven armed US Border Patrol agents were detained in Tijuana after crossing into Mexican territory. The agents were released to the US, and Border Patrol officials called the incursion an error.[47] Plans to integrate Mexican law enforcement into SWBI were largely frustrated. US electronic intelligence has identified numerous narco-*jefes* on the Mexican side of the border, but they are invariably tipped off by corrupt Mexican officers before they can be arrested, the DEA charges.[48]

The DEA is more reluctant to look at the growing co-optation of US law enforcement by the border cartels. The truth started to come out in the trial of Gulf Cartel kingpin Juan Garcia Abrego, arrested by Mexican federal forces and turned over to the FBI in 1996.

Carlos Rodriguez, former Gulf Cartel insider now doing sixty in US prison, testified in the Garcia Abrego trial that the Cartel had "a special deal" with a group in the Texas National Guard to truck cocaine and marijuana from South Texas to Houston. Juan Antonio Ortíz, who ran the Cartel's US transportation system before his 1993 arrest, testified it also used INS buses to ship tons of cocaine north from 1986 to 1990, when one of the INS staffers was caught. The drugs were stashed on buses used to transport captured migrants to Houston, 300 miles northeast, for flights back to Mexico. The beauty of the scheme, he testified, was that the INS buses were never stopped at road drug checkpoints. "They just waved them on," said Ortíz.[49]

The rival Juárez and Tijuana cartels wasted little time in rebuilding this kind of stateside infrastructure. At the small Arizona crossing of Douglas, Customs denied there was "evidence of systemic corruption" even after eight Customs, INS and Border Patrol agents there were found guilty of accepting bribes to wave through traffickers between 1992 and 1997. An under-the-border "drug tunnel" which emerged in a Douglas construction yard was discovered. Up to forty rigs a day (ostensibly hauling copper ore) continued to roll unsearched through Douglas—despite the fact that they were owned by the same businessman who owned the construction yard! The shenanigans were finally halted by the intervention of the Tucson Customs office, and subsequently exposed in the pages of *Insight*, a right-wing DC weekly.[50]

The tide of economic refugees is no more likely to slow. Clinton's spectacular Border Patrol operations—hundreds of agents deployed round-the-clock, backed up with flood lights and helicopters—only moved the problem around. 1994's Operation Gatekeeper succeeded in driving migrants inland from San Diego, to the harsh deserts of Imperial Valley and southern Arizona. Similarly, Operations Hold the Line and Blockade pushed migrants away from El Paso to Nogales. This prompted Operation Safeguard at Nogales, pushing the migrants into the empty spaces of the Sonoran Desert. Operation Rio Grande at Brownsville pumped the annual number of migrants intercepted in the McAllen Sector up 25 percent to over 200,000, but was protested by the local Valley Coalition for Justice as "just another example of a policy that will squeeze them out into more rural areas."[51]

The unscrupulous traffickers in human flesh known as *coyotes*, criminal types who smuggle migrants across the border for a fee, made out like the bandits that they are under these big operations. The fee they collect from the hapless *pollos* (cooked chickens, as they affectionately call their desperate clients) was jacked up well above the triple-digit dollar range in the San Diego area following Gatekeeper.[52]

On one occasion, a family suffocated to death after paying *coyotes* for the privilege of being locked into a northbound boxcar. Others were hidden in coffin-like wood boxes beneath a car hood, or jammed into portable toilets, over fifteen at a time. Three times in 1996, vehicles jammed with up to thirty migrants crashed while being pursued by authorities, killing ten and injuring twice as many.[53]

Bandits lurking in the canyons to prey on migrants make the border crossing an obstacle course with the threat of armed robbery or rape at every turn. Getting lost in the desert means risk of deadly hyperthermia under the harsh sun or hypothermia at night. Houston's Center for Immigration Research estimates that between 1993 and 1996, almost 1,200 people died while trying to cross into the US—mostly drowning in the Rio Grande.[54] And then, finally, is the gauntlet of law enforcement and vigilantes across the line in El Norte.

Roberto Martínez of the San Diego-based US–Mexico Border Project, a taskforce of the American Friends Service Committee, monitored human rights on the border for over ten years. Between 1984 and 1989, he said, the Border Crime Prevention Unit, a joint Border Patrol–San Diego Police Department task force, shot to death some forty migrants. In 1989, the unit was shut down after a wave of local protest. Three thousand San Diego area residents marched on the border to protest the militarization in 1986, and there was a wave of litigation by families of victims.[55]

"There have been at least six shooting deaths by the Border Patrol in California since 1989," Martínez told me in 1997. "Physical assaults, beatings, brutality have never stopped. Insults and body searches by INS, Customs and Border Patrol have never stopped. In the past two years, there have been three Border Patrol agents and one INS agent convicted of rape in San Diego. Two other Border Patrol rape cases are being investigated now in Arizona and El Paso."[56]

The Border Patrol had over five thousand troops on the Mexican border in 1997, with two thousand in the San Diego area alone. "There are probably somewhere upwards of two hundred military troops on the border now," said Martínez, despite the fallout since the Redford incident. "The military never really left. Only JTF 6 was suspended. The military still has covert operations all along the border."[57]

Martínez called the massive effort "absolutely ineffective" at stopping the flow of migrants. "Border Patrol estimates they apprehend a half-million a year, but it could be a lot of the same people coming back again."[58]

Ineffectiveness rarely stops governments from throwing good money after bad. If the politicians get their way, ever-growing numbers of troops could be mired in the Rio Grande quagmire for years to come.

The Immigration Reform Act signed by Clinton in October 1996 mandated a doubling of Border Patrol agents to over ten thousand by 2001, replacing Army troops. But Rep. James Trafficant of Ohio responded by pushing through a bill calling for dispatching ten thousand Army troops to the frontier *on top of* the new Border Patrol troops. The Senate failed to approve it; Trafficant vowed to try again.[59] Meanwhile, McCaffrey would assure thousands of National Guardsmen.

The new Immigration Reform law exempted the Border Patrol from complying with the Endangered Species Act and federal environmental regulations in 40 million acres along the southern frontier to construct new "fences." The regulation-free zone extends 80 kilometers into the US from San Diego to Brownsville, cutting through the sensitive Sonoran and Chihuahuan desert ecosystems.[60]

Desert ecologist Gary Paul Nabhan of Tucson's Native Seed Search had already warned of the toll on local biodiversity, and the culture of Indian groups whose homelands are dissected. "The Sonoran pronghorn—now numbering fewer than 500 individuals—is hit by trucks along the thoroughfare that parallels the US/ Mexican border," he writes. "Border officials regularly stop and harass O'odham and Cucupa citizens of Mexico as they attempt to visit their relatives in the US, and the Mexican *aduana* [customs] makes it just as difficult for American Indians to attend ceremonies and fiestas south of the border. Right-of-ways along the border promote the spread of weeds, like buffelgrass and Saharan mustards, which kill native species of plants along a quarter-mile strip on either side of the fence. The desert border becomes not merely a no-man's-land of drug trafficking and military surveillance; it also becomes a land of diminished culture, wildlife, and vegetation."[61]

In February 1999, shortly after the federal government finally granted the family of Ezequiel Hernández a $1 million annuity, the family of an 18-year-old migrant shot in the back by a DEA officer as he crossed the Rio Grande launched a $25 million suit against the US. Abecnego Monje Ortíz was struck between the shoulders as he ran through the brush of Maverick County, Texas, leaving him paralyzed. "I crossed the border in order to seek work in the United States, carrying nothing more than a jug of water," Monje said in the claim. "At the moment I was shot, I was running in the opposite direction from the man who shot me."[62]

THE GREAT FEAR

The US federal elite has been preparing for the social explosion in Mexico since the emergence of the revolutionary contagion in Central America in the 1980s. In 1984, the year of the chilling REX 84 ALPHA, CIA Director William Casey argued that if the US failed to prevent "another Cuba in Central America, Mexico will have a big problem, and we're going to have a massive wave of migration."[63] Of course it was Casey's own covert terror campaigns in the isthmus which were in fact sending refugees north.

In 1983, former CIA Director William Colby (author of the 1973 Chilean coup), termed Mexico's population explosion "the most obvious threat" to US national security. Predicting up to 20 million migrants by the year 2000 (the same figure McCaffrey would still be predicting as 2000 arrived), Colby warned that the Border Patrol "will not have enough bullets to stop them."[64]

The statement produced by a Latin American Strategy Development Workshop at the Pentagon in September 1990 found the US military's "extraordinarily positive" relations with Mexico faced a potential near-term danger: "a 'democracy opening' in Mexico could test the special relationship by bringing into office a government more interested in challenging the US on economic and nationalistic grounds."[65]

In his 1996 book *The Next War*, Reagan-era Defense Secretary Caspar Weinberger (who was indicted on charges of withholding information from the Congressional Contragate inquiry, and pardoned by President Bush as one of his last acts in office[66]) portrays a scenario in which border militarization to turn back the long-feared "flood of refugees" escalates into a US military invasion of its southern neighbor.

The book is a series of showdowns with Russia, China, Japan and Iran— Cold War and World War II scenarios updated for the new millennium, nuclear weapons going off like fireworks. The Mexico chapter begins with the US Army overwhelmed by the swarthy hordes at the Rio Grande.

The crisis is sparked when Mexico's "American-educated economist" president, "hailed as a symbol of political maturity," is assassinated. A "National Salvation Front"—sharing the EZLN's colors of red and black and led by a "radical populist" intellectual who smacks of Cuauhtémoc Cárdenas—takes power. The "forcible redistribution of farmland" triggers an economic crisis, unleashing the refugee hordes. Drug cartel wars lead to acts of terrorism in San Diego, and US intelligence links the National Salvation Front's populist strongman to the kingpins. In 2003, the White House authorizes an invasion.[67]

This time the US forces land at Tampico rather than at Veracruz as in 1847 and 1914. Air strikes take out the Federal District military bases, while PSYOP broadcasts effect the capitulation of the Mexican army. Weinberger shows a familiarity with Mexican military doctrine, even if he badly garbles the word "*campesino*." The National Salvation Front leadership takes to the Sierra Madre with a force of loyal officers and launches a guerilla resistance against the gringo occupation. A counter-insurgency war ensues.[68]

AMEXICA *VERSUS* AZTLAN

In the booming NAFTA investment zone of the expansive, arid Mexican north, local elites are impatient with the PRI's pace of neoliberal reform. Since 1989, the right-opposition PAN has gained governorship of three border states, Baja California, Chihuahua and Nuevo Leon—as well as the central states of Jalisco, Queretaro and Guanajuato. In 1998, the left-opposition PRD, traditionally stronger in the south, gained its first state: north-central Zacatecas.[69]

The PRI still nods to nationalism to hold Mexico together as the south and north pull in opposite directions. The south is the bastion of *maíz* agriculture, *campesino* pride and *México profundo;* the north is increasingly seen as *"Amexica"*: a hybrid culture more closely linked to the US than to the centralist PRI state.

The term Amexica was picked up approvingly by those international guardians of the Free Trade dogma at *The Economist* in a 1995 survey cheerleading "Mexico's Second Revolution"—meaning the counter-revolution. A map, coloring states with different shades of red to indicate levels of poverty, indicates the three emerging blocs: the deep red of misery in the South, the middle zones of the Center, and the light pink of Amexica in the North.[70] Of course such representations hide the pockets of agonizing poverty and hideous exploitation in the northern boom zone.

Driving from Laredo to Monterrey, it is easy to believe *Newsweek*'s 1993 year-end assessment that NAFTA Mexico is becoming a "US Sunbelt state"—another *faux pas* that failed to foresee the explosion in Chiapas.[71]

The Mexican North and the US Southwest are both frontier societies where Indians and cowboys alike are colonized by new industrial empires. The marginalization of the Mexican South is contrasted by the expansion of "edge cities" along the development corridors of Amexica. With the decay of central urban zones in the 1970s and 80s, the energy-and-water-intensive privatized space of the mall complex became the dominant model in the US Southwest, encompassing housing, office employment and shopping into integrated and controlled environments, designed around the automobile and inherently profligate in occupation of physical space. This model is increasingly exported over the border into the Mexican North, where elites need ever-greater insulation from the growing poverty, violence and ecological hazards.

This model renders the misery of the outsiders both more invisible and more convenient for the elites. As risks increase for illegal immigration, the *maquiladora* labor force swells and becomes more desperate. The expanded state and private security apparati provide more infrastructure for the cartels to co-opt, expanding their power. The more controlled environment for people inversely reflects the less controlled environment for capital.

The Mexican South—cradle of the EZLN—symbolizes the Indian past for contemporary Mexicans, while the north symbolizes the Free Trade future. From the Chichimec invasions of pre-Conquest times, to the "Sonoran Dynasty" established by Obregon and Calles in the Revolution's aftermath, the North has looked south to Central Mexico as the seat of an empire which can be usurped.[72] But another tendency looks north, seeking to wed itself to the American empire. In 1848, Jefferson Davis introduced a Senate measure to add Chihuahua, Coahuila, Nuevo Leon and Tamaulipas to the annexed territory.[73] The notion won sufficient sympathy among the Monterrey elites that Mexican federal authorities redrew the borders of Nuevo Leon to cut the state off from all but a sliver of access to the Rio Grande. Thanks to the *maquiladora* boom, Monterrey is today more economically tied to the US than to central Mexico.

Right-wing separatist movements supported by the business elite are already emerging in Amexica. A group of Nuevo Leon industrialists called for secession in 1996.[74] This strategy is echoed in corporate think-tank projections for the twenty-first century continent. In 1992, the International Geographical Union (IGU) released a "World Political Map" outlining the emerging new nations not only of Eurasia—but of North America. "Angelica," with Los Angeles as its capital, extends inland past El Paso and incorporates Baja California, Sonora and Chihuahua.[75] This Pacific Rim-oriented and corporate-dominated entity claims territory identified by Joel Garreau in his prescient 1981 book *The Nine Nations of North America* as "Mex-America."[76]

The divide between Amexica and *México profundo* is cultural as well as geographic, pervading every region of Mexico, and every sphere of life. It was evidenced in the January 1999 Mexican papal visit. The occasion prompted requisite calls by the Chiapas reactionaries for sacking the local bishop, and Zedillo's inner circle was deeply concerned that John Paul II would embarrass the regime by decrying repression in the southern state. Asked by a reporter about Chiapas, the Pontiff responded, "There will be no solution without recognition that the indigenous people were the first owners of the land." But he also warned against transforming the doctrinal distortions of Marxist-influenced Liberation Theology into an equally apostate "indigenous theology."[77]

The Pope, however, eagerly embraced a new corporate theology, with the Vatican cutting a host of deals with private companies to sponsor the visit. PepsiCo (sensing an opportunity to open a market long dominated by Coca-Cola) placed giant billboards throughout Mexico City, picturing His Holiness beside the logo. "Pepsi, always faithful," read the kicker. Mercedes-Benz, Hewlett Packard and the Sabritas potato chip manufacturer also became official papal sponsors.[78]

Amexica may soon have its own currency as well as theology. Economic experts warn that nations outside the three global currency zones of the dollar, euro and yen will be left behind. Argentina and Ecuador have already broached replacing their national currencies with the dollar—a move the experts applaud as a Free Trade tonic for all Latin America. Guillermo Calvo, director of the University of Maryland's Center for International Economics, has a recommendation on how to overcome nationalist resistance to the idea in Mexico: "The United States could send US dollars with the image of Zapata."[79]

The legacy of the Caudillo of the South, first usurped by the PRI state, now betrayed into the hands of gringo capital: the final death of Emiliano Zapata.

But the partisans of Amexica are not free of the revolutionary contagion even in their home turf of the northern boom zone. The very geographic mobility imposed by the mandates and dislocations of the Free Trade regime carries the spirit of the South's radical *campesino* movements into the industrial citadels of the North. Only two Nuevo Aguascalientes centers were built outside Chiapas when the Zapatistas put out the call in 1995—one in the Federal District, the other in a *barrio* of Tijuana, just below the US border.[80]

On July 4, 1996, a thousand migrant workers in Baja California's San Quintín Valley rioted, destroying four police cars and ransacking a score of local businesses. The workers, mostly young Mixtecos, were protesting the failure of the local Santa Anita ranch to pay them for three weeks. After police suppressed the protest, arresting at least sixty, the area was occupied by the army. *PANista* Gov. Hector Teran blamed radical groups for stirring up the workers.[81]

Just as the US Sunbelt development model extends south into Mexico, just as the hybrid cultural sphere of Amexica encompasses the border lands on both sides of the line, so do pockets of radical, indigenous Mexico, even *México profundo*, extend north into the United States. Mixtec migrants from Oaxaca also work the fields of Alta California, and Chicano communities in New Mexico, Colorado and Texas keep alive traditions that predate the 1848 annexation.

The same territory of the US Southwest which technocratic culture assigns as Amexica or Angelica is claimed by growing numbers of Mexican-Americans as Aztlan, the Chicano homeland. The name derives from the legendary homeland of the Aztecs, who as a wandering Chichimec people originated somewhere in the deserts of the north before arriving in Anahuac, usurping the Toltec empire and establishing their dominion over Central Mexico. The name Aztlan was originally revived by New Mexico's Territorial government in the 1880s to attract gringo settlers with the allure of Aztec grandeur.[82] In 1969, it was revived by Chicano activists in a Denver declaration, "The Spiritual Plan of Aztlan," to animate a movement for land and self-determination.[83]

THE SHADOW OF 1848

Over 400 miles up the Rio Grande Rift from El Paso lies San Luis, a town of nine hundred, mostly Spanish-speaking farmers descended from the Mexican pioneers who were Colorado's first settlers. San Luis is the seat of Costilla County, one of six that make up the San Luis Valley, a pocket of plains 8,000 feet high with imposing arms of the Rocky Mountains on either side. Traditional systems of communal land and water use contrasting sharply with those of the dominant culture persist there. The town lies below La Sierra Culebra, a branch of the Sangre de Cristo Range, now mostly covered by the 77,500-acre Taylor Ranch. This vast private holding is claimed as the usufructuary land of San Luis under terms protected by the 1848 Treaty of Guadalupe-Hidalgo. The conflict goes back generations, and has been termed by the local press a "range war."[84]

Taylor Ranch has been at odds with San Luis since John Taylor put up barbed-wire fences and armed guards to keep out the locals over a generation ago. When the old man's son Zachary started logging operations behind those fences in 1995, the battle heated up again.[85]

On June 10, 1997, six were arrested at gates on the access roads to Taylor Ranch, including Rocky Madrid, who was U-locked by the neck to a cattle guard almost continuously for seventy-seven hours. County workers nailed Rocky across the head with a bar from the cattle guard when cutting him loose. He was taken away unconscious.[86]

The others arrested were Anglo environmentalists from the group Ancient Forest Rescue, who blockaded the gates for several hours, two of them locked down, like Rocky. Protestors dug a trench in the road to block logging trucks; the sheriff called in a back-hoe to have it filled.[87]

The protest was led by the Land Rights Council, which came together to challenge Taylor on the land and in the courts. The Land Rights Council's Shirley Otero told me she wants to save "La Sierra, as we knew it. The Mexican government grant to our people, who were encouraged to settle the area, was recognized by the Treaty of Guadalupe-Hidalgo, including the right to communally graze, gather wood, and hunt elk and deer. Up until 1960, people used this land. Our community lacked legal knowledge and expertise to fight the land grab. But the resistance has always been alive. My grandmother was out there cutting fences."[88]

Between Taylor Ranch's 1995 announcement of a 10 million dollar timber sale to the Chicago-based multinational Stone Container and my visit to the valley in the summer of 1997, 10,000 acres had been decimated, the gates to the ranch had been blockaded numerous times, and over fifty arrested.[89]

The Sangre de Cristo Land Grant was awarded in 1844, following an appeal by Narcisco Beaubien, the young son of Charles Beaubien, a Canadian who had become a Mexican citizen and prominent Taos landowner. The younger Beaubien was killed in the Taos Revolt of 1847, an Indian-led uprising against Gen. Stephen Kearny's Army of the West, which had seized Nuevo Mexico the previous year. Charles inherited the land grant, and settlement continued as peace resumed.[90]

The Treaty of Guadalupe-Hidalgo read:

In the said territories, property of every kind, now belonging to Mexicans now established there shall be inviolately respected. The present owners, the heirs of these, and all Mexicans who may hereafter acquire said property by contract, shall enjoy with respect to it guarantees equally ample as if the same belonged to the citizens of the United States.[91]

By the turn of the century, over 80 percent of the Mexican and Spanish land grants in the United States—with their mineral and timber rights—had been usurped. Anglo land barons protected by the notorious Santa Fe Ring filled out patents on unsurveyed common lands and policed them with hired gunmen. The Santa Fe Ring would violently gain control of Charles Beaubien's earlier land grant in New Mexico's Colfax County after his death. The Santa Fe and Carson National Forests largely consist of *ejidos* the federal government appropriated under the theory that "public lands" should accrue to the "new sovereign." By the late 1890s, masked Chicano bands like Las Gorras Blancas and Las Manos Negras had emerged to defend against land grabs in northern New Mexico.[92]

But the claim in the San Luis Valley was well established from the start. Charles Beaubien parceled out the land grant—*la merced*—to arriving settlers, and gave the new community a common pasture land known as *la vega*. The Vega, just to the east of town toward the mountains, remains the last working commons in the United States. The Boston Commons is older, but is little more than a municipal park today. The Vega is still used for grazing by the families of San Luis.[93]

La Sierra was Beaubien's estate, but the people of San Luis were formally granted free access for summer grazing, winter wood gathering and game hunting. The forest remained intact, protecting the valley's watershed.[94]

In 1851, the first *acequias*, or irrigation ditches, were established, fed by the Rio Culebra coming down from La Sierra. The *pueblo*'s water rights were the first to be registered with the Colorado Territorial government.[95]

After Charles Beaubien's death in 1864, La Sierra and valley lands yet unsettled were sold to Col. William Gilpin, the first Territorial Governor. Gilpin signed an agreement with the heirs of Beaubien recognizing the rights of San Luis. By 1890, Gilpin and his partners had sold to other private owners. By 1902 these interests had formed a joint entity known as the Costilla Estate Development Company, or just *La Compañia*. The "Mountain Tract" became the last unfenced land in the Costilla Estate—and the last free area for the San Luis people's summer pasture and hunting grounds.[96]

La Compañia sold the Mountain Tract to North Carolina baron Jack Taylor in 1960 at the cut-rate 7-dollars-an-acre precisely because of the "cloud on the title." Taylor's deed provided that: "All of the land hereby conveyed . . . [is] also subject to claims of the local people . . . to rights of pasture, wood, and lumber and so-called settlement rights in, to and upon said land . . ."[97]

Taylor almost immediately went to court to "quiet title" to the land under the Torrens Title Registration Act, a Colorado law designed to wipe out indigenous land claims. In 1965, Colorado Federal District Court ruled in Taylor's favor. Judge Olin Hatfield Chilson found that "Spanish-Americans cannot make claims to another's land based on old Mexican law." The Tenth Circuit Court of Appeals upheld the decision, finding that the people of San Luis "have no rights of any kind or nature in and to the lands here involved . . ." The ink was hardly dry on the decision before Taylor placed gates and guards on all the roads leading into the property. Barbed-wire fences went up along the perimeter of the ranch.[98]

San Luis residents continued to sneak past guards and cut barbed wire to enter the Mountain Tract—but it was increasingly the young and reckless who were willing to risk it. Once, three young men were brutally beaten by Taylor's guards.[99]

Shoot-outs, mysterious fires, vandalism and cattle rustling continued until 1975, when Jack Taylor was shot in his bed on the ranch, his left ankle shattered. Taylor called on Gov. Stephen McNichols to call out the National Guard. The Governor refused, and Taylor moved back to North Carolina, never to return to his Sangre de Cristo land.[100]

Jack Taylor died in 1988, and Zachary inherited the ranch. Seven years later, he started logging it. The Land Rights Council brought a new lawsuit to gain access to the land and a hand in managing it—asserting that claimants had been denied the right to testify in the 1965 case. The road blockades were launched to slow the plunder.[101]

Zachary Taylor is a descendant of Gen. Zachary Taylor—commander of US forces in the war which brought the Southwest under gringo rule. The contemporary Zack Taylor admitted to the *Christian Science Monitor*: "It is ironic. These people must be wondering what it will take to get rid of me."[102]

A smaller section of the Land Grant to the north was bought by New York media mogul Malcolm Forbes Jr., who began subdividing it for luxury homes. The subdivision residents have formed a Concerned Property Owners to oppose the San Luis community's use of the land. "Communism is almost totally wiped out in the world, so why should we foster it in Costilla County?" opined their newsletter.[103]

San Luis feels like the town that time forgot, but the drain of the community's youth to the cities has begun to slow in recent years. "I think many of the old things are coming back," Corpus Gallegos said to me. The old man was running the oldest farm in the state of Colorado. The family has run the farm since 1851. "We're certified as an organic farm by the state of Colorado. We never used pesticides here."[104]

When I asked if the timber and real estate development in La Sierra has affected his farm in the valley, he responded, "Those are not developments to me, those are disruptive things, I don't call them developments. It has already started to show some effects in sand and topsoil coming down. Sometimes the water is black. This is new. I've been here a long time, and I've irrigated a long time."[105]

But the old farmer was also optimistic. "The community is pulling together around this issue," Corpus said.

Throughout the Southwest, land struggles are re-emerging a generation after the Chicano upsurge of the 1960s—as far as East Texas, where a Chicano family launched suit in 1997 to reclaim lands from the estate of the local Kenedy cattle clan.[106]

In the emblematic struggle of the 1960s movement, Reies López Tijerina and the Alianza Federal de Mercedes sparked a small local war in New Mexico's Rio Arriba county. In October 1966, some one hundred families with the Alianza began an occupation of the Echo Amphitheater campsite in the Santa Fe National Forest, declaring the "People's Republic of San Joaquin," with the local village of Tierra Amarilla as its capital. All the claimed land was a part of the San Joaquin del Rio Chama and Tierra Amarilla Land Grants, which had been usurped by a cattle company and then appropriated by the National Forest Service.[107]

The next summer, when the Alianza held a peaceful gathering in Coyote, state police waded in at night and arrested eleven for "illegal assembly" on a public campsite. A group of Alianzistas responded with an ill-conceived and adventurist attack on the Tierra Amarilla courthouse, in which two cops were shot and wounded. With the governor away, state Adjutant Gen. John Pershing Jolly mobilized the National Guard. Tierra Amarilla was occupied by troops and tanks. Alianzistas were rounded up in a barbed-wire pen. Most of those detained were women, children and elders. Troops combed the mountains for Tijerina and his partisans.[108]

The John Birch Society flooded the area with pamphlets warning of a "Communist plot to seize the Southwest." The fugitives were tracked down and stood trial. The Alianza offices were firebombed. Tijerina was imprisoned, but the movement continued.[109]

In the years to come, New Mexico villages such as Chilili and La Joya managed to legally recover lands which had been usurped by private interests, revive old land-use traditions and restore *acequias* long since filled in by erosion.[110]

In contemporary New Mexico, local support for a federal bill to finally address these issues, the Guadalupe-Hidalgo Treaty Land Claims Act, has divided Chicanos from some Anglo environmentalists, who fear the measure could be exploited by economic interests seeking privatization of National Forest lands. A recent wave of vandalism and sabotage against local Forest Service targets—including the bombing of a radio tower—is more likely the work of radical-right rednecks than Chicano militants. The bitter divide contrasts the Chicano–ecologist alliance just to the north in San Luis.[111]

THE PROSPECTS FOR TRANSNATIONAL RESISTANCE

In January 1998, twenty-two people from around the US—including veterans, clergy and a professor—were sentenced to six months in federal prison and fined $3,000 each for unlawful entry onto Fort Benning. They were among 601 arrested on November 16, 1997, as they entered the military base carrying crosses emblazoned with the names of civilians killed by School of the Americas graduates in Latin America. The twenty-two were "repeat offenders." They argued a "necessity defense" based on documentation of SOA complicity in human rights violations. The November protests are held each year to commemorate the massacre of six church workers by SOA graduates in El Salvador in 1989. Judge Robert Elliott, presiding over a packed courtroom, gave the protestors the maximum penalty.[112]

Defendant Rita Steinhagen, a 69-year-old nun from Minneapolis, said, "There's something wrong when we who participate in a solemn funeral procession are sent to prison, while the SOA graduates who did the killing get amnesty and will not spend one day behind bars."[113]

The recent Acteal massacre heightened the verisimilitude of this most massive action to shut down the SOA.

With the NAFTA architects looking to expand south—initially to Chile—the resources and future of the hemisphere, Alaska to Tierra del Fuego, depend on the challenge to forge effective ties of solidarity across borders.

Anti-racist and anti-corporate forces in the US face a challenge to reclaim the localist and populist agenda back from the organized radical right—which ultimately stands to betray those sentiments to corporate power and the most sinister elements of the federal government. The solidarity movement which mobilized in the US to defend the revolutions in Central America in the 1980s declined in the 1990s, even as new revolutionary movements have emerged in Mexico. Can a new solidarity effort find antidotes to the divide-and-conquer racism which pits the grassroots against the grassroots, Anglo-American workers and farmers against Mexican workers and *campesinos* similarly betrayed by NAFTA? Can it find the courage to repudiate the War on Drugs unequivocally, and oppose expansion of the federal "anti-terrorist" apparatus even when the expansion ostensibly targets the radical right?

Can it relentlessly expose how the integrated Free Trade regime works against popular interests on both sides of the border?

In the prelude to NAFTA, the agreement's proponents pushed computer simulations as proof that it would create lots of new jobs in all three signatory countries.[114]

In July 1997, the Clinton administration boasted NAFTA's "modest positive effect" on US net exports, income, investment and export-related jobs. Treasury Secretary Robert Rubin said, "NAFTA has served us well, and I believe NAFTA and trade liberalization more generally are critical to our economic future."[115]

"We're dead," Florida tomato grower Paul DiMare told Reuters, oblivious to the good news. "Congress has screwed the American people. They promised NAFTA would create jobs." Instead, twenty packing houses had closed and ten thousand workers been laid off within two years of NAFTA, farmland lying fallow.[116] In July 1996, the US International Trade Commission ruled that the surge in Mexican tomato imports was not unduly harming Florida growers.[117]

As the tomato and avocado wars gut Florida and California farmlands, the hemorrhage of investment from stateside manufacturing zones undercuts workforce bargaining power.

The election was drawing near in a 1997 United Auto Workers organizing drive at three ITT auto-parts plants in Michigan when management played the NAFTA card. The company brought in workers from Mexico to videotape employees in the plants. An assembly line was shut down, the equipment stacked onto flatbed trailers marked: "Mexico Transfer Job." The workers got the message and voted down the union. "The implication was, if you form a union, we will ship this stuff out to Mexico, and we can do it in a heartbeat," said UAW organizer Diane Ketola. ITT denied this, and appealed a National Labor Relations Board finding of unfair practices.[118]

According to a 1996 report of NAFTA's trinational Commission for Labor Cooperation, real wages for workers in the signatories had fallen, while the number of temporary workers had risen.[119]

In 1997, the US Chamber of Commerce called the first three years of NAFTA "a huge success." The Chamber's director David Hirschmann said, "Clearly the silver lining in Mexico's darkest hours has been the free trade agreement." A report by the Citizens Trade Campaign, *The Failed Experiment: NAFTA at Three Years*, claimed NAFTA had cost Mexico 2 million jobs, eliminated 28,000 small businesses and driven 8 million Mexicans into poverty.[120]

Mexico's most significant dissident industrial union, the Authentic Labor Front (FAT), has forged a strategic alliance with two US unions, the United Electrical Workers (UE) and the Teamsters. In 1994, the FAT gained enough support at a General Electric plant in Juárez to file a petition for a union election. When FAT supporters at the plant were fired after speaking to the press, UE organized demonstrations at GE's US plants. The dissident unionists charged GE used the firings—and threats to close the Juárez plant and blacklist workers—to frighten people before the election. The union lost the vote.[121]

Meanwhile in Rome, Georgia, a GE company town since 1954, more than three hundred workers were laid off when operations were moved down to Monterrey. GE denied the move was inspired by NAFTA, but the US Labor Department certified laid-off Rome workers for retraining and benefits designed for NAFTA's economic victims.[122] The Mexican *coyuntura* may yet jump the Rio Grande.

The civic sphere has also emerged as a theater of struggle north of the border. Resistance to transnational corporate rule in Canada has echoed the radical municipalism sweeping southern Mexico. In 1998, the Multilateral Agreements on Investment (MAI) was sent back to the OECD's drawing rooms following a wave of official protests by municipal governments around the world, but especially in Canada. In March 1996, after numerous proclamations by town councils that MAI represents an encroachment on local rights, the Federation of Canadian Municipalities passed a resolution demanding that Canada not sign unless the Agreements' binds on the nation were limited to "areas of federal jurisdiction."[123]

In July 1998, the EZLN's Fifth Declaration of the Lacandon Selva identified the resistance of indigenous peoples as a fundamental threat to NAFTA because, as a virtue of their very marginalization, they are the least psychically colonized by the industrial system: "Any reform which tries to break the bonds of historical and cultural solidarity which exist among the indigenous is condemned to failure and is, simply, an injustice and an historical denial."[124]

With the establishment of the International Network Against Neoliberalism following the Intergalactic Encuentro, the Maya rebels of Chiapas became the catalyst of a global movement. Marcos has called on what he terms his army of "moles" to lay the groundwork for resistance throughout the planet.[125]

This poses a question: whether globalization will merely destroy indigenous culture, further accelerating pauperization and eroding the ancient landbase—or if, through conscious struggle, it can be made reciprocal, bringing Maya rootedness in the land, community traditions of resistance, and intransigent insistence on dignity against all odds, to bear on a larger process of expanding democracy in Mexico and on planet Earth.

In August 1997, the International Network Against Neoliberalism held a Second Intergalactic Encuentro in Spain. The workshops were dispersed around various locales, including the Aragon village of Ruesta, where locals were fighting a planned nuclear waste dump. The Encuentro was attended by representatives from throughout Europe, as well as Comandantes Delia and Felipe from the EZLN.[126]

Declarations from the Spain gathering recognized the need to oppose both the Euro-unification of the Maastricht treaty, the emergence of a new imperialist bloc, as well as the neo-fascist forces which exploit the anti-Maastricht backlash.[127] As borders go down within the new Europe, Germany erects hi-tech walls on the Polish frontier, even enlisting neo-Nazi rabble to serve in patrol units, the Oder mirroring the Rio Grande.[128]

NAFTA was perceived by its chief architect George Bush as a pillar of his "New World Order"[129] in which the Pentagon polices an economically integrated planet, overseen by the WTO regime.

All restraints on exploitation are considered archaisms under the globalist dogma. As Pinochet's Chile and Fujimori's Peru indicated, neoliberal economics do not necessitate democracy. The tendency toward political democracy which supposedly accompanies economic liberalization is outweighed, even when it exists, by the concomitant consolidation of technocratic and privatized modes of social control. As control over resources shifts to the private sector, ostensibly democratic political structures become less relevant.

The right-wing militias and vigilante bands which now spread across the US, paradoxically exploiting both the libertarian and puritan traditions in US culture, represent one populist response to this reality—but in a form easily recuperated by ruling elites. The new militias in the US are a reverse image of the new rural movements in Mexico: similarly populist and militant, similarly drawing from both localism and nationalism, similarly claiming legitimacy in fundamental legal traditions—but rightist and racist rather than revolutionary and indigenous-based.

A radical populism which is rooted in human solidarity is the only possible antidote to the recuperable populism of ethnic scapegoating.

Contrary to the new nativist dogma, this antidote is deeply rooted in North American history. Those arrested at the SOA are the heirs of H. D. Thoreau, who went to jail to protest the war of annexation in 1846.[130] No less a personage than John Quincy Adams, viewing the war as a Southern slavocrat expansion strategy, urged soldiers to desert. Irish immigrants among the US troops did so, forming a "St. Patrick's Battalion"—the *San Patricios*—to resist the invader with their Mexican Catholic brothers.[131] After the war, Wild Cat, leader of the Black Seminoles who had resisted Zachary Taylor in the Florida swamplands, negotiated a pact with Mexico to settle in Coahuila with his warriors. For twenty years they defended the border from white fillibuster expeditions.[132]

The UE–FAT alliance begins to provide an antidote to the racist corporate populism of Pat Buchanan. The Ancient Forest Rescue activists who have made common cause with the farmers of San Luis have similarly crossed a cultural divide to advance human solidarity.

In October 1998, Texas authorities finally turned down a license for a nuclear waste dump in Sierra Blanca, Texas—just 25 kilometers north of the border—which was slated to receive "low-level" radioactive materials from various states. Citizens from both sides joined to repeatedly blockade the international bridge at Juárez–El Paso. Tarahumara Indians from Chihuahua even crossed the border to sit in at the state environmental bureaucracy offices in Austin. Such cross-border mobilizations are an antidote to the real and psychic walls which defy ecology on the international frontier.[133]

The Vermont-based Action for Community and Ecology in the Rainforests of Central America (ACERCA) does much work on Chiapas, and coordinates with the El Paso-based National Commission for Democracy in Mexico, the EZLN's stateside representatives. ACERCA sees solidarity with the indigenous inhabitants of the rainforests as the first responsibility of stateside environmentalists seeking rainforest preservation. Such work offers an antidote to neo-Malthusian eco-fascism which sees the demographic advance of the peasantry and poor, rather than corporate power and oligarchic concentrations of wealth, as the driving forces of ecological collapse.[134]

North Americans can learn much about themselves from how they are viewed by their southern neighbors. The cultural divide was vividly described by Mexico's most respected writer, Octavio Paz. No vulgar anti-American, Paz would by his later years actually become an apologist for US imperialism in the renewed Cold War of the 1980s.[135] In his classic work, *The Labyrinth of Solitude*, he wrote:

> Man is alone everywhere. But the solitude of the Mexican, under the great stone night of the high plateau that is still inhabited by insatiable gods, is very different from that of the North American, who wanders in an abstract world of machines, fellow citizens and moral precepts . . . North Americans consider the world to be something that can be perfected, and . . . we consider it something that can be redeemed . . . [T]he Puritan identified purity with health . . . Therefore . . . [e]very contact is a contamination. Foreign races, ideas, customs, and bodies carry within themselves the germs of perdition and impurity.[136]

This is the solitude of North America, behind the troops and electronic sensors that guard the imaginary line in the desert, behind the gated communities secured by rent-a-cops and video surveillance, behind the smiling façades of shopping malls and suburban sprawl, behind the soulless "renewed" urban centers gridded by police helicopters, behind the barbed wire, attack dogs and shotguns that uphold the prerogatives of private property in the countryside.

The Zapatistas broke Mexico's long solitude, and in the early days of 1994 were looked to as the catalyst that could redeem the nation with a renewed human solidarity. The revolutionary moment of 1994 still stands as a challenge to the hemisphere and the planet.

NOTES

INTRODUCTION

1 Julia Preston, *New York Times*, August 31, 1999.
2 Hermann Bellinghausen, *La Jornada*, August 16, 1999.
3 Ibid.
4 Ibid.
5 Ibid.
6 Ibid.
7 Angeles Mariscal, *La Jornada*, May 12, 1999.
8 Diego Cevallos, InterPress Service, May 4, 1999.
9 Juan Balboa, *La Jornada*, August 17, 1999.
10 Ibid.
11 Hermann Bellinghausen, *La Jornada*, August 16, 1999.
12 Ibid., August 16, 1999.
13 Ibid., August 19, 1999.
14 Reuters, August 26, 1999.
15 Diego Cevallos, InterPress Service, August 17, 1999.
16 Ibid.
17 Fray Bartolomé de Las Casas HRC Press Bulletin, August 19, 1999.
18 Ricardo Sandoval, *Miami Herald*, September 3, 1999.
19 Hermann Bellinghausen, *La Jornada*, August 17, 1999.
20 Ibid., August 19, 1999.
21 Julia Preston, *New York Times*, August 31, 1999.
22 Rene Villegas, Reuters, August 24, 1999.
23 Fiona Ortiz, Reuters, August 25, 1999.
24 San Manuel Autonomous Municipality press statement, September 2, 1999.
25 Reuters, April 19, 1999.
26 Susana Hayward, *San Antonio Express-News*, September 2, 1999.
27 EZLN communiqué, August 27, 1999.

28 Julia Preston, *New York Times*, August 31, 1999.
29 EZLN communiqué, August 27, 1999.
30 Julia Preston, *New York Times*, August 31, 1999.
31 Juan Balboa, *La Jornada*, September 4, 1999; Francisco Gomez Autonomous Municipality press statement, September 1, 1999.
32 Hermann Bellinghausen, *La Jornada*, June 23, 1999.
33 Jim Cason and David Brooks, *La Jornada*, August 21, 1999.
34 *Diario de Yucatan*, August 3, 1999.
35 Sam Dillon and Julia Preston, *New York Times*, August 2, 1999.
36 AP, September 13, 1999.
37 Jesus Ramirez Cuevas, *La Jornada*, March 15, 1999.
38 Julia Preston, *New York Times*, March 22, 1999.
39 Reuters, April 8, 1999.
40 Subcomandante Marcos.
41 *La Jornada*, July 21, 1999.
42 *Financial Times,* August 9, 1999.
43 AFP, October 3, 1999.
44 *Financial Times,* October 12, 1999; *Washington Post,* October 12, 1999.
45 *La Jornada,* October 16, 1999.
46 Ibid., May 18, 1999.
47 Ibid., December 12, 1999.
48 Ibid., November 21, 1999.
49 Ibid., December 31, 1999.
50 Ibid., January 16, 1999.
51 Notimex, December 17, 1999.
52 *The News* (Mexico City), January 3, 2000.
53 *La Jornada,* January 3, 2000.
54 Rural Advancement Foundation International (www.rafi.org) presss release, December 1, 1999.
55 *The News* (Mexico City), December 30, 1999.
56 *La Jornada,* December 23, 1999.
57 Ibid., January 3, 2000.

1 FIVE HUNDRED YEARS OF MAYA REBELLION

1 Traven, p. 3.
2 For the true story of B. Traven, see Zogbaum.
3 Traven, p. 3.
4 EZLN communiqué, March 1, 1994.
5 Bonfil, pp. 4–10.
6 Florescano, pp. 50–2.
7 Wolf 1959, pp. 135–6.
8 Browning, p. 54, quoted in Weinberg, p. 7.

9 Garcia de Leon, vol. 1, p. 27.

10 Recinos, pp. 30−1; Florescano, pp. 5−6.

11 Orozco Zuarth, pp. 14−30.

12 Florescano, p. 56; Schele and Freidel, p. 62; Perera and Bruce, p. 13.

13 Bonfil, p. 7.

14 Schele and Freidel, pp. 394−5.

15 Wolf 1959, p. 105.

16 Bricker, p. 147; Gosner, pp. 22−3; Wolf 1959, p. 105.

17 Thomas, pp. 184−5.

18 Bricker, pp. 3−10.

19 Ibid., p. 43.

20 Ibid., pp. 43−6.

21 Ibid., pp. 43−6.

22 Ibid., pp. 47−8; Garcia de Leon, vol. 1, pp. 40−3.

23 Bricker, pp. 50−1; Garcia de Leon, vol. 1, pp. 40−3.

24 Handy, pp. 20−1.

25 Bricker, pp. 24−7; Garcia de Leon, vol. 1, pp. 40−3; Reed 1964, pp. 48−9.

26 Bricker, pp. 13−29; Reed 1964, p. 49.

27 Bricker, p. 20; Perera and Bruce, p. 10.

28 Garcia de Leon, vol. 1, pp. 58−9; Wolf 1959, pp. 196−7.

29 Las Casas, p. 21; Gutiérrez, pp. 54, 369.

30 Gutiérrez, pp. 280−8, 316−19.

31 Ibid., p. 393; Handy, p. 23.

32 Wolf 1959, p. 220.

33 Ibid., pp. 189−91.

34 Krauze, p. 569.

35 Bonfil, pp. 78, 85.

36 Garcia de Leon, vol. 1, pp. 56−9; Wasserstrom, p. 91.

37 Schele and Freidel, pp. 394−5.

38 Paz, pp. 107−8.

39 Florescano, pp. 134−5; Eber, p. 25.

40 Schele and Freidel, pp. 68−9, 232; Wolf 1959, p. 170.

41 Bricker, pp. 55−7; Gosner, pp. 76, 114.

42 Bricker, pp. 55−6; Garcia de Leon, vol. 1, pp. 80−1.

43 Bricker, pp. 56−9; Garcia de Leon, vol. 1, pp. 80−1.

44 Bricker, pp. 55−68; Florescano, pp. 153−7; Garcia de Leon, vol. 1, pp. 82−3.

45 Bricker, pp. 55−68; Florescano, pp. 153−7; Wasserstrom, pp. 81−2.

46 Bricker, p. 57; Gibson, p. 117.

47 Bricker, pp. 55−68.

48 Ibid., pp. 55−68.

49 Ibid., pp. 70−6; Florescano, pp. 157−61.

50 Cockcroft 1983, pp. 46−7.

51 Hu-deHart, pp. 6−7.

52 Bricker, pp. 77−83.

53 Wasserstrom, p. 107; Wolf 1959, p. 245.

54 Hu-DeHart, pp. 7, 41.
55 Ibid.
56 Robert M. Laughlin, "Tzotzil and Tzeltal: Who in the World?" in Harris and Sartor, p. 20.
57 Reed 1964, pp. 33–40.
58 Bricker, pp. 87–9.
59 Ibid.; Reed 1964, pp. 34–59.
60 Reed 1964, pp. 72–80.
61 Bricker, pp. 89–93; Reed 1964, pp. 84–97.
62 Reed 1964, pp. 98–100.
63 Ibid., pp. 128–30.
64 Ibid., pp. 173–80.
65 Ibid., pp. 152–6.
66 Ibid., p. 156.
67 Ibid., p. 159.
68 Ibid., pp. 173–4.
69 Ibid., pp. 194–8.
70 Ibid., pp. 201–6.
71 Ibid., pp. 207–12.
72 Ibid., pp. 212–14.
73 Joseph 1988, pp. 29–30.
74 Reed 1964, pp. 238–41.
75 Ibid., p. 248.
76 Joseph 1988, pp. 93–120, 190–3, 219, 267.
77 Joseph 1986, pp. 105–25.
78 Reed 1964, pp. 250–3.
79 Bricker, pp. 119–26.
80 Ibid.; Harvey 1989, p. 45.
81 Bricker, pp. 119–20; Garcia de Leon, vol. 1, pp. 90–4.
82 Bricker, pp. 120–2; Garcia de Leon, vol. 1, pp. 90–4.
83 Bricker, pp. 122–3; Garcia de Leon, vol. 1, pp. 90–4.
84 Bricker, pp. 124–5; Garcia de Leon, vol. 1, pp. 90–4.
85 Bricker, p. 126; Garcia de Leon, vol. 1, pp. 90–4.
86 Harvey 1998, pp. 44–8.
87 Wasserstrom, pp. 158–9.
88 Ibid.
89 Ibid.; Knight, vol. 1, pp. 372–3; Robert M. Laughlin, "Tzotzil and Tzeltal: Who in the World?" in Harris and Sartor, p. 20.
90 Knight, vol. 2, pp. 240–2.
91 Nigh.
92 Wasserstrom, pp. 159–66.
93 Garcia de Leon, vol. 2, pp. 199–216; Wasserstrom, p. 164.
94 Colby and Dennett, pp. 83–6.
95 Garcia de Leon, vol. 2, pp. 216–18; Wasserstrom, p. 166.
96 Barry 1995, p. 178; Collier, pp. 35–6.
97 Nigh.

98 Reyes Ramos, pp. 84–5.
99 Human Rights Watch, p. 39.
100 Nations.
101 Zogbaum, p. 135.
102 Nations.
103 Reyes Ramos, p. 93.
104 Author's interview with Bishop Samuel Ruiz, San Cristóbal de Las Casas, Chis, December 1986.
105 Eber, pp. 31, 190.
106 Vogt, pp. 82–125.
107 Fazio 1994, pp. 49–51, 84–7; Womack 1999, pp. 23–9.
108 Harvey 1998, pp. 76–8.
109 Navarrete, pp. 45–58; author's interviews with Chamula residents, and Obispo Augustin Garcia, Iglesia de San Pascualito, Tuxtla Gutiérrez, Chis., March 1987.
110 Author's interview with Obispo Samuel Ruiz, March 1987.
111 Carlos Fazio, "Mexico: SIL Controversy Drags On," *Latinamerica Press*, Lima, April 1984; Colby and Dennett, p. 802.
112 Harvey 1998, pp. 78–9.
113 Harvey 1989, pp. 90–112.
114 Harvey 1998, pp. 126–30.
115 Amnesty International, p. 65.
116 Carlos Fazio, "Mexico: Guatemalan Refugees Resist Relocation," *Latinamerica Press*, Lima, June 21, 1984.
117 Weinberg, pp. 27–8, 49–50.
118 Harvey 1998, pp. 150–2.
119 Ross 1995, p. 266.
120 Harvey 1989, pp. 195–200; Ross 1995, pp. 155–6.
121 Ross 1995, p. 74.
122 Harvey 1998, p. 172.
123 Ross 1995, pp. 187, 280.
124 Ibid., p. 76.
125 Romero Jacobo, p. 100; Russell, pp. 36–7.

2 "MISERY IN THE NAME OF FREEDOM"

1 Charles Francis Adams, ed., *The Memoirs of John Quincy Adams*, Philadelphia, 1874, p. 323, cited in LaFeber, p. 24.
2 Paul L. Ford, ed., *Works of Thomas Jefferson*, New York, 1892, vol. 9, pp. 315–19, quoted in Merk, p. 9.
3 Julian Boyd, ed., *The Papers of Thomas Jefferson*, Princeton, 1950, vol. 9, p. 218, cited in LaFeber, p. 19.
4 Quoted in Arthur P. Whitaker, *The Western Hemisphere Idea*, Ithaca, NY, 1954, cited in LaFeber, p. 22.

5 Lynd, p. 75.
6 Letter to Robert Morris, December 25, 1783, cited in Lynd, pp. 69–70.
7 Boyd, ed., *The Papers of Thomas Jefferson*, vol. 8, pp. 681–2, cited in Lynd, p. 83.
8 Ibid., vol. 8, pp. 681–2, cited in Matthews, p. 27.
9 Ibid., vol. 15, pp. 392–3, cited in Matthews, p. 20.
10 Letter to John Cartwright, June 5, 1824, quoted in Arendt, p. 252.
11 Julian Boyd, ed., *The Papers of Thomas Jefferson*, Princeton 1950, vol. 12, pp. 8–9, cited in Matthews, p. 77.
12 Lavender, p. 149.
13 Ibid.
14 Karl Marx, "The North American Civil War," *Die Presse*, Vienna, October 20, 1861, reprinted in *Karl Marx, Frederick Engels: Collected Works*, International Publishers, New York, 1984, vol. 19, p. 39.
15 Lynd, p. 68.
16 "Notes on Virginia," 1787, cited in Thomas Jefferson, *Democracy*, Saul K. Padover, ed., Greenwood Press, New York, 1939, p. 60.
17 Parkes, p. 166.
18 Wolf 1969, p. 4.
19 Parkes, p. 166.
20 Ibid., p. 170.
21 Van Alstyne, p. 88.
22 Gerassi, p. 227.
23 Parkes, pp. 201–2.
24 Ibid., p. 203; Singletary, p. 16.
25 Ibid., p. 207.
26 Singletary, p. 9.
27 Merk, pp. 88, 117; Zinn, p. 149.
28 Caruso, p. 73.
29 Ibid., p. 100; Cockcroft 1998, p. 67; Singletary, pp. 37, 60, 72, 134.
30 Merk, pp. 99–100; Singletary, p. 116.
31 Lavender, p. 139.
32 Galeano, p. 135.
33 Lavender, pp. 154–5; Utley, p. 252.
34 Wurlitzer, p. 127; Walker, pp. 19–22, 29.
35 Selser, p. 17; Bourne, p. 178.
36 Marx, "The North American Civil War," p. 37.
37 Lavender, pp. 160–1; Starr, p. 103; Marx, "The North American Civil War," p. 36.
38 Frederick Engels, "The Movements of 1847," reprinted in *Karl Marx, Frederick Engels: Collected Works*, International Publishers, New York, 1984, vol. 6, p. 527.
39 Ibid.
40 Parkes, pp. 227–8.
41 Ibid., pp. 235, 239, 245.
42 Ibid., p. 235.
43 Ibid., pp. 255–8, 274.
44 Ibid., pp. 278–9.
45 Ibid., pp. 282–3.

46 Knight, vol. 1, p. 16.
47 Wolf 1969, pp. 15—18.
48 Parkes, pp. 298—9.
49 Cockcroft 1983, p. 87.
50 Parkes, p. 305.
51 Ibid., p. 306.
52 Wolf 1969, p. 19.
53 Parkes, pp. 308—9.
54 Ibid.
55 Wolf 1969, p. 38.
56 Cockcroft 1983, p. 93.
57 Turner, pp. 219, 223.
58 Parkes, p. 308.
59 Hart, p. 91.
60 Hu-DeHart, pp. 6—7.
61 Ibid., pp. 106, 159.
62 Ibid., pp. 128—9.
63 Ibid., pp. 180—1.
64 Karl Marx, "Speech on the Question of Free Trade," delivered to the Democratic Association of Brussels, January 9, 1848, reprinted in *Karl Marx, Frederick Engels: Collected Works*, International Publishers, New York, 1984, vol. 6, pp. 463—5.
65 Albro, pp. 5, 49, 90, 131, 149; Beezley, p. 11; Blaisdell, pp. 5, 142—62.
66 Knight, vol. 1, p. 77.
67 Parkes, p. 318.
68 Ibid., p. 321.
69 Knight, vol. 1, p. 218.
70 Ibid., p. 426.
71 Albro, p. 135; Hart, p. 102.
72 Knight, vol. 1, p. 419.
73 Asprey, p. 162.
74 Womack 1968, pp. 44—52.
75 Knight, vol. 1, 190; Krauze, pp. 280—1; Millon, p. 14.
76 Wolf 1969, p. 31.
77 Womack 1968, p. 127.
78 Parkes, p. 342.
79 Newell, p. 76.
80 Womack 1968, pp. 67—96.
81 Ibid., p. 204.
82 Ibid., pp. 226—7.
83 Millon, p. 39.
84 Ibid., p. 321.
85 Ibid., p. 315.
86 Galeano, p. 121.
87 Atkin, p. 188.
88 Knight, vol. 1, p. 472.

89 John Tutino, "Revolutionary Confrontation, 1913–1917," in Benjamin and Wasserman, p. 42.
90 Parkes, p. 337.
91 Knight, vol. 2, p. 13; Wright, p. 166.
92 Knight, vol. 2, p. 25.
93 Beezley, p. 158; Parkes, pp. 337–8.
94 Harris, pp. 27, 33, Parkes, p. 319.
95 Parkes, p. 321.
96 Katz 1981, pp. 136–8; Wolf 1969, p. 35.
97 Wolf 1969, p. 36; Katz 1998, pp. 17–35.
98 Harris, pp. 21–2.
99 Reed 1969, pp. 123, 132, 140.
100 Ibid., p. 145.
101 Ibid., p. 141.
102 Knight, vol. 2, p. 59.
103 Katz 1981, pp. 156–7.
104 Cary T. Grayson, *Woodrow Wilson: An Intimate Memoir*, Holt Rinehart Winston, New York, 1960, p. 30, quoted in Grieb, p. 41.
105 Langley, pp. 12–15.
106 Ibid.
107 Grayson, *Woodrow Wilson*, p. 31, quoted in Grieb, p. 154.
108 Knight, vol. 2, p. 155.
109 Asprey, p. 169.
110 Knight, vol. 2, pp. 169, 219.
111 Millon, p. 47.
112 Katz 1981, p. 268.
113 Tutino, "Revolutionary Confrontation, 1913–1917," in Benjamin and Wasserman, p. 60.
114 Ibid.; Krauze, p. 295; Newell, p. 114; Wright, p. 165.
115 Newell, p. 115.
116 Katz 1981, pp. 269–70; 1998, p. 526.
117 Parkes, pp. 358–9.
118 Katz 1981, p. 253.
119 Ibid., p. 299.
120 Ibid., p. 135.
121 Knight, vol. 2, p. 342.
122 MacLachlan, p. 57.
123 Nadelmann, p. 74; Sandos, pp. 78–100, 142–52.
124 Tuchman, pp. 7, 90–106.
125 Katz 1981, p. 303; Lister and Lister, p. 281.
126 Katz 1981, pp. 303–9; 1998, p. 569.
127 Harris, p. 93; Knight, vol. 2, pp. 350–1.
128 Wolf 1969, p. 41.
129 Hart, p. 133.
130 Knight, vol. 2, p. 433.
131 Hart, p. 155; Sandos, p. 154.
132 Parkes, pp. 360–1; *Constitucion Politica de Los Estados Unidos Mexicanos*, 1975 edition.

133　Atkin, p. 303; Womack 1968, pp. 252–7, 287; Newell, p. 128.
134　Womack 1968, p. 321.
135　Newell, pp. 52–5.
136　Romana Falcon, "Confiscated Estates—Revolutionary Conquest or Spoils?" in Benjamin and Wasserman, p. 157.
137　Parkes, pp. 366–7.
138　Ibid.
139　Wasserman, pp. 43, 77.
140　Cockcroft 1983, p. 105.
141　Langley, p. 17.
142　Fuentes, p. 43.
143　Langley, p. 18.
144　Barry 1992, pp. 17, 288.
145　Hamilton, p. 118.
146　Dorner, p. 40.
147　Barry 1995, p. 139; Stewart F. Voss, "Nationalizing the Revolution," in Benjamin and Wasserman, p. 293.
148　Hamilton, pp. 222–34.
149　Ibid., pp. 198, 227.
150　Wright, p. 171.
151　Hamilton, pp. 268–9.
152　Carr, pp. 167, 199, 200, 309.
153　Bartra, pp. 36–57; Hamilton, pp. 96–7, 261; Langley, p. 24.
154　Langley, p. 26.
155　Samson, pp. 102, 129.
156　Kennedy 1987, p. 343; Yergin, p. 13.
157　Pastor and Castañeda, p. 207.
158　Langley, pp. 45–7.
159　Warnock, p. 118; La Botz 1992, pp. 69–71.
160　Krauze, pp. 694–5; Langley, p. 68.
161　Langley, p. 68; Hodges, pp. 111–20.
162　Krauze, p. 706; Langley, pp. 68–71; Cockcroft 1983, p. 241.
163　Dorner, p. 40.
164　Cockcroft 1983, p. 243.
165　Langley, p. 75.
166　Pastor and Castañeda, p. 201.
167　Michael Garity, "Energy and Indian People," in Sklar, pp. 238–9.
168　Cockcroft 1983, p. 265; Langley, p. 79; Pastor and Castañeda, pp. 100–1.
169　Pastor and Castañeda, p. 104.
170　Cockcroft 1983, p. 265.
171　Riding, pp. 511–18.
172　Presidential Address to the Nation on the Situation in Nicaragua, March 16, 1986.
173　Barry 1992, p. 22.
174　Warnock, pp. 48–9.
175　Cockcroft 1983, p. 308.
176　Pastor and Castañeda, p. 145.

177 Warnock, p. 49.
178 Langley, p. 101.
179 Pastor and Castañeda, p. 201.
180 Ibid., pp. 226–7.
181 Ibid., pp. 229–30.
182 Ibid., p. 224.
183 Ibid., p. 208.
184 Barry 1992, pp. 96, 289.
185 La Botz 1995, p. 99.
186 Ibid., pp. 123, 130–1.
187 Warnock, p. 51.
188 Barry 1992, p. 87.
189 Warnock, p. 201.

3 SOUTHERN MEXICO IN THE FREE TRADE ORDER

1   EZLN communiqué, March 1, 1994.
2   Renner, p. 83.
3   Wollock.
4   Barry 1995, pp. 269–70; Article 27, *Constitucion Politica de los Estados Unidos Mexicanos*, Ediciones Delma, Mexico City, 1998.
5   Barry 1995, p. 117; Article 27, *Constitucion Politica de los Estados Unidos Mexicanos*.
6   Barry 1995, p. 270; Harvey 1998, p. 188.
7   Barry 1995, pp. 119, 269.
8   John Ross, "Big Pulp vs. Zapatistas," *Multinational Monitor*, April 1998.
9   Barry 1995, pp. 120–1.
10 Rodolfo Stavenhagen, Fernando Paz Sanchez, Cuauhtémoc Cardenas and Arturo Bonilla, *Neolatifundismo y Explotacion*, Mexico City, 1968, quoted in Galeano, p. 140.
11 Galeano, p. 135.
12 Barry 1995, pp. 123–4, 270.
13 Ibid., p. 66; Warnock, p. 201.
14 Harvey 1998, p. 181; Warnock p. 191.
15 *The Economist*, September 26, 1998.
16 Wollock; Lappé and Collins, p. 371.
17 Diego Cevallos, "Dying of Thirst Next to the Fountain," Interpress Service, May 27, 1996.
18 Janice Hughes, "ACTPN Draft Seeks Full Implementation of NAFTA Farm Provisions," *Inside US Trade*, June 12, 1996.
19 White House press release, "President Clinton Names Members to the Advisory Committee for Trade Policy and Negotiations," December 15, 1997.
20 Howard LaFranchi, "How Broccoli Might Stem Mexican Migration," *Christian Science Monitor*, January 21, 1997.
21 George A. Collier, Daniel Mountjoy and Ronald Nigh, "Peasant Agriculture and Global Change," *BioScience*, June 1994.

22 Harvey 1998, p. 179.
23 Warnock, p. 200.
24 Harvey 1998, pp. 182–4.
25 Nigh.
26 Dawkins, p. 19.
27 Wright, p. 35.
28 Ibid., pp. 41–2.
29 Ibid., p. 116.
30 Ibid., p. 43.
31 Shepard Barbash, "The Atomic War on Screwworms," *The Mexico City News*, February 3, 1987; author's visit to Tuxtla plant, January 1987.
32 John Nichols, Animal Plant Health Inspection Service, USDA, Tacoma Park, MD, in interview with author's assistant, September 10, 1999.
33 Autonomous Municipality San Pedro de Michoacan press statement, June 26, 1999.
34 Brinley Bruton, "Bolsa Ends Higher Despite Milk, Tortilla Price Hikes," *The Mexico City News*, December 27, 1996.
35 John Ward Anderson, *et al.*, "US Probes Mexico's Role in Drugs," *Washington Post*, May 11, 1997; Marisol Avena Cruz, "Tortillas contaminadas de maiz importado para animales, consumen milliones de mexicanos," *Quehacer Politico*, October 19, 1996; Mark Fineman, "Opposition Cries Foul as PRI Ends Investigation of State Firm," *Los Angeles Times*, September 27, 1996; Michelle Chi Chase, "CONASUPO Thefts Date to 1988 Says Commission," *The Mexico City News*, September 25, 1996.
36 Uriel Martinez, "Saquean Habitantes de Dos Colonias un Tren Cargado de Trigo," *La Jornada*, June 24, 1996; "Mexican Slum Dwellers Sack Corn Laden Train," Reuters, May 30, 1996.
37 Bonfil, pp. 17–18.
38 Barry 1995, pp. 220, 222.
39 Doyle, pp. 198–9; Fowler and Mooney, pp. 27–38; Lappé and Collins, p. 159.
40 Wollock.
41 Ibid.
42 Doyle, p. 39.
43 Wright, p. 173; Colby and Dennett, pp. 107–10, 266.
44 E. C. Stackman, Richard Bradfield and Paul Manglesorf, *Campaigns Against Hunger*, Belknap Press, Cambridge, MA, 1967, p. 316, quoted in Wright, pp. 174–6, 282.
45 Doyle, pp. 256–9, Shiva, pp. 33–7.
46 Wright, p. 8.
47 Ibid., p. 155.
48 Carl O. Sauer, *Agricultural Origins and Dispersals: The Domestication of Animals and Foodstuffs*, MIT Press, Boston, MA, 1969, p. 64, in Wright, p. 155.
49 Ibid.
50 Sauer in Bruce H. Jennings, *Foundations of International Agricultural Research*, Westview, Boulder CO 1988, p. 51, quoted by Wright, p. 178.
51 Shiva, p. 125.
52 Warnock, pp. 195–8.
53 Hu-DeHart, pp. 213–14.
54 Doyle, pp. 7, 13.
55 Wright, p. 214.

56 Doyle, p. 68.
57 Garrison Wilkes, "The Endangered Genetic Base of the World's Food Supply," *Bulletin of the Atomic Scientists*, February 1977, quoted in Jackson, p. 57.
58 Nabhan, p. 93.
59 Doyle, pp. 100, 311–12; Korten, p. 224.
60 Doyle, p. 149.
61 Shiva, p. 245; Wright, p. 210.
62 *Genetic Engineering and World Hunger*, Briefing 10, October 1998, The Corner House, Dorset, UK.
63 Michael Pollan, "Playing God in the Garden," *New York Times Magazine*, October 25, 1998.
64 Vandana Shiva, "The Seed and the Earth: Women, Ecology and Biotechnology," *The Ecologist* (London), January/February 1992.
65 Korten, p. 180.
66 Warnock, p. 160.
67 Quotes from Dr. Peter Raven, Missouri Botanical Garden, in presentation at the American Museum of Natural History, New York, October 5, 1998 (among numerous other sources).
68 World Commission on Environment and Development, p. 160.
69 SEMARNAP map, 1996.
70 Enrique Jardel, Eduardo Santana C. and Sergio Graf, "The Sierra de Manantlan Biosphere Reserve: Conservation and Regional Sustainable Development," *Parks*, International Union for the Conservation of Nature, February 1996.
71 Slideshow and presentation by Prof. Enrique J. Jardel, University of Guadalajara, at the American Museum of Natural History, New York, October 5, 1998; Galeano, p. 19.
72 Jardel presentation.
73 Author's telephone interview with Prof. Hugh Iltis, University of Wisconsin at Madison, October 16, 1998.
74 Author's telephone interview with Prof. Bruce Benz, Texas Wesleyan University, Ft. Worth, October 16, 1998.
75 Author's interview with Prof. Jardel at his presentation.
76 Greenpeace press release, May 25, 1999; Matilde Perez, *La Jornada*, June 24, 1999.
77 Published in *La Jornada*, January 27, 1994.
78 Nations.
79 Author's trip to jungle settlements, January 1984.
80 Nations.
81 Ibid.
82 Published in *La Jornada*, January 27, 1994.
83 Adriana Monteil Garcia, "El Impacto de la Construccion de la Presa Hidroelectrica Ing. Manuel Moreno Torres en el Municipio de Chicoasen, Chiapas" (thesis), Universidad Autonoma de Chiapas, 1991.
84 Harvey 1989, p. 79.
85 Author's interview with OCEZ militant José Magdaleno Velasco, San Cristóbal de Las Casas, April 1996.
86 Monteil Garcia, "El Impacto de la Construccion de la Presa Hidroelectrica."
87 Ibid.
88 Ibid.
89 Harvey 1989, p. 120.

90 S. Jeffrey and K. Wilkerson, "The Usumacinta River: Trouble on a Wild Frontier," *National Geographic*, October 1985; Larry Rohter, "A Threat Is Seen to Two Maya Sites," *New York Times*, March 26, 1987.

91 Published in *La Jornada*, January 27, 1994.

92 Orozco Zuarth, p. 110.

93 Collier, p. 16; Renner, p. 123.

94 "No Laughter in NAFTA," Institute for Policy Studies report, Washington DC, January 1996.

95 Jeremy Brecher, "Global Village or Global Pillage?" *The Nation*, New York, December 6, 1993.

96 Ibid.

97 Jill Hickson, "NAFTA Pollution Threat to US–Mexican Border," *Green Left Weekly*, December 6, 1995.

98 Korten, p. 129.

99 *Public Citizen*, p. 7.

100 Ibid., p. iii.

101 Hickson, "NAFTA Pollution Threat to US–Mexican Border."

102 *Public Citizen*, pp. 12–14.

103 Ibid., p. iv.

104 Ibid., p. 22.

105 Warnock, p. 221.

106 Ibid., p. 222.

107 Korten, p. 130.

108 *Public Citizen*, p. vi.

109 Ibid.

110 Juan Gonzalez, "Death Knell for Rio Grande," *New York Daily News*, June 10, 1993.

111 Hickson "NAFTA Pollution Threat to US-Mexican Border."

112 *Business Week*, August 4, 1997; *Wall Street Journal*, October 14, 1997; update on Metalclad case, August 1998, prepared by Michelle Sforza of Public Citizen's Global Trade Watch, Washington DC.

113 George Monbiot, "Running on MMT," *The Guardian* (London), August 13, 1998.

114 Keith Schneider, "Environmental Rift Emerges in Trade Pact," *New York Times*, September 15, 1992.

115 Dawkins, p. 13.

116 *Public Citizen*, p. ix.

117 Ray Sanchez, "No Cleanup From NAFTA," *New York Newsday*, April 21, 1996.

118 *Public Citizen*, p. xi.

119 Anthony DePalma, "Treaty Partners Study Fate of Birds at Polluted Mexican Lake," *New York Times*, August 1, 1995; *Public Citizen*, p. 60.

120 *Public Citizen*, p. 60.

121 Ibid.

122 "NAFTA Body Accuses Mexico Over Threat to Coral Reef," Reuters, June 7, 1996.

123 John Ross, "Titanic's Wake," *San Francisco Bay Guardian*, June 3, 1998.

124 La Botz 1992, pp. 27, 28, 163.

125 Ibid., p, 182.

126 David Bacon, "Rebellion on the Border," *San Francisco Bay Guardian*, March 5, 1997.

127 James Ledbetter, "Press Clips," *Village Voice*, New York, October 25, 1994.

128 La Botz 1992, p. 71.

129 Ibid., pp. 52–3; Warnock, p. 121.

130 Joseph Frazier, "As Legislators Bury One Scandal, Another Emerges," AP, September 27, 1996.

131 Bill Weinberg, "Laguna Verde: The Nuclear Debate in Mexico," *The Ecologist*, (London), November/December 1987.

132 Ibid.

133 Salvador Corro, *Proceso*, November 26, 1984; La Botz 1992, pp. 83–6.

134 Weinberg, "Laguna Verde: The Nuclear Debate in Mexico."

135 Warnock, p. 121.

136 Korten, p. 129; Warnock, p. 123.

137 Warnock, pp. 121–2.

138 La Botz 1992, pp. 114–26; Warnock, p. 122.

139 David Bacon, "Mexican Mine Strike Broken," *Connection to the Americas*, Resource Center of the Americas, Minneapolis, May 1999.

140 Warnock, p. 122.

141 Korten, p. 129; La Botz 1992, pp. 148–60; Warnock, p. 123.

142 Warnock, p. 122.

143 Korten, p. 129; Warnock, p. 122.

144 *Global Production*, April/May 1992.

145 *The Economist*, April 11, 1998.

146 Keith Bradsher, "Chile Test on Broader Free Trade," *New York Times*, May 2, 1992.

147 *NAFTA and Inter-American Trade Monitor*, Institute for Agriculture and Trade Policy, Minneapolis, May 17, 1996.

148 Chilean Forests Action Alert, January 29, 1999, via Internet (forest-americas@igc.org).

149 Korten, p. 180.

150 Ibid.

151 Vandana Shiva and Holla-Bhar Radha, "The Rise of the Farmers' Seed Movement," *Third World Resurgence*, Kuala Lumpur, no. 39.

152 *Deccan Herald*, Bangalore, December 4, 1998.

153 Barry Wilson, "Officials Favor Relaxed Labeling Guidelines," *Western Producer*, June 20, 1996.

154 Mark Ritchie, *Trading Away Our Environment: Global "Harmonization" of Pesticide Laws*, Institute for Agriculture and Trade Policy, Minneapolis, MN, 1990, p. 3.

155 Korten, p. 175.

156 Chris McGinn, "Trade Body Threatens Democracy," *Public Citizen News*, Washington DC, January/February 1998.

157 *The Economist*, October 3, 1998; author's e-mail interview with Michelle Sforza of *Public Citizen*, Washington DC, October 16, 1998.

158 *The Economist*, October 3, 1998.

159 Robert Evans, "Green Push Could Damage Trade Body—WTO Chief," Reuters, May 15, 1998.

160 *The Economist*, October 3, 1998.

161 "Global Trade Watch Backgrounder: The Alarming Multilateral Agreement on Investment," *Public Citizen*, Washington DC, 1997; "MAI: The Multilateral Agreement on Investment," OECD Policy Brief, 1997; "US Government Background Paper on the MAI," September 1997; "A Guide to the Multilateral Agreement on Investment," United States Council for International Business, Washington DC, January 1996.

162 *The Economist*, October 3, 1998.

163 Jeffrey E. Garten, "Needed: A Fed for the World," *New York Times*, September 23, 1998.

164 *International Finance*, November 17, 1975, cited in Sklar, p. 63.
165 Barry 1995, p. 43.
166 Bello, p. 28.
167 Cited in Castañeda 1995, p. 37, Korten, p. 201.
168 Bello, pp. 40, 52.
169 La Botz 1992, p. 165.
170 Barry 1995, p. 113.
171 *NAFTA and Inter-American Trade Monitor*, Institute for Agriculture and Trade Policy, Minneapolis, June 28, 1996.
172 *Wall Street Journal*, September 28, 1995.
173 *La Jornada*, September 25, 1997.
174 Barry 1995, p. 194.

4 ZAPATA LIVES

1 Fox.
 2 Amnesty International, pp. 64–72.
 3 Nations.
 4 Harvey 1998, pp. 48–50; Rita Balboa, "Colera en rios de Chiapas," *El Universal*, November 17, 1997.
 5 Collier, p. 109.
 6 Wollock.
 7 Author's interview with Bishop Samuel Ruiz, March 1987.
 8 Harvey 1998, pp. 150–2; James D. Nations, "The Lacandones, Gertrude Blom, and the Selva Lacandona," in Harris and Sartor, p. 38.
 9 Harvey 1998, pp. 148–50.
10 Ibid.
11 Fried, *et al.*, p. 287.
12 Weinberg, pp. 45–9.
13 Carlos Fazio, "Mexico: Guatemalan Refugees Resist Relocation," *Latinamerica Press*, Lima, June 21, 1984.
14 Bricker, p. 135.
15 Author's observations.
16 Fazio, "Mexico: Guatemalan Refugees Resist Relocation."
17 Margarita Nolasco, "Los Altos y La Selva," *La Reforma*, February 5, 1994.
18 Ibid.
19 Alma Guillermoprieto, "Zapata's Heirs," *The New Yorker*, May 16, 1994.
20 George A. Collier, "Roots of the Rebellion in Chiapas," *Cultural Survival Quarterly*, Cambridge, MA, Spring 1994.
21 Nations.
22 Harris and Sartor, pp. 7–15; author's interviews with Gertrude Blom, San Cristóbal de Las Casas, December 1984.
23 Luz Martin del Campo-Hermosillo, "Culture and Environment: Responding to Deforestation in the Lacandon Rainforest," City College, City University of New York, Applied Urban Anthropology, June 1998; Boremanse, pp. 9–12.

24 Nations.

25 Ibid.

26 Nations, "The Lacandones, Gertrude Blom, and the Selva Lacandona," in Alex and Sartor, p. 39.

27 Larry Rohter, "Tropical Rain Forest in Mexico Is Facing Destruction in Decade," *New York Times*, July 10, 1990.

28 Tim Golden, "Left Behind, Mexico's Indians Fight the Future," *New York Times*, January 9, 1994.

29 Mark Uhlig, "Mexican Debt Deal May Save Jungle," *New York Times*, February 26, 1991.

30 Gertrude Blom, "The Jungle Is Burning," in Harris and Sartor, pp. 147–8.

31 Nations.

32 Womack 1999, p. 39.

33 *La Jornada*, March 31, 1987.

34 Ibid.

35 La Botz 1992, p. 31.

36 *Diario El Dia*, Tuxtla Gutiérrez, January 8, 1987.

37 Ross 1995, pp. 74–5.

38 Fox.

39 Ross 1995, p. 76.

40 Gross, p. 111; *New York Times*, May 10, 1993.

41 Wilson T. Boots, "Uprising in Chiapas. Bishop Ruiz Sees a Moment of Grace," *Christian Century*, March 9, 1994; *El Financiero*, October 24, 1993.

42 Obituary, *New York Times*, December 29, 1993.

43 *Sintesis*, special edition, "La Guerra de los Olvidados," Puebla, January 1994, pp. 4–5.

44 Ibid.; author's interviews with witnesses, San Cristóbal de Las Casas, February 1994.

45 Russell, p. 21.

46 Ross 1995, p. 197.

47 Ibid., p. 20.

48 First Declaration of the Lacandon Selva, January 1994.

49 Russell, pp. 21–3.

50 *Sintesis*, special edition, "La Guerra de los Olvidados," Puebla, January 1994, p. 9.

51 Russell, pp. 25–6.

52 *Sintesis*, special edition, "La Guerra de los Olvidados," Puebla, January 1994, pp. 7, 9.

53 Ibid., pp. 10–11; *Excélsior*, January 5, 1994.

54 EZLN communiqué, January 6, 1998.

55 *La Reforma*, January 5, 1994, quoted in Russell, p. 22.

56 *Sintesis*, special edition, "La Guerra de los Olvidados," Puebla, January 1994, p. 19.

57 *Sintesis*, special edition, "La Guerra de los Olvidados II," Puebla, February 1994, p. 3.

58 Ibid., p. 5.

59 Ibid., p. 5.

60 Ibid., p. 6.

61 Ibid., p. 8.

62 Ibid., pp. 20–1.

63 Ibid., pp. 20–1.

64 Ibid., pp. 22–3.

65 *La Jornada*, January 19, 1994, quoted in Russell, p. 52.

66 *La Jornada*, January 31, 1994.

67 *Sintesis*, special edition, "La Guerra de los Olvidados II," Puebla, February 1994, pp. 22–3.
68 *Excélsior*, March 2, 1994, quoted in Russell, p. 57.
69 *Sintesis*, special edition, "La Guerra de los Olvidados III," Puebla, March 1994, pp. 22–3.
70 Ibid., p. 28.
71 Ross 1995, p. 212; *Sintesis*, special edition, "La Guerra de los Olvidados III," Puebla, March 1994, p. 19.
72 *La Jornada*, December 1, 1996.
73 Communiqué from forty-five Indigenous Campesino Organizations, San Cristóbal, February 17, 1994.
74 *Sintesis*, special edition, "La Guerra de los Olvidados III," Puebla, March 1994, p. 21.
75 *La Jornada*, March 7, 1994.
76 *Sintesis*, special edition, "La Guerra de los Olvidados III," Puebla, March 1994, p. 16.
77 Ibid., p. 3; *La Jornada*, February 15, 1994.
78 *Sintesis*, special edition, "La Guerra de los Olvidados III," Puebla, March 1994, p. 4; Russell, p. 62.
79 Russell, pp. 61–4.
80 Ross 1995, p. 19.
81 *Macropolis*, Mexico City, March 7, 1994, quoted in Russell, pp. 66–8.
82 *Reforma*, June 10, 1994, quoted in Russell, p. 68.
83 Russell, pp. 64–8.
84 Ibid., p. 69.
85 Evon Z. Vogt, "Possible Sacred Aspects of the Chiapas Rebellion," *Cultural Survival Quarterly*, Cambridge, MA, Spring 1994; *La Jornada*, March 19, 1994.
86 Communiqué from forty-five Indigenous Campesino Organizations, San Cristóbal, February 17, 1994.
87 *Diario de Chiapas*, Tuxtla, March 1, 1994.
88 *La Jornada*, April 1, 1994.
89 *La Jornada*, March 6, 1994; *High Times*, July 1994.
90 *Uno Mas Uno*, January 29, 1994.
91 *Proceso*, February 14, 1994.
92 *Proceso*, January 17, 1994.
93 *La Jornada*, February 26, 1994.
94 *Proceso*, February 21, 1994.
95 *La Jornada*, January 12, 1994.
96 *La Jornada*, March 15, 1994.
97 Author's interviews and observations.
98 *La Jornada*, March 15, 1994.
99 Harvey 1989, pp. 166–7.
100 *La Jornada*, March 3, 1994.
101 Harvey 1998, pp. 138–46.
102 *La Jornada*, March 12, 1994.
103 Ibid., February 2, 1994; March 10, 1994.
104 Ibid., November 13, 1994.
105 Human Rights Watch, p. 39.
106 *La Jornada*, November 6, 1994.
107 Robert M. Laughlin, "Tzotzil and Tzeltal: Who in the World?" in Harris and Sartor, p. 21.

108 *Excélsior*, March 10, 1994; *El Financiero*, March 9, 1994.
109 Mike Tangeman, "Mexican Bishop Threatened Following Peace Mediation," Catholic News Services, March 10, 1994.
110 *Sintesis*, special edition, "La Guerra de los Olvidados III," Puebla, March 1994, p. 24; author's interview with Bishop Ruiz, March 1994.
111 AP, March 26, 1994; *Washington Post*, March 27, 1994.

5 BEHIND LINES WITH MARCOS

1 *Sintesis*, special edition, "La Guerra de los Olvidados," Puebla, January 1994, p. 14.
2 *New York Times*, February 10, 1995.
3 This was also noted by journalists, through a comparison of photos. See Carlos Marin, *Proceso*, February 28, 1994.
4 This was also corroborated by the press, although the federal army death toll in this account may be inflated. See Ross 1995, pp. 26–30.

6 PARALLEL POWER

1 Third Declaration of the Lacandon Selva, January 1995.
2 *Proceso*, December 26, 1994.
3 *La Jornada*, April 10, 1994.
4 EZLN communiqué, June 10, 1994; Second Declaration of the Lacandon Selva, June 1994.
5 Ross 1995, pp. 379–81; Russell, pp. 92–3.
6 Ross 1995, pp. 374–6; Russell, pp. 88–90.
7 Ross 1995, pp. 374–6; Russell, pp. 88–90.
8 Ross 1995, pp. 374–6; Russell, pp. 88–90.
9 Ross 1995, pp. 374–6; Russell, pp. 88–90.
10 AFP, September 2, 1994.
11 *Transicion*, Organ of the State of Chiapas Rebel Government, San Cristóbal, January 8, 1995.
12 EZLN communiqué, December 19, 1994; *Siglo XXI*, San Cristóbal, December 19, 1994; *La Jornada*, December 20, 1994.
13 *Cuarto Poder*, Tuxtla Gutiérrez, December 23, 1994.
14 Hermann Bellinghausen, Marcos interview, *La Jornada*, December 20, 1994.
15 *La Jornada*, December 18, 1994.
16 Ibid.; *Siglo XXI*, San Cristóbal, December 19, 1994.
17 Author's interview with Amado Avendaño, San Cristóbal, December 1994.
18 *Diario de Chiapas*, Tuxtla Gutiérrez, December 22, 1994.
19 Ibid., December 17, 1994.
20 Ibid., December 22, 1994.
21 Ibid., December 31, 1994.
22 *Cuarto Poder*, Tuxtla, December 22, 1994.

23 Ibid.

24 *Expreso de Chiapas*, Tuxtla, December 29, 1994.

25 Amnesty International, pp. 117–18.

26 *New York Times*, December 9, 1994.

27 *Expreso de Chiapas*, Tuxtla, December 24, 1994.

28 *New York Times*, December 8, 1994.

29 *La Jornada*, August 31, 1994.

30 *Cuarto Poder*, Tuxtla, December 29, 1994; *La Jornada*, December 30, 1994.

31 AP, January 16, 1999.

32 *La Jornada*, December 24, 1994.

33 *Siglo XXI*, San Cristóbal, December 19, 1994.

34 Ibid., December 21, 1994; *La Jornada*, December 22, 1994; author's observations.

35 *Cuarto Poder*, Tuxtla, December 24, 1994; *La Jornada*, December 28, 1994.

36 *La Jornada*, January 18, 1995.

37 Author's interview.

38 *Proceso*, December 19, 1994.

39 Ibid.

40 San Cristóbal Diocese statement, published in *Cuarto Poder*, Tuxtla, December 20, 1994.

41 Tim Golden, "Mexico's New Offensive: Erasing Rebel's Mystique," *New York Times*, February 11, 1995.

42 *La Jornada*, February 10, 1995.

43 Ibid.; *New York Times*, February 11, 1995.

44 *New York Times*, February 11, 1995.

45 *La Jornada*, February 13, 1995; *New York Times*, February 14, 1995.

46 *La Jornada*, February 13, 1995.

47 *La Jornada*, February 12, 1994.

48 *The Financial Times*, February 1, 1995.

49 Marcos communiqué, February 9, 1995.

50 CCRI communiqué, February 9, 1995.

51 Ibid.

52 US State Department release, quoted in Monroy Gomez 1996, p. 12.

53 Reported in *Counterpunch*, Washington DC, February 1, 1995.

54 Address by Pres. Ernesto Zedillo, February 9, 1995, quoted in Monroy Gomez 1996, p. 11.

55 Donald M. Rothberg, "Chase Bank Denies Urging Elimination of Mexican Rebels," AP, February 14, 1995.

56 *La Jornada*, February 10, 1995.

57 *Proceso*, January 9, 1995.

58 Monroy Gomez, vol. 3, pp. 20–1.

59 *New York Times*, February 15, 1995.

60 *La Jornada*, August 25, 1995.

61 Monroy Gomez, vol. 3, p. 31.

62 Ibid., pp. 33–5; *La Jornada*, May 21, 1996.

63 Monroy Gomez, vol. 3, pp. 33–5.

64 Ibid.

65 *La Jornada*, April 16, 1995; *San Francisco Chronicle*, April 17, 1995.

66 *La Jornada*, May 11, 1995.
67 Ibid., May 14, 1995.
68 Monroy Gomez, vol. 3, p. 72.
69 John Ross, *Anderson Valley Advertiser*, Booneville, CA, May 17, 1995.
70 Reuters, AP, *San Francisco Chronicle*, May 2, 1995.
71 Mexican Labor News and Analysis (www.igc.apc.org/unitedelect), July 16, 1998.
72 Ross 1998, pp. 256–63.
73 *La Jornada*, July 16, 1995.
74 Ibid., October 16, 1994.
75 Third Declaration of the Lacandon Selva, January 1995.
76 Hodges, p. 88.
77 *Consulta* ballot, author's interviews with Alianza Civica activists.
78 Reuters, August 28, 1995; author's interviews with Alianza Civica activists.
79 Alianza Civica press release, Mexico City, August 29, 1995.
80 *New York Times*, August 28, 1995; *La Jornada*, August 27, 1995.
81 AP, October 18, 1995.
82 Reuters, October 23, 25, 1995.
83 AP, October 29, 1995.
84 NCDM press release, El Paso TX, November 1, 1995; Reuters, November 2, 1995.
85 *La Jornada*, January 7, 1996.
86 *New York Times*, November 26, 1995.
87 *La Jornada*, January 15, 1996.
88 Monroy Gomez, vol. 3, pp. 128–9.
89 Ibid., pp. 130–2.
90 Ibid., pp. 130 2.
91 Ibid., pp. 127, 131.
92 *La Jornada*, December 12, 1995.
93 Monroy Gomez, vol. 3, p. 135.
94 e.g., Fourth Declaration of the Lacandon Selva, January 1996.

7 THE CHALLENGE OF SAN ANDRÉS

1 *La Jornada*, December 24, 1995.
2 Ibid., December 31, 1995.
3 Ibid., December 24, 1995.
4 Reuters, January 3, 1996.
5 Hernandez and Vera, pp. 34–5.
6 *La Jornada*, December 31, 1995.
7 Fourth Declaration of the Lacandon Selva, January 1996.
8 *La Jornada*, September 14, 1997.
9 San Andrés Accords, quoted in Hernandez and Vera, p. 62.
10 Ibid., p. 82.
11 Hernandez and Vera, p. 223.

12 *La Jornada*, March 21, 23, 1996.
13 *Cuarto Poder*, Tuxtla Gutiérrez, June 5, 1996.
14 *La Jornada*, May 22, 1996.
15 Ibid., May 5, 1996.
16 Ibid.
17 EFE, May 8, 1996.
18 *La Jornada*, May 20, 1996.
19 *La Jornada*, May 30, 1996; author's observations.
20 Author's observations and interviews with witnesses, Oventic, May 1996.
21 *La Jornada*, May 21, 1996.
22 Reuters, May 20, 1996.
23 Juan Balboa, *La Jornada*, May 21, 1996.
24 Report by Terra Nuñez, Global Exchange volunteer, May 20, 1996.
25 Ibid.
26 Alejandro Angeles, *The News*, Mexico City, May 21, 1996.
27 *La Jornada*, May 14, 1996.
28 Reuters, February 6, 1996.
29 Tzoman Campesino Organization communiqué, Altamirano, May 23, 1996.
30 *La Jornada*, May 30, 1996.
31 Ibid., June 1, 1996.
32 Reuters, February 6, 1996.
33 Ibid.
34 *Cuarto Poder*, Tuxtla, June 7, 1996; *Diario de San Cristóbal*, June 7, 1996.
35 *La Jornada*, June 8, 1996.
36 *Expreso de Chiapas*, Tuxtla, June 9, 1996.
37 *El Universal*, June 10, 1996.
38 *La Republica en Chiapas*, Tuxtla, June 10, 1996.
39 *Diario de San Cristóbal*, June 9, 1996.
40 Ibid., June 7, 1996.
41 Reuters, April 14, 1996.
42 John Ross, *Mexico Barbaro*, electronic newsletter (johnross@igc.apc.org), April 15–23, 1996.
43 *La Jornada*, July 5, 1996; Hernandez and Vera, p. 223.
44 Ruggiero and Sahulka, introduction, p. 9; Ross, *Mexico Barbaro*, April 15–23.
45 Ross 1998, p. 215.
46 *La Jornada*, July 28, August 3, 1996.
47 Nestor Rodriguez Lobaina, Cuban Youth Network for Democracy, and Vladimir Roca, Democratic Socialist Current, letter to *La Jornada*, May 22, 1996.
48 Second Declaration of La Realidad, August 1996.
49 Ibid.
50 Jaime Aviles, *La Jornada*, November 12, 1996.
51 Ibid.
52 *La Jornada*, November 7, 1996.
53 Ibid., October 10, 1996; Hernandez and Vera, p. 224.
54 Ross, *Mexico Barbaro*, October 26, 1996; *La Jornada*, October 12, 1996.

55 *La Jornada*, August 4, 1996.

56 Catherine Ryan, *The Los Angeles View*, March 8, 1996.

57 Hernandez and Vera, p. 189.

58 CONPAZ press release, November 7, 1996, San Cristóbal de las Casas.

59 LIMEDDHH-FIDH press release, November 9, 1996, via Internet (limeddh@laneta.apc.org).

60 Reuters, November 7, 1996.

8 STEALTH COUNTERINSURGENCY

1   *Analisis Comparativo de la Propuesta del Ejecutivo Federal sobre Derechos Indigenas, a la Luz de Los Acuerdos de San Andrés*, Enlace Civil San Cristóbal, 1998, via Internet (www.enlacecivil.org.mx).

2   EZLN communiqué, January 11, 1997.

3   Reuters, January 23, 1997.

4   EZLN communiqué, January 24, 1997.

5   AP, March 16, 1997; *La Jornada*, March 20, 1997.

6   *La Jornada*, March 20, 1997.

7   AP, March 16, 1997; *La Jornada*, March 20, 1997.

8   *La Jornada*, April 3, 1997.

9   Weekly Bulletin of Human Rights in Mexico, March 11–17, 1997, Human Rights Center Miguel Agustin Pro Juarez (PRODH), Mexico City, via Internet (prodh@laneta.apc.org).

10 *La Jornada*, January 30, 1997.

11 Don Fitz, "The 1997 Elections in Mexico and the Rise of the Greens," *Synthesis/Regeneration*, St. Louis, Winter 1998.

12 *New York Times*, July 8, 1997.

13 AP, November 20, 1997.

14 *La Jornada*, July 20, 1997.

15 Ibid.

16 FZLN Special Post-Electoral News Update, July 5–16, 1997, via Internet (joshua@peak.org).

17 *La Jornada*, July 5, 1997.

18 FZLN Special Post-Electoral News Update, July 5–16, 1997.

19 Ibid.; *La Jornada*, July 9, 1997.

20 *La Jornada*, July 19, 1997.

21 *El Universal*, July 29, 1997.

22 Julia Preston, "Zapatista Caravan: Road Test for Peaceful Politics," *New York Times*, September 13, 1997.

23 Hernandez and Navarro, p. 230.

24 *La Jornada*, September 13, 1997.

25 Ibid., November 11, 1997.

26 Reuters, November 30, 1997.

27 Centro de Derechos Humanos Fray Bartolomé de Las Casas, pp. 94–116.

28 SIPAZ Action Alert, San Cristóbal, December 1, 1997, via Internet (www.nonviolence.org/sipaz).

29 Julia Preston, "Helmet Instead of a Miter for the Bishop of Chiapas," *New York Times*, June 16, 1998.
30 Centro de Derechos Humanos Fray Bartolomé de Las Casas, pp. 94–116.
31 Hermann Bellinghausen, *La Jornada*, December 1, 1998.
32 Chris Gilbreth, Global Exchange report, via Internet (globalexch@igc.org), November 1996.
33 *La Jornada*, March 31, 1997.
34 Ibid., January 23, 1998.
35 Ibid., November 24, 25, 26, 1997.
36 AP, January 16, 1999.
37 Author's telephone interview with George "Bud" Moore, United Church of Christ volunteer working in Chiapas at the time of the massacre, in Minneapolis, January 5, 1999.
38 *La Jornada*, December 30, 1997.
39 Ibid., December 28, 1997; Moore interview.
40 *La Jornada*, December 28, 1997.
41 Ibid., December 24, 1997.
42 Ibid., December 31, 1997.
43 Reuters, January 17, 1998.
44 Ibid.
45 Ibid.; *La Jornada*, January 2, 1998.
46 Julia Preston, "Mexican Police Blamed for Role in Massacre," *New York Times*, January 13, 1998.
47 Jesus Ramirez Cuevas, *Masiosare* (*La Jornada* Sunday magazine), February 22, 1998.
48 Ibid.
49 Julia Preston, "Chiapas Police Accused of Abetting Massacre," *New York Times*, January 24, 1998.
50 *La Jornada*, February 7, 1998.
51 Carlos Marin, "Plan del Ejercito en Chiapas . . ." *Proceso*, January 4, 1998.
52 Ibid.
53 Jaime Aviles, "Ruiz Ferro y los Paramilitares," *La Jornada/Masiosare*, December 21, 1997.
54 Brinley Bruton, *The News*, Mexico City, January 8, 1998.
55 Ross 1995, pp. 70–1, 157.
56 Darrin Wood, Nuevo Amanacer Press-Europa, December 28, 1997, via Internet (amanecer@aa.net).
57 *La Jornada*, December 26, 1997.
58 Jaime Aviles, *La Jornada*, January 10, 1998.
59 Ibid.
60 Centro de Infiormacion y Analisi de Chiapas (CIACH), Bulletin 81, November 19, 1997, via Internet (ciach@laneta.apc.org).
61 Congressman Joseph Kennedy, "Dear Colleague" letter, "SOA Graduates' Fingerprints On Mexico's Chiapas Policy," January 12, 1998.
62 Ibid.
63 Ibid.
64 Ibid.
65 AP, April 2, 1998; *La Jornada*, April 3, 1998; Reuters, April 4, 1998.
66 AP, January 23, 1998.
67 Ibid.
68 *La Jornada*, December 30, 1997.
69 *The News*, Mexico City, January 3, 1998.
70 EZLN communiqué, January 2, 1998.

9 DIRTY WAR OF ATTRITION

1 AFP, January 5, 1998; Reuters, January 4, 1998.
2 AFP, January 5, 1998; Reuters, January 4, 1998.
3 AFP, January 5, 1998; Reuters, January 4, 1998; AP, January 8, 1998.
4 *Acteal, Estrategia de Muerte* (video), Canal 6 de Julio, Mexico City, January 1998.
5 *La Jornada*, January 4, 9, 1998.
6 Reuters, January 12, 1998.
7 *La Jornada*, January 13, 1998.
8 Geoffrey Mohan, "Unraveling a Mexican Mystery," *Long Island Newsday*, October 2, 1998.
9 Ibid.
10 Blanche Petrich, *La Jornada*, November 24, 1997; *La Cronica*, December 26, 1997.
11 Barry 1992, p. 43.
12 *La Jornada*, December 27, 1997.
13 Ibid.
14 FZLN News Summaries, June 2, 1997, via Internet (joshua@peak.org).
15 FZLN News Summaries, February 14, 1997, via Internet (joshua@peak.org).
16 Ibid.
17 *La Jornada*, September 12, 1998.
18 Reuters, February 18, 1998.
19 *New York Times*, February 28, 1998.
20 *La Jornada*, September 15, 1998.
21 Reuters, May 13, 1998.
22 *Acteal, Estrategia de Muerte*, Canal 6 de Julio, Mexico City, January 1998.
23 Julia Preston, *New York Times*, July 12, 1998.
24 Womack 1999, p. 176.
25 Tom Buckley, *The News*, Mexico City, April 16, 1998.
26 AP, April 15, 1998.
27 Ibid.; Reuters, April 15, 1998.
28 Autonomous Municipality Ricardo Flores Magón communiqué, July 2, 1998.
29 Ibid., June 3, 1998.
30 *Mexpaz Weekly Bulletin*, April 30–May 6, Centro de Derechos Humanos Miguel Austin Pro-Juarez, Mexico City, via Internet (prodh@laneta.apc.org).
31 Michael McCaughan, *Irish Times*, May 3, 1998.
32 AP, July 6, 1998.
33 e.g., Autonomous Municipality San Pedro de Michoacan/Ejido Cruz del Rosario communiqué, June 14, 1998.
34 AP, June 3, 1998.
35 AP, June 11, 1998; *La Jornada*, June 11, 1998.
36 Molly Moore, *Washington Post*, August 3, 1998.
37 Ibid.
38 Reuters, January 9, 1998; *La Jornada*, January 14, 1998.
39 Author's observations.
40 John Ross, *Mexico Barbaro*, electronic newsletter (johnross@igc.apc.org), October 14, 1998.
41 Reuters, March 18, 1998.

42 Ross, *Mexico Barbaro*, October 14, 1998.
43 AP, May 20, 1998.
44 *Washington Post*, May 31, 1998.
45 *La Jornada*, May 17, 1998.
46 *New York Times*, May 18, 1998.
47 *La Jornada*, September 18, 1998.
48 William K. Stevens, "Storm Warning: Bigger Hurricanes and More of Them," *New York Times*, June 3, 1997.
49 *La Jornada*, September 13, 1998.
50 EZLN communiqué, September 12, 1998.
51 *Diario de Yucatan*, October 29, 1998.
52 *La Jornada*, November 29, 1998.
53 John Ross, "Big Pulp vs. Zapatistas," *Multinational Monitor*, April 1998.
54 *La Jornada*, November 23, 1998.
55 Julia Preston, *New York Times*, November 22, 1998.
56 Hermann Bellinghausen, *La Jornada*, November 24, 1998.
57 EZLN press release, November 26, 1998.
58 EZLN communiqué, October 27, 1998.
59 EZLN communiqué, December 14, 1998; *La Jornada*, December 15, 1998.
60 Molly Moore, *Washington Post*, July 29, 1998.
61 *La Jornada*, July 29, August 6, 1998.
62 Juan Balboa, *La Jornada*, December 16, 1998; Ginger Thompson, *New York Times*, December 23, 1998.
63 Ginger Thompson, *New York Times*, December 23, 1998.
64 Ibid.
65 Homily of Bishop Samuel Ruiz Garcia, Acteal, Chenalho, Chiapas, December 22, 1998.

10 "A REVOLUTION TO MAKE A REVOLUTION POSSIBLE"

1 EZLN communiqué, January 1998.
2 EZLN communiqué, July 1998.
3 EZLN communiqué, February 4, 1994.
4 LeBot, pp. 214–15.
5 Ibid., p. 241.
6 Ibid., pp. 256–7.
7 *New York Times*, February 27, 1994, quoted in Russell, p. 57.
8 Jesus Ramirez, "Rebel Leader Marcos Says 'Che Lives On' in Mexico," Reuters, August 28, 1997.
9 LeBot, p. 266.
10 Fourth Declaration of the Lacandon Selva, January 1996.
11 EZLN communiqué, August 29, 1996.
12 EZLN communiqué, June 1996.

13 EZLN communiqué, July 1, 1997.
14 "Durito IV: Neoliberalism and the Party-State System," Marcos communiqué, May 1995, printed in *La Jornada*, June 11, 1995.
15 "The Seven Loose Pieces of the Global Jigsaw Puzzle," Marcos communiqué, June 1997.
16 Riordan Roett, "Mexico—Political Update," Chase Manhattan Bank's Emerging Markets Group, January 13, 1995, reported in *Counterpunch*, Washington DC, February 1, 1995.
17 Ross 1995, p. 170; Marcos interview, *La Jornada*, February 4–7, 1994, reprinted in *La Palabra de los Armados de Verdad y Fuego*, p. 154.
18 Marcos interview, January 1997, videotaped and conducted by Kerry Appel, via Internet (kappel1@ix.netcom.com).
19 Tim Golden, "The Voice of the Rebels Has Mexicans in His Spell," *New York Times*, February 8, 1994.
20 *Proceso*, February 14, 1994.
21 *The Dallas Morning News*, July 24, 1998.
22 *¡Zapatistas! Documents of the New Mexican Revolution*, pp. 296, 300.
23 Marcos interview, *La Jornada*, February 4–7, 1994, reprinted in *La Palabra de los Armados de Verdad y Fuego*, p. 153.
24 *New York Times*, January 4, 1999.
25 e.g. EZLN communiqué, September 12, 1997.
26 *La Jornada*, February 25, 1997.
27 Maggie O'Kane, "The Hi-Tech Robin Hood," *The Guardian* (London), February 20, 1995.
28 EZLN communiqué, May 28, 1994.
29 Knight, vol. 2, p. 279; Lister and Lister, p. 271.
30 See Weinberg, pp. 88–90.
31 John Ross, "Save a Rainforest, Start a Revolution," *Sierra*, San Francisco, July/August 1994.
32 Revolutionary Laws, *¡Zapatistas! Documents of the New Mexican Revolution*, p. 53.
33 Weinberg, p. 72.
34 See ibid., pp. 114, 121.
35 See Andrew Revkin, *The Burning Season: The Murder of Chico Mendes and the Fight for the Amazon Rain Forest*, Houghton Mifflin, Boston 1990.
36 See Judith Kimerling, *Amazon Crude*, Natural Resources Defense Council, New York, 1991.
37 Alejandro Toledo Ocampo, "Hacia una economia politica de la biodiversidad y de los movimientos ecologicos comunitarios," *Chiapas #5*, Instituto de Investigaciones Economicas, UNAM 1998.
38 Revolutionary Laws, *¡Zapatistas! Documents of the New Mexican Revolution*, p. 52.
39 EZLN communiqué, January 26, 1994.
40 *¡Zapatistas! Documents of the New Mexican Revolution*, pp. 292–3.
41 EZLN communiqué, January 6, 1994.
42 EZLN communiqué, April 10, 1995.
43 Brundage, pp. 113–17.
44 Paz, p. 144.
45 "The Southeast in Two Winds: A Storm and a Prophecy," Marcos communiqué, published in *La Jornada*, January 27, 1994.
46 See Brundage, pp. 28–9; Schele and Freidel, pp. 429–30; Wolf 1959, pp. 144–5.
47 "The Southeast in Two Winds."
48 Ross 1995, p. 287; Castañeda 1995, p. 86.
49 Castañeda 1994, pp. 427–76.

50 *La Jornada*, May 5, 1995.

51 Comision Internacional de Enlace de la Consulta del EZLN statement, August 1995.

52 *La Jornada*, February 11, 1998.

53 Harry Cleaver, "The Zapatistas and the Electronic Fabric of Struggle" in Holloway, p. 99.

54 La Botz 1995, p. 65.

55 Ross 1998, p. 239.

11 OIL AND RESISTANCE IN TABASCO

1 Author's interviews, Villahermosa, January 1997.

2 *Los Derechos Humanos en Tabasco*, annual bulletin, CODEHUTAB, Villahermosa 1996; *La Verdad del Sureste*, Villahermosa, November 17, 1996.

3 Author's interviews with Raymundo Sauri, Santo Tomas Ecological Association, Villahermos, January 1997.

4 *Human Rights and Environment in Tabasco*, Global Exchange delegation report, San Francisco 1996; Moguel, pp. 1–5.

5 Ibid.; Raymundo Sauri interviews.

6 Ibid.; *Human Rights and Environment in Tabasco*.

7 *La Verdad del Sureste*, Villahermosa, March 6, 1996; Raymundo Sauri interview.

8 Moguel, p. 4.

9 Ibid., pp. 29–30; Raymundo Sauri interview.

10 *La Jornada*, February 19, 1996; *Presente*, Villahermosa, February 19, 1996; *Human Rights and Environment in Tabasco*.

11 Alvaro Delgado, Gerardo Albarran de Alba and Armando Guzmán, "PEMEX en Tabasco," *Proceso*, February 19, 1996; *Los Derechos Humanos en Tabasco*.

12 *Human Rights and Environment in Tabasco*.

13 *Los Derechos Humanos en Tabasco*, op cit.

14 Author's observation.

15 Delgado, *et al.*, *Proceso*, February 19, 1996.

16 Andres Oppenheimer, "Mexican Oil Company's Blasts Trigger National Debate," *Miami Herald*, November 15, 1996.

17 *New York Times*, April 27, 1992.

18 Andres Oppenheimer, *Miami Herald*, November 15, 1996; Riding, p. 243.

19 *La Verdad del Sureste*, Villahermosa, March 6, 1996.

20 *La Jornada*, September 5, 1996.

21 Moguel, p. 30.

22 CNDH Recommendation 100/92, May 21, 1990.

23 Ibid.; *Los Derechos Humanos en Tabasco*.

24 *Human Rights and Environment in Tabasco*.

25 UPI World Issues: "Oil Pollution in Mexico," April 10, 1996.

26 Ibid.

27 *La Verdad del Sureste*, Villahermosa, February 1, 1996.

28 *La Jornada*, September 5, 1996; *Los Derechos Humanos en Tabasco*.

29　*La Verdad del Sureste*, Villahermosa, March 6, 1996.

30　*Los Derechos Humanos en Tabasco.*

31　Sam Dillon, "Protestors Blockading Pemex Oil Wells," *New York Times*, February 1, 1996.

32　Sunita Chethik, "Campesinos in Tabasco Demand Compensation for Contamination by Pemex Oil Wells," Global Exchange report, February 17, 1996; Amnesty International Urgent Action Appeal, February 13, 1996; *La Verdad del Sureste*, Villahermosa, February 8, 1996.

33　*La Jornada*, February 6, 1996; *New York Times*, February 10, 1996; Reuters, January 31, 1996.

34　*La Jornada*, February 8, 1996; *Proceso*, February 19, 1996.

35　*La Verdad del Sureste*, Villahermosa, February 18, 1996.

36　*La Jornada*, February 6, 1996; *La Verdad del Sureste*, Villahermosa, February 9, 13, 1996.

37　*Presente*, Villahermosa, February 11, 1996.

38　Ibid., February 13, 1996.

39　"Opposition Protests Violently Repressed in Tabasco, Mexico," Fellowship of Reconciliation/ Resource Center for Nonviolence Action Alert, Santa Cruz, CA, February 1996; *New York Times*, February 10, 1996; *Presente*, Villahermosa, February 11, 1996.

40　*La Verdad del Sureste*, Villahermosa, February 23, 25, 1996.

41　Ibid., March 5, 1996.

42　Amnesty International Urgent Action Appeal, March 8, 1996; *Los Derechos Humanos en Tabasco.*

43　*Human Rights and Environment in Tabasco.*

44　*Cuarto Poder*, Tuxtla Gutiérrez, June 6, 1996.

45　*La Jornada*, June 26, 1996; AP, June 26, 1996; author's interviews with witnesses, Villahermosa, January 1997.

46　*La Jornada*, June 26, 1996.

47　*Analisis de Coyuntura del Mes de Julio de 1996*, CODEHUTAB bulletin.

48　Andres Oppenheimer, *Miami Herald*, November 15, 1996.

49　*La Jornada*, January 26, 1997.

50　Author's observations.

51　CODEHUTAB update, April 1997, via Internet (codehutab@laneta.apc.org).

52　Delgado, *et al.*, *Proceso*, February 19, 1996.

53　Author's interviews with witnesses, Simón Sarlat and Villahermosa, January 1997.

54　Raymundo Sauri interviews.

55　Moguel, pp. 14–18.

56　Ibid., pp. 35–6; "Oil Pollution in Mexico," UPI, April 10, 1996.

57　Roberto Thompson Gonzalez, *Explotacion Petrolera y Problematica Agraria en el Sureste de México*, Centro de Investigaciones Ecologicas del Sureste (CIES), San Cristóbal de Las Casas, Chiapas, 1980, pp. 156–66.

58　*La Jornada*, May 15, 1996.

59　*La Verdad del Sureste*, Villahermosa, July 3, 1996.

60　*La Jornada*, October 1, 1995.

61　*Analisis de Coyuntura del Mes de Julio de 1996*, CODEHUTAB bulletin.

62　*Reserva de la Biosfera Pantanos de Centla*, pamphlet, SEMARNAP, Delegacion Federal Tabasco.

63　*National Geographic*, October 1989.

64　*Reserva de la Biosfera Pantanos de Centla.*

65　Author's interviews; PROFEPA report on file with Hugo Ireta, Villahermosa.

66　Pemex maps on file with Hugo Ireta, Villahermosa.

67 Comision Para el Desarrollo de Las Zonas Petroleras del Estado de Tabasco, 1993, report on file with Hugo Ireta, Villahermosa.

68 PROFEPA finding on file with Hugo Ireta, Villahermosa.

69 "Programa de Perforacion, Pozo: Gualas I," internal Pemex map provided by confidential source.

70 *La Jornada*, July 9, 1996.

71 Ibid., January 20, 1995; *New York Times*, January 22, 1995.

72 AFP, June 3, 1995.

73 "Opposition Protests Violently Repressed in Tabasco, Mexico," Fellowship of Reconciliation/ Resource Center for Nonviolence Action Alert, Santa Cruz, CA, February 1996; *New York Times*, June 7, 1996.

74 Voice of America, August 21, 1995.

75 *New York Times*, June 7, 1996; *La Jornada*, July 16, 1996.

76 *La Verdad del Sureste*, Villahermosa, June 8, 1996.

77 *El Financiero International Edition*, September 12–18, 1994.

78 Ibid.

79 Ibid.

80 Christopher Whalen, *The Mexico Report*, Legal Research International, Washington DC, September 2, 1996.

81 *El Financiero International Edition*, September 12–18, 1994.

82 *New York Times*, June 21, 1990.

83 Bloomberg Business News Service, February 14, 1996.

84 Whalen, *The Mexico Report*, September 2, 1996; *Wall Street Journal*, January 23, 1997.

85 *El Financiero International Edition*, September 12–18, 1994.

86 *The Wall Street Journal*, January 23, 1997.

87 Ibid.; *Washington Post*, October 21, 1998.

88 Christopher Whalen, *The Mexico Report*, Legal Research International, Washington DC, October 7, 1994.

89 *Wall Street Journal*, January 23, 1997.

90 Bloomberg Business News Service, February 14, 1996.

91 Christopher Whalen, *The Mexico Report*, Legal Research International, Washington DC, October 7, 1994.

92 "Cronologia," *La Jornada*, January 20, 1997.

93 Ibid.; *La Reforma*, January 16, 1997; *La Jornada*, January 17, 1997.

94 *La Jornada*, January 20, 1997; *Tabasco Hoy*, Villahermosa, January 20, 1997; *The News*, Mexico City, January 26, 1997.

95 *La Verdad del Sureste*, Villahermosa, January 25, 1997.

96 Ibid., January 17, 1997.

97 *La Jornada*, February 26, 1996; *La Verdad del Sureste*, Villahermosa, February 26, 27, 1996.

98 *La Jornada*, April 12, 1996.

99 *La Verdad del Sureste*, Villahermosa, June 8, 1996.

100 *La Jornada*, May 14, 1996.

101 *Analisis de Coyuntura del Mes de Julio de 1996*, CODEHUTAB bulletin; author's interview with Manlio Cobos, CODEHUTAB, Villahermosa, January 1997.

102 Armando Guzman, *Proceso*, September 8, 1996.

103 *La Jornada*, September 5, 1996.

104 *Proceso*, September 8, 1996.

105 Ibid.

106 *La Jornada*, September 6, 1996.

107 Ibid., September 14, 1996.

108 Salvador Corro, "Operativos militares en casi todo el pais," *Proceso*, September 8, 1996; *La Jornada*, September 5, 1996.

109 Ibid., April 1, 1996.

110 Ibid., November 22, 1996.

111 *La Verdad del Sureste*, Villahermosa, February 21, 1996.

112 *The Economist*, March 4, 1995.

113 *Analisis de Coyuntura del Mes de Julio de 1996*, CODEHUTAB bulletin.

114 *Presente*, Villahermosa, March 21, 1996.

115 *Christian Science Monitor*, January 22, 1999.

116 Reuters, December 15, 1996.

117 Barry 1992, p. 136.

118 *Wall Street Journal*, January 20, 1992; Barry 1992, p. 138; Manzo Yépez, p. 109.

119 Manzo Yépez, p. 114.

120 *Wall Street Journal*, June 19, 1996.

121 *La Jornada*, January 15, 1995.

122 *New York Times*, January 12, 1989.

123 Ibid., December 17, 1997.

124 La Botz 1992, pp. 108–13; *La Jornada*, January 18, 1994; author's interviews with Francisco Castillo, Villahermosa, January 1997.

125 Siobhan McGrath, "'Workers in Trust' in Mexico: Neoliberalism's Re-definition," School for International Training, World Issues Program, Brattleboro VT, Spring 1998.

126 Author's interviews with Francisco Castillo, Villahermosa, January 1997.

127 Ibid.

128 Manzo Yépez, p. 38.

129 Thompson Gonzalez, *Explotacion Petrolera y Problematica Agraria en el Sureste de México*, p. 61.

130 Ibid.; Delgado, *et al.*, *Proceso*, February 19, 1996.

131 *El Universal*, February 3, 1997.

132 Wendy Call, "Corridor of Destruction," *Multinational Monitor*, November 1997.

133 *La Jornada*, January 22, 24, 1997.

134 *New York Times*, October 14, 1996.

135 *El Nacional*, February 3, 1997; *El Universal*, February 3, 1997.

136 Manzo Yépez, pp. 125–32.

137 *La Verdad del Sureste*, Villahermosa, March 2, 1996.

138 Ibid., March 1, 1996.

139 Robert Collier, *San Francisco Chronicle*, February 21, 1997.

140 *El Universal*, February 3, 1997.

141 *The News*, Mexico City, June 2, 1996.

142 Manzo Yépez, pp. 34–5, 83.

143 Ibid., pp. 76–7.

144 *Wall Street Journal*, June 19, 1996.

145 Manzo Yépez, pp. 78–81.

146 Ibid., p. 89.

147 Reuters, August 4, 1996; *San Francisco Examiner*, September 25, 1996.

148 *La Jornada*, January 16, 1997.

149 *La Reforma*, January 16, 1997.

150 John Saxe-Fernandez, *Petroleo y Estrategia, México y Estados Unidos en el Contexto de la Politica Global*, Siglo XXI, Mexico City, 1980, p. 31, cited in Manzo Yépez, p. 55.

151 Manzo Yépez, pp. 30–3; Barry 1992, pp. 286, 317.

152 Jonathan Kwitney, "The Mexican Connection: A Look at an Old George Bush Business Venture," *Barron's*, September 19, 1988; Riding, pp. 241–7.

153 *New York Times*, February 12, 1991; Manzo Yépez, p. 94.

154 *Washington Post*, March 21, 1998; *New York Times*, July 9, 1998.

155 *New York Times*, January 25, 1988.

156 *Time*, January 16, 1995.

157 *Time*, February 1, 1996.

158 *Presente*, Villahermosa, February 12, 1996.

159 Thompson Gonzalez, *Explotacion Petrolera y Problematica Agraria en el Sureste de Mexico*, p. 61.

160 Ibid., p. 64.

161 Barry 1992, p. 139.

162 Ross 1995, pp. 30, 266.

163 *Excelsior*, March 22, 1997, from Italian magazine *Limes*.

164 Reuters, August 23, 1999.

165 Sauri interview, op cit.

166 *La Verdad del Sureste*, Villahermosa, March 5, 1996.

167 Ibid., September 22, 1996.

168 UPI, July 14, 1996.

169 *La Jornada*, January 24, 1997; *Tabasco Hoy*, Villahermosa, January 24, 1997; *Novedades de Tabasco*, Villahermosa, January 24, 1997.

170 *Novedades de Tabasco*, Villahermosa, January 24, 1997.

171 Reuters, October 20, 1997.

172 Reuters, March 29, 1997.

173 LaborNet Action Alert, February 18, 1998 (www.labournet.org.uk).

174 Amnesty International Urgent Action Alert, December 9, 1998.

175 SERPAJ update, February 3, 1999.

176 Ibid.

177 *New York Times,* June 24, 1999.

178 *Washington Post,* December 26, 1999.

179 *New York Times,* October 25, 1999.

180 *Financial Times,* October 12, 1999; *Washington Post,* October 12, 1999.

181 Sauri interviews, op. cit.

12 GUARDIANS OF TEHUANTEPEC

1 Author's interviews with striking teachers, Oaxaca, December 1994.

2 *La Jornada*, February 29, 1996.

3 Ibid., November 25, 1995.

4 Ibid., February 29, 1996, June 1, 1997.
5 Serpaj Europa Action Alert, December 27, 1998.
6 Ibid., October 6, 1996.
7 Ibid., October 28, 1995.
8 Scott Robinson, "The Politics of Resettlement: Dams and Campesino Resistance to State Encroachment," in Howard and Ross, pp. 113–24.
9 Marcelino Diaz de Jesus, *et al.*, *La autonomia y el movimiento indigena en Guerrero*, Convergencia Socialista, Mexico City, 1997.
10 Ibid.; author's interview with Armando Mojica, Federal District Environment Secretariat, Mexico City, November 1998.
11 Reuters, April 7, 1996.
12 *La Jornada*, January 27, 1997.
13 Ibid., June 28, 1997.
14 Ce-Acatl, A.C. press release, Mexico City, June 1998.
15 Ibid.
16 Ayuntamiento Constitucional Indigena de Mazatlan Villa de Flores press release, June 18, 1998.
17 *La Jornada*, September 11, 1996, January 20, 1998.
18 Riding, p. 304.
19 Hodges, p. 39.
20 Ibid., p. 54.
21 Ibid., p. 57.
22 Ibid., pp. 58–61.
23 Ibid., pp. 61–2.
24 Ibid., pp. 63–4.
25 Ibid., pp. 65–7; Fuentes, pp. 45–59.
26 Hodges, pp. 94–7.
27 Ibid., pp. 28–9.
28 Ibid., pp. 28–9, 101; Miranda Ramirez, pp.11, 92.
29 Hodges, p. 97; Castañeda 1994, p. 88.
30 David LaFrance, "The Regional Nature of Maderismo," in Benjamin and Wasserman, p. 22.
31 Womack 1968, pp. 122–33.
32 Ibid., p. 171; LaFrance, "The Regional Nature of Maderismo," p. 33.
33 Thomas Benjamin, "Laboratories of the New State, 1920–1929," in Benjamin and Wasserman, p. 80.
34 Hodges, p. 99.
35 Ibid., p. 100.
36 Ibid., p. 103; Miranda Ramirez, p. 113.
37 Hodges, pp. 95, 100.
38 Poniatowska, p. 244.
39 Hodges, pp. 138–42.
40 Romero Jacobo, p. 140; Ross 1995, p. 273.
41 Ross 1995, p. 278.
42 Joseph Frazier, "Rights Commission Comes Down Hard on State Government after Massacre," AP, August 14, 1998.
43 Reuters, June 29, 1995; *Washington Post*, June 30, 1995.
44 Joseph Frazier, AP, August 14, 1998.

45 Ibid.

46 *La Jornada*, June 28, 1997.

47 Guerrero 500 Years of Indigenous Resistance Council press release, June 29, 1995.

48 Philip True, *San Antonio Express-News*, October 29, 1995.

49 *La Jornada*, March 10, 1996.

50 Ibid., February 20, 1996.

51 Ibid., January 16, 1997.

52 *El Diario,* Chihuahua, May 5, 1998.

53 John Ross, "Treasure of the Costa Grande," distributed by the Native Forest Network, Burlington, VT, September 6, 1996.

54 BBC, October 13, 1995; *Idaho Statesman*, December 18, 1998.

55 John Ross, "Treasure of the Costa Grande."

56 Ibid.

57 AP, October 15, 1997.

58 Parkes, p. 247.

59 John Tutino, "Ethnic Resistance: Juchitan in Mexican History," in Campbell, *et al.*, p. 57.

60 Parkes, p. 247.

61 Weinberg, pp. 74, 126.

62 Leigh Binford, "Irrigation, Land Tenure, and Class Struggle in Juchitan, Oaxaca," in Campbell, *et al.*, pp. 87–100.

63 Jeffrey Rubin, "COCEI Against the State: A Political History of Juchitan," in Campbell, *et al.*, pp. 157–75.

64 Frank Wadsworth, US Institute of Tropical Forestry, quoted in James D. Nations and H. Jeffrey Leonard, "Grounds of Conflict in Central America," in Maguire and Brown, cited in Weinberg, pp. 129–30.

65 Howard LaFranchi, "Mexico Wants Its Own 'Panama Canal'—Without US," *Christian Science Monitor*, Mexico edition, September 4, 1996.

66 Ibid.

67 Ibid.

68 Ibid.

69 Wendy Call, "Corridor of Destruction," *Multinational Monitor*, November 1997.

70 Ibid.

71 Humberto Rios Navarrete, "El megaproyecto de Tehuantepec," *Proceso*, May 10, 1998.

72 *Multinational Monitor*, November 1997.

73 John Ross, "Planners Aim for a 'Little Taiwan' in the Jungle," Gemeni News Service, July 26, 1996.

74 Ibid.

75 *Multinational Monitor*, November 1997.

76 "El Istmo ed Nuestro" declaration, February 22, 1997.

77 *La Jornada*, January 4, 1997.

78 Paul Garner, "Oaxaca: The Rise and Fall of State Sovereignty," in Benjamin and Wasserman, pp. 163–83; Macario Matus, "Juchitan Political Movements," in Campbell, *et al.*, pp. 125–8.

79 Binford, "Irrigation, Land Tenure, and Class Struggle in Juchitan, Oaxaca."

80 Rubin, "COCEI Against the State: A Political History of Juchitan."

81 Sergio Zermaño, "COCEI: Narodniks of Southern Mexico?" in Campbell, *et al.*, pp. 191–202.

82 Ibid.

83 Ibid.
84 Alejandro Toldedo Ocampo, "Hacia una economia politica de la biodiversidad y de los movimientos ecologicos comunitarios," *Chiapas #5*, Instituto de Investigaciones Economicas, UNAM, 1998.
85 Robinson, "The Politics of Resettlement: Dams and Campesino Resistance to State Encroachment."
86 Matilda Pérez U., *La Jornada*, February 3, 1997.
87 Luis Hernandez Navarro, *La Jornada*, December 27, 1995.
88 Robert Collier, *San Francisco Chronicle*, December 10, 1996.
89 Ibid., May 31, 1996.
90 *La Jornada*, June 28, 1996.
91 Robert Collier, *San Francisco Chronicle*, December 10, 1996.

13 THE GOLF WAR OF TEPOZTLAN

1 Lewis 1960, p. 16; Redfield, pp. 23–5.
2 Salvador Aguilar Benitez, *El Ecoturismo en el Estado de Morelos,* Centro de Estudios Historicos y Sociales del Estado de Morelos, Cuernavaca, 1994, p. 22.
3 Author's interview with ecologist Armando Mojica, Cuernavaca, April 1996.
4 Mallon, pp. 137 8.
5 Ibid., p. 139; Womack 1969, p. 162; Newell, p. 129.
6 Raul Benet, "Tepoztlan: saldos de una lucha social," *del Campo*, special supplement of *La Jornada*, May 3, 1996.
7 Benitez, *El Ecoturismo en el Estado de Morelos, Centro de Estudios Historicos y Sociales del Estado de Morelos*, pp. 37–40.
8 Ibid.; Armando Mojica interview.
9 Benitez, *El Ecoturismo en el Estado de Morelos, Centro de Estudios Historicos y Sociales del Estado de Morelos*, pp. 37–40; Armando Mojica interview.
10 Armando Mojica interview.
11 Author's interviews with Tepoztlan *ejidatarios* and Ayuntamiento Libre officials, April 1996.
12 "CUT Cronologia," *Tepoztlan Rebelde*, solidarity bulletin, Cuernavaca, May 1, 1996, distributed via Internet as "Brief History of the Struggle of the People of Tepoztlan," by Global Exchange, San Francisco, April 23, 1998 (globalexch@igc.apc.org).
13 Alberto Ruz Buenfil, "Tepoztlan: Eight Months Later . . . The Struggle Continues," Huehuecoyotl, Tepoztlan, April 14, 1996, via Internet (www.traverse.com).
14 Mojica interview.
15 CUT statement, Tepoztlan, October 1995; Mojica interview.
16 Armando Mojica Toldedo, "Los daños y efectos ambientales de un club de golf," Espacio Verde, Cuernavaca, October 1995.
17 CUT statement, Tepoztlan, October 1995.
18 *Tepoztlan Rebelde*; author's interview with Alberto Ruz Buenfil, Tepoztlan, April 1996.
19 *Tepoztlan Rebelde*; Ruz Buenfil interview.
20 *Tepoztlan Rebelde*; Ruz Buenfil interview.
21 *Tepoztlan Rebelde*; Ruz Buenfil interview.
22 *Tepoztlan Rebelde*; Ruz Buenfil interview.

23 *Tepoztlan Rebelde*; Ruz Buenfil interview.

24 *Tepoztlan Rebelde*; Ruz Buenfil interview.

25 *Tepoztlan Rebelde*; Ruz Buenfil interview.

26 CUT statement, Tepoztlan, October 1995.

27 *Tepoztlan Rebelde*.

28 Ibid.

29 *La Jornada*, October 1, 1995.

30 Author's observations.

31 See Redfield, pp. 69–132.

32 Author's observations, Tepoztlan, April 1996.

33 Rosas, p. 58.

34 Author's observations, Tepoztlan, April 1996.

35 Author's interview, Tepoztlan, April 1996.

36 Raul Benet, "Tepoztlan: saldos de una lucha social," *del Campo*, special supplement of *La Jornada*, May 3, 1996.

37 Francisco Ortiz Pinchetti, *Proceso*, April 29, 1996.

38 *Tepoztlan Rebelde*, op cit; author's interview with Ruz Buenfil, Tepoztlan, April 1996.

39 Laura Carlsen, "Sand Trapped in Paradise," *Business Mexico*, Houston, November 1995.

40 CUT statement, Tepoztlan, October 1995.

41 *Uno Mas Uno*, December 23, 1995.

42 Ibid.

43 Armando Mojica Toldedo, "Trampa en Tepoztlan: Argumentos técnico-administrivos para apoyar el rechazoal proyecto Club de Golf 'El Tepozteco,'" Espacio Verde, Cuernavaca, October 1995.

44 *Uno Mas Uno*, December 23, 1995.

45 *Tepoztlan Rebelde*.

46 *Proceso*, December 12, 1995.

47 Author's interview with Salvador Aguilar Benitez, Cuernavaca, April 1996.

48 *Tepoztlan Rebelde*.

49 Ruz Buenfil interview.

50 *La Jornada*, September 25, 1995.

51 Francisco Ortiz Pinchetti, *Proceso*, April 29, 1996.

52 *Tepoztlan Rebelde*; Ruz Buenfil interview.

53 *Tepoztlan Rebelde*; Ruz Buenfil interview.

54 *Tepoztlan Rebelde*; Ruz Buenfil interview.

55 *La Jornada*, January 20, 1996.

56 Ibid., December 26, 1995; *Tepoztlan Rebelde*.

57 *Tepoztlan Rebelde*.

58 Center for the Study of Responsive Law press release, Washington DC, February 14, 1996.

59 Ibid.

60 Ibid.

61 *Los Pueblos Indios en Morelos: Sus Derechos Tradicionales y la Imparticion de Justica*, Comision Independente de Derechos Humanos de Morelos, Cuernavaca, January/February 1996.

62 *La Jornada*, January 20, 1996.

63 *Tepoztlan Rebelde*.

64 John Ross, *Mexico Barbaro*, electronic newsletter (johnross@igc.apc.org), April 24–May 4, 1996.

65 Alberto Ruz Buenfil, "Tepoztlan: Eight Months Later . . . The Struggle Continues," Huehuecoyotl, Tepoztlan, April 14, 1996, via Internet (www.traverse.com).
66 Ibid.
67 Ibid.
68 Ibid.; Reuters, April 12, 1996; *La Jornada*, April 13, 1996.
69 Ruz Buenfil, "Tepoztlan: Eight Months Later . . . The Struggle Continues."
70 Augustin Ambriz and Fernando Ortega Pizarro, *Proceso*, April 15, 1996.
71 Reuters, April 12, 1996; *La Jornada*, April 13, 1996.
72 Ruz Buenfil, "Tepoztlan: Eight Months Later . . . The Struggle Continues."
73 *La Jornada*, April 13, 1996.
74 Ibid.; author's interview with Armando Mojica.
75 UPI, April 12, 1996.
76 Ruz Buenfil, "Tepoztlan: Eight Months Later . . . The Struggle Continues."
77 Global Anti-Golf Movement press release, Penang, Malaysia, 1996.
78 *La Jornada*, April 14, 1996.
79 *Diario de Morelos*, Cuernavaca, May 14, 1996.
80 Lewis 1951, pp. 114–17.
81 Mojica interview.
82 Ibid.
83 *Diario de Morelos*, Cuernavaca, May 22, 1996.
84 Ibid., May 25, 1996.
85 Mojica interview.
86 Miguel Angel Juarez, "Tepoztlan: un pueblo en resistencia," *La Reforma*, May 21, 1996.
87 Ibid.
88 Rodolfo Stavenhagen, *La Jornada*, December 26, 1995.
89 Jo Bedingfield, *San Francisco Chronicle*, November 12, 1995.
90 Ibid.
91 Mojica interview.
92 *Los Pueblos Indios en Morelos: Sus Derechos Tradicionales y la Imparticion de Justica*, Comision Independiente de Derechos Humanos de Morelos, Cuernavaca, January/February 1996.
93 Mojica interview.
94 Ibid.
95 Ibid.
96 Ibid.
97 Antonio Garcia de Leon, *La Jornada*, December 2, 1995; Mojica interview.
98 EZLN communiqué, September 10, 1995.
99 Fernando Meraz, "Narcolavado, el lado oscuro de El Teposteco," *El Financiero*, April 28, 1996.
100 Ibid.
101 Ibid.; Mojica interview.
102 Meraz, "Narcolavado, el lado oscuro de El Teposteco"; Alfonso Sanchez Luna, "Cuernavaca, refugio de narcos," *El Financiero*, April 28, 1996.
103 Meraz, "Narcolavado, el lado oscuro de El Teposteco."
104 Jesus Aranda, *La Jornada*, November 30, 1995; Mojica interview.
105 Antonio Garcia de Leon, *La Jornada*, April 13, 1996.
106 Mojica interview.

107 Ibid.; Antonio Garcia de Leon, *La Jornada*, December 1, 1995.

108 Mojica interview.

109 Ibid.; Espacio Verde press release, Cuernavaca, June 27, 1995.

110 Mojica interview.

111 *La Jornada*, February 3, 1997.

112 *New York Times*, February 23, 1997.

113 *La Reforma*, January 18, 1997.

114 *New York Times*, February 10, 1998.

115 Ibid.

116 *Los Angeles Times*, May 19, 1998.

117 *New York Times*, March 18, 1997; author's telephone interview with Armando Mojica, December 1998.

118 *New York Times*, March 18, 1997; author's telephone interview with Armando Mojica, December 1998.

119 Redfield, pp. 208–9.

120 Mojica interview.

121 Thomas Outerbridge, "The Disappearing Chinampas of Xochimilco," *The Ecologist* (London), 17, no. 2/3, 1987.

122 *La Jornada*, October 2, 1996.

123 Sam Dillon, "Capital's Downfall Caused by Drinking . . . of Water," *New York Times*, January 29, 1998.

124 SIPAZ Action Alert, Mexico City, January 30, 1997, via Internet (www.nonviolence.org/sipaz).

14 FIRE IN THE SIERRA MADRE DEL SUR

1 Fazio 1996, pp. 232–3; Ross 1998, p. 269.

2 Reuters, August 9, 30, 1996.

3 Fazio 1996, p. 233.

4 Julia Preston, "New Group in Mexico Affirms Rebel Status," *New York Times*, August 10, 1996.

5 Ibid.

6 Reuters, August 29, 1996.

7 Preston, "New Group in Mexico Affirms Rebel Status."

8 Sam Dillon, "Mexico Builds Picture of a Fanatical Rebel Group," *New York Times*, September 5, 1996.

9 Laurell, p. 19.

10 Dillon, "Mexico Builds Picture of a Fanatical Rebel Group."

11 Gross, pp. 123–4; Hodges, p. 194; Miranda, p. 172.

12 Gross, pp. 123–4.

13 Ibid.

14 Iganacio Ramirez, *Proceso*, September 1, 1996.

15 *La Jornada*, January 9, 1994.

16 EZLN communiqué, June 3, 1994.

17 *Proceso*, January 17, 1994.

18 Salvador Corr, "En una noche de terror, las fuerzas del EPR destruyeron el mito de la pantomima," *Proceso*, September 1, 1996.

19 Ibid.

20 Ibid.

21 Ibid.

22 Ibid.

23 Ibid.

24 *Wall Street Journal*, September 3, 1996.

25 Fazio 1996, p. 237; Alma Guillermoprieto, "The Unmasking," *The New Yorker*, March 13, 1995.

26 Reuters, July 5, 1998.

27 Dillon, "Mexico Builds Picture of a Fanatical Rebel Group."

28 Sam Dillon, "Rebel Group is Hunted in 7 States in Mexico," *New York Times*, August 31, 1996.

29 Anita Snow, AP, February 7, 1997.

30 Julia Preston, "Rebels in Mexico Resume Raids," *New York Times*, November 2, 1996.

31 Steve Fainaru, "Guerrillas Find Paradise," *Boston Globe*, September 10, 1996.

32 Julia Preston, "Mexican Leader Vows to Fight New Guerilla Violence," *New York Times*, September 2, 1996.

33 Julia Preston, "Mexico's Army Out of the Barracks," *New York Times*, September 14, 1996.

34 *La Jornada*, August 31, 1996.

35 *New York Times*, February 13, 1997.

36 Razhy Gonzalez, Reuters, June 30, 1997.

37 Harris Whitbeck, "Mexico's EPR Guerrillas Pressure Government at Gunpoint," CNN, July 1, 1997.

38 Che Guevara, "Guerilla Warfare: A Method," in Mallin, p. 92.

39 Joel Simon, "Mexican Army Escalates Patrols in Reputed Rebel Stronghold," Pacific News Service, August 28, 1996.

40 Aid and Defense Committee of Indigenous Pueblos and Communities (CODACPI) press release, Mexico City, March 27, 1998.

41 Hugo Pacheco Leon, *La Jornada*, January 14, 1997.

42 Francisco Lopez Barcenas, *La Jornada*, January 22, 1997.

43 José Gil Olmos, *La Jornada*, December 26, 1996; Mark Stevenson, AP, August 27, 1997.

44 Nuevo Amanacer Press, Madrid, November 10, 1996, via Internet (amanacer@cyberspace.com).

45 Robert Collier, "Mexico Casts Wide Net for Elusive Rebels," *San Francisco Chronicle*, December 10, 1996.

46 Ibid.

47 José Gil Olmos, *La Jornada*, December 26, 1996.

48 Maribel Gutiérrez, *La Jornada*, January 18, 1997.

49 *La Reforma*, January 28, 1997.

50 José Gil Olmos, *La Jornada*, December 26, 1996.

51 Joel Simon, "Government Targets Teachers Union as Backbone of Rebel Force," Pacific News Service, October 20, 1996.

52 Julia Preston, "Mexico Confronts Rebels with Limited Crackdown," *New York Times*, October 10, 1996.

53 Molly Moore, "Army War on Rebels Gives Jitters to Rural Townspeople," *Washington Post*, October 17, 1996.

54 Section 22, SNTE, Oaxaca, press release, *La Jornada*, March 24, 1997.
55 *La Jornada*, November 13, 1998.
56 AP, September 25, 1996.
57 Sam Dillon, "Shadowy Rebels Pose New Problems for Mexico," *New York Times*, July 17, 1996.
58 Amnesty International Urgent Action Bulletin, January 1997.
59 Blanche Petrich, *La Jornada*, June 29, 1997.
60 José Gil Olmos, "FAC-MLN: fuerte campaña de represion," *La Jornada*, February 2, 1997.
61 Kieran Murray, Reuters, November 23, 1995.
62 AP, December 7, 1996.
63 Bill Cormier, AP, January 29, 1997.
64 Blanche Petrich, *La Jornada*, June 29, 1997.
65 Ibid.
66 Julia Preston, "With Nonviolent Sallies, Rebels in Mexico Fight On," *New York Times*, February 13, 1997.
67 Victor Ruiz Arrazola, *La Jornada*, January 14, 1997.
68 EPR Periodico No. 17, April 20, 1998, via Internet (www.pengo.it/PDPR-EPR/).
69 EPR web site (www.pengo.it/PDPR-EPR/).
70 *Miami Herald*, June 9, 1998.
71 Reuters, August 10, 1998.
72 EPR communiqué, June 25, 1998, via Internet (www.pengo.it/PDPR-EPR/).
73 *La Jornada*, June 22, 1998.
74 Reuters, July 5, 1998.
75 Carlos Marin, "Paso a paso, en documentos, la fundacion del Ejercito Revolucionario del Pueblo Indigena," *Proceso*, June 28, 1998.
76 Juan Cervantes and Carlos Yañez, "Dividio al EPR la posibilidad de negociar con el regimen," *El Universal*, June 14, 1998.
77 *La Jornada*, January 10, 1996.
78 Ignacio Ramirez, *Proceso*, August 25, 1996.
79 Reuters, December 5, 1996.
80 Reuters, January 7, 1998.
81 Maribel Gutiérrez, *La Jornada*, November 12, 1998.
82 Ibid.
83 Javier Trujillo Juarez, *El Sol de Acapulco*, November 15, 1998.
84 Ibid.
85 All quotes from *Propuesta: tesis para el Cambio (nuestras planteamientos basicos)*, ERPI document, April 1999.
86 AP, April 1, 1999; author's interviews with Chilpancingo protestors, April 1999.
87 *La Jornada del Sur*, May 10, 1999; *La Jornada*, May 11, 1999.
88 *La Jornada del Sur*, May 9, 1999.
89 Tracy Eaton, *Dallas Morning News*, August 27, 1999.
90 *Novedades*, May 11, 1999.
91 AP, May 11, 14, 1999.
92 *Manifiesto de la Triple Alianza Guerrillera Indigena Nacional*, April 1999.
93 *La Jornada*, August 9, 1996.
94 *Proceso*, August 11, 1996.

95 *La Jornada*, September 3, 1996.
96 Ibid.
97 Ibid., October 25, 1999.
98 *Proceso,* October 31, 1999.
99 *El Universal,* October 28, 1999.
100 Ibid., October 27, 1999.
101 Ibid., October 28, 1999.
102 *La Jornada*, October 25, 1999.

15 ANATOMY OF THE NARCO-DICTATORSHIP

1 AP, February 10, 1997.
2 AP, November 24, 1995.
3 AFP, April 23, 1998.
4 Reuters, May 31, 1999
5 *New York Times*, October 7, 1997.
6 Ibid., February 19, 1997.
7 Ibid., March 18, 1997.
8 *Chicago Sun-Times*, March 13, 1997.
9 *New York Times*, January 16, 1996.
10 Ibid., September 16, 1996.
11 *The Economist*, November 15, 1997.
12 *Dallas Morning News,* November 29, 1997.
13 *La Jornada*, December 21, 1997.
14 *The Economist*, November 15, 1997.
15 *New York Times*, July 6, 1997; *La Jornada*, November 7, 1997.
16 *Washington Post*, November 7, 1997
17 *The Economist*, November 15, 1997.
18 *New York Times*, October 8, 1998.
19 *El Universal*, February 17, 1998.
20 AP, December 10, 1995.
21 AFP, December 5, 1995.
22 *New York Times*, March 26, 1998.
23 *La Reforma*, January 13, 1997.
24 *Long Island Newsday*, March 12, 1997.
25 Ibid.
26 Ibid.
27 Reuters, August 10, 1995.
28 Ibid.
29 *Los Angeles Times*, June 15, 1995.
30 AP, February 12, 1997.
31 Ibid.

32 *Quehacer Politico*, October 19, 1996.
33 *The News*, Mexico City, February 1, 1997.
34 *New York Times*, February 24, 1997.
35 *Quehacer Politico*, October 19, 1996.
36 *The News*, Mexico City, January 11, 1997.
37 *Long Island Newsday*, March 13, 1997.
38 *New York Times*, February 17, 1997.
39 Ibid., September 19, 1998.
40 *Washington Post*, October 21, 1998.
41 *New York Times*, January 22, 1999.
42 Ibid., January 14, 1999.
43 AP, September 15, 1999.
44 *The Economist*, November 15, 1997.
45 *La Jornada*, April 1, 1994.
46 *New York Times*, May 5, 1994.
47 *The Economist*, February 8, 1997.
48 *New York Times*, November 30, 1995.
49 *Washington Post*, April 30, May 5, 1994.
50 Ibid.
51 *New York Times*, August 3, 1995.
52 *Washington Post*, May 1, 1994; *La Jornada*, March 29, 1996; *El Financiero*, July 27, 1997.
53 Reuters, January 3, 1996; *New York Times*, January 4, 1996.
54 *Los Angeles Times*, June 15, 1995.
55 *Proceso*, August 15, 1994.
56 *La Jornada*, December 6, 1996.
57 Fazio 1996, p. 50.
58 *The News*, Mexico City, May 23, 1996.
59 Ibid., May 25, 1996.
60 *Ahi*, January 1997.
61 Knight-Ridder, May 11, 1995.
62 AP, September 27, 1996.
63 Ibid.
64 *New York Times*, April 23, 1998.
65 Ibid., April 23, 1998.
66 Ibid., April 23, 1998.
67 Ibid., March 9, 1997.
68 *Proceso*, January 26, 1997.
69 *New York Times*, January 30, 1998.
70 *Novedades*, May 11, 1999.
71 *San José Mercury News*, January 30, 1999.
72 Combined sources: Ricardo Sandoval, Knight-Ridder, September 19, 1998; Sam Dillon, *New York Times*, September 26, 1998; John Black, *Orange County Register*, September 26, 1998; Andew Downie, *Houston Chronicle*, November 11, 1998.
73 Ibid.
74 Ibid.

75 Dean Latimer, "Citibank and Your Drug War Dollars," *High Times*, February 1997.
76 *Wall Street Journal*, April 1, 1997.
77 *New York Times*, March 20, 1997.
78 Ibid., November 26, 1998.
79 *Long Island Newsday*, May 19, 1998.
80 Ibid.
81 *New York Times*, May 19, 1998.
82 Ibid.
83 Ibid.
84 *Long Island Newsday*, May 19, 1998.
85 *Washington Post*, May 20, 1998.
86 *New York Times*, June 9, 1998.
87 *New York Times*, March 16, 1999.
88 AP, April 10, 1997.
89 *The Financial Times*, March 17, 1998.
90 Ross 1998, pp. 136–7.
91 Pastor and Castañeda, p. 269.
92 Levine, pp. 304–8.
93 Ibid.
94 Carmelo Ruiz, "Green Protectionism," *Earth Island Journal*, Spring 1997.
95 Bill Weinberg, "Piracy on the Miskito Coast," *High Times*, September 1995.
96 Dick Russell, "Tuna, Dolphins and Drugs," *High Times*, January 1997.
97 Ibid.
98 John Ross, "Narco-Politics and the Tuna," *LA Weekly*, October 9, 1997.
99 AP, February 14, 1997.
100 Dick Russell, "Tuna, Dolphins, Whales and Drugs: The War Goes On," *High Times*, June 1997.
101 Ibid.
102 *New York Times*, November 26, 1998.
103 Ibid.
104 Reuters, March 31, 1999.
105 See, e.g., Scott and Marshall.
106 Weinberg, p. 134.
107 Dean Latimer, "Kill for the Love of Cali: The New Cartel Takes Over," *High Times*, June, 1995.
108 Paul DeRienzo, "Haiti's Nightmare: The Cocaine Coup and the CIA Connection," *High Times*, April, 1994.
109 *Los Angeles Times*, February 26, 1997.
110 Warnock, p. 232.
111 Linda Robinson, "The Bleeding Border," *US News and World Report*, February 24, 1997.
112 *Los Angeles Times*, September 15, 1996; *New York Times*, December 12, 1996.
113 *San Antonio Express-News*, May 2, 1997.
114 Ibid., January 31, 1997.
115 *New York Times*, December 29, 1997.
116 *El Financiero*, January 21, 1995.
117 *New York Times*, May 23, 1995.
118 Ibid., January 10, 1995.

119 *Washington Post*, May 11, 1997.
120 Warnock, p. 242.
121 *Dallas Morning News*, January 14, 1992.
122 Combined sources: *New York Times*, February 5, 9, 14, 1999, *Washington Post*, February 10, 1999, *Los Angeles Times*, February 5, 1999.
123 Ibid.
124 *New York Times*, June 9, 1999; *Miami Herald*, May 29, 1999.
125 Reuters, May 25, 1999.
126 *Orange County Register*, December 18, 1998.
127 Amnesty International press release, January 14, 1999.
128 UPI, April 13, 1998.
129 Ibid.

16 OPIUM FIELDS OF THE TARAHUMARA

1 Author's interview.
2 Ibid.
3 Original document signed by Baborigame *ejiditarios*, July 25, 1997.
4 Author's interviews, Coloradas de la Virgen, May 1998.
5 Ibid.
6 Alan Weisman, "The Deadly Harvest of the Sierra Madre," *Los Angeles Times Magazine*, January 9, 1994; Anthony DePalma, "Mexico's Indians Face New Conquistador: Drugs," *New York Times*, June 2, 1995.
7 Alejandro Gutiérrez, "El cacicazgo de los Fontes, la antesala de terror," *El Diario*, Chihuahua, October 21, 1996.
8 Author's interviews, Coloradas de la Virgen, May 1998.
9 Ibid.; *El Diario,* Chihuahua, October 21, 1996.
10 Author's interviews, Coloradas de la Virgen, May 1988.
11 Ibid.
12 Ibid.
13 Ibid.
14 Ibid., testimony of Samuel H. Hitt, Director, Forest Guardians, before US House of Representatives, Subcommittee on Foreign Relations, April 25, 1994.
15 *Los Angeles Times Magazine*, January 9, 1994.
16 Scott and Marshall, pp. 37–8.
17 Ibid.; author's interview with Randall Gingrich, Chihuahua, May 1998.
18 Alejandro Gutiérrez, *Proceso*, October 20, 1996; Alejandro Romero Ruiz, *La Jornada*, August 13, 1996.
19 Baum, p. 107.
20 Ibid., pp. 106–7, 126–7.
21 Roberto Tinoco, *et al.*, "Paraquat Poisoning in Southern Mexico: A Report of 25 Cases," *Archives of Environmental Health*, Washington DC, March/April 1993.

22 Wright, p. 4.

23 Maria Espino, *El Heraldo de Chihuahua*, September 20, 1994.

24 Author's interview with Edwin Bustillos, Chihuahua, May 1998.

25 Alejandro Gutiérrez, *El Diario*, Chihuahua, October 20, 1996.

26 *El Diario*, Chihuahua, October 21, 1996; *Los Angeles Times Magazine*, January 9, 1994.

27 Bustillos interview.

28 Alvarado, p. 112.

29 *El Diario,* Chihuahua, November 2, 1991.

30 Author's interview with reporter Alejandro Gutiérrez, *El Diario,* Chihuahua, May 1998.

31 Elias Montañez Alvarado, *Siete Dias*, political supplement of *El Diario,* Chihuahua, May 3, 1998.

32 Elva Gomez, COSYDDHAC, *Inventario de Vida*, Chihuahua, 1992.

33 Bustillos interview; Alvarado, p. 55.

34 *New York Times*, June 2, 1995.

35 Original document signed by Baborigame *ejiditarios*, January 25, 1996.

36 Conviction records, Departamento de Gobernacion, Estado de Chihuahua, November 8, 1995.

37 Bustillos interview.

38 Ibid.

39 Ibid.

40 Ibid.

41 Angelica Enciso, *La Jornada*, December 10, 1996.

42 Samuel Hitt testimony; *Los Angeles Times Magazine*, January 9, 1994.

43 Samuel Hitt testimony.

44 Author's interview with Randall Gingrich, Chihuahua, May 1998.

45 Ibid.

46 Ibid.

47 Daniel Garcia Monroy, "Denuncian saqueo en el ejido Pino Gordo," *El Diario,* Chihuahua, June 20, 1998; Sierra Madre Alliance update, June 5, 1999; *New York Times*, April 28, 1999.

48 Bustillos interview.

49 Building a Sierra Madre Biosphere Reserve: Conservation, Training and Baseline Studies, CASMAC, Chihuahua, 1998.

50 Ibid.; Gingrich interview.

51 Gingrich interview.

52 Ibid.

53 Ibid.

54 *El Diario,* Chihuahua, February 29, 1996, October 27, 1996, June 27, 1997; author's interview with Alejandra Esparsa, Escuela Nacional de Antropologia y Historia (ENAH), Chihuahua.

55 Kennedy 1978, pp. 15–17.

56 Ibid.

57 Ibid., pp. 22–3.

58 Knight, vol. 1, p. 199; vol. 2, p. 338.

59 Alejandro Gutiérrez, "Denuncia Diocesis de la Tarahumara engaños a indigenas," *El Diaro,* Chihuahua, May 6, 1998.

60 Bustillos interview; *Kwira*, Creel, Chihuahua, May 1998.

61 *Kwira*, ibid.

62 *New York Times*, July 7, 1998.

63 Author's telephone interview with Isela Gonzalez, advisor, Mujeres Indigenas Tarahumaras y Tepehuanes AC, Chihuahua, January 28, 1999.
64 *El Diario,* Chihuahua, May 23, 1997.
65 Blanche Petrich, *La Jornada*, July 9, 1996.
66 Hodges, pp. 26–30.
67 Ibid., pp. 26–30, 92–4.
68 Ibid.
69 Ross 1995, p. 278.
70 *La Jornada*, September 18, 1996.
71 *Proceso*, July 7, 1996.

17 NARCO-IMPERIALISM

1 Bill Weinberg, "Assassinations 'R' Us: Your Tax Dollars at Work," *High Times*, New York, April 1997.
2 *La Jornada*, September 20, 1996.
3 *New York Times*, February 16, 1999.
4 Ibid., October 24, 1995.
5 Fazio 1996, p. 179.
6 *The News*, Mexico City, October 28 1996.
7 Brad Peters, "The New Drug Czar Takes Over," *High Times*, New York, June 1996.
8 Ibid.
9 Ibid.
10 *New York Times*, May 8, 1996.
11 Hearst News Service, April 8, 1996; *La Jornada*, April 9, 1996.
12 *La Jornada*, March 17, 1996.
13 *The News*, Mexico City, October 28, 1996.
14 Ibid., March 30, 1996.
15 *La Jornada*, June 10, 13, 15, 1996.
16 Ibid., June 15, 1996.
17 Ibid., June 13, 1996; Letter to Secretary of State Warren Christopher signed by fifteen members of the US House of Representatives, September 20, 1996.
18 *La Jornada* , May 17, 1996.
19 Ibid., March 17, 1996.
20 EZLN communiqué, January 13, 1994.
21 Carlos Fazio and Samuel Blixen, *La Brecha*, Montevideo, October 28, 1995.
22 Ibid.
23 Ibid.
24 Scott and Marshall, pp. 47–9.
25 *Philadelphia Inquirer*, July 26, 1987.
26 *La Reforma*, May 8, 1994.
27 Fazio and Blixen.
28 Noticias de Guatemala, February 11–17, 1995.

29 *Washington Post*, September 21, 1996.
30 SOA Watch web site, www.derechos.org.
31 Jerry Meldon and Dean Latimer, "Bolivia Reelects 'Cocaine Coup' Jefe," *High Times*, New York, December 1997.
32 Darrin Wood, Nuevo Amanecer Press, Madrid, December 1997, via Internet (amanecer@cyberspace.com).
33 *La Jornada*, August 31, 1996.
34 Garance Burke, *El Financiero International*, August 3–9, 1998.
35 Ibid., June 25, 1998.
36 Barry 1992, pp. 53–74.
37 Pastor and Castañeda, p. 118.
38 Ibid.
39 Ross 1998, p. 139.
40 Pastor and Castañeda, p. 271.
41 Ross 1998, pp. 140, 162.
42 Scott and Marshall, pp. 41, 204.
43 Peter Dale Scott affidavit, September 30, 1996.
44 Scott and Marshall, pp. 34–5; Krüger, pp. 177–80.
45 Ross 1998, p. 161.
46 *New York Times*, February 13, 19, 1998.
47 Barry 1992, p. 53.
48 *La Jornada*, January 19, 1994.
49 AP, August 6, 1994.
50 Reuters, July 9, 1999.
51 *Quehacer Politico*, October 1992.
52 Informe 1997, Liga Mexicana por la Defensa de los Derechos Humanos-Federacion Internacional de los Derechos Humanos (LIMEDDH-FIDH), via Internet (limeddh@laneta.apc.org).
53 *The News*, Mexico City, January 25, 1994.
54 AP, April 8, 1997.
55 Ross 1998, p. 142.
56 Amnesty International, p. 101.
57 Gloria Leticia Diaz, *Proceso*, January 23, 2000.
58 Riding, p. 148.
59 *New York Times*, February 19, 1989.
60 Anderson and Anderson, pp. 72–81.
61 Ibid., p. 138; Buendia, p. 54.
62 Anderson and Anderson, p. 72.
63 Ibid., pp. 55, 139.
64 *La Extra*, January 15–21, 1995.
65 *The News*, Mexico City, July 1, 1997; Darrin Wood, Nuevo Amanecer Press, Madrid, June 1997, via Internet (amanecer@cyberspace.com).
66 Anderson and Anderson, p. 181; King, pp. 173–88.
67 Darrin Wood, Nuevo Amanecer Press, Madrid, January 22, 1998, via Internet (amanecer@cyberspace.com).
68 *La Jornada*, February 2, 1994.

69 *Patterns in Global Terrorism*, US State Department, 1996.

70 John Deutch, "Think Again: Terrorism," *Foreign Policy*, Fall 1997.

71 Graham H. Turbiville Jr., *Law Enforcement and the Mexican Armed Forces: The Military Undertakes New Internal Security Missions*, Foreign Military Studies Office, Fort Leavenworth KS, April 1997.

72 Pacific News Service, March 18, 1995.

73 Centro de Derechos Humanos Fray Bartolomé de Las Casas, pp. 156–7.

74 Gray, p. 178.

75 Ibid., p. 180.

76 Ibid., p 182.

77 Office of National Drug Control Policy, report to Congress, September 1997.

78 *Special Warfare*, Fort Bragg, NC, January 1996.

79 Michael Steinberg, "Massacre in Mexico: The North Carolina Connection," *The Prism*, Chapel Hill, NC, March 1998.

80 Pascal Beltran del Rio, *Proceso*, May 3, 1998.

81 Elizalde Trinfo, *La Jornada*, August 15, 1998.

82 *El Universal*, August 12, 1998; *Washington Post*, August 15, 1998.

83 Pascal Beltran del Rio, *Proceso*, May 3, 1998.

84 *Baltimore Sun*, January 27, 1997.

85 Fernando Ramirez de Aguilar L., *El Financiero*, January 25, 1998.

86 Reuters, March 15, 1998.

87 *Toronto Star*, July 7, 1999.

88 *Los Angeles Times*, December 22, 1998; AFP, December 22, 1998.

89 Reuters, December 24, 1998.

90 Ibid.

91 *Proceso*, January 19, 1997.

92 *The Guardian* (London), July 9, 1999.

18 BORDER WARS

1 *New York Times*, December 8, 1997.

2 Ibid., March 3, 1996.

3 *Washington Post*, July 30, 1997.

4 *Dallas Morning News*, May 23, 1997.

5 Robert Draper, "Soldiers of Misfortune," *Texas Monthly*, August 1997.

6 Ibid.; *Houston Chronicle*, June 20, 1997.

7 UPI, July 24, 1997.

8 *Austin American-Statesman*, June 29, 1997.

9 *Washington Post*, July 30, 1997.

10 *Texas Monthly*, August 1997.

11 Ibid.

12 Ibid.

13 Ibid.

14 *El Paso Herald-Post*, July 30, 1997.

15 *Washington Post*, July 30, 1997.
16 *Houston Chronicle*, August 14, 1997.
17 *New York Times*, August 16, 1997.
18 AP, August 16, 1997.
19 *Austin American-Statesman*, June 29, 1997.
20 Ibid.; *Texas Monthly*, August 1997.
21 *USA Today*, June 30, 1997.
22 Baum, p. 23.
23 Bertram, pp. 103–6; Pastor and Castañeda, p. 267.
24 *Dallas Morning News*, June 4, 1997.
25 *Washington Post*, July 30, 1997.
26 *Los Angeles Times*, November 8, 1997.
27 *Dallas Morning News*, August 25, 1997.
28 Ibid., June 4, 1997.
29 Ibid.
30 Dean Compton, "Operation: Protect America," National Alliance of Christian Militia press release, Redding, CA, October 1995.
31 Reuters, October 15, 1995.
32 *El Financiero*, November 11, 1995.
33 Ibid.
34 Sam Dillon, "US Tests Border Plan in Event of Crisis," *New York Times*, December 8, 1995.
35 *El Financiero*, November 11, 1995.
36 Donald Goldberg and Indy Badhwar, "Blueprint for Tyranny," *Penthouse*, August 1985; Keenen Peck, "The Take-Charge Gang," *The Progressive*, May 1985.
37 Alfonso Chardy, "Reagan Aides and the 'Secret' Government," *Miami Herald*, July 5, 1987.
38 Dave Lindorff, "Could It Happen Here?" *Mother Jones*, San Francisco, April 1988.
39 Flombe Brath, "Beyond Iran-Contragate: A Neofascist Oligarchy?" *The City Sun*, New York, August 5–11, 1987.
40 Ed Connolly, "A Highly Irregular Force: Scandals of the State Militias," *The Nation*, New York, March 18, 1991.
41 *The New York Times*, April 24, June 19, 1982.
42 Ibid., October 26, 1996.
43 Ibid., May 23, 1996.
44 *Soldiers* (www.dtic.mil/soldiers), November 1997.
45 UPI, January 29, 1997.
46 *New York Times*, April 24, 1997.
47 Notimex, January 24, 1997.
48 *New York Times*, April 24, 1997.
49 Reuters, September 30, 1996.
50 *Insight*, January 20, 1997.
51 *Dallas Morning News*, August 26, 1997; *San Francisco Chronicle*, October 6, 1997.
52 Wade Graham, "Masters of the Game," *Harpers*, July 1996.
53 *Philadelphia Inquirer*, May 12, 1996.
54 *New York Times*, August 24, 1997.
55 Author's telephone interview with Roberto Martínez, November 1997.

56 Ibid.
57 Ibid.
58 Ibid.
59 *Dallas Morning News*, August 14, 1998.
60 Landi Fernly, "Government Exempts Border from Environmental Law," *Earth First! Journal*, November/December 1996.
61 Gary Paul Nabhan, "Where Creatures and Cultures Recognize No Boundaries," *Orion*, Summer 1997.
62 AP, February 27, 1999.
63 *New York Times*, April 16, 1984, cited by Pastor and Castañeda, p. 343.
64 Carlos Rico in Vasquez, Carlos and Manuel Garcia y Griego, eds, *Mexican–US Relations: Conflict and Convergence*, UCLA, 1983, p. 150, cited in Pastor and Castañeda, p. 343.
65 Cited by Noam Chomsky in introduction to Dawkins.
66 Kornbluh and Byrne, pp. 410–11.
67 Weinberger, pp. 163–213.
68 Ibid.
69 *The Economist*, July 19, 1997; *New York Times*, July 7, 1998.
70 *The Economist*, October 28, 1995.
71 Cited in Castañeda 1995, p. 34.
72 Wright, p. 166.
73 Merk, p. 152.
74 *MacLeans*, September 23, 1996.
75 *Los Angeles Times*, August 30, 1992.
76 Garreau, pp. 207–44.
77 *Miami Herald*, January 23, 1999.
78 Reuters, January 19, 1999; *San Francisco Chronicle*, January 22, 1999.
79 *Miami Herald*, January 25, 1999.
80 *La Jornada*, December 26, 1995.
81 Ibid., July 22, 1996; Mexican Labor News and Analysis, July 16, 1996, via Internet (www.igc.apc.org/unitedelect/).
82 Ramon A. Gutiérrez, "Aztlan, Montezuma, and New Mexico: The Political Uses of American Indian Mythology," in Anaya and Lomeli, pp. 172–87.
83 Rudolfo A. Anaya, "Aztlan: A Homeland Without Boundaries," in Anaya and Lomeli, pp. 230–41.
84 Quote from *Rocky Mountain News*, August 1, 1993.
85 Bill Weinberg, "Contested Sierra: Development Threatens Pueblo-Hispano Land-Based Ways," *Native Americas*, Cornell University, Winter 1997.
86 Ibid.
87 Ibid.
88 Ibid.
89 Ibid.
90 Ron Sandoval, "The San Luis Vega," in Randall Teeuwen, ed., *La Cultura Constante de San Luis*, San Luis Museum Cultural and Commerical Center, San Luis, CO, 1985.
91 Quoted in Kutz, p. 51.
92 Kutz, p. 54; Lavender, pp. 223–9, 246–8.
93 Sandoval, "The San Luis Vega."

94 Ibid.
95 José Rivera and Devon G. Peña, "Historic Acequia Communities in the Upper Rio Grande," University of New Mexico, Albuquerque, 1997.
96 Sandoval, "The San Luis Vega."
97 Ibid.
98 Ibid.; Land Rights Council Chronology, San Luis, CO, 1994.
99 Calvin Trillin, "A Little Cloud on the Title," *The New Yorker*, April 26, 1976.
100 Ibid.
101 *Native Americas*, Winter 1997.
102 Julian Lloyd, "150-Year Old Land Dispute Intensified in Colorado," *Christian Science Monitor*, March 3, 1997.
103 *Gazette Telegraph*, Colorado Springs, June 6, 1993.
104 *Native Americas*, Winter 1997.
105 Ibid.
106 Sam Howe Verhovek, "Cattle Barons of Texas Yore Accused of Epic Land Grab," *New York Times*, July 14, 1997.
107 Kutz, pp. 55–8; Lavender, pp. 251–2.
108 Kutz, pp. 58–61.
109 Ibid., pp. 58–61.
110 Ibid., pp. 66–9.
111 James Brooke, "Hot Issue in Northern New Mexico: Fine Print of an 1848 Treaty," *New York Times*, 19 February 1998.
112 SOA Watch press release, January 20, 1998, via Internet (www.derechos.org).
113 Ibid.
114 Korten, p. 81.
115 UPI, July 1997.
116 Reuters, January 28, 1996.
117 AP, July 3, 1996.
118 *Business Week*, July 7, 1997.
119 *Journal of Commerce*, May 29, 1996.
120 *The News*, Mexico City, June 27, 1997.
121 David Bacon, "Rebellion on the Border," *San Francisco Bay Guardian*, March 5, 1997.
122 *Business Week*, July 7, 1997.
123 Resolution, Board of the Federation of Canadian Municipalities, March 6, 1998.
124 EZLN, Fifth Declaration of the Lacandon Selva, July 1998.
125 "An Inverted Periscope," Marcos communiqué, February 24, 1998.
126 *La Jornada*, July 31, 1997.
127 e.g, *Le Nuove Forme dell' Internazionalismo e dell' Antimperialismo nell' Epoca Della Globalizazione*, statement of Naples delegation, Second Intercontinental Encuentro for Humanity and Against Neoliberalism, August 1997.
128 Lee, p. 269.
129 George Bush presidential address, January 29, 1991.
130 Zinn, p. 154.
131 Cockcroft 1998, p. 67.
132 Katz 1997, pp. 67–75.

133 *Pacifica News*, July 6, 1998; *La Jornada*, October 23, 1998.

134 ACERCA mission statement, Burlington, VT, 1998.

135 See, e.g., "The Totalitarian Empire," in Octavio Paz, *One Earth, Four or Five Worlds: Reflections on Contemporary History,* Harcourt Brace Jovanovich, New York, 1985.

136 Paz, pp. 20–4.

BIBLIOGRAPHY

BOOKS, MONOGRAPHS AND ARTICLES

Albro, Ward S., *Always a Rebel: Ricardo Flores Magón and the Mexican Revolution*, Texas Christian University Press, Fort Worth, 1992

Alvarado, Carlos Mario, *La Tarahumara: Una Tierra Herida*, Talleres Graficos de Gobierno del Estado, Chihuahua, 1996

Anaya, Rudolfo A. and Francisco Lomeli, *Aztlan: Essays on the Chicano Homeland*, University of New Mexico Press, Albuquerque, 1989

Anderson, Scott and Jon Lee Anderson, *Inside the League*, Dodd, Mead, New York, 1986

Arendt, Hannah, *On Revolution*, Viking, New York, 1965

Asprey, Robert B., *War in the Shadows: The Guerrilla in History*, William Morrow, New York, 1994

Atkin, Ronald, *Revolution! Mexico 1910–1920*, John Day, New York, 1969

Barry, Tom, ed., *Mexico: A Country Guide*, Inter-Hemispheric Education Resource Center, Albuquerque, NM, 1992

Barry, Tom, *Zapata's Revenge: Free Trade and the Farm Crisis in Mexico*, South End Press, Boston, MA, 1995

Bartra, Armando, *Los Herederos de Zapata: Movimientos Campesinos Posrevolucionarios en México*, Ediciones Era, Mexico City, 1985

Baum, Dan, *Smoke and Mirrors: The War on Drugs and the Politics of Failure*, Little, Brown, New York, 1996

Beezley, William H., *Insurgent Governor: Abraham González and the Mexican Revolution in Chihuahua*, University of Nebraska, Lincoln, 1973

Bello, Walden, *Dark Victory: The United States, Structural Adjustment and Global Poverty*, Institute for Food and Development Policy, Oakland, CA, 1994

Benjamin, Thomas, *A Rich Land, A Poor People: Politics and Society in Modern Chiapas*, University of New Mexico, Albuquerque, 1989

Benjamin, Thomas and Mark Wasserman, eds, *Provinces of the Revolution: Essays on Regional Mexican History 1910–1929*, University of New Mexico, Albuquerque, 1990

Bertram, Eva, Morris Blachman, Kenneth Sharpe and Peter Andreas, eds, *Drug War Politics: The Price of Denial*, University of California Press, Berkeley, 1996

Blaisdell, Lowell L., *The Desert Revolution: Baja California, 1911*, University of Wisconsin Press, Madison, 1962

Bonfil Batalla, Guillermo, *México Profundo: Reclaiming A Civilization*, University of Texas Press, Austin, 1996

Boremanse, Didier, *Hach Winik: The Lacandon Map of Chiapas, Mexico*, Institute for Mesoamerican Studies, Albany, NY, 1998

Bourne, Kenneth, *Britain and the Balance of Power in North America*, University of California Press, Berkeley, 1967

Bricker, Victoria Reifler, *The Indian Christ, the Indian King: The Historical Substrate of Maya Myth and Ritual*, University of Texas Press, Austin, 1981

Browning, David, *El Salvador: Landscape and Society*, Oxford University Press, Oxford, 1971

Brundage, Burr Cartwright, *The Fifth Sun: Aztec Gods, Aztec World*, University of Texas Press, Austin, 1979

Buendia, Manuel, *La CIA en Mexico*, Ediciones Océano, Mexico City, 1986

Campbell, Howard, *et al.*, eds, *Zapotec Struggles: Histories, Politics and Representations from Juchitan, Oaxaca*, Smithsonian, Washington DC, 1993

Carr, Barry, *Marxism and Communism in Twentieth-Century Mexico*, University of Nebraska, Lincoln, 1992

Caruso, A. Brooke, *The Mexican Spy Company: United States Covert Operations in Mexico, 1845–1848*, McFarland and Co., Jefferson, NC, 1991

Castañeda, Jorge, *Utopia Unarmed: The Latin American Left After the Cold War*, Vintage, New York, 1994

—— *The Mexican Shock: Its Meaning for the US*, New Press, New York, 1995

Cockcroft, James D., *Mexico: Class Formation, Capital Accumulation, and the State*, Monthly Review, New York, 1983

—— *Mexico's Hope: An Encounter with Politics and History*, Monthly Review, New York, 1998

Colby, Gerard and Charlotte Dennett, *Thy Will Be Done: The Conquest of the Amazon*, HarperCollins, New York, 1995

Collier, George, *Basta! Land and the Zapatista Rebellion in Chiapas*, Institute for Food and Development Policy, Oakland, CA, 1994

Dawkins, Kristin, *NAFTA: The New Rules of Corporate Conquest*, Open Magazine Pamphlet Series, Westfield, NJ, 1993

Dorner, Peter, *Latin American Land Reforms in Theory and Practice*, University of Wisconsin Press, Madison, 1992

Doyle, Jack, *Altered Harvest: Agriculture, Genetics, and the Fate of the World's Food Supply*, Penguin, New York, 1985

Eber, Christine, *Water of Hope, Water of Sorrow: Women and Alcohol in a Highland Maya Town*, University of Texas Press, Austin, 1995

Fazio, Carlos, *Samuel Ruiz: El Caminante*, Espasa Calpe, Mexico City, 1994

—— *El Tercer Vinculo: De la Teoria del Caos a la Teoria de la Militarizacion*, Joaquin Mortiz, Mexico City, 1996

Florescano, Enrique, *Memory, Myth, and Time in Mexico*, University of Texas Press, Austin, 1994

Fowler, Cary and Pat Mooney, *Shattering: Food, Politics, and the Loss of Genetic Diversity*, University of Arizona Press, Tucson, 1990

Fox, Jonathan, *The Politics of Food in Mexico: State Power and Social Mobilization*, Cornell University Press, Ithaca, NY, 1993

—— "The Challenge of Democracy: Rebellion as Catalyst," *Chiapas: Challenging History*, special edition of *Akwe:kon Journal*, Cornell University, Summer 1994

Fried, Jonathan L., *et al.*, eds, *Guatemala in Rebellion: Unfinished History*, Grove Press, New York, 1983

Fuentes, Carlos, *A New Time for Mexico*, Farrar, Straus and Giroux, New York, 1996

Galeano, Eduardo, *Open Veins of Latin America: Five Centuries of the Pillage of a Continent*, Monthly Review, New York, 1973

Garcia de Leon, Antonio, *Resistencia y Utopia* (2 vols), Ediciones Era, Mexico City, 1993

Garreau, Joel, *The Nine Nations of North America*, Houghton Mifflin, Boston, MA, 1981

Gerassi, John, *The Great Fear in Latin America*, Collier, New York, 1965

Gibson, Charles, *The Aztecs Under Spanish Rule: A History of the Indians of the Valley of Mexico 1519–1810*, Stanford University Press, Stanford, CA, 1964

Gosner, Kevin, *Soldiers of the Virgin: The Moral Economy of a Colonial Maya Rebellion*, University of Arizona Press, Tucson, 1992

Gray, Chris Hables, *Postmodern War: The New Politics of Conflict*, Guilford Press, New York, 1997

Greene, Graham, *The Power and the Glory*, Viking, New York, 1946

Grieb, Kenneth, *The United States and Huerta*, University of Nebraska Press, Lincoln, 1969

Gross, Liza, *Handbook of Leftist Guerilla Groups in Latin America and the Caribbean*, Council on Hemispheric Affairs/Westview Press, Boulder, CO, 1995

Gutiérrez, Gustavo, *Las Casas: In Search of the Poor of Jesus Christ*, Orbis Books, New York, 1993

Hamilton, Nora, *The Limits of State Autonomy: Post-Revolutionary Mexico*, Princeton University Press, Princeton, NJ, 1982

Handy, Jim, *Gift of the Devil: A History of Guatemala*, South End Press, Boston, MA, 1984

Harris, Alex and Margaret Sartor, eds, *Gertude Blom· Bearing Witness*, University of North Carolina Press, Chapel Hill, 1984

Harris, Larry A., *Pancho Villa: Strong Man of the Revolution*, High-Lonesome Books, Silver City, NM, 1995

Hart, John M., *Anarchism and the Mexican Working Class, 1860–1931*, University of Texas Press, Austin, 1978

Harvey, Neil, "Corporatist Strategies and Popular Responses in Rural Mexico: State and Opposition in Chiapas, 1970–1988" (PhD thesis), University of Essex, 1989

—— *The Chiapas Rebellion: The Struggle for Land and Democracy*, Duke University Press, Durham, NC, 1998

Hodges, Donald C., *Mexican Anarchism After the Revolution*, University of Texas Press, Austin, 1995

Holloway, John and Eloína Peláez, *Zapatista! Reinventing Revolution in Mexico*, Pluto Press, London, 1998

Howard, Michael and Douglas Ross, eds, *Mexico's Second Revolution?*, Centre for International Studies, Simon Fraser University, Vancouver, 1991

Hu-DeHart, Evelyn, *Yaqui Resistance and Survival*, University of Wisconsin Press, Madison, 1984

Jackson, Ben, *Poverty and the Planet: A Question of Survival*, Penguin, New York, 1990

Joseph, Gilbert M., *Rediscovering the Past at Mexico's Periphery: Essays on the History of Modern Yucatan*, University of Alabama University Press, AL, 1986

—— *Revolution From Without: Yucatan, Mexico, and the United States, 1880–1924*, Duke University Press, Durham, NC, 1988

Katz, Friedrich, *The Secret War in Mexico: Europe, the United States and the Mexican Revolution*, University of Chicago Press, Chicago, 1981

—— *The Life and Times of Pancho Villa*, Stanford University Press, Stanford, CA, 1998

Katz, William Loren, *Black Indians: A Hidden Heritage*, Simon and Schuster, New York, 1997

Kennedy, John G., *Tarahumara of the Sierra Madre: Beer, Ecology, and Social Organization*, AHM Publishing, Arlington Heights, IL, 1978

Kennedy, Paul, *The Rise and Fall of the Great Powers*, Random House, New York, 1987

King, Dennis, *Lyndon LaRouche and the New American Fascism*, Doubleday, New York, 1989

Knight, Alan, *The Mexican Revolution* (2 vols), Cambridge University Press, Cambridge, 1986

Kornbluh, Peter and Malcolm Byrne, *The Iran-Contra Scandal: The Declassified History*, New Press, New York, 1993

Korten, David C., *When Corporations Rule the World*, Kumarian Press, West Hartford, CT/Berett-Koehler, San Francisco, CA, 1995

Krauze, Enrique, *Mexico: Biography of Power*, HarperCollins, New York, 1997

Krüger, Henrik, *The Great Heroin Coup: Drugs, Intelligence and International Fascism*, South End Press, Boston, MA, 1980

Kutz, Jack, *Grassroots New Mexico: A History of Citizen Action*, Inter-Hemispheric Education Resource Center, Albuquerque, NM, 1989

La Botz, Dan, *Mask of Democracy: Labor Suppression in Mexico Today*, South End Press, Boston, MA, 1992

—— *Democracy in Mexico: Peasant Rebellion and Political Reform*, South End Press, Boston, MA, 1995

LaFeber, Walter, *Inevitable Revolutions: The United States in Central America*, Norton, New York, 1984

Langley, Lester D., *Mexico and the United States: The Fragile Relationship*, Twayne Publishers, Boston, MA, 1991

Lappé, Frances Moore and Joseph Collins, *Food First: Beyond the Myth of Scarcity*, Ballantine, New York, 1977

Las Casas, Bartolomé, *The Devastation of the Indies: A Brief Account*, Seabury Press, New York, 1974

Laurell, Asa Cristina, *Mexico, a Restricted Democracy*, Casa del Sol, Mexico City, 1992

Lavender, David, *The Southwest*, University of New Mexico Press, Albuquerque, 1960

LeBot, Yvon, *Subcomandante Marcos: El Sueño Zapatista*, Plaza y Janés, Barcelona, 1997

Lee, Martin A., *The Beast Reawakens*, Little, Brown and Co., Boston, MA, 1995

Levine, Michael, *Deep Cover*, Delacorte Press, New York, 1990

Lewis, Oscar, *Life in a Mexican Village: Tepoztlan Restudied*, University of Illinois Press, Urbana, 1951

—— *Tepoztlan: Village in Mexico*, Holt Rinehart Winston, New York, 1960

Lister, Florence C. and Robert H. Lister, *Chihuahua: Storehouse of Storms*, University of New Mexico Press, Albuquerque, 1966

López y Rivas, Gilberto, *Nacion y Pueblos Indios en el Neoliberalismo*, Plaza y Valdez, Mexico City, 1995

Lynd, Staughton, *Intellectual Origins of American Radicalism*, Vintage, New York, 1968

MacLachlan, Colin M., *Anarchism and the Mexican Revolution: The Political Trials of Ricardo Flores Magón in the United States*, University of California Press, Berkeley, 1991

Maguire, Andrew and Janet Welsh Brown, eds, *Bordering on Trouble: Resources and Politics in Latin America*, World Resources Institute, Washington DC, 1986

Mallin, Jay, ed. *"Che" Guevara On Revolution*, Delta, New York, 1969

Mallon, Florencia E., *Peasant and Nation: The Making of Postcolonial Mexico and Peru*, University of California Press, Berkeley, 1995

Manzo Yépez, José Luis, *¿Que Hacer con Pemex? Una Alternativa a la Privatizacion*, Grijalbo, Mexico City, 1996

Matthews, Richard K., *The Radical Politics of Thomas Jefferson*, University of Kansas, 1984

Merk, Frederick, *Manifest Destiny and Mission in American History*, Vintage, New York, 1963

Millon, Robert P., *Zapata: The Ideology of a Peasant Revolutionary*, International Publishers, New York, 1969

Miranda Ramírez, Arturo, *El Otro Rostro de la Guerrilla: Genaro, Lucio y Carmelo*, Editorial El Machete, Mexico City, 1996

Moguel V., Julio, *La Violencia del Oro Negro en Mecoacan, Tabasco*, Friedrich, Ebert, Stiftung, Mexico City, 1994

Montemayor, Carlos, *Chiapas: La Rebelion Indígena de México*, Joaquin Mortiz, Mexico City, 1997

Nabhan, Gary Paul, *Enduring Seeds: Native American Agriculture and Wild Plant Conservation*, North Point Press, San Francisco, 1989

Nadelmann, Ethan A., *Cops Across Borders: The Internationalization of US Criminal Law Enforcement*, Pennsylvania State University Press, University Park, 1993

Nations, James D., "The Ecology of the Zapatista Revolt," *Cultural Survival Quarterly*, Cambridge, MA, Spring 1994

Navarrete, Carlos, *San Pascualito Rey y el Culto a la Muerte en Chiapas*, UNAM, Mexico City, 1982

Newell, Peter E., *Zapata of Mexico*, Black Thorn, Somerville, MA, 1979

Nigh, Ronald, "Zapata Rose in 1994: The Indian Rebellion in Chiapas," *Cultural Survival Quarterly*, Cambridge, MA, Spring 1994

Orozco Zuarth, Marco A., *Sintesis de Chiapas*, Edysis, Tuxtla Gutiérrez, 1994

Parkes, Henry Bamford, *A History of Mexico*, Houghton Mifflin, Boston, MA, 1960

Pastor, Robert A. and Jorge G. Castañeda, *Limits to Friendship: The United States and Mexico*, Knopf, New York, 1988

Paz, Octavio, *The Labyrinth of Solitude*, Grove Press, New York, 1961

Perera, Victor and Robert D. Bruce, *The Last Lords of Palenque: The Lacandon Maya of the Mexican Rainforest*, University of California Press, Berkeley, 1982

Poniatowska, Elena, *Fuerte es el Silencio*, Ediciones Era, Mexico City, 1997

Recinos, Adrian, trans. and ed., *El Popol Vuh: Las Antiguas Historias del Quiché*, Editorial Universitaria Centroamericana, Guatemala, 1978

Redfield, Robert, *Tepoztlan: A Mexican Village*, University of Chicago Press, Chicago, 1930

Reed, John, *Insurgent Mexico*, International Publishers, New York, 1969

Reed, Nelson, *The Caste War of Yucatan*, University of California Press, Stanford, 1964

Renner, Michael, *Fighting for Survival: Environmental Decline, Social Conflict, and the New Age of Insecurity*, Norton, New York, 1996

Reyes Ramos, Maria Eugenia, *El Reparto de Tierras y la Politica Agraria en Chiapas, 1914–1988*, UNAM, Mexico City, 1992

Riding, Alan, *Distant Neighbors: A Portrait of the Mexicans*, Vintage, New York, 1984

Romero Jacobo, César, *Los Altos de Chiapas: La Voz de las Armas*, Planeta, Mexico City, 1994

Rosas, Maria, *Tepoztlan: Cronica de Desacatos y Resistencia*, Ediciones Era, Mexico City, 1997

Ross, John, *Rebellion from the Roots: Indian Uprising in Chiapas*, Common Courage Press, Monroe, ME, 1995

—— *The Annexation of Mexico: From the Aztecs to the IMF*, Common Courage Press, Monroe, ME, 1998

Russell, Philip L., *The Chiapas Rebellion*, Mexico Resource Center, Austin, TX, 1995

Samson, Anthony, *The Seven Sisters: The Great Oil Companies and the World They Shaped*, Viking, New York, 1975

Sandos, James A., *Rebellion in the Borderlands: Anarchism and the Plan of San Diego, 1904–1923*, University of Oklahoma Press, Norman, 1992

Schele, Linda and David Freidel, *A Forest of Kings: The Untold Story of the Ancient Maya*, William Morrow, New York, 1990

Scott, Peter Dale and Jonathan Marshall, *Cocaine Politics: Drugs, Armies, and the CIA in Central America*, University of California Press, Berkeley, 1991

Selser, Gregorio; *Sandino: General of the Free*, Monthly Review, New York, 1981

Shiva, Vandana, *The Violence of the Green Revolution*, Zed Books, London, 1991

Simon, Joel, *Endangered Mexico: An Environment on the Edge*, Sierra Club, San Francisco, 1998

Singletary, Otis A., *The Mexican War*, University of Chicago Press, Chicago, 1960

Sklar, Holly, ed., *Trilateralism: The Trilateral Commission and Elite Planning for World Management*, South End Press, Boston, MA, 1980

Starr, Kevin, *Americans and the California Dream, 1850–1915*, Oxford University Press, Oxford, 1973

Thomas, Hugh, *Conquest: Montezuma, Cortés, and the Fall of Old Mexico*, Simon and Schuster, New York, 1993

Traven, B., *General from the Jungle*, Allison and Busby, London, 1985

Tuchman, Barbara W., *The Zimmerman Telegram*, Ballantine, New York, 1958

Turner, John Kenneth, *Barbarous Mexico*, 1910, reprinted by University of Texas Press, Austin, 1969

Utley, Robert M., *A Life Wild and Perilous: Mountain Men and the Paths to the Pacific*, Henry Holt, New York, 1997

Van Alstyne, Richard W., *The Rising American Empire*, Quadrangle, Chicago, 1960

Vogt, Evon Z., *Fieldwork among the Maya: Reflections on the Harvard Chiapas Project*, University of New Mexico Press, Albuquerque, 1994

Walker, William, *The War in Nicaragua*, University of Arizona Press, Tucson, 1985

Warnock, John, *The Other Mexico: The North American Triangle Completed*, Black Rose, Montreal, 1995

Wasserman, Mark, *Persistent Oligarchs: Elites and Politics in Chihuahua, Mexico 1910–1940*, Duke University Press, Durham, NC, 1993

Wasserstrom, Robert, *Class and Society in Central Chiapas*, University of California Press, Berkeley, 1983

Weinberg, Bill, *War on the Land: Ecology and Politics in Central America*, Zed Books, London, 1991

Weinberger, Caspar and Peter Schweizer, *The Next War*, Regnery, Washington DC, 1996

Wolf, Eric R., *Sons of the Shaking Earth: The People of Mexico and Guatemala*, University of Chicago Press, Chicago, 1959

—— *Peasant Wars of the Twentieth Century*, Harper, New York, 1969

Wollock, Jeffrey, "Globalizing Corn: Technocracy and the Indian Farmer," *Chiapas: Challenging History*, special edition of *Akwe:kon Journal*, Cornell University, Summer 1994

Womack, John Jr., *Zapata and the Mexican Revolution*, Vintage, New York, 1968

—— *Rebellion in Chiapas: An Historical Reader*, New Press, New York, 1999

World Commission on Environment and Development, *Our Common Future*, Oxford, 1987

Wright, Angus, *The Death of Ramon González: The Modern Agricultural Dilemma*, University of Texas Press, Austin, 1990

Wurlitzer, Rudy, *Walker: The True Story of the First American Invasion of Nicaragua*, Harper and Row, New York, 1987

Yergin, Daniel, *The Prize: The Epic Quest for Oil, Money and Power*, Touchstone, New York, 1992

Zinn, Howard, *A People's History of the United States*, Harper and Row, New York, 1980

Zogbaum, Heidi, *B. Traven: A Vision of Mexico*, Scholarly Resources, Inc., Wilmington, DE 1992

HUMAN RIGHTS REPORTS

Amnesty International, *Mexico: Human Rights in Rural Areas*, London, 1986

Centro de Derechos Humanos Fray Bartolomé de Las Casas, *Ni Paz Ni Justicia*, San Cristóbal de Las Casas, Chiapas, 1996

Human Rights Watch, *Implausible Deniability: State Responsibility for Rural Violence in Mexico*, New York, 1997

Public Citizen, *NAFTA's Broken Promises: The Border Betrayed*, Washington DC, 1996

ANTHOLOGIES OF EZLN COMMUNIQUÉS AND RELATED DOCUMENTS

Accion Zapatista Editorial Collective, eds, *Conversations with Don Durito*, Autonomedia, New York, 1999

Bardacke, Frank, *et al.*, eds, *Shadows of Tender Fury: The Letters and Communiqués of Subcomandante Marcos and the Zapatista Army of National Liberation*, Monthly Review, New York, 1995

Clarke, Ben and Clifton Ross, eds, *Voice of Fire: Communiqués and Interviews from the Zapatista National Liberation Army*, New Earth Publications, Berkeley, CA, 1994

Hernández Navarro, Luis and Ramon Vera Herrera, eds, *Acuedros de San Andrés*, Ediciones Era, Mexico City, 1998

Marcos, Subcomandante, *The Story of Colors: A Folktale from the Jungles of Chiapas*, Cinco Puntos Press, El Paso, 1999

Monroy Gómez, Mario B., *et al.*, eds, *Mujeres y Hombres sin Rostro* (3 vols, includes daily chronology), Servicios Informativos Procesados (SIPRO), Mexico City, 1994, 1995, 1996

La Palabra de los Armados de Verdad y Fuego: Entrevistas, Cartas y Communicados del EZLN, Editorial Fuenteovejuna, Mexico City, 1994

Ponce de Leon, Juana, ed., *Selected Writings of Subcommander Marcos*, Seven Stories Press, New York, 2000.

Ruggiero, Greg and Stuart Sahulka, eds, *Zapatista Encuentro: Documents from the 1996 Encounter for Humanity and Against Neoliberalism*, Open Media Pamphlet Series, Seven Stories Press, New York, 1998

¡Zapatistas! Documents of the New Mexican Revolution, Autonomedia, New York, 1994

INDEX

Ciudad Juárez, 50, 53, 83, 85, 87, 303, 312, 331,
341, 384, 386
Ciudad Pemex, 206, 216, 219, 229
Ciudad Real, 19, 21, 23, 28
Civic Alliance, *see* Alianza Civica
Clinton, Bill, 9, 82, 85, 90,91, 110, 130, 135, 145,
173,231, 302, 303, 314, 320, 347, 348, 361, 365,
367, 370, 371, 372, 372
CNA, *see* National Water Commission
CNC, 31, 34, 57, 58, 68, 99, 113, 114, 133
CNDH, *see* National Human Rights Commission
CNI, *see* National Indigenous Congress
Coahuila, 10, 40, 43, 45, 47, 50, 84, 376, 386
Coatzacoalcos, city and petrochemical complex,
228, 229, 230, 233, 248, 249, 251
Coca-Cola, 9, 69, 100, 242, 376
cocaine, 156, 157, 220, 222, 313, 315, 316, 317, 325,
331, 334, 351, 371
COCOPA, 7, 148, 154, 155, 160, 162, 164, 183–4,
285
CODEHUTAB, 209, 212, 224, 227
coffee, 28, 70, 129
coletos, 6, 98, 110, 116, 147, 355
Colombia, 7, 40, 74, 222, 248, 301, 303, 311, 315,
316, 318, 329, 331, 357, 359
Coloradas de la Virgen, 325–8, 329, 332, 333, 334,
335, 336, 337, 340
Colorado, 76, 331, 377, 378–81
Colosio, Luis Donaldo, 113, 117, 134, 267, 307–10,
321
Comitán, 121, 166, 172
Communist Party, Mexican, 34–5, 114, 241, 250, 281
CONAI, 138, 145, 147, 148, 158, 160, 166, 181, 184
CONPAZ, 148, 156–7, 163
Conservatives, 25, 40, 44
Constantine, Thomas, 318, 321, 346
Constitution, Mexican, 7, 55, 107, 154, 164, 207,
213, 229–30, 256, 259, 260, 283
Constitutionalist Army, 50–6; *see also* Carranzistas
consultas, 112, 149–51, 152, 154, 184, 190, 201
Contragate scandal, 318, 369, 374
contras, 62, 318, 348, 351, 354, 357
Coordinadora de Lucha Social, 206, 212, 213, 214,
217
corporatism 57, 58, 64, 191, 192, 352
Cortéz, Hernándo, 18, 19, 60, 298
Costa Rica, 62, 248, 318, 351, 352

Counter-Narotics Intelligence Center, 319, 320, 358
Coyuca de Benitez, 244–6, 252, 280, 286
coyuntura, 202, 292, 384
Cristero revolt, 31, 58, 354
Cruzob revolt, 26–8
CTM, 57, 58, 87, 89, 149, 191
Cuautla, 48, 50, 56, 257, 265
Cuba, 20, 25, 26, 28, 40, 41, 43, 128, 161, 189,
242–3, 291, 304, 351, 373
Cuernavaca, 10, 53, 55, 56, 241, 242, 243, 253, 255,
257, 261, 263, 264, 265, 268, 270, 271,272, 275
Culiacán, 70, 315, 331

DEA, *see* US Drug Enforcement Administration
Demesa Padilla, Gerardo, 264, 273
DF, *see* Mexico City
DFS, *see* Federal Security Directorate
Dialogue Law, 147, 151, 155, 158
Díaz, Porfirio, 27, 29, 30, 44–7, 48, 49, 88, 192, 301
dinosaurs (PRI faction), 170, 177, 191, 282, 309, 352
Duby Blom, Gertrude, 102, 103–4, 106
Durango state, 50, 56, 72, 324, 329, 331, 332

Echeverria, Luis, 60, 102, 267,270–1, 304, 351
ejidos, 21, 31, 32, 44, 45, 47, 49, 55, 57, 58, 64,
66–9, 76, 77–9, 80–1, 97, 100, 102, 114, 120–1,
124, 125, 136, 143, 148, 150, 157, 164, 191, 199,
207, 208, 209, 215, 216, 218–19, 235, 237, 239,
241, 242, 244, 246, 255, 266, 268, 290, 312,
324–8, 330, 331, 332–3, 334–6, 337, 379; *see also*
Article 27
El Bajio, *see* Bajio region
El Bosque, 6, 157, 165, 180, 184–5
El Paraiso, 245, 290, 291
El Paso, 331, 362, 371, 372, 376, 377, 386
El Paso Intelligence Center, 272, 366
El Salvador, 62, 99, 116, 130, 131, 173, 250, 349,
354, 357, 382
El Tepozteco archeological site, *see* Tepozteco National
Park
El Tepozteco development project, *see* Grupo KS
Elorriaga, Jorge Javier, 145, 148, 155, 159, 161–2
Emiliano Zapata Campesino Organization, *see* OCEZ
Emiliano Zapata Proletarian Organization, *see* OPEZ
encuentros, 3, 160–1, 183–4
Entzin, Sebastián, 148, 155, 159
EPR, *see* Popular Revolutionary Army